MARINE PROTECTED AREAS FOR WHALES, DOLPHINS AND PORPOISES

This book is dedicated to those who work on behalf of cetaceans and marine ecosystems, and to those who cannot speak, write and argue for their place in the sea: the whales, dolphins and porpoises and other marine species

'There is a tide in the affairs of men, which taken at the flood leads on to fortune... The flood is occurring regarding the high seas'

Graeme Kelleher (paraphrasing William Shakespeare in *Julius Caesar*) saying that now is the time to create and fight for high-seas marine protected areas

MARINE PROTECTED AREAS FOR WHALES, DOLPHINS AND PORPOISES

A World Handbook for Cetacean Habitat Conservation

Erich Hoyt

London • Sterling, VA

First published by Earthscan in the UK and USA in 2005

ISBN: 1-84407-064-6 paperback
         1-84407-063-8 hardback

Typesetting by MapSet Ltd, Gateshead, UK
Printed and bound in the UK by CPI Bath
Cover design by Anthony Waters
Cover photo: Sperm whale off Kamchatka, Russia, © Hal Sato, Far East Russia
Orca Project (WDCS)
Maps: Lesley Frampton
Illustrations: © Pieter Arend Folkens/A Higher Porpoise Design Group

For a full list of publications please contact:

Earthscan
8–12 Camden High Street
London, NW1 0JH, UK
Tel: +44 (0)20 7387 8558
Fax: +44 (0)20 7387 8998
Email: earthinfo@earthscan.co.uk
Web: **www.earthscan.co.uk**

22883 Quicksilver Drive, Sterling, VA 20166-2012, USA

Earthscan publishes in association with WWF-UK and the International Institute for
Environment and Development

The royalties from sales of this book will go toward the MPA work of WDCS, the
Whale and Dolphin Conservation Society.

A catalogue record for this book is available from the British Library

Library of Congress Cataloging-in-Publication Data

Hoyt, Erich.
    Marine protected areas for whales, dolphins, and porpoises : a world handbook for
cetacean habitat conservation / by Erich Hoyt.
        p. cm.
    Includes bibliographical references and index.
    ISBN 1-84407-063-8 (hardback) – ISBN 1-84407-064-6 (pbk.)
    1. Cetacean–Conservation. 2. Cetacea–Habitat. 3. Marine parks and reserves. I.
Title.

QL737.C4H675 2005
333.95'95–dc22

                                                                    2004016778

This book is printed on elemental chlorine-free paper

CONTENTS

List of Figures

LIST OF TABLES

LIST OF BOXES AND CASE STUDIES

BOXES

CASE STUDIES

Acknowledgements

First I must thank Margi Prideaux, Mark Simmonds, Michelle Grady, Sarah Dolman, Kate O'Connell, Chris Butler-Stroud, Nicolas Entrup, Cathy Williamson, Jess Feghali-Brown and everyone at WDCS, the Whale and Dolphin Conservation Society, for their patience during the lengthy gestation period required to research and write this work. In particular, Alison Wood and Vanessa Williams at WDCS saw the project through from the beginning and never stopped giving support and encouragement. To say that it started out as one thing and gradually metamorphosed into something else – typical of many books and detailed research projects – is to understate matters. There were long interruptions due to other books and reports with urgent deadlines, funding difficulties and delays for personal and family reasons. I never lost interest or faith in the project, though more than once I feared it might never be completed.

This document has seeds going back to my earliest writing and work on conservation. I want to remember the late American broadcaster–author–naturalist Roger Caras and the Nobel Laureate ethologist Niko Tinbergen for their past support, beginning with my first book, *Orca: The Whale Called Killer*, which they called a 'conservation tool; required reading' because of its focus on our battle for an early cetacean marine protected area. In many ways that – and many struggles over virgin forests in Canada – set me on a path. Those battles were reported in articles for *Equinox, Defenders, International Wildlife* and *National Geographic*, and I would like to recognize editors Jim Deane for commissioning 'Battle of the Bight' and Frank Edwards and Barry Estabrook for sending me to South Moresby in the Queen Charlotte Islands – one of the first large national marine protected areas in Canada. My work also benefited greatly from discussions over the years with both Professor Edward O Wilson, with his encyclopedic approach to cataloguing species and understanding ecosystems, and economist Francis Grey who turned his thinking to the underrated, largely unconsidered, value of marine protected areas and whales. Enormous credit and thanks must also be given to WDCS for providing primary support for my research, reports, workshop presentations and lectures in various countries since 1990.

I was fortunate to have two interns, Jean Blane (formerly of Dalhousie University, Marine Affairs Program, currently of the Canadian Environmental Assessment Agency) and Asuka Imai (formerly of McGill University and Boston University, and more recently working on biosphere reserves in Uzbekistan and the Democratic Republic of Congo) who spent separate two-month periods in my office doing research and summarizing data at an early stage. Jean Blane has continued to send useful information, and Asuka Imai specialized in GIS mapping as part of a graduate degree at Boston University to help with this and other projects. In addition, special thanks are due to Giuseppe Notarbartolo di Sciara, founder of the Tethys Research Institute and, among other things, coordinator of the Mediterranean Group of IUCN's World Commission on Protected Areas (WCPA), who led the long struggle to secure the landmark Pelagos Sanctuary for Mediterranean Marine Mammals – an inspiration by itself. Graeme Kelleher was very helpful in answering various questions drawing on his extensive knowledge and output on marine protected areas (MPAs). Toward the end of the project, Carole Carlson showed me a draft of her useful paper on cetacean sanctuaries for the International Fund for Animal Welfare (IFAW). Others who helped with valuable information, contacts or sources include Iain Orr, Patricia Birnie and Jackie Alder. All my colleagues on the Far East Russia Orca Project (FEROP) helped and inspired me in many ways, and I specifically mention my long-time collaborators and co-founders of the project, Hal Sato and Alexander M Burdin, as well as Karina Tarasyan who helped contact the many Russian zapovedniks.

This book was kindly reviewed by the following individuals who provided many helpful comments and corrections. For the Prologue, Introduction, Chapters 1–4 and the Epilogue: Margi Prideaux, Mark Simmonds, Vanessa Williams, Alison Wood and Jean Blane. Acknowledgements for the reviews of Chapter 5 are listed by marine region: Marine Region 1 (Antarctic): Sarah Dolman, David G Ainley; Marine Region 2 (Arctic): Gregoriy Tsidulko, Stefan Norris, Julian Woolford, Mai Britt Knoph, Doug Yurick; Marine Region 3 (Mediterranean): Giuseppe Notarbartolo di Sciara, Erika Urquiola Pascual; Marine Region 4 (Northwest Atlantic): Brad Barr, Nathalie Ward, Doug Yurick, Mary-Jean Comfort, Nadia Menard; Marine Region 5 (Northeast Atlantic): Mark Simmonds, Simon Berrow, Erika Urquiola Pascual, Marina Sequeira, Rui Prieto; Marine Region 6 (Baltic): Mark Simmonds, Rauno Lauhakangas, Julia Neider, Nicolas Entrup; Marine Region 7 (Wider Caribbean): Nathalie Ward; Marine Region 8 (West Africa): Erika Urquiola Pascual, Koen Van Waerebeek, Stephanie Lemm, Jenna Cains, Michel Vély; Marine Region 9 (South Atlantic): José Truda Palazzo, Jr, Mabel Augustowski, Miguel Iñíguez, Cristian de Haro, María del Valle Fathala; Marine Region 10 (Central Indian Ocean): Hiran Jayewardene, Brian D Smith; Marine Region 11 (Arabian Seas): Rob Baldwin; Marine Region 12 (East Africa): Omar A Amir, Michel Vély; Marine Region 13 (East Asian Seas): Benjamin Kahn, Ketut Sarjana Putra, Brian D Smith, AA Yaptinchay, José Ma Lorenzo Tan, Isabel Beasley, Ian G Baird; Marine Region 14 (South Pacific): Sue Miller, Nancy Daschbach, Allen Tom, Brad Barr, Margi Prideaux; Marine Region 15 (Northeast Pacific): Brad Barr, José Angel Sanchez Pacheco, Wendy Szaniszlo, Doug Yurick; Marine Region 16 (Northwest Pacific): Shigeki Komori, Grigoriy Tsidulko; Marine Region 17 (Southeast Pacific): Fernando Félix, Gian Paolo Sanino Vattier, Julio Reyes; and Marine Region 18 (Australia–New Zealand): Michelle Grady, Margi Prideaux, Philippa Brakes. Just before it went to press, Margi Prideaux read the entire manuscript and provided much-needed enthusiasm, as well as advice and comments.

Finally, besides WDCS support, primary funding for this project came from the John Ellerman Foundation, with additional funding from The Kleinwort

Charitable Trust, the Fishmongers' Company, the John Sacher Trust and Donna Balkan Litowitz. A special thanks goes to Eric Edwards, OBE, and Lord and Lady Antrim, for their help in fund raising. I am grateful to Jonathan Sinclair Wilson, Rob West, Akan Leander, Kim Allen, Gary Haley, Frances MacDermott, Ruth Mayo and everyone else at Earthscan for their help and encouragement as the book neared completion. Helen Johnston also helped considerably with the final editing. Moses Hoyt checked all the websites and many other last-minute details. The preparation of the maps was the meticulous and inspiring work of Lesley Frampton, with help from Steve Frampton. A big thanks to Pieter Folkens and the Higher Porpoise Design Group, for last minute heroics in preparing and letting us use Pieter's superb illustrations.

Finally, I must remember those who struggled through this long episode with me – Sarah, my wife, and children Moses, Magdalen, Jasmine and Max.

LIST OF ACRONYMS AND ABBREVIATIONS

ACCOBAMS	Agreement on the Conservation of Cetaceans of the Black Sea, Mediterranean Sea and Contiguous Atlantic Area
AEPS	Arctic Environmental Protection Strategy
AMAP	Arctic Monitoring and Assessment Program (Arctic Marine Region)
ASCI	area of special conservation interest
ASCOBANS	Agreement on the Conservation of Small Cetaceans of the Baltic and North Sea
ATBA	area to be avoided (IMO designation)
BAMP	Bazaruto Archipelago Master Plan (Mozambique)
CAFF	Conservation of Arctic Flora and Fauna (Arctic Marine Region)
CBA	cost–benefit analysis
CBD	Convention on Biological Diversity
CCAMLR	Convention on the Conservation of Antarctic Marine Living Resources
CEC	Commission for Environmental Cooperation
CI	Conservation International
CITES	Convention on International Trade in Endangered Species of Wild Fauna and Flora
CMS	Convention on the Conservation of Migratory Species of Wild Animals
CNSP	Convention on Conservation of Nature in the South Pacific
CONANP	Comisión Nacional de Áreas Naturales Protegidas (México)
COSEWIC	Committee on the Status of Endangered Wildlife in Canada
CPPS	Convention for the Protection of the Marine Environment and Coastal Areas of the South-East Pacific
CSG	Cetacean Specialist Group (IUCN)
DFO	Department of Fisheries and Oceans (Canada)
DNR	Department of Natural Resources (US)
EBM	ecosystem-based management
EC	European Commission
EEZ	exclusive economic zone
EIS	environmental impact statement
EPBC	Environmental Protection and Biodiversity Conservation Act (Australia)
EPPR	Emergency, Prevention, Preparedness and Response (Arctic Marine Region)
ESA	Endangered Species Act (US)
EU	European Union
EWT	Endangered Wildlife Trust
FEROP	Far East Russia Orca Project
FRPA	Fisheries Resources Protection Area (Japan)

GBRMP	Great Barrier Reef Marine Park
GIS	geographic information systems (for mapping)
HELCOM	Helsinki Convention (Convention for the Protection of the Baltic Environment against All Forms of Pollution)
HSMPA	high-seas MPA
HSUS	Humane Society of the United States
I	island
ICRAM	Instituto Centrale per la Ricerca Applicata al Mare (Italy)
ICRW	International Convention for the Regulation of Whaling
IFAW	International Fund for Animal Welfare
IMO	International Maritime Organization
INEFAN	National Institute of Forests and Natural Protected Areas (Ecuador)
IOMAC	Indian Ocean Marine Affairs Cooperation
ISACH	Indian and South Atlantic Consortium on the Humpback Whale
IUCN	The World Conservation Union
IWC	International Whaling Commission
IWDG	Irish Whale and Dolphin Group
LME	large marine ecosystem
MAB	Man and the Biosphere Programme (Unesco)
MARPOL	International Convention for the Prevention of Pollution from Ships (IMO convention)
MCEA	Convention for the Protection, Management and Development of the Marine and Coastal Environment of the Eastern African Region
MEP	Marine Environmental Police (US)
MPA	marine protected area
MR	marine region
MWA	marine wildlife area (Canada)
NAFO	Northwest Atlantic Fisheries Organization
NGO	non-governmental organization
NIPAS	National Integrated Protected Areas System (Philippines)
NMCA	national marine conservation area (Canada)
NMFS	National Marine Fisheries Service (US)
NMS	national marine sanctuary (US)
NOAA	National Oceanic and Atmospheric Administration (US)
NPAC	Natural Protected Areas Commission
NRSMPA	National Representative System of Marine Protected Areas (Australia)
NWA	national wildlife area (Canada)
NWR	National Wildlife Refuge (US)
OBIS	Ocean Biogeographic Information System
OSPAR	Oslo and Paris Convention for the Protection of the Marine Environment in the Northeast Atlantic
PA	protected area
PAME	Protection of the Arctic Marine Environment (Arctic Marine Region)

photo-ID	photographic identification
PMHL	Pacific Marine Heritage Legacy (Canada)
PSSA	Particularly Sensitive Sea Area (IMO designation)
Ramsar	Convention on Wetlands of International Importance Especially as Waterfowl Habitat
RMMCP	Regional Marine Mammal Conservation Programme (SPREP)
RMPs	Regional Marine Plans (Australia)
ROPME	Regional Organization for Protection of the Marine Environment (Arabian Seas Marine Region)
SAC	special area of conservation (EU)
SBSTTA	Subsidiary Body on Scientific, Technical and Technological Advice
SCI	site of community importance (EU)
SDWG	Sustainable Development Working Group (Arctic Marine Region)
SEMARNAT	Secretaria de Medio Ambiente y Recursos Naturales (México)
sp	species (singular)
SPA	Protocol for Special Protected Areas and Biological Diversity of the Barcelona Convention
SPAMI	Special Protected Areas of Mediterranean Interest
SPAW	Protocol Concerning Specially Protected Areas and Wildlife (part of the Cartagena Convention)
SPLASH	Structure of Populations, Levels of Abundance and Status of Humpbacks, 2004–2007 (Pacific Ocean)
spp	species (plural) or all species of a particular genus
SPREP	South Pacific Region Environment Program
SSA	special sea area
UNCED	United Nations Conference on Environment and Development
UNCLOS	United Nations Convention on the Law of the Sea
UNDP	United Nations Development Programme
UNEP	United Nations Environment Programme
Unesco	United Nations Educational, Scientific and Cultural Organization
WCMC	World Conservation Monitoring Centre (now called UNEP-WCMC)
WCPA	World Commission on Protected Areas
WCS	Wildlife Conservation Society (US)
WDCS	Whale and Dolphin Conservation Society (UK; also, US, Germany, Argentina, Australia)
WDFW	(State of) Washington Department of Fish & Wildlife
WHC	World Heritage Convention (Convention for the Protection of the World's Natural and Cultural Heritage) (Unesco)
WSSD	World Summit on Sustainable Development
WWF	World Wide Fund for Nature
YONAH	Years of the North Atlantic Humpback research programme

(See also acronyms used for MPAs in Table 1.3 on p19)

PROLOGUE

The publication of this handbook, *Marine Protected Areas for Whales, Dolphins and Porpoises*, will, it is hoped, mark the beginning of a new era in the worldwide research and protection of whales, dolphins and porpoises – the cetaceans. This work, sponsored by WDCS, the Whale and Dolphin Conservation Society, represents the first detailed investigation into the status, process and potential of instituting cetacean habitat protection.

This book is being completed as new findings about marine biodiversity quicken the pace of human interest in and development of the sea. At present, only 15 per cent of the estimated 1,650,000 (+150,000) catalogued species of plants and animals are marine. Yet recent research into deep-sea ecosystems reveals that an estimated 500,000 to 10 million, or even considerably more, marine species may exist, waiting to be named, studied and utilized (Gray, 1997; Wilson, 2002). Yet how little we know about these amazing marine ecosystems which are capable of producing such biodiversity.

Marine ecosystems contain substantial direct and indirect values for local communities who actively harness these resources, as well as for all people on Earth – but those values will be eroded if nations fail to protect a certain substantial portion of the world ocean.

According to the Sea Around Us project, 2.3 billion people – some 38 per cent of the world human population of about 6 billion – live within 62 miles (100 km) of the coast. And half of those – 1.15 billion people or 19 per cent of the world human population – live within 62 miles (100 km) of a marine protected area (Sea Around Us, forthcoming).

Our key goal with this work is to promote the creation of the best possible marine protected areas (MPAs) for cetaceans. Such areas stem from the identification of critical habitat: the areas that cetaceans use to feed, mate, reproduce and socialize, as well as the areas that protect essential ecosystem functions and the habitat that cetacean prey depends on. MPAs for cetaceans can have a far-reaching impact on marine conservation. In order to be effective, cetacean MPAs must also protect prime fish-rearing habitat and productive upwellings and other important ecosystem processes. Overall ecosystem-based management is essential to achieve these goals (see Boxes I.1, p2, and I.2, p4, for definitions of critical habitat and ecosystem-based management).

What is ecosystem-based management? A good starting point is the management of the uses and values of ecosystems. An ecosystem per se needs no management. It is the escalating human interactions with ecosystems and the damaging human impacts on ecosystems and species that we need to manage. Still, it has become clear that human uses must be accommodated within ecosystem capacities. Ecosystem-based management is a regime that recognizes that ecosystems are dynamic and inherently uncertain, yet seeks to manage these human interactions within ecosystems in order to protect and maintain ecological integrity and to minimize adverse impacts.

In order to achieve this goal, fundamental shifts in management thinking and research must take place:

- Management must move from a 'reactive' style to a 'proactive' style. This requires ongoing scientific analysis and the ability to adapt management practice quickly when new information signals a need for change.
- Research has to re-orient itself to view the ecosystem as a whole, using multiple components such as stability of reef or sea floor, predator presence and/or water quality as indicators of management success.
- Risk assessments of management choices must be reviewed regularly and adapted to new information.
- Multiple sectoral uses (commercial and sports fishing, fishing with cetacean bycatch, and other uses), as well as the resulting impacts, must be viewed as cumulative rather than isolated.
- Managers, policy-makers and the public must be alert to the misuse of the term 'ecosystem-based management', particularly by those seeking to justify the culling of predators. This is an abuse of the concept; ecosystem-based management must control human activities within or impacting upon the ecosystem.
- The ultimate aim is to maintain the ecosystem as it naturally occurs, not adapting it to human needs but enabling it to accommodate an acceptable level of human use. It is therefore important to understand more about the whole ecosystem, rather than focusing on one or other isolated area or species. Without doubt, these are major tasks to undertake in any large marine area, but they are necessary steps for humans in order to manage their involvement with marine ecosystems.

Ecosystem-based management requires that safeguards such as MPAs should be built into the system from an early stage to secure ecosystem integrity in the absence of full scientific certainty.

Ecosystem-based management leads to MPAs that are ideally part of networks of multi-zone areas. A useful model for such multi-zone protected areas is the 'biosphere reserve', which offers high protection to critical areas, intermediate protection to less important areas and provides a place and a means for people to participate in the MPA through educational low-impact whale watching and marine tourism, sustainable fishing and other activities. MPAs are best planned and maintained through efforts involving all stakeholders – local communities, conservation organizations, researchers, marine tourism operators, fishing and other industries and government ministries covering environment, fisheries, tourism and the ocean.

By adopting the concepts of critical habitat, ecosystem-based management and biosphere reserves, we – all of us who work to protect marine species and ecosystems – can make greater headway in MPA conservation. This book will take you step by step through these ideas, and it will explore the implications in terms of the situation with the world ocean that we find ourselves confronting today.

We at WDCS believe that MPAs, if well designed and managed, can play a key role in the conservation of cetaceans and marine ecosystems. Still, we recognize the importance of other conservation approaches and strategies, such as regulation of international trade and hunting, fisheries agreements, and promotion of whale watching, ecotourism and other compatible activities.

The first four chapters of this book outline the principles of good habitat conservation for whales, dolphins and porpoises. We reveal why this species-driven approach has considerable value in the ecosystem-oriented conservation world. The fifth and final chapter focuses on the world's 18 marine regions, providing an overview of MPA and cetacean conservation in each region, as well as detailed case studies and survey accounts of the more than 500 MPAs with cetacean habitat, both proposed and existing. There are many insights into conservation in action at the grass-roots level around the world.

In the 18 MPA tables, one for each marine region, we have tried to be as complete as possible, featuring both proposed and existing MPAs that offer a wide variety of habitat conservation measures ranging from protection from hunting and little else (for example, large-scale sanctuaries and 'paper parks') to full stakeholder-sanctioned protection with multi-use zones including highly protected reserves.

The MPA tables provide an easy way for people working on cetaceans or cetacean conservation in one area of the world to consider the larger picture, to be able to contact people in other parts of their own region or the world. Our hope is that this will lead to greater cross-fertilization, including the establishment of more networks of MPAs which are needed to protect cetaceans, many of which do not respect national or international boundaries and range seasonally and from year to year over large ocean areas.

We have also explored international cetacean sanctuaries and high-seas MPAs. Located in the 50 per cent of the ocean outside the limit of the 200 nautical mile (371 km) exclusive economic zones (EEZs), international sanctuaries represent weak examples of MPAs which may nevertheless have strategic conservation importance. More important are high-seas MPAs, though it may require determined political will and hard work by representatives of the world's nations to put into practice the United Nations Convention on the Law of the Sea (UNCLOS) and the Convention on Biological Diversity (CBD). Both of these treaties, for those who have read the fine print, require the world's nations to conserve whales, fish and biodiversity – to become, in effect, stewards of the high seas. It is also becoming clear that the Convention on the

Conservation of Migratory Species of Wild Animals (CMS) has a role to play in the protection of habitat on the high seas. The world's nations must come together with foresight and imagination to create a comprehensive network of precedent-breaking MPAs on the new frontier of the high seas.

Our inclusion of the widest range of MPAs in this book means neither that we seek nor that we approve of all types of supposed habitat protection. In fact, we believe that MPAs in most of the areas covered in this volume have a long way to go before they can meet the habitat needs of cetaceans and other marine biota, as well as the needs of the community stakeholders, and be called an effective contribution toward ecosystem-based management. But we recognize that many communities, nations and regions have been grappling with the idea of MPA conservation of one kind or another over the past few years, with greater or lesser success. And the best thing that we can do now is to start with what exists, and what has already been proposed, to build upon for the future.

Every proposed or existing MPA represents a work in progress. Our goal is to encourage each MPA to continue to improve, to identify critical habitat and to extend habitat conservation for cetaceans and the entire ecosystem, to learn from other areas' mistakes and successes, and to utilize new studies, legal protections, conventions, policies and directives as they become available.

The accounts of the MPAs in this book are changing even as this book goes to press. We plan to keep things up to date through the WDCS website (www.cetaceanhabitat.org) as new developments arise. We invite you to join us to help devise and refine strategies to help with marine conservation at the local as well as the international level. What is our ultimate goal? To have a world in which we can share our space – our marine habitat – with these long-lived, social mammals, animals of awesome size and complex behaviour, subjects of historical fascination and persistent mystery, animals that we are only beginning to understand – the whales, dolphins and porpoises.

Erich Hoyt
North Berwick
Scotland
August 2004

INTRODUCTION

There are three main driving forces behind this work. First, the habitat needs of cetaceans – the 84 species of whales, dolphins and porpoises – have been neglected. Marine habitat conservation has lagged behind land conservation. Within marine habitat conservation, cetaceans may be featured in certain reserves, but are their needs being adequately met? In most cases the answer is 'no'. We need to look carefully at identifying and protecting critical habitat for cetaceans (see Box I.1). The habitat of these wide-ranging animals is best protected through ecosystem-based management approaches (see Box I.2), using a carefully selected network of marine protected areas (MPAs), modelled along the lines of biosphere reserves, or zoned protected areas, which include both highly protected marine reserves as well as zones to allow human uses such as well-managed marine tourism and fishing. MPA regimes can address some or even most cetacean habitat protection needs, but it is useful to maintain a broad approach to conservation efforts on behalf of cetaceans to include other ecosystem-based protection and management strategies, international conventions and treaties, and other pragmatic approaches.

Second, there is more research and information on cetaceans than ever before – although large portions of it are difficult to access. The past three decades have seen the success of photographic identification (photo-ID) and other benign methods of studying cetaceans, including radio and satellite tagging and biopsy of skin and blubber for genetics and to measure contaminant loads and, most recently, diet. This has been the era of studying whales from live animals rather than carcasses, and with these studies, whales and dolphins have revealed certain details of their habitat needs, in many cases for the first time. There remain large gaps with most cetacean species, especially those that spend their lives in deep waters on the high seas, but the growing body of work is exciting, substantial and ready to be acted upon. Yet much cetacean habitat literature remains buried in unpublished reports, conference abstracts and proceedings, sighting databases, conservation organization newsletters, and papers in little-known journals that are not easily accessible or known to protected area managers and conservationists who focus on habitat issues. Research-compiling tools such as SEAMAP are starting to address this

Box I.1 Critical habitat

Critical habitat refers to those parts of a cetacean's range, either a whole species or a particular population of that species, that are essential for day-to-day survival, as well as for maintaining a healthy population growth rate. Areas that are regularly used for feeding (including hunting), breeding (all aspects of courtship) and raising calves, as well as, sometimes, migrating, are part of critical habitat, especially if these areas are regularly used.

Unlike land-based critical habitat, however, marine critical habitat boundaries may be less fixed, especially in terms of hunting and feeding areas which are dependent on upwelling and other ever-changing oceanographic conditions. Baleen whales, for example, are known to feed in and around upwellings, which vary depending on local and large-scale oceanographic conditions to some extent during a season and from year to year. The implication for MPA design is that more flexible definitions of MPAs for cetaceans are needed in some cases. This book argues for larger overall biosphere reserve-type areas which would include a number of highly protected 'core areas' corresponding to cetacean critical habitat with boundaries that can be adjusted as needed from year to year or even within seasons. Such adjustments should be adaptive, constantly reviewed and sensitive to signals from the wider environment. To achieve this fine-grained kind of critical habitat management, it will be necessary to unravel and understand ecosystem processes and the impacts that humans can have on such processes. An appropriate tool for this is ecosystem-based management (see Box I.2).

Critical habitat for cetaceans is a fairly new idea, yet to be fully explored, much less implemented. In the comprehensive US blueprint for MPAs, 'critical habitats' are areas 'such as spawning grounds, nursery grounds, or other areas harboring vulnerable life stages' (Commission on Geosciences, Environment, and Resources, 2000). According to this document, 'the primary consideration for implementing marine reserves should be the needs of each biogeographical region based on protecting critical habitats'. It is becoming clear that identifying the critical habitat of cetaceans, the crucial core areas, will be the first step towards good marine management of MPAs with cetaceans.

Critical habitat is identified under the US Endangered Species Act of 1973 but, to date, has mainly been applied to land-based endangered species. The Endangered Species Act prohibits federal government agencies from allowing activities that adversely affect critical habitat. Federal permits for fishing, oil and mineral development activities within critical habitat areas must show that critical habitat will not be harmed. Taylor et al (2004) showed that designation of critical habitat under the Endangered Species Act is significantly associated with improving population trends for species listed as endangered.

Much research over the next few decades will be focused on defining, locating and understanding the parameters for cetacean critical habitat. Some of these are conventional geographical aspects and others are the more fluid oceanographic parameters such as temperature, salinity and current. For example, a recent study attempting to quantify cetacean habitat patterns in the California Current using a broad suite of oceanographic data was 48 per cent successful in predicting cetacean presence, ranging from 70 per cent for Dall's porpoises to less than 10 per cent for fin whales (Reilly et al, 1997). As understanding and measurement of the appropriate parameters becomes sharper, this predictive ability should improve. Thus, critical habitat may be defined as not only the fixed and seasonally changing boundaries of the places cetaceans habitually use, but also as the less-

> or non-geographically based conditions that more precisely define such an area as critical habitat.
>
> What we need to do now, adopting a precautionary approach, is to conserve sufficiently large marine areas that include cetacean hot spots as well as the areas that we believe may have such conditions so that we can ensure that the options for future conservation are left open.

gap by making species distribution and oceanographic data fully available on the web (see p70). Still, there is much, much more that has never been collected or written down – the local knowledge and wisdom of field biologists who come into contact with cetaceans; whale watch operators and their teams of naturalists, researchers, volunteers and others who spend long days, year in and year out, with whales and dolphins at sea; as well as those who watch from fishing boats, cruise and container ships, private yachts and other ships. Finding, processing and using this knowledge is much more difficult. This book, with its basic details on each proposed or existing MPA, should be seen as a starting point – a grass-roots document to assist with local conservation and to forge new links and connections to existing networks.

Third, cetaceans, because of their educational, scientific and economic value, as well as, in general, their need for large conservation areas, may provide a key to protecting ocean habitats and bringing large new areas under conservation management (Hoyt, 1992; Agardy, 1997; Augustowski and Palazzo, 2003). Some cetaceans are rare or endangered and this provides the most basic conservation rationale. Still, it must be kept in mind that single species, or exclusively cetacean-oriented, approaches are generally of limited value. The best conservation projects consider the entire ecosystem, monitoring and protecting animals, plants and microorganisms, as well as considering people. They integrate marine areas with coastal communities. Such projects can only come from people with broad ecological and social perspectives. Unlike ocean management on a multijurisdictional basis, in which different species are managed separately by various agencies that apply regulations independently of each other, an ecosystem-based management model provides the best approach. That means managing human interactions with ecosystems in order to protect and maintain ecosystem integrity and to minimize adverse impacts. This requires a whole ecosystem approach through ongoing scientific analysis and a commitment to adapt management practice quickly when new information signals a need for change. However, in adopting an ecological, high biodiversity-oriented approach, whales and dolphins should not be overlooked as they have been in the past. Pragmatically, cetaceans attract public awareness and tourism, and they require a large habitat area, which can protect many other species. As long as calls for cetacean MPAs are underpinned by solid ecological studies, they may well produce great gains for many more – if not most – of the species involved, including humans.

In February 1992, I attended the IV World Parks Congress (World Congress on National Parks and Protected Areas) in Caracas, Venezuela, which

Box I.2 Ecosystem-based management (EBM)

Ecosystem-based management is a regime to manage the uses and values of ecosystems with all stakeholders to maintain ecological integrity in the face of the uncertain and ever-changing nature of ecosystems.

To maintain a healthy marine ecosystem, conservation management needs to use research to uncover and take into consideration all the key links within the ecosystem, as well as manage human activities and their impacts. It is necessary to manage fisheries, chemical and noise pollution, vessel traffic, climate change, agriculture and industrial activities that produce runoff, offshore oil, gas and other mineral industries, among other things, to minimize adverse impacts and to maintain a healthy functioning ecosystem.

Ecosystem-based management as a management regime grew out of the widely acknowledged failure of single-species management, primarily of fisheries. It is a management regime that seeks to include all the relevant stakeholders. In some countries, it is called 'ecosystem management'.

Ecosystem-based management requires an ongoing research commitment to unravel and model the complex linkages in marine ecosystems. And, where knowledge is lacking, a precautionary approach should be invoked to protect the ecosystems which nourish all life and life processes in the sea. The creation of effective MPAs is an important way to exercise the precautionary principle, protecting ecosystems while research is carried out.

In recent years, those in favour of marine mammal, shark and other large predator culling, as well as whaling, have sought to use the language and ideas of ecosystem-based management to argue for so-called fisheries protection – killing predators in a misguided attempt to protect commercial fish stocks. At the same time, some fisheries lobbies have also called for research into trophic interactions which would include killing animals to learn about what they eat and how they function in an ecosystem. Ecosystem research is desperately needed, but there are benign techniques available to study what animals eat and associated trophic interactions without killing those animals or disturbing or destroying the complex ecosystems that we are trying to understand. We are a long way from the approach of the Victorian era of killing animals to study their life history and ecology. Culling marine predators and other actions that seek to manipulate, disturb or destroy the ecosystem have no place in ecosystem-based management.

In *The Politics of Ecosystem Management*, authors Cortner and Moote (1999) comment that: 'Ecosystem management breaks new ground in resource management by making the social and political basis of natural resource management goals explicit and by encouraging their development through an inclusive and collaborative decision-making process. Ecosystem management is based on an ecosystem science that integrates many disciplinary approaches and addresses the ecological issues at very large temporal and spatial scales. Given the recognized complexity and dynamic nature of ecological and social systems, ecosystem management is adaptive management, constantly being re-assessed and revised as new information becomes available.'

focused world expertise on marine protected areas as one of the main themes. From more than 100 MPA theorists and practitioners in attendance, there were papers and reports on MPAs, but only two of them even mentioned whales and dolphins. At that time, whales and dolphins were not really on the habitat conservation agenda of countries, agencies or MPA practitioners. This was due in part to the move away from the idea of protecting species – even so-called charismatic megafauna – and a determination to follow ecological criteria. It was also because the relatively recent knowledge about cetaceans and cetacean habitat was just beginning to filter through to MPA workers. The expertise on MPAs, through IUCN (the World Conservation Union) and other international agencies, drew heavily on the personnel and experience from the Great Barrier Reef Marine Park, one of the first large MPAs and the best studied and managed. The problems of protecting shallow-water coral reef habitat for species fixed to the sea floor differ from the demands of trying to protect cetacean habitat for species that sometimes cross ocean basins. This publication is aimed at filling the gaps; it is the result of my own determination and that of WDCS, the Whale and Dolphin Conservation Society, to ensure that cetaceans receive the full benefits from MPA conservation.

By the time I started researching this book in the late 1990s, things had started to improve a little for cetacean habitat protection. Australia, New Zealand, Canada and the US have all gone through extended national debates on MPAs, and part of the result has been the identification and naming of a number of MPAs that feature or include cetaceans. The World Wide Fund for Nature (WWF) Arctic Programme has fostered a circumpolar MPA network that is showing results. The European Community, through its Habitats and Species Directive and the growing Natura 2000 network, has stimulated interest and work on small cetacean reserves in Europe. And the tremendous worldwide growth of whale watching (the number of whale watchers more than doubled between 1991 and 1998 from approximately 4 million to 9 million) has led to a number of MPA proposals with built-in socioeconomic rationales (Hoyt, 2001). In April 1999, in Peter GH Evans and Erika Urquiola Pascual's presentation on 'Protected Areas for Cetaceans' at the 13th Annual Meeting of the European Cetacean Society, held in Valencia, Spain, they reported that less than 3 per cent of all the 1300 MPAs around the world had been established with cetaceans primarily in mind, and that half of all 'cetacean MPAs' had been set up in the previous ten years (Evans and Urquiola, 2001). This works out to no more than 39 MPAs with cetaceans. In the *Encyclopedia of Marine Mammals*, Reeves (2002) prepared a list of 'protected or managed areas intended, at least in part, to benefit marine mammals'; nearly 50 areas specifically feature cetacean habitat. Using wider criteria than Evans, Urquiola and Reeves, and newer research, this book reveals that there are now many more existing and proposed MPAs that include cetacean habitat – more than 500 in all (see tables in Chapter 5, pp104–447, and the Epilogue, p449). Still, we remain at the dawn of habitat protection for cetaceans. The challenge will be to obtain high-quality habitat protection for cetaceans, improving on and extending the protection in existing MPAs, and building on various cetacean conservation initiatives.

To date, most MPAs have taken their lead from land-based protected areas (PAs) in terms of size, boundaries and management strategies. With few exceptions, MPAs tend to be of similar size to PAs. Yet the world ocean occupies nearly three times as much surface area as the land. Using this ratio as a guideline, MPAs ought to be at least three times the size of, or three times more numerous than, land-based parks. The Durban Accord and Action Plan from the V World Parks Congress in 2003 stated that approximately 12 per cent of the world's land area has protected status compared to less than 1 per cent of the world ocean and adjacent seas. This 'less than 1 per cent' may indicate some progress since 1995 when Kelleher et al reported only 0.5 (half a) per cent for all MPA protection, but the sea still lags well behind the land.

The sea differs fundamentally from the land and requires new ways of thinking and new approaches for conservation. Compared with land, the ocean is not only a horizontal but also a vertical, three-dimensional world, with different biomes, and accompanying species and ecosystems, occurring at different layers of the water column to a depth of seven miles (10 km) in the deepest trenches. Vast streams of water funnel across oceans, on the surface and at depth, carrying nutrients, planktonic life, larval forms, as well as contaminants, in isolated tubes or great fans of water. Columns of water sometimes flow from the sea bed to the surface, or vice versa, shifting on a seasonal basis or in response to climatic fluctuations. Land is comparatively static, while the oceans are mobile, active environments.

In view of all this, how large should MPAs be and what level of protection should they have? The larger and better protected they are, the more they will help replenish marine species and restore ecosystems, say Callum Roberts and Julie Hawkins (2000), citing considerable evidence in their excellent *Fully Protected Marine Reserves: A Guide*. Yet there is demonstrated value even for the smaller MPAs, as long as they contain substantial portions that are highly protected core areas, rated IUCN Category I, also known as no-take reserves (Ballantine, 1995). Still, if MPAs are smaller, then it is important that there are many more of them, forming effective networks, and that the protection is much greater in each one. The problem with MPAs today is that few of them contain highly, or fully, protected core areas. The father of MPAs in New Zealand and a strong proponent of full protection, Bill Ballantine, says that we should aim for 10 per cent of the world ocean to be in fully protected MPAs. And, in a recent joint statement entitled 'Troubled Waters: A Call to Action', more than 1600 scientists and conservationists declared that we should aim for 20 per cent of the sea as fully protected MPAs by the year 2020. Other calls, mainly to address the worldwide collapse of commercial fisheries, have suggested that between 20 and 50 per cent of the sea be protected to enable overexploited fish stocks to recover. But much depends on the degree of human impact (Roberts and Hawkins, 2000). Where human impact is low, 5 per cent may be enough; where it is high, 30 per cent may not be enough. Roberts and Hawkins and many other experts feel that 20 per cent is a minimum average goal, with some areas and habitats needing less protection and others more. The consensus from MPA practitioners around the world at the V World Parks Congress was that at least 20–30 per cent of each marine and coastal habitat should be in highly protected IUCN Category I areas. Yet, according to Roberts and Hawkins (2000), only an estimated 0.0001 (one ten-thousandth, or 0.01 per

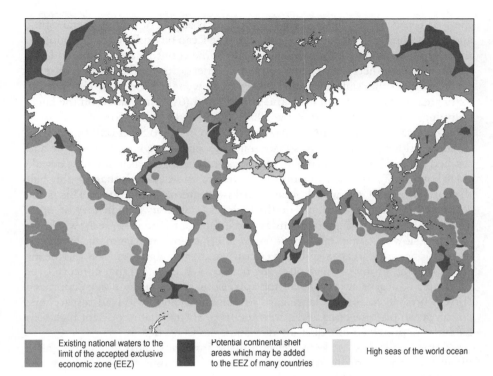

| | Existing national waters to the limit of the accepted exclusive economic zone (EEZ) | | Potential continental shelf areas which may be added to the EEZ of many countries | High seas of the world ocean |

This world map shows the limits of the exclusive economic zones (EEZs) of the nations of the world as of 2004, which generally extend from 12 nm (22.2 km) to 200 nm (371 km) of the coastline of every country. Some of these EEZs are due to expand over the next decade to up to 350 nm (649 km) depending on whether a country can prove that the continental shelf extends uninterrupted to this extended limit. The result is that more of the high seas will come under national jurisdiction in the future. Still, a substantial area remains on the high seas, and it will require international agreement and cooperation to designate MPAs with critical habitat protection for cetaceans using ecosystem-based management principles. Note that in the Mediterranean Sea and the Black Sea, there are no EEZ claims and thus the high seas start at 12 nm (22.2 km).
Source: Adapted from Malakoff (2002) and Cook and Carleton (2001).

Figure I.1 *The exclusive economic zones (EEZs) of the world ocean*

cent) of the world ocean exists in fully protected marine reserves. Even if this rough estimate is off by a power of ten, those who would protect the world ocean, restore exploited habitats and replenish depleted species have an awesome task in front of them.

The United Nations Conference on the Law of the Sea (1973–82) established territorial seas for coastal countries extending up to 12 nautical miles (22.2 km) from their coastlines. Furthermore, UNCLOS instituted the idea that countries could claim management jurisdiction of natural resources to the limits of an exclusive economic zone (EEZ) automatically extending from 12 nm (22.2 km) to 200 nm (371 km) and out to 350 nm (649 km) if the country can prove that the continental shelf extends uninterrupted. This means that the sea bed within these so-called 'EEZs' can be leased or given away as part of oil or mineral rights, and the fish and other resources in the water itself can be exploited. The countries themselves are responsible for management. Some countries have disputed EEZ claims, have conflicts with neighbouring countries or territories, or have not for one reason or other staked a claim. Others are now in the process of claiming the extra area between 200 nm (371 km) and 350 nm (649 km), based on the latest mapping, with all claims due by 2009 (Figure I.1). With continental shelf extension claims for as many as 60 countries amounting to 5 per cent of the total ocean sea floor, or 5.8 million square miles (15 million sq km), this marine and sea-bed grab will redefine national territories and the high seas in the next decade (Malakoff, 2002). Yet the situation for the rest of this decade is that roughly half the surface area of the world ocean remains in international waters. This is the so-called high seas. The culture of the high seas – with its long history of open access and its role as shipping highway and hunting ground (fish, seals, whales) – has been slow to come under national or international management. However, international laws, treaties and conventions are beginning to address the means for managing, or jointly managing, the high seas. It is hoped that concern over protecting critical cetacean habitat, and application of the precautionary approach (Box I.3) to allow for the large gaps in our knowledge, will lead researchers, conservation organizations and governments to ensure that important high-seas habitats are protected too, devising new strategies as needed.

Some scientists and conservationists involved with cetaceans have dismissed marine protected areas as being unsuitable and ineffective for protecting cetacean habitat. They have multiple objections:

- The size or scale required to protect cetaceans is not covered by conventional protected area models.
- Cetacean habitat needs are too fluid or difficult to define in terms of providing specific, defined habitat protection areas.
- Cetacean MPAs do little more than allow governments the chance to say that they are doing something for conservation when clearly they are not.

Yet, more than anything, a marine protected area for cetaceans becomes what stakeholders make of it. Better design and planning in the early stages helps – using ecosystem-based management and ensuring that critical habitats are protected. Of course, there will be limitations of size, legal recourse, and the need to share marine resources. Still, increasingly, MPAs are seen as 'works in progress' that have the capacity to improve and change. It is clear that MPAs require the support and leadership of all stakeholders – including scientists and conservationists – to make them work.

A declared MPA signifies a positive intention towards a piece of habitat. It is never an end point. In most cases, real protection requires more than the declaration or the declarer (government agency) ever imagined or intended. That is how it must be – if protection is ever to endure, adapt and function for the desired purpose. There are now, and will be in the future, many other uses for and competing interests in the sea.

Box I.3 The precautionary approach

An MPA may be seen as a demonstration of the 'precautionary approach'. This term which originated from debate over the so-called precautionary principle has been widely discussed and defined in recent years as a way to respond and act in the absence of information or scientific proof (Mayer and Simmonds, 1996). The precautionary approach considers and incorporates uncertainty to facilitate the decision-making process when knowledge or scientific proof is unavailable. It also ensures that a lack of certainty doesn't stop all action or decision-making.

The precautionary approach has become widely accepted across various scientific disciplines, in government as well as private and international arenas. Still, practical implementation of the precautionary approach in terms of conservation in general and ecosystems-based management and cetacean management in particular is still in the early stages.

A precautionary approach to decision-making for ecosystems-based management means that 'when in doubt, err on the side of conservation' (Sissenwine and Mace, 2001). It can be said that ecosystem-based MPAs and MPA networks, which assist in the management of the whole ecosystem, facilitate the multiple objectives of marine management, including the protection of habitat, biodiversity and fisheries. This approach is the best insurance against uncertainty, effectively embodying the precautionary approach.

For a precautionary approach to work, marine policy that includes ecosystem-based management and creation of MPAs must be set up to be explicitly precautionary. In addition, the assessment and periodic reassessment process must be fully precautionary. Finally, the burden of proof for showing that there are no unacceptable ecosystem risks or impacts rests with industry, including commercial fishing, shipping, mining and other resource extraction.

An example is El Vizcaino Biosphere Reserve (La Reserva de Biosfera El Vizcaíno) in México (Figure I.2). The Mitsubishi salt works lobbied the Mexican Government for expansion and was determined to push ahead with development in the gray whale's 'protected' habitat in the lagoons. Perhaps in another time, another country, the development would have proceeded without complaint. Certainly, it would have done so in México had there not been substantial protest. México's Grupo de los Cien (the Group of 100), together with international conservation groups and scientists, led a determined effort that eventually paid off when the Mitsubishi Corporation backed off. Today, the Vizcaino Biosphere Reserve is much stronger for the threats it has faced and overcome.

El Vizcaino Biosphere Reserve is a zoned MPA, assembled from several gray whale refuges dating from 1971 when Laguna Ojo de Liebre was made the first whale refuge by Presidential decree. Laguna San Ignacio, first protected in 1979, and also part of the biosphere reserve, is the core of the reserve – the only primary gray whale breeding/calving area in México that remains unaltered by industrial development. In November 1988, the entire lagoon complex was officially designated a United Nations Educational, Scientific and Cultural Organization (Unesco) Man and the Biosphere Programme (MAB) biosphere reserve and World Heritage site status followed in 1993.

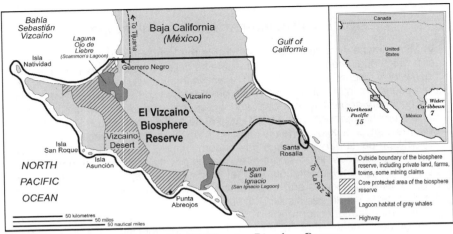

Figure I.2 *El Vizcaino Biosphere Reserve*

El Vizcaino Biosphere Reserve has a long history as a meeting place for gray whales and humans – from the whalers who almost made them extinct to the whale watchers who have presided over their return to their original numbers. It is not an MPA merely on paper. But even a 'paper MPA' can be better than no recognition, no MPA at all. Of course, there is the danger that MPAs encourage the public and government to feel that they are doing something for cetaceans and that cetacean habitat problems are being solved, when in many cases they are not. A paper MPA cannot be allowed to block real conservation efforts. Some paper MPAs were created in good faith without recognition that an effective MPA takes time and considerable effort to implement. Part of the problem is the length of time needed for the public process to develop and install a management plan. A paper MPA is at least a starting point. It is not just worth 'as little as the paper it's printed on'; it is something that represents the interest and effort of all the people who want to make the paper mean something, indeed much more even than what it may say.

Thus, the bottom line is that I believe that we must work within the system, as it were, to make protected areas work, as well as, at the same time, to do all the other things we can to assist with conservation: institute better laws; seek to develop networks of protection through international agreements, such as the Convention on the Conservation of Migratory Species of Wild Animals (CMS); ensure that the Convention on the International Trade in Endangered Species of Wild Fauna and Flora (CITES) and other trade laws and conventions are enforced; and promote education regarding cetacean hunting, incidental kills and pollution. Yet, despite my enthusiasm in general for MPAs, I will endeavour to be critical in my assessments of the proposed and existing MPAs described in the tables for each marine region in Chapter 5.

How well do the hundreds of existing MPAs in this volume conserve cetacean habitat? The answer is that, in a few limited areas, MPAs are trying to do an important job for cetaceans and cetacean habitat, but by and large, around the world, cetacean habitat, inside and outside protected areas and international sanctuaries, is little recognized, largely undescribed, marginally protected at best and being degraded every day. In some cases, the animals are being killed in conflicts with fisheries, shipping traffic or pollution of one kind or another such that any habitat protection is rendered almost worthless. In few areas is the management responsive to the seasonally changing habitat needs of cetaceans – if they are even known. It is depressing – but at least these MPAs are something to build on.

On the positive side, I see considerable ground for optimism in the numbers of people who are thinking and talking about MPAs for cetaceans. Some of this comes through the growing awareness of the need for more MPAs in general. But perhaps even more of it comes through cetacean tourism. The 10 million or more people a year who go whale watching have built a constituency for cetaceans and MPAs, particularly in the US, Canada, México and a few other countries (Table I.1). Whale watching occurs in 495 communities and each of these communities has a predictable, accessible population of cetaceans. Even though many of these areas have not been formally identified as cetacean habitat with the suite of studies necessary to confirm this, such predictable cetacean areas are a good indication of future possible cetacean MPA sites. Others, of course, are already MPAs and are using the 'brand name recognition' in various positive ways such as: Stellwagen Bank, in New England; Monterey Bay National Marine Sanctuary, in California; and Silver Bank Humpback Whale Sanctuary, which was renamed Marine Mammal Sanctuary of the Dominican Republic in 1996.

One of the most valuable ways for a marine protected area to earn money, including foreign exchange, is through sustainable tourism. In MPAs with cetaceans, whale watching has the power to bring significant revenues into nearby communities. Of course, whale or dolphin watching is successful in waters in many areas of the world that are not part of MPAs. But MPAs that feature or include cetaceans have the added attraction or lustre of a protected area designation. It gives the place where the whale watching occurs a name, an identity, a brand, rather than being an ordinary or nameless piece of ocean (IFAW, 1999). The MPA designation becomes a statement of the importance of the area and the whales that live there, as well as a way to sell whale watching and marine tourism. For those who believe that sustainable tourism is an important part of conserving marine ecosystems, MPAs provide a powerful, convincing method for marketing the marine environment.

Of course, not every part of every MPA should necessarily be open to tourism. Using the biosphere reserve model, or multi-zone approach, protected areas are commonly divided into various zones which include highly protected core areas, mixed zones allowing tourism and light use, and transition zones with more extensive use and development. Yet managing such areas can be complex. As with any MPA, managers cannot simply erect a fence around it. MPA practitioners must remain open to new management approaches and procedures, as well as scientific findings, as they arise.

Table I.1 *Top twelve whale watching countries and their MPAs with cetaceans*

Country	Whale watchers (land + sea)	Whale watching communities	Existing MPAs with cetaceans	Proposed MPAs with cetaceans	MPAs with cetaceans, proposed for expansion
1 US	4,316,537	90	18	3	1
2 Canada	1,075,304	78	9	12	3
3 Canary Islands	1,000,000	5	12	1	0
4 Australia	734,962	46	38	9	2
5 South Africa	510,000	20	18	3	1
6 New Zealand	230,000	30	2	3	1
7 Ireland	177,600	5	0	8	0
8 Brazil	167,107	14	16	1	0
9 UK	121,125	12	0	6	0
10 México	108,206	14	5	1	0
11 Japan	102,785	23	2	0	0
12 Argentina	84,164	9	17	0	2

Sources: Hoyt (2001) and data for this book. MPAs do not include national or international cetacean sanctuaries or MPAs found in overseas territories belonging to each country. Data for 2003 from the Canary Islands shows 500,000 whale watchers due to stricter controls and permits since the number in Hoyt (2001), while Australian numbers now surpass 1,500,000/year (Simon O'Connor, pers comm, 2004).

In the four-volume series *A Global Representative System of Marine Protected Areas*, the most common refrain, region by region, country by country, is that management programmes are lacking (Kelleher et al, 1995b). Since this series was written, awareness of the need for management plans – prepared through a public stakeholder process – has grown, yet, worldwide, most MPAs still require improved management to fulfil their mandates. This comment will be a common refrain in the assessments of individual MPAs in this volume. Besides more and better management, the overall feeling among cetacean scientists is that MPAs that would include cetaceans need more research, improved design, better protection and generally increased size in order to serve the often complex, wide-ranging needs of cetaceans. Some areas do address cetacean needs effectively but these are in the minority. At least, today, there is a growing realization of the importance of protecting cetacean habitat.

In Chapter 3, I will recommend a strategy for protecting cetacean habitat, presenting a step-by-step plan for making a good cetacean-based MPA. Some of the details, of course, will vary from place to place but this will provide specific goals to strive for. The key to the process will be determining the critical habitat needs of each population of each species, and ensuring overall ecosystem-based management.

Still, to the question of how well MPAs can ultimately protect cetacean habitat, there is no definitive answer. We are just learning the basics about most of the 84 species of cetaceans and their specific habitat needs. Certainly, postage-stamp size MPAs are not and will never be the answer for conserving cetaceans. And echoing concerns from various authors (Notarbartolo di Sciara and Birkun, 2002; Reeves, 2001), I agree that even large, well-designed and managed MPA networks will not be enough by themselves.

From within MPAs as well as outside them:

- We need to cut down on the amount of pollution flowing off the land and into rivers and seas.
- We need to ensure that human activities in the sea (fishing, shipping, large-scale whale watching and other marine tourism) do not make it difficult or impossible for cetaceans to live and thrive. We need good marine protection laws and good enforcement of these laws – in national as well as international waters.
- And with all these things, since we are still learning about the best management to maintain or improve an area, we need to invoke the precautionary approach often. We need to recognize that marine protection, as well as management, is an evolving, iterative process in which we learn by doing and then evaluating the results. It is particularly important that the management structures and limitations put in place at the creation of a new MPA do not restrict or hinder the evolution to better management.

The 21st century will almost certainly see unprecedented use of the world ocean for international shipping; fishing and mariculture; oil, gas and mineral development, as well as, unfortunately, its traditional use as a world dumping ground, primarily wastes from land. Much of this is fuelled by a growing world population – currently considered most likely to peak at around 9 billion in 2070 – 50 per cent more people than the 6 billion alive today (Lutz et al, 2001; Wilson, 2002). Another factor is human technological prowess that will enable exploration and development in the deep high seas. Our task, those of us who care about cetaceans, is to make a place for cetaceans in the sea – to ensure that what is rightfully theirs and has been for millennia – is well protected.

The main thing to say about MPAs is that we must start somewhere. MPAs, such as they are, provide one starting point for protecting cetacean habitat. It remains for us now to take up the challenge and build on this, to take these areas that appeal to tourism marketing boards as well as to ministries of the environment wanting to be seen to be doing something, and to extend them as needed, to help shape the policies and to participate actively in the management. Over time, it is only by taking up the challenge of each area, to fulfil the dreamed-of mandate, that we can hope to turn these into powerful, enduring marine conservation tools – not end points, but living, working tools – for local communities, for the world at large, for whales and dolphins.

1

OCEAN SANCTUARIES, MARINE RESERVES OR PARKS?

HISTORY OF MARINE PROTECTED AREAS AND CETACEANS

Glacier Bay, located in Alaska, has the distinction of being the oldest marine protected area (MPA) in the world to offer some protection to cetacean habitat. Glacier Bay National Monument was established in 1925, while Alaska was still a territory, some 34 years before it became the 49th state of the US in 1959. The national monument covered both land and adjacent water areas. The scenic beauty of the glacier and the bay were the main reasons for protection; whales were at most occasional visitors.

In the 1960s, it came to the notice of scientists that humpback whales were spending parts of the summer in and around Glacier Bay. The first humpback photographic identification (photo-ID) in Alaska was taken in Glacier Bay in 1964. The humpbacks arrive every June from tropical waters (Hawaii or México) to spend the northern summer feeding in and around the park. The popularity and high profile of humpbacks, with their bubblenet- and group-feeding activities, fuelled substantial tourism interest, as well as new scientific research and conservation initiatives, to try to give greater protection to the area by controlling fishing and tourism within the park.

The first MPA specifically aimed at protecting cetaceans was Laguna Ojo de Liebre (Scammon's Lagoon), established by the Mexican Government in January 1972 to protect a prime gray whale mating and calving lagoon. (This was the core of the area that in 1988 was expanded to include Laguna San Ignacio and part of Laguna Guerrero Negro, all of which together became El Vizcaino Biosphere Reserve.) Among cetaceans, gray whales have some of the most obvious habitat requirements because they bring their calves every winter to semi-enclosed salt-water lagoons on the west coast of Baja California,

México. Gray whales have also been among the most susceptible to decline due to human impact. In the mid 19th century, the whaler Capt Charles Scammon's discovery of the Baja lagoons almost drove gray whales to extinction in a matter of a few decades. They were easy pickings. More recently, it has become obvious that the lagoons must be protected not just from whaling but also from human encroachment due to excessive boat traffic, fishing gear and nets, pollution from local settlements, and industrial degradation of nearby land as well as marine areas.

As more has been learned about other cetaceans, marine habitats have been uncovered and new MPAs have been discussed and proposed. Cetacean scientists have discovered:

- the humpback whale's tropical mating and calving grounds in the Caribbean and in various locations across the Pacific;
- the deep water canyons off Nova Scotia where northern bottlenose whales live;
- the inshore feeding and breeding areas of bottlenose dolphins, tucuxi, Indo-Pacific hump-backed dolphins and harbor porpoises in dozens of locations; and
- the rubbing beaches and playing and resting areas of orcas around Vancouver Island in the North Pacific.

All of these discoveries have led to the creation of valuable MPAs. Most of this only began to happen, however, in the 1990s. There remains much to learn about the habitat needs of every population of every species of cetacean.

Over the years, there have also been moves, mainly within the International Whaling Commission (IWC), to declare large areas of the high seas, even entire ocean basins, as 'whale sanctuaries' (Table 1.1). In 1979, an IWC majority voted to create the Indian Ocean Sanctuary, based on a resolution put forward by the IWC representative of the Seychelles. This sanctuary, which covers nearly 4 million square miles (10 million km^2), is intended to protect whales from whaling on their mating and calving grounds as well as on some, but not all, of their feeding grounds. The precise species remit of the IWC continues to be debated, but the sanctuary is generally taken to cover only the large whales and not the small whales, dolphins and porpoises that are not listed on the IWC schedule and many of which continue to be killed in large numbers throughout the Indian Ocean as the bycatch of various fisheries (Leatherwood et al, 1984). Thus, the sanctuary designation falls short of providing comprehensive protection for cetacean habitat (Leatherwood and Donovan, 1991). However, the sanctuary has stimulated considerable research and some commercial whale watch operations. A 2002 review of the Indian Ocean Sanctuary by the IWC Scientific Committee featured a substantive paper detailing scientific work in the sanctuary (de Boer et al, 2002). Although, in general, research and conservation could be said to be at an early stage, the paper highlights the role of the Indian Ocean Sanctuary in furthering research, management plans, conservation strategies and other regional initiatives.

Table 1.1 *List of international cetacean sanctuaries and high-seas MPAs: existing and proposed*

Name of international sanctuary or MPA	Status	Location
Arctic Ring of Life International Marine Biocultural Reserve	proposed	Arctic Ocean region
Barents Sea International Marine Park	proposed	Barents Sea
Beringia Heritage International Park	proposed	Bering Strait, Bering and Chukchi seas
Celtic Shelf Break MPA	proposed	Celtic Sea, N Atlantic
Dogger Bank SAC	proposed	Dogger Bank, North Sea
Eastern Tropical Pacific Seascape	agreed 2004	existing MPAs in Costa Rica, Panamá, Colombia and Ecuador
Global Whale Sanctuary	proposed	World Ocean
Indian Ocean Sanctuary	agreed 1979	Indian Ocean
Orca Pass International Marine Stewardship Area	proposed	Georgia, Haro and Juan de Fuca straits, Puget Sound; US and Canadian waters
Pelagos Sanctuary for Mediterranean Marine Mammals	agreed 1999	Ligurian Sea (central Mediterranean – waters of Italy, France and Monaco)
South Atlantic Sanctuary	proposed	South Atlantic Ocean
South Pacific Whale Sanctuary	proposed	South Pacific Ocean
Southern Ocean Sanctuary	agreed 1994	Southern Ocean and Antarctica
Spratly Islands Marine Sanctuary	proposed	South China Sea
Wadden Sea Nature Reserve	agreed	coastal waters of Germany, Denmark and the Netherlands

Note: Table includes both existing and proposed cetacean sanctuaries and MPAs in the waters of two or more countries (transborder MPAs) and/or on the high seas.

Fifteen years after the designation of the Indian Ocean Sanctuary, in 1994, the IWC approved the Southern Ocean Whale Sanctuary, more commonly referred to as the Southern Ocean Sanctuary, which covers the waters of Antarctica (see p97). In 1999, a South Pacific Whale Sanctuary was proposed and turned down. The South Pacific proposal, as well as a subsequent South Atlantic Sanctuary proposal, have been kept alive by southern hemisphere nations. Also in 1999, Greenpeace, joined by other conservation organizations, began to circulate a petition on the Internet calling for 'a Global Whale Sanctuary by 2000' which they hoped would catch the spirit of the new millennium, but the idea was dropped after the South Pacific Whale Sanctuary was turned down for the second time.

According to Sidney Holt (2000): 'administratively speaking, it is difficult to see how [a world ocean sanctuary] would differ from the existing [IWC] moratorium [on whaling]. Both would be indefinite and require a three-fourths contrary majority to be over-turned. However, in the eyes of some, the idea of a sanctuary rather than an indefinite pause in commercial whaling may be weightier.'

Table 1.2 *List of national cetacean sanctuaries: existing and proposed*

Name of national sanctuary or MPA	Status	Location
American Samoa Whale and Turtle Sanctuary	designated 2003	EEZ limit
Australian Whale Sanctuary	designated 1980	EEZ limit of all claimed waters
Bermuda Whale Sanctuary	designated 2000	EEZ limit
Canary Islands Cetacean Marine Sanctuary	proposed 1990s	EEZ limit
Cook Islands Whale Sanctuary	designated 2001	EEZ limit
Falkland Islands Marine Mammal Sanctuary	designated 1992	EEZ limit
Fiji Whale Sanctuary	designated 2003	EEZ limit
French Polynesia Marine Mammal Sanctuary	designated 2002	EEZ limit
Guadeloupe Sanctuary, or Sanctuary of the South Antilles	proposed 2003	undetermined (EEZ limit of Guadeloupe?)
Indonesian Whale Sanctuary	proposed 1982	EEZ limit
Irish Whale and Dolphin Sanctuary	designated 1991	EEZ limit
Madeiran Marine Mammal Sanctuary	designated 1986	EEZ limit
Mexican Whale Refuge	designated 2002	EEZ limit
New Caledonia Whale Sanctuary	in effect late 1990s	EEZ limit
New Zealand Marine Mammal Sanctuary	in effect 1978	EEZ limit
Niue Whale Sanctuary	designated 2001	EEZ limit
Papua New Guinea Whale Sanctuary	designated 2002	EEZ limit
Samoa Whale, Turtle and Shark Sanctuary	announced 2002	EEZ limit
Seychelles Marine Mammal Sanctuary	designated 1979	EEZ limit
Tongan Whale Sanctuary	in effect 1989	EEZ limit
Tristan da Cunha Cetacean Sanctuary	designated 2001	EEZ limit of Tristan da Cunha and Gough I
Vanuatu Marine Mammal Sanctuary	designated 2003	EEZ limit
Whale Natural Refuge	designated 1990	EEZ limit of Ecuador

Another kind of cetacean sanctuary is the so-called 'national sanctuary', which some countries and territories have designated within their national waters, usually to the 200 nm (371 km) limit of the exclusive economic zone (EEZ) (Table 1.2). Many of these have come as part of the multinational effort to have the IWC turn the South Pacific into a whale sanctuary. The national waters and EEZs are so large in the South Pacific, with its sprawling island archipelagos, that, despite the IWC turning down the South Pacific Whale Sanctuary, more than half of the South Pacific is now covered by national cetacean sanctuaries (see Case Study 7, p188 and Box 5.9, p343).

Table 1.2 comprises a list of cetacean sanctuaries, both existing and proposed, that cover the national waters of a country or overseas territory. Since the late 1970s, 19 countries have designated their national waters as cetacean sanctuaries of one kind or another, with four other proposals still outstanding. More information about these national sanctuaries is provided under the specific marine region in Chapter 5, where the individual country or territory is found. 'In effect' status means that a sanctuary has not been declared as such, but that it has been referred to as a cetacean sanctuary and that laws protecting cetaceans in national waters are stringent enough to merit use of the word. 'Announced' means that the sanctuary has been announced but not yet formally declared.

Neither the national sanctuaries nor the large ocean sanctuaries, however, are considered marine protected areas by MPA practitioners, or under World Conservation Union (IUCN) definitions (IUCN, 1994) (see Box 1.1). Neither type of sanctuary is as important for cetacean habitat conservation as smaller, carefully regulated and managed MPAs. Still, the national and even the international sanctuaries deserve recognition, discussion and efforts for enhanced protection.

Finally, one of the hottest new areas of marine conservation, and one of the most important for cetaceans, is the move to promote and create MPAs on the high seas. In 1999, the Pelagos Sanctuary for Mediterranean Marine Mammals (originally called the Ligurian Sea Sanctuary) was designated by France, Monaco and Italy in national and international waters. This declaration, together with subsequent agreements and the management plans in preparation, effectively creates the world's first high-seas MPA. In this case, it is an important model for both transborder and high-seas cooperation and management. It establishes a positive precedent for high-seas MPAs which are being proposed in other parts of the world ocean. More discussion of this will come later (see Case Study 3, p135 and Figure 5.5, p134).

OCEAN SANCTUARIES, MARINE RESERVES OR PARKS – WHICH ONE AND WHY?

There is a bewildering array of names used for marine protected areas, or MPAs (Table 1.3). The most important definition is the one used by most MPA practitioners. An MPA is defined by the World Conservation Union (IUCN, 1994) as 'any area of intertidal or subtidal terrain, together with its overlying water and associated flora, fauna, historical and cultural features, which has been reserved by law or other effective means to protect part or all of the enclosed environment'.

The IUCN divides protected areas (PAs) into six main categories, representing a continuum from stricter protection to regimes designed for sustainable resource use:

- Category Ia – Strict nature reserve (managed mainly for science);
- Category Ib – Wilderness area (managed for wilderness protection);
- Category II – National park (managed for ecosystem protection and recreation);
- Category III – Natural monument (managed for conservation of specific natural or cultural features);

Table 1.3 *Marine protected areas – names in use around the world*

Name	Countries where in use (examples only) Notes regarding usage
Antarctic Specially Managed Area (ASMA)	Antarctic: IUCN Category V area (initiated 2002)
Antarctic Specially Protected Area (ASPA)	Antarctic: IUCN Category I area (initiated 2002)
area of special conservation interest (ASCI)	Europe: MPA created under the Bern Convention
area of special importance (ASI)	Baltic, North, Black and Mediterranean seas: MPA for small cetaceans under ASCOBANS; or for all cetaceans under ACCOBAMS
area to be avoided (ATBA)	world (states belonging to International Maritime Organization – IMO): area in which shipping is restricted; modest designation, more easily obtained than PSSAs
Baltic Sea Protected Area (BSPA)	Baltic Sea: MPA in the Baltic Sea created under HELCOM
biosphere reserve	world: UN designation for multi-zone area with architecture covering highly protected reserves, multi-use areas and transition areas; also, generic term
community fisheries conservation zone	Lao PDR: river only
country park (CP)	England, Hong Kong
fisheries resources protected area (FRPA)	China, Japan
habitat/species management area	world: IUCN Category IV
high-seas marine protected area (HSMPA)	world: MPA on the high seas
high-seas sanctuary	world: sanctuary on the high seas
international sanctuary	world: sanctuary on the high seas or involving the national waters of more than one country's waters
marine biosphere reserve	world: UN designation for biosphere reserve which includes or features marine waters (see biosphere reserve)
marine conservation area	various
marine ecological reserve	various: term implies highly protected 'no-take' area
marine park	various (Hong Kong, Jamaica, Kenya, Australia): but meaning varies, eg, in Kenya, an MPA closed to fishing. But generally a weaker designation than marine reserve. In the Australian media and public sphere, it is widely used to describe any marine protected area and is often assumed to mean a high level of protection. It can be confused with a marine zoo or aquarium which is also sometimes called a marine park
marine protected area (MPA)	world: generic term used by most MPA practitioners
Marine Protected Area (MPA)	Canada: federally protected marine area designated under the Oceans Act by the Dept of Fisheries and Oceans (DFO); South Africa: official name for all marine protected areas under the Marine Living Resources Act No 18 of 1998 (MLRA)
marine provincial park	various: emphasis on visitor or recreational use
marine reserve	various: IUCN use means strict protection (ie Category I) but meaning varies widely by country, often with legal definition, such as Belize where it is a multiple-use zoned area partly closed to extraction, or Kenya, an MPA where traditional fishing is allowed.
marine wilderness area	various: untouched marine area (see wilderness area)

Table 1.3 *continued*

Name	Countries where in use (examples only) / Notes regarding usage
marine wildlife area (MWA)	Canada: protected area created by Environment Canada under the Canada Wildlife Act
MPA (or mpa)	world: acronym in common use for 'marine protected area' (see also marine protected area)
nasjonalpark	Norway: national park
National Marine Conservation Area (NMCA)	Canada: Parks Canada marine area managed on partnership basis under federal government for sustainable use (allowing sustainable fishing but not mining, oil and gas exploration and ocean dumping) and containing smaller zones of high protection
National Marine Sanctuary (NMS)	US: MPA under flagship US MPA programme (IUCN Category VI)
national nature reserve	UK, China
national park (NP)	various: including US, Canada, Russia; IUCN Category II. Legal term in some countries such as Australia to apply to terrestrial management only (not used for MPAs)
national whale or cetacean sanctuary	various countries: large ocean area to stop hunting of whales or cetaceans to the limits of a nation's EEZ
natural monument	various including US, Russia: IUCN Category III
nature reserve, or strict nature reserve	world: IUCN Category Ia
naturreservat	Norway: nature reserve
no-take reserve	various: refers to highly protected reserve or core protected zone
parc national	France/French territories: national park
parc naturel régional	France/French territories: regional natural park
parque marino	Spain/Latin America: marine park
particularly sensitive sea area (PSSA)	world (states belonging to International Maritime Organization – IMO): areas which need special protection due to their significance for ecological, socioeconomic or scientific reasons and which may be vulnerable to damage by maritime activities
protected landscape/seascape	world: IUCN Category V
Ramsar site	world: refers to the Ramsar Convention set up to protect wetlands
raui	Cook Islands: MPA to protect fish and coral reef
reserva de biosfera	world: UN designation; Spanish for biosphere reserve
reserva marina	Spain/Latin America: marine reserve
reserva natural	Spain/Latin America: natural reserve
réserve naturelle	France: natural reserve
réserve naturelle volontaire	France: voluntary natural reserve
sanctuary, or marine sanctuary	world: large ocean area to stop hunting but may offer wider protection; can be national (to the EEZ limits) or international (high seas) or a mix of both

Name	Countries where in use (examples only) Notes regarding usage
site of community interest (SCI)	European Community: sites with EC-wide value
site of special scientific interest (SSSI)	UK, Hong Kong: usually small PA created for scientific purposes; also used in Antarctic (pre-2002)
sítio de interesse comunitário (SIC)	Portugal, Madeira, Azores: sites with EC-wide value
special area (SA)	Hong Kong: special conservation area
special area of conservation (SAC)	European Community (Habitats and Species Directive, Natura 2000 network)
special protected area (SPA)	Mediterranean: Barcelona Convention + SPA Protocol (1999); also refers to significant populations of wild birds and their respective habitats under the EU Birds Directive
specially protected area (SPA)	Antarctic: pre-2002 designation, now called ASPA
special protected area of Mediterranean interest (SPAMI)	Mediterranean: Barcelona Convention + SPA Protocol (1999)
specially reserved area (SRA)	Antarctic: pre-2002 designation, now called ASPA
strictly protected area	world: core protected zone or no-take reserve, highly protected area, IUCN Category I
sustainable use natural ecosystem	world: IUCN Category VI
wilderness area	mainly USA: untouched area; world: IUCN Category Ib
zakaznik or zakasnik	Russia: temporary wildlife reserve (IUCN Category IV)
zapovednik	Russia: scientific reserve (IUCN Category Ia)
zona de protecção especial (ZPE)	Portugal, Azores and Madeira: special area of protection (refers to significant populations of wild birds and their respective habitats under the EU Birds Directive)
zona especiais de conservação (ZEC)	Portugal, Azores and Madeira: special area of conservation (SAC) under the EU Habitats and Species Directive
zone de la conservation Ramsar	France and French territories: Ramsar conservation zone
zone de protection de biotopes	France and French territories: biotype protection zone
zone de protection spéciale	France and French territories: special protection zone (Bird Directive)

Sources: Numerous (eg Kelleher et al, 1995b; Salm and Clark, 2000)

- Category IV – Habitat/species management area (managed for conservation through management intervention);
- Category V – Protected landscape/seascape (managed for landscape/ seascape conservation and recreation); and
- Category VI – Managed resource protected area (managed for sustainable use of ecosystems).

For full definitions of each IUCN PA category, see Box 1.1. The management objectives of the various categories are charted in Table 1.4. Each IUCN protection category embraces multiple management objectives. In addition, a given MPA may contain several IUCN categories covering most if not all of the management objectives in a zoned protection scheme.

An area classified solely as Category VI is an incomplete MPA; to become a true MPA, it must contain areas of higher protection such as natural reserves or other IUCN Category I core areas to protect essential critical habitat for species found in the MPA. Unfortunately, some governments have misinterpreted the IUCN categories and have taken to declaring MPAs using Category VI alone, without including areas with a higher level of protection or any change in the management regime of the area (ie, essentially with all users and uses continuing on as they were before 'protection').

The IUCN protected area management categories have been used for MPAs as well as for the PAs for which they were originally established. Still, there is continuing debate about adapting or adjusting the categories specifically to fit MPAs because they are often comprised of various zone types and have varied, multiple objectives. Kelleher (pers comm 2003) strongly suggests keeping the categories the same. A useful refinement, suggested by Kelleher and Recchia (1998), would classify the Great Barrier Reef Marine Park, for example, as 'VI (Ia, Ib, II, III, IV)' which would show both the category VI for the overall area as well as the complex composition of the zones or core areas inside. Please note, however, that by itself the categorization of an MPA does not necessarily indicate size, design, degree of protection or even the full extent of management objectives, nor does it allow one to establish the degree of biological representation or effective management (UNEP/CBD/SBSTTA, 2003). Still, combined with other information, the categories do provide indications of the kind of protection intended. Also, note that outside the I–VI category system, there are several marine management areas that confer some measure of protection including fishing closures, restricted pollution areas, national and certain international high-seas sanctuaries. National and international high-seas sanctuaries are also covered in this book, as a category separate from MPAs.

MPA practitioners and conservationists most often use the name 'marine protected area' and the acronym 'MPA', but in practice there are numerous names used around the world, many of which have specific meanings or uses in particular countries or contexts. In some cases, as shown in Table 1.3, the same term can mean something different in another part of the world. For example, 'reserve' or 'marine reserve' is used interchangeably with MPA in some parts of the world, or it can mean an area strictly reserved, a no-take reserve, which is, in effect, the highly protected core area of a biosphere reserve-type MPA, which also includes zones to allow human uses such as marine tourism and fishing. I will adopt the more specific, highly protected area use of the word 'reserve' here, and use 'marine protected area' or 'MPA' as a generic term for a multi-use IUCN Category I–VI area (which may or may not contain reserves).

Another example of a term with disparate meanings is the word 'sanctuary'. 'Sanctuary' in the US is used to describe the flagship national marine protected areas, which are called 'US National Marine Sanctuaries'. Yet 'sanctuary' through much of the world, and in the sense I will mainly use here, refers to an animal sanctuary – an area where an animal can have a retreat, usually from hunting. To most cetacean researchers, 'sanctuary' has the connotation of a very large area which gives cetaceans protection from whaling but without either active multiple-use management or highly protected core areas. In practice, sanctuaries function mainly as national or international statements of good intention. They may forbid hunting, but for the most part there was no hunting of cetaceans in the recent histories of these sanctuaries anyway. And even as a sanctuary against hunting, there are various loopholes, such as 'scientific whaling', indigenous whaling, small cetacean hunting, and incidental kills associated with various fishing activities.

A number of papers and reports have focused on the meaning and rationale behind international whale sanctuaries (eg Holt, 2000; Leaper and Papastavrou, 2001; Phillips, 1996). Carlson (unpublished) listed 52 whale sanctuaries of all sizes, drawing on the more restricted definition of a cetacean sanctuary adopted by the IUCN/UNEP/WWF Workshop on Cetacean Sanctuaries, held in México in February 1979. This workshop defined a cetacean sanctuary as a place where:

- no cetacean may be killed, taken alive or harassed;
- the environmental qualities necessary for the biological functions that cetaceans perform there (such as breeding, calving, nursing, migrating, feeding) are not impaired by human activities;
- benign scientific research and observation by the public may be conducted under appropriate control; and
- public awareness of the significance of cetaceans in the natural environment can be enhanced (IUCN/UNEP/WWF, 1979).

Yet even this definition of sanctuary, making it into more of an MPA, is not enough to ensure true comprehensive protection for cetaceans, or for anything else, when the area to be covered is large, such as an entire ocean basin – most or all of which is on the high seas outside national waters. But the UN Convention on the Law of the Sea (UNCLOS), the Convention on Biological Diversity (CBD), the Convention on the Conservation of Migratory Species of Wild Animals (CMS) and various other fisheries agreements and conventions, all of which have come into force since this workshop, hold great promise in terms of creating effective large-scale MPAs for cetaceans. The Pelagos Sanctuary for Mediterranean Marine Mammals with its comprehensive list of conservation measures – and to a lesser extent the Indian Ocean Sanctuary and the more recent Southern Ocean Sanctuary – may provide the building blocks. But first let's look at the most effective and adaptable architecture for an MPA of any size: the biosphere reserve.

Box 1.1 IUCN management categories I–VI for protected areas (PAs), also applied to marine protected areas (MPAs)

According to the World Conservation Union (IUCN, 1994), a protected area (PA) is defined as 'an area of land and/or sea especially dedicated to the protection and maintenance of biological diversity, and of natural and associated cultural resources, and managed through legal or other effective means'. A marine protected area is defined as 'any area of intertidal or subtidal terrain, together with its overlying water and associated flora and fauna, historical and cultural features, which has been reserved by law or other effective means to protect part or all of the enclosed environment'.

The various categories of protected areas – also applicable to marine protected areas – are further defined as follows:

Category Ia – Strict nature reserve:
- a protected area managed mainly for science;
- an area of land and/or sea possessing some outstanding or representative ecosystems, geological or physiological features and/or species, available primarily for scientific research and/or environmental monitoring.

Category Ib – Wilderness area:
- a protected area managed mainly for wilderness protection;
- a large area of unmodified or slightly modified land and/or sea retaining its natural character and influence, without permanent or significant habitation, which is protected and managed so as to preserve its natural condition.

Category II – National park:
- a protected area managed mainly for ecosystem protection and recreation;
- a natural area of land and/or sea designated to (a) protect the ecological integrity of one or more ecosystems for present and future generations, (b) exclude exploitation or occupation inimical to the purposes of designation of the area, and (c) provide a foundation for spiritual, scientific, educational, recreational and visitor opportunities, all of which must be environmentally and culturally compatible.

Category III – Natural monument:
- a protected area managed mainly for conservation of specific natural features;
- an area containing one or more specific natural or natural/cultural features which is of outstanding or unique value because of its inherent rarity, representative or aesthetic qualities or cultural significance.

Category IV – Habitat/species management area:
- a protected area managed mainly for conservation through management intervention;
- an area of land and/or sea subject to active intervention for management purposes so as to ensure the maintenance of habitats and/or to meet the requirements of specific species.

Category V – Protected landscape/seascape:

- a protected area managed mainly for landscape/seascape conservation and recreation;
- an area of land, with coast and sea as appropriate, where the interaction of people and nature over time has produced an area of distinct character with significant aesthetic, ecological and/or cultural value, and often with high biological diversity. Safeguarding the integrity of this traditional interaction is vital to the protection, maintenance and evolution of such an area.

Category VI – Managed resource protected area:

- a protected area managed mainly for the sustainable use of natural ecosystems;
- an area containing predominantly unmodified natural systems, managed to ensure long-term protection and maintenance of biological diversity, while providing at the same time a sustainable flow of natural products and services to meet community needs.

Source: IUCN (1994)

BIOSPHERE RESERVES – A STRATEGY FOR THINKING ABOUT MPAS

The essence of an MPA is *protection* of marine ecosystems, species and other features. Protection is the key word. Thus, an MPA has to have at least part of its area in highly protected IUCN Category Ia or Ib reserves (see Box 1.1). It is often possible to combine two or more categories in the same MPA, as mentioned above for the Great Barrier Reef Marine Park. One of the best ways to combine categories, yet ensure protection, is through a biosphere reserve-type structure. It has proved an effective model (Batisse, 1990), even if biosphere reserves in certain parts of the world have failed to achieve their potential.

Initially applied to land only, biosphere reserves are being created in marine areas as well as in combined land and marine areas. The biosphere reserve concept is ideal for protecting cetacean critical habitat because it embraces the many existing non-invasive research programmes. At the same time, the high public profile of cetaceans stimulates the development of whale watching which, if well practised, can combine both ecotourism and an important research and educational activity. Also, habitat conservation works best when it has solid roots at the local level – in communities and among local conservation organizations, researchers and other stakeholders all working together. The biosphere reserve structure encourages this synergy.

The essence of a biosphere reserve can be summed up in the following three aspects, or roles:

1 a conservation role, including the conservation of genetic material, species and ecosystems;

Table 1.4 *The management objectives of the various IUCN MPA/PA categories*

Management objective	IUCN MPA/PA category						
	Ia	Ib	II	III	IV	V	VI
Pristine/wilderness protection	B	A	B	C	C	na	B
Scientific research	A	C	B	B	na	B	C
Species or genetic diversity	A	B	A	A	A	B	A
Environmental services	B	A	A	na	A	B	A
Natural or cultural features	na	na	B	A	C	A	C
Tourism, recreation, including commercial whale watching	na	B	A	A	C	A	C
Education	na	na	B	B	B	B	C
Sustainable use	na	C	C	na	B	B	A
Cultural attributes	na	na	na	na	na	A	B

Key
A = primary objective
B = secondary objective
C = may be applicable, but potentially not applicable
na = not applicable
Source: Adapted from Green and Paine (1997).

2   a logistic role, which means providing the interconnected facilities for research and monitoring in the framework of an internationally coordinated scientific programme; and

3   a development role, which means fostering a link with the human populations near the protected area through the rational and sustainable use of ecosystem resources.

The conservation role is primary, but the protected area must fulfil all three roles to be a biosphere reserve. An MPA that does not have highly protected core areas or does not integrate the needs of the population in surrounding regions through encouraging tourism, fishing or appropriate use of the MPA is not a biosphere reserve. Thus, for example, an IUCN Category VI reserve as interpreted by Australia for the Great Australian Bight Marine National Park, set up partly for southern right whales that spend part of every year off South Australia, cannot fit into the biosphere reserve model. Yet with greater protection through management, specifically with the addition of Category I core protection areas, it could become a real biosphere reserve. With its integration of development with conservation and logistic roles, the biosphere reserve concept is particularly suited to the often complex needs of stakeholders in the marine sector. But there do need to be highly protected core areas to make it work.

To foster these three roles, a biosphere reserve utilizes a special architecture (Figure 1.1). The simplest structure consists of one or more core areas devoted to strict nature reserve protection, surrounded by delineated buffer zones where only activities compatible with the conservation objectives can take place, which

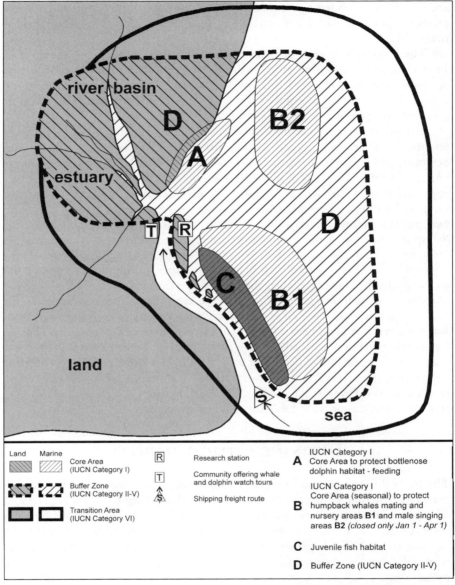

Note: This map shows the various zones of a hypothetical marine- and land-based biosphere reserve area. Core areas (IUCN Category I) are devoted to strict nature reserve protection; these are surrounded by buffer zones (Categories II–V) where activities compatible with the conservation objectives occur, and the buffer zones are in turn surrounded by a more or less defined transition zone (Category VI) which integrates the local people with sustainable resources management into the fabric of the overall reserve. To be effective, biosphere reserves must have zoned areas that are declared and enforced through legislation with management plans, formulated by the community, including all stakeholders.

Figure 1.1 *The architecture of a biosphere reserve*

are in turn surrounded by a more or less defined transition zone where there exists cooperation with local people and sustainable resources management is practised.

The geographical arrangement of the core area and the zones is adaptable. In marine areas, there might even be flexible, movable zones according to seasonal or annual changes in local conditions. Upwellings and other good fishing spots for cetaceans and humans sometimes change from year to year or even within a season.

Biosphere reserves are enshrined in international convention by the Man and the Biosphere Programme (MAB), part of the United Nations Educational, Scientific and Cultural Organization (Unesco). The first MAB report on Criteria and Guidelines for the Choice and Establishment of Biosphere Reserves appeared in 1974 (Unesco, 1974). Since the first biosphere reserves were named in 1976, hundreds of proposed and existing protected areas around the world have applied for and received the prestigious distinction of being able to use the 'biosphere reserve' name. And some protected areas that use other names, in fact, function as true biosphere reserves, demonstrating the value of the concept. It is also recognized that in a few countries, biosphere reserves are not well regarded by conservationists mainly because they fail to fulfil the protection mandate. The high profile 'biosphere reserve' designation may not always be the best protection available in a given situation for cetaceans or other species, or for ecosystems. A biosphere reserve that is just a theoretical concept and has no legislated protection is as useless as a paper reserve. Yet the biosphere reserve stands as a rugged model that has survived and been enhanced by considerable debate over the years. There are comparatively few marine biosphere reserves in name, and even fewer with cetaceans, but in the marine sector too, the biosphere reserve model can provide a valuable guiding concept.

DEFINING CRITICAL HABITAT

The most difficult scientific aspect of creating good biosphere reserves that feature or include cetaceans is defining and identifying the core areas. Core areas are equivalent to IUCN Category I, which is divided into Ia, strict nature reserves, and Ib, wilderness areas. For many species, including cetaceans, the key role of such highly protected core areas will be to preserve critical habitat while allowing for essential non-invasive scientific research and environmental monitoring.

What is critical habitat for cetaceans? The basic definition is a place or area regularly used by a cetacean group, population or species to perform tasks essential for survival and maintaining a healthy population growth rate. The most crucial areas are those where feeding, breeding and calving take place. But we must also look at the various important associated activities that precede or follow these and may require additional activity areas or habitats, or extensions of these areas. Thus, critical habitat must include areas not only for feeding, but also for hunting; not only for the act of breeding, but also for socializing and courtship; and not only for calving, but also for nursing, raising calves and resting. We may, in addition, need to include certain migration and travel corridors or 'rest stops'. Every population of every species has different, seasonally changing critical habitats for each type of behaviour. In many cases, even particular populations will have multiple critical habitats that may change as often as every few weeks, making the job of defining and prioritizing the protection of critical habitat complex and time consuming. In somewhat restricted habitats, however, researchers have been able to determine critical habitat through spatio-ecological analysis of observational data, such as in the case of bottlenose dolphins in Doubtful Sound, New Zealand (Lusseau and Higham, in press).

Cetacean critical habitat protection should extend to the critical habitat of cetacean prey as well as to areas where essential ecosystem processes occur. An area with upwellings that attracts various euphausiids and schooling fish would merit protection on both counts. Critical habitat located within proposed or existing MPAs should merit protection as a core area or areas while critical habitat located far afield may be protected in a separate reserve or ideally as part of an MPA network.

Unlike land-based critical habitat, marine critical habitat may be less fixed, especially in terms of hunting and feeding areas. Thus, it may be necessary to adjust the boundaries or zones in some seasons or years. This highlights the usefulness of the biosphere reserve model. With larger overall protection areas, it can be easier to adjust or move the boundaries of the core reserve or critical habitat zones. But how to recognize, manage and enforce flexible core areas? This surely takes more time and fine-tuning than with fixed, permanent boundaries. Still, it is less difficult than, for example, managing salmon and other fishing closures such as has been done for decades in the North American Pacific Northwest. Salmon fishing closures can vary day by day, even by the hour, with fisheries officers on site to modify and enforce the closures as needed and thus protect sufficient numbers of salmon returning to the rivers to spawn. The decline of Pacific salmon species goes back to widespread logging and damming of salmon rivers. There has been overfishing, too, and marine climatic cycles have been unfavourable to fish production (Bledsoe et al, 1989; Taylor, 2002). Critical habitat management at sea has sometimes been at fault but it is not the main cause of the decline.

Australia, a country on the leading edge of MPA declarations and also the conservation of cetaceans, has recently taken the approach of seeking to identify critical habitat for marine species, including whales and dolphins, before awarding formal habitat protection (Prideaux, 2003c; pers comm 2002) (see Box 5.12 on p419). This approach, as long as it does not become an excuse for delay, could significantly increase the potential value of future MPAs with cetaceans.

A suggested management regime for critical habitat core areas for cetaceans was outlined by Simmonds (1994). This useful proposal recognized the value of strict protection as well as zoning for cetacean protected areas, although the principles of stakeholder involvement are not as well developed as in the

BOX 1.2 ACTIVITIES EXCLUDED FROM CORE AREAS AND BUFFER ZONES: A PROPOSED MANAGEMENT REGIME FOR CETACEAN PROTECTED AREAS

These suggestions, adapted from Simmonds (1994), could provide a starting point for discussions with stakeholders regarding the critical habitat core areas and surrounding buffer zones of marine protected areas, including marine reserves and biosphere reserves.

A. In the core area(s), or inner zone(s), of full protection

All activities permitted within critical habitat core protection areas should be assessed and governed according to core conservation needs. Core areas or zones are usually equivalent to IUCN Category Ia or Ib. The following are guidelines:

- All fisheries activity should be prohibited.
- Commercial and military traffic should be prohibited.
- Organized whale/dolphin watching should be prohibited or limited and regulated under an agreed plan of management and subject to periodic review. Suggestions have been made to limit whale watching to one boat or aircraft for each core protected area and to require a licence subject to periodic review, but the extent of whale watching permitted must be agreed on a case-by-case basis depending on status of the population and species, the kind of critical habitat behaviour that the cetaceans engage in and the intensity of whale watching in adjacent areas, among other factors. In most cases, core areas should be seen as refuges where cetaceans can engage in their activities with no, or virtually no, possibility of disruption.
- Pleasure vessels must be prevented from harassing cetaceans. Vessels should be prohibited from approaching closer than 1650 ft (500 m) – although the animals do sometimes approach vessels (special procedures to mitigate disruption should then apply). Aircraft should not operate within a 1000-foot (300 m) radius of a cetacean.
- All conservation research activities and research vessels operating in the area should be regulated under an agreed plan of management and subject to periodic review. Exploration or extractive research in the zone should generally be prohibited.
- No discharges (industrial or domestic, vessel- or land-based) should be permitted directly into the zone or into waters draining into it.
- The extraction of, or exploration for, minerals or other large-scale industrial activities should be prohibited.
- Any and all other human interactions with cetaceans in the zone should be prohibited or regulated under an agreed plan of management and subject to periodic review.

B. In the buffer zone

All activities permitted within the buffer zone should be assessed and governed according to the requirements of the specific core protection area(s). This might mean that in some buffers certain uses would be permitted, whereas in others they might not be appropriate. Buffer zones are equivalent to IUCN Categories II–VI areas. The following are guidelines:

- All fisheries activity should be strictly controlled – gill nets should be prohibited and dredging, trawling and other fishery activity should be permitted only if regulated under an agreed plan of management and subject to periodic review. The situation with respect to other large-scale fisheries operations will be subject to review as further evidence about bycatch becomes available.
- Other commercial and military traffic should be regulated under an agreed plan of management, subject to periodic review.
- Organized whale/dolphin watching should be regulated under an agreed plan of management and subject to periodic review.
- Pleasure vessels must be prohibited from harassing cetaceans. Vessels should not approach closer than 1650 ft (500 m) – although the animals do sometimes approach vessels (special procedures to mitigate disruption should then apply). Aircraft should not operate within a 1000-foot (300 m) radius of a cetacean.
- All research activities and research vessels operating in the area should be regulated under an agreed management plan, subject to periodic review.
- No new discharges (industrial or domestic, vessel- or land-based) should be permitted directly into the zone or into waters draining into it if there is a possibility that these discharges will have an impact on the core protection zone. All existing discharges must comply fully with national and international legislation but special efforts should be made to minimize any impact on the core protection zone.
- Activities relating to mineral extraction and exploration should, if permitted, be regulated under an agreed plan of management and subject to periodic review.
- Any and all other human interactions with cetaceans in the zone should be prohibited or regulated under an agreed plan of management and subject to periodic review.

Adapted from Simmonds (1994) with permission, incorporating the suggestions of Mark Simmonds and Margi Prideaux (WDCS).

biosphere reserve model. Nevertheless, this management regime provides a useful basis upon which to outline our current understanding of core areas and buffer zones and the kinds of activity which may be permitted, regulated or excluded in each (Box 1.2).

NETWORKS OF MPAS

In recent years, increasing attention has been paid to the idea of developing networks of MPAs, rather than focusing simply on individual areas (Commission on Geosciences, Environment and Resources, 2000). Both the World Summit on Sustainable Development (Johannesburg, 2002) and the V World Parks Congress (Durban, 2003) have called for the development of a global system of MPA networks by 2012. This is partly in response to the postage-stamp nature of many MPAs. Especially if MPAs are small, but even if they are fairly large, there will need to be a number of them to forge an effective conservation plan for a species, as well as for ecosystems. Well-planned networks will take into account the promotion of genetic, species and ecosystem diversity. Networks also accommodate the needs of many ocean species that travel during their life histories, such as cetaceans which migrate or, in some cases, travel in search of food or mates. In addition, cetaceans depend on food webs whose critical habitats may be widely separated.

MPA networks help deliver the mandate of ecosystem-based management as they allow essential ecosystem processes and the important features of complex marine ecosystems to be protected. Still, the network idea is fairly new, especially as applied to cetaceans. In May 2000, in the US, a Presidential Executive Order directed the National Oceanic and Atmospheric Administration (NOAA), in cooperation with the Department of the Interior, to develop a national system of MPAs and to plan MPA networks in US coastal waters. This new focus on MPA networks was comprehensively reviewed by the Commission on Geosciences, Environment, and Resources (2000) in a report from the National Research Council. The commission recognized that the network approach has key implications for cetaceans as well as fish stocks, many of which require a network approach for best conservation. Thinking globally, the V World Parks Congress in 2003 envisioned building a worldwide system of marine and coastal protected area networks (for the full text of its Recommendation 5.22, see www.iucn.org/themes/wcpa/wpc2003/pdfs/ outputs/recommendations/approved/english/html/r22.htm).

To date, there are few attempts to develop networks of MPAs for cetaceans. Two that are notable, though not specifically for cetaceans, are in the Australian state of Victoria and in the Channel Islands of California, US. In 2002, both Victoria and California approved plans for representative networks of MPAs in their waters; Victoria will have 24 marine national parks and sanctuaries in its network, while the Channel Islands includes ten marine reserves and two marine conservation areas (*MPA News*, 2003a, 2003b). Victoria has 5.3 per cent of state waters set aside as 'no-take' areas (equivalent to highly protected IUCN Category I) while the Channel Islands National Marine Sanctuary strictly protects a minimum of 10 per cent of its 174 mi^2 (450 km^2) area, but if the proposed federal expansion to 425 mi^2 (1100 km^2) occurs, then the no-take area will expand to 25 per cent of the total area. (The percentage of California state waters that are highly protected has not been calculated, but it is considerably less than 25 per cent.)

Another fledgling attempt at an MPA network in the US and Canada can be found in the species recovery plans and habitat protection zones for North Atlantic right whales in which various MPAs, critical habitat and conservation areas are being seen as fulfilling vital aspects of the species' habitat protection needs during its annual migration around the western North Atlantic. Expert critical comment on these areas, with recommendations for improvement, can be found in Recchia et al (2001). Yet another networking attempt is in the initial overtures by sanctuary managers to link the Gerry E Studds Stellwagen Bank National Marine Sanctuary (off New England, in the US) with the Marine Mammal Sanctuary of the Dominican Republic, so that a key humpback whale feeding area in the north is linked to the key breeding area in the Caribbean, although both areas have fallen short of providing IUCN Category I critical habitat protection. Finally, in the European Community, the Natura 2000 Habitats and Species Directive is designed to provide a European network of MPAs for various habitats and species called special areas of conservation (SACs). To date, bottlenose dolphins are the main cetaceans included, so the idea of a real MPA network remains elusive for all other European cetacean species. Also, there are no IUCN Category I critical habitat designations. It remains to be seen whether the dolphin (and a few porpoise) SACs, many of which are in effect IUCN Category VI multiple-use management areas, will be sufficient to protect cetacean habitat in this region. Still, this big-picture, unified approach is an encouraging start. It is hoped that in these initial attempts to create MPA networks, there are the seeds for much more effective marine habitat conservation for the benefit of cetaceans and all marine species and ecosystems. (For more discussion on ecosystem-based management and MPA networks, see pp71–74.)

HIGH-SEAS MPAS

A final, important category to consider is that of MPAs on the high seas. These are not the ocean-wide sanctuaries related mainly to stopping whaling. Even so, the IWC whale sanctuaries provide a useful precedent of nations working together to agree upon conservation on the high seas. And of course, it would be technically possible for future IWC agreements to embrace, or even themselves create, highly protected high-seas MPAs, though current divisions in the IWC make this unlikely in the near future. In any case, among MPA practitioners, there is a growing movement to create real MPAs at sea that could be biosphere reserves with critical habitat core areas created as part of an MPA network. The main reason why few MPAs have been proposed on the high seas is because the high seas are located outside the 200 nm (371 km) EEZ limits of the countries of the world where no single state or authority has the power to designate MPAs, adopt management schemes or enforce any sort of compliance (see Figure I.1 on p7). Yet of the 84 species of cetaceans, some 31 species probably spend most of their lives on the high seas – including breeding, calving, nursing, feeding and migration. About 35 others have essential critical habitat in both high seas and national waters. Thus 79 per cent of all cetacean species have a strong high seas presence (see Table 1.5). In order to protect the critical habitat of cetaceans, and to follow the dictates of such international agreements as the United Nations Convention on the Law of the Sea (UNCLOS), the Convention on Biological Diversity (CBD) and the Convention on the Conservation of Migratory Species of Wild Animals (CMS) and its regional agreements, we must take steps to create MPAs in international waters.

In 1989, Maxine McCloskey presented a pioneer paper at the Thirteenth Northwest Wilderness Conference in Seattle, Washington, on the need to protect marine wilderness on the high seas. She updated and expanded this paper for the 1992 IV World Parks Congress in Caracas, Venezuela (McCloskey,

Table 1.5 *Cetacean species and the location of their critical habitat*

Cetacean species	Habitat inside 200 nm (371 km) national waters	Habitat on the high seas
1 North Atlantic right whale, *Eubalaena glacialis*	Breeding, calving, nursing, feeding, migration	Some migration and other activity
2 North Pacific right whale, *Eubalaena japonica*	Breeding, calving, nursing, feeding, migration	Some migration and other activity
3 southern right whale, *Eubalaena australis*	Breeding, calving, nursing, feeding, migration	Some migration and other activity
4 bowhead whale, *Balaena mysticetus*	Breeding, calving, nursing, feeding, migration	Some activity
5 pygmy right whale, *Caperea marginata*	Little known: some activity	Little known: some activity
6 gray whale, *Eschrictius robustus*	Breeding, calving, nursing, feeding, migration	Some activity
7 humpback whale, *Megaptera novaeangliae*	Breeding, calving, nursing, feeding, migration	Migration and some other activity
8 minke whale, *Balaenoptera acutorostrata*	Breeding, calving, nursing, feeding, migration	Breeding, calving, nursing, feeding, migration
9 Antarctic minke whale, *Balaenoptera bonaerensis*	Breeding, calving, nursing, feeding, migration	Breeding, calving, nursing, feeding, migration
10 Bryde's whale, *Balaenoptera brydei*	Breeding, calving, nursing, feeding, migration	Breeding, calving, nursing, feeding, migration
11 pygmy Bryde's whale, *Balaenoptera edeni*	Breeding, calving, nursing, feeding, migration	Breeding, calving, nursing, feeding, migration
12 sei whale, *Balaenoptera borealis*	Mainly feeding; otherwise unknown	Breeding, calving, nursing, feeding, migration
13 fin whale, *Balaenoptera physalus*	Mainly feeding; otherwise unknown	Breeding, calving, nursing, feeding, migration
14 blue whale, *Balaenoptera musculus*	Mainly feeding; otherwise unknown	Breeding, calving, nursing, feeding, migration
15 sperm whale, *Physeter macrocephalus*	Some breeding, calving, nursing, feeding	Breeding, calving, nursing, feeding
16 pygmy sperm whale, *Kogia breviceps*	Some breeding, calving, nursing, feeding	Breeding, calving, nursing, feeding
17 dwarf sperm whale, *Kogia sima*	Some breeding, calving, nursing, feeding	Breeding, calving, nursing, feeding
18 Cuvier's beaked whale, *Ziphius cavirostris*	Some breeding, calving, nursing, feeding	Breeding, calving, nursing, feeding
19 Arnoux's beaked whale, *Berardius arnuxii*	Probably some activity	Little known; most breeding, calving, nursing, feeding
20 Baird's beaked whale, *Berardius bairdii*	Some activity	Little known; most breeding, calving, nursing, feeding
21 Shepherd's beaked whale, *Tasmacetus shepherdi*	Probably some activity	Little known; probably most breeding, calving, nursing, feeding
22 Indo-Pacific beaked whale, *Indopacetus pacificus*	Probably some activity	Little known; probably most breeding, calving, nursing, feeding

Cetacean species	Habitat inside 200 nm (371 km) national waters	Habitat on the high seas
23 northern bottlenose whale, *Hyperoodon ampullatus*	Breeding, calving, nursing, feeding	Breeding, calving, nursing, feeding
24 southern bottlenose whale, *Hyperoodon planifrons*	Breeding, calving, nursing, feeding	Little known; most breeding, calving, nursing, feeding; migration
25 Hector's beaked whale, *Mesoplodon hectori*	Probably some activity	Little known; probably most breeding, calving, nursing, feeding
26 Perrin's beaked whale, *Mesoplodon perrini*	Probably some activity	Little known; probably most breeding, calving, nursing, feeding
27 True's beaked whale, *Mesoplodon mirus*	Probably some activity	Little known; probably most breeding, calving, nursing, feeding
28 Gervais' beaked whale, *Mesoplodon europaeus*	Probably some activity	Little known; probably most breeding, calving, nursing, feeding
29 Sowerby's beaked whale, *Mesoplodon bidens*	Probably some activity	Little known; probably most breeding, calving, nursing, feeding
30 Gray's beaked whale, *Mesoplodon grayi*	Some activity	Little known; most breeding, calving, nursing, feeding
31 pygmy beaked whale, *Mesoplodon peruvianus*	Probably some activity	Little known; probably most breeding, calving, nursing, feeding
32 Andrew's beaked whale, *Mesoplodon bowdoini*	Probably some activity	Little known; probably most breeding, calving, nursing, feeding
33 spade-toothed whale, *Mesoplodon traversii*	Probably some activity	Little known; probably most breeding, calving, nursing, feeding
34 Hubbs' beaked whale, *Mesoplodon carlhubbsi*	Probably some activity	Little known; probably most breeding, calving, nursing, feeding
35 ginkgo-toothed beaked whale, *Mesoplodon ginkgodens*	Probably some activity	Little known; probably most breeding, calving, nursing, feeding
36 Stejneger's beaked whale, *Mesoplodon stejnegeri*	Probably some activity	Little known; probably most breeding, calving, nursing, feeding
37 strap-toothed whale, *Mesoplodon layardii*	Probably some activity	Little known; probably most breeding, calving, nursing, feeding
38 Blainville's beaked whale, *Mesoplodon densirostris*	Some activity	Little known; most breeding, calving, nursing, feeding
39 Ganges and Indus River dolphins, *Platanista gangetica*	Breeding, calving, nursing, feeding, migration – rivers	Not present
40 Amazon River dolphin, or boto, *Inia geoffrensis*	Breeding, calving, nursing, feeding – rivers	Not present
41 Yangtze River dolphin, or baiji, *Lipotes vexillifer*	Breeding, calving, nursing, feeding – rivers	Not present
42 La Plata dolphin, or franciscana, *Pontoporia blainvillei*	Breeding, calving, nursing, feeding – rivers and inshore	Rarely present
43 beluga, *Delphinapterus leucas*	Breeding, calving, nursing, feeding, migration	Rarely present
44 narwhal, *Monodon monoceros*	Breeding, calving, nursing, feeding, migration	Some activity
45 Commerson's dolphin, *Cephalorhynchus commersonnii*	Breeding, calving, nursing, feeding – inshore	Not present

Table 1.5 *continued*

Cetacean species	Habitat inside 200 nm (371 km) national waters	Habitat on the high seas
46 Chilean dolphin, *Cephalorhynchus eutropia*	Breeding, calving, nursing, feeding – inshore	Not present
47 Heaviside's dolphin, *Cephalorhynchus heavisidii*	Breeding, calving, nursing, feeding – inshore	Not present
48 Hector's dolphin, *Cephalorhynchus hectori*	Breeding, calving, nursing, feeding – inshore	Not present
49 rough-toothed dolphin, *Steno bredanensis*	Some activity	Little known; most breeding, calving, nursing, feeding
50 Atlantic hump-backed dolphin, *Sousa teuszii*	Breeding, calving, nursing, feeding – inshore	Not present
51 Indo-Pacific hump-backed dolphin, *Sousa chinensis*	Breeding, calving, nursing, feeding – inshore	Not present
52 tucuxi, *Sotalia fluviatilis*	Breeding, calving, nursing, feeding – rivers and inshore	Not present
53 bottlenose dolphin, *Tursiops truncatus*	Most breeding, calving, nursing, feeding	Some breeding, calving, nursing, feeding
54 Indo-Pacific bottlenose dolphin, *Tursiops aduncus*	Most breeding, calving, nursing, feeding	Some breeding, calving, nursing, feeding
55 pantropical spotted dolphin, *Stenella attenuata*	Breeding, calving, nursing, feeding	Breeding, calving, nursing, feeding
56 Atlantic spotted dolphin, *Stenella frontalis*	Breeding, calving, nursing, feeding	Breeding, calving, nursing, feeding
57 spinner dolphin, *Stenella longirostris*	Breeding, calving, nursing, feeding	Breeding, calving, nursing, feeding
58 Clymene dolphin, *Stenella clymene*	Breeding, calving, nursing, feeding	Breeding, calving, nursing, feeding
59 striped dolphin, *Stenella coeruleoalba*	Breeding, calving, nursing, feeding	Breeding, calving, nursing, feeding
60 short-beaked common dolphin, *Delphinus delphis*	Breeding, calving, nursing, feeding	Breeding, calving, nursing, feeding
61 long-beaked common dolphin, *Delphinus capensis*	Breeding, calving, nursing, feeding	Breeding, calving, nursing, feeding
62 Fraser's dolphin, *Lagenodelphis hosei*	Breeding, calving, nursing, feeding	Breeding, calving, nursing, feeding
63 white-beaked dolphin, *Lagenorhynchus albirostris*	Breeding, calving, nursing, feeding	Breeding, calving, nursing, feeding
64 Atlantic white-sided dolphin, *Lagenorhynchus acutus*	Breeding, calving, nursing, feeding	Breeding, calving, nursing, feeding
65 Pacific white-sided dolphin, *Lagenorhynchus obliquidens*	Breeding, calving, nursing, feeding	Breeding, calving, nursing, feeding
66 dusky dolphin, *Lagenorhynchus obscurus*	Most breeding, calving, nursing, feeding	Some breeding, calving, nursing, feeding
67 Peale's dolphin, *Lagenorhynchus australis*	Most breeding, calving, nursing, feeding	Probably some breeding, calving, nursing, feeding

Cetacean species	Habitat inside 200 nm (371 km) national waters	Habitat on the high seas
68 hourglass dolphin, *Lagenorhynchus cruciger*	Some activity	Most breeding, calving, nursing, feeding
69 northern right whale dolphin, *Lissodelphis borealis*	Some breeding, calving, nursing, feeding	Probably most breeding, calving, nursing, feeding
70 southern right whale dolphin, *Lissodelphis peronii*	Some breeding, calving, nursing, feeding	Probably most breeding, calving, nursing, feeding
71 Risso's dolphin, *Grampus griseus*	Breeding, calving, nursing, feeding	Breeding, calving, nursing, feeding
72 melon-headed whale, *Peponocephala electra*	Breeding, calving, nursing, feeding	Breeding, calving, nursing, feeding
73 pygmy killer whale, *Feresa attenuata*	Breeding, calving, nursing, feeding	Breeding, calving, nursing, feeding
74 false killer whale, *Pseudorca crassidens*	Breeding, calving, nursing, feeding	Breeding, calving, nursing, feeding
75 orca, or killer whale, *Orcinus orca*	Breeding, calving, nursing, feeding; long-range foraging and migratory movements	Breeding, calving, nursing, feeding; long-range foraging and migratory movements
76 long-finned pilot whale, *Globicephala melas*	Breeding, calving, nursing, feeding	Probably most breeding, calving, nursing, feeding
77 short-finned pilot whale, *Globicephala macrorhynchus*	Breeding, calving, nursing, feeding	Probably most breeding, calving, nursing, feeding
78 Irrawaddy dolphin, *Orcaella brevirostris*	Breeding, calving, nursing, feeding – rivers and inshore	Not present
79 finless porpoise, *Neophocaena phocaenoides*	Breeding, calving, nursing, feeding	Not present
80 harbor porpoise, *Phocoena phocoena*	Breeding, calving, nursing, feeding	Not usually present
81 vaquita, *Phocoena sinus*	Breeding, calving, nursing, feeding – inshore	Not present
82 Burmeister's porpoise, *Phocoena spinipinnis*	Breeding, calving, nursing, feeding	Not present
83 spectacled porpoise, *Phocoena dioptrica*	Breeding, calving, nursing, feeding	Not present
84 Dall's porpoise, *Phocoenoides dalli*	Breeding, calving, nursing, feeding	Breeding, calving, nursing, feeding

Note: Cetacean species are listed according to Rice (1998), with amendments from the IWC Scientific Committee (IWC, 2001), Perrin et al (2002), Dalebout et al (2002), van Helden et al (2002) and Reeves et al (2003). Habitat assessments are derived from Klinowska (1991), Jefferson et al (1993), Reeves et al (2002, 2003) and information obtained for this volume in Chapter 5: Habitat protection for cetaceans around the world: status and prospects. A more detailed listing of cetacean species, subspecies and key populations with IUCN Red List assessments and distribution according to marine region is in Chapter 2, pp59–65.

1992, 1997). She was adapting the idea of land-based wilderness as envisioned by the US Wilderness Act (1973), which has set aside large land areas in pristine form. She did not address the political implications of high-seas MPAs or go into detail regarding mechanisms for conservation, but she chaired a working group that initiated scientific discussion on the idea of high-seas MPAs.

In October 2000, at IUCN's Second World Conservation Congress held in Amman, Jordan, Resolution 2.20 was adopted, calling on the Director General of the IUCN to work with members and multilateral agencies to explore an appropriate range of tools, including high-seas MPAs, with the objective of implementing effective protection, restoration and sustainable use of biodiversity and ecosystem processes on the high seas. The IUCN Amman Resolution on High Seas MPAs also asked national governments, conservation organizations and international agencies to improve the integration of established multilateral agencies and existing legal mechanisms in order to identify high-seas areas suitable for collaborative management action and to reach agreement by consensus on regimes for their conservation and management.

From these seeds, a movement has arisen to create MPAs on the high seas. In an effort to clarify and advance matters, in February 2001, a broad group of scientists and legal experts met for five days in Vilm, Germany, for the 'Expert Workshop on Managing Risks to Biodiversity and the Environment on the High-seas, including Tools such as Marine Protected Areas – Scientific Requirements and Legal Aspects'. The papers from this workshop explore new ways to think and act on the high seas in order to put into practice the principles of UNCLOS, CBD and other international agreements, using high-seas MPAs as a tool (eg Cripps and Christiansen, 2001; Fonteneau, 2001; Gjerde, 2001; Kimball, 2001; Osborn, 2001; Platzoder, 2001; Thiel, 2001; Warner, 2001; summary and analysis in de Fontaubert, 2001.)

The driving force for high-seas conservation through MPAs is the disastrous state of the world's fishing industry. According to UN Food and Agriculture Organization (FAO) statistics, 69 per cent of world fish stocks are fully exploited, depleted or slowly recovering. As of 2001, 10 per cent of the world fish catch was being harvested on the high seas, with 90 per cent within the national waters (to the EEZ limits) of coastal states. Since the Law of the Sea came into force in 1994, high-seas fishing has started moving from what is now a country's EEZ to areas immediately outside the 200 nm (371 km) limit. This has intensified the call for protective measures for pelagic fish stocks.

Besides fishing, high-seas threats include the potential exploitation of polymetallic nodules, cold seeps and pockmarks, as well as gas hydrates (Baker et al, 2001). For many years, the abyssal plains and deep-sea trenches beneath the high seas have been used as a dumping ground for nuclear and other hazardous waste. A key protective measure and means of management for future conservation could be the high-seas MPA. An MPA is a concrete demonstration of the precautionary approach (see Box I.3, p9). According to the 2001 high-seas workshop in Vilm, Germany, international law through the United Nations Law of the Sea certainly does not discourage countries from getting together to set up high-seas MPAs. On the contrary, the scientists and experts argued that the provisions for conservation of marine resources in UNCLOS and in the widely adopted CBD demand that countries take action that would include the creation of MPAs. There are many other provisions from fishing and other international conventions that can be used to help make high-seas MPAs work. What is needed is the political will – and stamina – to push through international agreements for such protection, and then to work to get them accepted and to enforce them.

The Pelagos Sanctuary for Mediterranean Marine Mammals, which was designated in late 1999 by Italy, France and Monaco, has set an important, exciting precedent (Notarbartolo di Sciara et al, 1992; Notarbartolo di Sciara, 2000). Here we have an area in the national waters and on the high seas off Italy, France and Monaco. (The EEZs in the Mediterranean have not been declared, making everything outside of 12 nm [22.2 km] from the coasts high seas.) It took some ten years to get the countries to agree on the sanctuary and sign the papers. The preparation of the management plan is underway. It could take several years for this to start to function as a valuable conservation tool. The cetaceans of the Mediterranean are important of course, but no less important may be the worldwide significance of the designation and the implications for other potential areas and cooperation by states. For these reasons, it is hoped that the management plan put in place will employ ecosystem-based management principles and be effective in terms of identifying and protecting cetacean critical habitat core areas as well as responsive to new data and management strategies as they arise in future.

Summing up key provisions of the United Nations Convention on the Law of the Sea relevant to the high seas, Charlotte de Fontaubert (2001) says that 'by combining the fisheries regime and the protection of the marine environment component [of UNCLOS], states are … in a position to take strong conservation measures on the high seas, as long as they cooperate with other states, show that the measures they want to take would enhance the conservation of resources and that they are based on the best scientific evidence available.'

Margi Prideaux (2003a) also emphasizes the role of UNCLOS, arguing that it has already established a mandate for high-seas protected areas through Article 194 which stipulates measures to protect 'rare and fragile ecosystems as well as the habitat of depleted, threatened or endangered species and other forms of marine life'; this is further reinforced by the Article 197 requirement for cooperation on a global basis.

Another key treaty, the Convention on Biological Diversity (CBD), has, with the work of its scientific advisors, the Subsidiary Body on Scientific, Technical and Technological Advice (SBSTTA), planned a programme of work to enhance marine conservation, including the creation of high-seas MPAs. De Fontaubert (2001) says that the CBD presents 'a strong mandate for the establishment of MPAs on the high seas, constrained only by the need to negotiate with other parties in areas beyond national jurisdiction'. Still, de Fontaubert believes that the United Nations Conference on Environment and Development statement, UNCED: Agenda 21, 'may well be the most important soft-law instrument that recognizes the possibility of enacting MPAs on the high seas.'

CMS is also becoming as an important instrument for high-seas critical habitat protection, according to Prideaux (2003b), especially with the harmonization of work plans between CBD and CMS. According to plans put forward during the 5th CBD Conference of the Parties, the work of CMS and migratory species would be integrated into the work programme and implementation of CBD 'with regard to, inter alia, the ecosystem approach; the Global Taxonomy Initiative; indicators, assessments and monitoring; protected areas; public education and awareness; and sustainable use, including tourism'.

CMS has a useful 'threat mitigation trend' running through its existing work (Prideaux, 2003b). CMS agreements specifically address multiple issues with on-the-ground programmes and scientific investigation. In addition, CMS focuses on the establishment of regional agreements through which conservation work proceeds, which increases its adaptability to regional circumstances. If high-seas and multijurisdictional cetacean critical habitats are to be protected within a biosphere reserve model, CMS with CBD and CMS regional agreements may be the most appropriate framework to develop this regime (Prideaux, 2003b, 2003c).

Besides all of the above approaches (UNCLOS, CBD, CMS, UNCED: Agenda 21, international whale sanctuaries and the precautionary approach), there is a range of other high-seas conventions, treaties and fishing agreements which provide precedents and offer promise for the creation of effective high-seas MPAs for cetaceans, fish and various resources. In sum, there is no simple legal framework covering high-seas waters outside national jurisdictions. Still, there exists a useful if complex mosaic of different treaties, action programmes and other instruments that can be said to comprise the legal regime of the high seas. It includes global and regional conventions, legally binding documents and 'soft law' (de Fontaubert, 2001). According to de Fontaubert, the international legal regime applicable to the high seas strongly advocates cooperation among governments, does not prohibit and in some ways encourages the establishment of MPAs and is subject to evolution including the possibility that high-seas MPAs could be endorsed more explicitly and promoted in future through the existing agreements.

A full list of legal instruments applicable to the high seas, as well as to the creation of MPAs within national waters, is detailed in Table 1.6. It is important to recognize that those states that are not party to these various conventions and treaties are not bound by them. Yet most states now recognize or are party to at least two of the important conventions for future high-seas MPA development: the United Nations Convention on the Law of the Sea (UNCLOS) and the Convention on Biological Diversity (CBD).

It is important to recognize that those states that are not party to these various conventions and treaties are not bound by them, although most states now recognize or are party to UNCLOS and the CBD.

The main hope for the future of MPAs on the high seas is that a few bold, brave states will get together on their own, regionally or through one of these conventions or treaties, and proceed to designate a few high-seas MPAs. The pioneer states must show that they are willing to restrict their own uses on the high seas in order that others will follow suit (de Fontaubert, 2001). Of course, there is also the danger that certain states will take advantage of the conservation measures of other states by exploiting the good fishing or whaling areas which have been identified, but this should not preclude conservation moves.

Ensuring compliance and providing enforcement capability for MPAs on the high seas will be exponentially more difficult than enforcing provisions for existing coastal MPAs (*MPA News*, 2003c). It is not just a question of being outside of national jurisdictions, but also of the sheer distance from land, in most cases at least 200 nm plus (371 km). For this reason, Carl Gustav Lundin, head of the IUCN Global Marine Programme, thinks that a combination of employing the latest satellite technology, as well as harnessing the capability of the underutilized national navies, could provide the necessary combination of good monitoring and enforcement. To do this, Lundin envisions the mass deployment of satellite transponders on the high-seas fishing fleet. Such transponders, already in use in national waters, send a signal from boat to shore indicating the location and general activity pattern of the vessel. Fishing boats entering closed areas could be apprehended – on site by navies, or later back in port.

Of course, such a programme would require international agreements. Kristina Gjerde, IUCN Global Marine Programme advisor, estimates that it may take more than five years to negotiate high-seas compliance mechanisms through UNCLOS and other agreements. Equally important, however, will be the abolition of flags of convenience for fishing and other vessels which opportunistically seek to dodge international agreements (*MPA News*, 2003c).

It is also recognized that the application of various diplomatic measures and economic pressures will help to encourage compliance. Of course, this depends on the political will and commitment of the participating states. But if regions or groups of states have gone through the effort of agreeing to protect an important high-seas area, they should be willing to take various means to enforce it.

The whale conservationist or MPA practitioner should use all the instruments available for conservation on the high seas (see Chapter 4). An example of a good high-seas strategy is the United Nations General Assembly Drift-net Resolution (1991), which has helped alleviate a serious problem that could not have been solved or certainly solved as well through MPAs. After this resolution took effect in 1992, more than 1000 vessels were withdrawn from large-scale (2.5 km+) drift-net fishing with its large bycatch of marine mammals (Reeves, 2002). In some cases, diplomatic wording regarding the conservation of an area may achieve more than by giving it the high profile MPA name, whether it goes by 'marine protected area', 'sanctuary', 'biosphere reserve' or 'marine reserve'.

Since the 2001 Vilm, Germany, workshop on the high seas, there have been additional workshops which have continued and enhanced the debate, notably the 2003 Malaga Workshop on High Seas Marine Protected Areas (see www.iucn.org/themes/marine/pdf/GjerdeBreideHSMPA.pdf).

At the V World Parks Congress in September 2003, a target was set for five ecologically significant, high-seas MPAs to be created by 2008, as well as a global system of MPA networks by 2012, including strictly protected areas that amount to at least 20–30 per cent of each habitat, the implementation of an ecosystem-based approach to fisheries management and marine biodiversity conservation through MPAs integrated with marine and coastal governance and management actions (see recommendations at www.iucn.org.themes/ wcpa/wpc2003/pdfs/outputs/recommendations/approved/english/html/r2 2.htm and www...r23.htm).

The consensus is that urgent as well as long-term action is needed to conserve marine living resources on the high seas. Some of that should take the form of MPAs as part of a broad suite of necessary actions. Important for cetaceans as an outcome of the Congress was the overt recognition that species protection is a core objective of MPA declaration and that MPAs should provide a framework that can contribute significantly to the management of species with special management needs including highly migratory species, ecosystems and habitats.

There is a growing realization that it may be possible to use cetaceans, with their world-ranging habitats – at least some of them closely allied with fishing hot spots – and international cetacean agreements, to develop much better conservation on the high seas. Despite limited legal jurisdiction over the high seas, the Congress recognized the establishment of MPAs through existing international agreements including UNCLOS, CBD, the UN Fish Stocks Agreement and CMS. Further, the 'Message of the V World Parks Congress to the CBD,' which identifies actions for the Programme of Work under the Convention, called for the promotion of synergies between CBD and other processes including CMS. Of particular note in Recommendation 23 was the call for immediate and urgent action to protect large-scale, persistent oceanographic features such as currents and frontal systems which constitute critical habitat for many cetacean and other species listed in the IUCN Red List and the appendices of CITES, CMS and related agreements.

Table 1.6 *International and regional treaties, conventions and other agreements with a bearing on MPAs and the conservation of cetaceans*

Name of treaty, convention, agreement Coverage	Main provisions and specific use in MPA creation	For more information
ACCOBAMS – Agreement on the Conservation of Cetaceans of the Black Sea, Mediterranean Sea and Contiguous Atlantic Area *Mediterranean and Black Seas: national waters (declared only to 12 nm) and high seas*	• Signed 1996, under the Bonn Convention (CMS), ACCOBAMS entered into force in 2001. It applies to coastal Mediterranean and Black Sea countries. • Annex 1 lists the cetaceans of the Mediterranean, Black Sea and Atlantic Contiguous Area. • It specifically aims to establish a network of 'specially protected areas to conserve cetaceans'. • It prohibits the deliberate killing of cetaceans in national waters.	• web: www.accobams.org; www.wcmc.org.uk/cms/ • see Cetaceans of the Mediterranean and Black Seas: State of Knowledge and Conservation Strategies (web: www.accobams.mc/Accob/Wacco.nsf/Fram1FrDown?OpenFrameSet)
ASCOBANS – Agreement on the Conservation of Small Cetaceans of the Baltic and North Sea *Baltic Sea and North Sea, western European seas: to EEZ limits*	• Signed 1991, under the Bonn Convention (CMS), ASCOBANS entered into force in 1994. • It originally covered small cetaceans in the Baltic Sea and North Sea but it has been extended to waters of Western Europe, including several non-signatory countries. • MPAs are called 'areas of special importance' (ASI).	• web: www.ascobans.org; www.wcmc.org.uk/cms/
Barcelona Convention – Convention for the Protection of the Marine Environment and Littoral of the Mediterranean Sea against Pollution *Mediterranean: national waters (declared only to 12 nm) and high seas*	• Established under UNEP in 1975, the Barcelona Convention was amended in 1995. The 'Mediterranean Action Plan' (UNEP/MAP) applies to all Mediterranean coastal states.	• web: www.unepmap.org

Table 1.6 *continued*

Name of treaty, convention, agreement Coverage	Main provisions and specific use in MPA creation	For more information
Bern Convention – The Emerald Network; Convention on the Conservation of European Wildlife and Natural Habitats *European seas: national waters to EEZ limits (declared and undeclared)*	• Formulated under the aegis of European Community Council September 1979, it has been in force since 1982 and covers European states. • Cetaceans are listed in Appendix II (List of strictly protected species) and in Appendix III (List of protected species).	• web: www.coe.int/english/cadres/bern.htm
Cartagena Convention (the Convention for the Protection and Development of the Marine Environment of the Wider Caribbean Region) and the Protocol Concerning Specially Protected Areas and Wildlife (SPAW) *Greater Caribbean Sea: national waters to EEZ limits and high seas*	• This regional association of Greater Caribbean countries was formed with the adoption of the Cartagena Convention in 1983 but not ratified until 1986. It is the key environmental treaty in the wider Caribbean. • The Cartagena Convention set up the Caribbean Environment Program under the 1990 (SPAW) Protocol on Specially Protected Areas and Wildlife. The SPAW Protocol, which entered into force in June 2000, recommends the establishment of protected areas and recommends specific measures, providing a framework for developing a regional network of MPAs that would allow protection at the ecosystem level. The implementation is up to the individual states. The SPAW Protocol is also recognized as an instrument to help implement the CBD signed by most states.	• web: www.cep.unep.org/pubs/legislation/cartxt.html; www.cep.unep.org/pubs/legislation/spaw.html; www.cep.unep.org/pubs/legislation/oilspill.html; www.cep.unep.org/pubs/legislation/cartstatus.html www.cep.unep.org;
CCAMLR – Convention on the Conservation of Antarctic Marine Living Resources *Antarctic: high seas*	• Formulated in Canberra, Australia, in May 1980, CCAMLR has been in force since April 1982. • The objective is to conserve living resources in the Southern Ocean. • CCAMLR is an important tool as it promotes research and analysis, partly through an ecosystem-based management approach. • The Madrid Protocol (Protocol on Environmental Protection to the Antarctic Treaty) regulates environmental protection in Antarctica and, in its Annex V, allows for the development of MPAs called ASPAs (Antarctic Specially Protected Areas). ASPAs include specially protected areas (SPAs), sites of special scientific interest (SSSIs) and specially reserved areas.	• Kimball (1999) • web: www.ccamlr.org • see also the Antarctica and Southern Ocean Coalition site: web: www.asoc.org

CITES – Convention on International Trade in Endangered Species of Wild Fauna and Flora *World Ocean: national waters to EEZ limits and high seas*	• Formulated under UNEP in 1973, CITES has been in force since July 1975 and has worldwide application. • CITES regulates international trade (all international movements for whatever purpose) of species listed in three appendices. • Cetaceans are listed in Appendix 1 (Species threatened with extinction), Appendix 2 (Species not threatened with extinction, but in danger if their commerce is not subject to restraints), and Appendix 3 (Single state protected species, entered into the appendix to regulate exports from their territory).	• web: www.unep-wcmc.org • To contact CITES Trade Database Team, UNEP-WCMC; email: species@unep-wcmc.org
CMS or Bonn Convention – Convention on the Conservation of Migratory Species of Wild Animals *World Ocean: national waters to EEZ limits and high seas*	• Established by UNEP in June 1979 and entering into force in 1983, CMS conserves 'entire populations or any geographically separate part of the population of any species or lower taxon … a significant proportion of whose members cyclically and predictably cross one or more national boundaries'. • For cetaceans, see Appendix I (Migratory species in danger) and Appendix II (Migratory species with an unfavourable conservation status requiring international cooperation for conservation and management).	• web: www.cms.int
CNSP – Convention on Conservation of Nature in the South Pacific *South Pacific: national waters to EEZ limits and possibly high seas*	• Formulated in Apia in June 1976, CNSP entered into force June 1990. • CNSP may offer potential for protection of cetaceans and their habitat in the South Pacific Commission area.	
The Convention on Biological Diversity (CBD) and the Jakarta Mandate *World Ocean: national waters to EEZ limits and high seas*	• The CBD, legally binding since 1994, is the most widely supported of all international agreements, with more than 145 countries now party to the convention. It is the first comprehensive international agreement committing governments to protect Earth's biological resources through the conservation and sustainable use of biodiversity. • The CBD, in Article 8, calls on parties to 'as far as possible and as appropriate, establish a system of protected areas or areas where special measures need to be taken to conserve biological diversity'. • State parties are asked to take measures to ensure the conservation and sustainable use of biodiversity, to monitor biodiversity in their territories, to identify and take measures for the control of destructive activities, and to integrate consideration of biodiversity into national decision-making. • Article 4 states that the CBD applies in areas within national jurisdiction, the EEZs, as well as beyond the limits of national jurisdiction for processes and activities carried out by a	• web: www.biodiv.org/

Table 1.6 *continued*

Name of treaty, convention, agreement Coverage	Main provisions and specific use in MPA creation	For more information
	member state, regardless of where their effects occur, such as on the high seas. Article 5 adds that states must cooperate with other contracting states, as far as possible and appropriate, in areas beyond national jurisdiction. • In 1995, the Jakarta Mandate developed a programme of action for implementing the CBD in terms of marine and coastal biodiversity. Establishing marine and coastal protected areas is one of the five main tenets of the agreement, allied to provisions calling upon states to implement integrated coastal area management and to ensure the sustainable use of coastal and marine living resources. • The CBD established the Subsidiary Body on Scientific, Technical and Technological Advice (SBSTTA) as an expert scientific body to develop the programme of work on marine and coastal biodiversity, including marine protected areas. • According to de Fontaubert (2001), the CBD presents 'a strong mandate for the establishment of MPAs on the high seas, constrained only by the need to negotiate with other parties in areas beyond national jurisdiction'.	
CPPS – Convention for the Protection of the Marine Environment and Coastal Areas of the South-East Pacific *Southeast Pacific: national waters to EEZ limits and possibly high seas*	• In force since May 1986, CPPS is implemented under the guidelines of UNEP OCA/PAC's Action Plan for the Protection of the Marine Environment and Coastal Areas of the South-East Pacific. • CPPS is aimed at stopping marine pollution and could help protect cetacean prey and habitat. • The Coordinated Programme on Marine Pollution Monitoring and control in the South-East Pacific (CONPACSE) is a monitoring and assessment programme under CPPS. • CPPS includes the countries of Chile, Colombia, Ecuador, Panama and Peru.	• CPPS (2000) • web: www.gsf.de/UNEP/con1.html
EU Habitats and Species Directive (Natura 2000) *EC waters: national waters to EEZ limits*	• Formulated by the European Community Council in 1992, the EU Habitats and Species Directive applies to all EU states. • Parts relevant to cetaceans include: Annex II (Animal and plant species of community interest whose conservation requires the designation of special areas of conservation – SACs) which, for cetaceans, has only bottlenose dolphins and harbor porpoises; Annex IV (Animal and plant species of community interest in need of strict protection) covers all the	• web: www.ecnc.nl/doc/europe/legislat/habidire.html

	cetacean species in the marine areas of the EC; and Annex V (Animal and plant species of community interest whose taking in the wild and exploitation may be subject to management measures). • Natura 2000 is the programme to create a network of protected areas across the entire European Community. • The EU Habitats and Species Directive provides a first framework for the protection of coastal and marine wildlife. However, the protection afforded to the offshore, pelagic and deep-sea marine environment in this context is extremely limited.	
HELCOM or Helsinki Convention – Convention for the Protection of the Baltic Environment against All Forms of Pollution *Baltic Sea: national waters to EEZ limits and possibly high seas*	• This 1992 convention protects Baltic marine waters from pollution partly through creating a system of marine and coastal protected areas. • Signed by countries bordering the Baltic Sea and by the European Community, HELCOM stipulates that all contracting parties must establish a system of coastal and marine protected areas. Environmental Action Programme has guidelines for offshore protected areas in the Baltic Sea.	• web: www.helcom.fi
ICRW – International Convention for the Regulation of Whaling (convention responsible for establishing the International Whaling Commission – IWC) *World Ocean: high seas*	• Signed in Washington, DC, December 1946 and in force since 10 November 1948, ICRW currently has more than 40 nation members who are parties to the convention and belong to the International Whaling Commission (IWC). • According to ICRW, whale species are protected from overfishing, but there is debate over the definition of 'whale' and whether it includes small cetaceans. • The convention provides for the adoption of regulations designed to open and close waters, including the designation of sanctuaries on the high seas where no whaling is allowed, under Article V of the Convention. Approval of a sanctuary through an amendment to the schedule requires a 3/4 majority vote. Currently, two ocean sanctuaries are in place: the Indian Ocean and Southern Ocean. • IWC sanctuaries only prohibit whaling although there is evidence that these sanctuaries have promoted other conservation measures and research. Perhaps most useful, this agreement provides precedent, since 1946, of nations working together on the high seas.	• web: www.iwcoffice.org
MARPOL Agreement – International Convention for the Prevention of Pollution from Ships; put into practice by IMO –	• Drafted 1973 and in force since 1978, IMO is a UN forum on shipping issues which formulates international regulations on shipping. • IMO recognizes its responsibilities to limit the adverse environmental impacts from shipping. IMO can designate Particularly Sensitive Sea Areas (PSSAs) within EEZs or on the	• *MPA News* (2002a) details PSSAs vs ATBAs and tells how to apply for PSSA designation; web: cwss.www.de/news/

Table 1.6 *continued*

Name of treaty, convention, agreement Coverage	Main provisions and specific use in MPA creation	For more information
International Maritime Organization *World Ocean: national waters to EEZ limits and high seas*	• high seas to protect significant ecological, socioeconomic or scientific features which may be vulnerable to damage by maritime activities (*MPA News*, 2002a). • Candidate PSSAs can be suggested by member states, and are then reviewed by the Marine Environment Protection Committee. • Guidelines list ecological, social, cultural, economic and scientific criteria to be met before an area can be designated a PSSA. • Three PSSAs proposed or existing are located in/near MPAs which already have some measure of protection: Florida Keys National Marine Sanctuary, Wadden Sea Conservation Area, and the Great Barrier Reef Marine Park Authority. • Designated PSSAs may have traffic separation schemes, pilotage, vessel traffic services and no-discharge areas to avoid the risk of collision, grounding and other adverse impacts from shipping. The measures are legally binding to the vessels belonging to all IMO members.	documents/pssa/PSSA-report.pdf • web: www.fknms.nos.noaa.gov
MCEA – Convention for the Protection, Management and Development of the Marine and Coastal Environment of the Eastern African Region *East African/western Indian Ocean countries: national waters to EEZ limits and possibly high seas*	• The Protocol Concerning Protected Areas and Wild Fauna and Flora in the Eastern African Region was signed in Nairobi, in June 1985. • Protocol applies to regional waters, gives protection to listed species including migratory species (such as blue and humpback whales) and ecosystems.	• web: www.unep.org/eaf/
NAFO – Northwest Atlantic Fisheries Organization and Convention on Future Multilateral Cooperation in the Northwest Atlantic Fisheries *Northwest Atlantic: national waters to EEZ limits and high seas*	• Instituted October 1978 in Ottawa, NAFO has been in force since January 1979. • NAFO covers all fisheries in the convention area. • It is supposed to include cetaceans not covered by IWC.	• web: www.nafo.ca

OSPAR Convention – Oslo and Paris Convention for the Protection of the Marine Environment in the Northeast Atlantic *Northeast Atlantic Ocean: EEZs and high seas*	• Environment Ministers of 15 Northeast Atlantic states and the members of the European Commission agreed in 1998 to identify marine species, habitats or ecosystems that need protection and to 'promote the establishment of a network of marine protected areas to ensure the sustainable use and protection and conservation of marine biological diversity and its ecosystems'. They signed Annex V to the OSPAR Convention and adopted the Strategy on the Protection and Conservation of Ecosystems and Biological Diversity of the Maritime Area. • The components of an MPA network are due to be put in place by 2010. • Annex V (on the Protection and Conservation of the Ecosystems and Biological Diversity of the Maritime Area) promotes the establishment of specific areas needing protection and management of human activities in these areas, while Appendix 3 provides the Criteria for Identifying Human Activities for the Purpose of Annex V. • The OSPAR maritime area covers territorial waters from the 12–200 nm (22.2–371 km) EEZ and beyond, on the high seas of the Northeast Atlantic. • Also relevant to this area are the EU Common Fisheries Policy, the Norwegian Fisheries Policy and the Icelandic Fisheries Policy.	• Nijkamp and Bijvoet (1996); Evans (1999); Evans and Urquiola (2001); Urquiola and Evans (2001) • web: www.ospar.org
PCSP – Permanent Commission of the Conference on the Use and Conservation of the Marine Resources of the South Pacific and Agreements of the Conference on the Use and Conservation of the Marine Resources of the South Pacific *South Pacific: national waters to EEZ limits*	• Initiated August 1952 to regulate catching of large baleen and sperm whales in the South Pacific, PCSP was the first international agreement to claim jurisdiction over all marine resources including the sea floor within 200 nm (371 km) of the coast. • This agreement has not been actively pursued since Chile and Peru joined the IWC in 1979 and Colombia and Ecuador stopped whaling, but it is said that this agreement may have potential for dealing with the conservation and management of any cetacean species in PCSP waters.	
Ramsar – Convention on Wetlands of International Importance Especially as Waterfowl Habitat	• Formulated February 1971, Ramsar has been in force since December 1975. • This convention can protect wetlands, including marine water of not more than 20 feet (6 m) deep at low tide, which are of international importance to riverine and coastal cetaceans and to more pelagic species using inshore areas, for example for breeding or feeding.	• web: www.ramsar.org/

Table 1.6 *continued*

Name of treaty, convention, agreement Coverage	Main provisions and specific use in MPA creation	For more information
World Ocean: *inshore portions of national waters only*	Many proposed or existing wetlands conservation areas already listed in Appendix II contain, or are likely to contain, cetacean habitat, but all have been listed for other reasons. Ramsar areas may protect the critical habitat of species in the food chain important as cetacean prey and are critical for ecosystem-based management.	
UNEP Regional Seas Programme	• Initiated in 1974 as a global programme to be implemented regionally, the Regional Seas Programme seeks to combat environmental problems through the rational management of marine and coastal areas. As of 2004, there are 13 separate regions and more than 140 participating coastal states and territories. Each regional seas programme is organized around a framework treaty which operates under the UN Environment Programme (UNEP). Existing protocols include: the Mediterranean (Barcelona Convention); the South Pacific (Noumea Convention); the Wider Caribbean (Cartagena Convention); the East Africa (Nairobi Convention); and the Northeast Pacific (Antigua Convention). The protocols refer to protective measures which include MPAs to serve a variety of objectives. For the most part, the terms of the conventions apply both in areas of national jurisdiction and on the high seas in the region.	• web: www.unep.ch/seas/; www.gpa.unep.org/seas/strategy.htm; www.gpa.unep.org/seas/seas.htm • For more on each regional programme, see separate entries in this table and the following websites: Northwest Pacific (NOWPAP) – web: merrac.nowpap.org/; Black Sea (BSEP) – web: www.blacksea-environment.org/; East Asian Seas – web: 206.67.58.208/uneproap/; South Pacific Region (SPREP) – web: www.sprep.org.ws
SPA Protocol – Protocol for Special Protected Areas and Biological Diversity of the Barcelona Convention *Mediterranean: national waters (declared only to 12 nm) and high seas*	• Established under UNEP in 1995 to apply to coastal states in the Mediterranean, this protocol has been in force since 1999. • Appendix 2 lists threatened species contains certain cetaceans. • There is a list of Special Protected Areas of Mediterranean Interest (SPAMI).	• web: www.rac-spa.org.tn

The UN Agreement on Stradling Fish Stocks (1995) *World Ocean: national waters to EEZ limits and high seas*	• The full title of the UN Fish Stocks Agreement is 'The United Nations Agreement for the Implementation of the Provisions of the United Nations Convention on the Law of the Sea of 10 December 1982 relating to the Conservation and Management of Straddling Fish Stocks and Highly Migratory Fish Stocks'. It builds upon and fills gaps in UNCLOS to manage fish species throughout their range between EEZs and the high seas, or migrating over long distances in the high seas. It recognizes the 'biological unity of the stocks'. • Article 6 emphasizes the precautionary approach or principle and insists that states act with protective management to ensure that fish stocks are not damaged. One of the recognized ways to apply the precautionary approach is through MPAs. • The agreement came into force in December 2001.	• web: www.un.org/Depts/los/convention_agreements/convention_overview_fish_stocks.htm
Unesco Man and the Biosphere Programme (MAB) *World Ocean: national waters to EEZ limits and possibly high seas*	• Man and the Biosphere Programme (MAB) was set up through the United Nations Educational, Scientific and Cultural Organization (Unesco) • Biosphere reserves provide a valuable model for MPA conservation by combining the conservation, logistic and development roles and by using a combination of highly protected IUCN Category I core areas, along with surrounding areas which integrate the needs of local populations and are less protected, transition areas. • Originally envisioned for land-based protected areas, biosphere reserves now include marine areas. Some sites have protected cetacean habitat.	• Batisse (1990); Unesco (1974) • web: www.unesco.org/mab/
United Nations Conference on Environment and Development – UNCED: Agenda 21 *World Ocean: national waters to EEZ limits and high seas*	• Called 'Earth's Action Plan', Agenda 21 is a practical manual and blueprint for sustainable development negotiated and adopted by all participating states at the UN Conference on Environment and Development (UNCED), in June 1992. • Chapter 17, on the protection of the oceans, calls on states to undertake measures to maintain biological diversity and productivity of marine species under national jurisdiction, including establishing and managing protected areas. It also calls for states to conserve marine living resources on the high seas, specifying the protection and restoration of endangered marine species and the preservation of habitats and other ecologically sensitive areas. • According to de Fontaubert (2001), 'Agenda 21 may well be the most important soft-law instrument that recognizes the possibility of enacting MPAs on the high seas.'	• web: http://habitat.igc.org/agenda21/index.htm

Table 1.6 *continued*

Name of treaty, convention, agreement Coverage	Main provisions and specific use in MPA creation	For more information
UNCLOS – United Nations Convention on the Law of the Sea: General provisions *World Ocean: national waters to EEZ limits and high seas*	• Initiated April 1982 in New York, UNCLOS entered into force in 1994, after ratification by 60 countries. • UNCLOS, often referred to as the 'Law of the Sea', gives all coastal states the right to extend their territorial sea from the former 3 nm (5.5 km) to 12 nm (22.2 km); in practice many nations had already done this. Most important, it also gives countries the right to declare a marine Exclusive Economic Zone (EEZ) up to 200 nm (371 km) from the coast as well as from national islands off the coast, and up to 350 nm (649 km) from the coast where a continental shelf extension can be established. Coastal states have management jurisdiction over their EEZ including the management of both living and non-living marine resources. Other norms of high-seas law, such as right of passage, apply. • The regime of the high seas (outside the EEZs) dictates that all states have the right to engage in fishing, subject to treaty obligations and the rights of other states. • UNCLOS also has relevance to areas outside the national EEZs and to high-seas MPA creation. UNCLOS is a living treaty, subject to modifications and elaboration. • Marine mammals are specifically exempted from the general requirement to promote optimum utilization of living resources within the EEZs and on the high seas. According to Article 65, states are required to prohibit or regulate their exploitation more strictly than with other marine species. 'States shall cooperate with a view to the conservation of marine mammals and in the case of cetaceans shall in particular work through the appropriate international organizations for [their] conservation, management and study.' Article 120 extends this principle to the high seas.	• web: www.un.org/Depts/los/index.htm
UNCLOS: The Environment Regime *World Ocean: national waters to EEZ limits and high seas*	• 'States have the obligation to protect and preserve the marine environment' (Article 192). • States have the right to exploit their natural resources but it must be done in accordance with their environmental policies and duty to protect and preserve the marine environment. • States shall act individually or jointly as appropriate to take all measures necessary for conservation, using the best practical means at their disposal. • States shall take measures to ensure that activities under their jurisdiction or control are so	

conducted as not to cause damage by pollution 'beyond the areas where they exercise sovereign rights'. This also means that a state is responsible for the activities of vessels flying its flag on the high seas.

- States shall take measures to deal with all sources of pollution of the marine environment.
- States must take measures to protect and preserve 'rare or fragile ecosystems as well as the habitat of depleted, threatened or endangered species and other forms of marine life'.
- States shall refrain from unjustifiable interference with activities carried out by other states in the exercise of their rights and in pursuance of their duties in conformity with this Convention. Thus UNCLOS protects the rights of other states but holds them accountable for their obligations under the Convention – one of which is the Article 192 duty to protect the marine environment.

UNCLOS: The Fisheries Regime
World Ocean: national waters to EEZ limits and high seas

- The states' freedom to fish on the high seas is limited both by the right of other states to fish and their duty to cooperate 'as may be necessary for the conservation of the living resources of the sea'.
- With the right to fish comes the responsibility to respect the rights of other states and to ensure that the stocks do not become depleted. Overfishing is not permitted.
- States shall cooperate to establish subregional or regional fisheries management organizations and take measures 'which are designed, on the best scientific evidence available ... to maintain or restore populations of harvested species at levels which can produce the maximum sustainable yield'.
- States, together and/or through the regional fisheries management organizations, can adopt any measures negotiated and deemed necessary for the conservation of fish stocks.
- States should take measures on the high seas that take into account the interdependence of stocks and associated species, which can be achieved through the protection of a whole area rather than a mere target stock.

WHC World Heritage Convention – Convention for the Protection of the World's Natural and Cultural Heritage
World Ocean: national waters to EEZ limits and high seas

- Formulated through Unesco in Paris, November 1972, WHC has been in force since December 1975.
- WHC is responsible for helping to protect cultural heritage as well as the world's most important natural habitats of threatened animals, and sites of outstanding scientific or conservation value.
- Sites included on the World Heritage List and the List of World Heritage in Danger qualify for the World Heritage Fund, administered by the World Heritage Committee.
- Some sites have cetacean habitat, although they have been listed for other reasons.

- web: www.whc.unesco.org/nwhc/pages/home/pages/homepage.htm

Table 1.6 *continued*

Name of treaty, convention, agreement Coverage	Main provisions and specific use in MPA creation	For more information
World Summit on Sustainable Development (WSSD): Plan of Implementation *World Ocean: national waters to EEZ limits and high seas*	• Action plan was agreed to by 189 countries attending the 26 August–4 September 2002 meeting in Johannesburg, South Africa. • WSSD recommended establishment of MPAs worldwide under international law and based on scientific information, including representative networks of MPAs, by 2012. • WSSD recommended depleted fish stocks to be restored by 2015, with elimination of all subsidies contributing to illegal, unreported and unregulated fishing. • Ecosystem approach for sustainable development of the oceans is to be applied by 2010. To facilitate this, the White Water to Blue Water Partnership will start in the Wider Caribbean in 2003, followed by Africa and the South Pacific. • Regular reporting and assessments of the state of the marine environment are to be made a regular process under the UN. • 'Global Forum on Oceans, Coasts, and Islands' is to be formed with national and international conservation groups and other organizations, and government representatives working on marine initiatives, to confer regularly to ensure that the initiatives, targets and timetables of WSSD are met. • According to Bud Ehler, IUCN World Commission on Protected Areas, 'The targets and timetables found in the WSSD Plan of Implementation represent an important advance over actions taken in Chapter 17 of Agenda 21 at the 1992 Earth Summit that had provided few specific targets and timetables for action.' (see UNCED: Agenda 21 above)	• web: www.johannesburgsummit.org

Note: Besides the websites listed above for each agreement, the Wildlife Interest Group of the American Society of International Law lists many cetacean and other wildlife laws and agreements – international, regional and country by country – on its website. Check on the web: http://eelink.net/~asilwildlife/legislat.shtml.

2

WHY SPOTLIGHT WHALES, DOLPHINS AND PORPOISES?

INTRODUCTION

There are two main reasons to spotlight cetaceans in the creating of marine protected areas (MPAs): cetaceans have intrinsic value as species in themselves, and they have value and play an important role in terms of conserving other species and whole ecosystems.

The idea that whales, dolphins and porpoises need protected habitat is still fairly new, even among MPA practitioners. The impression persists among portions of the general public that whales were 'saved' when the whaling moratorium was put in place in the mid-1980s. In fact, the IUCN Red List status of more than a third of all great whale species remains 'endangered' (5 of 14 species), followed by 'lower risk but conservation dependent' (4 species); one species is 'vulnerable', one is 'near threatened', and two are 'data deficient'. Only one is of 'least concern', the pygmy right whale which has a comparatively small range, but was never hunted by whalers.

Among all 84 species of whales and dolphins, 42 (50 per cent) have the status of 'data deficient' or 'not evaluated' – we simply do not know enough to be able to say whether populations are healthy or not (see Tables 2.3–2.7). A further eight species have their major populations or subspecies listed as data deficient or not evaluated, leaving only 34 of 84 species (40 per cent) with known designations. Of these 34, 9 are critically endangered or endangered, and a further 5 are vulnerable, for a total of 14 endangered and vulnerable (17 per cent of the total 84 species). Of course, an endangered, critically endangered or vulnerable status is in itself a rationale for MPA conservation (Agardy, 1997), while a precautionary approach strongly indicates that a classification of 'data deficient' or 'not evaluated' is also grounds for MPA conservation. Thus, nearly all cetacean species qualify for habitat protection through MPAs on the basis of their Red List status alone.

Creating MPAs to protect probable cetacean critical habitat provides an added rationale as well as a practical means to learn much more about cetaceans and how we might assist in their survival. The research into living whale populations is only three decades old at most. The substantial results of these studies are just starting to come in. The tools of photographic identification (photo-ID), in which individual animals can be identified through natural markings, plus satellite and radio tracking, aerial- and boat-based surveys, acoustic and biopsy work have opened the door to understanding the lives and thus the habitat needs of animals that spend about 95 per cent of their lives underwater (Bigg, 1982; Bigg et al, 1987; Darling, 1977; Payne et al, 1990; Sears, 1983; Wells et al, 1987; many others). Still, this is long-term research.

Most cetacean species travel constantly, yet have periods of the year in which they range through one or more fairly localized areas. In general, the more that is learned about cetaceans, the more it becomes evident that populations of some species favour or return regularly to familiar places (Bigg, 1982; Darling et al, 1983; Dorsey et al, 1990; Sears, 1983; Wells et al, 1987; many others).

These localized areas for whales and dolphins – whether they are called home ranges, or mating, breeding or feeding grounds – exist on a much larger scale than comparable areas for all but the largest social land mammals. But it will take much more scientific research to determine the critical habitat needs of most cetaceans, all but the most commonly studied dozen or so species. Meanwhile, we have the precautionary approach, and a certain pragmatic value in 'using' cetaceans as a vehicle for MPA conservation in general. To the MPA practitioner or mainstream conservationist, what can adopting a cetacean-oriented approach for certain MPAs contribute to MPA conservation in general? Before answering this question, I will first look at the intrinsic values of cetaceans as well as their particular conservation needs.

What is the worldwide status of each cetacean species, as well as that of key subspecies and populations? Where do these species, subspecies and populations live? The section and accompanying tables below aim to provide the essential status and distribution information as a starting point for MPA managers and researchers who are preparing proposals or management plans for cetacean habitat conservation in MPAs.

RED LIST ASSESSMENT OF CETACEAN SPECIES, SUBSPECIES AND POPULATIONS

The World Conservation Union (IUCN) Red List (Hilton-Taylor, 2000 or www.redlist.org), along with the 2002–2010 IUCN Cetacean Action Plan (Reeves et al, 2003), provides a basic indication of the status of cetacean species as well as certain subspecies and populations. This information has been developing over the past two decades with the IUCN Red Data Book covering cetaceans (Klinowska, 1991) and previous cetacean action plans (Perrin, 1988, 1989; Reeves and Leatherwood, 1994). There are reviews of certain cetacean species available through International Whaling Commission (IWC) special volumes – for example, porpoises in Bjørge and Donovan (1995) and northern hemisphere pilot whales in Donovan et al (1993). A number of national, regional and conservation organization cetacean action plans have also been produced.

The Red List designations for cetacean species, subspecies and populations, presented below, follow the 2000 Categories and Criteria (IUCN, 2001) except for retaining the LR(cd), or Lower Risk (conservation dependent), category until new evaluations are available, as suggested by Reeves et al (2003). See Table 2.1.

The word 'stock', used in the tables below, means essentially a population and refers to a largely isolated unit with little or no genetic exchange, as used in IWC assessments. Of course, definitions for stocks and populations can be highly contentious for various reasons, including the management implications for hunting as well as the conservation implications of endangered species and populations. Yet, within the IWC and other international bodies and forums, the term 'stock' is used even in the absence of a biologically coherent or generally accepted definition (Donovan, 1991). I have adopted the designations suggested in Reeves et al (2003) as followed and in some cases proposed from within the IUCN Cetacean Specialist Group (CSG).

The distribution of each cetacean species, subspecies and population, as shown in Tables 2.3–2.7, is separated into the world's 18 marine regions, as defined by the IUCN World Commission on Protected Areas (WCPA, formerly CNPPA) (Kelleher et al, 1995b). Neither the IUCN Red List nor the various cetacean action plans divide cetacean distribution into marine regions. Yet, because of its value in terms of identifying and securing protection and management for cetacean habitat, it was done for this book (using Reeves et al, 2002, 2003). A list of the 18 marine regions is shown in Table 2.2, and full descriptions of each marine region are provided in Chapter 5.

THE VALUE OF CETACEANS FOR MARINE-BASED CONSERVATION

Aside from their intrinsic value, whales and dolphins are proving to be valuable assets for planning, promoting and implementing marine conservation initiatives such as MPAs. There are four main reasons for employing cetaceans to help create, define and manage MPAs:

1 Cetaceans can spearhead successful public marine education and help forge a positive community identity

Most of the sea is invisible to humans. Marine ecosystems, with their great diversity of marine species, ecosystem processes and habitats, cannot, for the

Table 2.1 *IUCN Red List status designations*

Many species have had no systematic evaluation or the data are deficient:			
NE	Not Evaluated	DD	Data Deficient – formerly called Insufficiently Known
If there are sufficient data, then a species, subspecies or population can be:			
CR	Critically Endangered	EN	Endangered
VU	Vulnerable	NT	Near Threatened – formerly called Lower Risk (near threatened)
LR(cd)	Lower Risk (conservation dependent)	LC	Least Concern – formerly called Lower Risk (least concern)
There are also two categories for extinction:			
EX	Extinct	EW	Extinct in the Wild (can be some captives)

Note: This table provides the key for IUCN Red List status for cetacean species, subspecies and populations as used in the text and in Tables 2.3–2.7.

Table 2.2 *Key to world Marine Regions 1–18*

1 Antarctic	10 Central Indian Ocean
2 Arctic	11 Arabian Seas
3 Mediterranean	12 East Africa
4 Northwest Atlantic	13 East Asian Seas
5 Northeast Atlantic	14 South Pacific
6 Baltic	15 Northeast Pacific
7 Wider Caribbean	16 Northwest Pacific
8 West Africa	17 Southeast Pacific
9 South Atlantic	18 Australia–New Zealand

This table provides the key for the 18 marine regions as used in Tables 2.3–2.7.
For maps and detailed information on each of the marine regions of the world, see Chapter 5.
Figure 5.1 is a world map showing the boundaries of all the marine regions (p88).

most part, be seen. Whales and dolphins, as large, air-breathing animals linked to the surface and to the air we breathe, are fellow social mammals who provide our closest link to the world ocean. Evidence of our interest in this link is the substantial worldwide popularity of whale watching (Hoyt, 2001). Establishing a cetacean reserve around a target species can provide a strong image for a community or region. Cetaceans are not only the high profile attractions that bring people to the sea but, by their presence, they advertise the health of that part of the sea, since they are known to the public as inhabitants of clean, healthy waters. The tourism and local community benefits from cetaceans, as well as the economic impact, can be substantial (Hoyt, 2002; Hoyt and Hvenegaard, 1999, 2002; IFAW, 1999). Further, whales, as 'flagship' species, can be a tool for raising awareness about the role of MPAs in marine conservation initiatives (Augustowski and Palazzo, 2003).

Table 2.3 *Baleen whales. World distribution and status of species, subspecies and key populations*

Baleen whales (suborder Mysticeti) in the families Balaenidae, Right Whales (1–4); Neobalaenidae, Pygmy Right Whale (5); Eschrichtidae, Gray Whales (6); Balaenopteridae, Rorquals (7–14)

Species, subspecies, key populations	Red List status	1	2	3	4	5	6	7	8	9	10	11	12	13	14	15	16	17	18
1. North Atlantic right whale, *Eubalaena glacialis*	EN		■			■		■	?										
2. North Pacific right whale, *Eubalaena japonica*	EN														?	■	■		
3. southern right whale, *Eubalaena australis*	LR(cd)	■			■				■							■			■
4. bowhead whale, *Balaena mysticetus*	LR(cd)		■	■									■		■		■		
a. bowhead: Bering–Chukchi–Beaufort stock	LR(cd)		■																
b. bowhead: Okhotsk Sea stock	EN		■														■		
c. bowhead: Baffin Bay–Davis Strait stock	EN				■											■			
d. bowhead: Hudson Bay–Foxe Basin stock	VU				■														
e. bowhead: Svalbard–Barents Sea stock	CR		■																
5. pygmy right whale, *Caperea marginata*	LC		■		■					■							■		
6. gray whale, *Eschrichtius robustus*	LR(cd)		■		■												■		
a. gray: Northeast Pacific (American) stock	LR(cd)				■											■			
b. gray: Northwest Pacific (Asian) stock	CR															■			
c. gray: North Atlantic	EX																		
7. humpback whale, *Megaptera novaeangliae*	VU	■	■	■	■	■	■	■	■	■	■	■	■	■	■	■	■	■	■
8. minke whale, *Balaenoptera acutorostrata*	NT	■	■	■	■	■	■	■	■	■	■	■	■	■	■	■	■	■	■
a. minke: North Atlantic, *B. acutorostrata acutorostrata*	NE								■	■									
b. minke: North Pacific, *B. acutorostrata scammoni*	NE									?	?	?	?					■	
c. minke: dwarf-form, *B. acutorostrata subsp*	NE	■							■							■			■

Key: ■ Indicates species is present in a marine region

Table 2.3 *continued*

Baleen whales (suborder Mysticeti) in the families Balaenidae, Right Whales (1–4); Neobalaenidae, Pygmy Right Whale (5); Exchrichtidae, Gray Whales (6); Balaenopteridae, Rorquals (7–14)

Species, subspecies, key populations	Red List status	1	2	3	4	5	6	7	8	9	10	11	12	13	14	15	16	17	18
9. Antarctic minke whale, *Balaenoptera bonaerensis*	LR(cd)	■																■	■
10. Bryde's whale, *Balaenoptera brydei*	DD							■										■	■
11. pygmy Bryde's whale, *Balaenoptera edeni*	DD																	■	
12. sei whale, *Balaenoptera borealis*	EN				■	■					?	?	?					■	■
a. sei: northern hemisphere, *B. borealis borealis*	NE										?	?	?						
b. sei: southern hemisphere, *B. borealis schlegellii*	NE	■	■			■					?	?	?					■	■
13. fin whale, *Balaenoptera physalus*	EN				■	■					?	?	?					■	■
a. fin: northern hemisphere, *B. physalus physalus*	NE								?						?				
b. fin: southern hemisphere, *B. physalus quoyi*	NE	■	■			■		■										■	■
14. blue whale, *Balaenoptera musculus*	EN																	■	■
a. blue: North Atlantic stock, *B. musculus musculus*	VU														?				
b. blue: North Pacific stock, *B. musculus musculus*	LR(cd)																		
c. blue: Indian Ocean, *B. musculus indica*	NE											?			?				
d. pygmy blue whale, *B. musculus brevicauda*	DD		■							■									
e. Antarctic blue whale, *B. musculus intermedia*	EN												?					■	■

Key: ■ Indicates species is present in a marine region

Table 2.4 *Toothed whales: sperm and beaked whales. World distribution and status of species, subspecies and key populations*

Toothed whales (suborder Odontoceti) in the families Physeteridae, Sperm Whales (15); Kogiidae, Pygmy and Dwarf Sperm Whales (16–17); Ziphiidae, Beaked Whales (18–38)

Species, subspecies, key populations	Red List status	1	2	3	4	5	6	7	8	9	10	11	12	13	14	15	16	17	18
15. sperm whale, *Physeter macrocephalus*	VU	■	■	■	■	■		■	■	■	■	■	■	■	■	■	■	■	■
16. pygmy sperm whale, *Kogia breviceps*	LC	■	■	■	■	■										■	■	■	■
17. dwarf sperm whale, *Kogia sima*	LC	■	■	?	■	■										■	■	■	■
18. Cuvier's beaked whale, *Ziphius cavirostris*	DD	■	■	■	■	■										■	■	■	■
19. Arnoux's beaked whale, *Berardius arnuxii*	LR(cd)									■					■	■			■
20. Baird's beaked whale, *Berardius bairdii*	LR(cd)												■	■			■		
21. Shepherd's beaked whale, *Tasmacetus shepherdi*	DD								■										
22. Indo-Pacific beaked whale, *Indopacetus pacificus*	DD							?			?	?	?	?	?			?	
23. northern bottlenose whale, *Hyperoodon ampullatus*	LR(cd)		■			■											■		■
24. southern bottlenose whale, *Hyperoodon planifrons*	LR(cd)								■	■	?		?	?	?				■
25. Hector's beaked whale, *Mesoplodon hectori*	DD								■						?				
26. Perrin's beaked whale, *Mesoplodon perrini*	NE																■		
27. True's beaked whale, *Mesoplodon mirus*	DD								■			?							■
28. Gervais' beaked whale, *Mesoplodon europaeus*	DD												?						■
29. Sowerby's beaked whale, *Mesoplodon bidens*	DD						?			■							■		■
30. Gray's beaked whale, *Mesoplodon grayi*	DD							?	?										■
31. pygmy beaked whale, *Mesoplodon peruvianus*	DD	■							?										
32. Andrew's beaked whale, *Mesoplodon bowdoini*	DD									■			?		?			?	
33. spade-toothed whale, *Mesoplodon traversii*	NE																		
34. Hubbs' beaked whale, *Mesoplodon carlhubbsi*	DD																■		
35. ginkgo-toothed beaked whale, *Mesoplodon ginkgodens*	DD				■										?				
36. Stejneger's beaked whale, *Mesoplodon stejnegeri*	DD																■		
37. strap-toothed whale, *Mesoplodon layardii*	DD					■					■								■
38. Blainville's beaked whale, *Mesoplodon densirostris*	DD	■	■	■	■	■			?		■	■	■		■	■	■		■

Key: ■ Indicates species is present in a marine region

Table 2.5 *Toothed whales: river dolphins, belugas and narwhals. World distribution and status of species, subspecies and key populations*

Toothed whales (suborder Odontoceti) in the families Platanistidae, Indian River Dolphin (39); Iniidae, Amazon River Dolphin (40); Lipotidae, Yangtze River Dolphin (41); Pontoporiidae, La Plata Dolphin (42); Monodontidae, Beluga and Narwhal (43–44)

Species, subspecies, key populations	Red List status	1	2	3	4	5	6	7	8	9	10	11	12	13	14	15	16	17	18
39. Ganges and Indus River dolphins, *Platanista gangetica*	EN										■		■						
a. Ganges River dolphin, or susu, *P. gangetica gangetica*	EN										■								
b. Indus River dolphin, or bhulan, *P. gangetica minor*	EN												■						
40. Amazon River dolphin, or boto, *Inia geoffrensis*	VU								■	■									
a. Orinoco dolphin, or tonina, *I. geoffrensis humboldtiana*	NE								■										
b. Bolivian dolphin, or bufeo, *I. geoffrensis boliviensis*	NE									■									
c. Amazon River dolphin, or boto, *I. geoffrensis geoffrensis*	NE									■									
41. Yangtze River dolphin, or baiji, *Lipotes vexillifer*	CR																		
42. La Plata dolphin, or franciscana, *Pontoporia blainvillei*	DD		■		■														
43. beluga, *Delphinapterus leucas*	VU																■		
44. narwhal, *Monodon monoceros*	DD																	■	

Key: ■ Indicates species is present in a marine region

Note: The Red List currently recognizes two species of *Platanista gangetica*, the Ganges River and the Indus River dolphins. Both of these river dolphins from South Asia are listed as EN, but river dolphin experts concur that even considered as one species with two populations, the species should still be EN (Reeves et al, 2003). Please also note that common names for the subspecies of Amazon River dolphins are somewhat fluid and the names do not directly correspond to the subspecies as listed above, with the name 'boto' being used largely by Brazilian-speakers and 'bufeo' outside Brazil, except Venezuela where it is frequently 'tonina'.

Table 2.6 *Toothed whales: ocean dolphins. World distribution and status of species, subspecies and key populations*

Toothed whales (suborder Odontoceti) in the family Delphinidae, Ocean Dolphins (45–78)

Species, subspecies, key populations	Red List status	1	2	3	4	5	6	7	8	9	10	11	12	13	14	15	16	17	18
45. Commerson's dolphin, *Cephalorhynchus commersonii*	DD	■																	
a. Commerson's: S America, *C. commersonnii commersonnii*	NE									■								■	
b. Commerson's: Kerguelen, *C. commersonnii subsp*	NE																	■	
46. Chilean dolphin, *Cephalorhynchus eutropia*	DD																		■
47. Heaviside's dolphin, *Cephalorhynchus heavisidii*	DD								■										
48. Hector's dolphin, *Cephalorhynchus hectori*	EN																		■
a. Hector's dolphin: South Island populations	EN																		■
b. Hector's dolphin: North Island population	CR																		■
49. rough-toothed dolphin, *Steno bredanensis*	DD			■		■				■	■	■	■	■	■	■	■		
50. Atlantic hump-backed dolphin, *Sousa teuszii*	DD							■											
51. Indo-Pacific hump-backed dolphin, *Sousa chinensis*	DD															■			
52. tucuxi, *Sotalia fluviatilis*	DD																		
a. tucuxi: marine, *S. fluviatilis guianensis*	NE					■													
b. tucuxi: freshwater, *S. fluviatilis fluviatilis*	NE			■															
53. bottlenose dolphin, *Tursiops truncatus*	DD					■				■	■	■	■	■	■	■	■	■	■
54. Indo-Pacific bottlenose dolphin, *Tursiops aduncus*	DD				■														
55. pantropical spotted dolphin, *Stenella attenuata*	LR(cd)					■				■	■						■		■
a. E Pacific offshore spotted dolphin: subsp A (Perrin 1975)	NE					■													
b. Hawaiian spotted dolphin: subsp B (Perrin 1975)	NE										■								
c. Eastern Pacific coastal spotted, *S. attenuata graffmani*	NE				■														
56. Atlantic spotted dolphin, *Stenella frontalis*	DD							■	■	■									
57. spinner dolphin, *Stenella longirostris*	LR(cd)									■							■	■	■
a. Gray's spinner, *S. longirostris longirostris*	NE									■				■				■	
b. Eastern (whitebelly) spinner, *S. longirostris orientalis*	NE					■												■	
c. Costa Rican spinner, *S. longirostris centroamericana*	NE					■													
d. dwarf spinner dolphin, *S. longirostris roseiventris*	NE?													■					

Key: ■ Indicates species is present in a marine region

Table 2.6 *continued*

Toothed whales (suborder Odontoceti) in the family Delphinidae, Ocean Dolphins (45–78)

Species, subspecies, key populations	Red List status	1	2	3	4	5	6	7	8	9	10	11	12	13	14	15	16	17	18
58. Clymene dolphin, *Stenella clymene*	DD							■	■	■								■	■
59. striped dolphin, *Stenella coeruleoalba*	LR(cd)		■	■	■	■		■	■	■		■	■					■	■
60. short-beaked common dolphin, *Delphinus delphis*	LC							■	■			■	■		?			■	■
61. long-beaked common dolphin, *Delphinus capensis*	LC									■				■					■
a. Arabian common dolphin, *D. capensis tropicalis*	LC?																		
62. Fraser's dolphin, *Lagenodelphis hosei*	DD									■									■
63. white-beaked dolphin, *Lagenorhynchus albirostris*	LC			■				■											
64. Atlantic white-sided dolphin, *Lagenorhynchus acutus*	LC							■											
65. Pacific white-sided dolphin, *Lagenorhynchus obliquidens*	LC									■							■		
66. dusky dolphin, *Lagenorhynchus obscurus*	DD				■	■													
a. dusky dolphin: South America, *L. obscurus fitzroyi*	NE				■	■													
b. dusky dolphin: Indian Ocean, *L. obscurus obscurus*	NE																		■
c. dusky dolphin: New Zealand, *L. obscurus subsp*	NE															■	■		
67. Peale's dolphin, *Lagenorhynchus australis*	DD				■														
68. hourglass dolphin, *Lagenorhynchus cruciger*	LC	■							■	■						■	■		
69. northern right whale dolphin, *Lissodelphis borealis*	LC									■							■		
70. southern right whale dolphin, *Lissodelphis peronii*	DD	■			■	■			■										
71. Risso's dolphin, *Grampus griseus*	DD							■	■	■		■						■	■
72. melon-headed whale, *Peponocephala electra*	LC					■				■									■
73. pygmy killer whale, *Feresa attenuata*	DD					■				■									■
74. false killer whale, *Pseudorca crassidens*	LC					■				■			■						■
75. orca, or killer whale, *Orcinus orca*	LR(cd)	■			■	■		■	■	■								■	■
76. long-finned pilot whale, *Globicephala melas*	LC	■			■	■		■	■										
a. long-finned pilot whale: North Atlantic, *G. melas melas*	NE							■	■										
b. long-finned pilot whale: North Pacific, *G. melas subsp*	NE-EX?																		
c. long-finned pilot whale: s hemisphere, *G. melas edwardii*	NE	■			■	■			■										
77. short-finned pilot whale, *Globicephala macrorhynchus*	LR(cd)								■	■		■						■	■
78. Irrawaddy dolphin, *Orcaella brevirostris*	DD																		■
a. Mahakam River (Irrawaddy) dolphin	CR																		

Key: ■ Indicates species is present in a marine region

Table 2.7 *Toothed whales: porpoises. World distribution and status of species, subspecies and key populations*

Toothed whales (suborder Odontoceti) in the family Phocoenidae, Porpoises (79–84)

Species, subspecies, key populations	Red List status	1	2	3	4	5	6	7	8	9	10	11	12	13	14	15	16	17	18
79. finless porpoise, *Neophocaena phocaenoides*	DD																■		
a. finless porpoise: Indian O, *N. phocaenoides phocaenoides*	NE										■	■							
b. finless porpoise: W Pacific, *N. phocaenoides sunameri*	NE													■	■				
c. finless porpoise: Yangtze, *N. phocaenoides asiaeorientalis*	EN				■														
80. harbor porpoise, *Phocoena phocoena*	VU					■	■	■	■										
a. harbor porpoise: North Atlantic, *P. phocoena phocoena*	NE															■	■		
b. harbor porpoise: Baltic Sea	VU															■			
c. harbor porpoise: Black Sea, *P. phocoena relicta*	VU			■															
d. harbor porpoise: E North Pacific, *P. phocoena vomerina*	NE						■												
e. harbor porpoise: W North Pacific, *P. phocoena (vomerina)*	NE															■	■		
81. vaquita, *Phocoena sinus*	CR	■																	
82. Burmeister's porpoise, *Phocoena spinipinnis*	DD									■									
83. spectacled porpoise, *Phocoena dioptrica*	DD	■								■									
84. Dall's porpoise, *Phocoenoides dalli*	LR(cd)																	■	
a. Dall's porpoise: dalli-phase, *P. dalli dalli*	NE																■		
b. Dall's porpoise: truei-phase, *P. dalli truei*	NE																		■

Key: ■ Indicates species is present in a marine region

2 Good cetacean-based MPA conservation means ecosystem-based conservation

Protecting cetaceans effectively means protecting all marine organisms living in the ecosystem and the ecosystem itself (Prideaux, 2003a). Since cetaceans typically occupy large habitats, there is the strong potential that effective programmes to conserve cetacean habitat will include protection of much more – sometimes even a network of MPAs – including a wide variety of other species, ecosystems and ecosystem processes.

3 Cetaceans provide an ecological monitor for the health of the marine environment

In every ecosystem with whales and dolphins, as the most visible species, cetaceans help to provide an effective monitoring system for the health of the environment. Toothed whales, and to some extent baleen whales, are good biological indicators of the status of the environment that they live in. As predators at the top of the marine food chain with a long lifespan measured in decades, they accumulate man-made polluting substances such as organochlorine compounds and heavy metals, which have implications not only for cetacean and human health but for the basic health of the ocean's ecosystems (Martineau et al, 1987; Martineau et al, 1994; O'Shea, 1999; O'Shea et al, 1999; Rejinders et al, 1999; Simmonds and Hutchinson, 1996). Cetaceans are also a good indicator of problems in the food chain brought on by overfishing or other factors, or in changes in marine environmental conditions. The El Niño phenomenon, for example, produced changes in cetacean distribution (Simmonds, pers comm 2002). Although the El Niño phenomenon is well known and has many indicators, cetacean distribution was immediately and dramatically affected, indicating broad ecological changes.

4 Cetacean popularity can be harnessed to extend management and increase funding for MPAs, thereby bringing larger areas of the ocean under ecosystem-based management

Habitats for toothed whales, plus baleen whale feeding areas, are typically productive marine habitats that support large populations of various fish, krill, copepods and other planktonic invertebrates. These areas may support commercial fishing industries, as well as whale watching, associated marine tourism and other human uses of the ecosystem. At a sustainable level, these uses are compatible, although carefully prepared management plans are needed. Ecosystem-based management should include not only protection of species, ecosystems and ecosystem processes but also management of human uses of the ecosystem. Identification of whale habitats, and attempts to create MPAs, could bring larger areas of the sea under ecosystem-based management plans. Further, the popularity of whales and dolphins with the public means that they can help promote education as well as attract interest and funding support for such management.

Obtaining MPAs and MPA networks using cetaceans as a key element in an overall plan of protecting larger ecosystems has almost untapped potential. Of course, much remains to be learned about how effectively a cetacean-focused approach will work to improve the conservation of other species, particularly in ecologically disturbed areas (Hooker and Gerber, 2004). In any case, we must not ignore or abandon the many other reasons for marine habitat conservation including coral reefs, mangroves, estuaries, seagrass beds and protection of the breeding and juvenile habitats for many fish and marine invertebrates – even if they are not part of cetacean MPAs.

3

Creating Better Marine Protected Areas for Cetaceans: Steps towards the Design, Establishment and Management of Marine Protected Areas for Cetaceans

Basic principles

The bible of marine protected area (MPA) planning and management is Salm and Clark's *Marine and Coastal Protected Areas: A Guide for Planners and Managers*, first published in 1984, revised in 1989 and 2000. This book is also useful in planning and managing areas which include cetaceans. Kelleher (1999, 2001) and Kelleher and Kenchington (1992) provide additional perspective on the development and establishment of MPAs, with many practical suggestions, drawing on Graeme Kelleher's valuable hindsight analysis from his time as head of the Great Barrier Reef Marine Park Authority from 1979 to 1994. In Meffe et al (1999), there is a stimulating 'big picture' discussion of what ought to be the guiding principles of marine mammal conservation and its implementation in view of the human relationship to nature. Below, I have expanded on some of Salm and Clark's, as well as Kelleher's and Meffe et al's, suggestions, specifically tailoring them to fit cetaceans and cetacean habitat. They are also incorporated in the 'Steps to creating better MPAs for cetaceans' section later in this chapter.

Early in their book, Salm and Clark highlight two important premises to keep in mind regarding the planning and management of all MPAs.

First is the fundamental linkage of marine with coastal and terrestrial ecosystems. MPAs cannot be considered or properly managed as separate from nearby terrestrial ecosystems. Several examples of key linkages are:

- most marine pollution comes from the land;
- a large portion of the biological productivity occurs in coastal waters which are modified by the flow of fresh water into the sea; and

- land-based humans have a dominating influence on the sea in terms of marine commerce, recreation, scientific exploration and other activities.

Second, marine systems and linkages occur on a global scale; occurrences in one part of the world ocean can have an impact far away, though the time scale for such events can be long – years to decades. For example, the bomb tests over Siberia that ended with the Test Ban Treaty in 1962 put the radioactive by-product tritium into the rivers of Siberia in the 1950s, which subsequently moved into surface waters and crossed the Arctic Ocean. Off Greenland, the tritium became part of deep water formation and was transported to the North Atlantic Deep Water. This tritium-tagged deep water began moving south and was off Bermuda by the early 1980s. Although the half-life for tritium means that it is no longer an environmental threat, the tritium-tagged water will soon be curving round South America en route to the North Pacific where the deep water will eventually rise and return to the surface. There is only one world ocean system and all the water circulates throughout it. Deep water transport is only one rather sluggish part of world ocean circulation, but it hints at the effects over space and time.

CETACEAN HABITAT NEEDS

Few cetacean scientists have considered and made evaluations of MPAs for cetaceans in terms of specific habitat needs. In 1999, Peter Evans and Erika Urquiola Pascual (2001) identified 39 such MPAs as part of their presentation to the European Cetacean Society. They outlined the prerequisites for creating MPAs for cetaceans and gave useful worldwide examples of different types of protection based on various cetacean habitat needs. Prideaux (2003b, 2003c) establishes a strong case for cetacean critical habitat and examines in detail the value to cetaceans of an ecosystem-based and regional management approach. Her work shows that protecting cetacean critical habitat using ecosystem-based management provides benefits to the focal species as well as to ecosystems and human communities.

Evaluating cetacean habitat needs with the idea of creating and extending MPAs and enforcing the management provisions in existing MPAs is a complex, time-consuming, continual process. First, one needs to accumulate the literature for cetaceans found in such journals as *Marine Mammal Science, Canadian Journal of Zoology, Coastal Management, Conservation Biology, Journal of Cetacean Research and Management*, and *Environmental Conservation*, as well as from conferences and workshops (Society of Marine Mammalogy, European Cetacean Society, Latin American Marine Mammal Society, South American Specialists in Aquatic Mammals, Society of Latin American Specialists in Aquatic Mammals, and many other regional and national societies). There are also a number of volumes in the marine mammal field which gather and synthesize the data from key papers (for example, Mann et al, 2000; Perrin et al, 2002; Reynolds and Rommel, 1999; Simmonds and Hutchinson, 1996; Twiss and Reeves, 1999).

The International Whaling Commission (IWC) special volumes, on the *Cephalorhynchus* dolphins, northern hemisphere pilot whales, porpoises and others provide reviews of cetacean status (for example, Bjørge and Donovan, 1995; Brownell and Donovan, 1988; Donovan et al, 1993). In addition, Klinowska (1991), in the IUCN Red Data book on cetaceans, takes a species-by-species approach and includes sections for each species' habitat needs and status. This book should be updated regularly. Meantime, the Red List website has the latest status list of cetacean species as well as certain subspecies and populations (see www.redlist.org).

One valuable approach, in terms of evaluating the most pressing cetacean habitat needs, is the periodic IUCN Species Survival Commission prescription for the conservation of cetaceans. The most recent cetacean action plan covers 2002–2010 (Reeves et al, 2003). These action plans aim to cover all cetaceans but there are many admitted gaps. They focus on prescriptions for rare and endangered species and populations, but as this is part of the rationale of making MPAs, this alone would make the work valuable for cetacean-based MPA creation or ecosystem-based conservation which features or includes cetaceans.

A web-based tool called SEAMAP has great potential for enabling the selection of MPA sites that will best meet particular cetacean habitat needs. This project of the Ocean Biogeographic Information System (OBIS) has compiled taxonomic and geo-referenced data on nearly 200 species of marine mammals, sea turtles and seabirds. It allows easy access to physical oceanographic data at regional and global scales as well as software tools for biogeographic analysis and site selection (*MPA News*, 2004). (Access to the OBIS-SEAMAP database and software tools is free; see http://obismap.env.duke.edu.)

Another essential tool, which is being updated, is the detailed Kelleher et al (1995b) *A Global Representative System of Marine Protected Areas*. Whales and dolphins are only briefly considered in its four volumes, but it provides a superb overview of each region and most coastal countries' MPA status. Because it was prepared with national and regional advisory committees, it also carries considerable weight in its evaluations of existing MPAs and recommendations for possible new MPAs and better management. Some countries have seen considerable progress toward MPA conservation since 1995; the situation for others remains the same or worse. This, too, is an effort that needs re-evaluation and updating every 5–10 years at minimum.

Yet all of the above are only part of our knowledge base on cetaceans. A largely untapped resource in evaluating cetacean habitat lies in the everyday experiences of the biologists, knowledgeable fishing crews, lighthouse keepers, whale watch operators, naturalists and others who spend their days – at least part of them – in the presence of cetaceans. The era of photographic identification (photo-ID) work, which started on orcas, bottlenose dolphins and gray, humpback and right whales in the early 1970s, along with the steady growth of whale watching in 495 communities in 87 countries and overseas territories, has meant that large numbers of people are aware of, and making useful observations of, cetaceans. It is the accumulated wealth of this knowledge, much of which is unpublished and even unwritten, that we need to consider. We need to start to combine the published work on cetacean habitat with the unpublished and unwritten that may be valuable in terms of identifying cetacean critical habitat and creating MPAs for cetaceans. Of course, we also need more targeted systematic studies to define cetacean habitat needs such as Lusseau and Higham's (in press) work on defining critical habitats for bottlenose dolphins in New Zealand.

This book is designed to provide an easy way for people working on cetaceans or cetacean conservation in one area of the world to consider the larger picture, to be able to contact people in other parts of their own country or the world, and then to devise the networks of MPAs that are going to be needed to protect cetaceans, many of which do not respect national or international boundaries and which range seasonally and annually over large ocean areas.

Chapter 5 of this book has extensive tables for each of the 18 marine regions of the world. Each table lists not only existing MPAs but also those which have been proposed by government bodies, conservation organizations and, in some cases, researchers. Each entry details what is known about the MPA and the rationale for protection. There are also key contacts and websites for further information. In sum, this is designed to be a first effort to create not only a grass-roots directory of all the MPAs, proposed and existing, which feature or include cetaceans, but to make a start towards gathering the accumulated expertise for each of these areas. With each person and group working in so many corners of the sea for MPA conservation, much can be accomplished for whales and dolphins and ecosystems. The challenge now is for people to start to work together more effectively.

THE VALUE OF ECOSYSTEM-BASED MANAGEMENT

There is much to be gained for cetaceans and other marine species by using an ecosystem-based management approach to marine conservation. In the words of Graeme Kelleher (2001): 'Because of the highly connected nature of the sea, which efficiently transmits substances and forcing factors, an MPA will rarely succeed unless it is embedded in, or is so large that it constitutes, an integrated ecosystem management regime.' Ecosystem-based management has been employed in terrestrial ecosystems for some years but it is fairly new as applied to the ocean.

The history of the management of the world ocean, in both national (to the limit of EEZs) and international (high-seas) waters, is mostly no management, or almost unrestrained exploitation. The minimal management that has existed has been multijurisdictional, with industries and nations largely operating independently (and sometimes at cross-purposes) to each other. The intertwined stories of the exploitation of world fish, seal and whale resources provide many examples of the failure of such management. Ecosystem-based management, though much more complex and requiring substantial scientific expertise, holds the promise of at least delivering to the future healthy ocean ecosystems that are capable of sustaining a rich diversity of phytoplankton, zooplankton, fish and whales.

This ecosystem-based approach has its roots in an understanding that the ecosystem is the key element for conservation, and it cements the shift from species to ecosystem protection that most protected area thinkers, strategists and managers undertook during the 1980s. Although countries have been slow to take up this idea, marine protected area practitioners now realize that the best way to protect and restore marine habitats is through ecosystem-based management using networks of zoned MPAs which include core protection areas or highly protected reserves.

An ecosystem-based management model manages human interactions with ecosystems in order to protect and maintain ecosystem integrity and to minimize adverse impacts. This requires a whole ecosystem approach through ongoing scientific analysis and a commitment to adapt management practice quickly when new information signals a need for change.

One key approach is to adopt large marine ecosystems (LMEs) as the principal assessment and management units for ecosystem-based management. LMEs are large regions of the sea – typically 77,000 mi^2 (200,000 km^2) or greater – characterized by distinct bathymetry, hydrography, productivity and trophically dependent populations. The 64 LMEs of the world ocean, which are listed by marine region in Chapter 5, are responsible for an estimated 95 per cent of the world's fisheries, measured according to biomass. Recognizing the importance of researching and understanding LMEs, IUCN and NOAA (the US National Oceanic and Atmospheric Administration) have recently joined forces in an action programme to assist developing countries in planning and implementing an ecosystem-based strategy focused on LMEs.

Ecosystem-based MPAs and MPA networks help orient management towards the whole ecosystem, rather than single species, stocks or resources. This approach facilitates the multiple objectives of marine management, including the protection of habitat, biodiversity and fisheries. This approach is also the best insurance against uncertainty, effectively embodying the precautionary approach.

In terms of an ecosystem-based strategy, MPAs provide a place as well as the reason to institute basic, long-term scientific research programmes. The research needed for ecosystem-based management should be a priority but it can be conducted alongside the work to define and design MPAs, and work on studying cetacean and other wildlife critical habitat needs. Yet it is unlikely that this kind of research can be done in depth before, or as a condition to, making a protected area. The research to support and fully implement ecosystem-based management as part of an MPA is long-term research that will require detailed biological inventories, baseline studies, experimental research and monitoring schemes, all requiring considerable time and expense, as well as regular assessments and re-evaluation and the development of new techniques and expertise. Marine ecosystem-based management is in its infancy. Some of the difficulties and challenges are spelled out in Jay Barlow's (2002) article on 'Management' in the *Encyclopedia of Marine Mammals*.

Ecosystem management refers to approaches ranging from simply considering the impact of a management decision on other elements of the ecosystem to the simultaneous optimization of management strategies to meet management goals of all elements of an ecosystem. There are no examples of the latter approach, although … the signatory nations of the Convention for the Conservation of Antarctic Marine Living Resources (CCAMLR) are pursuing this goal … it is unarguably true that improvements can be made in resource management by considering ecosystem interactions [but] predicting the implications of even a simple ecosystem perturbation is far beyond our current capabilities. Significant progress in implementing ecosystem management may be left to future generations (Barlow, 2002, pp708–9).

Yet Barlow underestimates the extent of the work being done by CCAMLR, whose Ecosystem Monitoring Program focuses on the management of the ecosystem, including fisheries, and uses selected sites and species as indicators in the study of long-term trends. As well, calls for ecosystem-based management have been made in the US through the National Research Council report on marine protected areas (Commission on Geosciences, Environment and Resources, 2000). Worldwide, the 189 countries that sent representatives to the World Summit on Sustainable Development (WSSD) in 2002 included in their 'Plan of Implementation' the provision to encourage the application of the ecosystem approach for the sustainable development of the ocean by 2010. To accomplish this, the 'White Water to Blue Water' Partnership was set up to promote integrated watershed and marine ecosystem-based management through existing treaties and conventions, and the Wider Caribbean marine region was selected as the first project area, attracting significant funding and expertise.

Meanwhile, in Australia, ecosystem-based management has already become a central part of its new, comprehensive 'Oceans Policy' (Commonwealth of Australia, 1998). In 2002, WWF Australia unveiled a valuable policy paper outlining the principles for developing ecosystem-based management of world ocean capture fisheries 'as a first step in developing an internationally accepted, ecologically-based framework for the sustainable management of human activities' in the world ocean (Ward et al, 2002). The WWF paper does not claim to provide a quick fix for all problems facing the marine environment and the extraction of resources from it, nor does it attempt to establish a comprehensive framework for all ecosystem-based management, but it effectively presents a way forward, building for the most part on existing fishery management approaches, to be adapted and improved over time through continuous monitoring and community stakeholder involvement.

In 2003, the Australian Conservation Foundation, Victorian National Parks Association, Australian Marine Conservation Society and the Whale and Dolphin Conservation Society launched *Oceans Eleven* which builds on the previous work of WWF and details an eleven-step approach for ecosystem-based management of large marine regions (Smyth et al, 2003). This work focuses on the cross-jurisdictional management of marine regions in Australia and makes key recommendations including the development of appropriate legislation, the creation of a research coordination body, the planning and creation of representative marine protected areas and the commitment to community capacity building and involvement. Throughout the process, there would be an ongoing, iterative, ecosystem-based management regime, which would address multiple and cumulative impacts.

The work in Australia, as well as in the Antarctic, the Caribbean and the US, has just begun, and it holds great promise for what may be possible elsewhere. It is clearly time to invest in the idea of ecosystem-based management, and the best way to do this is to try to put it into action, exploring the process and learning from the mistakes of others.

STEPS TO CREATING BETTER MPAS FOR CETACEANS

The basic requirements for MPAs in general are summarized in Box 3.1. There is no one ideal MPA for cetaceans, as cetacean needs vary by species, population and location, and must be evaluated in view of existing and possible future human uses of an area. The aim here is to provide a road map to identify and obtain the best possible cetacean MPAs in a given area or for the particular cetacean whose habitat is to be protected.

There are a number of steps that need to be undertaken in order to achieve the desired high level of conservation for cetaceans using MPAs. In the steps that follow, it is important to remember that marine or any type of conservation is best achieved through an integration of expertise from various fields including economics, policy development, communication, political science, adaptive management, conflict resolution, law, human behaviour, clarification of property rights issues, sociology, statistical uncertainty, philosophy and ethics (Meffe et al, 1999). Useful and appropriate findings from these various areas must then be integrated with good biological and ecological knowledge, and a generous application of the precautionary approach. Finally, we must keep in mind the pressure from increasing human population and corresponding resource use, both of which impart a keen sense of urgency to MPA conservation.

The key steps to creating an MPA mainly or partly for cetaceans can be broken down as follows:

1 Do a literature review and tap existing expertise to uncover critical habitat, as far as is known, for a given area or for the given cetacean species or population(s). Check the OBIS SEAMAP database to see what may be available on cetacean and other marine species distribution (see http://obismap. env.duke.edu).

2 Examine the literature and case studies on MPAs. Chapter 5 of this book could be used as a starting point, with the case studies provided along with contacts and references for further information and follow-up. A full bibliography, with many key references on MPAs, is provided at the back of the book. A 2001 workshop on 'Improving Applications of Science in MPA Design

---

BOX 3.1 SUMMARY OF BASIC REQUIREMENTS FOR AN MPA

For best results, a marine protected area must have:

- scientific background research into critical habitat requirements of cetaceans and other species, as well as the marine ecology and an inventory of the area;
- early multidisciplinary input to choose, plan, implement and review the MPA;
- a good relationship with local communities and all stakeholders who participate in the MPA process because they see tangible benefits for themselves and others;
- sensible boundaries or networks in view of the species, ecosystems and ecosystem processes that are being protected;
- good MPA design, built around substantial IUCN Category I core areas, with additional zones or levels of protection such as in the biosphere reserve model;
- a comprehensive ecosystem-based and socioeconomic management plan;
- legal recognition as well as broad public acceptance;
- an educational programme which is interactive, reciprocal and continuous for those who will use, travel through or visit the protected area, directed at communities living near the area, fishermen, tourists and other commercial users of the sea within and outside the MPA;
- management of pollution, both marine and land-based (from nearby or adjacent land areas);
- an enforcement programme; and
- reassessment and re-evaluation (both self and third-party) at periodic intervals with stakeholder input.

---

and Management' provides some up-to-date expertise and contacts (see www.gcfi.org).

3 Identify funding sources for surveys, research, planning, development and other phases of MPA identification and creation, as well as potentially for management. Funding sources can be local, national, regional and international. The largest international source of funding for biodiversity conservation including MPAs is the Global Environment Facility (GEF), administered by the World Bank, the United Nations Environment Programme (UNEP) and the United Nations Development Programme (UNDP). In recent years, more than 30 countries have shared approximately US$100 million per year for marine conservation projects (UNEP/CBD/SBSTTA, 2003). Other international sources include the UNDP, bilateral-aid agencies, conservation groups and other non-governmental organizations (NGOs) and the various regional development banks such as the Asian Development Bank. Useful publications on raising revenues for MPAs include Lindberg (2001) and Offen (2003). A study on the costs of managing MPAs was prepared by Gravestock (2002). Publications from a June 2000 'Economics of Marine Protected Areas' conference (Vancouver, BC, Canada) have appeared in the journals *Natural Resource Modeling* (15:3 and 15:4) and *Coastal Management* (30:2).

This step will likely need to be revisited several times during the process of MPA development, creation and management. According to Graeme Kelleher (2001): 'Financial sustainability needs to be built in from the beginning. Socioeconomic considerations usually determine the success or failure of MPAs. In addition to biophysical factors, these considerations should be addressed from the outset in identifying sites for, selecting and managing MPAs.'

4 Commission field surveys for cetaceans and other rare, endangered and important species, as needed. Conduct research into wild whale and dolphin populations using air and shipboard surveys, radio and satellite tracking (using benign methods), hydrophone recording and photo-ID studies to:

- establish movements, migration and seasonal patterns;
- determine hunting behaviour and food preferences;
- establish critical habitat 'home range', including feeding, mating and calving grounds, as well as areas important for social and cultural activities, including but not limited to resting, singing, socializing, and rubbing on rocks; and
- monitor populations throughout the year and, ideally for at least two to three years, to determine if area use is consistent.

Full population biology studies can take several to many years depending on the size of the area, logistics, level of funding, and so forth, but there are available strategies for rapidly obtaining a reasonable amount of data. In Indonesian parks, for example, 'rapid ecological assessment' studies for cetaceans have provided broad stroke details on cetacean abundance and distribution within and outside the park boundaries in a single season. With experienced cetacean observers, this could be enough to propose working boundaries for critical habitat and other areas or zones.

5 Identify the critical habitat needs specific to the population or group to be protected using the general guidelines, literature reviews and case studies but giving the most weight to the results of the particular field surveys (see key step 4 above).

6 Following an ecosystem-based approach to conservation, examine the food chains of cetaceans and other key species and establish a strategy for critical habitat protection for these species too, not all of which would be located in the immediate area being considered for an MPA. The strategy could include the creation or enhancement of proposed or other existing MPAs, formulating fishing agreements and investigating other treaties and conventions. Make sure that essential ecosystem processes, such as upwellings and other processes responsible for high biological productivity, are protected – both within and outside the MPA. Identify and take note of LMEs, as identified for each marine region in Chapter 5. It will not be possible to protect these in their entirety but knowing the big picture helps ensure that the ecological issues and ecosystems are considered within large spatial scales as well as in detail.

7 Research national and provincial or state laws, as well as regional and international conventions, to determine existing national, regional and international frameworks that might allow for creating an MPA. For most countries, the most important legal instruments for MPAs are provincial (or state) and particularly national regulations – the laws of each country. However, there are also a considerable number of regional and international conventions and treaties which may be used to create or enhance marine protected areas, and some of these conventions provide detailed guidance, confer international prestige and interest, and/or help fulfil international responsibilities through their protection. At the regional level, there are initiatives such as OSPAR (for northwest Europe), ACCOBAMS (the Mediterranean and Black seas) and the European Community (EC countries), which have various marine habitat protection plans or options to which member countries subscribe. The Convention on the Conservation of Migratory Species of Wild Animals (CMS), in particular, may prove valuable for regional protection mechanisms (Prideaux, 2003b). On the other hand, and at a completely different scale, cetacean sanctuaries have been proposed and approved at the international level, primarily on the high seas, through international bodies such as the IWC. (See Table 1.6, p43, for a list of international treaties, conventions and other agreements with a bearing on MPAs and the conservation of cetaceans.)

Further detail and discussion of the legal instruments can be found in Salm and Clark (1989, 2000), Kelleher et al (1995b) and Scovazzi (1999). Urquiola and Evans (2001) conducted a review of the various legal instruments for setting up MPAs in Europe. A good summary of all US regulations relating to marine mammals, including MPAs, can be found in Twiss and Reeves (1999). This same volume has a summary of legal instruments pertaining to Antarctica. There is also useful background information related to cetaceans, whale watching and protected areas in Birnie and Moscrop (2000) and on cetacean and wildlife legal agreements on the website of the Wildlife Interest Group of the American Society of International Law (see http://eelink.net/~asilwildlife/legislat.shtml).

8 Determine and evaluate all human uses of the area: commercial and sports fishing; whale watching and marine tourism; recreational boating; shipping and other marine traffic; mineral, oil and gas leases; and other activities. It is essential to be aware of the full socioeconomic consequences of any proposed MPA. A cost–benefit analysis (CBA) such as that suggested in Dixon and Sherman (1990), IFAW (1999), IUCN (2000) and Wells (1997) will go far in terms of allowing the various existing and potential users and conservers of an area to be able to create an effective MPA appropriately balanced in size and scope. Conservationists should not be afraid of such an analysis if it is conducted by an economist skilled in environmental assessments; a complete CBA will give full weight to many biodiversity and ecosystem values that few MPA users or management plans ever consider. The true social, environmental and economic costs of overfishing, whaling, ocean dumping and the mining of the sea bed are carefully weighed and accounted for (Jackson et al, 2001). The ecosystem services from proposed protected areas should also be evaluated, given a number value and included in these assessments (see Costanza et al, 1997; IFAW, 1999; IUCN, 2000).

The socioeconomic evaluation process can be sophisticated and detailed, as well as local and responsive to users of the potential MPA and local communities, and the results will help determine choice of site, boundaries, zoning and the appropriate kind and extent of protection. The stakeholders should be involved in the evaluation process, as well as in the subsequent management plan which benefits from the evaluation (see key step 11 below).

9 Determine areas that can be used for mixed human and cetacean use and core protection areas, where cetaceans or their fish prey should be left alone. If this is a proposal for a zoned area, prepare a zoning plan. A detailed schematic of all the details needed for an effective zoning plan can be found in Kelleher and Kenchington (1992).

10 Consider the prevailing oceanography of the area, including influence from the land and terrestrial water systems, existing and potential marine pollution sources and patterns, shipping traffic, and other problems.

11 Consider the following factors or criteria (A–H below) to decide whether an area should be proposed as a cetacean MPA. These criteria, adapted and expanded from Kelleher and Kenchington (1992), are also useful in determining the boundaries for any proposed MPA. They feature many of the key critical habitat considerations but they also contain elements essential for the logistic and developmental aspects and roles of biosphere reserves. There are also some points of strategic value.

A Ecological importance

Does the proposed MPA:

- contain cetacean feeding, breeding, nursery or rest areas?
- contain habitat for rare or endangered cetacean species?
- contain rare or unique habitat for cetacean species?
- have a useful or valuable variety of cetacean and other habitats?
- contain any of the above cetacean habitats which could be proposed as IUCN Category I core areas?
- contribute to maintenance of essential ecological processes or life-support systems (eg, upwellings and habitat for fish larvae important as prey, which could be protected in IUCN Category I core areas)?
- preserve key cetacean genetic diversity?
- have integrity (the degree to which the area either by itself or in association with other protected areas encompasses a complete ecosystem)?

B Scientific importance

Does the proposed MPA:

- have value for research and monitoring of cetaceans?

C Economic importance

Does the proposed MPA:

- have a potential to make a contribution to economic value (or to enhance the existing value) through protection as an MPA?
- enhance effective management of whale watching tourism and overall protection of the area for recreation?

D Social importance

Does the proposed MPA:

- have existing or potential value to local communities and at the national and international level because of its aesthetic, educational, recreational, heritage, historical and/or cultural value?

E Biogeographic importance

Does the proposed MPA:

- contain rare biogeographic qualities?
- represent an example of a biogeographic type or types?
- contain unique or unusual geological features?

F Naturalness

Does the proposed MPA:

- have a natural quality (the extent to which the area has been protected from, or has not been subject to, human-induced change)?

G National or international significance

Does the proposed MPA:

- have the potential to be included in national 'protected area' legislation (see the various country boxes in Chapter 5)?
- have the potential to gain recognition from international forums or conventions, such as listing on the World Heritage List, or could it be declared as a biosphere reserve, or other type of international designation (see Table 1.6)?

H Feasibility and practicality

Is the proposed MPA:

- in a country with laws that can be used to make an effective MPA?
- broadly supported by the public in general and specifically local communities?
- politically acceptable?
- compatible with existing use of the area, or can it be argued that protection is preferable?
- insulated from external destructive influences, or can such influences be controlled or removed?
- compatible with existing management regimes and/or can it be managed effectively, including enforcement of provisions?

12 As early as possible, get together with all stakeholders and appropriate international supporters, as well as those with professional expertise, and formulate a draft management plan. Try to involve the fullest range of disciplines from the start. In terms of stakeholders, it is usually easy to invite and meet with conservation organizations, researchers, appropriate government representatives, whale watch and marine tourism operators and local community officials. It may be more difficult, but essential, to involve commercial fishermen, indigenous or aboriginal groups, local residents and potential or existing polluters. If any groups are past or future stakeholders, special effort should be made to seek out and support their participation, too. All stakeholders must be made aware of benefits that will accrue from MPA creation. For a guide to involving fishermen in the MPA process, see Bernstein (2002). Other valuable lessons on the problems and pitfalls of MPA creation due to the failure to engage local communities can be learned from Jon Lien's analysis of a failed MPA in northeast Newfoundland in the 1990s (Lien, 1999).

Following what will often be an extended consultation process, the draft management plan needs to be circulated for public and user input. Then, as time passes, it must be modified in light of changes in whale distribution, visitor numbers, and other findings and changes that come to light. A detailed schematic of all the details needed to prepare an effective management plan can be found in Kelleher and Kenchington (1992).

13 As part of the management plan, set up education programmes for all stakeholders including users and local communities to teach about the behaviour of whales and dolphins, how to live and work around them and how best to conserve them (see IFAW, WWF and WDCS, 1997). Keep in mind a guiding principle of conservation from Meffe et al (1999): The best communication and conservation education programmes are interactive, reciprocal and continuous (this also applies to steps 8, 12, 14, 16 and 17 in this list).

Part of making a working MPA system is having an educated electorate, researchers and managers who are focused toward ecosystem-based, critical habitat approaches, as well as stakeholders in every community who are involved in the process. As with other issues, depending on the country, government can initiate the education process. Still, as a practical matter, it will take the concerted efforts of researchers, local and national conservation organizations and international groups such as Conservation International, Greenpeace, WWF, the International Fund for Animal Welfare (IFAW) and WDCS in order to get the public to become aware of the importance of conserving specific ocean habitats through marine protected areas.

The job of informing the public is considerable. In 1999, for example, SeaWeb, an American project to raise public awareness of the ocean, commissioned The Mellman Group to do a public survey of American attitudes toward MPAs (*MPA News*, 2000a). There were some disturbing findings:

- Only a third of those surveyed were even aware of the US National Marine Sanctuary Program (which originated in 1972) or its 13 flagship sanctuaries.
- 43 per cent of those surveyed believed that the ocean was a homogeneous body of water and that protecting one particular area of it from pollution or overfishing was useless.

The survey did find that people generally favour increased protection of ocean habitat, but the information gap has important conservation implications. For those who wish to promote and try to create a new MPA, they must first explain to the public, policy-makers, bureaucrats and others what an MPA is and why they are needed.

By 2002, there were indications in certain parts of the world that MPAs were becoming better known and supported. In a public poll of research in British Columbia, Canada, 75 per cent of recipients supported the idea of setting aside territorial waters as reserves to protect more species and ecosystem processes.

14 As part of the management plan, determine how enforcement will be organized. Recognize that a good education programme, in addition to its value in promoting and planning MPAs, is an essential component of effective management and enforcement.

15 Following on from step 7 above, work to obtain the legal status for the proposed marine protected area, recognizing that a combination of local, state/provincial and national legislation and international convention and recognition may be the best solution, and that any official status may take years to obtain. Therefore, a pragmatic approach may be necessary, with working plans and strategies for various scenarios and levels of protection.

16 Continue to develop, manage and enhance the human relationship to the MPA. Address changing socioeconomic needs. The 2001 workshop 'Human

System Connectivity: A Need for MPA Management Effectiveness' provides useful tips (*MPA News*, 2002b).

17 Consider achieving protection status not as a final goal but as a first stage or step towards conservation. Creating effective protected areas, whether they are marine- (MPAs) or land-based, is an iterative, participatory process, subject to change, and is bound to fail if the management plan is seen as set in stone or as a fixed law imposed from the outside. As with MPA design, management must be both top-down and bottom-up. An MPA must have clearly defined objectives against which its performance is regularly checked, and a monitoring programme to assess management effectiveness and recommend changes (Kelleher, 2001).

18 Don't give up and don't stop working for the best MPA possible. The battle for marine protection, once enjoined, is permanent and continuous. However, as Graeme Kelleher (2001) advises: 'It is better to have an MPA that is not ideal in an ecological sense but which meets the primary objective than to strive vainly to create the "perfect" MPA. It is usually a mistake to postpone action on the establishment of an MPA because biophysical information is incomplete. There will usually be sufficient existing information to indicate whether the MPA is justified ecologically and to set reasonable boundaries.'

4

STRATEGIES FOR PROTECTING CETACEANS TO COMPLEMENT AND SUPPLEMENT MARINE PROTECTED AREAS

CONSERVATION STRATEGIES FOR CETACEANS BESIDES MPAs

Networks of marine protected areas (MPAs), if well organized as part of ecosystem-based management to protect the critical habitat of cetaceans, would ideally form the centrepiece for cetacean conservation. However, various complementary and supplementary measures should also be taken – partly because network planning is rarely comprehensive and, even if it is, additional measures provide insurance against habitat or other degradation in future. In practice, most MPAs fall short of the desired comprehensive level of protection, which means that other conservation strategies are essential.

MPAs must be considered in the broader context of a general management plan for coastal and marine resources, that is, an umbrella programme for conservation of renewable resources as well as implementation of ecosystem-based management principles (Salm and Clark, 1989, 2000; Augustowski and Palazzo, 2003). Each cetacean population as well as each ecosystem should have its own 'survival plan'. Some species survival plans do exist, particularly for endangered cetaceans such as North Atlantic right and blue whales in the US. Also useful is the broad survey featuring some of the more endangered cetacean species in the Cetacean Action Plan of the IUCN Species Survival Commission's Cetacean Specialist Group (Reeves et al, 2003). But for many cetacean populations and species there is little analysis even if there are data available. Cetacean survival plans would start with the fundamental importance of habitat but would also include a consideration of all of the following:

1 Laws are needed to prevent harassment, hunting, capturing and killing, including the direct taking or the incidental killing of cetaceans in fishermen's nets or in other gear.

2 Pollution must be reduced or preferably eliminated in waters within, all around and from the land and rivers affecting given MPAs.

3 No MPAs, or even networks of MPAs, are able to conserve the entire range of a cetacean population or to cover the entire range of possible impacts. Therefore, research must be undertaken to determine the extent of other threats within the population's range, and to mitigate these as much as possible. Obviously, the most important areas are feeding, calving and breeding grounds, but negative factors can also damage a population using an area as a migration corridor. Ship traffic, particularly in known whale habitats, should be subject to legislation that requires posting watches and even slowing down in certain areas. The problem of North Atlantic right whales that are hit by shipping traffic is serious enough now to be considered the difference in the species' ultimate survival (Kraus, 1990). Right whales are hit wherever they are found, although they may be particularly vulnerable on their northern feeding grounds, some of which are in or near shipping lanes. MPAs and special conservation zones are imposing marine traffic speed zones, but the fear is that it may not be enough unless ships are able to avoid striking North Atlantic right whales throughout their entire range.

4 Within the MPA and nearby areas there must be educational activities aimed at fishermen, whale watch operators, commercial shipping operators and recreational boaters, as well as the general public. The programme should include not only users of the MPA, but those who pass through the area or who use nearby areas.

5 Adequate fishing regulations and management must be established in and near the MPA to prevent overfishing particularly of species that may have an impact on cetacean food chains.

6 A scientific programme is essential to monitor and study the ecology of the marine protected area, as well as the important species including other cetaceans and top predators, prey species, and the plankton – the entire ecosystem. This ecosystem-based research programme must include regular data collection and analysis covering biology, behaviour, range and habitat use, among other things. The scientific information must then be publicized both through professional journals to researchers and wildlife managers, as well as to MPA users, including whale watchers, fishermen, boaters, appropriate industry and the general public.

7 National laws and international agreements – not just those pertaining to MPAs but those concerning species protection, trade and other matters – should be researched and utilized for the additional protections they can offer (see Table 1.6 on p43).

8 Some countries, states and provinces have established regimes of land use planning and coastal zone management that can provide useful management tools for wildlife corridors and transition zones.

9 A big part of any conservation strategy is the political dimension. This means that campaigning conservationists with good lobbying and overall communication skills can help create an awareness of and constituency for cetacean needs. In dealing with politicians and bureaucrats, remember the power of the people. Building broad public support for all kinds of cetacean conservation especially through expansion of items 4 and 6 above (educational and scientific aspects) can go a long way towards creating the depth of sympathy for cetaceans that can move or, if necessary, force politicians and bureaucrats to act.

OTHER PRAGMATIC APPROACHES

In some countries, there have been calls to direct marine conservation efforts away from MPAs towards a purely ecosystem-based management approach, with MPAs an occasional or incidental part of conservation. In other parts of the world, MPAs may be difficult or impossible to obtain. This may be because of a prejudice against designating protected areas. Sometimes, local extractive marine industries such as whaling, dolphin hunting and sealing make serious habitat conservation an unpopular suggestion. Japan, for example, has been criticized by marine conservationists and scientists for having one of the weakest MPA programmes of all developed countries and for neglecting to consider marine mammals in biodiversity conservation plans (see Box 5.10 Do MPAs really exist in Japan?, p379). And in some countries with MPA programmes, it is clear that MPAs are not always the answer for marine ecosystem protection in general or cetacean habitat protection in particular. The bottom line is that whatever kind of management helps the situation, even a little, is better than nothing at all. The hope is that the 'powers that be' will take these suggestions to heart and work to improve the situation. Yet, at the same time, we the people must drive the powers that be to do a good job.

Of course, national policies and cultural beliefs are subject to change. There is no doubt that for most of the world the idea of MPAs has gained some acceptance, even powerful currency, as a tool for marine conservation, although it has a long way to go before it becomes meaningfully enshrined in every country's environmental policy. In the absence of better or more widely accepted alternative regimes for protecting essential ecosystems and species habitat, MPAs are here to stay. What is needed, for each country, is a determination to work for both high quality MPAs, as well as towards a high quality integrated national marine policy and legal framework.

5

HABITAT PROTECTION FOR CETACEANS AROUND THE WORLD: STATUS AND PROSPECTS

INTRODUCTION

To evaluate the present status of habitat protection for cetaceans, I have examined each of the 18 marine regions of the world ocean following the scheme adopted by the IUCN World Commission on Protected Areas (WCPA, formerly CNPPA) (Kelleher et al, 1995c). The 18 marine regions were devised mainly on the basis of biogeographic criteria but, for practical reasons, also pay heed to political or pragmatic boundaries. For example, South Africa, extends from the Atlantic to the Indian oceans but is all included in Marine Region 8, West Africa. In addition, Central America, minus México, is included as part of the Southeast Pacific Marine Region, and a large part of the Arctic of northern Alaska and Canada is included with the Northwest Atlantic. Despite these and a few other incongruities, I have used the WCPA system of dividing the 18 regions, mainly for practical reasons of consistency for MPA practitioners (see Figure 5.1).

Initially, I began preparing country accounts for each of the 151 coastal countries and 47 island territories, describing cetacean habitat in each. This too-detailed approach was soon abandoned in favour of a marine region approach. The rationale is that few cetaceans reside entirely in the waters of a single country; exceptions are the Yangtze River dolphin in China, vaquita in México and Hector's dolphin in New Zealand. Therefore, conservation issues are primarily a regional matter. The regional approach also lends itself to discussion

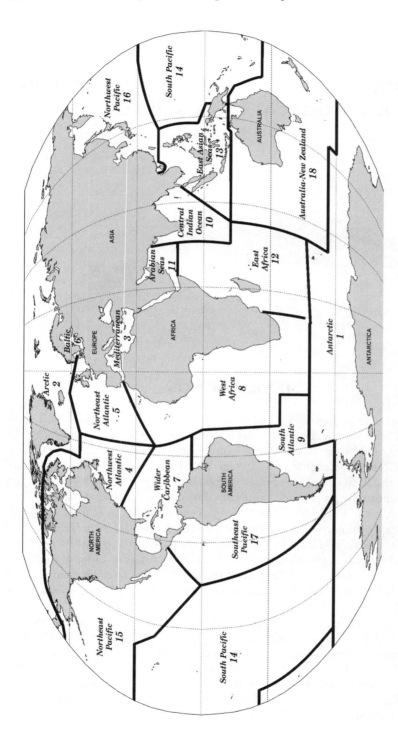

Figure 5.1 *Map of the 18 marine regions of the world*

The IUCN World Commission on Protected Areas (WCPA) divides the world ocean into 18 marine regions. See Table 5.1 for a complete listing of the countries and territories in each marine region.

Table 5.1 *Marine regions: countries, biogeographic zones and key treaties*

MARINE REGION	1 Antarctic	Biogeographic zones	No division into biogeographic zones

Countries and territories
Antarctica, Balleny Island Archipelago (various country bases but no government); South Georgia Island and South Sandwich Islands (UK), Bouvet (Norway), Prince Edward Island and Marion Island (South Africa), Crozet Islands and Kerguelen Islands (France), Heard Island and McDonald Islands (Australia)

Key regional treaties and conventions
CCAMLR – Convention on the Conservation of Antarctic Marine Living Resources; The Madrid Protocol (Protocol on Environmental Protection to the Antarctic Treaty)

MARINE REGION	2 Arctic	Biogeographic zones	Five biogeographic zones: High Arctic Oceanic, High Arctic Coastal, Arctic Coastal, Arctic Maritime, Norwegian Coast

Countries and territories
Canada (far north only), Faeroe Islands (Denmark), Greenland (Denmark), Iceland, Norway, Russia (north only), Shetland Islands (UK), Svalbard (Norway)

Key regional treaties and conventions
Protection of the Arctic Marine Environment (PAME), Conservation of Arctic Flora and Fauna (CAFF), OSPAR Convention

MARINE REGION	3 Mediterranean	Biogeographic zones	Ten biogeographic zones: Alborán Sea, Algerian Basin, Tyrrhenian Basin, Ionian Basin, Levantine Basin, Aegean Sea, Adriatic Sea, Marmara Sea, Black Sea, Azov Sea

Countries and territories
Mediterranean: Albania, Algeria, Bosnia-Herzogovina, Croatia, Cyprus, Egypt, France, Gibraltar (UK), Greece, Israel, Italy, Lebanon, Libya, Malta, Monaco, Montenegro, Morocco, Slovenia, Spain, Syria, Tunisia, Turkey, Yugoslavia; Black Sea: Bulgaria, Georgia, Romania, Russia, Turkey, Ukraine

Key regional treaties and conventions
ACCOBAMS, EU Habitats and Species Directive, SPA Protocol (Protocol for Special Protected Areas and Biological Diversity of the Barcelona Convention), Mediterranean Action Plan (UNEP/MAP); Strategic Action Plan for the Rehabilitation and Protection of the Black Sea, Black Sea Environmental Programme

MARINE REGION	4 Northwest Atlantic	Biogeographic zones	Ten biogeographic zones: four Polar Zones: Viscount Melville Sound, Lancaster Sound, Hudson Strait, Hudson-James Bay; three Subpolar Zones: North Slope/Beaufort Sea, Labrador Shelf, Gulf of St Lawrence; three Eastern Temperate Zones: Grand Banks/Scotian Shelf, Acadian, Virginian

Countries and territories
US (northeast: North Carolina to New England, northern Alaska), Canada (east and most of north and Arctic), St Pierre and Miquelon (France), Bermuda (UK)

Key regional treaties and conventions
Northwest Atlantic Fisheries Organization and Convention on Future Multilateral Cooperation in the Northwest Atlantic Fisheries (NAFO); no UNEP regional treaties but there are national programmes in the US, Canada and Bermuda (UK)

Table 5.1 *continued*

MARINE REGION	5 Northeast Atlantic	Biogeographic zones	Six biogeographic zones: Boreal Region, Boreal-Arctic, Boreal-Lusitanean, Lusitanean, Lusitanean-Boreal, Azores-Madeira

Countries and territories
Azores and Madeira (Portugal), Belgium, Denmark (west side), France (Atlantic side), Germany (west side), Ireland, The Netherlands, Portugal, Spain (Atlantic side), UK

Key regional treaties and conventions
Mainly OSPAR Convention and EU Habitats and Species Directive; some countries also participate in HELCOM (the Helsinki Convention), ASCOBANS and ACCOBAMS

MARINE REGION	6 Baltic	Biogeographic zones	Nine biogeographic zones: Skagerrak, Kattegat, Sound (Oresund) and Belt Sea, Baltic proper, Gulf of Finland, Åland Sea and Archipelago Sea, Bothnian Sea, Bothnian Threshold, Bothnian Bay

Countries and territories
Denmark (east side), Estonia, Finland, Germany (east side), Latvia, Lithuania, Norway (southeast side), Poland, Russia (Kaliningrad; Gulf of Finland), Sweden

Key regional treaties and conventions
Mainly ASCOBANS and HELCOM (the Helsinki Convention); also EU Habitats and Species Directive and OSPAR Convention

MARINE REGION	7 Wider Caribbean	Biogeographic zones	Six biogeographic zones: Antillian, Continental, Northwest, Gulf, Bahamian, Guianan

Countries and territories
Anguilla (UK), Antigua and Barbuda (UK), Bahamas, Barbados, Belize, Cayman Islands (UK), Colombia, Costa Rica, Cuba, Dominica, Dominican Republic, French Guiana, Grenada, Guadeloupe (France), Guatemala, Guyana, Haiti, Honduras, Jamaica, Martinique (France), México, Montserrat (UK), Netherlands Antilles (Curaçao, Bonaire, Aruba, St Maarten, St Eustatius and Saba) (Netherlands), Nicaragua, Panamá, Puerto Rico (US), St-Barthélemy (France), St Kitts and Nevis (UK), St Lucia, St-Martin (France), St Vincent and the Grenadines, Suriname, Trinidad and Tobago, Turks and Caicos Islands (UK), Venezuela, Virgin Islands (UK), Virgin Islands (US), southeast US: the Gulf coast from Texas to Florida and north to North Carolina

Key regional treaties and conventions
Cartagena Convention and SPAW Protocol on Specially Protected Areas and Wildlife; Caribbean Environment Programme (CAR/RCU, UNEP)

MARINE REGION	8 West Africa	Biogeographic zones	Five biogeographic zones: Western Tropical, Western Intertropical, Western Subtropical (North), Western Subtropical (South), Eastern Subtropical

Countries and territories
Angola, Ascension (UK), Benin, Bouvet (Norway), Cameroon, Canary Islands (Spain), Cape Verdes (Portugal), Congo, Côte d'Ivoire, Equatorial Guinea, Gabon, The Gambia, Ghana, Guinea, Guinea-Bissau, Liberia, Mauritania, Morocco, Namibia, Nigeria, St Helena (UK), São Tomé and Príncipe, Senegal, Sierra Leone, South Africa, Togo, Tristan da Cunha (UK), Western Sahara (Morocco)

Key regional treaties and conventions
Convention for Cooperation in the Protection and Development of the Marine and Coastal Environment of the West and Central African Regions (UNEP regional programme for the West and Central African region includes all countries listed except Morocco, Namibia and South Africa); Morocco belongs to ACCOBAMS (see Marine Region 3)

MARINE REGION	9 South Atlantic	**Biogeographic zones**	Five biogeographic zones: Eastern Tropical, Eastern Intertropical, Eastern Subtropical, Eastern Temperate, Other Oceanic Areas (Falkland/Malvinas Islands)

Countries and territories
Argentina, Brazil, Falkland Islands (Malvinas) (UK), Uruguay

Key regional treaties and conventions
A UNEP regional seas programme is in its early stages

MARINE REGION	10 Central Indian Ocean	**Biogeographic zones**	Five biogeographic zones: Western Indian Ocean, Eastern Indian Ocean, Northern Bay of Bengal, East Bay of Bengal, Central Indian Ocean

Countries and territories
Andaman and Nicobar Islands (India), Bangladesh, British Indian Ocean Territory (Chagos Territory) (UK), India, Maldives, Myanmar, Sri Lanka

Key regional treaties and conventions
A UNEP regional seas programme has been established – the South Asia Cooperative Environment Programme (SACEP); includes all the countries of the region plus Pakistan in Marine Region 11

MARINE REGION	11 Arabian Seas	**Biogeographic zones**	13 biogeographic zones: Gulf of Aden, Southern Red Sea, Central Red Sea, Northern Red Sea, Gulf of Aqaba, Gulf of Suez, Southern Oman, Indo-Pacific, Arabian Gulf Basin, Shatt al Arab, Southern Coastal Arabian Gulf, Gulf of Salwa, Qatar-UAE Coastal

Countries and territories
Egypt, Eritrea, Iran, Jordan, Kuwait, Oman, Pakistan, Saudi Arabia, Sudan, United Arab Emirates, Yemen

Key regional treaties and conventions
Two UNEP regional seas programmes for the Red Sea and Gulf of Aden (PERSGA), as well as for all Gulf countries under the Kuwait Action Plan (ROPME)

MARINE REGION	12 East Africa	**Biogeographic zones**	Five biogeographic zones: Red Sea–Indian Ocean Interface, Northern Area, Central Area, Southern Area, Oceanic Islands (Seychelles, Mauritius, Comoros)

Countries and territories
Comoros, Kenya, Madagascar, Mauritius, Mayotte (France), Mozambique, La Réunion (France), Seychelles, Somalia, Tanzania

Key regional treaties and conventions
MCEA – Convention for the Protection, Management and Development of the Marine and Coastal Environment of the Eastern African Region, Protocol Concerning Protected Areas and Wild Fauna and Flora in the Eastern African Region (Nairobi Convention); Somalia belongs to PERSGA (see Marine Region 11)

MARINE REGION	13 East Asian Seas	**Biogeographic zones**	22 second-order biogeographic zones: North Vietnam, South Vietnam, East Coast – Gulf of Thailand, Inner Gulf of Thailand, West Coast – Gulf of Thailand, Northeast Coast – Peninsula Malaysia, Southeast Coast – Peninsula Malaysia, West Coast – Eastern Malaysia, Jawa Sea, Makassar Sea, Flores Sea (west), Flores Sea (east), Banda Sea, Arafura Sea, Malaku Sea, Sulawesi Sea, Sulu Sea, East Coast,

Table 5.1 *continued*

Eastern Malaysia, Indian Ocean, Straits of Molucca, Andaman Sea – Inner Coast, West Coast – Peninsula Malaysia

Countries and territories
Brunei, Cambodia, Indonesia, Malaysia, Philippines, Singapore, Spratly Islands (disputed), Thailand, Vietnam

Key regional treaties and conventions
East Asian Seas Action Plan (UNEP regional seas programme) applies to all but Brunei and also includes several nations outside the region (Australia, China and RO Korea)

MARINE REGION	14 South Pacific	Biogeographic zones	20 biogeographic zones: Southern Papua New Guinea, Northern Papua New Guinea, Solomon Islands, New Caledonia, Vanuatu, Fiji, Tonga, Western Samoa, Tuvalu, Nauru, Guam-Northern Mariana Islands, Federated States of Micronesia, Marshall Islands, Kiribati, Cook Islands, Western French Polynesia, Eastern French Polynesia, Northern French Polynesia, Pitcairn, Hawaii Archipelago (including Midway and Johnston Atoll)

Countries and territories
American Samoa (US), Cook Islands (New Zealand), Easter Island (Chile), Federated States of Micronesia, French Polynesia (France), Fiji, Guam (US), Hawaii (US), Johnston Atoll (US), Kiribati, Marshall Islands, Nauru, New Caledonia (France), Niue, Northern Mariana Islands (US), Northwestern Hawaiian Islands (including Midway) (US), Palau, Palmyra Atoll (US), Papua New Guinea, Pitcairn Islands (UK), Samoa, Solomon Islands, Tokelau (New Zealand), Tonga, Tuvalu, Vanuatu, Wake Island (US), Wallis and Futuna (France)

Key regional treaties and conventions
Apia Convention, SPREP Convention includes all the countries of the region plus Australia and New Zealand

MARINE REGION	15 Northeast Pacific	Biogeographic zones	Nine biogeographic zones: three subpolar zones: Beringian, Aleutian, West Coast Fjords; one temperate zone: Oregonian; three subtropical zones: Montereyan, San Diegan, Cortezian; two tropical zones: Mexican, Panamanian

Countries and territories
US (West Coast and Alaska south of the Bering Strait), Canada (West Coast), México (West Coast)

Key regional treaties and conventions
No UNEP regional treaty but various academic and regional links provide some basis for cooperation on MPAs and other cetacean issues

MARINE REGION	16 Northwest Pacific	Biogeographic zones	Eight biogeographic zones: Tropical, Subtropical, Warm Temperate: Closed Sea, Warm Temperate: Open Sea, Cold Temperate: Closed Sea, Cold Temperate: Open Sea, Subarctic and Arctic

Countries and territories
China (including Hong Kong and Macao), Taiwan, Japan, PDR Korea, RO Korea, Russia

Key regional treaties and conventions
NOWPAP – UNEP regional seas programme for the Northwest Pacific; RO Korea and China are also
involved with the UNEP regional seas programme for East Asian Seas and the East Asian Seas Action Plan

MARINE REGION	17 Southeast Pacific	**Biogeographic zones**	Six biogeographic zones in the coastal realm: Western Tropical, Western Intertropical, Western Subtropical, Western Temperate, Subpolar, Subpolar Archipelagic, plus three oceanic areas: Galápagos Archipelago, Cocos Island and Juan Fernández Archipelago

Countries and territories
Guatemala, Honduras, El Salvador, Nicaragua, Costa Rica (including Cocos Island), Panamá, Colombia,
Ecuador (including the Galápagos archipelago), Perú, Chile (including Juan Fernández Archipelago)

Key regional treaties and conventions
Countries in central America (plus México) are signatories to the UNEP Convention for Cooperation in the
Protection and Sustainable Development of the Marine and Coastal Environment of the Northeast Pacific
(Antigua Convention); UNEP's Southeast Pacific Region (CPPS) includes all the countries of western South
America plus Panamá and they have agreed to the Action Plan for Protection of the Marine Environment
and Coastal Areas of the Southeast Pacific (1981) and Action Plan for the Conservation of Marine Mammals
in the Southeast Pacific (PNUMA 1992)

MARINE REGION	18 Australia– New Zealand	**Biogeographic zones**	40 biogeographic zones. In Australia, there are 14 coastal zones: North Coast, Northwest Coast, Central West Coast, Lower West Coast, Southwest Coast, Great Australian Bight, South Gulf Coast, Bass Strait, Tasmanian Coast, Lower East Coast, Central East Coast, Northeast Coast, Great Barrier Reef, Gulf of Carpentaria; five oceanic zones: Northwest Oceanic, West Oceanic, South Oceanic, Southeast Oceanic and Northeast Oceanic; four ocean zones: Indian Ocean, Southern Ocean, Tasman Sea and Coral Sea. There are also nine External Territories Zones: Christmas Island, Cocos-Keeling, Ashmore-Cartier, Coral Sea Islands, Norfolk Island, Lord Howe Island, Macquarie Island, Antarctic Territory and Heard and Macdonald Island. New Zealand has eight marine biogeographic zones: Kermadec Island, Three Kings Island/North Cape, Northeastern, Central, Chatham Island, Southern, Snares Island, Subantarctic (Auckland Island, Campbell Island, Antipodes Island and Bounty Island)

Countries and territories
Australia (including Christmas, Cocos-Keeling, Macquarie and Norfolk islands) and New Zealand (including
Auckland, Campbell, Antipodes and Bounty islands)

Key regional treaties and conventions
Australia and New Zealand are part of the UNEP regional seas programme for the South Pacific – SPREP;
Australia is also involved with the UNEP regional seas programme for East Asian Seas with the East Asian
Seas Action Plan (UNEP regional seas programme)

of the various regional treaties and conservation initiatives of the UNEP regional seas programmes and other regional conventions and programmes. Thus, the Cartagena Convention which established the Caribbean Environment Program under the Protocol Concerning Specially Protected Areas and Wildlife (SPAW) includes the same countries (with almost the same marine boundaries) as those found in the WCPA marine region. There are a few marine regions not yet covered by regional treaties or other agreements, and there are some marine regions covered by two or more treaties. Still, most of them correspond closely to the WCPA marine region divisions.

Soon, it may be possible to pursue more international marine initiatives such as the UN Law of the Sea, but for the most part, it is easier and faster to make progress at the regional level, harnessing more closely shared aspirations and interests, pursuing joint research and action plans. In addition to SPAW in the Caribbean, ACCOBAMS produced by Mediterranean Sea, Black Sea and contiguous Atlantic countries is a landmark agreement that has greatly advanced the prospects for marine conservation and habitat protection in this area, although there is still much work to be done. (Other regional groups and agreements which would do well to emulate ACCOBAMS include ASCOBANS for the Baltic and North seas and SPREP in the South Pacific.) This chapter will show what these and other agreements are achieving in the 18 marine regions of the world.

Of course, in terms of cetacean conservation, it remains important for nations, especially those with large exclusive economic zones (EEZs) and with substantial parts of cetacean populations within national boundaries, to push for marine conservation and the designation of MPAs. This applies particularly to Russia, Australia, New Zealand, Indonesia, Canada and the US. MPA conservation can be accomplished in some cases unilaterally as well as within the regional framework, but MPAs will often be more effective if they are part of a network and are the result of strategic national and regional planning.

The WCPA further divides each marine region into biogeographic zones – some 150 in all. The WCPA rationale behind the further divisions into biogeographic zones is mainly the drive to protect representative areas within each zone. With cetaceans, there are some species or populations that are closely identified with particular biogeographic zones. But this is the exception. Most cetaceans are found across several or many biogeographic zones. In terms of assessing the overall representativeness of all MPAs up to 1995, Kelleher et al (1995c) determined that 118 out of 150 zones (79 per cent) had at least one MPA; some 32 zones (21 per cent) had no MPAs. Even for those biogeographic zones with MPAs, however, the median number was only four MPAs per zone and, for the most part, these were very small in comparison to the entire zone. In most zones, the area in MPAs amounted to much less than 1 per cent of the total marine area of the zone. The guideline figure at the IV World Parks Congress was for 10 per cent of each biogeographical zone to be in a protected area.

Table 5.1, which provides a quick guide to the 18 marine regions, lists the countries, territories and biogeographic zones in each marine region, as well as

---

Box 5.1 Notes about the marine region tables (5.2–5.22) in Chapter 5

Please note the following style conventions for the numbering of each MPA or sanctuary in the tables and accompanying maps for each of the 18 marine regions:

- The large international sanctuaries employ Roman numerals for the map codes (I, II, III, IV and so on).
- The national sanctuaries, which usually extend to the EEZ limit of a nation or national territory, use letters (A–Z).
- The MPAs are listed using numbers or Arabic numerals (1, 2, 3 and so on).
- Those sanctuaries or MPAs with proposed extensions, or newly proposed as MPAs, can be found at the end of the list for each country, with the numbers or letters in italics.

The three different numbering systems reflect the varying levels of protection and management afforded by national and international sanctuaries and MPAs.

The information in the tables is designed to provide a simple snapshot of MPAs and sanctuaries with cetaceans, both existing and proposed. For each listing, there is basic information on location, size, species lists, special features, rationale for protection, comments on management and level of protection, and contact details for further information. This information has been culled from a wide variety of sources and it is constantly changing; for the latest information, please follow the contact details and/or check the WDCS website on MPAs (www.cetaceanhabitat.org).

---

the key regional treaties and conventions. For detailed information on each treaty and convention, see Table 1.6.

All 18 marine regions have cetacean populations, although our level of knowledge and the degree of protection vary considerably. For each of the marine region sections that follow, there is a general discussion of cetaceans found and whether they are indigenous, vulnerable or endangered, their known critical habitats and background on notable MPAs, as well as regional and certain key national conservation initiatives. The 64 known large marine ecosystems (LMEs) are identified according to region (eg, Sherman and Alexander, 1986, 1989; see www.edc.uri.edu/lme/intro.htm). LMEs can provide keys to understanding a region, useful for ecosystem-based management, as well as suggesting productive locations for future MPAs. Efforts to monitor, assess and manage these ecosystems, underway in most of the world's LMEs, are crucial to the future health, productivity and sustainability of the sea.

For each marine region there is also a map showing proposed and existing MPAs that feature cetaceans. In some marine regions, cetaceans move into rivers on the adjacent continents, and in certain cases, as with most of the river dolphins, reside year-round in rivers. Included on the MPA lists are river reserves, which are loosely considered here as MPAs. Properly they are PAs – land-based protected areas – but we include them because of their importance for river dolphins, as well as for some of the ocean dolphins which have seasonal or permanent river-based populations.

Finally, this chapter identifies priorities for research, education and conservation in each region according to the IUCN 2002–2010 Conservation Action Plan for the World's Cetaceans (Reeves et al, 2003). These priorities are determined by a worldwide network of cetacean specialists, with particular attention being paid to endangered species and populations. It is not complete; it leaves out many species and populations which arguably are as endangered or which have needs equal to some of those listed, but it is a useful worldwide action plan which makes a good starting point toward conservation initiatives in each marine region.

MARINE REGION 1: ANTARCTIC

The blue whale, the world's largest animal, once flourished in the vast feeding grounds of the Antarctic, especially around the massive upwellings of the Antarctic Slope Front and the southern boundary of the Antarctic Circumpolar Current. This was the blue whale's rich, untouched domain before the whalers arrived and killed some 360,000 blues, mainly in the first half of the 20th century.

Today, the blue whale around Antarctica may number as low as only a few hundred. Still, the Southern Ocean has a variety of baleen and toothed whale populations to protect, as well as extraordinarily productive ecosystems which continue to make this region one of the world's premier feeding areas for whales, dolphins, pinnipeds, fish and seabirds. Besides the blue whale, six other baleen whale species come to feed in the region: humpback, fin, sei, minke, Antarctic minke and southern right whales. In addition, there are thirteen toothed whale species: the sperm whale, five beaked whale species, six oceanic dolphin and one porpoise species (Bannister et al, 1996; Bowles et al, 1994; de Boer and Simmonds, 2001; Stewardson, 1997). There may be indigenous subspecies or distinctive populations of a number of these including minke and blue whales and orcas (eg, Pitman and Ensor, 2003). The baleen whales are mainly summer-only residents, migrating north to Marine Regions 8, 9, 10, 12, 14, 17 and 18 for the winter. Yet minke whales have been seen in winter at the outer edge of the pack ice and both blue and minke whale calls have been recorded year-round in the West Antarctic Peninsula region (Moore et al, 2003). The toothed whales and dolphins may also remain year-round but still must retreat with the ice formation to the outer edges of Marine Region 1, although not necessarily leaving the region entirely.

Antarctica is unique and full of stark contrasts. It is a land mass with no native humans surrounded by a great ocean brimming with marine life, the Southern Ocean. It is not a country, yet many countries have bases on it. It is as close as we have on Earth to the sort of shared international management that may one day be required on the moon or on other planets, as well as on the 50 per cent of the world ocean that is outside national regulation.

The story of protecting the Antarctic and its surrounding waters goes back to the first half of the 20th century. When the International Whaling Commission (IWC) was formed in 1946, it inherited a whale sanctuary in the Antarctic dating from 1938. This sanctuary consisted of the South Pacific sector of the Southern Ocean (approximately one-quarter of the Antarctic) and applied to pelagic whaling of baleen whales only. Holt (2000) called it a 'symbolic' sanctuary and, in any case, it was abolished in 1955 when the whaling countries needed more whales.

In 1992, a French proposal for an Antarctic whale sanctuary was submitted to the IWC; it was approved in 1994 during the IWC meeting in Puerto Vallarta, México. The resulting Southern Ocean Whale Sanctuary, more commonly referred to as the Southern Ocean Sanctuary, is recognized as part of a portfolio of treaties and other measures to protect Antarctica and its surrounding seas, but it is legally binding only upon the more than 40 member nations of the IWC. Of note, Japan has hunted several hundred minke whales a year in the sanctuary, invoking a clause in the IWC Convention allowing a long-term scientific research programme (Leaper and Papastavrou, 2001). Most cetacean researchers and the governments of their respective countries contend that it is not necessary to kill whales to do research and that Japan's research is just a commercial hunt in the guise of science. For this reason, Japan's research programme is called 'scientific whaling'. In any case, it proves the point that an international sanctuary is only effective when countries and their nationals respect it. The conservation efforts of a majority of countries and the 'global common' can be put at risk by the arrogant actions of a single country.

The boundaries of the Antarctic Marine Region lie roughly along the Antarctic Polar Front (formerly called Antarctic Convergence), and correspond to the Convention on the Conservation of Antarctic Marine Living Resources (CCAMLR) boundary as agreed by Antarctic Treaty parties. Besides the Antarctic continent and the main waters surrounding it, the region includes South Georgia Island and South Sandwich Islands (UK), Bouvet (Norway), Prince Edward Island and Marion Island (South Africa), Crozet Islands and Kerguelen Islands (France), and Heard Island and McDonald Islands (Australia).

Along with the Southern Ocean Sanctuary of the IWC, Antarctic treaties and conventions that provide a certain amount of protection to ecosystems – and potentially to cetaceans – include:

- The 1961 Antarctic Treaty and associated additional agreements referred to as the Antarctic Treaty System. These govern all activities south of latitude 60° S covering the continent and immediately surrounding waters. The treaty system has been negotiated in two dozen meetings over the past more than 40 years.
- Agreed Measures for the Conservation of Antarctic Fauna and Flora (1964). This agreement introduced strong regulations to protect fauna and flora. However, it has been superseded and updated by the Environmental Protocol below.

- The Convention for the Conservation of Antarctic Seals (CCAS) (1972), which regulates possible future commercial sealing operations south of 60° S.
- The Convention on the Conservation of Antarctic Marine Living Resources (CCAMLR) (1982), which has created a conservation organization to institute ecosystem-based management in fisheries. Its mandate may prove a landmark not just for Antarctica but for the world. The 29 nations signing this convention are bound to a proactive approach, investigating the impact of not only targeted species, but also the predators and prey of that species. This convention extends to the natural boundary of the Antarctic Polar Front, thus covering the high seas in much of the Southern Ocean Sanctuary (to 60° S in the Pacific sector; 55° S in the eastern Indian Ocean; 50° S in most of the South Atlantic; and 45° S in the western Indian Ocean).
- The Protocol on Environmental Protection to the Antarctic Treaty (1998). This sets out regulations to ensure the environmental protection of Antarctica, using a precautionary approach. The so-called Madrid, or Environmental, Protocol – partly a result of the failure of an Antarctic treaty on commercial mining and mineral extraction – effectively bans all mineral resource activity for at least 50 years other than scientific research and makes Antarctica a 'natural reserve devoted to peace and science' with some of the strongest environmental protection regimes found anywhere in the world (see Kimball, 1999, for more information on the Antarctic Treaty System).

The Environmental Protocol and CCAMLR are the most crucial to protecting the waters of the Southern Ocean Sanctuary as important cetacean habitat. The Environmental Protocol has gone part way toward the long-standing Greenpeace–Australian–French vision of Antarctica as a World Park (Szabo, 1994), while CCAMLR aims to extend management into the surrounding marine waters, providing a crucial ecosystem management regime for the Southern Ocean Sanctuary. Initially, only 12 nations participated in the Antarctic Treaty but signatories now include 43 countries representing 80 per cent of the world's population.

The Environmental Protocol, in its Annex V on Area Protection and Management, has provisions for the establishment of marine or land-based protected areas called ASPAs (Antarctic specially protected areas) and ASMAs (Antarctic specially managed areas). ASPAs are roughly equivalent to IUCN Category I and ASMAs to Category V, according to the Second Antarctic Protected Areas Workshop Report 2000. Included in ASPAs are the previous (pre-2002) categories of specially protected areas (SPAs), sites of special scientific interest (SSSIs) and specially reserved areas (SRAs). Approval via CCAMLR of any protected area is required before acceptance by the Antarctic Treaty Consultative Meeting (ATCM).

In 2000, the World Conservation Congress agreed to Resolution 2.54, which calls for the development of a comprehensive network of Antarctic and

Southern Ocean protected areas as set out in Annex V of the Protocol. This network should include appropriate representation of the principal habitats and biological diversity of the region as well as other values, and it should consider new kinds of Antarctic protected areas, with special emphasis on marine sites. At a meeting of Antarctic specialists at the V World Parks Congress in 2003, Antarctic Treaty Parties were asked to ensure the establishment of a representative system of MPAs and to give particular attention to areas south of 60° S, with the largely intact Ross Sea area highlighted as a priority for protection.

The waters surrounding Antarctica make up the largest cetacean feeding grounds in the world, and for some of the most depleted large-whale populations. Given the principles of ecosystem-based management enshrined in CCAMLR, the common aim of 'Peace and Science' in the Antarctic Treaty and the intrinsic value of Antarctica to all nations and peoples, adequate protection of such cetacean critical habitat in this region could set a valuable global precedent. Yet, to date, marine habitat protection is limited and lacking in cohesive management, and there is no protection for cetacean critical habitat. The overall marine habitat conservation effort has been very disappointing.

As of 1995, there was a total of 17 comparatively small MPAs of all kinds across the entire marine region (Antarctic Division, Australian Department of the Environment and Dingwall, 1995). By 2004, the total was approximately 20, mostly very small, protected areas with a marine component, only six of which were entirely marine. Of these, just three ASPAs are of a size – 66–425 mi^2 (170–1100 km^2) – that could even make a difference to cetaceans, although there is no mention of cetaceans or cetacean habitat in the management plans of these or any other ASPAs.

Two subantarctic archipelagos outside of CCAMLR 'jurisdiction', however, have large MPAs that are protecting at least some cetacean critical habitat. The first is the Australian Heard Island and MacDonald Islands Marine Reserve which, in 2002, was created as the world's largest fully protected (IUCN Category I) MPA, at 25,000 mi^2 (65,000 km^2). In addition, two protected areas in the Prince Edward Islands of South Africa – at Prince Edward Island Reserve and Marion Island Reserve – are thought to include southern right whale habitat.

In 1999, the New Zealand delegation led an arguably ill-prepared attempt through CCAMLR to create an 'international MPA' for the Balleny Islands Archipelago. It met with resistance from nations with strong fisheries interests. The proposal revealed problems with the lack of process within CCAMLR to assess and approve management plans for proposed MPAs. It is clear that future proposals for MPAs that may include cetacean habitat will have to be argued with care and determination. In 2003, New Zealand again raised the Balleny Islands idea, this time as an ASPA (under the new designations) and the plan is to submit a Balleny Islands proposal in 2004.

The Southern Ocean Sanctuary received its first ten-year review by the IWC in 2004. More research into Antarctic cetaceans – non-lethal research that respects the sanctuary intentions instead of 'scientific whaling' – should be funded by governments and conservation organizations to help strengthen the sanctuary. Specific proposals for important critical habitats functioning as core areas in a marine biosphere reserve or as part of a network of MPA reserves would help lay significant additional groundwork toward making an effective international or high-seas MPA. One such proposal is for the Ross Sea (see Case Study 1, p101), and a number of others are expected to be developed, some of which may include cetacean habitat. As of 2004, except for the 'broad brush' protection from whaling in the Southern Ocean Sanctuary, there are only three existing and one proposed MPAs which feature cetacean habitat (as shown in Table 5.2).

The Antarctic Marine Region is considered to have one large marine ecosystem (LME) called the Antarctic marine ecosystem which refers to the waters around the Antarctic continent. The Antarctic Polar Front, which has an average position of about 58° S, provides the main biogeographic boundary between the Antarctic and the Southern Ocean. More recently, various publications have referred to the Ross Sea Shelf Ecosystem and the Weddell Sea Ecosystem, but there is still no agreement on biogeographic classifications.

Understanding the oceanography of the Southern Ocean is crucial to explaining its high productivity and its important role in the world ocean, as well as the potential impacts from global warming and world climate change. The Antarctic Circumpolar Current is the primary way that surface waters are exchanged between the world ocean basins (Antarctic Division, Australian Department of the Environment and Dingwall, 1995). In Antarctic waters, there is a dramatic exchange of heat, fresh water and carbon dioxide and other gases, between the layers of the sea and between the ocean and atmosphere. Massive upwellings at the Antarctic Divergence, close to the Antarctic continent at about 65° S, introduce an abundance of nutrients into the surface layer that fuel the tremendous plankton explosion during the Antarctic spring and summer. Antarctic krill, *Euphausia superba*, which plays a central role in the food web of the slope and water overlying deeper areas, exists in extremely high abundance along and outward from the continental shelf break, and helps to sustain blue and other baleen whale species.

The strict protection of critical habitat and the maintenance of healthy ecosystems in the Antarctic is important for cetacean and other marine species, as well as being crucial for global ocean circulation, world climate and many other factors. It may be that cetaceans prove to be the environmental monitors for this region of global importance. Will cetaceans ever return to pre-whaling numbers in the Antarctic? No one knows, but if they do, it would be the most optimistic sign that the Antarctic ecosystem is healthy and capable of supporting not only cetaceans but the future of all life in this region.

The ultimate success of the conservation regime for Antarctica will depend on political will and resources – international cooperation – to fulfil and enforce the provisions of various treaties. The Southern Ocean Sanctuary, with the various treaties and protocols and a network of MPA reserves within it, has at least a chance of being the stepping stone toward effective, significant protection for cetaceans as well as for the entire ecosystem.

Case Study 1: Ross Sea – time for nations to act

Ross Sea MPA, *may be proposed*

Type: May be proposed as an Antarctic Specially Protected Area (ASPA) or other type of international MPA offering protection to the neritic ecosystem and food web, including certain fish, whales, dolphins and the ecosystem.

Location: The Ross Sea, off Antarctica, Southern Ocean. Specifically, the waters south of the 10,000 ft (3000 m) isobath, which extends from 69° S, 170° E (off Cape Adare, Victoria Land) to 76° S, 155° W (off King Edward VII Peninsula, Marie Byrd Land). Included would be a northward jog of the 3 m isobath, around Iselin Bank, to about 69° S, 175° W. It would include the continental slope 1600–10,000 ft (500–3000 m) and the continental shelf of the Ross Sea.

Cetacean species: Antarctic minke whale, *Balaenoptera bonaerensis*; orca, *Orcinus orca* (including three possible forms according to Pitman and Ensor, 2003); sei whale, *Balaenoptera borealis*; Arnoux's beaked whale, *Berardius arnuxii*. Seaward of the slope live the southern bottlenose whale, *Hyperoodon planifrons*, and, further north, the hourglass dolphin, *Lagenorhynchus cruciger*. Historically, before the intensive 20th century whaling, the blue whale, *Balaenoptera musculus*, and the southern right whale, *Eubalaena australis*, occurred along the Ross Sea continental slope.

Additional species and other features: Measures of primary productivity and plankton standing stocks indicate the Ross Sea to be the richest stretch of water of comparable size in the Southern Ocean. Middle-trophic-level species include, principally, crystal krill, *Euphausia crystallorophias*; and Antarctic silverfish, *Pleuragramma antarcticum*. There is a fishery for Antarctic toothfish, *Dissostichus mawsoni*. About 943,000 pairs (38 per cent of the world population) of Adélie penguins, *Pygoscelis adeliae* and 52,000 pairs (26 per cent) of emperor penguins (*Aptenodytes forsteri*) nest along its shores. Several million Antarctic petrels (*Thalassoica antarctica*) feed within the Ross Sea Slope Ecosystem during summer, one of the greatest concentrations in the Southern Ocean. Among seals, Ross Sea numbers contribute the following to Pacific Sector populations: Weddell seals, *Leptonychotes weddellii*, 32,000 individuals (45 per cent); leopard seals, *Hydrurga leptonyx*, 8000 (11 per cent); and crabeater seals, *Lobodon carcinophagus*, 205,000 (12 per cent). For additional information and references, see CCAMLR Document WG-EMM 02/60 and Ainley (2002).

Possible size of protected area: 231,000 square miles (598,000 km^2).

Rationale: To protect the largest remaining minimally changed marine ecosystem on Earth.

The Ross Sea is a 'well-defined embayment of Antarctica about the size of southern Europe, bounded by Victoria Land to the west; King Edward VII Peninsula, Marie Byrd Land, to the east; the Ross Ice Shelf to the south; and the Southern Ocean, Pacific Sector, to the north'.

So begins Antarctic researcher David Ainley's 2002 proposal in support of a Ross Sea protection regime: 'Its waters comprise two related biotic systems: the Ross Sea Shelf Ecosystem (RSShE) and the Ross Sea Slope Ecosystem (RSSlE). The RSShE is the last sizeable marine ecosystem on Earth (except the Weddell Sea) that has escaped direct anthropogenic alteration; the RSSlE, similar to all of Earth's other marine ecosystems, has lost most or all of its large baleen whales but otherwise is intact. A huge multidisciplinary, international scientific effort, at great expense, has been invested in studies of the geology, physics and biology of the Ross Sea over the past 45 years. The successful result is an incredible wealth of knowledge, including long-term biological data sets unduplicated anywhere else in the Antarctic that have documented climate forcing, as well as top-down influences, not confused by human exploitation or activity. Ironically, much remains unknown about how these ecosystems function. The Ross Sea is currently off limits to mineral extraction, but pressure on its biological resources is growing. The food web is not complex and, therefore, easily perturbed. Before it is too late, one of the last places on Earth where both top-down and bottom-up ecosystem processes can be studied, should be protected from human exploitation. Establishment of an MPA would further that end.'

WDCS, among other groups, supports the highest level of protection for the Ross Sea, whether this is by an MPA or through ecosystem-based management or a combination of methods. In 2002, additional support for the MPA idea came from the Pacific Seabird Group and the SCAR Subcommittee on Bird Biology as well as in discussions in CCAMLR meetings. WDCS concurs with Ainley's proposal that there should be 'no commercial or other intensive take of biotic resources allowed in the absence of full knowledge of the effect of any level of take on ecosystem processes and food web balances'. Currently, two fisheries are underway, one involving Antarctic toothfish (*Dissostichus mawsoni*) which CCAMLR attempts to regulate in a knowledge vacuum, though the species is of critical importance to the Ross Sea ecosystem and has demographic traits that reveal sensitivity to adult mortality. The danger is that the relatively small-scale fishing will expand to the uncontrollable take levels exhibited on *Dissostichus* stocks elsewhere in the Southern Ocean, which have led to rapid depletion. The second fishery involves a 'scientific' catch of Antarctic minke whales (*Balaenoptera bonaerensis*) by the Japanese Research Program in the Antarctic (JARPA). According to Ainley, the catch, which has removed more than 4500 whales − a third in the Ross Sea and vicinity − since the scientific study's inception in 1988, is 'being exercised on a long-lived species also critical to the Ross Sea food web balance... Fundamental knowledge of this species' natural history is lacking, but the scientific data being gathered by JARPA is not necessary to minke whale management and what is being gathered is obtainable by non-lethal methods.'

In October 2002, two proposals to protect small portions of the Ross Sea were tabled at CCAMLR meetings: Terra Nova Bay, a small area on the

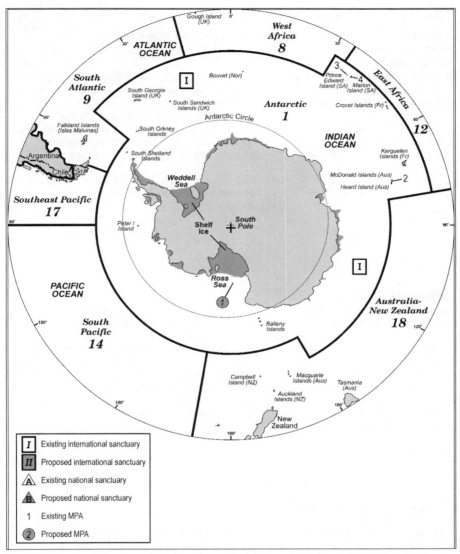

The roman numerals, letters and numbers correspond to the sanctuaries and MPAs listed and described in Table 5.2.

Figure 5.2 *Map of Marine Region 1: Antarctic MPAs and sanctuaries*

Victoria Land coast of the Ross Sea, and the marine waters bordering Cape Royds in McMurdo Sound (marine areas some 1640 ft (500 m) from shore). Orcas and minke whales do visit these areas. Both of these sites are valuable for various reasons but, in terms of specifically protecting significant cetacean habitat or the Ross Sea ecosystems, these proposals are inadequate.

Table 5.2 *Marine Region 1: Antarctic MPAs and sanctuaries*

Name of MPA or sanctuary, location and size	Cetacean and other notable species
INTERNATIONAL **(I) Southern Ocean Sanctuary** (including Antarctica), also known as the **Southern Ocean Whale Sanctuary** • Southern Ocean • 19.3 million mi^2 (50 million km^2). The land area of Antarctica itself is 5.4 million mi^2 (13.9 million km^2)	• 7 baleen and 13 toothed whale species, including humpback whale, *Megaptera novaeangliae*; Antarctic minke whale, *Balaenoptera bonaerensis*; blue whale, *Balaenoptera musculus*; sperm whale, *Physeter macrocephalus*; Arnoux's beaked whale, *Berardius arnuxii*; southern bottlenose whale, *Hyperoodon planifrons*; hourglass dolphin, *Lagenorhynchus cruciger*; orca, *Orcinus orca* • also: Antarctic fur seals; Ross, Weddell, crabeater and leopard seals; elephant seals; various penguins; euphausiids
ANTARCTICA **(1) Ross Sea MPA, *may be proposed*** • the Ross Sea, off Antarctica: waters south of the 1640 fathom (10,000 ft or 3000 m) isobath, which extends from 69° S, 170° E (off Cape Adare, Victoria Land) to 76° S, 155° W (off King Edward VII Peninsula, Marie Byrd Land); includes continental slope 1640–10,000 ft (500–3000 m) deep and the continental shelf of the Ross Sea • 231,000 mi^2 (598,000 km^2) **See Case Study 1.**	• Antarctic minke whale, *Balaenoptera bonaerensis;* orca, *Orcinus orca* (including possible new fish-eating species or ecotype of orca); sei whale, *Balaenoptera borealis* • Measures of primary productivity and plankton standing stocks indicate the Ross Sea is the richest stretch of water of comparable size in the entire Southern Ocean. Species include crystal krill, Antarctic silverfish, Antarctic toothfish; Adélie and emperor penguins; several million Antarctic petrels; Weddell, leopard and crabeater seals
HEARD ISLAND and MCDONALD ISLANDS (Australia) **(2) Heard Island and McDonald Islands Marine Reserve** • located 2800 mi (4500 km) southwest of Australia and 900 mi (1500 km) north of Antarctica within Australian territory waters in the Indian Ocean sector of the Southern Ocean (53° 05' S and 73° 30' E) • 25,000 mi^2 (65,000 km^2)	• some seasonal or sporadic: southern right whale, *Eubalaena australis*; humpback whale, *Megaptera novaeangliae*; blue whale, *Balaenoptera musculus*; fin whale, *Balaenoptera physalus*; Antarctic minke whale, *Balaenoptera bonaerensis*; sperm whale, *Physeter macrocephalus*; southern bottlenose whale, *Hyperoodon planifrons*; Arnoux's beaked whale, *Berardius arnuxii*; strap-toothed whale, *Mesoplodon layardii*; dusky dolphin, *Lagenorhynchus obscurus*; Commerson's dolphin, *Cephalorhynchus commersonnii*; hourglass dolphin, *Lagenorhynchus cruciger*; orca, *Orcinus orca*; long-finned pilot whale, *Globicephala melas*; spectacled porpoise, *Phocoena dioptrica* • also: southern elephant seal, subantarctic fur seal, leopard seal, macaroni penguin (world's largest colony), Patagonian toothfish

Notes and rationale	For more information
<ul><li>In 1992, a French proposal for an Antarctic whale sanctuary was first submitted to the IWC and it was approved by 3/4 majority in 1994 during the IWC meeting in Puerto Vallarta, México. The resulting Southern Ocean Sanctuary has become widely recognized as part of a portfolio of treaties and other measures to protect Antarctica and its surrounding seas, but it is legally binding only upon the more than 40 member nations of the IWC.</li><li>Rationale is to protect large whales from commercial whaling, to monitor whale populations and study the effects on whales of not whaling as well as the effects of environmental change on whale populations. As the issue of global warming increases in importance, this last point has achieved considerable prominence due to the evidence of climatic changes in the Antarctic ice.</li><li>In addition, the entire Antarctic Marine Region is considered by some to be an MPA on the basis of the protective measures found in the Antarctic Treaty System (Antarctic Div/Australia and Dingwall, 1995).</li></ul>	<ul><li>Boyd, 2002; Holt, 2000; Leaper and Papastavrou, 2001; Szabo, 1994</li><li>Contact: WDCS – Australasia; email: info@wdcs.org.au; web: www.wdcs.org.au</li><li>International Whaling Commission (IWC), The Red House, Station Road, Histon, Cambridge CB4 4NP UK; web: www.iwcoffice.org</li></ul>
<ul><li>To protect the largest virtually untouched marine ecosystem on Earth.</li><li>In 2002, two proposals were made to the CCAMLR meetings to protect tiny areas of the Ross Sea: Terra Nova Bay and Cape Royds, both of which were approved.</li><li>A huge multidisciplinary scientific effort has been invested in studies of the geology, physics and biology of the Ross Sea over the past 45 years. The successful result is an incredible wealth of knowledge, including long-term biological data sets unduplicated anywhere else in the Antarctic. Yet much remains unknown about how these ecosystems function.</li><li>WDCS, among other groups, supports the highest level of protection for the Ross Sea, whether by an MPA or through ecosystem-based management or other methods. In 2002, support for the MPA idea came from the Pacific Seabird Group and the SCAR Subcommittee on Bird Biology as well as in talks at CCAMLR meetings.</li></ul>	<ul><li>Ainley, 2002; Boyd, 2002</li><li>Contact: WDCS – Australasia; email: info@wdcs.org.au; web: www.wdcs.org.au</li><li>David Ainley; email: dainley@harvey ecology.com; web: www.penguin science.com</li></ul>
<ul><li>In 1997 the islands (land portion) were put on the World Heritage List. In Oct 2002 the Australian government declared the extensive MPA – said to be world's largest 'fully protected' marine reserve (classed as IUCN Category Ia); it is administered by the Australian Antarctic Division which is preparing management plans.</li><li>Rationale for protection includes the unique features of the benthic and pelagic environments, the representative marine habitat types and the cultural values of the two islands; cetacean research needs to be done to determine species present and their habitat use within the area.</li><li>Not designed specifically around cetacean habitat, but because of its size it almost certainly contains some significant cetacean habitat.</li></ul>	<ul><li>Contact: Heard Island and McDonald Islands Marine Reserve; web: www.deh.gov.au/ coasts/mpa/heard/; www.deh.gov.au/ minister/env/2002/ mr09oct02.html</li><li>WDCS – Australasia; email: info@wdcs.org.au; web: www.wdcs.org.au</li></ul>

Table 5.2 *continued*

Name of MPA or sanctuary, location and size	Cetacean and other notable species
PRINCE EDWARD ISLANDS (South Africa) **(3) Prince Edward Island Reserve** • 1680 mi (2700 km) southeast of Cape Town • 17 mi² (44 km²), includes land areas	• southern right whale, *Eubalaena australis* • also: southern elephant seal, subantarctic fur seal, four species of penguin, six species of seabirds in South African Red Data Book
(4) Marion Island Reserve • 1680 mi (2700 km) southeast of Cape Town, part of 'Prince Edward Islands' • 116 mi² (300 km²), includes land areas	• southern right whale, *Eubalaena australis*; orca, *Orcinus orca* • also: southern elephant seal, subantarctic fur seal, four species of penguin, six species of seabirds in South African Red Data Book

At the V World Parks Congress in 2003, at a 'side event' meeting by Antarctic experts, special mention was made of the Ross Sea and the value of protecting it as the 'largest remaining ecosystem on Earth that has so far virtually escaped human impact'. A key recommendation from the discussion was that Treaty Parties should make the Ross Sea area a priority for protection.

The Environmental Protocol and CCAMLR are crucial to protecting the waters of the Southern Ocean Sanctuary as important whale habitat. Yet specific provisions must be made for the Ross Sea so that the rich ecosystem there is not degraded. A highly protected ASPA is one option but there are others that may be politically more acceptable that would forestall or prevent all-out development.

If fully protected, the Ross Sea MPA would form the jewel of the Southern Ocean Sanctuary, and stand as a shining example of what can be accomplished amid all the treaties and conventions designed to conserve the last continent and its marine ecology.

Notes and rationale	For more information
• Established in 1947 as a strict nature reserve (IUCN Category I) with total protection granted under the Prince Edward Islands Act and the Sea Birds and Seals Protection Act 46 of 1973. • Degree or appropriateness of protection for right whale habitat is yet to be clarified.	• Klinowska, 1991; Robinson and De Graaff, 1994 • Contact: South African Scientific Committee for Antarctic Research, Dept of Transport, PB X193, Pretoria 0001, South Africa
• Established in 1948 as a strict nature reserve (IUCN Category I) with total protection granted under the Prince Edward Islands Act and the Sea Birds and Seals Protection Act 46 of 1973. • Degree or appropriateness of protection for right whale habitat is yet to be clarified.	• Klinowska, 1991; Robinson and De Graaff, 1994 • Contact: South African Scientific Committee for Antarctic Research, Dept of Transport, PB X193, Pretoria 0001, South Africa

MARINE REGION 2: ARCTIC

The Arctic Marine Region has two emblematic toothed-whale cetaceans as year-round residents – the narwhal and beluga. There is also the bowhead whale, an Arctic baleen whale that does not migrate into temperate or tropical waters, but undertakes shorter migrations within the Arctic following or retreating from the ever-changing ice edge. In addition, various other baleen whales, such as humpback and minke whales, migrate into Arctic or subarctic waters to feed in summer. Toothed whales include sperm whales, orcas, Atlantic white-sided and white-beaked dolphins and harbor porpoises.

The Arctic Marine Region has a number of MPAs that include cetaceans but none that have been designed specifically for cetaceans. Some hunting of cetaceans occurs inside MPAs, such as within Greenland's huge Northeast Greenland National Park and in the Melville Bay Wildlife Sanctuary. For Svalbard, northwest of Norway, in 2003, the original system of national parks and nature reserves dating from 1973 was expanded with new protected areas and the marine boundaries for Svalbard's protected areas were extended from 4 nm (7.4 km) to 12 nm (22.2 km).

Three more far-reaching proposals dating from the mid-1990s could offer substantial benefits for cetacean habitat. All three are large, transborder and partly high-seas MPAs: the Arctic Ring of Life International Marine Biocultural Reserve, the Barents Sea International Marine Park and the Beringia Heritage International Park (Bleakley and Alexander, 1995). Unfortunately, none of these proposals has been realized yet, although all were identified as 'priorities' by Bleakley and Alexander.

Four countries – Canada, Russia, Iceland and Norway – plus the Danish territories of Greenland and the Faeroes and the Shetland Islands (UK) have marine borders in the Arctic Marine Region. The region features a portion of subarctic and cold temperate waters south of the Arctic Circle in the North Atlantic off southern Greenland, all around Iceland and off the entire west coast of Norway with its ice-free fjords. It includes the entire marine northern Arctic coast of Russia but not Alaskan waters or much of what is generally considered the Canadian Arctic. Instead, northern Alaska and almost all of the Canadian Arctic except the northernmost islands are included in the Northwest Atlantic Marine Region. With the highly endangered bowheads, only three of the five stocks, or breeding populations, are partly or mainly within the Arctic Marine Region; the others are in the Northwest Atlantic, Northwest Pacific and/or Northeast Pacific marine regions. Certain populations of belugas are also partly or completely outside the region – mainly in the Northwest Atlantic.

Polar opposite region to the Antarctic, the Arctic has many dramatic differences and aspects unique to itself. Most of all, it has three native cetacean species while the Antarctic has none. The Arctic is an ocean without a large continental land mass. It is politically complex, and for many years was part of the Cold War battleground. Nuclear-powered submarines and icebreakers have made the region passable despite the ice formations. By contrast, the Antarctic has largely existed free from power struggles.

In terms of whales, both Arctic and Antarctic have been important feeding grounds. The Arctic was the first to be discovered and heavily whaled – beginning in the early 17th century, while the Antarctic whale feeding grounds were mainly exploited in the 20th century. Baleen whales feeding in the Arctic, though reduced to low numbers for some species, continue to be hunted from Norway, Canada, Alaska (US), Russia, Greenland and, most recently, with whaling having restarted, Iceland.

In the Arctic Marine Region, ten large marine ecosystems (LMEs), have been identified: West Greenland Shelf, East Greenland Shelf, Barents Sea, Norwegian Shelf, Iceland Shelf, Arctic Ocean, Kara Sea, Laptev Sea, East Siberian Sea and Chukchi Sea. The overall oceanography includes upper current flows from Russia across the Arctic to the Norwegian-Greenland Sea. The Norwegian-Greenland Sea and Davis Strait between Greenland and Labrador, Canada, are two of the three main areas where the world ocean's deep water is created (the other is off Antarctica). Warm salty water flows up from the Mediterranean and is rapidly cooled as it flows northward by winds coming off Labrador and Greenland. The result is dense, cold water that sinks to the bottom in massive vertical flows. This North Atlantic Bottom Water then flows south through the North and South Atlantic.

The Arctic Environmental Protection Strategy (AEPS), set up under the Arctic Council established in 1996, has five working groups which focus on the marine and terrestrial environment:

- The Protection of the Arctic Marine Environment (PAME) works on policy measures related to marine protection from both land- and sea-based

---

BOX 5.2 THE VIEW ON MPAs IN ICELAND

Iceland is an active member of the OSPAR Convention (Oslo and Paris Convention for the Protection of the Marine Environment in the Northeast Atlantic) (Nijkamp and Bijvoet, 1996). According to the wider OSPAR definition of marine protected areas (any maritime area under management which results in some level of protection for at least a part of the ecosystem), Iceland has some 39 'marine protected areas', half of which regulate fisheries, including 11 relatively large areas and 16 offshore areas. These areas are closed year-round or seasonally or have restricted access for fisheries management purposes. Iceland is the only OSPAR partner having such large offshore areas controlled in this manner. Most closures are aimed at restricting demersal and pelagic trawling and Danish seine netting, but, according to Sigmar Arnar Steingrímsson, who has attended the OSPAR meetings representing Iceland's Marine Research Institute, these 'might benefit cetaceans'. But colleague Gisli Vikingsson, who has focused on whale studies for some years, notes that any move to protect cetaceans would require surveys to determine habitat. 'If [any] such areas should be chosen on the grounds that they are important habitat to cetaceans it would require some systematic evaluation based on the available knowledge on distribution and abundance of the different species. I am not aware of any such process going on' (Vikingsson, pers comm, 2003).

There is little doubt that the outer area of Breidafjördur and Skjalfandi Bay, possibly extending west to cover parts of Eyjafjördur, among other areas around Iceland, would be celebrated in many other countries as national and international treasures because of their resident whale populations, and made into protected areas or parks or biosphere reserves. Iceland has not shown the political will to designate protected habitat for cetaceans through such MPAs, although there is discussion about this possibility in the future among local and international conservation groups, tourism officials and some researchers. Officially, however, there is no talk of making MPAs for cetaceans. And with Iceland resuming whaling activities in August 2003, taking minke whales near some of these areas, the possibility for protecting cetacean habitat seems ever more remote.

---

activities, including impacts from shipping, offshore oil and gas and the efficacy of existing international agreements related to protection of the marine environment;

- Arctic Monitoring and Assessment Program (AMAP) identifies and assesses problems;
- Conservation of Arctic Flora and Fauna (CAFF) works on habitat protection and biodiversity;
- Emergency, Prevention, Preparedness and Response (EPPR) focuses on pollution prevention and control; and
- Sustainable Development Working Group (SDWG), the newest working group, is looking into sustainable development and environmental protection.

PAME and CAFF are the two working mostly on conservation aspects of the marine environment. The European part of the region (Norway and Iceland) also comes under the OSPAR Convention which has a programme of MPA

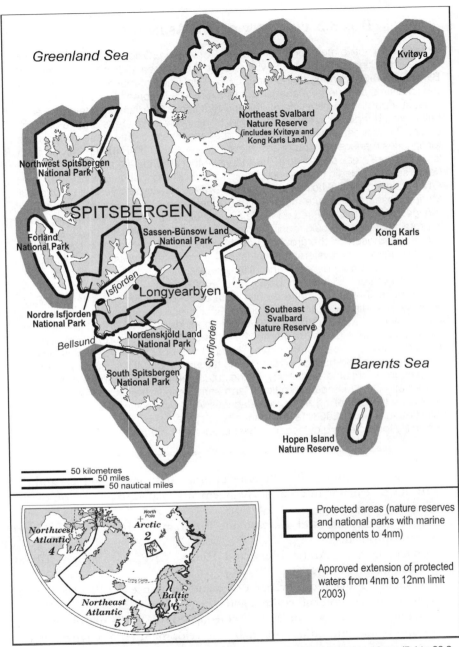

In December 2003, the marine boundaries of Svalbard were extended from 4 to 12 nm (7.4 to 22.2 km), adding some 15,830 mi² (41,000 km²) of coastal waters to the protected areas of Svalbard, an area the size of Switzerland. See Case Study 2, for more information.

Figure 5.3 *Map of Svalbard*

conservation in the region from 12 nm (22.2 km) to 200 nm (371 km) and beyond, on the high seas of the Northeast Atlantic.

In 1995, there was a total of 16 MPAs of all kinds in this marine region (Bleakley and Alexander, 1995). The region is divided into five biogeographic zones, four of which were represented by at least one MPA. As of 2004, according to Table 5.3 prepared for this book, there are three proposed international MPAs, 23 existing and 16 proposed MPAs (including 11 unnamed Russian Arctic areas) – all of which feature cetacean habitat. Two of the existing MPAs are proposed for a higher protection level.

The IUCN 2002–2010 Conservation Action Plan for the World's Cetaceans recommends a number of research and education initiatives for the Arctic Marine Region (Reeves et al, 2003):

- to assess the status of the Svalbard-Barents Sea stock of bowhead whales between East Greenland and Russia and identify threats to their survival and recovery; and
- to promote intensive field research on bowhead whales in the eastern Canadian Arctic (also applies to Marine Region 4).

Both of these initiatives are of highest priority as they focus on endangered species in the region, and the Svalbard-Barents Sea stock of bowhead whales is critically endangered.

Case Study 2: Svalbard – a complicated protection regime

Svalbard National Parks, Nature Reserves and Other Protected Areas

Type: National parks, nature reserves and other protected areas which include mainly land with coastal and marine areas.

Location: Svalbard including territorial waters bordering the Barents Sea, Greenland Sea and Arctic Ocean. Spitsbergen, which is often used interchangeably with Svalbard, is actually the largest island in the Svalbard archipelago.

Cetacean species: common: beluga, *Delphinapterus leucas*; also: narwhal, *Monodon monoceros*; minke whale, *Balaenoptera acutorostrata*; white-beaked dolphin, *Lagenorhynchus albirostris*; fin whale, *Balaenoptera physalus*; humpback whale, *Megaptera novaeangliae*; blue whale, *Balaenoptera musculus*; orca, *Orcinus orca*; Atlantic white-sided dolphin, *Lagenorhynchus acutus*; usually more offshore: northern bottlenose whale, *Hyperoodon ampullatus*; sperm whale, *Physeter macrocephalus*; sei whale, *Balaenoptera borealis*.

Additional species and other features: polar bear, *Ursus maritimus*; walrus, *Odobenus rosmarus*; harp seal, *Phoca groenlandica*; ringed seal, *Phoca hispida*; gray seal, *Halichoerus grypus*; bearded seal, *Erignathus barbatus*; hooded seal, *Cystophora cristata*; harbour seal, *Phoca vitulina*; various important seabird staging and feeding areas; more than 50 fish species; around 175 species of bryozoans (aquatic invertebrates called sea mats); 200 species of polychaetes (worms); 150 species of poriferans (sponges). Other features include an ice-edge zone with high primary production. About 80 per cent of the water entering and leaving the Arctic basin moves through the narrow channel between Greenland and Spitsbergen. This means that the Arctic has not only a strong hydrographic and climatic connection to the North Atlantic, but also extensive faunal exchanges. Spitsbergen is thus important as a major island group between the Arctic and Atlantic.

Size of existing protected area: The size of Svalbard's three national parks and nature reserves (and additional plant sanctuaries), created in 1973, is 25,640 mi^2 (66,424 km^2), including 13,510 mi^2 (35,000 km^2) of land and 12,130 mi^2 (31,424 km^2) of water. In 2003, land areas amounting to 1717 mi^2 (4449 km^2) were added to the protection zone for a total of 15,088 mi^2 (39,088 km^2) – about 63 per cent of Svalbard's land area. In addition, the expansion of Svalbard's boundaries from 4 nm (7.4 km) to 12 nm (22.2 km), announced in December 2003, adds up to 15,830 mi^2 (41,000 sq km^2) of marine waters to the Svalbard system of protected areas. The total marine area protected around Svalbard is estimated at 27,956 mi^2 (72,424 km^2).

Rationale: To make Svalbard – its ecology, habitats with rare plants and outstanding wildlife populations, including high densities of seabirds and marine mammals – 'the best-managed wilderness area' in the Arctic.

The story of Svalbard – including various protected parks and reserves and an idea for a 'Svalbard National Park' – shows the importance of a bold proposal for achieving conservation goals. It is an example of how long and tangled the conservation process can become. The 'one national park' idea was a failure but the hoped-for, desperately needed, protection regime became, in 2004, very nearly a reality.

The Svalbard Treaty of 1920 gave Norway sovereignty and responsibility over the entire Svalbard archipelago, although Russia as a signatory nation was granted equal rights to exploit natural resources in the archipelago (Prokosch, 1999).

Svalbard was one of the early whaling centres in the North Atlantic–Arctic. Beginning in the late 1600s, thousands of bowhead whales were caught until the population collapsed around 1860. Reeves (1980) estimates that there were 25,000 bowheads in 1679; in recent decades, however, there have been only a handful of sightings and some writers consider the Spitsbergen stock locally extinct around Svalbard (McQuaid, 1986). Other whales were taken as well, including smaller whales such as belugas, dating back to the 1700s. In 1818, a wintering Russian crew reportedly took 1200 belugas from a base at the southernmost tip of the island of Spitsbergen (the main island in the Svalbard archipelago) (Gjertz and Wiig, 1994). According to this report, many more than 15,000 belugas (recorded minimum) were taken between the 1700s and the early 1960s in Svalbard, when the fishery ended. Today, beluga numbers are considered fairly healthy and they are the most commonly sighted whale in the area.

In 1973, the Norwegian government created three national parks and two nature reserves. They also made 15 small bird sanctuaries, a special reserve for seabirds and walruses, a flora conservation area and two areas for plant species protection. As of December 2003, the five main protected areas have a marine component of 12 nautical miles (13.8 miles or 22.2 km) from shore which includes some beluga habitat as well as occasional or partial feeding grounds for other cetaceans. Orcas follow fish into the fjords along the west coast, especially in autumn. Minkes and fins are also sometimes seen in the fjords through the summer, though they are more common a little offshore. Humpback whales often feed along the west coast of Spitsbergen. Blue whales are also sometimes seen but they are rare. White-beaked dolphins are common along the southwest coast of Spitsbergen and southwards into the Barents Sea, including around Bear Island. Narwhals were historically found off northwest Spitsbergen but cannot be counted on. Sei whales are only found in the southern part of the archipelago, closer to Bear Island. Finally, sperm whales and northern bottlenose whales might sometimes be seen within the deepest waters of the territorial limit but they are normally found at the edge of the continental slope, some miles further out from shore.

According to regulations for Svalbard's national parks and nature reserves: 'The sea bed is protected against catching or gathering by diving or by use of bottom trawl or scrape. Shrimp trawling is allowed in waters with depths of 100 metres or more... Mammals or birds and their habitat and nests are protected against damage and destruction of any kind that are not due to ordinary traffic.' This last point also includes sea mammals in the protected areas and thus means that whales and dolphins are safe from hunting if they are found within the waters of the protected area.

In 1995, the Norwegian parliament called for the government to propose new protected areas on Svalbard and to preserve 'important land areas with biological production' (Prokosch, 1999). Most researchers and others involved with Svalbard agreed that the protection level was not representative and not secure enough to prevent the physical degradation particularly of the wildlife-rich tundra. The Norwegian government set a goal that Svalbard should be the best-managed wilderness area in the world. Following this, the Norwegian Polar Institute evaluated Svalbard and made various proposals for additional protected areas that would be more representative of ecosystems and habitats (Prokosch, 1999). The Norwegian Polar Institute's 1998 report stated that 'despite its significant extension, the national parks and the large nature reserves together do not safeguard a representative cross-section of Svalbard's natural and cultural environment. The most productive and species rich land areas of the island group are least represented within the protected areas.' Following this report, the Governor of Svalbard proposed nine new areas for protection covering a total of approximately 1578 square miles (4088 km²).

Since 1996, the World Wide Fund for Nature, through WWF Norway and WWF's Arctic Programme, has joined with other NGOs to work actively on better protection for Svalbard. In 1999, responding to the government's proposal for a new Svalbard environmental law and the proposals for new protected areas, WWF initiated a campaign to protect all of Svalbard as one national park which would protect the entire archipelago under a single management regime.

Reaction to the Svalbard National Park proposal was predictably mixed, but the Norwegian parliament in 2000 affirmed the planned improvement of the environmental protection of the archipelago and left the door open to significant further protection, without accepting the 'one national park' proposal (Humphreys and Prokosch, 2000; Hansson, 2000).

Meantime, a new Svalbard Environmental Protection Act has been put in place which brings together all environmental regulations for Svalbard under one act and, among other things, gives protection to sea mammal species 'belonging to the ecosystem' which includes belugas. Belugas are also protected under the Game Regulation for Svalbard and Jan Mayen. Migrating sea mammal species, however, such as minke whales and harp seals, are not included but are protected within the territorial waters surrounding protected areas. At present, the hunting of minke whales occurs mainly off the Norwegian mainland.

Since 2000, the Svalbard 'one national park' idea has quietly receded into the background but it fulfilled an important role, helping to push the issue of more comprehensive protection. WWF's goal with the 'one national park' proposal was to save Svalbard's wilderness from being fragmented and destroyed. That is, arguably, now close to being achieved (Norris, 2003).

In late 2003, news came that five new protected areas were being created in Svalbard, including three national parks and an important island nature reserve at Hopen Island. This has effectively extended the land-based protection to a further 1717 mi^2 (4449 km^2) of Svalbard. However, more good news came in December 2003 with Norway's decision to extend the territorial boundaries of Svalbard from 4 to 12 nm (7.4 to 22.2 km). This effectively expands all of Svalbard's coastal national park and nature reserves, adding 15,830 mi^2 (41,000 km^2) of coastal waters to the protected areas of Svalbard, an area the size of Switzerland. This important Arctic MPA development could benefit Svalbard's cetaceans.

Much work remains to be done to sort out boundaries, management, enforcement and other issues. Svalbard, with its assortment of national parks, nature reserves and other protected areas, may have a complicated protection regime. But it nevertheless appears that the unsuccessful 'one national park' proposed for Svalbard has become a success story for marine and land-based protection in the Arctic. Svalbard is on its way to becoming the dreamed-of 'best-managed Arctic wilderness'.

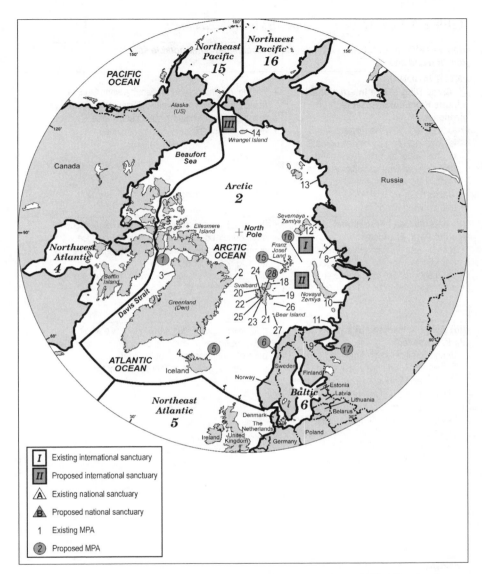

The roman numerals, letters and numbers correspond to the sanctuaries and MPAs listed and described in Table 5.3.

Figure 5.4 *Map of Marine Region 2: Arctic MPAs and sanctuaries*

Table 5.3 *Marine Region 2: Arctic MPAs and sanctuaries*

Name of MPA or sanctuary, location and size	Cetacean and other notable species
INTERNATIONAL *(I)* **Arctic Ring of Life International Marine Biocultural Reserve,** *proposed* • located along the permanent Arctic ice cap including the zones or leads of open water and polynyas in the Arctic Ocean waters of Canada, Russia, Norway, Greenland and Alaska (US) • size undetermined	• beluga, *Delphinapterus leucas*; narwhal, *Monodon monoceros*; bowhead whale, *Balaena mysticetus*; various feeding baleen whales; orca, *Orcinus orca* • also: seals, seabirds
(II) **Barents Sea International Marine Park,** *proposed* • Barents Sea including Svalbard, Bear Island, Novaya Zemlya, Franz Josef Land and the sea area between • size undetermined	• beluga, *Delphinapterus leucas*; narwhal, *Monodon monoceros*; bowhead whale, *Balaena mysticetus*; humpback whale, *Megaptera novaeangliae*; various feeding baleen whales • also: seals, polar bears, seabirds; key growing and feeding area for fish
(III) **Beringia Heritage International Park,** *proposed* • Bering Strait between Chukotsk Peninsula, Russia and Alaska – the Bering Land Bridge – including portions of the Bering and Chukchi Seas • size undetermined but plan is to include existing monuments, preserves and parks around Bering Strait as well as a 60-mile-wide (97 km) strip of coast on the Bering and Chukchi seas	• gray whale, *Eschrictius robustus*; minke whale, *Balaenoptera acutorostrata*; orca, *Orcinus orca*; Dall's porpoise, *Phocoenoides dalli*; others • also: walrus, more than 200 species of bird
CANADA *(1)* **Nirjutiqavvik National Wildlife Area,** *proposed for higher protection level* • Coburg Island, Nunavut • 68.7 mi^2 (178 km^2) total; 55.4 mi^2 (143.5 km^2) marine component	• bowhead whale, *Balaena mysticetus*; narwhal, *Monodon monoceros*; beluga, *Delphinapterus leucas* • extensive seabird populations nest on the south coast of Coburg Island: thick-billed murres, kittiwakes, fulmars, black guillemots

Notes and rationale	For more information
• Rationale is to create a biocultural marine reserve to protect diverse and fragile Arctic ecosystems including extensive critical habitat for marine mammals and seabirds along the polar ice; polar ice supports the basis of the Arctic marine food web. • In 1995, Bleakley and Alexander made a strong recommendation for the creation of this land- and marine-based park. • Conflicts and problems in the area include oil and gas exploration and development, marine traffic, mining, military activities including nuclear-powered transport and nuclear waste disposal.	• Bleakley and Alexander, 1995
• Rationale is to protect diverse Arctic ecosystems and the Barents Sea, one of the most productive areas in the Arctic. • Special features include the productive ice edge. • Initially proposed by Norwegian NGOs, the Barents Sea park was also a regional priority recommendation in Bleakley and Alexander (1995). • Conflicts and problems in the area include oil and gas exploration and development, marine traffic and dumping of nuclear wastes.	• Bleakley and Alexander, 1995
• Rationale is that the Bering Strait between Alaska and Russia serves as an international crossroads for wildlife and indigenous people and is one of the most biologically productive ecosystems in the region. • In 1988, IUCN member nations passed a resolution to encourage the US and Russia to designate the area as a World Heritage Site, and the protection of the area was endorsed by US and Russian leaders at the 1990 and 1992 summits. US portion of the park would include the existing Bering Land Bridge and Noatak national preserves and the Cape Krustenstern and Kobuk Valley national monuments, while a new park on the Chukotsk Peninsula would form part of the Russian contribution. Both Bleakley and Alexander (1995) and Newell and Wilson (1996) recommend creating this land- and marine-based park and note that the park would include several biodiversity hot spots, including Providenskiye Fjords and Tundra, Bol'shoy Diomid and Maliy Diomid Islands. In 2003, Stepanitsky (2003) wrote that Beringia National Park is planned for designation in 2010.	• Bleakley and Alexander, 1995; Melnikov and Zagrebin, 2000; Newell and Wilson, 1996; Stepanitsky, 2003
• Coburg Island and the surrounding waters were made an NWA in 1995; in 1997 WWF Canada proposed that this area be upgraded to provide effective protection for marine wildlife and habitats. They called for banning of bottom trawling and dragging, large-scale dredging and non-renewable resource development which under the current system can be done through permits.	See also Tables 5.7 and 5.19 for more Canadian MPAs. • Contact: Nirjutiqavvik NWA; web: www.newparks north.org/nirjucws.htm • WWF Canada, 245 Eglinton Ave E, 410, Toronto, Ont M4P 2Z7, Canada; web: www.wwf.ca

Table 5.3 *continued*

Name of MPA or sanctuary, location and size	Cetacean and other notable species
GREENLAND (Denmark) **(2) Northeast Greenland National Park** • northern and northeastern Greenland, where the Arctic Ocean (Lincoln Sea, Wandel Sea, Independence Fjord) meets the Greenland Sea (north from Kong Oscar Fjord) • 375,000 mi² (956,700 km²) includes both terrestrial (primarily) and marine areas; sea area alone is 42,692 mi² (110,600 km²)	• beluga, *Delphinapterus leucas*; narwhal, *Monodon monoceros*; also, fin whale, *Balaenoptera physalus*; minke whale, *Balaenoptera acutorostrata*; white-beaked dolphin, *Lagenorhynchus albirostris*; occasionally, sperm whale, *Physeter macrocephalus*; orca, *Orcinus orca*; others • also: polar bear, walrus, numerous seabirds
(3) Melville Bay Wildlife Sanctuary • northwest Greenland, stretching along the coast for 155 mi (250 km) between north of Upernavik and south of Thule, on Baffin Bay • 3071 mi² (7957 km²), including coastal land and a marine area of 2004 mi² (5193 km²)	• beluga, *Delphinapterus leucas*; narwhal, *Monodon monoceros*; also, fin whale, *Balaenoptera physalus*; minke whale, *Balaenoptera acutorostrata*; occasionally, sperm whale, *Physeter macrocephalus*; orca, *Orcinus orca*; others • also: walrus, polar bear, pink-footed and barnacle geese, seabirds, various seals, numerous commercial fish species

Notes and rationale	For more information
• Established in 1974 and expanded in 1988, this park and Unesco biosphere reserve, called the world's largest national park, has significant Arctic cetacean populations. There are also huge problems with hunting. It was known that hunting at a basic level would be part of the activities in the transition zones or outside the park but that it would be carefully managed. However, the high numbers taken without sufficient research and a management plan have caused acute concern since the mid-1990s. Since then, research has started on the exploitation levels of marine mammals in the area, but Greenland Home Rule and local managers also need to manage and set up an effective enforcement regime. • Rationale was to set aside a large Arctic ecosystem with outstanding bird, marine mammal and fish populations and to conserve resources for subsistence hunting and fishing.	• Born and Böcher, 1999; Hansen, 2002; Mikkelsen, 1996a, 1996b • WWF Arctic Programme, PO Box 6784, St Olavsplass, N-0130 Oslo, Norway; email: arctic@wwf.no • Greenland Institute of Natural Resources, PO Box 570, 3900 Nuuk, Greenland; web: http://esb.natur forvaltning.no/ GinstNatres.htm • Greenland Home Rule, PO Box 269, 3900 Nuuk, Greenland
• Established shortly after home-rule government began by act of Ministry of Greenland on 27 May 1980, the Melville Bay Wildlife Sanctuary was renewed in 1989 by Greenland Home Rule. The act says that the sanctuary should protect polar bears, seals, belugas, narwhals and walruses from exploitation, disturbance and other human activities but management details are unclear. WWF Arctic considers the reserve 'partially protected'. The reserve excludes all hunting in an inner zone closest to the ice, and restricts hunting in the outer zone, but hunting often occurs (Mikkelsen, 1996b). Indeed, Melville Bay is a traditional hunting ground for the people of Thule district. The Greenland Home Rule Government has been called upon by WWF and others involved in the Circumpolar Protected Area Network Plan to sponsor new research, 'implement stronger protective regulations and intensify its efforts to enforce those that already exist' (Mikkelsen, 1996b). Since 1996 when the above comments were made, more research has been done on the exploitation levels of marine mammals in the area and this work should continue. But Greenland Home Rule and local managers also need to manage and set up an effective enforcement regime. • Heide-Jorgensen and Dietz (1995) report that satellite tracking shows the sanctuary to be seasonally important for protecting narwhals from exploitation. Some narwhals from the Baffin Bay population spend the two-month open water season feeding in the sanctuary before moving offshore into pack ice in late October.	• Heide-Jorgensen and Dietz, 1995; Mikkelsen, 1996b • Contact: MP Heide-Jorgensen, Greenland Fisheries Research Institute, Tagensvej 135, 2200 Copenhagen N, Denmark • WWF Arctic Programme, PO Box 6784, St Olavsplass, N-0130 Oslo, Norway; email: arctic@wwf.no • Greenland Institute of Natural Resources, PO Box 570, 3900 Nuuk, Greenland; web: http://esb.natur forvaltning.no/ GinstNatres.htm • Greenland Home Rule, PO Box 269, 3900 Nuuk, Greenland • Zackenberg Ecological Research Operations (ZERO), Danish Polar Center, Copehagen K, Denmark; web: www.dpc.dk

Table 5.3 *continued*

Name of MPA or sanctuary, location and size	Cetacean and other notable species
ICELAND Lyveldi Island **(4) Breidafjördur MPA** • Breidafjördur, northwest Iceland • 1042 mi² (2700 km²) includes islands and surrounding waters	• most common: white-beaked dolphin, *Lagenorhynchus albirostris*; harbor porpoise, *Phocoena phocoena*; also present: minke whale, *Balaenoptera acutorostrata*; long-finned pilot whale, *Globicephala melas*; orca, *Orcinus orca* • also: large assortment of seabirds, with many nesting on rocks in the reserve, such as cormorant, guillemot, fulmar, puffin, kittiwake, as well as the rare white-tailed eagle; numerous seals
(5) Skjalfandi Bay MPA, *under discussion* • Skjalfandi Bay, northeast Iceland • size undetermined	• common residents: minke whale, *Balaenoptera acutorostrata*; white-beaked dolphin, *Lagenorhynchus albirostris*; harbor porpoise, *Phocoena phocoena*; visitors: humpback whale, *Megaptera novaeangliae*; sei whale, *Balaenoptera borealis*; blue whale, *Balaenoptera musculus*; northern bottlenose whale, *Hyperoodon ampullatus*
NORWAY Kongeriket Norge **(6) Tysfjord and Hellemofjord MPA, *proposed*** • Tysfjord and Hellemofjord, Nordland county, Norwegian Sea • 121 mi² (314 km²)	• orca, *Orcinus orca* • also: herring spend their winters in the fjord

Notes and rationale	For more information
• Established in 1995, Breidafjördur is by far the largest MPA in Iceland (rated IUCN Category IV with elements of Ib and V). Regular bird watching trips out of Stykkisholmur travel through the MPA, and the same operator offers whale watch trips outside the MPA to the outer areas of Breidafjördur, where blue and humpback whales, orcas, harbor porpoises, white-beaked dolphins and other cetaceans occur in much greater numbers than in the reserve itself. To date, however, there has been no discussion of extending the MPA to include this outer area which stands as, arguably, one of the best blue whale and orca habitats in the North Atlantic. • Rationale is to protect an area of outstanding natural beauty with the most diverse marine and intertidal habitats in Iceland; islands contain bird staging areas; numerous fish and invertebrates of commercial value. • In terms of research, no organized surveys have been carried out in the Breidafjördur area on species, numbers and distribution of cetaceans. However, whale watch operators are keeping records of whale sightings, mainly outside the reserve but also with some sightings inside, and these are sent to the Marine Research Institute. • The Nature Conservancy Council administers the national parks and reserves in Iceland. There are only four relatively small MPAs in Iceland.	• Björgvinsson, 1999; Nijkamp and Bijvoet, 1996; Petersen and Gudmundsson, 1995; Petersen et al, 1998 • Contact: Nature Conservancy Council, Náttúruverndarráð Hverfisgata 26, Hlemmur 3, Reykjavík, Iceland • Sigmar Arnar Steingrímsson, Hafrannsóknastofnuninni/ Marine Research Institute, PO Box 1390, Skúlagata 4, 121 Reykjavík, Iceland; web: www.hafro.is/ • Arni Finnsson, c/o Iceland Nature Conservation Association, Thverholt 15, 105 Reykjavík, Iceland; web: www.mmedia.is/nsi
• Rationale is to protect an area of outstanding natural beauty which serves as a summer nearshore feeding ground for resident minke whales, white-beaked dolphins and harbor porpoises and sometimes other cetaceans; MPA could add appeal, publicity and 'branding' to Husavik, the whale watch capital of northern Europe. • There is little doubt that Skjalfandi Bay would be celebrated in many other countries as a national treasure and made into a protected area or park. Iceland has not shown the political will to propose protected habitat for its cetacean populations through MPAs, although there is some discussion among conservation groups, tourism officials and some researchers about this as a future possibility. Officially, however, there is no talk of making MPAs for cetaceans.	• Asbjorn Björgvinsson, The Whale Centre, PO Box 172, 640 Husavik, Iceland; email: icewhale@centrum.is; web: www.icewhale.is
• This area is considered a possible candidate MPA for a number of reasons including the autumn–winter presence of orca which come to feed on the herring. • Since the early 1990s, whale watching has grown steadily; this tourism brings substantial mainly foreign revenues to the region (hotels, restaurants, shops, supporting up to ten tour operators). • In 2000, the Institute of Marine Research in Bergen started a project to map the occurrence of small cetaceans in the fjords and coastal waters of mainland Norway. For orcas, the prime important foraging grounds are in the Vestfjorden-Lofoten area, including Tysfjorden. In 2001, a national advisory committee on MPAs was established in Norway. In 2003 this area was among 36 proposed by the committee to be included in the national MPA network; the formal proposal is still in process as of 2004.	• DeNardo, 1998; Hoyt, 2001; Simila, 1997 • Contact: WWF Norway, PO Box 6784, St Olavsplass, N-0130 Oslo, Norway • Mai Britt Knoph, Ministry of the Environment, PO Box 8013 Dep N-0030 Oslo, Norway; email: mbk@md.dep.no; web: http://odin.dep.no/md/ • Arne Bjørge, Institute of Marine Research, Bergen, Norway; email: arne.bjoerge@imr.no

Table 5.3 *continued*

Name of MPA or sanctuary, location and size	Cetacean and other notable species
RUSSIA Russian Federation Rossiskaya Federatsiya	
(7) Great Arctic Nature Reserve (Bolshoy Arktichesky Zapovednik) • Karskoye Sea along the Taimyr peninsula, including the deltas of the Taymura and Pyasina rivers • 16,093 mi^2 (41,692 km^2), includes land areas; marine part is 3786 mi^2 (9809 km^2)	• beluga, *Delphinapterus leucas* • also: seals, walrus, polar bear, reindeer, seabirds, northernmost source of migratory flyways
(8) Gydanskiy Nature Reserve (Zapovednik) • northern coast of the Gydan peninsula, Karskoye Sea • 3390 mi^2 (8782 km^2), plus 232 mi^2 (600 km^2) marine buffer zone and 347 mi^2 (900 km^2) land buffer zone	• beluga, *Delphinapterus leucas* • also: walrus, polar bear, seabirds
(9) Kandalakshskiy Nature Reserve (Zapovednik) • White Sea and Barentsevo (Barents) Sea • 272 mi^2 (705 km^2), includes land areas; marine part is 191 mi^2 (496 km^2)	• beluga, *Delphinapterus leucas*; orca, *Orcinus orca*; harbor porpoise, *Phocoena phocoena*
(10) Nenetskiy Nature Reserve (Zapovednik) • 60 mi (100 km) north of Naryan-Mar town, Pechorskoye Sea, Barentsevo (Barents) Sea • total area is 1210 mi^2 (3134 km^2), with marine area of 702 mi^2 (1819 km^2)	• resident: beluga, *Delphinapterus leucas*; orca, *Orcinus orca* (near border of reserve); transient, Jun–Aug: Atlantic white-sided dolphin, *Lagenorhynchus acutus*; white-beaked dolphin, *Lagenorhynchus albirostris*; harbor porpoise, *Phocoena phocoena*; narwhal, *Monodon monoceros*; others (total 19 cetacean species)
(11) Shoynenskiy National Park • White Sea, Nenetskiy Territory, northwest Russia • 63 mi^2 164 km^2), includes land areas	• probable cetacean habitat – beluga and other whales
(12) Taymirskiy Biosphere Reserve (Zapovednik) • biopshere zapovednik on the Taymir peninsula in the Laptevih Sea • 10,498 mi^2 (27,197 km^2), mainly land areas	• beluga, *Delphinapterus leucas*

Notes and rationale	For more information
• This coastal and marine area was proposed by WWF and the Institute for Evolutionary Morphology and Animal Ecology of the Russian Academy of Sciences, after a joint biological expedition to northern Taymyr in 1989. In 1993, the Great Arctic Zapovednik was created. Approximately the size of Switzerland and rated IUCN Category Ia, it is the world's largest highly protected area. The reserve has substantial marine areas. Cetacean surveys and habitat assessments would help to define the extent of cetacean habitat use, but belugas are known to use inshore areas extensively in summer months. • Ecotourism activity is possible in this reserve.	See also Tables 5.6, 5.9 and 5.19 for more Russian MPAs; see Box 5.11 for explanation of Russian protected areas. • Contact: Chuprov Valeriy Leonidovich, Schorsa Str, 1, a/box 126, Dudinka, Taymyrskiy Territory, 663210 Russia; email: reserve@dudinka.ru • WWF Russian Programme Office; web: www.wwf.ru
• Created in 1996 as a coastal zapovednik (IUCN Category Ia), this reserve includes small marine areas and the islands of Oleniy, Velkitskogo, Neupokoyeva and Shokolskogo. • The marine portion extends only 0.6 mi (1 km) from the zapovednik's coastal line; cetacean surveys and habitat assessments are required to determine cetacean habitat use.	• Contact: Golosenko Nikolay Alexeevich, Geophisiks Str, 18, GosKomEcology of Tazovskiy region (for GPZ), Tazovskiy village, Jamalo-Nenetskiy Territory, Russia
• Designated in 1932 as a coastal zapovednik which includes marine areas (IUCN Category Ia). • Cetacean surveys and habitat assessments are needed to determine cetacean habitat use.	• Contact: Chavgun Alexander Stepanovich, Lineynaya Str 35, Kandalaksha, Murmanskaya Territory, 184040 Russia
• Designated in 1997 as a coastal zapovednik which includes marine areas (IUCN Category Ia). • No dedicated cetacean research but observations are recorded. Belugas are found in the core part of the reserve for foraging and travel some 10 mi (15 km) up the Pechora River estuary. • Cetacean surveys and habitat assessments are needed to determine cetacean habitat use for orcas and other cetaceans; beluga use of estuary is well documented. • 19 marine mammal species are found in the Pechorskoye Sea, according to Murman Marine Biological Institute of Russian Academy of Science.	• Contact: AS Glotov and AG Kuznetsov, Nenetskiy Zapovednik, Fakel, ul Gazovikov, 2, Naryan-Mar, Arkhangelskaya, Russia; email: kazarka@atnet.ru
• National park which includes marine areas (IUCN Category II). • Marine component thought to include cetacean habitat; surveys and habitat assessments are needed.	
• Coastal zapovednik (IUCN Category Ia). • Cetacean surveys and habitat assessments are needed to determine cetacean habitat use.	• Contact: Karbainov Juriy Mikhailovich, Taymyrskaya Territory, Khatanga, a/box 31, 663260 Russia, a/box 31; email: taimyr@orc.ru

Table 5.3 *continued*

Name of MPA or sanctuary, location and size	Cetacean and other notable species
(13) Ust'-Lenskiy Nature Reserve (Zapovednik) • Laptevih Sea • 5531 mi² (14,330 km²), includes marine areas	• beluga, *Delphinapterus leucas*
(14) Wrangel Island (Ostrov Vrangelya) Nature Reserve (Zapovednik) • north of Chukotka mainland, Chukotskoye (Chukchi) Sea • 8591 mi² (22,256 km²) includes land areas on both Wrangel and Herald islands; marine part is 5520 mi² (14,300 km²)	• bowhead whale, *Balaena mysticetus*; gray whale, *Eschrictius robustus*; humpback whale, *Megaptera novaeangliae*; fin whale, *Balaenoptera physalus*; beluga, *Delphinapterus leucas*; orca, *Orcinus orca* • also: largest concentration of breeding polar bears and huge walrus rookeries; extensive seabird colonies
[MPAs 15–16] ***(15) Franz Josef Land Wildlife Refuge (Zakaznik), proposed for extension and protection as a national park*** • Franz Josef Land, north of Novaya Zemlya, Arctic Russia • size of 1994 zakaznik is 16,200 mi² (42,000 km²), 62 per cent marine ***(16) Russian Arctic National Park (Russkaya Arktika), proposed*** • Franz Josef Land, northern Novaya Zemlya and marine areas • size undetermined	• beluga, *Delphinapterus leucas*; narwhal, *Monodon monoceros*; bowhead whale, *Balaena mysticetus*; others • also: polar bear, various Arctic seals
(17) Solovetskiy Islands Biosphere Reserve (Zapovednik), proposed • off Cape Beluzhiy, White Sea • no size data	• beluga, *Delphinapterus leucas* • largha and bearded seals
Various Russian Arctic MPAs	• beluga, *Delphinapterus leucas*; narwhal, *Monodon monoceros*; bowhead whale, *Balaena mysticetus*; orca, *Orcinus orca*; minke whale, *Balaenoptera acutorostrata*; others

Notes and rationale	For more information
• Designated in 1985 as a coastal zapovednik which includes marine areas (IUCN Category Ia). • Cetacean surveys and habitat assessments are needed to determine cetacean habitat use.	• Contact: Gorokhov Dmitriy Nikolaevich, Academik Phedorov Str 28, Tixi, Bulunskiy, Sakha republic (Yakutiya), 678400 Russia
• Designated in 1976 to protect Arctic island ecosystems, this island zapovednik (IUCN Category Ia) includes marine areas in a 3.1 mi (5 km) buffer zone around the nature reserve on Wrangel Island. • Cetacean surveys and habitat assessments needed to determine cetacean habitat use.	• Kochnev, 2000; Newell and Wilson, 1996 • Contact: Bove Leonid Leonidovich, Naberezhnaya Str, 27, Mys Shmidta, Shmidtovskiy, Chukotskiy Territory, 686870 Russia; email: wisnr@chrues.chukotka.ru
• In 1994 a temporary marine and terrestrial wildlife refuge or zakaznik was created at Franz Josef Land. WWF then proposed it for expansion as the 'Russian Arctic National Park'. The first step in the process occurred in 1999 when the Arkhangelsk Legislative Assembly approved the national park idea. In 2003, it was announced that the Russian Arctic National Park would be designated in 2010. • The large marine component of the proposed national park would include substantial cetacean habitat but surveys and habitat assessments are needed to determine which areas require Category I core area protection. • Ecotourism will be allowed in the national park.	• Stepanitsky, 2003 • WWF Russian Programme Office; web: www.wwf.ru • Environmental Education Center 'Zapovedniks'; email: chipmunk@online.ru
• Goal of MPA would be to control ecotourism impact and vessel traffic within critical beluga habitat. • The land area is currently protected as a natural reserve. IFAW is trying to make the Solovetskiy archipelago and adjacent waters a protected Unesco biosphere reserve. • Beluga research has been carried on here and around the White Sea for many years; surveys and habitat assessments over the past few years have found nearshore areas which belugas use for reproductive purposes.	• Belkovich, 2002; Ognetov and Svetocheva, 2000 • Contact: Gregoriy Tsidulko, IFAW; email: gtsidulko@ifaw.org
• Eleven large new areas in the Russian Arctic (including entire west coast waters of Novaya Zemlya and three different locations in the White Sea) have been suggested as 'marine protected areas' by WWF and other groups (see map published in *Arctic Bulletin*, no 4, 2003, p24). • Marine component would certainly include cetacean habitat; surveys and habitat assessments required.	• Contact: WWF Russian Programme Office; web: www.wwf.ru

Table 5.3 *continued*

Name of MPA or sanctuary, location and size	Cetacean and other notable species
SVALBARD ARCHIPELAGO (Norway) [MPAs 18–22] **(18) Northeast Svalbard Nature Reserve (Nordaust-Svalbard Naturreservat)** • northeast Svalbard including territorial waters to 12 nm (13.8 mi or 22.2 km), Barents Sea • size of this area is unavailable but the size of all three national parks, plus nature reserves and additional plant sanctuaries, in Svalbard is 25,640 mi² (66,424 km²), including 13,510 mi² (35,000 km²) of land and 12,130 mi² (31,424 km²) of water; in 2003, Svalbard's territorial boundaries were expanded to 12 nm (22.2 km), adding 15,830 mi² (41,000 km²) to the area conserved **(19) Southeast Svalbard Nature Reserve (Søraust-Svalbard Naturreservat)** • Southeast Svalbard including territorial waters **(20) Northwest Spitsbergen National Park (Nordvest-Spitsbergen Nasjonalpark)** • northwestern Svalbard including territorial waters **(21) South Spitsbergen National Park (Sør-Spitsbergen Nasjonalpark)** • southwest Svalbard including territorial waters **(22) Forland National Park (Forlandet Nasjonalpark)** • Prins Karls Forland, large island off western Spitsbergen in the Svalbard archipelago, including territorial waters	• common: beluga, *Delphinapterus leucas*; occasionally: minke whale, *Balaenoptera acutorostrata*; white-beaked dolphin, *Lagenorhynchus albirostris*; Atlantic white-sided dolphin, *Lagenorhynchus acutus*; humpback whale, *Megaptera novaeangliae*; fin whale, *Balaenoptera physalus*; blue whale, *Balaenoptera musculus*; orca, *Orcinus orca*; in northern areas: narwhal, *Monodon monoceros* • also: polar bear; walrus; harp, ringed, gray, bearded, hooded and harbour seals; important seabird staging and feeding areas; more than 50 fish species; 175 species of bryozoans; 200 species of polychaetes (worms); 150 species of poriferans (sponges)

Notes and rationale	For more information
• Established in 1973, these various nature reserves and national parks originally had a marine component of only 4 nm (4.6 mi or 7.4 km) from shore. This was expanded in Dec 2003 to 12 nm (13.8 mi or 22.2 km), which includes beluga habitat as well as other cetacean feeding grounds. Orcas follow fish into the fjords especially in autumn. Minkes and fins are also sometimes seen in the fjords through the summer, though they are more common a little out to sea. Humpback whales often feed along the west coast of the main island of Spitsbergen. There is some tourism to Svalbard and future potential for whale watching (Hoyt, 1997a). • Rationale is for the protection of Svalbard, its ecology and outstanding wildlife populations. • According to regulations for Svalbard's nature reserves and national parks, 'the sea bed is protected against catching or gathering by diving or by use of bottom trawl or scrape. Shrimp trawling is allowed in waters with depths of 100 m or more... Mammals or birds and their habitat and nests are protected against damage and destruction of any kind that are not due to ordinary traffic.' This last point also includes sea mammals in the protected areas and thus means that cetaceans are protected if they stay within 12 nm (13.8 mi or 22.2 km) of the coast of the protected area. However, a new Environmental Protection Act is being established for Svalbard which awards protection to sea mammal species 'belonging to the ecosystem', including belugas. Belugas are also protected under the Game Regulation for Svalbard and Jan Mayen. Migrating sea mammal species, however, such as minke whales and harp seals, are not included. Thus, minke whale catching could technically be allowed just outside of Svalbard's territorial waters or in those parts of Svalbard's waters outside the protected areas. Such protection by Norway recognizes the archipelago's outstanding natural value. Still, some feel the area should be larger with uniform management and regulations. **See Case Study 2**, Svalbard – A complicated protection regime, for a fuller discussion.	• Gjertz, 1991; Gjertz and Wiig, 1994; Hoyt, 1997a; Norris, 2003; Prokosch, 1999; Schandy, 2000 • Contact: WWF Arctic Programme, PO Box 6784, St Olavsplass, N-0130 Oslo, Norway; email: arctic@wwf.no • Fredrik Juell Theisen, Miljøverndepartementet (Ministry of the Environment), PO Box 8013 Dep, N-0030 Oslo, Norway; email: FJT@md.dep.no; web: http://odin.dep.no/md/

Table 5.3 *continued*

Name of MPA or sanctuary, location and size	Cetacean and other notable species
[MPAs 23–26] **(23) Nordenskjöld Land National Park (Nordenskjöld Land Nasjonalpark)** • southwest Svalbard, territorial waters on Bellsund and Van Mijenfjorden, Greenland Sea **(24) Nordre Isfjorden National Park (Nordre Isfjorden Nasjonalpark)** • inner Isfjorden, including Nordfjorden, western Svalbard, off the Greenland Sea **(25) Sassen-Bünsow Land National Park (Sassen-Bünsow Land Nasjonalpark)** • at eastern end of inner Isfjorden, western Svalbard, off the Greenland Sea **(26) Hopen Island Nature Reserve (Hopen Naturreservat)** • Hopen Island, southeastern Svalbard, Barents Sea	• common: beluga, *Delphinapterus leucas*; occasionally in some areas: minke whale, *Balaenoptera acutorostrata*; humpback whale, *Megaptera novaeangliae*; fin whale, *Balaenoptera physalus*; orca, *Orcinus orca* • also: various seabirds and polar bear in some areas
(27) Bear Island Nature Reserve (Bjørnøya Naturreservat) • Bear Island (Bjørnøya), southernmost point of Svalbard archipelago, on Bjornoy-banken, Norwegian Sea • 347 mi² (900 km²) total, 68 mi² (175 km²) land	• humpback whale, *Megaptera novaeangliae*; minke whale, *Balaenoptera acutorostrata*; sei whale, *Balaenoptera borealis*; white-beaked dolphin, *Lagenorhynchus albirostris*
(28) Svalbard National Park (Svalbard Nasjonalpark), *proposed* • Svalbard including territorial waters on the Barents Sea, Greenland Sea and Arctic Ocean • size of proposed area was originally 40,972 mi² (106,144 km²) (59 per cent land and 41 per cent water), most of which is now protected in national parks, nature reserves and plant sanctuaries; an additional marine area of 15,830 mi² (41,000 km²) is also protected as of 2003	• common: beluga, *Delphinapterus leucas*; also: narwhal, *Monodon monoceros*; minke whale, *Balaenoptera acutorostrata*; white-beaked dolphin, *Lagenorhynchus albirostris*; fin whale, *Balaenoptera physalus*; humpback whale, *Megaptera novaeangliae*; blue whale, *Balaenoptera musculus*; orca, *Orcinus orca*; Atlantic white-sided dolphin, *Lagenorhynchus acutus* • also: polar bear; walrus; harp, ringed, grey, bearded and hooded seals; seabird staging and feeding areas

Notes and rationale	For more information
• In 1998, the Norwegian Polar Institute evaluated Svalbard's current protected areas and made various proposals for additional protected areas that would be more representative of ecosystems and habitats (Prokosch, 1999). The 1998 report stated that 'despite its significant extension, the national parks and the large nature reserves together do not safeguard a representative cross-section of Svalbard's natural and cultural environment. The most productive and species-rich land areas of the island group are *least* represented within the protected areas.' Based on this report, in 2003, five new protected areas were created in Svalbard, including the four with a marine component at left (23–26). Total size is 1717 mi^2 (4449 km^2) of Svalbard's land area. This means that 15,088 mi^2 (39,088 km^2) of Svalbard's land area is now protected (about 63 per cent). In late 2003, the extension of the park boundaries from 4 to 12 nm (7.4 to 22.2 km) means that the total Svalbard marine protected zone now amounts to nearly 27,956 mi^2 (72,424 km^2). • Rationale is to protect rich tundra with wetland birds and plants; these areas also include some prime beluga habitat.	• Norris, 2003; Prokosch, 1999 • Contact: WWF Arctic Programme, PO Box 6784, St Olavsplass, N-0130 Oslo, Norway; email: arctic@wwf.no • Fredrik Juell Theisen, Miljøverndepartementet (Ministry of the Environment), PO Box 8013 Dep, N-0030 Oslo, Norway; email: FJT@md.dep.no; web: http://odin.dep.no/md/
• Proposed as a nature reserve by Norwegian authorities, Bear Island Nature Reserve including territorial waters was created in 2002 as an important staging post for birds migrating to and from the Arctic. All animal life is to be protected, although sea fishing will be allowed under Ministry of Fisheries regulations. • The protected area does not include prime upwelling areas at the edge of the continental slope where feeding whales are commonly found. In addition to the cetaceans listed at left, sperm whales are also seen offshore.	• Gjertz, 1991; Gjertz and Wiig, 1994; Prokosch, 1999; Schandy, 2000; Norris, 2002 • Contact: WWF Arctic Programme, PO Box 6784, St Olavsplass, N-0130 Oslo, Norway; email: arctic@wwf.no
• In the late 1990s, WWF's Norway and Arctic programmes campaigned for 'one national park' for Svalbard which would protect all of Svalbard and the surrounding water, as well as its ecology and outstanding wildlife populations, including high densities of seabirds and marine mammals, under a single protection and management scheme. This campaign was unsuccessful but with the 2003 creation of five new protected areas covering 1717 mi^2 (4449 km^2) of Svalbard's land area and the extension of the park boundaries from 4 to 12 nm (7.4–22.2 km), the original 'one park' goal is close to being realized. With the 12 nm (22.2 km) marine boundaries, the Svalbard marine protected zone has added up to 15,830 mi^2 (41,000 km^2) to Svalbard protected areas. **See Case Study 2**, Svalbard – A complicated protection regime, for a fuller discussion.	• Gjertz, 1991; Gjertz and Wiig, 1994; Hansson, 2000; Hoyt, 1997a; Humphreys and Prokosch, 2000; McQuaid, 1986; Mørkved and Gjertz, 1994; Norris, 2003; Prokosch, 1999; Reeves, 1980; Schandy, 2000 • Contact: WWF Arctic Programme, PO Box 6784, St Olavsplass, N-0130 Oslo, Norway; email: arctic@wwf.no • Fredrik Juell Theisen, Miljøverndepartementet (Ministry of the Environment), PO Box 8013 Dep, N-0030 Oslo, Norway; email: FJT@md.dep.no; web: http://odin.dep.no/md/

MARINE REGION 3: MEDITERRANEAN

In the 1980s cetacean researchers were surprised to find resident populations of several large species of whales in the Mediterranean Sea despite busy shipping traffic, pollution problems and exotic marine invaders. Yet populations of fin, sperm and Cuvier's beaked whales are living close to tourist hot spots along the Spanish, French and Italian coasts, and in the Greek islands. And there are long-finned pilot whales and orcas, as well as Risso's, striped, bottlenose and common dolphins in these waters. The most productive and diverse area is near the entry to the Strait of Gibraltar and in the western part of the Mediterranean around the Ligurian Sea, but there are also sperm whale and dolphin populations in the eastern Mediterranean, such as in the Ionian and Aegean seas.

On the other hand, common dolphins are clearly in trouble and another cetacean, the harbor porpoise, appears to have been driven out of the Mediterranean, although it still lives in the Black Sea. The Black Sea, joined to the Mediterranean (Marmara Sea) through the narrow Bosphorus Strait, is considered part of the Mediterranean Marine Region. The Black Sea also has resident bottlenose and short-beaked common dolphins.

In the early 1990s, soon after the discovery of resident fin and sperm whales and various dolphins in the Ligurian Sea off Italy, France and Monaco, representatives of these three countries agreed to consider a proposal for a cetacean sanctuary. The Pelagos Sanctuary for Mediterranean Marine Mammals was approved in 1999. A landmark sanctuary and MPA, it is the first high-seas MPA, including both national and high-seas waters. The fact that three countries are working together also makes it important in terms of the prospects for future international cooperation. Such cooperation in the Mediterranean is facilitated by the Protocol for Special Protected Areas and Biological Diversity (SPA Protocol) of the Barcelona Convention. Awarding the sanctuary special designation as a Special Protected Area of Mediterranean Interest (SPAMI), which is designed for MPAs on the high seas of the Mediterranean (outside 12 nm), means that all other Mediterranean countries belonging to the Barcelona Convention must respect the designation. The sanctuary is fairly large – 33,772 mi^2 (87,492 km^2) – yet still only a quarter the size of one of the world's largest MPAs, the Great Barrier Reef Marine Park.

In addition to the 'Pelagos Sanctuary', the Mediterranean has a number of much smaller areas proposed as MPAs which include dolphin habitat. Most are proposed special areas of conservation (SACs), under the EU Habitats and Species Directive, or small marine nature reserves or coastal parks which may protect at least some dolphin habitat. These areas are mainly found at present in Spain and Italy. A proposed marine park in Croatia would be established partly to conserve resident bottlenose dolphins studied since the early 1990s.

Compared to the European coast of the Mediterranean, much less is known about cetaceans and cetacean habitats on the African side. No MPAs with known cetacean habitat have been created on the Mediterranean coast of

North Africa. As of 2004, however, Tunisia was considering proposals for nine MPAs in national waters, none of which have been created for cetaceans, but six of which are known to have cetacean presence. Surveys have just begun and are reportedly showing some cetacean habitat. There are known resident bottlenose and possibly other dolphin populations in Tunisian waters.

With the intensive cetacean field work on a range of species led by Spanish scientists in the Strait of Gibraltar, possibly soon with the collaboration of Moroccan scientists, there may well be cetacean habitat protection proposals in the near future. The Pelagos Sanctuary for Mediterranean Marine Mammals should be used as a model for multi-country agreements in the region and around the world.

The Mediterranean Marine Region has two large marine ecosystems (LMEs) that have been identified: the Mediterranean Sea and Black Sea. There are substantial upwelling areas along the coast of North Africa and between the Ligurian Sea and the Golfe du Lion. The Mediterranean is almost a closed sea yet it is subject to outside influences, especially in the western portion. The narrow Strait of Gibraltar, only 12 miles (20 km) wide and 1050 feet (320 m) deep, limits the inflow of surface waters from the North Atlantic and the outflow of salty Mediterranean water. It takes about a century for the Mediterranean to replace its water.

Politically, the Mediterranean and Black Sea have some 27 countries and one territory within the region (see Table 5.1 on p89). Some 130 million people live along the 29,000 miles (46,000 km) of Mediterranean coastline alone, and the land areas of the region are visited by 150 million tourists a year. Large populations and industry located close to the coast contribute to marine pollution from agricultural runoff and sewage, and visiting ships carry oil and other risky cargo. Also worrying is *Caulerpa* grass, the mutant invader that kills algae and everything else; it stands as a threat to the future of marine life in the Mediterranean.

Mediterranean researchers across many disciplines have worked to address these problems with substantial cooperative efforts. A case in point is the pioneering ACCOBAMS agreement (the Agreement on the Conservation of Cetaceans of the Black Sea, Mediterranean Sea and Contiguous Atlantic Area). Entering into force in 2001, ACCOBAMS has encouraged the establishment of a network of specially protected areas to conserve habitats and species, including cetaceans. The agreement of the parties includes a wide range of protections for cetaceans. Some argue that the comprehensive range of protections included under ACCOBAMS in effect makes the entire Mediterranean at least a Category VI MPA. If so, it would be too physically and culturally sprawling to offer real habitat protection to cetaceans or other marine species. In any case, ACCOBAMS is certain to become a model for marine and other agreements in other marine regions. A comprehensive status report for the Mediterranean and Black Sea Marine Region to the ACCOBAMS Secretariat was released in February 2002. Entitled 'Cetaceans of the Mediterranean and Black Seas: state of knowledge and conservation strategies' (Notarbartolo di Sciara, 2002), it can be obtained at www.accobams.org.

In addition, for the Black Sea alone, in 1996 all six governments adopted the 'Strategic Action Plan for the Rehabilitation and Protection of the Black Sea'. This action plan promotes positive action to conserve biological diversity, reduce pollution and improve habitat protection for marine mammals, among other things. For more information on Mediterranean Sea and Black Sea agreements pertaining to cetaceans see Table 5.4.

In 1995, there was a total of 53 MPAs of all kinds in this marine region (Batisse and de Grissac, 1995). The region is divided into ten biogeographic zones, only six of which were represented by more than one MPA. Many more MPAs have been created in this region since the late 1990s. In the Black Sea alone, as of 2002, there were some 63 existing and 43 proposed coastal and marine protected areas, none created for cetaceans, but some of which may well include cetacean habitat. Surveys need to be done to determine which areas can help protect cetacean habitat together with other conservation measures identified and implemented through ACCOBAMS (Notarbartolo di Sciara and Birkun, 2002).

As of 2004, according to Table 5.6 prepared for this book, there are 24 existing (three of which are proposed for expansion) and 35 proposed MPAs which feature cetacean habitat, as well as one existing high-seas, multi-country sanctuary, the Pelagos Sanctuary for Mediterranean Marine Mammals. Potential new MPAs depend on finding critical habitat areas but, if such areas can be identified, new MPAs may form a useful component of conservation strategies for sperm whales along the Aegean Arch; bottlenose dolphins in predictable, known hot spots; and short-beaked common dolphins wherever they occur regularly (Notarbartolo di Sciara and Birkun, 2002).

The IUCN 2002–2010 Conservation Action Plan for the World's Cetaceans recommends a number of research and education initiatives for this region (Reeves et al, 2003):

- to assess abundance and threats to survival of harbor porpoises in the Black Sea and surrounding waters;
- to investigate the distribution, abundance, population structure and factors threatening the conservation of short-beaked common dolphins in the Mediterranean and Black Seas;
- to investigate the distribution and abundance of bottlenose dolphins in the Mediterranean Sea and Black Sea, and evaluate threats to their survival;
- to develop and test approaches to reducing conflicts between bottlenose dolphins and small-scale fisheries in the Mediterranean Sea; and
- to conduct a basin-wide assessment of sperm whale abundance and distribution in the Mediterranean Sea.

An IUCN-suggested initiative directly related to marine habitat conservation is:

- to implement pilot conservation and management projects for short-beaked common dolphins around the known areas of Kalamos, Greece and Ischia, Italy where there is critical habitat, in order to reverse their

Table 5.4 *Mediterranean and Black Sea cetaceans belonging to appendices of international conventions, directives and agreements*

Common name	Species name	Applicable appendices of international conventions, directives and agreements (see notes below)								
		CMS1	CMS2	Be2	Ha2	Ha4	SPA2	C1	C2	ACC
fin whale	*Balaenoptera physalus*	X		X		X	X	X		X
short-beaked common dolphin	*Delphinus delphis*		X	X		X	X		X	X
Striped dolphin	*Stenella coeruleoalba*		X	X		X	X		X	X
bottlenose dolphin	*Tursiops truncatus*		X	X	X	X	X		X	X
Risso's dolphin	*Grampus griseus*			X		X	X		X	X
long-finned pilot whale	*Globicephala melas*			X		X	X		X	X
sperm whale	*Physeter macrocephalus*	X		X		X	X	X		X
Cuvier's beaked whale	*Ziphius cavirostris*			X		X	X		X	X
harbor porpoise	*Phocoena phocoena*		X	X	X	X	X		X	X
orca	*Orcinus orca*			X		X	X		X	X
false killer whale	*Pseudorca crassidens*			X		X	X		X	X
minke whale	*Balaenoptera acutorostrata*			X		X	X	X		X
humpback whale	*Megaptera novaeangliae*	X		X		X	X	X		X
rough-toothed dolphin	*Steno bredanensis*			X		X	X		X	X

Notes:
CMS1 = Appendix I: Migratory species in danger, from CMS or the Bonn Convention (Convention on the Conservation of Migratory Species of Wild Animals)
CMS2 = Appendix II: Migratory species which have an unfavourable conservation status and require international agreements for their conservation and management, from CMS
Be2 = Appendix 2: List of strictly protected species, from the Bern Convention (Convention on the Conservation of European Wildlife and Natural Habitats)
Ha2 = Annex II: Animal and plant species of community interest whose conservation requires the designation of special areas of conservation, from the EU Habitats and Species Directive
Ha4 = Annex IV: Animal and plant species of community interest in need of strict protection, from the EU Habitats and Species Directive
SPA2 = Appendix 2: List of threatened species, from the Protocol for Special Protected Areas and Biological Diversity of the Barcelona Convention (SPA Protocol)
C1 = Appendix 1: Species Threatened with Extinction, from CITES (Convention on International Trade in Endangered Species of Wild Fauna and Flora)
C2 = Appendix 2: Species not threatened with extinction but in danger if their commerce is not subject to restraints, from CITES
ACC = Annex 1: Indicative list of Cetaceans of the Mediterranean and Black Sea and Atlantic Contiguous Area, from ACCOBAMS
Source: Table adapted, courtesy of Barbara Mussi and Giuseppe Notarbartolo di Sciara

The Pelagos Sanctuary for Mediterranean Marine Mammals was designated in 1999 as a transborder MPA in the national waters of France, Italy and Monaco, as well as on the high seas of the Mediterranean. It is also a Special Protected Area of Mediterranean Interest (SPAMI). See Case Study 3.

Figure 5.5 *Map of the Pelagos Sanctuary for Mediterranean Marine Mammals*

decline in the Mediterranean (Bearzi et al, 2003). 'The immediate establishment of protected areas should be accompanied by experimental management plans that include intensive monitoring of the dolphins, restrictions on vessel traffic and fishing activity, education efforts directed at the local fishing communities and recreational users, and focused research' (Reeves et al, 2003).

The above priority actions are also included in the ACCOBAMS report (Notarbartolo di Sciara, 2002) but other useful actions mentioned are the identification of new Mediterranean sites of conservation importance for fin whales, in addition to the Ligurian Sea, and an assessment of the various sites with respect to the species' total habitat needs. In the same report, Notarbartolo and Birkun (2002) add several points particularly relevant to MPAs in the region:

- All MPA managers within the region should be made aware of the possibility of cetacean critical habitat within their borders in order to harness scientific support and implement cetacean conservation measures.
- An inventory of the region's MPAs should be maintained in order to help assess and enhance their real and potential effectiveness for cetacean conservation. This could be used to help form a regional MPA network focused on common cetacean monitoring and conservation protocols.
- When important critical habitats are identified, there should be specific MPA measures under the SPA Protocol of the Barcelona Convention.

Case Study 3: Pelagos Sanctuary for Mediterranean Marine Mammals

Pelagos Sanctuary for Mediterranean Marine Mammals

Type: Existing international sanctuary affording protection for large whales.

Location: Corsico-Provencal-Ligurian Basin, central Mediterranean Sea, west of central Italy, south of France and Monaco. The waters of the sanctuary are 47 per cent in the national waters of the three countries, and 53 per cent in international waters.

Cetacean species: fin whale, *Balaenoptera physalus*; sperm whale, *Physeter macrocephalus*; striped dolphin, *Stenella coeruleoalba*; bottlenose dolphin, *Tursiops truncatus*; short-beaked common dolphin, *Delphinus delphis*; Risso's dolphin, *Grampus griseus*; long-finned pilot whale, *Globicephala melas*; Cuvier's beaked whale, *Ziphius cavirostris*; occasional presence: minke whale, *Balaenoptera acutorostrata*; humpback whale, *Megaptera novaeangliae*; orca, *Orcinus orca*; false killer whale, *Pseudorca crassidens*; rough-toothed dolphin, *Steno bredanensis*.

Additional species and other features: Rich pelagic diversity including tunas, swordfish, sunfish, sharks and giant devil rays. Prevailing oceanographic conditions in the area feature a permanent front which favours primary marine productivity. Key basis of this productive ecosystem is a mesopelagic zooplankton biomass, especially krill, *Meganyctiphanes norvegica*, likely the exclusive food of Mediterranean fin whales (Notarbartolo di Sciara et al, 2003).

Size of designated protected area: 33,772 square miles (87,492 km^2). Water area only from nearshore to pelagic.

Rationale: To protect the whales and dolphins in prime cetacean habitat in the Mediterranean waters of France, Monaco and Italy. The habitat, located from nearshore to deep-water, pelagic areas, includes cetacean feeding grounds as well as areas used by migrating and breeding cetaceans.

The motivation for creating the Pelagos Sanctuary for Mediterranean Marine Mammals – originally called the Ligurian Sea Sanctuary – came from information obtained during research cruises conducted since the late 1980s. These cruises revealed the presence of substantial cetacean concentrations within the area coupled with a conspicuous variety of other pelagic species such as tunas, swordfish, sunfish, sharks and giant devil rays – a high degree of marine diversity in a productive ecosystem with a large krill and other zooplankton biomass. A summary of cetacean research in the sanctuary is presented in Table 5.5.

In 1989, Tethys Research Institute and Greenpeace requested that the area be given protection. In 1991, Project Pelagos was presented, followed by lobbying through conservation and scientific research institutes, led by Tethys. These activities garnered widespread public and eventually government support. In 1998, the area was included in the list of putative Italian MPAs thereby laying the initial legal groundwork for a procedure toward its establishment. Finally, in 1999, the three countries signed the agreement to create the Pelagos Sanctuary for Mediterranean Marine Mammals, the first of its kind. A 'cetacean sanctuary' in name only, it aims to be a transborder MPA. It took most of a decade for the three countries to agree to the designation. In February 2000, at an international IFAW-ICRAM workshop on whale watching, ICRAM scientists presented a symposium on the sanctuary. In 2001, an inventory of biological, cultural and other features was prepared for the area.

It was originally envisaged that the sanctuary would follow the biosphere reserve architecture with multiple zone areas, including highly protected core zones (IUCN Category I) for cetacean critical habitat (Notarbartolo di Sciara et al, 1991). When the sanctuary was designated in 1999, however, there was no mention of the biosphere reserve idea. In February 2003, shortly after Italy became the last to ratify its signature, the first Meeting of the Parties began to discuss the preparation of a management plan. There is hope that the sanctuary will become a true MPA with effective biosphere reserve zoning. The extensive data over more than a decade from Tethys and other cruises will be used to identify critical habitat areas deserving of IUCN Category I protection.

The sanctuary has also been entered into the list of Special Protected Areas of Mediterranean Interest (SPAMI) within the Protocol for Special Protected Areas and Biological Diversity of the Barcelona Convention. Under the auspices of the Barcelona Convention's Protocol, high-seas areas identified as a SPAMI gain legal protection as the Protocol requires all parties adhering to the Convention (as of April 2001, 19 Mediterranean coastal states and the European Community) to respect the protection measures established within each individual SPAMI.

The story of the Pelagos Sanctuary for Mediterranean Marine Mammals illustrates the long process required for effective MPA conservation. At all stages in the process, politics, economic considerations and apathy had the power to derail the process and damage or even destroy the efforts of many people over many years. 'Paper park' or real cetacean habitat protection? By 2005 or 2006, we should know.

Table 5.5 *Cetacean research in the Mediterranean, focusing on the Pelagos Sanctuary for Mediterranean Marine Mammals*

Cetacean species in the sanctuary	Data on population estimates and genetics	References
fin whale, *Balaenoptera physalus*	• approximately 1000 individuals in the sanctuary, 350 of which have been identified • population estimate in the western Mediterranean is >3500 individuals • Mediterranean population is genetically isolated from Atlantic conspecifics	Bérubé et al, 1998; Forcada et al, 1995, 1996; Notarbartolo di Sciara et al, 2003; Zanardelli et al, 1998
sperm whale, *Physeter macrocephalus*	• present at low densities within the sanctuary • no information is available on either sperm whale population size or the relationship between Mediterranean and Atlantic populations	Drouot, 2003
striped dolphin, *Stenella coeruleoalba*	• approximately 25,000 individuals in the sanctuary • Mediterranean population (>126,000) is likely to be reproductively isolated from Atlantic conspecifics	Aguilar, 2000; Forcada and Hammond, 1998; Garcia-Martinez et al, 1999
bottlenose dolphin, *Tursiops truncatus*	• present in the sanctuary throughout the continental shelf (but rare off Liguria) • no population estimate exists for the Mediterranean Sea	
short-beaked common dolphin, *Delphinus delphis*	• very rare, but present throughout the sanctuary • population estimate in the southwestern Alborán Sea is 15,000 individuals	Bearzi et al, 2003; Forcada, 1995
Risso's dolphin, *Grampus griseus*	• 300 photo-identified and currently resighted individuals in the sanctuary	Airoldi et al, 1999
long-finned pilot whale, *Globicephala melas*	• intermittently present in the sanctuary's offshore waters	
Cuvier's beaked whale, *Ziphius cavirostris*	• present in the sanctuary; regularly seen in specific locations (eg, off Imperia)	

Source: Adapted from Notarbartolo di Sciara (2000). Courtesy, Giuseppe Notarbartolo di Sciara and Giulia Mo.

Case Study 4: Regno di Nettuno MPA

Regno di Nettuno *proposed MPA* (Regno di Nettuno area di reperimento)

Type: Proposed marine protected area.

Location: Pontino Campano archipelago, between the islands of Ischia, Procida, Vivara and the mainland, southern Tyrrhenian Sea, near Napoli, Italy.

Cetacean species: striped dolphin, *Stenella coeruleoalba* (year-round; frequent spring and summer); bottlenose dolphin, *Tursiops truncatus* (year-round; frequent spring and summer); Risso's dolphin, *Grampus griseus* (April–October); long-finned pilot whale, *Globicephala melas*; short-beaked common dolphin, *Delphinus delphis* (mainly July–August); fin whale, *Balaenoptera physalus* (year-round, mainly July–August); sperm whale, *Physeter macrocephalus* (all year but rare).

Additional species and other features: Pelagic fishes such as *Mobula mobular*, *Thunnus* species, *Xiphias gladius* and open-water seabirds including *Calonectris diomedea*, *Puffinus puffinus* and *Larus ridibundus*. StudioMare cetacean surveys have also led to analysis of fin whale faecal material which has revealed the presence of crustacean exoskeletons belonging to the euphausiid *Meganyctiphanes norvegica*, a key species in the pelagic trophic web. The coastal area of the park is characterized by *Posidonia oceanica* (seagrass beds), rocky banks and cliffs. The area proposed for protection is the coastal part of the Cuma submarine canyon in the northern waters off Ischia Island; the canyon was first described by M Pennetta in 1998 who revealed how the continental slope is penetrated by submarine canyons, of which the deepest is Cuma.

Size of proposed protected area: Undecided as marine area is in proposal stage.

Rationale: To protect the biodiversity around this deep canyon incursion into the continental slope, including cetaceans.

Regno di Nettuno was first proposed as an MPA in 1991 through the Ministry of the Environment under legislation L 394/91. It is not being considered as part of a public process but is based on an agreement between the local administration and the Ministry of Environment. As of 2001, the Ministry of Environment had completed the first and second phases of studies for the institution of the MPA. There is no management plan prepared but there are plans for one. Jurisdiction over the MPA may be municipal.

Regno di Nettuno is part of a larger area (the archipelago Pontino and Campano) which has been the object of a long-term study on cetaceans that began around the same time as the MPA was proposed in 1991. In this area, researchers from StudioMare have regularly recorded six species of cetaceans: striped, bottlenose, short-beaked common and Risso's dolphins, plus sperm and fin whales (Mussi et al, 1998). They have taken photo-ID data of fin whales (Mussi et al, 1999), common and striped dolphins (data in process), bottlenose dolphins (Mussi et al, 1997a, 1997b, 1998) and Risso's dolphins (data in process). In addition, acoustic recordings have been made of striped, common, bottlenose and Risso's dolphins, sperm whale and long-finned pilot whale. Pilot whale recording and sighting data reveal a single stable pod of six free-ranging individuals that are seasonally resident off the southern coast of Ventotene Island, bordering the Isole di Ventotene e Santo Stefano MPA.

Since cetaceans had never been studied in the area before, StudioMare began with a year-round census. From June 1991 to June 1993, data were collected from ferries, cargo ships and fishing boats crossing the area. The recordings were sometimes sporadic but they enabled documentation of the winter presence of cetaceans in the area (Mussi et al, 1997a, 1997b, 1998).

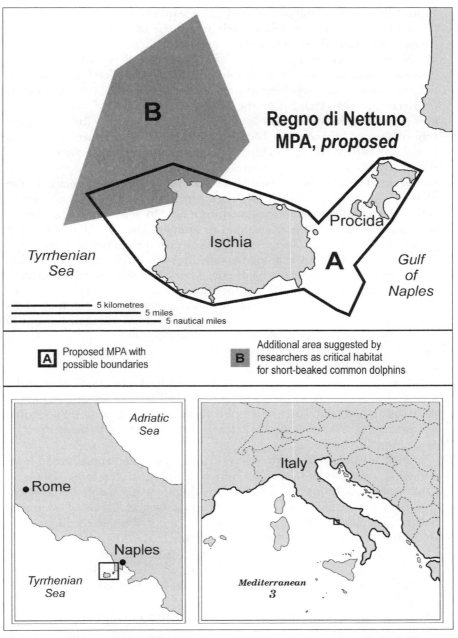

The proposed Regno di Nettuno MPA offers frequent sightings of various whales and dolphins including the increasingly rare short-beaked common dolphin. However, the currently proposed MPA does not cover the dolphins' main critical habitat areas as defined by researchers. See Case Study 4.

Figure 5.6 *Map of Regno di Nettuno*

From 1993 to 1999, StudioMare used the research vessel *Barbarian*, a 48-foot (15-m) schooner equipped as a ketch, which has been transformed into a floating laboratory devoted to cetacean research.

Above Cuma canyon, studying acoustic and surface behaviour of mixed groups of common and striped dolphins, StudioMare has observed how dolphins utilize coastal habitat close to shore especially in July and August (Mussi et al, 1999). Ischia is on the outskirts of the Gulf of Naples, a busy area particularly in summer. In 2000, StudioMare reported a Risso's dolphin school harassed by pleasure boaters, hinting at potential problems from casual, unlicensed whale watching. The group also recorded collisions and deaths from boat strikes for fin whales and striped dolphins.

StudioMare's biologists have observed feeding and mating behaviour in all the dolphin species in the proposed protected area. Newborn dolphin calves of various species were sighted from June to September. The animals were monitored to determine variations in their behaviour during the day, with underwater and surface video synchronized to acoustic recordings.

The area of the Cuma submarine canyon is also used as a feeding ground by fin whales. The feeding whales engage in circle swimming with flukes showing above the surface. When they dive, fin whales often create bubble clouds. Most of the time the whales spend at the surface is at sunset, which is probably associated with the vertical migrations of Euphausiid prey at night. On these occasions the whales often emerge, mouth open, employing vertical lunges. Whales are sometimes sighted close to the Ischia coast – 3.5 miles (5.6 km) the closest.

After their initial research, StudioMare decided to work to protect the area and to focus attention on the role played by submarine canyons in distribution and abundance of trophic resources for cetaceans. Submarine canyons are clearly an important cetacean habitat where a particular pelagic assemblage can be found.

Currently the most urgent aspect of the research and conservation work surrounds the short-beaked common dolphin. Literature, data and osteological collections indicate that these dolphins were a common resident species of the Mediterranean Sea. The species, however, has faced a dramatic decline in numbers in recent decades, and has almost completely disappeared from large portions of its former range (Bearzi et al, 2003).

Key known areas of common dolphin distribution include the Alborán Sea, the eastern Ionian Sea and the northern Aegean Sea. The Cuma submarine canyon is the only Italian area studied where common dolphins are seasonally resident (Mussi et al, 1999).

Mediterranean short-beaked common dolphins and their critical habitats are probably threatened by the combined effect of high contamination levels, intentional and incidental takes, overfishing and decreasing food resources, high noise levels and overall habitat degradation. Industrial activities in or near the Cuma submarine canyon include shipping traffic, sports and pleasure boats, as well as possible use by NATO ships and submarines. Based on available data, the species appears to be facing a high risk of extinction in

BOX 5.3 LEGISLATION ON MPAS AND CETACEANS IN ITALY

Marine Protected Areas in Italy have been proposed on the basis of specific national legislation that identifies areas of the Italian coastline where MPAs may be established. The relevant laws are as follows:

- L 979/82, 'Disposizioni per la difesa del mare', identifies 21 marine areas which may be awarded protection measures.
- L 394/91, 'Legge quadro sulle aree protette', identifies another 26 marine areas which require potential protection measures.
- L 344/97, 'Disposizioni per lo sviluppo e la qualificazione degli interventi e dell'occupazione in campo ambientale', adds one more marine area to the list – Parco Marino Torre del Cerrano.
- L 426/98, 'Nuovi interventi in campo ambientale', puts the Pelagos Sanctuary for Mediterranean Marine Mammals on the MPA list.

As of 2002, 15 MPAs had been established according to the process identified by the Servizio Difesa Mare, Ministero dell'Ambiente (the Marine Protection Service of the Ministry of the Environment) which is the national legal body in charge of marine resource protection. Eight of these 15 MPAs are managed by local management bodies, two are managed by national parks (which are terrestrial and institutionally connected to the Ministry's Nature Conservation Service rather than the Marine Protection Service), one MPA is managed by WWF Italy and the remaining four, for which a management body has not yet been designated, are being managed temporarily by the local Coast Guard offices (Capitanerie di Porto).

Most Italian MPAs are zoned according to the biosphere reserve strategy of having one or more highly protected IUCN Category I core zones, surrounded by buffer zones where limited human activities are allowed. These are in turn surrounded by boundary transition zones with less protection.

The establishment of an MPA does not require that cetacean habitats be studied or verified. Most MPA zoning processes, which were established at a time when little attention was paid to cetaceans, predominantly take into account the geological formation of the seabottom and the characterization of specific habitats rather than the presence of coastal or pelagic species. The exceptions to this rule are the more recent MPAs of the Asinara and Maddalena national parks whose studies for the zoning process took into account, among many other factors, the presence of cetacean species in the area.

Cetaceans have been protected in Italy since the ratification of CITES (1975), the Bern (1981) and Bonn (1983) conventions, the regulation of the EU Habitats and Species Directive (1997) and the ratification of the Barcelona Convention Protocol for Special Protected Areas and Biological Diversity (1999). According to a 1992 national law, fines and sanctions have been established to prevent the harming or trading of cetaceans.

As of 2002, according to data compiled by the Italian government's Central Institute for Applied Marine Research (ICRAM), there are 11 MPAs in the process of being established, four of which have some cetacean populations and are listed below. Out of the 11, four were proposed under L 394/91 and seven were under L 979/82. In addition, 22 other areas are proposed for protection under L 394/91 and could be classified as 'areas in which legislation foresees the establishment of an MPA', two of which include cetaceans.

As a member of the European Community, Italy follows the EU Habitats and Species Directive (1992) which requires that a network (called Natura 2000) of so-called special areas of conservation (SACs) be designated to conserve outstanding natural habitats and prime examples of habitat types, as well as rare, vulnerable or endangered species. The regulation of the directive was passed in Italy in 1997. Bottlenose dolphins are the only cetacean species found around Italy that are included on Annex II of the Habitats and Species Directive.

Implementation of the Habitats and Species Directive in Italy is the responsibility of the Nature Conservation Service of the Ministry of the Environment which handles terrestrial conservation. This may pose a problem for the marine SACs in that some sort of legal national regulation should probably be passed to sort out who is responsible for which aspect (marine vs terrestrial) of the SAC.

In any case, as of 2004, the list of SACs from the Nature Conservation Service had yet to be released. This list should include land- as well as marine-based SACs. However, Italy already has a comprehensive series of proposals for MPAs under existing national legislation that are generally larger than SACs and which protect bottlenose dolphins, so there may not be any others to be submitted specifically for bottlenose dolphins (see Table 5.6).

In 2003, ICRAM announced the development of a new system to bring Italian MPAs into a cohesive network. 'Sistema Afrodite', as it is called, is a pioneer method for standardizing the research in all MPAs, bringing them effectively into a cohesive network and improving the ability to monitor MPAs effectively and to determine large-scale network effectiveness.

most Mediterranean areas in the near future. Appropriate levels of protection must be immediately put in place for the species in order to prevent further damage to Mediterranean populations. There is also a need in Cuma to link a study on common dolphins there to other key areas in the Mediterranean (such as the Alborán Sea and Greece). It is vital to compare data in order to determine the overall status of such little-known populations. In the IUCN 2002–2010 Cetacean Action Plan for the World's Cetaceans, detailed research and conservation measures are recommended to help save Mediterranean populations of short-beaked common dolphins (Reeves et al, 2003).

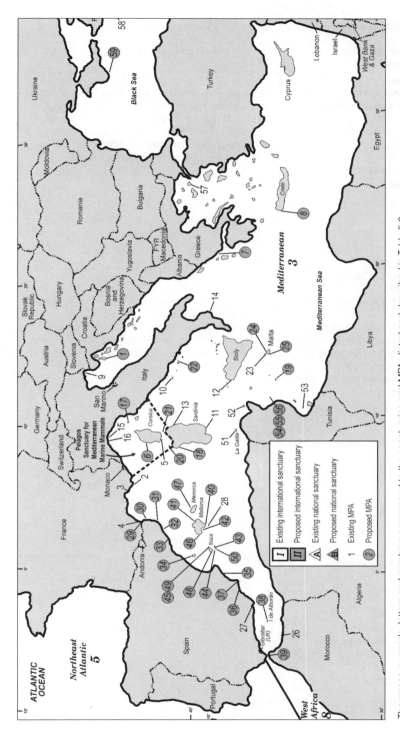

The roman numerals, letters and numbers correspond to the sanctuaries and MPAs listed and described in Table 5.6.

Figure 5.7 *Map of Marine Region 3: Mediterranean MPAs and sanctuaries*

Table 5.6 *Marine Region 3: Mediterranean MPAs and sanctuaries*

Name of MPA or sanctuary, location and size	Cetacean and other notable species
INTERNATIONAL **(I) Pelagos Sanctuary for Mediterranean Marine Mammals** • Ligurian, Corsican and northern Tyrrhenian Sea; in the waters of France, Italy and Monaco and the adjacent high seas • 33,772 mi^2 (87,492 km^2) **See Case Study 3.**	• fin whale, *Balaenoptera physalus*; striped dolphin, *Stenella coeruleoalba*; sperm whale, *Physeter macrocephalus*; bottlenose dolphin, *Tursiops truncatus*; short-beaked common dolphin, *Delphinus delphis*; Risso's dolphin, *Grampus griseus*; long-finned pilot whale, *Globicephala melas*; Cuvier's beaked whale, *Ziphius cavirostris*
CROATIA Republic of Croatia Republika Hrvatska **(1) Losinj Dolphin Reserve, proposed** • waters adjacent to west coast of the islands of Losinj and Cres, Cres-Losinj Archipelago, northern Adriatic Sea • 2002 proposal was for 386 mi^2 (1000 km^2) but there are still no definite borders as of early 2004	• bottlenose dolphin, *Tursiops truncatus* (resident – about 120 photo-IDed animals) • also: Griffon vultures on cliffs, marine turtles, at least 95 species of fish (large predators such as sharks, tunas and swordfishes), marine invertebrates and seaweeds in high diversity
FRANCE République Française **(2) Port Cros National Park (Le Parc national de Port-Cros)** • Iles d'Hyères, 25 mi (40 km) southeast of Toulon • 9 mi^2 (24 km^2) including 7 mi^2 (18 km^2) marine waters	• bottlenose dolphin, *Tursiops truncatus*

Notes and rationale	For more information
• First identified as a prime cetacean area in 1989, the sanctuary received protection in 1999 (ratified 2002) with the agreement of the governments of France, Monaco and Italy. Rationale is to protect prime cetacean habitat located from nearshore to deep pelagic areas, including seasonal and year-round feeding and breeding areas. • A management plan was underway in 2003 with the hope that the sanctuary will become a true MPA following the zoned biosphere reserve model and including IUCN Category I areas to protect critical habitat of cetaceans and fish. • Also listed in 2001 as a Special Protected Area of Mediterranean Interest (SPAMI) which requires all parties to the SPA Protocol of the Barcelona Convention to follow sanctuary rules, even on the high seas.	• Fossi et al, 1992, 1999; Fossi and Marsili, 1997 Marsili et al, 1996, 1998; Notarbartolo di Sciara, 2000, 2001; Notarbartolo di Sciara et al, 1992; Panigada et al, 1999; Relini et al, 1994; others • Contact: Giuseppe Notarbartolo di Sciara; email: disciara@tin.it • Giovanni Bearzi, Tethys Research Institute; email: bearzi@inwind.it
• This nearshore area is one of the few places in the Mediterranean where bottlenose dolphins are being studied; research shows that these dolphins suffer from high contaminant levels; the dolphin reserve could be part of larger conservation efforts focusing on local fauna, flora and preservation of Croatian cultural heritage which includes both marine and terrestrial areas in the Cres-Losinj Archipelago. • In 1987, Tethys Research Institute (TRI) began studying the dolphins, using photo-ID, acoustic tracking, abundance, distribution and behavioural work and analyses of stranded carcasses; in 1993, with growing data on the year-round residence of the dolphins off Croatia, TRI biologists Giovanni Bearzi and Giuseppe Notarbartolo di Sciara proposed that the dolphins' habitat be conserved, in a special document for the Cres-Losinj Management Plan. Since then, more comprehensive protection was proposed in 2002 – a submission to the Croatian government for an MPA around the island of Losinj. The Blue World Institute of Marine Research and Conservation, in Veli Losinj, has led the effort to create the reserve. As well, the reserve suggestion was adopted at the first Meeting of the Parties of ACCOBAMS as one of two pilot dolphin MPAs in the Mediterranean.	• Bearzi, 1995; Bearzi and Notarbartolo, 1997; Bearzi et al, 1993; Hoyt, 1997a; • Contact: Drasko Holcer, Blue World/Adriatic Dolphin Project; email: Drasko.Holcer@ blue-world.org; web: www.blue-world.org • Peter Mackelworth, email: pcm@pmackelworth. freeserve.co.uk; ucfapcm@ucl.ac.uk • Giovanni Bearzi, Tethys Research Institute; email: bearzi@inwind.it
• In Dec 1963, Port Cros National Park became the first national marine park in Europe, set up to conserve a representative sample of western Mediterannean island and marine species.	See Pelagos Sanctuary for Mediterranean Marine Mammals and Case Study 3. See also Table 5.8 for additional French MPAs. • Batisse and de Grissac, 1995 • Contact: Le Parc national de Port-Cros; web: www.portcros parcnational.fr

Table 5.6 *continued*

Name of MPA or sanctuary, location and size	Cetacean and other notable species
(3) Côte Bleue Marine Park (Parc Marin Côte Bleue) • Côte Bleue coastline between Marseille and Fos, Provence • park is 38.6 mi² (100 km²) with 15.5 mi (25 km) coastline extending 2 nm (4 km) offshore	• sporadic: bottlenose dolphin, *Tursiops truncatus*; striped dolphin, *Stenella coeruleoalba*; long-finned pilot whale, *Globicephala melas*
(4) Cerbère-Banyuls Natural Marine Reserve (Réserve Naturelle Marine de Cerbère-Banyuls) • near Spanish border opposite the villages of Cerbère and Banyuls, Pyrénées-Orientales • 2.5 mi² (6.5 km²) marine area	• bottlenose dolphin, *Tursiops truncatus*; striped dolphin, *Stenella coeruleoalba*; short-beaked common dolphin, *Delphinus delphis*
(5) Bonifaccio Marine Reserve (Réserve Marin Bouches de Bonifacio) • Corsica, Mediterranean Sea	• bottlenose dolphin, *Tursiops truncatus*
(6) Scandola Nature Reserve (Réserve Naturelle de Scandola), *proposed* • west Corsica, near Porto • proposal includes 3.5 mi² (9.2 km²) land and 3.9 mi² (10 km²) marine waters	• bottlenose dolphin, *Tursiops truncatus*
GREECE Hellenic Republic Elliniki Dimokratia **(7) Kalamos MPA,** *proposed* • coastal waters around the island of Kalamos, western Greece, Ionian Sea • size undetermined	• short-beaked common dolphin, *Delphinus delphis*; bottlenose dolphin, *Tursiops truncatus*
(8) Southern Crete Sperm Whale MPA, *proposed* • offshore waters of southwest Crete, Greece • size undetermined	• sperm whale, *Physeter macrocephalus*

Notes and rationale	For more information
• Designated in 1983, the park includes two small fully protected marine reserves of 0.33 mi² (0.85 km²) at Carry and 0.81 mi² (2.1 km²) at Couronne. • There have been no cetacean studies in the park.	• Contact: Parc Marin Côte Bleue; email: syndicatmixte@parc marincotebleue.fr; web: www.parcmarin cotebleue.fr
• This natural marine reserve was designated in 1974 to protect fauna, flora and artisanal fisheries. • Cetaceans are seen regularly near the reserve but not so often within the reserve, but they are on the species list for the reserve and are noted as part of a Natura 2000 study.	• Contact: Marie-Laure Licari, Réserve Naturelle Marine de Cerbère-Banyuls, 66650 Banyuls-sur-Mer, France; email: marielaure. licari@cg66.fr
• This marine reserve has dolphin sightings and may include dolphin habitat; studies need to be done to determine cetacean habitat.	• Contact: Bonifaccio Marine Reserve; email: culioli@oec.fr
• MPA would manage marine environment in order to conserve its biodiversity. • This reserve is included in the Pelagos Sanctuary for Mediterranean Marine Mammals. There may be an opportunity for the sanctuary management plan to incorporate and utilize the protection afforded to dolphin habitat here. There are some 20 resident dolphins but studies are needed to determine if the reserve protects habitat.	• Augier, 1985; Evans, 1999; Batisse and de Grissac, 1995; Liret et al, 2001 • Contact: Réserve Naturelle de Scandola, BP 417, 20184 Ajaccio cedex, Corse, France
• Proposed as a possible MPA at first Meeting of the Parties of ACCOBAMS; proposal must be considered first by Greece after it becomes a party to ACCOBAMS. • Rationale would be to protect known cetacean habitat. • Proposed by Tethys Research Institute and Pelagos Cetacean Research Institute to protect small, declining population of common dolphins (fewer than 100 left).	• Contact: Tethys Research Institute; web: www.tethys.org • Pelagos Cetacean Research Institute; email: afrantzis@otenet.gr; web: www.pelagosinstitute.gr
• Proposed as a possible MPA at first Meeting of the Parties of ACCOBAMS; proposal must be considered first by Greece after it becomes a party to ACCOBAMS. • Rationale would be to protect known cetacean habitat. • Pelagos Cetacean Research Institute has been working with sperm whales since 1997; they helped to identify southwest Crete as a prime habitat area, although there are other possible areas all along the Hellenic Trench and some may be important in terms of social groups with calves.	• Contact: Alexandros Frantzis, Pelagos Cetacean Research Institute; email: afrantzis@otenet.gr; web: www.pelagosinstitute.gr

Table 5.6 *continued*

Name of MPA or sanctuary, location and size	Cetacean and other notable species
ITALY Repubblica Italiana **(9) Gulf of Trieste (Golfo di Trieste) Miramare MPA** • near Trieste, Friuli-Venezia-Giulia, Gulf of Trieste, northern Adriatic Sea • 0.5 mi² (1.27 km²)	• common: bottlenose dolphin, *Tursiops truncatus*; sporadic: Risso's dolphin, *Grampus griseus*; striped dolphin, *Stenella coeruleoalba*
(10) Ventotene and Santo Stefano Islands (Isola di Ventotene e Santo Stefano) MPA • near Lazio, Latina, Pontine Archipelago, central Tyrrhenian Sea • 10.8 mi² (27.9 km²)	• summer: bottlenose dolphin, *Tursiops truncatus*; spring-summer: striped dolphin, *Stenella coeruleoalba*; uncommon: short-beaked common dolphin, *Delphinus delphis*; Risso's dolphin, *Grampus griseus*; summer and seasonal: long-finned pilot whale, *Globicephala melas*; fin whale, *Balaenoptera physalus*
(11) Capo Carbonara MPA • Capo Carbonara, near Villasimius, including the islands of Serpentara and Cavoli, southeast Sardinia, southwestern Tyrrhenian Sea • 34.2 mi² (88.6 km²)	• bottlenose dolphin, *Tursiops truncatus* (year-round); fin whale, *Balaenoptera physalus*; and sperm whale, *Physeter macrocephalus* (observed outside the MPA boundaries) • also: monk seal
(12) Egadi Islands (Isole Egadi) MPA • off Trápani, northwest Sicily, northeastern Sicilian Channel • 207.7 mi² (538.1 km²)	• bottlenose dolphin, *Tursiops truncatus*; striped dolphin, *Stenella coeruleoalba* (observed in Sicilian channel); short-beaked common dolphin, *Delphinus delphis* (observed in Sicilian channel area, not necessarily in the MPA)

Notes and rationale	For more information
• Proposed through national legislation (L 979/82) in 1982 and established in 1986, this MPA is managed by WWF Italy. • Rationale is to protect nearshore marine waters/sea floor with biological, geological and cultural features. • Entire MPA is an IUCN Category I core zone where fishing and commercial boating activities are not allowed. MPA staff have identified the three dolphin species present but more research is needed to determine status and habitat use within as well as all around this small reserve.	See Pelagos Sanctuary for Mediterranean Marine Mammals above and Case Study 3. • Francese et al, 1999 • Marco Francese and Maurizio Spoto, Riserva Marina di Miramare, Viale Miramare 349, 34014 Trieste, Italy • Giuseppe Notarbartolo di Sciara; email: disciara@tin.it • Giovanni Bearzi, Tethys Research Institute; email: bearzi@inwind.it
• Proposed through national legislation in 1982 (L 979/82) and established in 1997, this MPA is managed as part of a terrestrial natural reserve by the Municipality of Ventotene. No management plan but a zoning plan created three zones: a highly protected core zone – A, a B zone and a C zone. A copy of the MPA feasibility study can be obtained from the Ministry of the Environment. • Rationale is to protect nearshore and some deep marine waters and the sea floor with biological, geological and cultural features. • Research on cetaceans includes photo-ID of bottlenose dolphins, acoustic tracking and recording. Further cetacean research must verify that the area is used as a feeding and summering ground as well as the implications of habitat use outside MPA boundaries.	• Mussi et al, 1997a, 1997b, 1998, 2000 • Contact: ICRAM; email: comunicazione@icram.org • Giuseppe Notarbartolo di Sciara; email: disciara@tin.it • StudioMare; email: info@delphismdc.org; web: www.delphismdc.org/
• Proposed through national legislation (L 394/91) in 1991 and established in 1999, this MPA has no management plan, only a zoning plan. The area is managed by the Villasimius municipality. Inside the core zone, no fishing or navigation is allowed, only limited diving. A marine geomorphological map has been prepared as part of the zoning process. • Rationale is to protect nearshore waters and sea floor including biological, geological and cultural features. • Cetacean research has been photo-ID, acoustic tracking and recording of bottlenose dolphins. More studies needed to specify cetacean habitat use, as well as to monitor interactions with human activities.	• Arcangeli and Marini, 1999 • Contact: ICRAM; email: comunicazione@icram.org • Giuseppe Notarbartolo di Sciara; email: disciara@tin.it • Caterina Fortuna; email: fortuna.cm@tiscalinet.it
• Proposed through national legislation in 1982 (L 979/82) and established in 1996 by ministerial decree, this MPA has been managed by the coast guard (Capitaneria di Porto) offices in Trápani. Management is being handed over to the municipality of Favignana. The Marine Protection Service will update the MPA's status based on proposals from the new management body. • Rationale is to protect marine waters and the sea floor with biological, geological and cultural features. • Research on bottlenose dolphins includes photo-ID and acoustics. Suggested future research should examine dolphin interactions with fishing gear, relative abundance and distribution of *Tursiops* in MPA. Use of AHDs (acoustic devices to drive dolphins away from nets) needs to be evaluated for harm to dolphins (Notarbartolo di Sciara and Birkun, 2002) and possibly banned at least from the MPA.	• Chiofalo et al, 2000; Mazzola et al, 1995; Quero et al, 2000; • Contact: ICRAM; email: comunicazione@icram.org • Giuseppe Notarbartolo di Sciara; email: disciara@tin.it • Giovanni Bearzi, Tethys Research Institute; email: bearzi@inwind.it

Table 5.6 *continued*

Name of MPA or sanctuary, location and size	Cetacean and other notable species
(13) Tavolara and Punta Coda Cavallo (Tavolara – Punta Coda Cavallo) MPA • near Porto San Paolo (Olbia), northeast Sardinia, western Tyrrhenian Sea • 58.3 mi² (150.9 km²)	• bottlenose dolphin, *Tursiops truncatus*
(14) Capo Rizzuto Island (Isola Capo Rizzuto) MPA • Capo Rizzuto, near Crotone, Calabria, Golfo di Squillace and western Ionian Sea	• bottlenose dolphin, *Tursiops truncatus*
[MPAs 15–18] **(15) Cinque Terre National Park** • between Levanto and Riomaggiore, near La Spezia, Liguria, Ligurian Sea **(16) Gulf of Portofino (Golfo di Portofino) MPA** • near Portofino, Liguria, Ligurian Sea **(17) Tuscan Archipelago (Arcipelago Toscano) National Park with *proposed* marine extension, *in process of designation*** • Tuscan Archipelago, Ligurian Sea **(18) Capo Testa-Punta Falcone MPA, *proposed*** • near Capo Testa-Punta Falcone, northwestern Sardinia	• These four existing and proposed MPAs, which have not been specifically surveyed for cetaceans, form a small coastal part of the Mediterranean Sanctuary for Cetaceans. Cetaceans in the sanctuary include the fin whale, *Balaenoptera physalus*; striped dolphin, *Stenella coeruleoalba*; sperm whale, *Physeter macrocephalus*; bottlenose dolphin, *Tursiops truncatus*; short-beaked common dolphin, *Delphinus delphis*; Risso's dolphin, *Grampus griseus*; long-finned pilot whale, *Globicephala melas*; Cuvier's beaked whale, *Ziphius cavirostris*. However, the cetaceans found in these MPAs would most likely be restricted to dolphins moving close to shore.
(19) Pelagie Islands MPA (Isole Pelagie area di reperimento) *proposed, in process of designation* • waters around Lampedusa, Lampione and Linosa, southwest of Sicily (midway between Malta and Tunisia), southwest Sicilian Channel • no size data	• bottlenose dolphin, *Tursiops truncatus* (little information on extent of species' presence – 12 individuals photo-IDed as of 1998); fin whale, *Balaenoptera physalus* (observed off Lampedusa) • Lampedusa and Linosa are loggerhead turtle nesting grounds

Notes and rationale	For more information
• This nearshore MPA was proposed through national legislation in 1982 (L 979/82) and established in 1997 by ministerial decree. The area has been managed by the coast guard (Capitaneria di Porto) offices in Olbia but management is being handed over to a local management body assigned to a consortium of the municipalities of Olbia, Loiri, Porto San Paolo and San Teodoro. The Marine Protection Service will update the status of the MPA based on proposals from the new management body. There is no management plan but one may be prepared later. Cetacean research has been photo-ID studies of bottlenose dolphins. Future useful research could help establish the extent of habitat use. • Rationale is to protect marine waters and the sea floor with biological, geological and cultural features.	• Bearzi and Notarbartolo di Sciara, 1992; Consiglio et al, 1992; Marini et al, 1995 • Contact: ICRAM; email: comunicazione@icram.org • Giuseppe Notarbartolo di Sciara; email: disciara@tin.it • Giovanni Bearzi, Tethys Research Institute; email: bearzi@inwind.it
• Established in 1991 through legislation L 979/82, this MPA is managed by the Province of Crotone. There has been no research on cetaceans here, but local MPA personnel see dolphins. • Rationale is ecological, not specifically for cetaceans.	• Contact: ICRAM; email: comunicazione@icram.org • Giuseppe Notarbartolo di Sciara; email: disciara@tin.it • Giovanni Bearzi, Tethys Research Institute; email: bearzi@inwind.it
• The rationale for these areas is ecological, not specifically for cetaceans. • More research is needed to determine cetacean habitat use within as well as all around these proposed and existing MPAs.	• Contact: ICRAM; email: comunicazione@icram.org • Giuseppe Notarbartolo di Sciara; email: disciara@tin.it • Giovanni Bearzi, Tethys Research Institute; email: bearzi@inwind.it
• This MPA was proposed in 1982 (legislation L 979/82). • Rationale is to protect marine waters and sea floor including biological, geological and cultural features. • Research on cetaceans includes photo-ID studies of bottlenose dolphins and tracking of fin whales near Lampedusa Island, but there is limited information on the two species' presence and habitat use. There have been only 12 individual dolphins photo-IDed here.	• Marini et al, 1995; Pace et al, 1998 • Contact: ICRAM; email: comunicazione@icram.org • Giuseppe Notarbartolo di Sciara; email: disciara@tin.it • Giovanni Bearzi, Tethys Research Institute; email: bearzi@inwind.it

Table 5.6 *continued*

Name of MPA or sanctuary, location and size	Cetacean and other notable species
(20) **Asinara Island (Isola dell'Asinara) National Park** *with proposed marine extension, in process of designation* • around Asinara Island, northwest Sardinia, Sardinian Sea • no size data	• year-round: bottlenose dolphin, *Tursiops truncatus*; striped dolphin, *Stenella coeruleoalba*; short-beaked common dolphin, *Delphinus delphis*; Risso's dolphin, *Grampus griseus*; off external northwestern limits of the MPA: fin whale, *Balaenoptera physalus*; sperm whale, *Physeter macrocephalus*
(21) **Maddalena Archipelago (Arcipelago della Maddalena) National Park** *with proposed marine extension, in process of designation* • Maddalena archipelago, between Sardinia and Corsica, including the middle of the Strait of Bonifacio; expanded transborder proposal would include adjacent French (Corsican) waters • no size data	• common: bottlenose dolphin, *Tursiops truncatus*; possible: fin whale, *Balaenoptera physalus*; sperm whale, *Physeter macrocephalus*; Risso's dolphin, *Grampus griseus*; striped dolphin, *Stenella coeruleoalba*
(22) **Regno di Nettuno MPA, (Regno di Nettuno area di reperimento),** *proposed* • Pontino Campano archipelago, between the islands of Ischia, Procida, Vivara and the mainland, southern Tyrrhenian Sea, near Napoli • no size data **See Case Study 4.**	• striped dolphin, *Stenella coeruleoalba*; bottlenose dolphin, *Tursiops truncatus*; Risso's dolphin, *Grampus griseus*; long-finned pilot whale, *Globicephala melas*; short-beaked common dolphin, *Delphinus delphis*; fin whale, *Balaenoptera physalus*; sperm whale, *Physeter macrocephalus*
MALTA Repubblika Ta' Malta **(23) Dwejra Marine Conservation Area** • northwestern Gozo, includes land and marine area, sister island to Malta • no size data	• bottlenose dolphin, *Tursiops truncatus*
(24) Cirkewwa Marine Conservation Area, *proposed* • northern tip of Malta • 1.2 mi² (3 km²)	• year-round, but common Apr–Jul: bottlenose dolphin, *Tursiops truncatus*; short-beaked common dolphin, *Delphinus delphis*; rare: striped dolphin, *Stenella coeruleoalba*

Notes and rationale	For more information
• This MPA was proposed in 1991 using legislation L 394/91. The basic abundance and distribution research on cetaceans here has utilized photo-ID studies of bottlenose dolphins, as well as acoustic tracking and recording. A detailed inventory of the area has been prepared covering biological and cultural features. There has also been a study to look at possible zoning in the marine area, but there are no definite plans for a management plan. The management of the MPA will likely be assigned to the existing terrestrial national park. • Rationale is to extend an existing national park to include marine waters and sea floor with biological, geological and cultural features worth protecting.	• Ferreccio et al, 1993; Lauriano, 1997a, 1997b; Lauriano and Notarbartolo di Sciara, 1995; Lauriano et al, 1999; Pavan et al, 1995 • Contact: ICRAM; email: comunicazione@icram.org • Giuseppe Notarbartolo di Sciara; email: disciara@tin.it
• First proposed in 1991 under legislation L 394/91, this MPA includes a proposed marine extension to a national park that is in the process of designation. There is also discussion between Italy and France about combining Maddalena Archipelago National Park with Lavezzi Marine Reserve as a single transborder MPA. • Rationale is not stated but not specifically cetaceans. • Research on cetaceans includes photo-ID studies of bottlenose dolphins, as well as basic abundance and distribution (tracking) studies. • There is a basic inventory of the biological, cultural and other features of the proposed MPA, and a zoning study has been conducted to determine how the area should be managed.	• Arcangeli et al, 1997; Consiglio et al, 1992; Lauriano and Notarbartolo di Sciara, 1995; Marini et al, 1996 • Contact: Giuseppe Notarbartolo di Sciara; email: disciara@tin.it • ICRAM; email: comunicazione@icram.org
• This marine protected area was first proposed in 1991 through the Ministry of the Environment under legislation L 394/91. The MPA is based on an agreement between the local administration and the Ministry of Environment. Jurisdiction over the proposed protected area may be municipal. A management plan will be developed. • Rationale is to protect the biodiversity around the deep canyon incursion into the continental slope, including cetaceans (with known habitat for short-beaked common dolphins).	• Diaz Lopez et al, 2000; Mussi et al, 1997a, 1997b, 1998, 1999; Mussi and Miragliuolo, 1999 • Contact: StudioMare; email: info@delphismdc.org; web: www.delphismdc.org/ • Giuseppe Notarbartolo di Sciara; email: disciara@tin.it
• Nature Trust have received LIFE funds and are managing the project starting with an inventory in 2004 (undertaken by PJ Schembri, Marine Institute, Univ of Malta) with work on conservation and zonation to start in 2005, followed in 2006–2007 by guiding and use of a warden; final zonation will depend on the data collected. • Research will define dolphin habitat needs.	• Contact: Nature Trust (Malta), PO Box 9, Valletta CMR 01, Malta; email: mlcg@waldonet.net.mt; web: www.naturetrustmalta.org
• Rationale is partly that this is feeding and breeding habitat for bottlenose and short-beaked common dolphins. • Proposed 1991 by the planning authority of Malta; monitoring and research underway to define dolphin habitat; Nature Trust has been appointed partners with Malta Environment Protection Authority on the project.	• Contact: Nature Trust (Malta), PO Box 9, Valletta CMR 01, Malta; email: mlcg@waldonet.net.mt; web: www.naturetrustmalta.org

Table 5.6 *continued*

Name of MPA or sanctuary, location and size	Cetacean and other notable species
(25) Delimara Marine Conservation Area, *proposed* • southern tip of Malta • no size data	• common: bottlenose dolphin, *Tursiops truncatus*; short-beaked common dolphin, *Delphinus delphis*; sporadic: striped dolphin, *Stenella coeruleoalba*
MONACO Principality of Monaco Principauté de Monaco	
MOROCCO al-Mamlaka al-Maghrebia **(26) Al Hocemia National Park (Parc National D'Al Hoceima)** • near town of al Hoceima, northeastern Morocco, on the Mediterranean coast • total size is 167.5 mi^2 (434 km^2), of which 66.4 mi^2 (172 km^2) is marine	• bottlenose dolphin, *Tursiops truncatus*; possibly: short-beaked common dolphin, *Delphinus delphis*; striped dolphin, *Stenella coeruleoalba*; and other cetaceans resident and migratory
SPAIN Reino de España **(27) Cabo de Gata-Nijar Natural Park (Parque Natural Cabo de Gata-Nijar)** • off Cabo de Gata, Andalucia, southeast Spain	• bottlenose dolphin, *Tursiops truncatus*; other cetacean species possible
(28) Marine and Land National Park of the Cabrera Archipelago (Parque Nacional Maritimo-Territorio del Archipielago de Cabrera) • Baleares Archipelago	• bottlenose dolphin, *Tursiops truncatus*; and other cetaceans resident and migratory

Notes and rationale	For more information
• This proposed conservation area is in the process of being confirmed. • Cetacean records are mainly based on strandings.	• Contact: Nature Trust (Malta), PO Box 9, Valletta CMR 01, Malta; email: mlcg@waldonet.net.mt; web: www.naturetrustmalta.org
	See Pelagos Sanctuary for Mediterranean Marine Mammals above and Case Study 3.
• Park covers marine and terrestrial area with a substantial buffer zone roughly the same size as the park. • Inventory and planning are still at an early stage; cetacean distribution studies need to be done to determine habitat. • An earthquake in February 2004 devastated the region and the local infrastructure.	• Batisse and de Grissac, 1995 • Contact: Abdellatif Bayed, Université Mohammed V - Agdal Institut Scientifique, Unité d'Océanologie Biologique; email: bayed@israbat.ac.ma
• Rationale is protection of scenic natural landscape and biological diversity. • Existing land-based natural park will protect coast with some marine component. • This natural park was designated in 1989; more recently, it has been found that various dolphin and possibly whale species are found in or near park waters; there is also a fisheries reserve, designated in 1995, the Cabo de Gata-Nijar Fisheries Reserve.	See also Table 5.8 for additional Spanish MPAs. • Sociedad Española de Cetáceos 2000 • Contact: Erika Urquiola, Sociedad Española de Cetáceos – SEC (Spanish Cetacean Society); email: urquiola@cetaceos.com or sec@cetaceos.com; web: www.cetaceos.com
• Rationale is protection of scenic natural landscape and biological diversity on unique islands. • Land- and marine-based national park, one of Spain's newest, designated in 1991; portions of it are also being considered for SAC protection which would include bottlenose dolphins (see 11 areas listed below, entries 40–50).	• Sociedad Española de Cetáceos 2000 • Contact: Erika Urquiola, Sociedad Española de Cetáceos – SEC (Spanish Cetacean Society); email: urquiola@cetaceos.com or sec@cetaceos.com; web: www.cetaceos.com

Table 5.6 *continued*

Name of MPA or sanctuary, location and size	Cetacean and other notable species
[MPAs 29–50] ***(29)* Cabo de Creus SAC**, *proposed* • Cabo de Creus, Cataluña, eastern Spain ***(30)* El Montegrí-Illes Medes SAC,** *proposed* • off Illes Medeas, Cataluña, eastern Spain • 19.7 mi^2 (51 km^2) ***(31)* Muntanyes de Begur SAC,** *proposed* • off Cataluña, eastern Spain • 8.2 mi^2 (21.2 km^2) ***(32)* Cap de Santa Creus SAC**, *proposed* • off Cataluña, eastern Spain • 0.84 mi^2 (2.2 km^2) ***(33)* Litoral de Tarragona SAC,** *proposed* • off Cataluña, eastern Spain • 4.6 mi^2 (11.8 km^2) ***(34)* Islas Columbretes SAC,** *proposed* • Islas Columbretes, Golfo de Valencia, eastern Spain • 47.5 mi^2 (12.3 km^2) ***(35)* Isla de Tabarca SAC,** *proposed* • Isla de Tabarca, Valenciana, eastern Spain • 55.8 mi^2 (144.6 km^2) ***(36)* Escarpe de Mazarrón SAC,** *proposed* • Golfo de Mazarrón, Murcia, southeast Spain • 11.6 mi^2 (30 km^2) ***(37)* Medio Marino de Murcia SAC,** *proposed* • Murcia, southeast Spain • 614 mi^2 (1590.7 km^2) ***(38)* Isla de Alborán SAC,** *proposed* • Isla de Alborán, 120 mi (190 km) east of the Strait of Gibraltar, midway between Spain and Morocco • 102.1 mi^2 (246.6 km^2) ***(39)* Frente Litoral del Estrecho de Gibraltar SAC,** *proposed* • Strait of Gibraltar • 29.9 mi^2 (77.5 km^2)	• bottlenose dolphin, *Tursiops truncatus* • also (only at Islas Columbretes): fin whale, *Balaenoptera physalus* (on migration)

Notes and rationale	For more information
• As of 2000, these areas (MPAs 29–39) were identified and proposed as special areas of conservation (SACs) under Annex 1 habitat criteria of EU legislation. • Rationale is not usually specifically for bottlenose dolphins but dolphins are sometimes found in the SAC and the management plan could help with habitat protection. In some cases, extensions were proposed by SEC using Alnitak and CIRCE databases, or proposals were part of the 'Mediterranean Project' to identify SACs for cetaceans in the Mediterranean marine region, a project financed by Spain's Environment Ministry. • Some of these areas are located within 'fisheries reserves'.	• Sociedad Española de Cetáceos, 2000 • Contact: Erika Urquiola, Sociedad Española de Cetáceos – SEC (Spanish Cetacean Society); email: urquiola@cetaceos.com or sec@cetaceos.com; web: www.cetaceos.com • Juan Antonio Raga, 'Proyecto Mediterráneo', Dirección General de Conservación de la Naturaleza, Universitat de Valencia, Valencia, Spain; email: toni.raga@uv.es • Javier Pantoja (Marine Programme Director) and Miguel Aymerich (Sub-Director of Biodiversity), Dirección General de Conservación de la Naturaleza, Ministerio de Medio Ambiente, Madrid, Spain; email: JPantoja@mma.es; miguel.aymerich@ gvsf.mma.es

Table 5.6 *continued*

Name of MPA or sanctuary, location and size	Cetacean and other notable species
All remaining areas in this section are located in the Baleares Archipelago: *(40)* **Cabrera y Mignorn SAC,** *proposed* • 74 mi² (191.7 km²) *(41)* **Bahía de Alcudia SAC,** *proposed* • 65.6 mi² (170 km²) *(42)* **Cap Blank SAC,** *proposed* • 12.4 mi² (32 km²) *(43)* **Salinas de Ibiza y Formentera SAC,** *proposed* • 75.9 mi² (196.7 km²) *(44)* **Islas del Poniente de Ibiza SAC,** *proposed* • 9.8 mi² (25.4 km²) *(45)* **Punta de Sa Creu SAC,** *proposed* • 4.5 mi² (11.8 km²) *(46)* **Sa Dragonera SAC,** *proposed* • 6 mi² (15.4 km²) *(47)* **Es Grau-Favaritx SAC,** *proposed* • 12.8 mi² (33.2 km²) *(48)* **Es Vedrà I Vedranell SAC,** *proposed* • 2.5 mi² (6.4 km²) *(49)* **Tagomago SAC,** *proposed* • 2.1 mi² (5.5 km²) *(50)* **Cap de Barbaria SAC,** *proposed* • 6.6 mi² (17 km²)	• bottlenose dolphin, *Tursiops truncatus*
TUNISIA Tunisian Republic al-Jumhuriya at-Tunisiya **(51) La Galite MPA and SPAMI** • Tunisian national and high-seas waters outside 12 nm (22.2 km) • no size data	• bottlenose dolphin, *Tursiops truncatus*; possibly: short-beaked common dolphin, *Delphinus delphis*; striped dolphin, *Stenella coeruleoalba*
(52) Zembra and Zembretta MPA and SPAMI • Tunisian national and high-seas waters outside 12 nm (22.2 km) • no size data	• bottlenose dolphin, *Tursiops truncatus*; possibly: short-beaked common dolphin, *Delphinus delphis*; striped dolphin, *Stenella coeruleoalba*
(53) Kneiss MPA and SPAMI • Tunisian national and high seas waters outside 12 nm (22.2 km) • no size data	• bottlenose dolphin, *Tursiops truncatus*; possibly: short-beaked common dolphin, *Delphinus delphis*; striped dolphin, *Stenella coeruleoalba*

Notes and rationale	For more information
• As of 2000, these areas (MPAs 40–50) were identified and proposed as special areas of conservation (SACs) under Annex 1 habitat criteria of EU legislation. • Rationale is not usually specifically for bottlenose dolphins but dolphins are sometimes found in the SAC and the management plan could help with habitat protection. In some cases, extensions were proposed by SEC using Alnitak and CIRCE databases, or proposals were part of the 'Mediterranean Project' to identify SACs for cetaceans in the Mediterranean marine region, a project financed by Spain's Environment Ministry. • Some of these areas are located within 'fisheries reserves'.	• Sociedad Española de Cetáceos, 2000 Contact: Erika Urquiola, Sociedad Española de Cetáceos – SEC (Spanish Cetacean Society); email: urquiola@cetaceos.com web: www.cetaceos.com • Juan Antonio Raga, 'Proyecto Mediterráneo', Dirección General de Conservación de la Naturaleza, Universitat de Valencia, Valencia, Spain; email: toni.raga@uv.es • Javier Pantoja (Marine Programme Director) and Miguel Aymerich (Sub-Director of Biodiversity), Dirección General de Conservación de la Naturaleza, Ministerio de Medio Ambiente, Madrid, Spain; email: JPantoja@mma.es; miguel.aymerich@ gvsf.mma.es
• MPA in national and high-seas waters that includes bottlenose dolphin habitat. • Area is also listed as a SPAMI under the SPA Protocol of the Barcelona Convention, which requires all signatory countries to respect this partly high-seas MPA.	• Contact: Karim Ben Mustapha; email: Karim.Benmustapha@ instm.rnrt.tn
• MPA in national and high-seas waters that includes bottlenose dolphin habitat. • Area is also listed as a SPAMI under the SPA Protocol of the Barcelona Convention, which requires all signatory countries to respect this partly high-seas MPA.	• Contact: Karim Ben Mustapha; email: Karim.Benmustapha@ instm.rnrt.tn
• This MPA in national and high-seas waters includes bottlenose dolphin habitat. • Area is also listed as a SPAMI under the SPA Protocol of the Barcelona Convention, which requires all signatory countries to respect this partly high-seas MPA.	• Contact: Karim Ben Mustapha; email: Karim.Benmustapha@ instm.rnrt.tn

Table 5.6 *continued*

Name of MPA or sanctuary, location and size	Cetacean and other notable species
(54–56) Three additional MPAs proposed with cetaceans • Tunisian waters • no size data	• bottlenose dolphin, *Tursiops truncatus* (inshore); possibly: short-beaked common dolphin, *Delphinus delphis*; striped dolphin, *Stenella coeruleoalba*
TURKEY Republic of Turkey Türkiye Cumhuriyeti **(57) Gökçeada Marine Reserve** • between Yıldız Bay and Yelken Rock, North Aegean Sea • size 0.14 mi² (0.37 km²)	• bottlenose dolphin, *Tursiops truncatus*; short-beaked common dolphin, *Delphinus delphis*; possibly up to six other cetacean species • also: Mediterranean monk seal, loggerhead sea turtle, endemic seagrass, sponges, cephalopods, fish
BLACK SEA COUNTRIES: Bulgaria, Georgia, Romania, Russia, Turkey, Ukraine **Various existing and proposed biosphere reserves, marine protected areas and marine reserves along the Black Sea** • especially on the north coast of the Black Sea in the Ukraine and Romania with fewer in Bulgaria, Georgia and Russia and the fewest along the Turkish coast	• common (inshore): bottlenose dolphin, *Tursiops truncatus*; harbor porpoise, *Phocoena phocoena*; sporadic (inshore): short-beaked common dolphin, *Delphinus delphis*
RUSSIA Russian Federation Rossiskaya Federatsiya **(58) Sochinskiy National Nature Park** • Russian Black Sea coast on border with Georgia • 749 mi² (1,940 km²) includes mainly land areas	• possibly bottlenose dolphin, *Tursiops truncatus*; harbor porpoise, *Phocoena phocoena*
UKRAINE **(59) Cape Sarych to Cape Khersones MPA**, *proposed* • coastal area of southern Crimea, between Cape Sarych and Cape Khersones, Ukraine, in the Black Sea • no size data	• harbor porpoise, *Phocoena phocoena*; bottlenose dolphin, *Tursiops truncatus*

Notes and rationale	For more information
• As of 2004, there were proposals for a number of MPAs in Tunisian waters, none of which have been created for cetaceans, but at least three of which are known to have cetacean presence.	• Contact: Karim Ben Mustapha; email: Karim.Benmustapha@ instm.rnrt.tn
• Established in 1999 to protect habitat diversity, this park has a small core region with two buffer zones, but overall size is too small at present to provide significant protection to cetaceans. All fishing and diving activity and marine traffic is prohibited. • Cetaceans are under legal protection since 1983 in the Turkish waters. According to Bayram Öztürk, the main threats to cetaceans in Turkish-water MPAs are fishing and pollution. Economic difficulties for fishermen impede cooperation with NGOs and other stakeholders. Turkey has signed the SPA Protocol but implementation is, so far, insufficent. Turkey may need external expertise for MPAs due to lack of experience in this field. • Research is needed to define cetacean habitat in the vast coastal and island areas of Turkey covering four seas: Mediterranean, Aegean, Marmara and Black seas. This work is envisioned as part of the Turkish National Action Plan for the Conservation of Cetacean Species in the Turkish Waters of the Aegean and Mediterranean Seas, as part of the Mediterranean Action Plan, and additional cetacean MPAs are expected to come from this work.	• Öztürk 1996, 1998; Öztürk and Öztürk, 2003 • Contact: Bayram Öztürk, Faculty of Fisheries, Istanbul Univ, and Turkish Marine Research Foundation; email: ozturkb@istanbul.edu.tr
• There are 63 existing and 43 proposed coastal and marine protected areas around the Black Sea; the marine component, for several of the large MPAs particularly, may include cetacean habitat; surveys and habitat assessments are required to determine if these MPAs can contribute to cetacean habitat protection in the region. • Some possible areas may be: Danube Delta Biosphere Reserve, Dunaiskie Plavni Biosphere Reserve, Cheromorskiy Biosphere Reserve, Zernov's Phillophora Field MPA, Abrau Peninsula National Park, Supsa MPA, Kolkheti National Park and Prebosphoric Marine Reserve, all *proposed*.	See also separate Black Sea listing for Russia below. • Birkun and Krivohizchin, 2000; Notarbartolo di Sciara and Birkun, 2002 • Contact: Alexei Birkun, Jr, Lab of Ecology and Experimental Pathology, Crimean State Medical Univ; email: AlexeiBirkun@home.cris.net
• In 1983 Sochinskiy became a national nature park (IUCN Category II). • Marine component thought to include cetacean habitat; surveys and habitat assessments required.	See also Tables 5.3, 5.9 and 5.19 for more Russian MPAs. • Birkun and Krivohizchin, 2000 • Contact: Penkovskiy Nikolay Dmitrievich, Moscovskaya Str, 21, Sochi, 354000 Russia; email: forest@sochi.ru
• Proposed as an MPA at first Meeting of the Parties of ACCOBAMS. Suggestion was adopted to create an MPA for these waters, with the proposal to be taken up at future ACCOBAMS meetings. • Rationale is to protect known cetacean habitat through ACCOBAMS.	• Birkun and Krivohizchin, 2000; Notarbartolo di Sciara and Birkun, 2002 • Contact: Alexei Birkun, Jr, Lab of Ecology and Experimental Pathology, Crimean State Medical Univ; email: AlexeiBirkun@home.cris.net

MARINE REGION 4: NORTHWEST ATLANTIC

The Northwest Atlantic Marine Region is one of the best known, most highly productive feeding areas for cetaceans in the world ocean. Situated close to the large population centres of northeast US and eastern Canada, this region attracts a quarter of the world's whale watchers – some 2.5 million people – who watch whales largely in the waters of the Gulf of Maine, the Bay of Fundy and in the St Lawrence River and Gulf. The whales in this region have been studied intensively for more than three decades and their habits as well as their inshore habitats are becoming well known.

From April to October, humpback, fin and minke whales feed in the upwellings and other productive areas in the Gulf of Maine, the St Lawrence and off eastern Canada. Blue whales can be seen feeding in the upwellings of the North Shore of the St Lawrence River and Gulf from August to October, although a few remain into the winter. Some 372 blue whales have been photo-identified in the St Lawrence since 1980. Only an estimated maximum of 1500 blues remain in the entire North Atlantic, divided between Marine Regions 2, 4 and 5.

Off Nova Scotia, above a submarine canyon called The Gully, northern bottlenose whales live in one of the few defined habitats in the world for the lesser-known group of beaked whale species. Beaked whales are offshore, deep-diving species whose lives, habits and habitats remain largely hidden.

In the northern parts of the region, in the Canadian and US (Alaskan) Arctic, resident arctic whales are found: belugas, narwhals and bowhead whales. All are year-round residents of this region and the adjacent Arctic Marine Region 2, following or retreating from the ever-shifting ice edge. Approximately 75 per cent of the world's remaining bowhead whales and more than 10,000 belugas make seasonal migrations across the Beaufort Sea in the most westerly part of the region.

Other frequent visitors throughout much of the region inshore and offshore include Atlantic white-sided and white-beaked dolphins, harbor porpoises, pilot whales and orcas.

Finally, this region is the last stand and remaining hope of the North Atlantic right whale. Centuries ago, this species became the first whale to be commercially hunted and the first to be driven to very low levels. In 1980, what were thought to be a few stragglers of the species were discovered to be using the Bay of Fundy; the intensive studies that followed showed that some 325 animals remained (Katona and Kraus, 1999). Besides the Bay of Fundy, a mother and calf feeding and nursery area, the whales use Brown's Bank–Roseway Basin off southern Nova Scotia as a courting and feeding area. Massachusetts Bay and Great South Channel east of Cape Cod are mainly used as springtime feeding areas. There is also a winter warm-water calving area that has been found off southern Georgia/northern Florida which is in the Wider Caribbean, Marine Region 7.

This region has a number of important MPAs set aside or proposed that would help protect cetacean habitat, although for both Canada and the US,

MPA protection of cetaceans is but one among several objectives. The hallmark of Canada's national marine conservation area (NMCA) programme is the representation of natural regions. However, in Canadian waters, The Gully MPA for northern bottlenose whales and the proposed Igalirtuuq National Wildlife Area for bowhead whales, as well as, in US waters, the Gerry E Studds Stellwagen Bank National Marine Sanctuary for a wide range of cetaceans, are all strongly oriented toward cetacean habitat. The Saguenay–St Lawrence Marine Park with its resident endangered St Lawrence belugas, and seasonal minke, fin, blue and humpback whales, will also help protect important habitat for endangered cetaceans.

The Northwest Atlantic Marine Region has six large marine ecosystems (LMEs) that have been identified: Southeast US Continental Shelf, Northeast US Continental Shelf, Scotian Shelf and Newfoundland–Labrador Shelf, all in the North Atlantic; and Hudson Bay and Beaufort Sea in the northern part of the region, usually considered the Arctic. The oceanography of the region is complex and diverse, ranging from polar and subpolar waters from the Beaufort Sea and across the Canadian Arctic to temperate waters off the east coast of the US. The US east coast waters are dominated by the warm offshore Gulf Current which comes up from the Gulf of Mexico and turns northeast toward Britain and northern Europe, missing the Gulf of Maine and Nova Scotia. The cold Labrador Current moves south along the coast of Labrador and has a pervasive impact on the oceanography and biological productivity of the Gulf of St Lawrence as well as on the broad shelf from Labrador south to the Gulf of Maine. The various large and small banks, including the Georges, Browns, Baccaro, Stellwagen and Grand banks, are particularly productive, with areas of upwelling. Along the some 500 miles (800 km) north shore of the St Lawrence River and Gulf, the incursions of cold water funnelled at depth along the Laurentian Trough to the north shore cause massive upwellings that attract hungry blue, fin, minke and humpback whales and dolphins.

This zone is nearly all inside US and Canadian waters, and adjacent high seas. The only small exceptions are the territories of St Pierre and Miquelon (France), south of Newfoundland, and Bermuda (UK). There is no UNEP regional seas programme for this region. Instead, MPAs here are mainly the responsibility of the US and Canadian federal governments (see Boxes 5.4 and 5.5 on pp166–172 for a brief summary of these programmes). In 1995 there was a total of 88 MPAs of all kinds in this marine region (Mondor et al, 1995). This region is divided into ten biogeographic zones all of which are represented by at least one MPA but two of which have only bare representation in very small MPAs. In 2004, there were 11 existing and 7 proposed MPAs which feature cetacean habitat, as well as an EEZ cetacean sanctuary around Bermuda.

The IUCN 2002–2010 Conservation Action Plan for the World's Cetaceans has largely left conservation initiatives for this region to the US and Canada. However, there are two research and education initiatives based in Marine Region 2 which also extend into this region (Reeves et al, 2003):

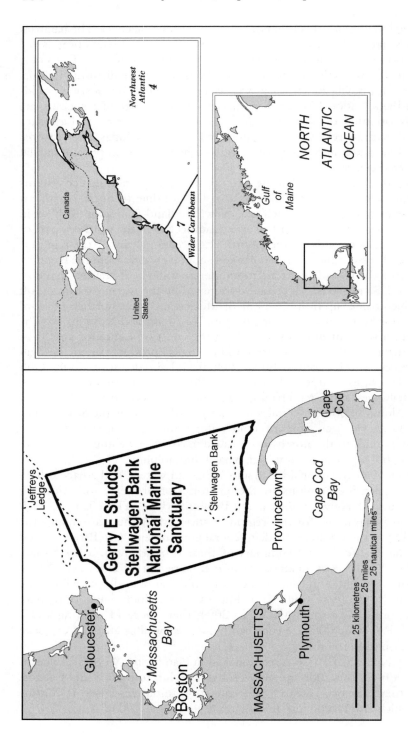

Figure 5.8 *Map of Gerry E Studds Stellwagen Bank National Marine Sanctuary*

The Stellwagen Bank National Marine Sanctuary was designated in 1992 partly to protect the toothed and baleen whales feeding on the bank. See Case Study 5.

- to promote intensive field research on bowhead whales in the eastern Canadian Arctic; and
- to investigate the status of narwhal populations subject to hunting, and ensure that regulations are adequate for conservation.

Case Study 5: Gerry E Studds Stellwagen Bank National Marine Sanctuary

Gerry E Studds Stellwagen Bank National Marine Sanctuary

Type: Existing marine protected area, nearshore waters, federal management.

Location: 25 miles (40 km) east of Boston, 3 miles (5 km) southeast of Cape Ann, and 3 miles (5 km) north of Provincetown, Cape Cod, Massachusetts, in the southern Gulf of Maine.

Cetacean species: common, April–October: humpback whale, *Megaptera novaeangliae*; fin whale, *Balaenoptera physalus*; minke whale, *Balaenoptera acutorostrata*; January–April (possible other months): North Atlantic right whale, *Eubalaena glacialis*; year-round: Atlantic white-sided dolphin, *Lagenorhynchus acutus*; long-finned pilot whale, *Globicephala melas* (especially September–April); harbor porpoise, *Phocoena phocoena* (mainly September–April); sporadic or rare: sei whale, *Balaenoptera borealis*; blue whale, *Balaenoptera musculus*; orca, *Orcinus orca* (mainly July–September); white-beaked dolphin, *Lagenorhynchus albirostris* (mainly April–November); bottlenose dolphin, *Tursiops truncatus*; common dolphin, *Delphinus* spp; striped dolphin, *Stenella coeruleoalba*.

Additional species and other features: Four species of sea turtles; harbor and gray seals; more than 40 species of coastal and pelagic seabirds including roseate tern, storm petrel and northern gannet; bluefin tuna (accounts for more than half of the total revenue generated by commercial landings from Stellwagen Bank), Atlantic cod, winter flounder, sea scallop and northern lobster. Formed by the retreat of glaciers from the last Ice Age, Stellwagen Bank consists primarily of coarse sand and gravel. Its position at the mouth of Massachusetts Bay forces an upwelling of nutrient-rich water from the Gulf of Maine over the bank leading to high productivity. At least ten historic shipwrecks have been identified within or adjacent to the sanctuary boundary, but more are likely to be discovered when the cultural resource inventory is completed.

Size of protected area: 842 square miles (2181 km^2).

Rationale: Stellwagen Bank was selected as a sanctuary based on outstanding biological, geological, oceanographic and cultural features. The bank supports a wealth of marine life including various marine mammal species, several endangered or threatened sea turtles and seabirds and various commercial fish species. The area also supports a high level of human use that was lacking comprehensive and coordinated management. It was felt that sanctuary designation would provide both coordination of ongoing and planned human activities, and the mechanisms for long-term protection of the ecosystem. In terms of cetaceans, the sanctuary helps protect feeding habitat for humpback and other baleen whales and dolphins and it is part of the migration corridor for the endangered North Atlantic right whale.

Box 5.4 The flagship US national marine sanctuaries programme

National marine sanctuaries form the centrepiece of the American effort to protect marine ecosystems. As of 2002, there were 13 in total, ranging in size from the Fagatele Bay National Marine Sanctuary in American Samoa, a quarter of a square mile (0.66 km^2), to Monterey Bay National Marine Sanctuary off California with 5328 mi^2 (13,802 km^2). These protected areas should not be confused with sanctuaries in other parts of the world that only restrict hunting; they are in effect multiple-use resource management areas (IUCN Category VI protection). The US national marine sanctuaries are seen as areas of the ocean and coast that are protected from some or all human activities to conserve biodiversity, fisheries, cultural and recreational resources, and to provide valuable natural laboratories for scientific research.

In 1972, the US Congress passed Title III of the Marine Protection, Research and Sanctuaries Act, now called the 'National Marine Sanctuary Act', in response to public concern about the effects of pollution on the health of marine resources. The Act authorizes the designation of 'areas of special national significance due to their resource or human use values' as national marine sanctuaries to promote comprehensive management of their special 'conservation, recreation, ecological, historical, research, educational or aesthetic' resources. National marine sanctuaries may be designated in coastal and ocean waters, in submerged lands and in the Great Lakes and their connecting waters. The Act is administered by the Sanctuaries and Reserves Division of the National Oceanic and Atmospheric Administration (NOAA).

The National Marine Sanctuaries programme is designed to provide leadership and act as a catalyst to link assets and resources of government and NGOs to focus attention on the need to manage and protect marine resources. Its mandate includes:

- a diversity of nationally significant marine areas;
- providing enhanced resource protection through conservation and management;
- coordinating research on, and monitoring of, the site-specific marine resources of the sanctuaries;
- enhancing public awareness, understanding, appreciation and wise use of the marine environment;
- promoting management practices that further marine conservation and ecologically sustainable uses of marine resources outside sanctuary boundaries; and
- facilitating, to the extent compatible with the primary objective of resource protection, multiple uses of the sanctuaries.

Sanctuary designation is generally preceded by many months, in some cases years, of public meetings and consultations. The intent is to arrive at a regional consensus as to whether the site should be designated, and if it is, how the management framework is to be constructed (Barr, 1995). Education and outreach programmes, enforcement and compliance, as well as research, are all part of each management plan.

Managing and regulating the activities in each sanctuary is accomplished through sanctuary regulations, permits and consultations. Certain activities determined to be incompatible with resource protection, such as ocean dumping and mineral development, are prohibited outright. Special use permits may be issued for commercial activities that do not damage sanctuary resources. Sanctuary managers have the authority to ensure that all permits for activities proposed within or affecting the sanctuary are consistent with the management plan.

In addition to the 13 sanctuaries already designated, as of early 2004, one more was under active consideration, the large Northwestern Hawaiian Islands Coral Reef Ecosystem Reserve which has been proposed as a national marine sanctuary which would cover some 131,240 mi^2 (340,000 km^2).

Most of the sanctuaries have resident or migratory cetacean populations, and a number have sanctuary-specific cetacean guidelines or regulations. While some sanctuaries do not specifically regulate activities concerning cetaceans, they are managed using an ecosystem-based approach and may indirectly address many of the issues related to cetaceans and their use of their habitats within the sanctuaries.

Education and outreach efforts attempt to meet the programme's mandate for resource protection through enhanced public awareness, understanding, appreciation and careful use of the coastal and marine environments. Education programmes include student curricula, field trips, adult lectures, resource user and teacher workshops, volunteer programmes, interpretive law enforcement and a wide variety of print media.

Constraints to NOAA's ability to manage the sanctuaries include inadequacy of funding for the programme, lack of regulatory authority over activities outside the sanctuary that affect the sites' resources, minimal to modest enforcement capabilities and lack of regulatory flexibility. Florida Keys National Marine Sanctuary, for example, operates on a budget one-tenth that of Yellowstone National Park, although both are roughly the same size, and each attracts millions of visitors a year.

In the mid-1990s, the sanctuary programme began work on a long-range research plan to identify national system-wide priorities for management-oriented research and monitoring, recently completed, as well as regional themes of particular concern for individual sanctuaries. The hope was that this might serve as a stimulus for obtaining significant future funding for research. Sanctuary managers are now evaluating what information is needed to address specific management problems. In addition, system-wide monitoring standards and protocols are now being developed, as monitoring programmes vary considerably from site to site, mainly due to extreme differences in sanctuary resources and environments.

The emphasis on a democratic public and industry participation process in the creation and development of MPAs and their management plans is a positive and necessary prerequisite as it allows the various stakeholders to 'buy in' to the MPA idea. However, in the effort to reach consensus in an often drawn-out public process, MPAs tend to become IUCN Category VI (mixed-use) areas. In this process, Category I critical habitat core protection areas are difficult to establish, even as part of biosphere-type reserves (a model not often considered in the US), although cetacean biologists as well as fisheries and other ecologists increasingly see highly protected core areas as crucial to the success of every MPA. It is clear that the benefits of Category I core zones have to be better sold to industry, the public and other stakeholders.

Currently, less than 0.1 per cent of US marine waters is highly, or fully, protected in Category I areas. In response to this, and as part of an effort to evaluate the sanctuaries, the National Academy of Public Administration reviewed the US National Marine Sanctuaries programme in 2000. It determined that the sanctuaries 'need to take more steps to protect marine resources within their boundaries, including regulating and prohibiting fishing or other activities when appropriate'. Subsequently, National Marine Sanctuaries amendments specifically included a restriction on designating new sites until the programme could show it had the resources to manage effectively the existing sites. The Commission on Geosciences, Environment, and Resources (2000), in a report from the National Research Council, was generally critical of the US sanctuaries, stating that they 'contain a variety of marine environments that constitute neither a representative system of MPAs nor a network'. The Commission has called for 20 per cent of US marine waters to be highly protected, IUCN Category I reserves – 200 times more than currently protected. However, the Commission was positive about the sanctuary programme's overall mandate to exclude oil and gas development, dredging, placement of structures and dumping, and celebrated its ability to facilitate conflict resolution among users (Commission on Geosciences, Environment, and Resources, 2000).

In May 2000, in the US, a Presidential Executive Order from Bill Clinton directed NOAA, in cooperation with the Department of the Interior, to develop a national system of MPAs and a plan for MPA networks in US coastal waters. This new focus on MPA networks was comprehensively reviewed in the Commission on Geosciences, Environment, and Resources report. Conservationists and conservation organizations hope that refocusing the effort in terms of a national system will result in the protection of more and much larger areas. A system-wide approach can only help species such as whales and dolphins which travel over large areas. In any case, this network approach has key implications for cetaceans as well as fish stocks, many of which require a network approach for best conservation.

In addition to its flagship national marine sanctuaries, the US has available a variety of other means of protecting marine waters, mainly as extensions of land-based regimes such as national parks, monuments, wildlife refuges and others. These are typically much smaller areas than the national marine sanctuaries. At the state level, for the coastal states, most notably California, there are various provisions for protecting state coastal waters as part of state parks, beaches and other nature designations, most of which are fragmentary in terms of protecting cetacean habitat, but which could be useful in future if targeted toward cetacean habitat protection.

A recent comprehensive assessment of US laws governing marine mammal conservation is provided by Baur et al (1999). For more information on the strategy to create networks of MPAs and a national system, see www.mcbi.org. For further insights on the status, shortcomings and future needs of US MPAs, using the Gulf of Maine, New England, as a case study, see Recchia et al (2001).

In 1982, Charles 'Stormy' Mayo of the Center for Coastal Studies, together with Sherrard Foster for Defenders of Wildlife, nominated Stellwagen Bank for consideration as a national marine sanctuary. Based on biological productivity, and ecological and economic resource values, NOAA acknowledged Stellwagen Bank as a potential sanctuary in the early 1980s. The decision to designate Stellwagen Bank as a sanctuary did not gain impetus until 1988, when a developer proposed to place a 144-acre (58 ha) fixed platform on the bank. The platform would have housed a major resort, including one of the largest casinos in the world. Prompted by growing concern over the type and amount of human activity on the bank and its possible effects on biological productivity, the US government called for a study of the site in 1989. The site was designated in November 1992, and final sanctuary regulations became effective on 20 March 1994.

Activities prohibited within the sanctuary include: exploring for, developing or producing sand and gravel products; discharging or depositing any materials; altering the seabed or constructing any structures on the seabed; moving, injuring or possessing historical resources; injuring or harassing marine mammals, turtles and seabirds; incineration of any material from onboard any vessel; and 'lightening' (the transfer of petroleum-based products/materials from vessel to vessel). Vessel operation, mariculture and the exploration, development and production of oil and gas resources may be subject to future sanctuary regulations.

Research activities include: side-scan sonar survey and geological characterization; fishery habitat research; sanctuary-user surveys; and the 'aquanaut' programme for student research on benthic communities and acoustics being conducted with the National Undersea Research Center at University of Connecticut. Behavioural ecology and habitat studies are being conducted in nearby Cape Cod and Massachusetts bays to explore the relationship between these habitats and the endangered whales that use them. The studies also document the current state of these waters in terms of disposal of waste effluent and dredged materials. In addition to all this research, there is an extensive survey of human uses of Stellwagen Bank, focusing on fishing activities and looking at changes from 1998 to the present.

Whale population studies in the area have focused on long-term investigations of humpback, minke and North Atlantic right whales in the Stellwagen area, Great South Channel, and in the wider Gulf of Maine. The foundation of this work is one of the world's largest and most accurate databases on individually identified whales in the form of several species photo-ID catalogues, most notably the North Atlantic humpback whale catalogue. As part of the Years of the North Atlantic Humpback (YONAH) programme, an investigation of humpback whales throughout the North Atlantic, researchers in the Stellwagen and Gulf of Maine area collaborated with humpback whale researchers in Canada, Iceland, Norway, the Dominican Republic and other countries to gain an ocean-wide perspective on humpback whales (Smith et al, 1999). Additional YONAH and other publications have looked at site use by the various components of the humpback whale population.

The sanctuary programme provides the means to coordinate the various human activities with the regulatory authority. Sanctuary staff work with the US Coast Guard, National Marine Fisheries Service and the Commonwealth of Massachusetts Division of Law Enforcement to enforce sanctuary regulations. There is special as well as routine surveillance of the sanctuary by ship and air patrols. Sanctuary staff and the Marine Environmental Police (MEP) also enlist public support to help monitor the sanctuary, distribute guidelines for whale watching to boaters, and broadcast radio warnings of endangered species sightings.

In 1985 and 1986, humpback whales shifted their distribution and, initially, researchers and the public feared they might have left Stellwagen Bank completely. In 1993 and 1995, there was a decrease in the number of humpbacks in the Stellwagen area. These temporary shifts in distribution appear to be due to ecosystem changes producing a sharp decline in the 'building block' sand lance populations on the bank. It is essential to understand the reasons for these periodic changes and to protect the critical habitat of humpback whales and their prey – both within and outside the sanctuary, adopting a precautionary approach. It may be that several habitat areas, rather than just the primary Stellwagen habitat, need to be protected to accommodate year-to-year ecosystem variability. It is also important to continue to monitor activities such as whale watching and other habitat uses, to monitor the waste site, and keep track of contaminants in stranded whales and dolphins as well as fish species that are caught in the area.

Sanctuary creation has helped raise awareness of other ocean uses. Industries operating in or near the area include whale watching (an estimated 1 million whale watchers per year) and recreational boating, and commercial and recreational fishing also occur in the sanctuary. Heavily used shipping lanes cross the sanctuary and, as of 1995, included some 2700 commercial vessels, principally carrying refined petroleum products, in and out of the Port of Boston annually. The proximity to urban areas (including metropolitan Boston) has put pressure on Stellwagen Bank from pollution loading. Only three miles (5 km) from the bank is the Massachusetts Bay Disposal Site, an undersea dump site used since the 1940s, where up to 80,000 barrels of toxic waste including atomic waste have been dumped. Between 1940 and 1970, some industrial and radioactive waste was also disposed of at several other sites within Massachusetts Bay, largely unrecorded and unregulated. The most frequently used site was the so-called Industrial Waste Site located near the western edge of the sanctuary boundary. While toxic dumping has not taken place recently, rusting barrels remain on the ocean floor. The dump site is being used for disposal of dredged harbour sediments, which have the potential to carry high pollution loads. And, more recently, increasing traffic from cruise ships has made the issue of ship discharge from these 'floating cities' a mounting concern.

Stellwagen Bank has been and continues to be an important inshore fishing ground for commercial fish including groundfish, scallops and bluefin tuna. The area is a restricted mesh area, designated to protect juvenile haddock which use the bank as a nursery ground. The sanctuary has targeted fish and fish habitat as one of its primary research focuses. One potential goal is to try to identify an area, or areas, within the sanctuary where dragging would be prohibited, allowing study of the long-term recovery of heavily dragged areas. There is also a closed area called the 'Western Gulf of Maine Closure' where fishing of groundfish has been prohibited. This closure

Box 5.5 MPA developments in Canada

The second largest country with the world's longest coastline and one of the few countries bounded by three oceans (Arctic, North Atlantic and North Pacific), Canada has substantial cetacean populations which spend all or part of the year within Canada's vast national waters. Yet, despite this strong marine focus, Canada has been comparatively slow to come to grips with its responsibility for MPA conservation (Lien, 1999). Canada has mostly small marine protected areas, and only a handful contain significant cetacean habitat. Several, however, are in the process of introducing, or are having discussion about, protection, which could improve the prospects for cetacean habitat conservation in Canada.

There are three main mechanisms for protecting marine areas in Canada:

1 Parks Canada, which has separate agency status reporting to the Minister of Environment, designates representative marine areas as national marine conservation areas (NMCAs) with conservation, public understanding and enjoyment objectives. The National Marine Conservation Areas Policy was articulated in 1994 with the system plan described in detail in 1995 (Mercier and Mondor, 1995). These documents outlined the development of a system of NMCAs with enabling legislation, the Canada National Marine Conservation Areas Act, following in June 2002.

The NMCA system plan (called 'Sea to Sea to Sea') divides Canada's Great Lakes and ocean expanses into 29 distinct regions, 24 of them in the oceans. An NMCA is defined as a marine area managed by Parks Canada and partner federal or provincial agencies for sustainable use (allowing sustainable fishing but not mining, oil and gas exploration and development, or ocean dumping), while also containing zones of high protection.

The five steps toward establishing a new NMCA are:

Step One: Identifying representative marine areas within a marine region.

Step Two: Selecting potential NMCAs from among the representative areas.

Step Three: Assessing NMCA feasibility.

Step Four: Negotiating a new NMCA establishment agreement.

Step Five: Establishing a new NMCA formally by placing it under legislation (Mercier and Mondor, 1995).

In September 2002, former Prime Minister Jean Chrétien announced at the World Summit on Sustainable Development in Johannesburg that the Canadian government would create ten new national parks and five new marine conservation areas over the next several years, and invest in ensuring the ecological health of existing national parks. Two proposed NMCAs in British Columbia with significant cetacean populations are included: Southern Strait of Georgia, off southeastern Vancouver Island, and Gwaii Haanas, in the southern Queen Charlotte Islands.

Canada's systematic biogeographic approach in the NMCA system plan has been admired by MPA practitioners in other countries. If truly representative NMCAs can be established in all regions, then Canada will have the makings of an excellent MPA network which can be complemented by the developing programmes of Environment Canada, and Fisheries and Oceans Canada, described below as the second and third mechanisms for creating MPAs.

2 Environment Canada, under the Canada Wildlife Act, can create national wildlife areas (NWAs) and marine wildlife areas (MWAs) to protect nationally significant habitats for wildlife conservation, research and interpretation. NWAs can be established out to 12 nm (22.2 km) while MWAs can be created beyond that, to the limits of Canada's EEZ. Along with the Migratory Birds Act, the Canada Wildlife Act has been used mainly for the protection of migratory and seabird habitats. The act does not require inclusion of the seabed, making it more difficult to exclude activities such as oil and gas development and mining. In early 2004, the Scott Islands Marine Wildlife Area was announced as the first pilot project (see listing in Table 5.19, on p362).

3 The Department of Fisheries and Oceans (DFO), through the Fisheries Act, is responsible for the management of marine mammal populations. Also, since the adoption of the Oceans Act in 1997, DFO has the authority to establish MPAs for the protection of marine species and habitats. For areas where vulnerable or particularly significant populations of cetaceans warrant protection and are outside of representative areas that might qualify for NMCA status, DFO is the most logical department to take the lead in obtaining legal MPA status. In addition, DFO has the ultimate responsibility for cetaceans in Canada, as well as jurisdiction over fisheries. In terms of all Canadian MPAs, however, critics claim that DFO has made slow progress in its role as the coordinating agency for MPA programmes in Canada. Since the passage of the Oceans Act, proposed MPAs have included The Gully (off Nova Scotia), Leading Tickles, Gilberts Bay and Eastport (in Newfoundland), Musquash Estuary (New Brunswick), Manicouagan Peninsula (Québec) and Race Rocks, Gabriola Passage, Endeavour Hydrothermal Vents area and Bowie Seamount (all in British Columbia waters), several of which include cetacean habitat. Of these, only The Gully and Endeavour Hydrothermal Vents have now attained designated MPA status.

Please note that in Canada only, the term 'marine protected area' denotes a DFO protected marine area as designated under the Oceans Act. To distinguish from the generic MPA, Canadian DFO MPAs will be written with 'marine protected area' or 'MPA' in quotes.

In terms of species protection, COSEWIC (Committee on the Status of Endangered Wildlife in Canada) determines the national status of wild species, subspecies and important populations in Canada. At least 15 whale and dolphin populations have been assessed as warranting vulnerable, threatened or endangered status. In June 2002, Canada's long-awaited endangered species legislation, talked about since the 1970s when the landmark US Endangered Species Act was passed, became law as the Species at Risk Act (SARA).

overlaps part of the sanctuary and is being used as a site to support extensive research on the effects of closure on these important fish habitats.

In June 2002, the sanctuary began a management plan review, including a series of public scoping meetings to obtain suggestions on how NOAA should be managing the Sanctuary. A primer on the Sanctuary entitled 'Stellwagen Bank National Marine Sanctuary, state of the sanctuary: a progress report' was made widely available (the management plan review process can be followed by going to www.sbnms.nos.noaa.gov).

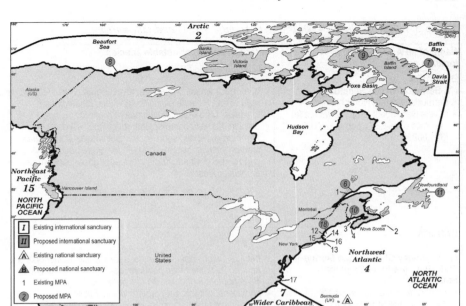

The roman numerals, letters and numbers correspond to the sanctuaries and MPAs listed and described in Table 5.7.

Figure 5.9 *Map of Marine Region 4: Northwest Atlantic MPAs and sanctuaries*

In addition to the management plan review, there have been frequent suggestions to expand the sanctuary or to create one or two new ones in adjacent waters used by the same populations of whales. These include Jeffreys Ledge and Great South Channel. Most years on Stellwagen Bank, the whales and dolphins divide much of their spring and summer feeding time between the three areas, and in the summers, when the whales disappear from Stellwagen Bank, they are sometimes found in these other areas.

Table 5.7 *Marine Region 4: Northwest Atlantic MPAs and sanctuaries*

Name of MPA or sanctuary, location and size	Cetacean and other notable species
BERMUDA **(A) Bermuda Whale Sanctuary** • Bermuda, western North Atlantic • covers Bermuda's territorial waters (to the limits of its EEZ), some 125,000 mi^2 (324,000 km^2)	• humpback whale, *Megaptera novaeangliae*; North Atlantic right whale, *Balaena glacialis*; fin whale, *Balaenoptera physalus*; blue whale, *Balaenoptera musculus*; striped dolphin, *Stenella coeruleoalba*; rough-toothed dolphin, *Steno bredanensis*; short-finned pilot whale, *Globicephala macrorhynchus*; sperm whale, *Physeter macrocephalus*; pygmy sperm whale, *Kogia breviceps*; goosebeak whale, *Ziphius cavirostris*
CANADA **(1) Saguenay-St Lawrence Marine Park (Parc marin du Saguenay-St-Laurent)** • located at the confluence of the Saguenay and St Lawrence rivers • 439 sq mi^2 (1,138 sq km^2)	• beluga, *Delphinapterus leucas*; minke whale, *Balaenoptera acutorostrata;* fin whale, *Balaenoptera physalus;* blue whale, *Balaenoptera musculus;* harbor porpoise, *Phocoena phocoena;* occasionally: sperm whale, *Physeter macrocephalus;* humpback whale, *Megaptera novaeangliae;* Atlantic white-sided dolphin, *Lagenorhynchus acutus* • also: harbor, gray and harp seals
(2) The Gully 'Marine Protected Area' • Scotian Shelf, 25 mi (40 km) southeast of Sable Island, Nova Scotia, 124 mi (200 km) southeast of Halifax, Nova Scotia, in the open North Atlantic • 912.5 mi^2 (2364 km^2). The Gully itself is the largest submarine canyon off eastern Canada, reaching a width of 6 mi (10 km) and depths of 6500 ft (2000 m) – about as wide and deep as the Grand Canyon.	• all months: northern bottlenose whale, *Hyperoodon ampullatus*; occasional, mainly Jul–Sept: blue whale, *Balaenoptera musculus*; fin whale, *Balaenoptera physalus*; minke whale, *Balaenoptera acutorostrata*; humpback whale, *Megaptera novaeangliae*; long-finned pilot whale, *Globicephala melas*; short-beaked common dolphin, *Delphinus delphis*; Atlantic white-sided dolphin, *Lagenorhynchus acutus*; bottlenose dolphin, *Tursiops truncatus*; harbor porpoise, *Phocoena phocoena* • also: seabirds such as greater shearwater and Leach's storm petrel

Notes and rationale	For more information
• A cetacean refuge or sanctuary was announced for Bermuda's territorial waters on 3 July 2000; all Bermuda Fisheries legislation applies, offering complete protection for every marine mammal species. • Bermudan waters are important for migrating humpback whales; some of the earliest humpback song recordings were made here; there is evidence that blue and other large whales may use Bermuda, with its distinctive topography, as a 'beacon' for navigating through the North Atlantic. • Sanctuary covers cetaceans only but has extraordinary features which include the Bermuda Seamount with its coral reefs, numerous important shipwrecks and wide diversity of marine species.	• Min of Environment, Govt of Bermuda, 2000; Sterrer, 1992 • Contact: John A Barnes, Director, Dept of Agriculture and Fisheries, Govt of Bermuda, PO Box HM 834, Hamilton HM CX, Bermuda • Bermuda Zoological Society, Box 145, The Flatts, Smith's 3, Bermuda
• In 1990, the governments of Canada and Québec signed a federal–provincial agreement to create a marine park; the management plan was produced in 1995 and approved in 1996. The joint federal–provincial marine park was established under 'mirror' provincial (Québec) and federal Parks Canada legislation. Technically, Québec retains jurisdiction over the seabed, while the federal government controls the water column and species found in the water. Thus the cetaceans and their habitat are the responsibility of Parks Canada and the federal government. • Rationale is to protect a representative portion of the St Lawrence estuary with high marine biodiversity, but the protection of the endangered St Lawrence beluga was the catalyst for creating the park; one objective is to protect critical habitat for belugas and other cetaceans. • Protection of marine species and ecosystems requires commitment to responsible management of the large whale watch industry within and around the park. In 2002 whale watch regulations for the park were adopted and a zoning plan, in progress, would protect core habitats of whales and other wildlife. • In 2003, DFO was considering further plans to protect the St Lawrence Estuary, including cetacean habitat, to complement the Saguenay-St Lawrence Marine Park, but as of 2004 the proposal had not been made public.	See also Tables 5.3 and 5.19 for additional Canadian MPAs. • *Canada Gazette*, 1979, 1993; Dept of Canadian Heritage et al, 1995; Hoyt, 1985a; Michaud and Gilbert, 1993; Mingelbier and Michaud, 1996; St Lawrence Beluga Recovery Team, 1995 • Contact: Parc marin du Saguenay-St-Laurent, Tadoussac, PQ, Canada: web: www.pc.gc.ca/amnc-nmca/qc/saguenay/index_f.asp • Guy Cantin, DFO; email: canting@dfo-mpo.gc.ca
• Critical offshore habitat for 230 northern bottlenose whales, the majority of which are seen in a 5 x 12.4 mi (8 x 20 km) core area at the entrance to the canyon in the central upwelling waters, although they also forage east and west along the Scotian Shelf (Faucher and Whitehead, 1995). The Gully is the only place where a population or species of beaked whale has been systematically researched. Also provides habitat for other cetaceans: a feeding as well as a mating-breeding area. • Marine fish biodiversity monitoring has shown The Gully to be an area of high marine productivity – one of the most richly biodiverse regions of the Scotian Shelf. • Announced as a proposed site for a DFO 'MPA' under the Oceans Act in 1998; draft regulations were published for comment in Dec 2003 proposing the banning of fishing and gas exploration in one of three zones, with restricted activities in the other two zones. Researcher Hal Whitehead said that the regulations don't go far enough toward ensuring the whales' health and safety. • The Gully became Canada's second Oceans Act 'MPA' in 2004.	• Faucher and Weilgart, 1992; Faucher and Whitehead, 1995; Hooker et al, 2001; Reeves et al, 1993; Whitehead et al, 1997, 1998 • Contact: Hal Whitehead, Dept of Biology, Dalhousie University, Halifax NS B3H 4J1 Canada; web: www.dal.ca/~whitelab/ • DFO; web: www.dfo-mpo.gc.ca/canwaters-eauxcan/oceans/mpa-zpm/mpa_e.asp • WWF Canada, 90 Eglinton Ave E, #504, Toronto, Ont M4P 2Z7 Canada; web: www.wwf.ca

Table 5.7 *continued*

Name of MPA or sanctuary, location and size	Cetacean and other notable species
(3) Bay of Fundy Right Whale Conservation Area • Grand Manan Basin, between Digby and Grand Manan islands in the Bay of Fundy, New Brunswick **(4) Roseway Basin Right Whale Conservation Area** • south of Cape Sable Island on the eastern edge of the Gulf of Maine, between Browns and Baccaro Banks, off southwest Nova Scotia (42°45'–43°05'N; 65°03'–65°40'W)	• Jun–Dec: North Atlantic right whale, *Eubalaena glacialis*; fin whale, *Balaenoptera physalus*; humpback whale, *Megaptera novaeangliae*; Jun–Oct: harbor porpoise, *Phocoena phocoena*; Atlantic white-sided dolphin, *Lagenorhynchus acutus*; in Roseway Basin only: sperm whale, *Physeter macrocephalus*; sei whale, *Balaenoptera borealis* • also: harbor seal, basking shark, seabirds
(5) Auyuittug National Park • Cumberland Peninsula, Baffin Island, Nunavut • 7697 mi^2 (19,707 km^2), mostly land based	• narwhal, *Monodon monoceros*
(6) Manicouagan 'Marine Protected Area', proposed • Manicouagan Peninsula, west of Baie-Comeau on the north shore of the St Lawrence Estuary extending south into the Laurentian Channel (downstream from existing Saguenay-St Lawrence Marine Park) • approximately 270 mi^2 (700 km^2)	• beluga, *Delphinapterus leucas*; minke whale, *Balaenoptera acutorostrata*; fin whale, *Balaenoptera physalus*; blue whale, *Balaenoptera musculus*; harbor porpoise, *Phocoena phocoena*; occasionally: sperm whale, *Physeter macrocephalus*; humpback whale, *Megaptera novaeangliae*; Atlantic white-sided dolphin, *Lagenorhynchus acutus*
(7) Igaliqtuuq National Wildlife Area and Biosphere Reserve, proposed • Isabella Bay on Baffin Island, Nunavut, from coast out to 12 nm (22 km) • no size data	• Jul–Sept: bowhead whale, *Balaena mysticetus*; orca, *Orcinus orca*; narwhal, *Monodon monoceros* (migratory) • also: harp seals, ringed seals and polar bears

Notes and rationale	For more information
• These critical habitats (the main nursery areas as well as mating areas) for the right whale, located in the Bay of Fundy and Roseway Basin, as well as feeding areas, are conservation areas with guidelines but no legislated regulation; however, recent change of shipping lanes may help protect whales. • First proposed as areas requiring protection in 1991 by Moira Brown, East Coast Ecosystems. In 1993, special pilot directions were instituted to try to get ships to slow down when travelling through this area due to large number of right whale mortalities from shipping. In July 2003, in the Bay of Fundy and Roseway Basin, whales were given right of way by the Canadian government with recognition from the International Maritime Organization (IMO), to protect them from ship collisions, the main cause of their decline. Canada's Right Whale Recovery Plan (2000) will move two major shipping lanes 4 mi (6 km) to the east and north, reducing the probability of a whale being hit by 80 per cent. • Right whale research includes photo-ID and biopsy studies, acoustic tracking and recording, abundance and distribution studies (satellite tagging). The conservation area boundaries were derived from survey sighting data.	• Brown et al, 1995; Hoyt, 1993a; Kraus, 1990; Kraus and Brown, 1992; Kraus and Kenny, 1991 • Contact: Moira Brown, New England Aquarium, Central Wharf, Boston, MA 02110 USA; email: mwbrown@neaq.org • Francine Mercier, Parks Canada, 4th Fl, 25 Eddy St, Hull, Quebec K1A 0M5 Canada; web: www.pc.gc.ca/default.html
• This national terrestrial park with a marine component was established in 1972; in 1993 an agreement was forged between the government and the Inuit to negotiate the formal establishment of the reserve to a national park. • Narwhals are found in the northern fjords of the park.	• Contact: Auyuittuq National Park; web: www.canadianparks.com/nunavut/auyutnp/index.htm
• Proposed 'MPA' by DFO, listed as an 'area of interest' in 1998 to protect estuarine (salt marshes, eelgrass beds, sand flats) and marine ecosystems; three rivers (Betsiamites, Outardes and Manicouagan) converge with the salt water of the lower St Lawrence estuary to create a highly productive marine environment supporting invertebrates, fish and marine mammals. • Site was initially proposed as an MPA by the NGO Pointe-aux-Outardes Nature Park. • Area is visited by cetaceans, used for feeding and protects ecosystem important for cetacean prey.	• Contact: DFO; web: www.dfo-mpo.gc.ca/canwaters-eauxcan/oceans/mpa-zpm/mpa_e.asp
• First proposed for an MPA in 1987 by WWF Canada and Clyde River community groups; now in process of probable designation with territorial, aboriginal and federal (Environment Canada) management under the Canada Wildlife Act as an NWA; a much more extensive marine-based area (extending north and south into Davis Strait) is also being proposed as a biosphere reserve. • Proposed in part to protect critical habitat in Isabella Bay used by a large proportion of the endangered Baffin Bay/Davis Strait bowhead whales for feeding and resting, especially in late summer and autumn. • Bowhead photo-ID work is being conducted, with studies of food availability and feeding ecology; three-year broad-based Inuit project to study whales lasted from 2001 to 2003. • Serious conflicts may develop with oil and gas development if allowed in the critical bowhead whale habitat in the bay.	• Wheeler, 2003 • Contact: Canadian Wildlife Service, Environment Canada; web: www.newparksnorth.org/igaliq.htm • WWF Canada, 245 Eglinton Ave E, 410, Toronto, Ont M4P 2Z7 Canada; web: www.wwf.ca

Table 5.7 *continued*

Name of MPA or sanctuary, location and size	Cetacean and other notable species
(8) Beaufort Sea Beluga 'Marine Protected Area', *proposed* • Shallow Bay, east Mackenzie Bay, Kugmallit Bay and near Kendall Island, Northwest Territories and Yukon, Beaufort Sea • no size data	• beluga, *Delphinapterus leucas*
(9) Lancaster Sound National Marine Conservation Area, *proposed but suspended* • Lancaster Sound, Nunavut • size undetermined	• narwhal, *Monodon monoceros*; beluga, *Delphinapterus leucas*; orca, *Orcinus orca*; bowhead whale, *Balaena mysticetus* • also: ringed seals, walrus, a third of Eastern Canada's colonial seabirds breed and feed here (thick-billed murres, black-legged kittiwakes, northern fulmars and others)
(10) West Isles National Marine Conservation Area, *proposed but discontinued* • located in the West Isles, New Brunswick, on the Bay of Fundy • size undetermined	• Jul–Oct: North Atlantic right whale, *Eubalaena glacialis*; minke whale, *Balaenoptera acutorostrata*; harbor porpoise, *Phocoena phocoena*; humpback whale, *Megaptera novaeangliae*. • also: harbour seals and diverse fish and benthic invertebrate fauna
(11) Bonavista-Notre Dame Bays National Marine Conservation Area, *proposed but discontinued* • northeast Newfoundland • proposed size was 1160 mi^2 (3000 km^2)	• humpback whale, *Megaptera novaeangliae*; fin whale, *Balaenoptera physalus*; minke whale, *Balaenoptera acutorostrata*; white-beaked dolphin, *Lagenorhynchus albirostris*; Atlantic white-sided dolphin, *Lagenorhynchus acutus*; long-finned pilot whale, *Globicephala melas*; harbor porpoise, *Phocoena phocoena* • also: seabirds, six seal species
UNITED STATES OF AMERICA (US) **(12) Gerry E Studds Stellwagen Bank National Marine Sanctuary** • east of Massachusetts on Stellwagen Bank, Gulf of Maine • 842 mi^2 (2181 km^2) **See Case Study 5.**	• humpback whale, *Megaptera novaeangliae*; North Atlantic right whale, *Eubalaena glacialis*; fin whale, *Balaenoptera physalus*; minke whale, *Balaenoptera acutorostrata*; Atlantic white-sided dolphin, *Lagenorhynchus acutus*; long-finned pilot whale, *Globicephala melas*; harbor porpoise, *Phocoena phocoena*; six others sporadic or rare (see Case Study 5 for more about cetacean species and periods of habitat use)

Notes and rationale	For more information
• Proposed 'MPA' by DFO includes beluga habitat; currently identified as an 'area of interest' being considered in conjunction with the Inuvialuit peoples of the western Arctic. • The Beaufort Sea Beluga Management Plan, prepared with the local community Hunters and Trappers Committees and DFO, manages the area in four separate zones for the beluga subsistence hunt, excluding oil, gas, mining and tourism from the prime nearshore hunting areas where belugas are found in the most accessible numbers; this is the only known traditional summer concentration of the Beaufort Sea beluga stock. • To date, hunting is not excluded from any part of the area. Thus, habitat protection does not stop hunting but only excludes industry.	• Fisheries Joint Management Committee, 2001
• National marine conservation area proposal for Lancaster Sound area was prepared in 1987 and identified as a priority in Mondor et al (1995) but the feasibility assessment for the proposed NMCA was suspended at the request of local Inuit. • Rationale for proposed NMCA is that this is an area of high primary productivity as well as a crucial migratory and feeding area. • Lancaster Sound has the single largest summer concentration of narwhal in the world; nearly half of the world population of 20,000 is found in Prince Regent Inlet, west of Baffin Island, every year.	• Mercier and Mondor, 1995 • Contact: Parks Canada; web: www.pc.gc.ca/progs/amnc-nmca/index_E.asp
• Critical habitat for the North Atlantic right whale and harbor porpoise. • Proposed as an NMCA in the mid-1980s by Parks Canada but met with significant local opposition; an NMCA proposal in the Bay of Fundy may be reactivated in future.	• Contact: Parks Canada; web: www.pc.gc.ca/progs/amnc-nmca/index_E.asp
• Site remains of tremendous value with the greatest diversity of representative oceanographic, geological, biological and cultural features of the South Labrador Shelf marine region. • Proposed in 1997 as a national marine conservation area but not well received by local people; abandoned 1999 by Parks Canada. According to Jon Lien (1999): 'Canada's policy and legislation seemed to poorly fit the NE Newfoundland Coast situation; it certainly did not provide assistance or options that were obvious to hard-pressed fishing communities.' • The failure of this proposal provides a lesson in the importance of strategic planning and public process in working for MPAs.	• Lien, 1999; Mercier, 1995 • Contact: Jon Lien, Whale Research Group, 230 Mount Scio Rd, St John's, NF, A1C 5S7 Canada; email: jlien@morgan.ucs.mun.ca • Contact: Parks Canada; web: www.pc.gc.ca/progs/amnc-nmca/index_E.asp
• MPA designated in 1992 with federal management under NMS programme, IUCN Category VI. • Outstanding biological, geological, oceanographic and cultural features, including wealth of marine life: various marine mammal species, sea turtles and seabirds, and many commercial fish species. With a high level of human use, it was hoped that an NMS could help coordinate management. In 2002, the sanctuary had a public review of the management plan. • Considerable cetacean and other research has revealed feeding habitat for humpback and other baleen whales and dolphins; part of migration corridor and feeding area for endangered North Atlantic right whale. • NMS regulations limit marine discharges and dumping and non-renewable resource development; fishing is permitted.	See also Tables 5.10 and 5.19 for additional US MPAs. • Gerry E Studds Stellwagen NMS, 2002; Recchia et al, 2001; Smith et al, 1999; Ward, 1995 • Contact: Sanctuary Superintendent, Gerry E Studds Stellwagen Bank National Marine Sanctuary, Scituate, MA 02066 USA; web: www.sbnms.nos.noaa.gov

Table 5.7 *continued*

Name of MPA or sanctuary, location and size	Cetacean and other notable species
(13) Great South Channel Northern Right Whale Critical Habitat Area • east of Cape Cod, Massachusetts, Great South Channel, Gulf of Maine • 3231 mi² (8371 km²)	• North Atlantic right whale, *Eubalaena glacialis*; also, humpback whale, *Megaptera novaeangliae*; Atlantic white-sided dolphin, *Lagenorhynchus acutus*; and others
(14) Cape Cod Bay Northern Right Whale Critical Habitat Area • north end of Cape Cod Bay, Massachusetts • 643 mi² (1666 km²)	• North Atlantic right whale, *Eubalaena glacialis*; also: humpback whale, *Megaptera novaeangliae*; Atlantic white-sided dolphin, *Lagenorhynchus acutus*, and others
[MPAs 15–16] **(15) Cape Cod Bay Ocean Sanctuary** • Cape Cod Bay, Massachusetts • 616 mi² (1596 km²) **(16) Cape Cod Ocean Sanctuary** • east of Cape Cod, along entire outer Cape Cod peninsula • 189 mi² (490 km²)	• North Atlantic right whale, *Eubalaena glacialis*; also: humpback whale, *Megaptera novaeangliae*; Atlantic white-sided dolphin, *Lagenorhynchus acutus*, and others
(17) Monitor National Marine Sanctuary • 16 mi (26 km) SE of Cape Hatteras, North Carolina • 1.3 mi² (3.4 km²)	• bottlenose dolphin, *Tursiops truncatus* • the wreck functions as a productive artificial reef, supporting temperate and tropical fish species; dolphins occur due to this productivity
(18) Jeffreys Ledge *proposed* **MPA or** *proposed extension* **to Stellwagen Bank NMS** • north of Stellwagen Bank, Gulf of Maine • size undetermined	• humpback whale, *Megaptera novaeangliae*; North Atlantic right whale, *Eubalaena glacialis*; fin whale, *Balaenoptera physalus*; minke whale, *Balaenoptera acutorostrata*; Atlantic white-sided dolphin, *Lagenorhynchus acutus*; harbor porpoise, *Phocoena phocoena*

Notes and rationale	For more information
• Federal endangered species protected area, IUCN Category IV, established 1997, managed by the National Marine Fisheries Service (NMFS, part of NOAA).	• Recchia et al, 2001
• Federal endangered species protected area, IUCN Category IV, established 1997, managed by the National Marine Fisheries Service (NMFS, part of NOAA).	• Recchia et al, 2001
• State ocean sanctuaries managed by the Massachusetts Dept of Environmental Management, IUCN Category V, established 1971. • These state ocean sanctuaries are not designed to protect cetaceans but they do limit marine discharges, dumping, non-renewable resource development and other activities that disturb benthic habitats, other than fishing.	• Recchia et al, 2001
• Existing MPA, federal management, designated because of historical significance of the wreck of the *USS Monitor*, a Civil War vessel. • Although bottlenose dolphins are regularly found in the area, the sanctuary itself is too small to afford real protection without considerable expansion of its size and effective mandate.	• Contact: Monitor National Marine Sanctuary, Fort Eustis, VA 23604-5544 USA; web: http://monitor.nos.noaa.gov
• Proposal would extend Stellwagen Bank sanctuary to cover additional area of whale distribution and habitat, or it could form a new national marine sanctuary or other MPA.	• Recchia et al, 2001 • Contact: Mason Weinrich; email: mason@whalecenter.org • Gerry E Studds Stellwagen Bank National Marine Sanctuary; web: www.sbnms.nos.noaa.gov

MARINE REGION 5: NORTHEAST ATLANTIC

The Northeast Atlantic Marine Region is where commercial whaling started, around 1000 AD in the Bay of Biscay, and where it flourished for centuries before moving north into the Arctic. The big, slow whales, particularly North Atlantic right whales, were nearly eliminated; they are still rarely seen in the region's waters. However, 28 other cetacean species are often found in various parts of the region. The Bay of Biscay has been found to be one of the region's most productive areas and the centre of highest cetacean diversity.

In the northern part of the Bay of Biscay, southwest of the Brittany coast of France, live bottlenose dolphins, harbor porpoises and minke whales, with common and striped dolphins and long-finned pilot whales more common in deeper waters. The prime habitat for other cetaceans begins roughly half way between the Brittany coast of France and northern Spain, including the abyssal plain and canyons, off the continental shelf. The species here include fin, sei, blue, sperm, short-finned pilot and false killer whales; orcas; Risso's, Atlantic white-sided and white-beaked dolphins; as well as beaked whale species including the northern bottlenose whale and Cuvier's, Sowerby's and True's beaked whales.

In the British isles, northern France and Denmark, the five main cetacean species are minke whales, harbor porpoises and bottlenose, common and white-beaked dolphins. In the productive waters at the edges of the region, however, off the Northern and Western Isles of Scotland and southwest Ireland, these species are often found feeding along with fin whales (seasonal), Risso's dolphins and orcas.

The Azores has a wide variety of pelagic cetaceans due to the islands' central Atlantic position on the mid-Atlantic Ridge and the sheer drop-off close to shore. Hunting in the canyons around the volcanic Azores are sperm, blue, fin and sei whales; northern bottlenose and the rarer beaked whales including Cuvier's; false killer and pilot whales; orcas; plus bottlenose, Atlantic spotted, common, Risso's and striped dolphins.

There are two main regional initiatives that apply to the Northeast Atlantic:

- The European Union Habitats and Species Directive, in its Natura 2000 programme, is designed to provide a network of marine- and land-based protected areas in the European Community, including the Portuguese island territories of Madeira and the Azores. A number of special areas of conservation, or SACs, have been proposed as candidate areas to protect bottlenose dolphin and harbor porpoise habitat in several of the member countries.
- The OSPAR Convention for the Protection of the Marine Environment of the Northeast Atlantic, formulated in 1992, has since been signed by all the contracting parties. As part of OSPAR, the parties are identifying marine species, habitats and ecosystems that need to be protected, conserved or restored. There is a mandate to promote the establishment of an MPA network to be put in place by 2010. Most OSPAR countries are in this region, although several are located in the Arctic Marine Region.

In addition, several countries in the region participate in the Helsinki Convention for the Baltic Sea, as well as ASCOBANS which originally focused on the Baltic Sea and North Sea, and recently has been extended to most of western Europe, and ACCOBAMS, which covers the Mediterranean Sea and Black Sea and Atlantic contiguous countries.

Marine protected areas for cetaceans are only in their infancy in this region. A number of SACs are being designed to protect resident inshore populations of bottlenose dolphins: in the Sado River estuary, south of Lisbon; in the Shannon River estuary in Ireland; in the Moray Firth in Scotland; and in Cardigan Bay, Wales, among other areas. The question is whether the habitat protection is substantial enough – in terms of size and quality of critical habitat protection. In most cases the answer is no. Also, SACs apply to only two cetacean species: the bottlenose dolphin and the harbor porpoise, and harbor porpoises only to a limited extent with SACs proposed, to date, in Germany and Ireland. Marine conservation programmes in Europe urgently need to be expanded to include other cetaceans and much larger areas, through a rethinking of the EU Habitats and Species Directive, plus application of the OSPAR Convention and other regional agreements, as well as through national programmes. At the time the EU Habitats and Species Directive was being written in the early 1990s, bottlenose dolphins and harbor porpoises were the only cetaceans known to live in inshore waters. Since then, the number of cetacean populations and species being studied in the region has increased steadily. Cetacean distribution and habitat needs are becoming increasingly well known and certainly well enough known that species such as short-beaked common, Atlantic white-sided and Risso's dolphins, among others, should be able to have their habitats protected as well.

There is one national cetacean sanctuary, located in the national waters of Ireland, but to date it has largely been a token designation and requires additional cetacean protection measures to achieve its potential (see Case Study 7 on p188).

The Northeast Atlantic Marine Region has four large marine ecosystems that have been identified: North Sea, Celtic-Biscay Shelf, Iberian Coastal and Faroe Plateau. The region covers the waters of the eastern North Atlantic, but not including the Norwegian–Greenland Sea or the inland Baltic Sea and Mediterranean Sea. Politically, it includes the waters of nine countries from Denmark, the UK and Ireland in the north to Spain and Portugal in the south, including the two Portuguese oceanic territories of Madeira and the Azores (see Table 5.1 on p89).

The oceanography of the region is dominated by the Gulf Stream, and its eastern extension, the North Atlantic Drift, which brings warm water to the more northerly latitudes of Europe, before returning in a clockwise gyre. As well, an infusion of even warmer, saltier water pours into the North Atlantic from the Mediterranean. This warm water flows north and when it encounters cold Arctic winds in winter, cools rapidly and sinks, forming a large part of the cold deep waters of the North and South Atlantic. These two large-scale water movements are responsible for the dynamic nature of the North Atlantic and have an impact on biological productivity as well as short- and medium-term climate change over the entire region.

In 1995, there was a total of 41 MPAs of all kinds in this marine region (Gubbay, 1995). The region has been divided into six biogeographic zones, five of which were represented by at least one MPA. In 2004, there were 25 existing (eight of which are proposed for expansion) and 25 proposed MPAs which feature cetacean habitat. Many of these are the SACs which may include bottlenose dolphin habitat. Some of the areas listed in Table 5.8 as SACs with probable dolphin habitat will no doubt prove, after more study, to have insufficient habitat worth protecting for cetaceans, although many have ecological or other importance to conservation. Still, these and other areas, with some expansion, may yet prove to be valuable for conserving dolphin and other cetacean habitat. Equally important, if SACs can incorporate the biosphere reserve idea of having IUCN Category I core areas, their value for conserving cetacean critical habitat will greatly increase. In addition to the MPAs, this marine region has one existing and two proposed international sanctuaries or MPAs of possible benefit to cetaceans as well as two existing national cetacean sanctuaries.

Case Study 6: Shannon River Estuary Special Area of Conservation

---

Shannon River Estuary Special Area of Conservation, *nominated*

Type: MPA officially nominated as a candidate special area of conservation (cSAC) under the EU Habitats and Species Directive (1992).

Location: Shannon River estuary on the west coast of Ireland: from Loop Head (County Clare) and Kerry Head (County Kerry) to Killaloe (County Clare), including the lower freshwater reaches of the rivers Kilmastulla, Mulcear, Fergus and Cloon and the tidal areas of the rivers Cashen and Deel.

Cetacean species: bottlenose dolphin, *Tursiops truncatus* (year-round); also: harbor porpoise, *Phocoena phocoena*; short-beaked common dolphin, *Delphinus delphis*; minke whale, *Balaenoptera acutorostrata* (all found in the waters adjacent to Lower River Shannon and occasionally entering the western boundary off Loop Head).

Additional species and other features: Seals, otters, herons, large colonies of guillemots and razorbills, ravens, choughs and peregrine. This important estuarine ecosystem has 14 Annex I habitats, including one priority habitat, and six Annex II species (such as, freshwater pearl mussel, sea lamprey, river lamprey and otter), as listed in annexes to the EU Habitats and Species Directive. Napoleonic coastal defences (five batteries) and promontory forts; monastic settlements date from the 6th century.

Size of protected area: 247.7 square miles (641.8 km^2).

Rationale: The area serves as a mating, breeding and feeding ground for a resident population of bottlenose dolphins, as well as wintering waterfowl, breeding seabirds and other species and habitats.

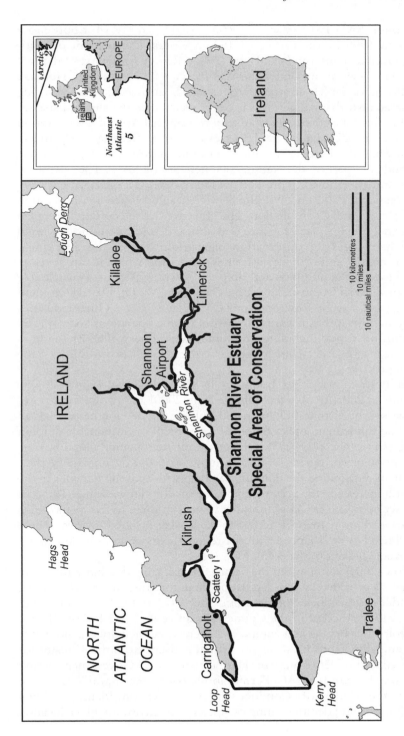

Bottlenose dolphins resident in the Shannon River are the main reason this area was proposed for protection as a special area of conservation under the EU Habitats and Species Directive. See Case Study 6.

Figure 5.10 *Map of the Shannon River Estuary SAC*

The Shannon River Estuary was first proposed as an MPA for bottlenose dolphins in 1995 by the Office of Public Works, Department of Arts, Culture, Gaeltacht and the Islands. In 1997, a Refuge for Fauna Order was drafted. This legislation, under the Wildlife Act (1976) and the Heritage Order (1994), was largely an attempt to regulate boat-based dolphin watching to minimize disturbance, but 'it was never enacted as the site and species involved fulfilled the criteria for nomination as Special Area of Conservation (SAC) under the EU Habitats and Species Directive' (Berrow, 2000). In late 1999, the Shannon Estuary was made a candidate SAC (cSAC) and it was then included as part of the Natura 2000 network of SACs. The operators, scientists and government representatives have devised a management plan, and the National Parks and Wildlife Service has developed a conservation plan, subject to public consultation. The objectives of the conservation plan are to manage the estuary for rare and annexed wildlife and to maintain annexed habitats. The conservation plan acknowledges the developing tourism potential and provides a framework within which it can develop. The goal is to make dolphins and dolphin watching part of a sustainable tourism product in County Clare (Brady Shipman Martin, David Pryor and Associates, and Natural Environmental Consultants, 1999). Other industries operating in or near the area are commercial fishing operations and some 50 manufacturing firms, including an aluminium refinery. The Shannon is Ireland's main river, its catchment area covering as much as two-thirds of the entire country.

With dolphin watching booming in the estuary – 15,000–20,000 participants in 2003 (double the number from 2000) and two new purpose-built vessels – the Shannon Dolphin and Wildlife Foundation has worked to prepare and implement a plan for the development of sustainable dolphin watching (Berrow, 2000, 2003). Objectives include maintaining a healthy dolphin population, raising public awareness of the dolphins and their environment, integrating the dolphin watching with ecotour activities in the region, and increasing the volume and value of dolphin watching. The goal is to attract up to 25,000 dolphin watch visitors in three to five years which would be worth more than €1 million to the local economy. Obviously, these goals will need to be balanced with the requirements under SAC legislation for the overall benefit to the dolphins.

Berrow (2003) summarized the details for managing dolphin watching in the estuary as provided by SAC legislation (Statutory Instrument 94 of 1997, made under the European Communities Act 1972 and in accordance with the obligations inherent in the Council Directive 92/43/EEC of 21 May 1992). Dolphin watching as a commercial recreational activity is a 'notifiable activity' and all persons must obtain written consent from the Minister for the Department of Environment, Heritage and Local Government before dolphin watching in the SAC. Permission is contingent upon agreeing to abide by the Codes of Conduct and Conservation Plan, providing monitoring data and demonstrating competence in environmental education and species identification. The National Parks and Wildlife Service is attempting to control the total time allowed watching dolphins. Operators complying with all requirements will be accredited under a special scheme and allowed to fly a dolphin flag from their vessels. These operators will be officially sanctioned.

SACs are still a young 'work in progress' and they hold great potential to improve dolphin habitat conservation. Still, certain other matters may need to be addressed if the proposed SACs in Ireland, the UK and around Europe are going to be effective for long-term marine habitat and cetacean conservation. First is the matter of size: are they large enough to protect cetaceans? The second, closely related, issue is zoning. One principle, advanced in this book, is that all MPAs will benefit from the identification and protection of IUCN Category I core habitat and by having generous transition and border areas, such as are found in the best biosphere reserves. To date, in the EU countries where SACs are being proposed, most appear to be IUCN Category VI areas with MPA management being imposed on areas which function as shipping corridors or even harbours, with already established urban, industrial or other uses. With such a mix of users all being catered for to some degree, marine habitat conservation becomes more difficult than, for example, in the southern hemisphere, the Americas or in parts of the Pacific where zoning of MPAs can be accomplished free from or less influenced by prior ownership or control, or by entrenched commercial pressures. Finally, as argued elsewhere in this book, the full application of ecosystem-based management principles is the best way to ensure that an ecosystem stays healthy long into the future.

The UK and Irish SACs are showing some early evidence of initiatives from researchers and other stakeholders, as well as management agencies, to consider all aspects for the management of the ecosystem. The Shannon River in Ireland has become the first region in Ireland to implement the Water Framework Directive, through River Basin Management Plans, to maintain water quality. Land-based sources of pollution around the Shannon River are being identified and brought under local management. The success of these efforts will be just as important as the more immediate and obvious impacts from modification and management of shipping and fishing, as well as dolphin watching and other marine-based tourism. But for an ecosystem-based management approach to work, it needs a comprehensive, coordinated approach and an appropriate legal framework, including the force of law and the necessary economic backing, to control and manage competing human uses so that the ecosystem can support dolphins and other species.

Case Study 7: Irish Whale and Dolphin Sanctuary

Irish Whale and Dolphin Sanctuary

Type: Large refuge or sanctuary comprising entire national waters with a ban on hunting.

Location: Coastal waters around Ireland to the EEZ limit which is generally up to 200 nautical miles (371 km) from shore or from national island groups, in the eastern North Atlantic.

Cetacean species: 24 species of cetaceans have been recorded in Irish waters. Eleven species are regularly recorded, according to Rogan and Berrow (1995): minke whale, *Balaenoptera acutorostrata*; fin whale, *Balaenoptera physalus*; bottlenose dolphin, *Tursiops truncatus*; striped dolphin, *Stenella coeruleoalba*; short-beaked common dolphin, *Delphinus delphis*; white-beaked dolphin, *Lagenorhynchus albirostris*; Atlantic white-sided dolphin, *Lagenorhynchus acutus*; Risso's dolphin, *Grampus griseus*; long-finned pilot whale, *Globicephala melas*; orca, *Orcinus orca*; and harbor porpoise, *Phocoena phocoena*.

Additional species and other features: Covers cetaceans only. There are many excellent shore-based lookouts and headlands for watching and enjoying cetaceans in the sanctuary (Hoyt, 2003).

Size of designated protected area: 146,800 square miles (380,300 km^2).

Rationale: Blanket protection for cetaceans from activities that threaten their lives. The creation of the sanctuary was an international statement from Ireland's government regarding whales residing in or travelling through national waters.

On 7 June 1991 the Irish Government declared Irish waters a whale and dolphin sanctuary. This is an extension of the legal framework already in place in Irish law that bans the hunting of all whale species, including dolphins and porpoises, within the exclusive fishery limits of 200 nm (371 km) of the coast (Rogan and Berrow, 1995).

The sanctuary does not have the legal status of a reserve or refuge, but protects cetaceans only through the Whale Fisheries Act and the Wildlife Act. The Whale Fisheries Act (1937) prohibits the hunting of baleen whales within the exclusive fishery limits of the state. In 1982, this was extended to protect all species of cetaceans, including dolphins and porpoises. The Wildlife Act (1976) provides additional protection to cetaceans from 'wilful interference', which includes interference within their habitat and destruction of their breeding places within the 12 nm (22.2 km) limit.

The Irish Sanctuary was created at a time when Ireland was immersed in international debates on whaling within the International Whaling Commission (IWC). In general, putting aside the IWC connection, the designation of national whale sanctuaries is seen by some as a token move by governments wishing to appear sympathetic to the environment either

The Irish Whale and Dolphin Sanctuary, declared in 1991, extends to the EEZ limits of Irish waters.
See Case Study 7.

Figure 5.11 *Map of the Irish Whale and Dolphin Sanctuary*

for internal (environmental perception) or external reasons (trade, tourism). Still, many Irish citizens learned for the first time through this publicity that Ireland had significant numbers of whales around its coasts and, indeed, that Ireland had a whaling past and this has contributed to an environmental awareness in Ireland (Rogan and Berrow, 1995). At the same time, research has been stimulated, including the funding of a number of offshore expeditions as well as an increase in coastal-based activity to explore the sanctuary and quantify the number of cetacean species and their seasonal presence in Irish waters (Gordon et al, 2000). Also, research has begun to quantify incidental captures of cetaceans associated with certain fisheries and has measured pollution levels. Finally, there has been economic impact: through international press and promotion, cetaceans are now part of the reason for people visiting Ireland and spending extra days; the sanctuary helps provide brand-name recognition (Hoyt, 2001).

From the start, the Irish Whale and Dolphin Group has worked with the National Parks and Wildlife Service, the fishing industry and others to make the sanctuary a reality. Still, it has a long way to go to become more than a paper sanctuary. Over the past few years, the Irish government has not enhanced its conservation reputation by repeatedly opposing certain cetacean sanctuaries in the South Pacific Ocean and South Atlantic Ocean at the IWC meetings. Also, there is a rapacious salmon fishery off the west coast of Ireland which requires better management, as well as a looming problem of potential dolphin mortalities from the development of a larger trawler fishery. A checklist for future management of the Irish Whale and Dolphin Sanctuary might include:

- more monitoring of cetaceans within Irish waters (including support of the national stranding and sighting scheme; publishing all verifiable strandings; using sighting data to identify important calving and feeding grounds);
- monitoring, quantifying and reducing any incidental mortality in existing and future fisheries;
- monitoring, evaluating and mitigating the impact of contaminants on cetaceans;
- evaluating the food needs of Irish cetaceans in light of the current state and history of fisheries exploitation;
- stock assessments for cetaceans determined to be endangered or vulnerable in Irish waters – especially for those species that have been exploited in Irish waters;
- monitoring and evaluating the impact of whale watching on cetaceans, should the industry grow much larger; and
- monitoring and evaluating the impact of global warming on cetaceans.

Many of the above might well be done as part of existing research, monitoring or other management programmes, with appropriate fine-tuning so that important cetacean questions can be answered too.

In the Irish Whale and Dolphin Sanctuary, as well as in the recently declared national cetacean sanctuaries in Papua New Guinea, the Cook Islands, Ecuador, México and other countries and territories (see Table 1.2 on p17), an opportunity now exists to enhance cetacean conservation by identifying the critical habitat of cetaceans and using ecosystem-based management principles. Most of these sanctuaries were created in response to IWC debates, and currently protect cetaceans mainly from hunting. Some national sanctuaries mandate additional modest protection or monitoring and research provisions, yet all areas fall well short of being an MPA.

A fresh, useful strategy for national whale sanctuaries would be to adopt the principles and architecture of marine biosphere reserves (see p25). For the smaller national waters of island countries and territories, most or all of the area, even to the limit of the EEZ, could be turned into a biosphere

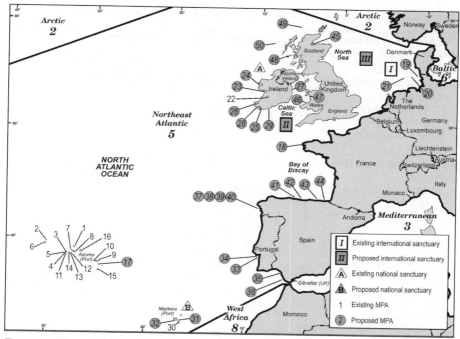

The roman numerals, letters and numbers correspond to the sanctuaries and MPAs listed and described in Table 5.8.

Figure 5.12 *Map of Marine Region 5: Northeast Atlantic MPAs and sanctuaries*

reserve, with smaller highly productive and fragile key areas set aside in legally binding, highly protected critical habitat core areas. Most of the biosphere reserve would consist of transition areas where sustainable fishing, whale watching and other commercial activities would continue to occur.

A biosphere reserve is a vehicle for engaging the public, researchers and government in conservation, providing a strong incentive for conservation as well as encouraging sustainable commercial activities. Although biosphere reserves are in many ways a kind of MPA, they have a proven scientific and conservation value for species, ecosystems and the people who interact with them, making them appear to be a fresh solution without the 'baggage' of the MPA label. Moreover, the Unesco-conferred 'biosphere' tag provides an attractive, high quality international label which can promote tourism far beyond a country's waters and marine attractions. Going for a 'biosphere reserve' confers a distinctive profile which can help with funding. Most of all, the real protection afforded by successful management of a biosphere reserve, together with strong legal protection of its core areas, is a means or at least a large step towards ensuring that marine resources will be put on a sustainable basis. Adopting a biosphere reserve approach would be a way to make the 'cetacean sanctuary' designation truly meaningful, turning a country's waters into significant, well-managed conservation areas.

Table 5.8 *Marine Region 5: Northeast Atlantic MPAs and sanctuaries*

Name of MPA or sanctuary, location and size	Cetacean and other notable species
INTERNATIONAL **(I) Wadden Sea (Waddensee) Nature Reserve** • in the coastal waters of Denmark (southwest), Germany and The Netherlands, extending 12 nm (22.2 km) from the coast	• harbor porpoise, *Phocoena phocoena* • also: gray seal, scoters and other seabirds
(II) **Celtic Shelf Break MPA,** *proposed* • located in the Celtic Sea, SW of England, W of France and S of Ireland, extending from 48°30'N and 52°N to 4°W and the 1000 m contour at the edge of the continental slope. It is bounded to the east by the English Channel, and to the south and west by the continental slope; depending on the precise boundaries, it would include parts of the EEZs of the UK, Ireland and France • no definite size proposed yet	• Atlantic white-sided dolphin, *Lagenorhynchus acutus*; short-beaked common dolphin, *Delphinus delphis*; harbor porpoise, *Phocoena phocoena* • also: basking sharks; leatherback turtles; commercial fish species such as hake, megrim, blue whiting and mackerel; diverse ichthyoplankton assemblages with more than 70 species identified; seabirds include gannets, fulmars, kittiwakes, petrels and shearwaters. The number of planktonic, benthic and other fish species currently recorded include 13 species considered common or abundant, 14 considered uncommon and 51 considered rare
(III) **Dogger Bank SAC,** *proposed* • Dogger Bank, North Sea, in the waters of Germany, Denmark, The Netherlands and the UK • 656 mi² (1,700 km²)	• harbor porpoise, *Phocoena phocoena* (high percentage of mother–calf groups); various other dolphins present • also: sandbank feeding area for birds, fishes and marine mammals

Notes and rationale	For more information
• This international reserve administered tri-nationally by Denmark, Germany and The Netherlands contains three national parks in all. • Not designed to protect cetaceans, but this reserve does include some harbor porpoise habitat (see also 'Harbor Porpoise Sanctuary' and Sylter Außenriff SAC, *proposed*, both listed under Germany below).	• Contact: Stephan Lutter, WWF North-East Atlantic Programme; email: lutter@wwfneap.org • WDCS Deutschland; email: info.de@wdcs.org; web: www.wdcs-de.org
• Proposed offshore marine protected area where small cetacean populations are currently believed to be under threat due to bycatch. The area is known to have a relatively diverse assemblage of planktonic, benthic and other fish species, with highly productive upwellings. • The Celtic Sea/southwestern approaches represent a key marine area without specific protection. The Celtic Sea may be a migration corridor for basking shark, and it is a spawning ground for various commercial fish (megrim, blue whiting and mackerel). Still, little is known about the marine ecology here, and further studies would be necessary to quantify the area's importance. • Work on cetaceans includes Hammond et al, 1995 and other references at right. Celtic Sea estimates include: harbor porpoises – 36,000 (confidence limits 13,000–103,000); 800 (130–5,500) Atlantic white-sided dolphins and 75,000 (23,000–285,000) common dolphins. These small cetaceans are known to be subject to a high mortality rate from bycatch in set-net and pelagic trawl fisheries in the area. • Future conflicts include potential offshore oil and gas development; some exploration activity has already been licensed by the UK and Irish Governments.	• Angel (unpbl); Evans, 1980; Hammond et al, 1995; Horstman and Fives, 1994; Northridge et al, 1995; Pingree and Mardell, 1981; Tregenza et al, 1997; Walton, 1997 • Contact: Stephan Lutter, WWF North-East Atlantic Programme; email: lutter@wwfneap.org; web: www.ngo.grida.no/wwfneap/Publication/briefings/CelticShelf.pdf
• In 2003, the German Federal Agency for Nature Conservation proposed part of the Dogger Bank as a special area of conservation (SAC) under the EU Habitats and Species Directive (DE 1003-301). • Rationale for protection is that this is the largest sandbank in the North Sea with well-preserved structure and function and importance as a feeding area for birds, fishes and marine mammals. • Largest part of the area is in UK waters, but substantial portions are also in German, Dutch and Danish waters; an 'international' SAC should be jointly agreed by all. • SACs only cover bottlenose dolphins and harbor porpoises under Annex II of the EU Habitats and Species Directive. This area may include important habitat for other cetacean species. Cetacean surveys for these areas could identify additional useful habitat to be set aside in highly protected core areas (IUCN Category I).	• Gubbay et al, 2002 • Contact: WDCS Deutschland; email: info@wdcs-de.org; web: www.wdcs-de.org; *see* also on the web: www.habitatmare natura2000.de • Stephan Lutter, WWF North-East Atlantic Programme; email: lutter@wwfneap.org; web: www.ngo.grida.no/wwfneap/Publication/briefings/Dogger.pdf

Table 5.8 *continued*

Name of MPA or sanctuary, location and size	Cetacean and other notable species
AZORES (Portugal) Arquipélago dos Açores **[MPAs 1–16]** **(1) Ilhéu de Baixo – Restinga Ilha Graciosa ZEC** • Ilhéu de Baixo and southeastern Ilha Graciosa (27°57'0"W, 39°0'50"N) • 0.9 mi² (2.4 km²), includes 16 per cent land **(2) Costa e Caldeirão – Ilha do Corvo ZEC** • Costa e Caldeirão (31°6'0"W, 39°42'0"N), west, north and east coasts of Ilha do Corvo • 3.8 mi² (9.8 km²) includes 82 per cent land **(3) Caldeira e Capelinhos – Ilha do Faial ZEC** • Caldeira e Capelinhos (28°45'W, 38°35'N), Faial • 0.9 mi² (20.4 km²), includes 90 per cent land **(4) Monte da Guia – Ilha do Faial ZEC** • Monte da Guia (28°37'21"W, 38°31'15"N), southeastern Faial • 1.4 mi² (3.6 km²), includes 30 per cent land **(5) Morro de Castelo Branco – Ilha do Faial ZEC** • Morro de Castelo Branco (28°45'15"W, 38°31'21"N), southwestern Faial • 0.5 mi² (1.4 km²), includes 24 per cent land **(6) Costa Nordeste – Ilha das Flores ZEC** • Costa Nordeste (31°10'W, 39°30'N), northeastern Flores • 4.8 mi² (12.4 km²), includes 25 per cent land **(7) Ponta dos Rosais – Ilha de S Jorge ZEC** • Ponta dos Rosais (28°18'36"W, 38°45'12"N), northwestern S Jorge island • 1.1 mi² (2.9 km²), includes 54 per cent land area	• bottlenose dolphin, *Tursiops truncatus*; also, in some areas: short-beaked common dolphin, *Delphinus delphis*; others • also: some sites have important seabird colonies including Cory's, Manx and little shearwater, Madeiran storm petrel, common and roseate tern

Notes and rationale	For more information
• Proposed as special areas of conservation (SACs) under the EU Habitats and Species Directive (also known as zona especial de conservação – ZEC) and received EU approval in Dec 2001. • Rationale for protection is that these sites offer important representative habitat with some evidence of bottlenose dolphin presence. However, at most sites, dolphins have only been seen in passing and in most cases it is not known whether they are resident or not. Current studies suggest the presence of at least one resident *Tursiops* population off Faial island, but more studies are needed. Because of the diversity of cetaceans found around the Azores, it is possible that some of the areas may offer some habitat protection for other cetacean species, if fragmentary. • Sites are part land, part marine and range from 9 to 100 per cent marine. Some of these sites already have some protection as natural forest or other reserves that is now being enhanced through ZEC proposals. • In many cases the marine parts of these sites will almost certainly be too small to conserve cetacean habitat. Cetacean research needs to be conducted as part of surveys for these areas and if important habitat can be identified, larger areas should be set aside in highly protected core areas (IUCN Category I). • These ZECs only cover bottlenose dolphins, as this is the only Azores cetacean presently included on Annex II of the EU Habitats and Species Directive. The Azores has outstanding cetacean habitat within its national waters, to the limit of its EEZ, as demonstrated by the reliable whale watch tours which are offered all around the islands (Hoyt, 2001, Viallelle, 1997). Sperm whales, various dolphin species and even beaked whales have habitat that could be defined and protected with the assistance of whale watch operators and the various researchers working with them.	• Hoyt, 2001; Prieto et al, 2001; Viallelle, 1997 • Contact: Ricardo Serrão Santos, Oceanography & Fisheries Dept, Univ of the Azores; email: ricardo@notes.horta.uac.pt; web: www.horta.uac.pt/projectos/life/mare.html; www.horta.uac.pt/projectos/life/hrsic.html • Secretaria Regional Do Ambiente, 9900-014 Horta, Açores, Portugal; web: http://sra.azores.gov.pt • Rui Prieto; email: rui.prieto@wapicode.com

Table 5.8 *continued*

Name of MPA or sanctuary, location and size	Cetacean and other notable species
(8) Costa NE e Ponta do Topo – Ilha de S Jorge ZEC • northern coast of the eastern end of the island of S Jorge (27°51'W, 38°35'N) • 14.3 mi² (37.1 km²), includes 91 per cent land	• bottlenose dolphin, *Tursiops truncatus*; also, in some areas: short-beaked common dolphin, *Dophinus delphis*; others • also: some sites have important seabird colonies including Cory's, Manx and little shearwater, Madeiran storm petrel, common and roseate tern
(9) Caloura-Ponta da Galera – Ilha de S Miguel ZEC • Caloura-Ponta da Galera (25°30'30"W, 37°42'30"N), S Miguel island • 0.14 mi² (0.36 km²), includes 17 per cent land	
(10) Banco D João de Castro (Canal Terceira – S Miguel) ZEC • Banco D João de Castro, Canal Terceira (26°36'30"W, 38°13'55"N), S Miguel island • 5.79 mi² (15 km²)	
(11) Baixa do Sul (Canal do Faial) ZEC • Baixa do Sul (28°35'24"W, 38°30'35"N), between Faial and Pico islands • 2.02 mi² (5.24 km²)	
(12) Ponta da Ilha – Ilha do Pico ZEC • Ponta da Ilha (28°2'W, 38°25'N), eastern Pico island • 1.56 mi² (4.03 km²), includes 35 per cent land	
(13) Lajes do Pico – Ilha do Pico ZEC • Lajes do Pico (28°15'22"W, 38°23'25"N), southern Pico • 0.49 mi² (1.28 km²), includes 17 per cent land	
(14) Ilhéus da Madalena – Ilha do Pico ZEC • Ilhéus da Madalena (28°32'50"W, 38°32'0"N), west of Pico Island • 0.59 mi² (1.52 km²), includes 14 per cent land	
(15) Ponta do Castelo – Ilha de Sta Maria ZEC • Ponta do Castelo (25°2'3"W, 36°55'47"N), Sta Maria island • 1.2 mi² (3 km²), includes 35 per cent land	
(16) Costa das Quatro Ribeiras – Ilha da Terceira ZEC • Costa das Quatro Ribeiras (27°126"W, 38°48'0"N), northern Terceira island • 1.01 mi² (2.61 km²), includes 40 per cent land	

Notes and rationale	*For more information*
• Proposed as special areas of conservation (SACs) under the EU Habitats et al, and Species Directive (also known as zona especial de conservação – ZEC) and received EU approval in Dec 2001. • Rationale for protection is that these sites offer important representative habitat with some evidence of bottlenose dolphin presence. However, at most sites, dolphins have only been seen in passing and in most cases it is not known whether they are resident or not. Current studies suggest the presence of at least one resident *Tursiops* population off Faial island, but more studies are needed. Because of the diversity of cetaceans found around the Azores, it is possible that some of the areas may offer some habitat protection for other cetacean species, if fragmentary. • Sites are part land, part marine and range from 9 to 100 per cent marine. Some of these sites already have some protection as natural forest or other reserves that is now being enhanced through ZEC proposals. • In many cases the marine parts of these sites will almost certainly be too small to conserve cetacean habitat. Cetacean research needs to be conducted as part of surveys for these areas and if important habitat can be identified, larger areas should be set aside in highly protected core areas (IUCN Category I). • These ZECs only cover bottlenose dolphins, as this is the only Azores cetacean presently included on Annex II of the EU Habitats and Species Directive. The Azores has outstanding cetacean habitat within its national waters, to the limit of its EEZ, as demonstrated by the reliable whale watch tours which are offered all around the islands (Hoyt, 2001, Viallelle, 1997). Sperm whales, various dolphin species and even beaked whales have habitat that could be defined and protected with the assistance of whale watch operators and the various researchers working with them.	• Hoyt, 2001; Pietro 2001; Viallelle, 1997 • Contact: Ricardo Serrão Santos, Oceanography & Fisheries Dept, Univ of the Azores; email: Ricardo@notes.horta. uac.pt; web: www.horta.uac.pt/ projectos/life/hrsic.html • Secretaria Regional Do Ambiente, 9900-014 Horta, Açores, Portugal; web: http://sra.azores.gov.pt • Rui Prieto; email: rui.prieto@wapicode.com

Table 5.8 *continued*

Name of MPA or sanctuary, location and size	Cetacean and other notable species
(17) **Formigas Islets and Dollabarat Reef (Canal S Miguel-Sta Maria) Natural Reserve (Reserva Natural Ilhéu das Formigas e Recife Dollabarat),** *proposed as an* **OSPAR MPA and ZEC** • Ilhéu das Formigas e Recife Dollabarat (25°45'W, 37°15'N), between S Miguel and Sta Maria • 14.7 mi² (38 km²)	• bottlenose dolphin, *Tursiops truncatus*; possibly other cetaceans • also: loggerhead turtles, black coral, pelagic fish
FRANCE République Française	
(18) **Iroise Marine National Park (Parc National Marin d'Iroise),** *proposed* • western tip of Britanny, France, at 48°25'N, 5°W including islands of Ouessant and Sein and Molène archipelago, eastern North Atlantic Ocean • 772 mi² (2000 km²)	• bottlenose dolphin, *Tursiops truncatus*; transient: long-finned pilot whale, *Globicephala melas* and short-beaked common dolphin, *Delphinus delphis* • also: breeding Atlantic gray seal, common seal; seven fish species and eight birds are on national red list; area is known for abundant algal communities, seagrass and colonies of nesting seabirds
GERMANY Federal Republic of Germany Bundesrepublik Deutschland *(19)* **Harbor Porpoise Sanctuary and SAC, National Park Wadden Sea of Schleswig-Holstein,** *proposed extension* • West of the islands of Sylt and Amrum, northern German Wadden Sea, northern German Bight, off the southern North Sea, within 12 nm (22.2 km) limit; extension would be outside of the 12 nm (22.2 km) limit	• harbor porpoise, *Phocoena phocoena* • also: gray seal; up to 200,000 scoters

Notes and rationale	For more information
• A nature reserve since 1988, this site is partly a European Site of Community Importance (SCI) and is proposed for protection as an OSPAR Convention MPA. • Rationale is that it is a seamount with shallow reefs and important feeding grounds, spawning and nursery areas for many fish species. • Management and protection regime still has to be put in place.	• Contact: Stephan Lutter, WWF North-East Atlantic Programme; email: lutter@wwfneap.org; web: www.ngo.grida.no/ wwfneap/Publication/ briefings/FormigasBank.pdf • Rui Prieto; email: rui.prieto@wapicode.com
• Proposed as a marine national park, Iroise Marine National Park has been considered for a regional nature park, a natural reserve, a candidate biosphere reserve and an EC Birds Directive site, with the main goal of preserving biodiversity. A marine national park would limit human disturbance and pressures, though present levels are considered very low. • In France, the role of a marine national park is to manage the marine environment to conserve its biodiversity. To create a marine national park, a special decree is needed that defines the park in terms of species and habitats. Also, there must be a management plan with a biological and habitat inventory. Human activities must be integrated into the plan if they form part of the conservation objective. The application of the management plan must include enforcement (through marine patrols and implementing educational programmes). • Studies by Liret et al (2001) have charted dolphin habitat use and home ranges over more than four years.	*See also* Table 5.6 for additional French MPAs • Liret et al, 2001 • Contact: Celine Liret, Laboratoire d'Étude des Mammifères Marins Ocèanopolis, BP 411, 29275 Brest cedex, France; email: celine.liret@oceanopolis.com • Iroise Marine National Park; email: philippe.le-niliot@ bretagne.environnement. gouv.fr
• On 15 Oct 1999, the parliament of Schleswig-Holstein state, Germany, voted to create a small cetacean sanctuary within the existing National Park Wadden Sea of Schleswig-Holstein. This park is part of the Wadden Sea Nature Reserve – an international reserve administered jointly by Germany, The Netherlands and Denmark (see Wadden Sea Nature Reserve above). • Since 1999, the sanctuary has been nominated as an SAC and, in 2001, scientists and WWF proposed for protection the adjacent waters as they serve as a key porpoise corridor (see Sylter Außenriff SAC and other proposed SACs below). • More than 4500 harbor porpoises reside in the area; up to 15 per cent of the sightings are calves; this is the first porpoise calving ground found in the North Sea. • A variety of bottom fauna and a highly productive food web are based on the nutrient-rich effluents of the river Elbe which mix with the coastal current.	See also Table 5.9 for additional German MPAs. • Hammond et al, 1995; IUCN, 1997; Prochnow, 2001; Schmidt and Hussel, 1994, 1995; Sonntag et al, 1999 • Contact: WDCS Deutschland; email: info.de@wdcs.org; web: www.wdcs-de.org • Stephan Lutter, WWF North-East Atlantic Programme; email: lutter@wwfneap.org; web: www.ngo.grida.no/ wwfneap/Projects/ MPAmap.htm

Table 5.8 *continued*

Name of MPA or sanctuary, location and size	Cetacean and other notable species
(20) **Sylter Außenriff SAC,** *proposed* • North Sea waters west of Sylt and Amrum islands • 2052 mi² (5317 km²)	• harbor porpoise, *Phocoena phocoena* (high percentage of mother–calf groups); other cetaceans present
(21) **Borkum-Riffgrund SAC,** *proposed* • west of the German Bight, North Sea, German waters • 230 mi² (595 km²)	• year-round: harbor porpoise, *Phocoena phocoena*; other cetaceans may be present
IRELAND Eire **(A) Irish Whale and Dolphin Sanctuary** • coastal waters of Ireland to 200 nm (371 km) • 146,800 mi² (380,300 km²) **See Case Study 7.**	• 24 cetacean species seen in Irish waters, 11 regularly (Berrow and Rogan, 1997; Berrow et al, 2002): minke whale, *Balaenoptera acutorostrata*; fin whale, *Balaenoptera physalus*; bottlenose dolphin, *Tursiops truncatus*; striped dolphin, *Stenella coeruleoalba*; short-beaked common dolphin, *Delphinus delphis*; white-beaked dolphin, *Lagenorhynchus albirostris*; Atlantic white-sided dolphin, *Lagenorhynchus acutus*; Risso's dolphin, *Grampus griseus*; long-finned pilot whale, *Globicephala melas*; orca, *Orcinus orca*; harbor porpoise, *Phocoena phocoena*
(22) Shannon River Estuary SAC • Shannon River Estuary, counties Clare, Kerry, Limerick and Tipperary, west coast of Ireland • 247.7 mi² (641.8 km²) **See Case Study 6.**	• bottlenose dolphin, *Tursiops truncatus* (year-round); sporadic: short-beaked common dolphin, *Delphinus delphis*; minke whale, *Balaenoptera acutorostrata* • also: seals, otters, herons, large colonies of guillemots and razorbills, ravens, choughs and peregrines

Notes and rationale	For more information
• Proposed in 2003 by the German Federal Agency for Nature Conservation as an SAC under the EU Habitats and Species Directive (DE 1209-301). • Rationale for protection is that this is the largest known concentration of harbor porpoises in German waters (porpoise population estimated at 4000–6500). It also has a reef habitat and typical sandbank.	• Contact: WDCS Deutschland; email: info.de@wdcs.org; web: www.wdcs-de.org; also: www.habitatmare natura2000.de
• Proposed as SAC under the EU Habitats and Species Directive (DE 2104-301). • Rationale for protection is that this area is a flat sandbank with reef areas; harbor porpoises live in the area year-round and may belong to small western North Sea population (centred off the coast of The Netherlands).	• Contact: WDCS Deutschland; email: info.de@wdcs.org; web: www.wdcs-de.org; also: www.habitatmare natura2000.de
• Established June 1991, the Irish Whale and Dolphin Sanctuary is a large refuge or sanctuary comprising the entire national waters of Ireland with a ban on hunting cetaceans. • Created with great optimism, the sanctuary has led to increased awareness and research into cetaceans, but the level of cetacean and ecosystem protection could be greatly increased through real management as an MPA, perhaps along the lines of a biosphere reserve with highly protected core areas for cetacean critical habitats.	• Berrow, 2001; Berrow and Petch, 1998; Berrow and Rogan, 1997; Berrow et al, 2002; Evans, 1980; Hoyt, 2001; Rogan and Berrow, 1995 • Contact: Simon Berrow; email: simon.berrow@iwdg.ie • Emer Rogan, Dept of Zoology, University College Cork, Prospect Row, Cork, Ireland; email: e.rogan@ucc.ie • Irish Whale and Dolphin Group; web: www.iwdg.ie • See also references (some of which may be downloaded as PDFs) at www.iwdg.ie/ downloads.asp?cat=26 and www.iwdg.ie/ categories.asp?cat=51
• First proposed as an MPA in 1995; in 1999, the area was officially nominated as an SAC under the EU Habitats and Species Directive (1992) and is now in the process of designation. • Rationale for protection is that this is a prime area with an estuarine ecosystem which serves as a mating, breeding and feeding ground for a resident population of bottlenose dolphins. • Dolphin watching is popular with this population; management strategies are discussed in Case Study 6.	• Berrow, 2000; Berrow and Holmes, 1999; Berrow et al, 1996; Brady Shipman Martin et al, 1999; IWDG, 2000 • Contact: Simon Berrow; email: sdwf@oceanfree.net • Irish Whale and Dolphin Group; web: www.iwdg.ie; www.shannondolphins.ie

Table 5.8 *continued*

Name of MPA or sanctuary, location and size	Cetacean and other notable species
(23) Galway Bay SAC, *proposed* • Galway Bay, Co Galway	• bottlenose dolphin, *Tursiops truncatus*; harbor porpoise, *Phocoena phocoena*; other cetaceans sporadic
(24) North Connemara SAC, *proposed* • off North Connemara coast, Co Galway	• bottlenose dolphin, *Tursiops truncatus*
[MPAs 25–26] **(25) Roaringwater Bay SAC,** *proposed* • Roaringwater Bay, Co Cork **(26) Blasket Islands SAC,** *proposed* • Blasket Islands, Co Kerry	• harbor porpoise, *Phocoena phocoena*; other cetaceans sporadic
[MPAs 27–28] **(27) Dublin Bay SAC,** *proposed* • Dublin Bay, Co Dublin **(28) Dursey Island SAC,** *proposed* • Dursey Island, Co Cork	• harbor porpoise, *Phocoena phocoena*; other cetaceans sporadic
(29) Old Head of Kinsale SAC, *proposed* • Old Head of Kinsale, Co Cork • no size data	• harbor porpoise, *Phocoena phocoena*; short-beaked common dolphin, *Delphinus delphis*; Risso's dolphin, *Grampus griseus*; minke whale, *Balaenoptera acutorostrata*; fin whale, *Balaenoptera physalus;* other species sporadic • also: breeding seabirds
MADEIRA (Portugal) **(B) Madeiran 'Marine Mammal Sanctuary'** • coastal waters of the Madeira Islands, 615 mi (990 km) southwest of Lisbon, Portugal, to the limits of Madeira's EEZ • 166,000+ mi^2 (430,000+ km^2)	• sperm whale, *Physeter macrocephalus*; pygmy sperm whale, *Kogia breviceps*; blue whale, *Balaenoptera musculus*; fin whale, *Balaenoptera physalus*; sei whale, *Balaenoptera borealis*; minke whale, *Balaenoptera acutorostrata*; humpback whale, *Megaptera novaeangliae*; bottlenose dolphin, *Tursiops truncatus*; rough-toothed dolphin, *Steno bredanensis*; seven other dolphin species; three beaked whales • also: Mediterranean monk seal

Notes and rationale	For more information
• Proposed MPA under EU legislation as an SAC under Annex 1 habitat criteria. • Rationale for protection is that the area is thought to provide habitat that is part of the ecological requirements of bottlenose dolphins and in some cases harbor porpoises.	• IWDG, 2000 • Contact: Irish Whale and Dolphin Group; web: www.iwdg.ie • Simon Berrow; email: simon.berrow@iwdg.ie
• Proposed MPA under EU legislation as an SAC under Annex 1 habitat criteria. • Rationale for protection is that the area is thought to provide habitat that is part of the ecological requirements of bottlenose dolphins.	• IWDG, 2000 • Contact: Irish Whale and Dolphin Group; web: www.iwdg.ie • Simon Berrow; email: simon.berrow@iwdg.ie
• Proposed MPA under EU legislation as an SAC for harbor porpoises. • Rationale for protection is that the area is thought to provide habitat that is part of the ecological requirements of harbor porpoises.	• IWDG, 2000 • Contact: Irish Whale and Dolphin Group; web: www.iwdg.ie • Simon Berrow; email: simon.berrow@iwdg.ie
• Proposed MPA under EU legislation as an SAC under Annex 1 habitat criteria. • Rationale for protection is that the area is thought to provide habitat that is part of the ecological requirements of harbor porpoises.	• IWDG, 2000 • Contact: Irish Whale and Dolphin Group; web: www.iwdg.ie • Simon Berrow; email: simon.berrow@iwdg.ie
• Proposed MPA under EU legislation as an SAC under Annex 1 habitat criteria. • Rationale for protection is that the area is thought to provide habitat that is part of the ecological requirements of harbor porpoises. • This area also supports other cetacean and seabird populations in near- to offshore waters and may be worth expanding as a larger cetacean MPA.	• IWDG, 2000 • Contact: Irish Whale and Dolphin Group; web: www.iwdg.ie • Simon Berrow; email: simon.berrow@iwdg.ie
• On 16 Apr 1986, the Madeiran Parliament declared Madeiran waters, to the limits of its EEZ, to be protected for all marine mammals (whales and dolphins as well as seals, and especially the Mediterranean monk seal). • Rationale is to protect the marine mammals of the Madeira Islands, including the endangered Mediterranean monk seal. • Madeiran whalers gave up whaling in the early 1980s. Some now fashion harpoons and whaling ships for souvenirs and museum pieces. Industries operating in the area include shipping traffic and commercial fishing. • Although not formally called a marine mammal sanctuary, all marine mammal species are legally protected from direct catches, killing and capture to the limit of Madeira's EEZ.	• Contact: Luís Freitas, Director of the Whale Museum of Madeira, Largo Manuel Alves,9200-032 Caniçal, Madeira; email: lfreitasmb@mail.telepac.pt

Table 5.8 *continued*

Name of MPA or sanctuary, location and size	Cetacean and other notable species
[MPAs 30–32] **(30) Ilhas Desertas Natural Reserve (Reserva Natural das Ilhas Desertas) and ZEC** • Ilhas Desertas (16°29'30"W, 32°30'0"N) • 37.3 mi² (96.7 km²) **(31) Ponta de S. Lourenço ZEC,** *proposed* • Ponta de S. Lourenço, (16°41'0"W, 32°44'20"N) • 7.2 mi² (18.6 km²) **(32) Ilhéu da Viúva Natural Reserve (Reserva Natural das Ilhéu da Viúva) and ZEC,** *proposed* • Ilhéu da Viúva (16°51'50"W, 32°48'25"N) • 6.6 mi² (17.1 km²)	• bottlenose dolphin, *Tursiops truncatus* • also: includes habitat for the Mediterranean monk seal and (on land) many species of plants including endemics of the Madeiran archipelago
PORTUGAL República Portuguesa **(33) Sado Estuary Natural Reserve (Reserva Natural Estuário do Sado) and Ramsar area,** *proposed* **for ZEC** • Sado Estuary (8°43'29"W, 38°27'48"N) • existing size is 92.5 mi² (239.7 km²) • proposed extension would join the areas of the natural reserve and RAMSAR site and add an extra area to create a ZEC of 120 mi² (309.7 km²)	• resident: bottlenose dolphin, *Tursiops truncatus*; occasionally: harbor porpoise, *Phocoena phocoena* • also: abundant bird species in the estuary
(34) Arrábida Natural Park (Parque Natural da Arrábida) and Marine Natural Reserve, *proposed* **for expansion as ZEC** • between Praia da Foz (north of Cape Espichel) and Forte de Albarquel, west of Sado Estuary • land-based protected area: 42.7 mi² (110.5 km²) with small marine component; proposed ZEC (land + marine): 79.7 mi² (206.6 km²)	• resident: bottlenose dolphin, *Tursiops truncatus*; occasionally: harbor porpoise, *Phocoena phocoena*; short-beaked common dolphin, *Delphinus delphis*; striped dolphin, *Stenella coeruleoalba* • also: diverse, outstanding range of fauna and flora
SPAIN Reino de España **(35) Doñana National Park (Parque Nacional de Doñana) and** *proposed* **SAC** • off Andalucia, southwest Spain	• various cetaceans, migratory at minimum, possibly some resident

Notes and rationale	For more information
• Proposed as an SAC under the EU Habitats and Species Directive (also known as zona especial de conservação – ZEC). • Rationale for protection is that this is important representative habitat with some evidence of bottlenose dolphin presence. • Ilhas Desertas Natural Reserve is zoned for strict protection as a 'reserva integral' (IUCN Category I) on land and 50 per cent of the sea area. These islands are the main habitat of the Mediterranean monk seal for feeding and reproduction. The other two reserves are also areas used by the Mediterranean monk seal as well as bottlenose dolphins. • All three MPAs include 15 per cent land area.	• Contact: Luís Freitas, Director of the Whale Museum of Madeira, Largo Manuel Alves, 9200-032 Caniçal, Madeira; email: lfreitasmb@mail.telepac.pt
• Originally designated as a natural reserve, followed by protection as a Ramsar site, and now proposed as a ZEC which is equivalent to an SAC. • Rationale for protection is the resident dolphin population plus birds and fish in the estuary. • In the 1980s researchers began studying the Sado Estuary dolphins, applying photo-ID techniques. This population, resident in the Sado Estuary, has been followed for some two decades. The additional areas, proposed along the coast in the ZEC application, are important both as part of the bottlenose dolphin habitat and for protecting adjacent land areas to help regulate runoff and other land-based pollution effects. Besides pollution, considerable ship traffic and urban congestion present serious risks to this estuarine ecosystem.	• Freitas and dos Santos, 1999; Gaspar, 1999 • Contact: Marina Sequeira, Instituto da Conservação da Natureza, Lisboa, Portugal; email: sequeiram@icn.pt; web: www.icn.pt
• Marine natural reserve created in 2000; habitat-based proposal for a ZEC. • Rationale for protection is the resident dolphin population plus birds and fish and providing additional protection and status for water extension to the existing park.	• Contact: Parque Natural da Arrábida, Praca da República, 2900-587 Setúbal, Portugal; web: www.icn.pt • Marina Sequeira, Instituto da Conservação da Natureza, Lisboa, Portugal; email: sequeiram@icn.pt
• Rationale is protection of scenic natural landscape and biological diversity. • Existing land-based national park was designated in 1978 to protect coast with some nearshore marine component; as of late 2000, a marine portion of this area, plus an additional area, has been identified and proposed as an SAC under Annex 1 habitat criteria of EU legislation, but not as a cetacean SAC. Proposal to include cetaceans in the species criteria is being made by the Sociedad Española de Cetáceos – SEC (Spanish Cetacean Society).	See also Table 5.6 for additional Spanish MPAs. • Sociedad Española de Cetáceos, 2000 • Contact: Erika Urquiola, Sociedad Española de Cetáceos – SEC (Spanish Cetacean Society); email: urquiola@cetaceos.com or sec@cetaceos.com; web: www.cetaceos.com

Table 5.8 *continued*

Name of MPA or sanctuary, location and size	Cetacean and other notable species
(36) Breña y Marismas de Barbate Natural Park (Parque Natural de la Breña y Marismas de Barbate) and *proposed* SAC • off Andalucia, southwest Spain	• bottlenose dolphin, *Tursiops truncatus*; harbor porpoise, *Phocoena phocoena*; various cetaceans, migratory and possibly resident
[MPAs 37–38] **(37–38) Islas Cies and Complex Ons-Ogrove National Park (Parque Nacional Islas Cies y Complex Ons-Ogrove) with two *proposed* SACs** • off Galicia	• bottlenose dolphin, *Tursiops truncatus*
[MPAs 39–40] **(39) Islas Cies SAC, *proposed*** • off Galicia • 3.7 mi^2 (9.7 km^2) **(40) Complex Ons-Ogrove SAC, *proposed*** • off Galicia • 16.3 mi^2 (42.3 km^2)	• bottlenose dolphin, *Tursiops truncatus*
(41–44) Four additional SACs, *proposed* • two in Asturias and two in Pais Vasco • sizes undetermined	• bottlenose dolphin, *Tursiops truncatus*

Notes and rationale	For more information
• Rationale is protection of scenic natural landscape and biological diversity. • This natural park was designated for scenic and tourism purposes. It is a land-based natural park with coastline and nearshore waters protected. As of late 2000, a land and marine portion of this area, plus an additional area, has been identified and proposed as an SAC under Annex 1 habitat criteria of EU legislation, but not as a cetacean SAC. A proposal to extend the SAC of Frente Litoral del Estrecho de Gibraltar SAC (see Table 5.6 on p156) to include this natural park has been made by the SEC and also under the conclusions of the 'Mediterranean Project', financed by Spain's Environment Ministry.	• Sociedad Española de Cetáceos, 2000 • Contact: Erika Urquiola, Sociedad Española de Cetáceos – SEC (Spanish Cetacean Society); email: urquiola@cetaceos.com or sec@cetaceos.com; web: www.cetaceos.com • Mario Morcillo, BALAENA, Barbate, Spain; email: orcamar@iname.com
• Part of this area became a natural park in 1980. Currently it is in the process of becoming a much larger national park with both land and marine areas. As of late 2000, two parts of this area have also been identified and proposed as an SAC under Annex 1 habitat criteria of EU legislation. Nominations to include bottlenose dolphins under Annex I criteria are being made by the Sociedad Española de Cetáceos – SEC (Spanish Cetacean Society) following its efforts to identify ceacean populations around mainland Spain (see immediately below for more information on these two SACs). • Marine mammal research group CEMMA works here.	• Sociedad Española de Cetáceos, 2000 • Contact: Erika Urquiola, Sociedad Española de Cetáceos – SEC (Spanish Cetacean Society); email: urquiola@cetaceos.com or sec@cetaceos.com; web: www.cetaceos.com • Alfredo Lopez, CEMMA; email: cemma@arrakis.es
• As of late 2000, these proposed MPAs have been identified and proposed as an SAC under Annex 1 habitat criteria of EU legislation. The nominations to include bottlenose dolphins under Annex II criteria are being made by the SEC following its efforts to identify cetacean populations around mainland Spain. These two proposals are in addition to those listed above (MPAs 37–38). • Rationale is not specifically for bottlenose dolphins but dolphins are sometimes found in the SAC. • Marine mammal research group CEMMA works here.	• Sociedad Española de Cetáceos, 2000 • Contact: Erika Urquiola, Sociedad Española de Cetáceos – SEC (Spanish Cetacean Society); email: urquiola@cetaceos.com or sec@cetaceos.com; web: www.cetaceos.com • Alfredo Lopez, CEMMA; email: cemma@arrakis.es
• Four more areas have been proposed as SACs which include bottlenose dolphin habitat by the SEC following its efforts to identify ceacean populations around mainland Spain. As of late 2003, the two regions involved, Asturias and Pais Vasco, had not decided whether to present the proposals.	• Contact: Erika Urquiola, Sociedad Española de Cetáceos – SEC (Spanish Cetacean Society); email: urquiola@cetaceos.com or sec@cetaceos.com; web: www.cetaceos.com

Table 5.8 *continued*

Name of MPA or sanctuary, location and size	Cetacean and other notable species
UNITED KINGDOM United Kingdom of Great Britain and Northern Ireland (UK) *(45)* **Moray Firth Candidate SAC,** *proposed* • inner Moray Firth, northeast Scotland, North Sea; includes the Beauly/ Inverness Firths and the outer reaches of the Dornoch and Cromarty Firths • 584.2 mi² (1513.4 km²)	• bottlenose dolphin, *Tursiops truncatus*; occasionally: minke whale, *Balaenoptera acutorostrata*; harbor porpoise, *Phocoena phocoena* • additional species found in the subtidal sandbanks include communities of amphipods, bivalves and polychaetes, as well as spawning grounds and nursery area for juvenile fish species
(46) **Cardigan Bay Candidate SAC,** *proposed* • Cardigan Bay, west Wales • 370 mi² (958.6 km²)	• bottlenose dolphin, *Tursiops truncatus*; harbor porpoise, *Phocoena phocoena*; occasionally: short-beaked common dolphin, *Delphinus delphis* • also: gray seal, various seabirds
(47) **Lleyn Peninsula and the Sarnau (Pen Llyn a`r Sarnau) SAC,** *proposed* • northern Cardigan Bay, west Wales • 563.7 mi² (1460.2 km²)	• bottlenose dolphin, *Tursiops truncatus*; harbor porpoise, *Phocoena phocoena* • also: gray seal, various seabirds

Notes and rationale	For more information
• In 1996, part of the inner Moray Firth was proposed under the EU Habitats and Species Directive as an SAC to protect the resident bottlenose dolphin population, the northernmost bottlenose dolphins and the only population in the North Sea. • As part of a public process, a management scheme (first revision, 2003) has proposed measures to protect the dolphins and their habitat, to manage the area's marine environment for the benefit of the dolphins, their habitat and the submerged sandbanks, as well as to raise awareness about the dolphins and the benefits of having an SAC, and to enhance and promote the area's social and economic resources. • A compliance monitoring process has been put in place whereby relevant authorities who agree to be part of the process constantly review and report on their actions; these authorities have formed the Moray Firth Partnership and the Moray Firth cSAC Management Group.	• Arnold, 1997; Curran et al, 1996; Janik and Thompson, 1996; more information from www.morayfirth-partnership.org • Contact: Ben Leyshon, Scottish Natural Heritage; email: ben.leyshon@snh.gov.uk • Ellie Dickson, WDCS; email: ellie.dickson@wdcs.org • Joint Nature Conservation Committee (JNCC); web: www.jncc.gov.uk/ ProtectedSites/SACs election/default.htm
• Proposed under the EU Habitats and Species Directive as an SAC to protect the resident bottlenose dolphins, the only known population living off England and Wales. • The bottlenose dolphin population is estimated to be 130 animals. Bottlenose dolphins have been seen all round the Welsh coast, but mainly in Cardigan Bay where a small group, including calves, appears to be resident within the candidate SAC, as well as in the northern part of the bay. Part of this population also ranges around southwest England. The Cardigan Bay dolphins appear to use the area for all essential activities including feeding and breeding. • In late 1999, a management plan was prepared by a partnership of statutory authorities and local people. In 2003, a management plan review was undertaken. • Currently, a number of proposed SACs are found along the Cardigan Bay coast. WDCS researchers believe that the distribution of dolphins, as well as porpoises, throughout the bay means that at minimum these various coastal SACs could be linked and, even better, the entire bay should be made an SAC.	• Contact: Mark Simmonds, WDCS, email: mark.simmonds@wdcs.org; web: www.wdcs.org • For management plans, research papers, details of public meetings and contacts, see: www.cardiganbaysac.org.uk • Joint Nature Conservation Committee (JNCC); web: www.jncc.gov.uk/ ProtectedSites/ SACselection/default.htm
• Proposed under the EU Habitats and Species Directive as an SAC primarily to protect sandbanks, estuaries, coastal lagoons, reefs, large shallow inlets and bays but bottlenose dolphins are a 'qualifying feature'. • This area forms part of the range of the Cardigan Bay resident bottlenose dolphin population which is estimated to number 130 animals. Currently, a number of proposed SACs are found along the Cardigan Bay coast. WDCS researchers believe that the distribution of dolphins, as well as porpoises, throughout the bay means that at minimum these various coastal SACs could be linked and, even better, the entire bay should be made an SAC.	• Contact: Mark Simmonds, WDCS, email: mark.simmonds@wdcs.org; web: www.wdcs.org • Joint Nature Conservation Committee (JNCC); web: www.jncc.gov.uk/ ProtectedSites/ SACselection/default.htm

Table 5.8 *continued*

Name of MPA or sanctuary, location and size	Cetacean and other notable species
(48) **Hebridean Marine National Park,** *proposed* • Inner Hebrides, northwest Scotland, including the seas around Rum, Eigg, Muck, Coll and Tiree, as well as along the coast of the northwest Highlands from Mallaig to Crinan • size undetermined	• minke whale, *Balaenoptera acutorostrata*; white-beaked dolphin, *Lagenorhynchus albirostris*; short-beaked common dolphin, *Delphinus delphis*; bottlenose dolphin, *Tursiops truncatus*; Risso's dolphin, *Grampus griseus*; harbor porpoise, *Phocoena phocoena*; occasional, orca, *Orcinus orca* • also: basking sharks, golden eagle, white-tailed sea eagle
[MPAs 49–50] *(49)* **Atlantic Frontier MPA and World Heritage Site,** *proposed* • located on Atlantic Frontier continental shelf, northwest of Scotland • size undetermined *(50)* **St Kilda Archipelago SAC,** *proposed* • located around St Kilda, west of outer Hebrides, Scotland • 98.3 mi^2 (254.7 km^2) includes land and marine waters	• common: harbor porpoise, *Phocoena phocoena*; white-beaked dolphin, *Lagenorhynchus albirostris*; Altantic white-sided dolphin, *Lagenorhynchus acutus*; minke whale, *Balaenoptera acutorostrata*; occasional, long-finned pilot whale, *Globicephala melas*; short-beaked common dolphin, *Delphinus dephis*; Risso's dolphin, *Grampus griseus*; sperm whale, *Physeter macrocephalus*; orca, *Orcinus orca*; bottlenose dolphin, *Tursiops truncatus*; sei whale, *Balaenoptera borealis*; fin whale, *Balaenoptera physalus*; humpback whale, *Megaptera novaeangliae*; northern bottlenose whale, *Hyperoodon ampullatus*; Sowerby's beaked whale, *Mesoplodon bidens*; at least three other species including blue whale, *Balaenoptera musculus*, are classifed 'rare' • also: harbor, gray and hooded seals; pelagic and continental-shelf fishes

Notes and rationale	For more information
• This idea for a marine national park is being proposed under the National Parks Scotland Act 2000 to protect habitats, fauna and flora, including cetacean and fish species. • As Britain's first marine national park, this proposed MPA would bring together educational programmes, promote sustainable use, enable strengthened planning controls, better fisheries management, rerouting of oil tankers away from inshore routes and improve the value of tourism, fish and other products from the area by creating a high quality national park 'brand'.	• Contact: Hebridean Marine National Park Partnership, Kinvara, Bonawe, Oban PA37 1RL Scotland; email: hebridean.partnership@ virgin.net; web: www.hmnpp.org.uk
• This proposed offshore MPA could include habitat for some 15–20 cetacean species and their foodwebs. • Harwood and Wilson (2001) detail the implications of developments for cetaceans including oil exploration and extraction, as well as acoustic impacts. A protected area could bring these developments and threats under management. • In 1998, the Atlantic Frontier was proposed by Greenpeace as a World Heritage Site and supported by WDCS and other NGOs. Despite support in the UK parliament, however, the UK government decided not to include the Atlantic Frontier on its list of World Heritage nominations to be presented to Unesco. This does not preclude it from being presented at a later date and WDCS remains convinced of the value of this area for protecting cetacean habitat. • St Kilda Archipelago, situated in the Atlantic Frontier, is already a World Heritage Site and the area is proposed as an SAC. An SAC would extend protection to the waters around St Kilda, possibly including some cetacean habitat, and could be the nucleus of an Atlantic Frontier MPA. However, the current St Kilda SAC proposal seeks only to protect the habitats in and around the island. • In 1999, the prospects of massive oil exploration and production in the Atlantic Frontier, along with seismic testing (shown to have negative effects on whales and dolphins) as well the prospects of increasing shuttle tanker traffic to service new oil fields led to the St Kilda World Heritage Site being considered as a case for inclusion on the List of World Heritage in Danger, although it was not in the end placed on the list.	• Evans, 1980; Weir et al, 2001; Harwood and Wilson, 2001 • Contact: Mark Simmonds, WDCS, email: mark.simmonds@wdcs.org; web: www.wdcs.org • Joint Nature Conservation Committee (JNCC); web: www.jncc.gov.uk/ ProtectedSites/ SACselection/default.htm

MARINE REGION 6: BALTIC

In the Baltic Marine Region, the harbor porpoise is the main resident cetacean. Near the edge of its border with the Northeast Atlantic Marine Region (a line drawn from the northern tip of Denmark to the tip of southern Norway) white-beaked dolphins and minke whales are also found. Historically, other toothed whale species such as orcas were found in the Baltic, but are rarely seen today. Harbor porpoises, too, have suffered declines. In the Skagerrak Sea, for example, Swedish gill-netters (bottom-set gill nets for cod) were shown to have a high, unsustainable bycatch of harbor porpoises (Carlström and Berggren, 1996). In the southern Baltic Sea, since the 1950s, harbor porpoises have declined to a tenth of the original numbers probably due to toxic pollutants (Esping and Grönqvist, 1995). There are three species of seal present, mainly ringed and gray seals, followed by a small number of harbor or common seals.

The region has an active marine habitat conservation programme but it does not feature cetaceans. Some of the existing MPAs may cover some harbor porpoise habitat but none are known prime cetacean areas. The existing MPAs are mostly very small.

The Baltic Marine Region is considered to have one large marine ecosystem (LME): the Baltic Sea. It also includes the neighbouring sea, the Skagerrak, which is usually considered part of the North Sea. In many respects, the Baltic is similar to an inland sea or a massive estuary, and in the past 12,000 years has several times alternated between being a large freshwater lake and a brackish marine area as it is today. It is linked to the open sea circulation only by the narrow straits of the Sound (Oresund) and the Danish Belts (the Great and Little Belts) east of Denmark. These have a strong outflow of brackish water at the surface. Most of the inflow comes from rivers in the region, although there is also an incoming salty water bottom current from the North Sea.

Some ten countries border the Baltic Marine Region, from Norway, Denmark and Germany in the west to Sweden, Finland, Poland, Russia and the Baltic republics in the east. Most are party to various non-UNEP regional seas programmes which feature or include the Baltic Sea:

- In 1992, every Baltic Sea country, as well as the European Community, signed the Helsinki Convention, the full name of which is the Convention for the Protection of the Marine Environment of the Baltic Sea Area. As part of the convention, the contracting parties are obliged to establish a system of coastal and marine Baltic Sea protected areas.
- Baltic Sea countries are also party to the OSPAR Convention for the Protection of the Marine Environment of the Northeast Atlantic and some also participate in the EU Habitats and Species Directive, following the mandate to establish SACs.
- Finally, there is ASCOBANS, the Agreement on the Conservation of Small Cetaceans of the Baltic and North Sea. Entering into force in 1994, it is concerned with the conservation of small cetaceans and their habitat. ASCOBANS serves as a regional agreement of the Convention on

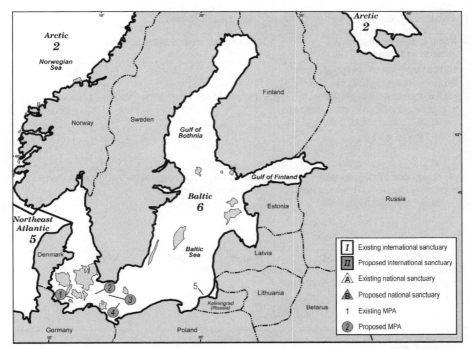

The roman numerals, letters and numbers correspond to the sanctuaries and MPAs listed and described in Table 5.9.

Figure 5.13 *Map of Marine Region 6: Baltic MPAs and sanctuaries*

Migratory Species (CMS) and has the power to set aside 'areas of special importance'.

To summarize, as of 1995, there was a total of 43 MPAs of all kinds in this marine region (Esping and Grönqvist, 1995). This region is divided into nine biogeographic zones with seven represented by more than one MPA and one zone with no MPA. In 2004, there were one existing and four proposed MPAs with cetacean habitat (see Table 5.9).

The IUCN 2002–2010 Conservation Action Plan for the World's Cetaceans has recommended one research and conservation initiative for this region (Reeves et al, 2003):

- to assess the abundance, distribution and population structure of harbor porpoises in the Baltic Sea and support efforts to promote their recovery.

Table 5.9 *Marine Region 6: Baltic MPAs and sanctuaries*

Name of MPA or sanctuary, location and size	Cetacean and other notable species
GERMANY Federal Republic of Germany Bundesrepublik Deutschland **(1) Fehmarnbelt SAC, *proposed*** • strait between German island Fehmarn and the Danish Lolland, Baltic Sea • 108 mi² (281 km²)	• year-round: harbor porpoise, *Phocoena phocoena*
(2) Kadetrinne SAC, *proposed* • central Baltic Sea, in German waters outside 12 nm (22.2 km) limit	• year-round (resident and migratory): harbor porpoise, *Phocoena phocoena*
(3) Westliche Rönnebank SAC, *proposed* • eastern Baltic Sea, in German waters outside 12 nm (22.2 km) limit	• migratory: harbor porpoise, *Phocoena phocoena*
(4) Pommersche Bucht mit Oderbank SAC, *proposed* • Oderbank, eastern Baltic Sea, in German waters outside 12 nm (22.2 km) limit • 427 mi² (1107 km²)	• year-round: harbor porpoise, *Phocoena phocoena*
RUSSIA Russian Federation Rossiskaya Federatsiya **(5) Kurshskaya Kosa National Park** • national park on the Baltiyskoye (Baltic Sea) • current size of marine portion is 26 mi² (66 km²); land part is smaller	• possible cetacean habitat: harbor porpoise, *Phocoena phocoena*

Notes and rationale	For more information
• Proposed as a special area of conservation (SAC) under the EU Habitats and Species Directive (DE 1332-301). • Harbor porpoises (maximum population 500) occur in the proposed SAC and surrounding waters and swim regularly through the Fehmarnbelt. For porpoises, it may be a recreational as well as partly a reproductive area.	See also Table 5.8 for additional German MPAs. • Contact: WDCS Deutschland; email: info.de@wdcs.org; web: www.wdcs-de.org; also: www.habitatmare natura2000.de
• Proposed as an SAC under the EU Habitats and Species Directive (DE 1339-301). • Harbor porpoises are regularly found in this region, as well as on migration. Acoustic porpoise detectors (PODs), first used in 2002, document regular porpoise presence.	• Contact: WDCS Deutschland; email: info.de@wdcs.org; web: www.wdcs-de.org; also: www.habitatmare natura2000.de
• Proposed as an SAC under the EU Habitats and Species Directive (DE 1249-301). • The eastern Baltic population of harbor porpoises may use this area as a migration route.	• Contact: WDCS Deutschland; email: info.de@wdcs.org; web: www.wdcs-de.org; also: www.habitatmare natura2000.de
• Proposed as an SAC under the EU Habitats and Species Directive (DE 1652-301). • Harbor porpoises here are probably part of the Eastern Baltic Sea population which numbers only about 600 individuals and is separate from the western Baltic. • On monitoring flights east and west of Rügen in May and July 2002, there were sightings of 79 animals during the reproductive and breeding period. Especially in July, hot spots were found on the Oderbank.	• Contact: WDCS Deutschland; email: info.de@wdcs.org; web: www.wdcs-de.org; also: www.habitatmare natura2000.de
• Established 1987, this coastal national park includes marine areas, equivalent to IUCN Category II. • Marine component thought to include cetacean habitat; surveys and habitat assessments required. • No information on surveys but harbor porpoises may be present.	See also Tables 5.3, 5.6 and 5.19 for additional Russian MPAs. • Contact: Teplyakov Gennadiy Nikolaevich, Kaliningradskaya Territory, Zelenogradskiy region, Rybachiy village, 238535 Russia; email: root@kknp.koenig.su or postmaster@ kknp.koenig.su

MARINE REGION 7: WIDER CARIBBEAN

In all, some 30 cetacean species use the Caribbean for seasonal or year-round habitat. Cetacean habitat in the Wider Caribbean Marine Region includes the year-round mating, calving and feeding grounds for many toothed whales and dolphins such as sperm whales (throughout the region), spotted and bottlenose dolphins in the Bahamas, various beaked whale species (in the Bahamas, St Lucia and Dominica, among other places). Also important are the seasonal mating, calving and/or nursery grounds for baleen whales such as humpback whales and possibly Bryde's whales. The North Atlantic right whales have important nursery areas in the far north of the region, along the US coast of Florida and Georgia. Both humpback and right whales have habitat that is in shallow water, and sometimes close to shore. The humpbacks are vulnerable, although they appear to be recovering. The North Atlantic right whale, with about 325 individuals left, is endangered and numbers are not increasing, mainly due to boat collisions.

One of the first high profile Caribbean MPAs was the Silver Bank Humpback Whale Marine Sanctuary, designated in 1986 by the Dominican Republic and expanded in 1996 and renamed the Marine Mammal Sanctuary of the Dominican Republic. It was established to protect the mating, calving and nursery ground of humpback whales in three of the key areas where they spend their winters (Navidad Bank, Samaná Bay as well as Silver Bank). Since then, other humpback wintering areas have been discussed as possible proposals, such as around Mouchoir Bank in the Turks and Caicos Islands. In the eastern Caribbean, the Soufrière Marine Management Area in St Lucia is a model community MPA managed mainly for protection of fishing resources but various toothed whales also gain some protected habitat. Nearby Dominica has the Soufrière/Scotts Head Marine Reserve with its special zoned activity areas; it is oriented toward protecting fishing as well as diving and other recreational resources, including whale watching for the local sperm whales and various dolphins. If cetacean critical habitat areas can be located and given IUCN Category I protection, this area could offer significant habitat protection to cetaceans. In 2002, México designated all of its national waters as a cetacean sanctuary, both Caribbean and Pacific coasts. Since then, researchers in both Guadeloupe and Venezuela have suggested sanctuaries.

Some 28 national governments have a role in Wider Caribbean marine conservation (see Table 5.1 on p89). The Wider Caribbean Marine Region covers the Caribbean Sea and Gulf of Mexico, with a small adjacent portion of the southwest North Atlantic Ocean. The region has two large marine ecosystems (LMEs) that have been identified: the Caribbean Sea and the Gulf of Mexico. In the northeast, the Bahamas and Turks and Caicos Islands form a boundary that extends around the Greater and Lesser Antilles to include the Caribbean coasts of South and Central America from French Guiana west. Moving clockwise, the region then extends west and northwest to the Gulf coasts of México and the US. Finally, the southeast US Atlantic coast is included from Florida north to Cape Hatteras, North Carolina. The inclusion of this portion of the North Atlantic makes the region slightly larger than the UNEP definition of the Caribbean used in regional treaties.

The warm surface Guiana Current flowing out of Brazilian waters defines and links the Wider Caribbean oceanography. From Brazil, this current joins the North Equatorial Current which then flows through the Lesser Antilles, around the western tip of Cuba, and into the Gulf of Mexico. In the Gulf, it loops around and flows east through the Florida Straits, turning into the Gulf Stream above the Bahama Bank. The deepest trench in the North Atlantic is southeast of here; the Puerto Rican Trench plunges to 28,232 feet (8605 m). As in most of the world ocean and all of the tropics, there is a slow flow of cold deep water at abyssal depths that does not mix with the warmer upper layers.

The Caribbean is noted for some of the most diverse coral reef faunas in the world, with about 14 per cent of the world's coral reefs located in the region (Stanley, 1995). There are mangroves on almost every coastline and extensive seagrass beds both of which show considerable diversity. The continental coast has coastal lagoons.

A regional association of Greater Caribbean countries was formed with the adoption of the Cartagena Convention in 1983, ratified in 1986. The key environmental treaty in the wider Caribbean, the Cartagena Convention, then set up the Caribbean Environment Program under the 1990 (SPAW) Protocol on Specially Protected Areas and Wildlife. The SPAW Protocol, which entered into force in June 2000, recommends the establishment of protected areas and other specific measures to provide a framework for developing a regional network of MPAs with ecosystem-level protection. The implementation is up to the individual states. The SPAW Protocol is also recognized as an instrument to help implement the Convention on Biological Diversity (CBD) signed by most states within the region. In 2003, the White Water to Blue Water Partnership, an initiative of the World Summit on Sustainable Development (WSSD), began working to help facilitate integrated watershed and marine ecosystem-based management.

In 1995, Stanley listed 104 MPAs of all kinds representing 7.9 per cent of the world total, with five out of six biogeographic zones within the region having at least one MPA. Fuelled by the SPAW Protocol, the Caribbean has become one of the more active areas for MPA conservation, with some 300 MPAs listed in a regional database. Few of these, however, have documentation of cetacean habitat. As of 2004, according to Table 5.10 prepared for this book, there are 33 existing and 15 proposed MPAs which feature cetacean habitat. Two of the 33 existing MPAs are proposed for expansion.

The Wider Caribbean is on Annex V of the International Convention for the Prevention of Pollution from Ships (MARPOL 73/78) and is defined as a special sea area (SSA) with more stringent standards for discharge of garbage. In addition, under the IMO General Provision on Ships Routing, the Florida coast is an 'area to be avoided'.

The IUCN 2002–2010 Conservation Action Plan for the World's Cetaceans recommends a number of research, education and conservation initiatives for this region (Reeves et al, 2003):

- to investigate interactions between river dolphins and fisheries in Amazonia and Orinoquia (also applies to Marine Region 9);
- to assess existing and planned water development projects and gold mining in the Amazon and Orinoco basins (also for Marine Region 9);
- to develop a conservation strategy for South American river dolphins (also for Marine Region 9);
- to investigate live-capture fisheries for bottlenose dolphins in México and Cuba; and
- to conduct cetacean abundance estimation workshops in Latin America (also for Marine Regions 9 and 17).

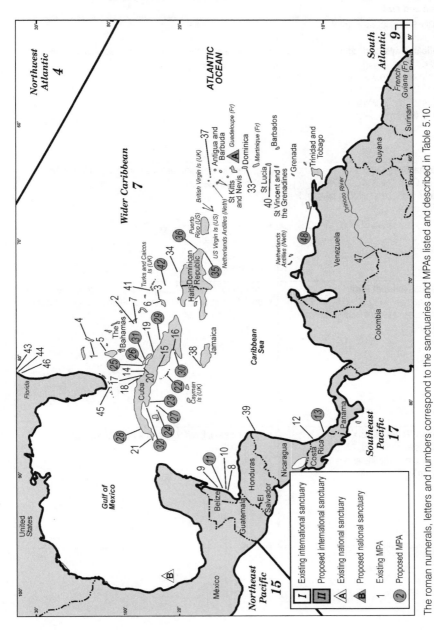

Figure 5.14 *Map of Marine Region 7: Caribbean MPAs and sanctuaries*

The roman numerals, letters and numbers correspond to the sanctuaries and MPAs listed and described in Table 5.10.

Table 5.10 *Marine Region 7: Caribbean MPAs and sanctuaries*

Name of MPA or sanctuary, location and size	Cetacean and other notable species
BAHAMAS Commonwealth of the Bahamas **(1) Pelican Cays Land and Sea Park** • located in Abaco, marine boundaries extend to the barrier island chain (26°24'27"N, 77°0'W) • 2.7 mi² (8.5 km²)	• bottlenose dolphin, *Tursiops truncatus*; various others • also: coral reefs
(2) Exuma Cays Land and Sea Park • Exuma Cays (24°31'N, 76°39'W) • 176 mi² (456 km²) includes land and marine areas	• bottlenose dolphin, *Tursiops truncatus*; various others • also: coral reefs
(3) Inagua National Park • Great Inagua Island (21°5'N, 73°21'W) • total land and marine size is 287 mi² (743 km²)	• bottlenose dolphin, *Tursiops truncatus*; various others • also: largest breeding colony of West Indian flamingos (50,000); coral reefs
(4) Abaco National Park • Abaco Island (26°0'N, 77°15'W) • total land and marine size is 79 mi² (205 km²)	• bottlenose dolphin, *Tursiops truncatus*; various others

Notes and rationale	For more information
• Established 1981 as a national park, IUCN Category II. • Rationale is to protect coastal, intertidal and marine habitats. Rationale is ecosystem-based but bottlenose dolphins and other cetaceans in nearshore waters are protected too. • The NGO Bahamas National Trust manages Bahamian national parks; management plan is being developed.	• Contact: Bahamas National Trust; web: www.bahamas nationaltrust.com • Diane Claridge, Bahamas Marine Mammal Survey; email: bmms@oii.net; web: www.bahamaswhales.org
• Established 1958 as a national park, IUCN Category II. • Rationale is to protect mangrove, coastal, intertidal and marine habitats. • Regular patrols to protect park species. • Marine boundaries extend only to the 100 fathom contour – 600 ft (180 m) depth. • The NGO Bahamas National Trust manages Bahamian national parks; management plan is being developed. • Cetacean surveys need to be done to determine habitat.	• Contact: Bahamas National Trust; web: www.bahamas nationaltrust.com • Diane Claridge, Bahamas Marine Mammal Survey; email: bmms@oii.net; web: www.bahamaswhales.org
• Established 1965 as a national park, IUCN Category II, in 1997, it was designated a Wetland of International Importance and in 2002 an Important Bird Area (Birdlife International); rationale is to protect mangrove, coastal, intertidal and marine habitats. • Marine boundaries extend only to the 100 fathom contour – 600 ft (180 m) depth. • The NGO Bahamas National Trust manages Bahamian national parks; management plan is being developed. • Cetacean surveys need to be done to determine habitat. • Bahamas National Trust is working with Ministry of Tourism to teach local residents how to be bird guides.	• Contact: Bahamas National Trust; web: www.bahamas nationaltrust.com • Diane Claridge, Bahamas Marine Mammal Survey; email: bmms@oii.net; web: www.bahamaswhales.org
• Established 1994 as a national park, IUCN Category II. • Rationale is to protect island, coastal and marine habitats. • Marine boundaries extend only to the 100 fathom contour – 600 ft (180 m) depth. • The NGO Bahamas National Trust manages Bahamian national parks; management plan is being developed. • Cetacean surveys need to be done to determine habitat.	• Contact: Bahamas National Trust; web: www.bahamas nationaltrust.com • Diane Claridge, Bahamas Marine Mammal Survey; email: bmms@oii.net; web: www.bahamaswhales.org

Table 5.10 *continued*

Name of MPA or sanctuary, location and size	Cetacean and other notable species
(5) Central Andros National Parks • several locations in the Central Andros islands (24°18'N, 77°52'W) • total land and marine size is 447 mi² (1158 km²) **(6) Little Inagua National Park** • Little Inagua (21°28'N, 72°57'W) • total land and marine size is 49 mi² (128 km²) **(7) Moriah Harbour Cay National Park** • Great Exuma (23°28'N, 75°39'W) • 21 mi² (54 km²)	• bottlenose dolphin, *Tursiops truncatus*; other cetaceans seen regularly in less than 100 fathoms or 600 ft (180 m) in the Bahamas (courtesy Diane Claridge, BMMS) are: minke whale, *Balaenoptera acutorostrata*; fin whale, *Balaenoptera physalus*; humpback whale, *Megaptera novaeangliae*; sperm whale, *Physeter macrocephalus*; dwarf sperm whale, *Kogia sima*; Blainville's beaked whale, *Mesoplodon densirostris*; Cuvier's beaked whale, *Ziphius cavirostris*; Atlantic spotted dolphin, *Stenella frontalis*; pantropical spotted dolphin, *Stenella attenuata*; Risso's dolphin, *Grampus griseus*; false killer whale, *Pseudorca crassidens*; orca, *Orcinus orca*; short-finned pilot whale, *Globicephala macrorhynchus* • also: manatee, coral reefs
BELIZE **(8) Port Honduras Marine Reserve** • north of Punta Gorda Town (16°12'52"N, 88°36'22"W) • 157 mi² (406 km²)	• bottlenose dolphin, *Tursiops truncatus*; other dolphin species possible • also: West Indian manatee
(9) Belize Barrier Reef Reserve System World Heritage Site • extends 160 mi (260 km) from the border of México in the north to the Guatemalan border to the south • 372 mi² (963 km²)	• bottlenose dolphin, *Tursiops truncatus*; other dolphin species possible • also: West Indian manatee, 500 fish species
(10) Swallow Cay Wildlife Sanctuary • Drowned Cayes area • 14 mi² (36.3 km²)	• bottlenose dolphin, *Tursiops truncatus* • also: West Indian manatee
(11) Turneffe Atoll MPA and Biosphere Reserve, *proposed* • Turneffe Atoll • no size data	• bottlenose dolphin, *Tursiops truncatus* • also: West Indian manatee, American crocodile and roseate tern

Notes and rationale	For more information
• Established in 2002 as one of ten new National Parks, protecting both marine and terrestrial areas and doubling the national system of protected areas to more than 700,000 acres or 1100 mi² (2850 km²). • Central Andros National Parks has extensive wetland with critical habitat for birds, crabs and iguanas; one of world's longest and best-preserved barrier reefs with the world's highest density of blue holes. Initial protection here is focusing on Central Andros with additional protection to be created in the north and south. • Rationale is to protect island forest, coastal, intertidal, mangrove and marine habitats. • Marine boundaries extend only to the 100 fathom contour – 600 ft (180 m) depth. • The NGO Bahamas National Trust manages Bahamian national parks; management plan is being developed. • Cetacean surveys need to be done to determine habitat.	• Contact: Bahamas National Trust; web: www.bahamas nationaltrust.com • Diane Claridge, Bahamas Marine Mammal Survey; email: bmms@oii.net; web: www.bahamaswhales.org • More information; web: www.bsc-eoc.org/ download/BNT-newsletter_ June02.pdf
• Declared a marine reserve (rated IUCN Category IV) in Jan 2000 to protect an important fish nursery but also includes 135 small mangrove islands, hundreds of protective cays and a barrier reef. • Use of gill nets is illegal. Cetacean distribution and habitat needs should be studied.	• Contact: Port Honduras Marine Reserve; web: www.southernbelize.com/ honduras.html
• Declared a World Heritage Site in 1996 with IUCN Category II, III and IV protection, this site includes seven existing marine reserves, national parks and natural monuments created 1977–1996 under the Fisheries Act (Chapter 174 of the Laws of Belize) and covering a wide range of typical coastal and marine ecosystems of Belize. • Areas include: Bacalar Chico National Park and Marine Reserve, Laughing Bird Caye National Park, Half Moon Cay Natural Monument, Blue Hole Natural Monument, Glovers Reef Marine Reserve, South Water Cay Marine Reserve and Sapodilla Cayes Marine Reserve. • Cetaceans are not specifically mentioned for protection but area would almost certainly offer some habitat protection; cetacean studies need to be done.	• Contact: Belize Barrier Reef Reserve System World Heritage Site; web: www.wcmc.org.uk:80/ protected_areas/data/wh/ reef.html
• Declared a wildlife sanctuary in Jan 2002, this area is rated IUCN Category IV.	• Contact: Birgit Winning, OSE, Fort Mason Center, Bldg E, San Francisco, CA 94123-1394 USA; email: winning@oceanic-society.org
• Specific areas within the atoll have been proposed as marine reserves but no protection exists currently; as of Oct 2002, the entire area has now been proposed as a biosphere reserve (the Turneffe Islands Advisory Committee to the Coastal Zone Institute and Authority adopted it is as a formal motion). • Rationale includes protection of both resident dolphins and manatees in the large, biologically diverse coral atoll. • Oceanic Society Expeditions (OSE) maintains a year-round research station and has conducted research expeditions since 1992, helping to promote conservation.	• Contact: Birgit Winning, OSE, Fort Mason Center, Bldg E, San Francisco, CA 94123-1394 USA; email: winning@oceanic-society.org

Table 5.10 *continued*

Name of MPA or sanctuary, location and size	Cetacean and other notable species
COSTA RICA República de Costa Rica **(12) Tortuguero National Park** • northeast Costa Rica • 73 mi² (189.5 km²)	• common: bottlenose dolphin, *Tursiops truncatus* • also: green, leatherback and hawksbill turtles, West Indian manatee
(13) **Gondoca-Manzanillo Wildlife Reserve**, *proposed for expansion* • located near Panamá border • no size data	• tucuxi, *Sotalia fluviatilis*; bottlenose dolphin, *Tursiops truncatus*; offshore: pantropical spotted dolphin, *Stenella attenuata*
CUBA República de Cuba **Cuban national natural parks, reserves and wildlife refuges with probable cetacean habitat: (14) Caguanes PN, (15) Cayos de Ana María RF, (16) Delta del Cauto RF, (17) Lanzanillo Pajonal Fragoso RF, (18) Las Picúas RF, (19) Río Máximo RF, (20) Buena Vista RB, (21) Guanahacabibes RB** • see map, Figure 5.14, for locations • sizes of marine areas are (14) 46 mi² (120 km²); (15) 70 mi² (181 km²); (16) 39 mi² (100 km²); (17) 295 mi² (765 km²); (18) 155 mi² (402 km²); (19) 56 mi² (144 km²); (20) 874 mi² (2263 km²); (21) 191 mi² (495 km²)	• inshore species in many areas include: bottlenose dolphin, *Tursiops truncatus*; Atlantic spotted dolphin, *Stenella frontalis*; pantropical spotted dolphin, *Stenella attenuata*; offshore: sperm whale, *Physeter macrocephalus*; others: humpback whale, *Megaptera novaeangliae*; dwarf sperm whale, *Kogia sima*; Cuvier's beaked whale, *Ziphius cavirostris*; Risso's dolphin, *Grampus griseus*; short-finned pilot whale, *Globicephala macrochynchus*; false killer whale, *Pseudorca crassidens*; at least 15 cetacean species total, based on counts for Gulf of Mexico and Bahamas
Cuban national natural parks, reserves and wildlife refuges, *proposed and in process of likely approval:* **(22) Jardines de la Reina PN, (23) Ciénaga de Zapata PN y RB, (24) Cayo Cantiles – Avalo – Rosario PN, (25) Los Caimanes PN, (26) Cayo Coco RE, (27) Cayo Largo ANT, (28) Cayo Levisa, (29) Bahía Malagueta RF, (30) Banco de Buena Esperanza RF, (31) Cayo Cruz RF, (32) Cayos Juan Ruiz, Cristóbal y Providencia RF** • see map, Figure 5.14, for locations • sizes of marine areas are (22) 776 mi² (2,010 km²); (23) 594 mi² (1540 km²); (24) 196 mi² (508 km²); (25) 111 mi² (287 km²); (26) 71 mi² (184 km²); (27) 263 mi² (682 km²); (28) 119 mi² (308 km²); (29) 36 mi² (92 km²); (30) 64 mi² (165 km²); (31) 68 mi² (175 km²); (32) 63 mi² (164 km²)	• inshore species in many areas include: bottlenose dolphin, *Tursiops truncatus*; Atlantic spotted dolphin, *Stenella frontalis*; pantropical spotted dolphin, *Stenella attenuata*; offshore: sperm whale, *Physeter macrocephalus*; others: humpback whale, *Megaptera novaeangliae*; dwarf sperm whale, *Kogia sima*; Cuvier's beaked whale, *Ziphius cavirostris*; Risso's dolphin, *Grampus griseus*; short-finned pilot whale, *Globicephala macrochynchus*; false killer whale, *Pseudorca crassidens*; at least 15 cetacean species total, based on counts for Gulf of Mexico and Bahamas

Notes and rationale	For more information
• Designated in 1970, this national park was set aside mainly to protect prime nesting site for the green turtle in the Caribbean.	See also Table 5.21 for additional Costa Rican MPAs. • Contact: Tortuguero National Park; web: www.costaricabureau.com/ nationalparks/tortuguero.htm
• This existing coastal Caribbean reserve is being proposed for expansion as an MPA. • As of Feb 2001, an effort was underway to extend the reserve's borders in order to manage commercial fishing, which may be having an impact on the dolphins, as well as to include offshore spotted dolphins. • Court battle is trying to stop Harkins Oil Exploration Co from seismic exploration for oil in the reserve.	• Contact: Paul Forestell, Social Science Division, Southampton College, Southampton, NY 11968, USA
• Dedicated cetacean surveys and research need to be done to quantify cetaceans present and habitat use of the various areas. • Cuba has an ambitious protected area programme which includes considerable marine protected areas, usually protected as part of larger natural parks or reserves. The programme is managed by the national Centro Nacional de Áreas Protegidas de Cuba which has the following categories of protection featuring marine areas: natural park or parque natural (PN); natural reserve or reserva natural (RN); ecological reserve or reserva ecológica (RE); área protegida de recursos manejados or protected area of managed resources (APRM) which includes Ramsar sites with wetlands of international importance; wildlife refuge or refugio de fauna (RF); touristic natural area or área natural turística (ANT); biosphere reserve or la reserva de biosfera (RB). Estimated protection level ranges from IUCN Category II for PN, RN, RE; Category IV for RF; Category V for ANT; other areas are unrated.	• Jefferson and Lynn, 1994; Schmidly, 1981 • Contact: Reinaldo Estrada Estrada, Director, Centro Nacional de Areas Protegidas, Ministerio del Medio Ambiente, Calle 18A e/4114, La Habana 11300, Cuba; email: rey@ama.cu; web: www.cuba.cu/ciencia/ citma/ama/cnap/mapa3.htm
• Dedicated cetacean surveys and research need to be done to quantify cetaceans present and habitat use of the various areas. • Cuba has an ambitious protected area programme which includes considerable marine protected areas, usually protected as part of larger natural parks or reserves. The programme is managed by the national Centro Nacional de Áreas Protegidas de Cuba which has the following categories of protection featuring marine areas: natural park or parque natural (PN); natural reserve or reserva natural (RN); ecological reserve or reserva ecológica (RE); área protegida de recursos manejados or protected area of human resources (APRM); wildlife refuge or refugio de fauna (RF); área natural turística or touristic natural area (ANT). Estimated protection level ranges from IUCN Category II for PN, RN, RE; Category IV for RF; Category V for ANT; other areas are unrated.	• Jefferson and Lynn, 1994; Schmidly, 1981 • Contact: Reinaldo Estrada Estrada, Director, Centro Nacional de Areas Protegidas, Ministerio del Medio Ambiente, Calle 1 8A e/4114, La Habana 11300, Cuba; email: rey@ama.cu; web: www.cuba.cu/ciencia/ citma/ama/cnap/mapa3.htm

Table 5.10 *continued*

Name of MPA or sanctuary, location and size	Cetacean and other notable species
DOMINICA Commonwealth of Dominica **(33) Soufrière/Scotts Head Marine Reserve** • between Scotts Head peninsula and Anse Bateaux, west coast of Dominica, eastern Caribbean • no size information	• common: spinner dolphin, *Stenella longirostris*: pantropical spotted dolphin, *Stenella attenuata*; dwarf sperm whale, *Kogia sima*; pygmy sperm whale, *Kogia breviceps*; sporadic: sperm whale, *Physeter macrocephalus*; false killer whale, *Pseudorca crassidens* • also: coral reef with hard and soft corals and reef fish
DOMINICAN REPUBLIC República Dominicana **(34) Marine Mammal Sanctuary of the Dominican Republic (Santuario de Mamíferos Marinos de la República Dominicana)** • northeast of the Dominican Republic including Silver Bank, Navidad Bank and part of Samaná Bay • total size 965 mi² (2500 km²) Includes the former MPA: **Silver Bank Humpback Whale Sanctuary (Santuario de las Ballenas Jorobadas del Banco de La Plata)**	• Dec–Apr: humpback whale, *Megaptera novaeangliae*; Bryde's whale, *Balaenoptera brydei*; pilot whale, *Globicephala* sp; sperm whale, *Physeter macrocephalus*; bottlenose dolphin, *Tursiops truncatus*; pantropical spotted dolphin, *Stenella attenuata* • humpback mothers with calves stay in coral areas in the north, solitary singing males in 65–130 ft (20–40 m) deep waters • also: commercial fish, manatee and marine turtles
(35) East National Park (Parque Nacional del Este), *proposed for expansion* • eastern Dominican Republic • expanded size undetermined	• bottlenose dolphin, *Tursiops truncatus*
(36) Bayahibe Marine Sanctuary (Santuario de Marino Bayahibe), *proposed* • near East National Park • no size data	• bottlenose dolphin, *Tursiops truncatus*

Notes and rationale	For more information
• Plans for the reserve date to 1987, but the area only became a reserve in 2003. • Managed as a multi-use, zoned marine area, with some restrictions on fishing, diving, whale watching and other uses; main rationale is to protect reef fish. • If cetacean critical habitat areas can be located and given IUCN Category I protection, this area could provide an important model for cetacean habitat conservation in the eastern Caribbean.	• Contact: Arun Madisetti; email: ssmrdominica@ hotmail.com; web: www.avirtual dominica.com/ssmr
• Marine mammal sanctuary designated as the Silver Bank Humpback Whale Sanctuary in 1986 (Presidential Decree No 319-86); in 1996, the sanctuary was extended to include Navidad Bank and part of Samaná Bay, thus covering the three main humpback breeding grounds in DR waters. Administered by a multi-institutional organization, the sanctuary is supposed to protect not only humpback whales, but also various dolphins, whales and manatees. The 2000 Law of the Environment and Natural Resources of the Dominican Republic (64-00) strengthens overall environmental standards, as well as protection and conservation of marine mammals. • Sanctuary protects shallow platform coral reef systems with mating and calving areas for humpback whales. From Feb to Apr, Silver Bank itself has the densest concentration of humpbacks found in the North Atlantic with up to 3000 humpback whales present at one time; humpbacks from each of five discrete feeding stocks in the western North Atlantic are known to aggregate on the bank; many shipwrecks on the bank include the *Concepción de la Flota de Nueva España,* shipwrecked in 1641, which contained a large cargo of gold and silver, and is origin of the name Silver Bank. • Samaná Bay is a site of high biological productivity along the coast and a key winter habitat area for humpback whales with a high proportion of use by mothers with newborns; management regime is needed for substantial whale watching industry, commercial and artisanal fishing and potential hydrocarbon exploration and production.	• Bonnelly de Calventi, 1994; CEBSE, 1993; Whitehead, 1981 • Contact: Comisión Rectora del Banco de La Plata (Governing Committee of the Silver Bank Sanctuary), Museo National de Historia Natural, Plaza de La Cultura, Santo Domingo, DR; Idelisa Bonnelly de Calventi; email: ibonnelly@ verizon.net.do
• Dolphins appear to be present at Saona Island and on the park's west coast; dolphin research is trying to quantify extent of critical habitat in and near park waters. • Idelisa Bonnelly de Calventi and others recommend that dolphins be protected within park waters, especially around Saona Island, and that the marine boundaries be expanded as needed to fit dolphin habitat.	• Contact: Idelisa Bonnelly de Calventi; email: ibonnelly@ verizon.net.do
• Dolphin research is trying to quantify distribution in the park's waters. • Idelisa Bonnelly de Calventi recommends that dolphins be protected here and that the boundaries be designed to fit dolphin habitat.	• Contact: Idelisa Bonnelly de Calventi; email: ibonnelly@ verizon.net.do

Table 5.10 *continued*

Name of MPA or sanctuary, location and size	Cetacean and other notable species
GUADELOUPE and ST-BARTHÉLEMY (France) **(A) Guadeloupe Sanctuary, or Sanctuary of the South Antilles (Sanctuaire Caribéain du Sud Antilles),** *proposed* • around Guadeloupe, eastern Caribbean • waters to the 12nm limit around Guadeloupe; some discussion about trying to include waters of Martinique and Dominica	• Jan–May: humpback whale, *Megaptera novaeangliae*; others year-round, some sporadic: sperm whale, *Physeter macrocephalus*; pantropical spotted dolphin, *Stenella attenuata*; bottlenose dolphin, *Tursiops truncatus*; false killer whale, *Pseudorca crassidens*; pygmy killer whale, *Feresa attenuata*; short-finned pilot whale, *Globicephala macrorhynchus* • also: marine turtles, many birds, fish
(37) St-Barthélemy MPA • St-Barthélemy, Leeward Islands • 4.6 mi^2 (12 km^2) MPA to protect rich tropical reef ecology	• humpback whale, *Megaptera novaeangliae*; various dolphins
JAMAICA **(38) Montego Bay Marine Park** • Montego Bay, northwest Jamaica • 10 mi^2 (26 km^2)	• common: bottlenose dolphins, *Tursiops truncatus*; sporadic: pilot whale, *Globicephala* sp
MÉXICO Estados Unidos Mexicanos **(B) Mexican Whale Refuge** • national waters of México in Marine Regions 7 and 15, to the limits of México's EEZ • 1,157,112 mi^2 (2,997,700 km^2) Also listed under Marine Region 15.	• bottlenose dolphin, *Tursiops truncatus*; and some 38 other cetacean species found mostly in the Mexican Pacific
NICARAGUA República de Nicaragua **(39) Miskito Coast Protected Area** • Miskito Coast from Walpasiksa north to Old Cape at the Honduras border • 4246 mi^2 (11,000 km^2), includes land and sea areas	• tucuxi, *Sotalia fluviatilis* • also: West Indian manatee, sea turtles

Notes and rationale	For more information
• Proposal for an MPA or cetacean sanctuary still to be defined but aimed to protect cetacean feeding and breeding grounds as well as habitat for marine turtles. • Guadeloupe's regional environment ministry (DIREN) supports the proposal along with IFAW and the Caribwhale Association (whale watch operator association) as part of SPAW Protocol from the Cartagena Convention which encourages initiatives from member states for enhanced habitat conservation, but it would be organized initially at the provincial (Préfecture) and national (Ministère) level. • Cetacean research to date has been photo-ID, genetic, acoustic tracking, abundance and distribution studies. • Cetacean threats include accidental netting from fishing boats and growing boat and shipping traffic.	• Contact: Caroline and Renato Rinaldi, Association Evasion Tropicale, Étude Recensement Protection Tortues Marines and Cétacés; email: evastropic@wanadoo.fr
• Precise cetacean use of the MPA is not quantified but about 100 humpback whales are seen in the general area every year.	• Hoyt, 1999 • Contact: Arnaud Apremont, Saint-Barths Cétacés; email: stbarth.cetaces@ wanadoo.fr
• Supports outstanding mangroves, seagrass beds and coral. • Adjacent to popular visitor beaches, boating and watersport areas but some zoned use. • Cetacean habitat use of the area has not been quantified.	• Contact: Montego Bay Marine Park, Montego Bay, Jamaica; web: www.montego-bay-jamaica.com/mbmp/
• Rationale is for a refuge or sanctuary for cetaceans that protects them from hunting but may go further. • Designated in 2002; legislation published in Federal Register requires protection plan (equivalent to MPA management plan) to be defined for México's national waters under a new territorial species legal protection regime established by new Wildlife Law in 2000 (which will take responsibility for maintaining necessary environmental conditions for whales). • Commercial and recreational activities will not be restricted inside the zone, but efforts will be undertaken to provide users with information on whale species and their significance in maintaining ecological balance.	See also Table 5.19 for additional Mexican MPAs. • Contact: Juan Bezaury Creel, WWF México; web: www.wwf.org.mx/ • Greenpeace México, México, DF 03400, México; web: www.greenpeace. org.mx
• Initiated as a project in 1990, and awarded national protection in 1991, this grass-roots, locally managed protected area was set up with outside NGO support (WWF, Cultural Survival, MacArthur Foundation, USAID and Liz Claiborne Foundation) to some 23 communities. • Biological importance is partly to protect prime nesting site for sea turtles in the Caribbean. While not designed for cetaceans, there may be some cetacean habitat protection.	

Table 5.10 *continued*

Name of MPA or sanctuary, location and size	Cetacean and other notable species
ST LUCIA **(40) Soufrière Marine Management Area** • Soufrière Bay, southwest coast of St Lucia, eastern Caribbean • no data on size	• spinner dolphin, *Stenella longirostris*; pantropical spotted dolphin, *Stenella attenuata*; short-finned pilot whale, *Globicephala macrorhynchus*; sometimes: sperm whale, *Physeter macrocephalus*; dwarf sperm whale, *Kogia sima*; pygmy sperm whale, *Kogia breviceps*; false killer whale, *Pseudorca crassidens*
TURKS AND CAICOS ISLANDS (UK) **(41) Princess Alexandra Marine National Park** • located on the north side of Provo	• bottlenose dolphin, *Tursiops truncatus*
(42) Mouchoir Bank Marine Sanctuary, *discussed as possible proposal* • large shallow bank located southeast of the Turks Islands and north of the Dominican Republic • size undetermined	• humpback whale, *Megaptera novaeangliae*; other cetaceans would be similar to those included under Silver Bank Humpback Whale Sanctuary in the Dominican Republic, listed above
UNITED STATES OF AMERICA (US) **(43) Gray's Reef National Marine Sanctuary and Biosphere Reserve** • 17 mi (27.4 km) east of Sapelo Island, Georgia • 23 mi² (59.6 km²)	• North Atlantic right whale, *Eubalaena glacialis* • also: loggerhead sea turtle, black sea bass, grouper, angelfish, barrel sponge, ivory bush coral and sea whips

Notes and rationale	For more information
• Existing zoned community MPA managed mainly for fishing; includes four different marine reserves, with a balanced overall programme modelled on the biosphere reserve concept which includes protection, management and local education but allows some tourism and fishing. • Within the management area, all coral and sponges are protected from collection, spearguns are illegal and boats are not allowed to anchor on the reefs. Instead, yachts and other boats are required to use moorings. In addition, the collection of marine mammals is specifically prohibited, either dead or alive. The Soufrière Marine Management Association is in charge of enforcement, coordinating the movements and activities of local fishing boats, yachts and divers.	• Contact: Soufrière Marine Management Association; web: www.smma.org.lc/
• MPA has some dolphin use, including by the lone, sociable dolphin JoJo, but precise dolphin use has not been quantified. • There is tourism use by resorts in the area. • Management plan needs to be devised with bottlenose dolphin use considered.	• Contact: Turks and Caicos Department of Environment and Coastal Resources (DECR); email: decr@tciway.tc; Dean Bernal; web: www.jojo.tc
• First proposed as an MPA to protect one of the main humpback whale calving and mating areas by Howard Wynn, University of Rhode Island, in the 1970s; in 2000 the TCI Marine Mammal Conference agreed that the first step toward a formal proposal would be a multidisciplinary study to learn more about the humpbacks' use of the area, to see which other cetaceans are present, and to find out about other biological and cultural features that might be part of the proposal and to help to determine the reserve size and boundaries. • An MPA could serve the dual function of publicizing TCI waters as a natural marine paradise with abundant marine mammals and other wildlife as well as protecting Mouchoir Bank from regional fishermen and others who may exploit fishing and other resources. • Patrol boats to Mouchoir Bank as well as whale watch boats are trying to control fishing and to collect data to help shape MPA proposal.	• Hoyt, 2000 • Contact: Turks and Caicos Department of Environment and Coastal Resources (DECR); email: decr@tciway.tc
• Achieved NMS designation in 1981, Gray's Reef became a Unesco biosphere reserve in 1986. • Designated to protect a productive 'sandstone reef ecosystem' with a wide variety of species from corals to sea turtles, site is now thought to be part of critical winter calving habitat for North Atlantic right whales. • Restricted activities include fishing, military, mineral extraction, dumping or discharge, seabed alteration and use of wire fish traps, bottom trawls and explosives.	See also Tables 5.7 and 5.19 for additional US MPAs. • Contact: Gray's Reef National Marine Sanctuary, 30 Ocean Science Circle, Savannah, GA 31411 USA; web: www.graysreef.nos. noaa.gov/

Table 5.10 *continued*

Name of MPA or sanctuary, location and size	Cetacean and other notable species
(44) Southeastern Right Whale Critical Habitat • located offshore northern Florida and southern Georgia • no size information	• winter: North Atlantic right whale, *Eubalaena glacialis*
(45) Florida Keys National Marine Sanctuary • Florida Keys, southern tip of Florida • marine area is 3698 mi² (9580 km²)	• bottlenose dolphin, *Tursiops truncatus*; Atlantic spotted dolphin, *Stenella frontalis*; short-beaked common dolphin, *Delphinus delphis* • also: Florida manatee
(46) Fort Clinch State Park Aquatic Preserve • north end of Amelia Island, Nassau County, northeastern Florida • 14 mi² (36.4 km²)	• seasonal: North Atlantic right whale, *Eubalaena glacialis*; humpback whale, *Megaptera novaeangliae* • also: Florida manatee, 5 sea turtle species, American alligator, many bird species
VENEZUELA República de Venezuela **(47) Caño Guaritico Wildlife Refuge** • located in Apure State	• boto, or Amazon River dolphin, *Inia geoffrensis* • also: tropical rain forest species
(48) Venezuelan Cetacean Sanctuary, *proposed* • located along the states of Anzoategui, Sucre, Nueva Esparta and several small islands which are federal dependences • about 216 mi² (560 km²)	• May–Nov: pygmy Bryde's whale, *Balaenoptera edeni*; also: humpback whale, *Megaptera novaeangliae*; various dolphin species; in all Venzuelan waters, some 23 cetacean species are found • also: manta rays, whale shark

Notes and rationale	For more information
• Rationale is to protect the winter nursery habitat for North Atlantic right whales, especially from the impacts of commercial fishing and vessel traffic. • Federal threatened/endangered critical habitat site under NMFS established in 1994.	• Contact: Marine Protected Areas of the United States; web: http://mpa.gov/
• Designated in 1990 to protect the coral reef ecosystem, this national marine sanctuary also has some dolphin habitat. • Management includes multiple use (commercial and recreational fishing, boating, diving) and zoning with highly protected core areas.	• Contact: Florida Keys NMS; web: http://mpa.gov/
• Fort Clinch State Park Aquatic Preserve and adjacent Nassau River-St Johns Marshes Aquatic Preserve are state aesthetic and biological reserves that are designed to help protect critical habitat for various fish and wildlife centred on a salt marsh area. Public access for sport fishing, boating and other activities is permitted under permit and subject to closures.	• Contact: Fort Clinch State Park Aquatic Preserve; email: Amy.Kalmbacher@ dep.state.fl.us; web: www.dep.state.fl.us/ coastal/sites/northeast/ ftclinch/info.htm
• Existing freshwater and land-based reserve. • Rationale for this reserve was as a wildlife refuge to protect a number of threatened and endangered species including boto, the Amazon River dolphin.	• Caranto and Gonzalez-Fernandez, 1998 • Contact: TM Caranto and AJ Gonzalez-Fernandez, Universidad de los Llanos 'Ezequiel Zamora' (UNELLEZ), Postgrado en Manejo de Fauna Silvestre y Acuatica, Guanare 3310, Venezuela
• Sanctuary was proposed in 1990 by researchers from Fundacetacea to protect all cetaceans in a limited portion of the national waters of Venezuela which is known for its high concentration of cetaceans. • Sanctuary is a first attempt to address the fact that there are no MPAs for cetaceans in Venezuela, but the sanctuary idea is not under formal consideration. In other work, since 1996, Profauna (the Venezuelan Fish and Wildlife Service) has been conducting field research in the State of Aragua on the central coast of Venezuela, in order to obtain baseline information to devise an action plan for conservation and research on marine mammals (Bolaños and Campo, 1998); cetaceans are also found in the waters adjacent to Mochima Bay National Park and Los Roques Archipelago National Park.	• Romero et al, 1997 • Contact: Fundacetacea; email: iagudo@lycos.com • For more information on cetaceans in Venezuela, contact: Centro de Investigación de Cetáceos (CIC); email: drstenella@hotmail.com; cic_ne@cantv.net

MARINE REGION 8: WEST AFRICA

Cetacean habitat in the West African Marine Region includes year-round extensive inshore and nearshore dolphin populations around the mangroves, while offshore upwellings support regular seasonal feeding areas for both baleen and toothed whales. A search for the former breeding grounds of the North Atlantic right whale around Cintra Bay, Western Sahara (Morocco), in the mid-1990s, turned up no right whale sightings, but the southern right whales do come to give birth and raise their calves in the nearshore waters of South Africa and Namibia. Humpback whales have been identified over the past decade on the breeding grounds of the Cape Verde Islands. The Canary Islands have some of the richest and most accessible cetacean fauna in the world, with at least 26 species of cetaceans, including various beaked whales. Research and conservation in the Canary Islands have proceeded rapidly in recent years, following the improved management of the local whale watching industry – based largely on resident short-finned pilot whales and bottlenose dolphins.

A few species such as the Heaviside's dolphin and the Atlantic hump-backed dolphin are found only in this region, while the pygmy right whale is associated with the waters around South Africa, although it also lives in other southern hemisphere waters.

In the Canary Islands, the European Commission in December 2001 approved 11 special areas of conservation (SACs) to protect mainly bottlenose dolphin habitat. Total dolphin habitat protected amounts to 573 mi^2 (1486 km^2). In addition, the Natural Marine Park of the Whales in west Tenerife is in the process of being approved, and there are proposals to turn the waters off southeast Fuerteventura into a beaked whale and other cetaceans MPA, as well as one to make all Canary Islands waters into a marine mammal sanctuary. Other MPAs in the region that offer habitat protection to cetaceans include the Banc d'Arguin National Park and Biosphere Reserve in Mauritania and the Saloum Delta National Park and Biosphere Reserve in Senegal, both of which have resident dolphin populations, as well as the De Hoop, Tsitsikamma and other MPAs designated under South Africa's 1998 MPA legislation partly to protect southern right whale habitat.

The West African Marine Region has three large marine ecosystems (LMEs) that have been identified: the Canary Current, Guinea Current and Benguela Current. The region covers the waters of the southeast North Atlantic, the eastern South Atlantic and a small adjacent portion of the southwestern Indian Ocean. Politically, it includes 21 countries and 7 territories along the western and southern coast of Africa from Morocco, at the Strait of Gibraltar, in the North, to the east coast of South Africa at the border of Mozambique (see Table 5.1 on p89).

Five main oceanic currents dominate the region:

- From the north, the cool-water Canary Current flows southwest along the north African coast.

- The South Equatorial Current flows west from the coast south of the Equator.
- The Guinea Current moves east and southeast toward the coast of the Gulf of Guinea, carrying warm water.
- The Benguela Current brings cool water in along the coast of the southwest African zone before turning offshore at about 6° S.
- Finally, on South Africa's east coast, the Agulhas Current carries warm water southwest to the southern tip of Africa.

These and other oceanographic and atmospheric factors create a band of upwellings along extensive parts of the African coastline, a few tens of kilometres from land, at different times of year. Off northwest Africa, upwellings mainly occur from October to April. Offshore Senegal has areas of particularly high productivity. In the Gulf of Guinea, especially in the northern part, some upwellings occur from June to September. Southern Africa, especially off Namibia, has strong upwellings in August and weak upwellings from November to February.

A dominant coastal and nearshore feature from Angola to Mauritania is the mangrove forest which in some areas forms a dense band up to 30 miles (50 km) out from the coast, in addition to substantial extensions up rivers. The densest mangroves are in Cameroon, Gabon, The Gambia, Guinea, Guinea-Bissau, Nigeria and Sierra Leone, although much has been cleared in recent years. There are numerous river deltas along the west coast, such as the River Gambia, the Volta River in Ghana, the Niger in Nigeria and the Congo River in the Democratic Republic of the Congo. Some have permanent tidal swamps which extend up to 124 mi (200 km) upstream, many containing mangroves and supporting various dolphin populations besides the important marine and freshwater fish and bird species. The west coast of Africa has no true coral reefs and only isolated coral communities.

A regional conservation treaty, as part of the UNEP Regional Seas Programme, came into force in 1984: The Convention for Cooperation in the Protection and Development of the Marine and Coastal Environment of the West and Central African Regions, along with the Protocol on Combating Pollution in Cases of Emergency. Initiatives have focused on efforts to control pollution and to develop the infrastructure to manage the marine environment.

In 1995, there was a total of 42 MPAs of all kinds in this marine region (Wells and Bleakley, 1995). The region is divided into five biogeographic zones, all but one of which was represented by at least one MPA. As of 2004, according to Table 5.11 prepared for this book, there are 41 existing and 6 proposed MPAs which feature cetacean habitat. The area also forms part of a proposed international cetacean sanctuary for the South Atlantic Ocean, initiated through the IWC, which has yet to be approved. It would serve as a sanctuary from whaling and could be a stepping stone here towards greater protection and recognition of cetacean habitat needs.

The IUCN 2002–2010 Conservation Action Plan for the World's Cetaceans recommends a number of research initiatives for this region (Reeves et al, 2003):

- to investigate bycatches and directed takes of small cetaceans in Ghana, West Africa;
- to investigate bycatches and directed takes of small cetaceans in Senegal and The Gambia, northwestern Africa;
- to investigate the status of Atlantic hump-backed dolphins in northwestern Africa;
- to investigate cetacean mortality in the eastern tropical Atlantic tuna purse-seine fishery; and
- to investigate the potential effects of oil and gas development on humpback whales and other cetaceans in the coastal waters of West Africa.

Blainville's Beaked Whale
Mesoplodon densirostris

Ginkgo-toothed Beaked Whale
Mesoplodon ginkgodens

Andrew's Beaked Whale
Mesoplodon bowdoini

Hubbs' Beaked Whale
Mesoplodon carlhubbsi

Longman's Beaked Whale
Mesoplodon pacificus

Strap-toothed Whale
Mesoplodon layardii

Gray's Beaked Whale
Mesoplodon grayi

Arnoux's Beaked Whale
Berardius arnuxii

Tasman Beaked Whale
Tasmacetus shepherdi

Northern Bottlenose Whale
Hyperoodon ampullatus

Pygmy Sperm Whale
Kogia breviceps

Sowerby's Beaked Whale
Mesoplodon bidens

Stejneger's Beaked Whale
Mesoplodon stejnegeri

True's Beaked Whale
Mesoplodon mirus

Pygmy Beaked Whale
Mesoplodon peruvianus

Gervais' Beaked Whale
Mesoplodon europaeus

Cuvier's Beaked Whale
Ziphius cavirostris

Dwarf Sperm Whale
Kogia sima

Hector's Beaked Whale
Mesoplodon hectori

Baird's Beaked Whale
Berardius bairdii

Bowhead Whale
Balaena mysticetus

Sperm Whale
Physeter macrocephalus

Northern Right Whale
Eubalaena glacialis

Mesoplodon species A
Mesoplodon sp

Southern Right Whale
Eubalaena australis

Blue Whale
Balaenoptera musculus

Pygmy Right Whale
Caperea marginata

Southern Bottlenose Whale
Hyperoodon planifrons

Gray Whale
Eschrichtius robustus

Humpback Whale
Megaptera novaeangliae

Sei Whale
Balaenoptera borealis

Bryde's Whale
Balaenoptera brydei

Fin Whale
Balaenoptera physalus

Minke Whale
Balaenoptera acutorostrata

Whales of the world ocean by Pieter Arend Folkens/A Higher Porpoise Design Group

Resident orcas, *Orcinus orca*, at left, off southeast Kamchatka, Russia, are found in the Nalychevo and Kronotskiy Reserves (Zapovedniks). On the other side of the Pacific (this page), the Robson Bight/Michael Bigg Ecological Reserve in British Columbia, Canada, is a small reserve that helps protect rubbing and resting areas for orcas. Photo at far left by Hal Sato, Far East Russia Orca Project (WDCS). Photographs on this page by Erich Hoyt.

Resident Atlantic spotted dolphins, *Stenella plagiodon* (below), live in the coastal waters of the Bahamas in the Wider Caribbean Marine Region. Various national and 'land and sea' parks are being set up to protect ecosystems which include dolphin habitat. In southeastern Brazil (above), the Right Whale Environmental Protection Area offers excellent land-based whale watching and has a tradition of more than two decades of southern right whale, *Eubalaena australis*, research, A September 2000 Brazilian government decree protects this southern right whale birthing and nursery site. Photographs (below) by William W Rossiter, Cetacean Society International, and (above) by José T Palazzo, Jr, International Wildlife Coalition

The gray whale, *Eschrictius robustus*, (above) was the first whale to have a dedicated protected area with the creation of Laguna Ojo de Liebre (Scammon's Lagoon) National Gray Whale Refuge in 1971. In November 1988 the complex of Mexican Pacific gray whale breeding lagoons was named as El Vizcaino Biosphere Reserve. Photograph by Stephen Leatherwood, courtesy Oceanic Society Expeditions

Some 230 northern bottlenose whales, *Hyperoodon ampullatus*, live above a submarine canyon (above) called The Gully, 124 miles (200 km) southeast of Halifax, Nova Scotia. The Gully 'Marine Protected Area', the first marine protected area for any species of beaked whale, was declared Canada's second Ocean's Act 'MPA' in 2004. Watching the humpback whale, *Megaptera novaeangliae*, (opposite, below) and Atlantic white-sided dolphins, *Lagenorhynchus acutus*, (opposite, above) is an important economic activity in the Gerry E Studds Humpback Whale National Marine Sanctuary, off New England, US. Photograph on this page by Hal Whitehead. Photographs opposite by William W Rossiter, Cetacean Society International.

Dolphins and porpoises of the world ocean by Pieter Arend Folkens/A Higher Propoise Design Group

1   Dall's Porpoise, *Phocoenoides dalli*
2   Spectacled Porpoise, *Phocoena dioptrica*
3   Finless Porpoise, *Neophocaena phocaenoides*
4   Burmeister's Porpoise, *Phocoena spinipinnis*
5   Harbor Porpoise, *Phocoena phocoena*
6   Vaquita, *Phocoena sinus*
7   Long-finned Pilot Whale, *Globicephala melas*
8   Northern Right Whale Dolphin, *Lissodelphis borealis*
9   Southern Right Whale Dolphin, *Lissodelphis peronii*
10 White-beaked Dolphin, *Lagenorhynchus albirostris*

11 Boto (Amazon River Dolphin), *Inia geoffrensis*
12 Pygmy Killer Whale, *Feresa attenuata*
13 False Killer Whale, *Pseudorca crassidens*
14 Melon-headed Whale, *Peponocephala electra*
15 Spinner Dolphin, *Stenella longirostris*
16 Atlantic White-sided Dolphin, *Lagenorhynchus acutus*

17 Baiji (Yangtze River Dolphin), *Lipotes vexillifer*
18 Orca, Killer Whale, *Orcinus orca*
19 Risso's Dolphin, *Grampus griseus*
20 Spinner Dolphin (Hawaiian form), *Stenella longirostris*
21 Pacific White-sided Dolphin, *Lagenorhynchus obliquidens*

22 Indus Susu, *Platanista minor*
23 Ganges Susu, *Platanista gangetica*
24 Irrawaddy Dolphin, *Orcaella brevirostris*
25 Beluga, *Delphinapterus leucas*
26 Narwhal, *Monodon monoceros*
27 Clymene Dolphin, *Stenella clymene*
28 Dusky Dolphin, *Lagenorhynchus obscurus*
29 Atlantic Spotted Dolphin, *Stenella frontalis*
30 Hourglass Dolphin, *Lagenorhynchus cruciger*

31 Franciscana (La Plata Dolphin), *Pontoporia blainvillei*
32 Short-finned Pilot Whale, *Globicephala macrorhynchus*
33 Rough-toothed Dolphin, *Steno bredanensis*
34 Bottlenose Dolphin, *Tursiops truncatus*
35 Black Dolphin, *Cephalorhynchus eutropia*
36 Commerson's Dolphin, *Cephalorhynchus commersonnii*
37 Pantropical Spotted Dolphin, *Stenella attenuata*
38 Peale's Dolphin, *Lagenorhynchus australis*

39 Indo-Pacific Hump-backed Dolphin, *Sousa chinensis*
40 Atlantic Hump-backed Dolphin, *Sousa teuszii*
41 Tucuxi, *Sotalia fluviatilis*
42 Heaviside's Dolphin, *Cephalorhynchus heavisidii*
43 Hector's Dolphin, *Cephalorhynchus hectori*
44 Common Dolphin, *Delphinus delphis*
45 Striped Dolphin, *Stenella coeruleoalba*
46 Fraser's Dolphin, *Lagenodelphis hosei*

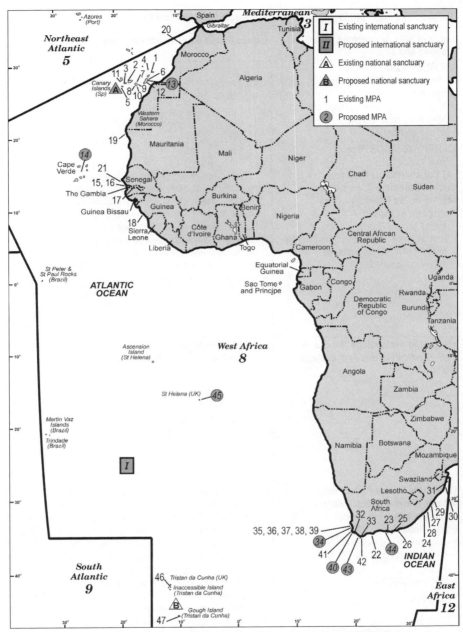

The roman numerals, letters and numbers correspond to the sanctuaries and MPAs listed and described in Table 5.11.

Figure 5.15 *Map of Marine Region 8: West African MPAs and sanctuaries*

Table 5.11 *Marine Region 8: West African MPAs and sanctuaries*

Name of MPA or sanctuary, location and size	Cetacean and other notable species
INTERNATIONAL *(I)* **South Atlantic Sanctuary,** *proposed* • South Atlantic Ocean, spread across Marine Regions 8 and 9 • size undetermined	• in total, the South Atlantic Ocean has some 53 species of cetaceans
CANARY ISLANDS (Spain) Islas Canarias *(A)* **Canary Islands Cetacean Marine Sanctuary (Sanctuario Marino de las Ballenas – Islas Canarias),** *proposed* • waters around Canary Islands, all or portion of national waters to the limit of the EEZ of the Canary Islands • size undetermined	• inshore: short-finned pilot whale, *Globicephala macrorhynchus*; bottlenose dolphin, *Tursiops truncatus*; offshore: sperm whale, *Physeter macrocephalus*; minke whale, *Balaenoptera acutorostrata*; Bryde's whale, *Balaenoptera brydei*; Cuvier's beaked whale, *Ziphius cavirostris*; Blainville's beaked whale, *Mesoplodon densirostris*; and various other beaked whales; at least 26 cetacean species in all (Urquiola, 1998) • also: loggerhead turtles
(1) Chinijo Archipelago Natural Park (Parque Natural Archipielago Chinijo) • north Lanzarote • 35 mi^2 (91 km^2)	• bottlenose dolphin, *Tursiops truncatus*; and others (see Natural Marine Park of the Whales, below)
(2) Natural Marine Park of the Whales (Parque Natural Marino de las Ballenas) and Franja Marina Teno Rasca SAC • west Tenerife extending out about 5 mi (8 km) from shore (28°16'N, 16°53'W) • 268.3 mi^2 (695 km^2)	• common (Annex II): bottlenose dolphin, *Tursiops truncatus*; common (Annex IV): rough-toothed dolphin, *Steno bredanensis*; Atlantic spotted dolphin, *Stenella frontalis*; short-beaked common dolphin, *Delphinus delphis*; striped dolphin, *Stenella coeruleoalba*; Risso's dolphin, *Grampus griseus*; short-finned pilot whale, *Globicephala macrorhynchus*; sperm whale, *Physeter macrocephalus*; pygmy Bryde's whale, *Balaenoptera edeni*; other species found here but not officially protected: humpback whale, *Megaptera novaeangliae*; fin whale, *Balaenoptera physalus*; sei whale, *Balaenoptera borealis*; North Atlantic right whale, *Eubalaena glacialis*; Blainville's beaked whale, *Mesoplodon densirostris*; Cuvier's beaked whale, *Ziphius cavirostris*; orca, *Orcinus orca*; false killer whale, *Pseudorca crassidens* • also: loggerhead turtle

Notes and rationale	For more information
• Rationale is to protect large whales from commercial whaling and to stimulate whale watching for the benefit of local communities as well as cetacean research and conservation.	• See full account in Marine Region 9, Table 5.12.
• For some years there has been the idea of creating a marine sanctuary for cetaceans which would cover all the islands, or some large portion of them. A proposal exists, but there is no word on when or if it is going to be formally considered. In 1999, WWF Spain began actively promoting the idea of a whale sanctuary for the islands and helped push through ecological research, a threats analysis and conservation needs assessment, along with the proposal; the sanctuary could encompass either all of the waters of the Canary Islands, or possibly the waters between the islands, with or without the main whale watch areas off southwest Tenerife and La Gomera. • Rationale would be to protect the exceptional cetacean populations of the Canary Islands.	
• Rationale is for the protection of scenic natural landscape and biological diversity. • This land-based coastal area was designated as a natural park in 1994. More recently, it has been found that bottlenose dolphins are resident in the inshore waters of the park. In late 2000, part of the park was identified and proposed as a special area of conservation (SAC) under EU legislation Annex 1 habitat and Annex II species criteria for bottlenose dolphins (see Sebadades de La Graciosa SAC, below). Part of the archipelago waters are also protected in a fisheries reserve – Isla Graciosa e Islotes del Norte de Lanzarote – which was set aside in 1995.	• Contact: Erika Urquiola, Sociedad Española de Cetáceos – SEC (Spanish Cetacean Society), Islas Canarias, Spain; email: urquiola@cetaceos.com or sec@cetaceos.com; web: www.cetaceos.com
• Approved Dec 2001 as an SAC under EU Habitats and Species Directive in part to protect bottlenose dolphin and loggerhead turtle habitat (Annex II criteria); also protects Annex IV species. • Process of declaration as a natural protected area was initiated under Decreto Legislativo 1/2000 in Apr 2002 by order of the Consejería of the Canary Islands and the Dept of the Environment. • Sociedad para el Estudio de los Cetáceos en el Archipielago Canario (SECAC) and Tenerife Conservación have been working in this area.	• Urquiola, 1998 • Contact: Erika Urquiola, Sociedad Española de Cetáceos – SEC (Spanish Cetacean Society), Islas Canarias, Spain; email: urquiola@cetaceos.com or sec@cetaceos.com; web: www.cetaceos.com • Vidal Martín, SECAC; email: ziphius@teide.net; web: www.cetaceos.org • Manuel Carrillo, Tenerife Conservación; email: monachus@mixmail.com

Table 5.11 *continued*

Name of MPA or sanctuary, location and size	Cetacean and other notable species
(3) Franja Marina Santiago – Valle Gran Rey SAC • off southwestern La Gomera (28°2'N, 17°18'W) • 50.7 mi² (131.4 km²)	• common (Annex II): bottlenose dolphin, *Tursiops truncatus*; common (Annex IV): striped dolphin, *Stenella coeruleoalba*; Atlantic spotted dolphin, *Stenella frontalis*; short-finned pilot whale, *Globicephala macrorhynchus*; other species found here but not officially protected: rough-toothed dolphin, *Steno bredanensis*; short-beaked common dolphin, *Delphinus delphis*; Blainville's beaked whale, *Mesoplodon densirostris*; sporadic: blue whale, *Balaenoptera musculus*; fin whale, *Balaenoptera physalus*; pygmy Bryde's whale, *Balaenoptera edeni*; North Atlantic right whale, *Eubalaena glacialis*; sperm whale, *Physeter macrocephalus*; pygmy sperm whale, *Kogia breviceps*; orca, *Orcinus orca*; Risso's dolphin, *Grampus griseus* • also: loggerhead turtles
(4) Sebadales de La Graciosa SAC • north Lanzarote (29°13'N, 13°30'W) • 4.6 mi² (11.9 km²)	• common (Annex II): bottlenose dolphin, *Tursiops truncatus*
(5) Mar de las Calmas SAC • southwest El Hierro (27°38'N, 18°3'W) • 38.2 mi² (99 km²)	• common (Annex II): bottlenose dolphin, *Tursiops truncatus*; (Annex IV): striped dolphin, *Stenella coeruleoalba*; Atlantic spotted dolphin, *Stenella frontalis*; short-finned pilot whale, *Globicephala macrorhynchus*; short-beaked common dolphin, *Delphinus delphis*; other species found here but not officially protected: fin whale, *Balaenoptera physalus*; Cuvier's beaked whale, *Ziphius cavirostris*; Blainville's beaked whale, *Mesoplodon densirostris* • also: loggerhead turtle
(6) Sebadales de Corralejo SAC • northeast Fuerteventura (28°42'N, 13°49'W) • 7.5 mi² (19.4 km²)	• common (Annex II): bottlenose dolphin, *Tursiops truncatus*; common (Annex IV): Risso's dolphin, *Grampus griseus* • also: loggerhead turtle

Notes and rationale	For more information
• Approved Dec 2001 as an SAC under EU Habitats and Species Directive in part to protect bottlenose dolphin and loggerhead turtle habitat (Annex II criteria); also protects Annex IV species. • SECAC is developing a management plan as part of a Life Naturaleza project. • Other groups working in the area include Atlantic Blue, Tenerife Conservación and MEER; habitat protection is supported by work from Project MEER La Gomera.	• Ritter, 1996; Ritter and Brederlau, 1999 • Contact: Erika Urquiola, Sociedad Española de Cetáceos – SEC (Spanish Cetacean Society), Islas Canarias, Spain; email: urquiola@cetaceos.com or sec@cetaceos.com; web: www.cetaceos.com • Bern Brederlau, Atlantic Blue; email: atlanticblue@airtel.net • Vidal Martín, SECAC; email: ziphius@teide.net; web: www.cetaceos.org
• Approved Dec 2001 as an SAC under EU Habitats and Species Directive in part to protect bottlenose dolphin habitat (Annex II criteria). • SECAC has been working in this area. • Cetacean surveys and research are needed to quantify habitat use.	• Contact: Erika Urquiola, Sociedad Española de Cetáceos – SEC (Spanish Cetacean Society), Islas Canarias, Spain; email: urquiola@cetaceos.com or sec@cetaceos.com; web: www.cetaceos.com
• Approved Dec 2001 as an SAC under EU Habitats and Species Directive in part to protect bottlenose dolphin and loggerhead turtle habitat (Annex II criteria); also protects Annex IV species. • The University of La Laguna is working in this area on beaked whale (*Ziphiidae*) distribution and ecology; more cetacean surveys and research will help quantify habitat use.	• Contact: Erika Urquiola, Sociedad Española de Cetáceos – SEC (Spanish Cetacean Society), Islas Canarias, Spain; email: urquiola@cetaceos.com or sec@cetaceos.com; web: www.cetaceos.com
• Approved Dec 2001 as an SAC under EU Habitats and Species Directive in part to protect bottlenose dolphin and loggerhead turtle habitat (Annex II criteria); also protects Annex IV species. • SECAC has been working in this area. • Cetacean surveys and research are needed to quantify habitat use.	• Contact: Erika Urquiola, Sociedad Española de Cetáceos – SEC (Spanish Cetacean Society), Islas Canarias, Spain; email: urquiola@cetaceos.com or sec@cetaceos.com; web: www.cetaceos.com

Table 5.11 *continued*

Name of MPA or sanctuary, location and size	Cetacean and other notable species
(7) Área Marina de la Isleta SAC • northeast Gran Canaria (28°10'N, 15°27'W) • 33 mi² (85.6 km²)	• common (Annex II): bottlenose dolphin, *Tursiops truncatus*; common (Annex IV): sperm whale, *Physeter macrocephalus*; striped dolphin, *Stenella coeruleoalba*; Atlantic spotted dolphin, *Stenella frontalis*; Risso's dolphin, *Grampus griseus*; short-finned pilot whale, *Globicephala macrorhynchus* • also: loggerhead turtle
(8) Franja Marina de Mogán SAC • southwest Gran Canaria • 115.8 mi² (299.9 km²)	• common (Annex II): bottlenose dolphin, *Tursiops truncatus*; common (Annex IV): Atlantic spotted dolphin, *Stenella frontalis*; other species found here but not officially protected: Risso's dolphin, *Grampus griseus*; striped dolphin, *Stenella coeruleoalba*; rough-toothed dolphin; *Steno bredanensis*; Blainville's beaked whale, *Mesoplodon densirostris*; Gervais' beaked whale, *Mesoplodon europaeus*; sei whale, *Balaenoptera borealis*; fin whale, *Balaenoptera physalus*; pygmy Bryde's whale, *Balaenoptera edeni*; sperm whale, *Physeter macrocephalus* • also: loggerhead turtle
(9) Bahía del Confital SAC • northeast Gran Canaria (28°8'N, 15°27'W) • 2.4 mi² (6.3 km²)	• common (Annex II): bottlenose dolphin, *Tursiops truncatus;* common (Annex IV): Risso's dolphin, *Grampus griseus*
(10) Sebadales de Playa del Inglés SAC • southeast Gran Canaria (27°45'N, 15°33'W) • 4.6 mi² (11.9 km²)	• common (Annex II): bottlenose dolphin, *Tursiops truncatus*
(11) Franja Marina de Fuencaliente SAC • south La Palma (28°32'N, 17°53'W) • 27.2 mi² (70.6 km²)	• common (Annex II): bottlenose dolphin, *Tursiops truncatus;* common (Annex IV): Atlantic spotted dolphin, *Stenella frontalis;* Risso's dolphin, *Grampus griseus;* striped dolphin, *Stenella coeruleoalba* • also: loggerhead turtle

Notes and rationale	For more information
• Approved Dec 2001 as an SAC under EU Habitats and Species Directive in part to protect bottlenose dolphin and loggerhead turtle habitat (Annex II criteria); also protects Annex IV species. • SECAC is working in this area, in some years as part of a Life Naturaleza project • Cetacean surveys and research are needed to quantify habitat use.	• Contact: Erika Urquiola, Sociedad Española de Cetáceos – SEC (Spanish Cetacean Society), Islas Canarias, Spain; email: urquiola@cetaceos.com or sec@cetaceos.com; web: www.cetaceos.com • Vidal Martín, SECAC; email: ziphius@teide.net; web: www.cetaceos.org
• Approved Dec 2001 as an SAC under EU Habitats and Species Directive in part to protect bottlenose dolphin and loggerhead turtle habitat (Annex II criteria); also protects Annex IV species. • SECAC has been working in this area since 1996, in some years as part of a Life Naturaleza project and at other times for the Canaries government.	• Contact: Erika Urquiola, Sociedad Española de Cetáceos – SEC (Spanish Cetacean Society), Islas Canarias, Spain; email: urquiola@cetaceos.com or sec@cetaceos.com; web: www.cetaceos.com • Vidal Martín, SECAC; email: ziphius@teide.net; web: www.cetaceos.org
• Approved Dec 2001 as an SAC under EU Habitats and Species Directive in part to protect bottlenose dolphin habitat (Annex II criteria); also protects Annex IV species. • Cetacean surveys and research are needed to quantify habitat use.	• Contact: Erika Urquiola, Sociedad Española de Cetáceos – SEC (Spanish Cetacean Society), Islas Canarias, Spain; email: urquiola@cetaceos.com or sec@cetaceos.com; web: www.cetaceos.com
• Approved Dec 2001 as an SAC under EU Habitats and Species Directive in part to protect bottlenose dolphin habitat (Annex II criteria). • Cetacean surveys and research are needed to quantify habitat use.	• Contact: Erika Urquiola, Sociedad Española de Cetáceos – SEC (Spanish Cetacean Society), Islas Canarias, Spain; email: urquiola@cetaceos.com or sec@cetaceos.com; web: www.cetaceos.com
• Approved Dec 2001 as an SAC under EU Habitats and Species Directive in part to protect bottlenose dolphin and loggerhead turtle habitat (Annex II criteria); also protects Annex IV species. • Cetacean surveys and research are needed to quantify habitat use.	• Contact: Erika Urquiola, Sociedad Española de Cetáceos – SEC (Spanish Cetacean Society), Islas Canarias, Spain; email: urquiola@cetaceos.com or sec@cetaceos.com; web: www.cetaceos.com

Table 5.11 *continued*

Name of MPA or sanctuary, location and size	Cetacean and other notable species
(12) Playa de Sotavento de Jandía SAC • southeast Fuerteventura (28°9'N, 14°12'W), extending one mile out to sea • 21.1 mi² (54.6 km²)	• common (Annex II): bottlenose dolphin, *Tursiops truncatus*; common (Annex IV): short-beaked common dolphin, *Delphinus delphis*; other species found here but not officially protected: striped dolphin, *Stenella coeruleoalba*; Cuvier's beaked whale, *Ziphius cavirostris*; Blainville's beaked whale, *Mesoplodon densirostris* • also: loggerhead turtle
(13)* Southeastern Fuerteventura (unnamed) MPA, *proposed • southeast Fuerteventura, overlaps Playa de Sotavento de Jandía SAC above but would extend much farther out to sea • size undetermined	• Cuvier's beaked whale, *Ziphius cavirostris*; Blainville's beaked whale, *Mesoplodon densirostris*; plus other whales and dolphins
CAPE VERDE República de Cabo Verde ***(14)* Cape Verde Humpback Whale MPA, *proposed*** • nearshore waters around Cape Verde Islands • size undetermined	• humpback whale, *Megaptera novaeangliae*
THE GAMBIA Republic of Gambia **(15) Niumi National Park** • occupies northwest Atlantic coast of The Gambia, on the north bank of the Gambia River mouth	• year-round: Atlantic hump-backed dolphin, *Sousa teuszii*; bottlenose dolphin, *Tursiops truncatus* • also: West African manatee, clawless otters
(16) Tanji Bird Reserve • southwest Atlantic coast of The Gambia	• year-round: bottlenose dolphin, *Tursiops truncatus*; suspected: Atlantic hump-backed dolphin, *Sousa teuszii*
(17) Kiang West National Park • located more than 50 mi (80 km) up river, near Tendaba • 10 mi² (26 km²)	• Dec–Mar (dry season): bottlenose dolphin, *Tursiops truncatus* • also: probably West African manatee

Notes and rationale	For more information
• Approved Dec 2001 as an SAC under EU Habitats and Species Directive in part to protect bottlenose dolphin and loggerhead turtle habitat (Annex II criteria); also protects Annex IV species. • SECAC has been working in this area. • Cetacean surveys and research are needed to quantify habitat use.	• Contact: Erika Urquiola, Sociedad Española de Cetáceos – SEC (Spanish Cetacean Society), Islas Canarias, Spain; email: urquiola@cetaceos.com or sec@cetaceos.com; web: www.cetaceos.com
• In 2002 a special committee was created to study the causes and origin of the mass strandings of 14 beaked whales (*Ziphius* and *Mesoplodon* species) on Fuerteventura and Lanzarote in Sept 2002, and to decide what to do; in Nov 2003, the committee decided to promote the declaration of southeastern Fuerteventura as an MPA for cetaceans but especially for beaked whales. This would be only the second beaked whale protected area in the world, following the designation of The Gully off Nova Scotia, Canada, for northern bottlenose whales.	• Contact: Erika Urquiola, Sociedad Española de Cetáceos – SEC (Spanish Cetacean Society), Islas Canarias, Spain; email: urquiola@cetaceos.com or sec@cetaceos.com; web: www.cetaceos.com
• This special nursery area in shallow waters and reefs, identified for humpback whale mothers and calves by German research group, may require protection in view of large-scale tourism developments planned for the islands.	• Contact: Michael Schneider; email: delpharion@aol.com; mischnei@aol.com
• Land and nearshore national park created in 1986. • Rationale is to protect diverse habitat including salt marsh, mudflats, dunes, mangrove, swamp, lagoon and ocean as well as native species. • 'Poaching of manatees and bycatch of dolphins and manatees in fisheries occurs, but these and other harmful activities would be worse without the protection provided by park staff' (Reeves, 2002).	• Reeves, 2002; Van Waerebeek et al, 2000 • Contact: Koen Van Waerebeek; email: k.van.waerebeek@skynet.be; cepec.dir@terra.com.pe
• Land and nearshore bird reserve which includes the Bijol islands and associated inshore waters where there is some dolphin habitat.	• Van Waerebeek et al, 2000 • Contact: Koen Van Waerebeek; email: k.van.waerebeek@skynet.be; cepec.dir@terra.com.pe
• Largest national park in The Gambia, created in 1987; includes riverine habitat and 'off limits' reserve areas. • 'Poaching of manatees and bycatch of dolphins and manatees in fisheries occurs, but these and other harmful activities would be worse without the protection provided by park staff' (Reeves, 2002). • Some commercial dolphin watching in the park helps provide economic incentive for protection (Hoyt, 2001).	• Reeves, 2002; Van Waerebeek et al, 2000 • Contact: Koen Van Waerebeek; email: k.van.waerebeek@skynet.be; cepec.dir@terra.com.pe

Table 5.11 *continued*

Name of MPA or sanctuary, location and size	Cetacean and other notable species
GUINEA Republic of Guinea République de Guinée **(18) Konkoure Estuary (Delta du Konkoure) MPA** • Konkoure Estuary (9°45'N, 13°41'W)	• dolphins, probably Atlantic hump-backed dolphin, *Sousa teuszii*; bottlenose dolphin, *Tursiops truncatus* • also: West African manatee
MAURITANIA Islamic Republic of Mauritania; République Islamique Arabe et Africaine de Mauritanie **(19) Banc d'Arguin National Park (Parc National du Banc d'Arguin) and Biosphere Reserve** • northern Mauritania, south of Nouadhibou (Pt Étienne) • includes land and nearshore areas of 4632 mi^2 (12,000 km^2)	• all year: bottlenose dolphin, *Tursiops truncatus*; Atlantic hump-backed dolphin, *Sousa teuszii*; orca, *Orcinus orca*; harbor porpoise, *Phocoena phocoena*; pilot whales, *Globicephala* sp, live mainly in coastal waters by the park, but can also be seen in the park • also: Mediterranean monk seal, although main Cap Blanc colony is just outside the park
MOROCCO al-Mamlaka al-Maghrebia **(20) Dakhla National Park (Parc National de Dakhla)** • Dakhla province, western Morocco, on the Atlantic coast • total size uknown but includes marine areas all along the Dahkhla province shoreline	• various cetaceans resident and migratory • also: Mediterranean monk seal
SENEGAL République de Sénégal **(21) Saloum Delta National Park and Siné-Saloum Biosphere Reserve (Parc du Delta du Saloum)** • Siné-Saloum Delta, opposite northern border of The Gambia and the open Atlantic • 695 mi^2 (1800 km^2)	• Atlantic hump-backed dolphin, *Sousa teuszii*; bottlenose dolphin, *Tursiops truncatus* • also: West African manatee

Notes and rationale	For more information
• Protected as Ramsar site no 575, since Nov 1992. • Rationale is to protect diverse habitat including salt marsh, mudflats, dunes, mangrove, swamp, lagoon and ocean as well as native species. • Cetacean research would help quantify habitat use.	• Contact: Koen Van Waerebeek; email: k.van.waerebeek@skynet.be; cepec.dir@terra.com.pe
• Existing MPA since 1976 designated under Unesco Biosphere Reserve programme, includes desert shore, mudflats, mangroves, islands and shallow seas, which serve as spawning ground and nursery for massive concentrations of fish, crustaceans and molluscs. • Area is site of traditional mullet fishery; Imraguen fishers are helped by bottlenose dolphins from Sept–Dec; cetacean studies since mid-1990s reveal that resident dolphins use area for feeding, mating and breeding. • Artisanal fishing permitted; industrial fishing excluded but high level of offshore- and shark-fishing in the park has substantial dolphin bycatch which threatens cooperative fishing, as well as future dolphin watching and marine tourism. • Management plan has minimal public involvement.	• Cooperation Francaise, 1993; Price et al, 1992; Vely et al, 1995 • Ba Abou Sidi, CNROP (National Oceanic and Fisheries Research Ctr), BP 22, Nouadhibou, Nouakchott, Mauritania • Parc National du Banc d'Arguin, BP 58541, Nouakchott, Mauritania • Michel Vely; l'association Megaptera; email: mvely@megaptera-oi.org; web: www.megaptera-oi.org
• Park covers marine and terrestrial areas, set up largely to protect the monk seals. • Inventory and planning are still at an early stage; cetacean distribution studies need to be done to determine habitat.	• Contact: Abdellatif Bayed, Université Mohammed V – Agdal Institut Scientifique, Unité d'Océanologie Biologique; email: bayed@israbat.ac.ma
• Existing land and nearshore national park (open forest, mangroves, lagoons, sand dunes, ocean islands) which was made a biosphere reserve under Unesco Biosphere Reserve programme in 1980. • 'Poaching of manatees and bycatch of dolphins and manatees in fisheries occurs, but these and other harmful activities would be worse without the protection provided by park staff' (Reeves, 2002).	• Reeves, 2002; Van Waerebeek et al, 2000 • Contact: Koen Van Waerebeek; email: k.van.waerebeek@skynet.be or cepec.dir@terra.com.pe

Table 5.11 *continued*

Name of MPA or sanctuary, location and size	Cetacean and other notable species
SOUTH AFRICA Republiek van Suid-Afrika **(22) De Hoop MPA** • east of Arniston for 31.7 mi (51 km) along the coast to Cape Infanta, Western Cape • 121.6 mi² (315 km²)	• Jun–Nov: southern right whale, *Eubalaena australis*; Apr–Dec, migratory: humpback whale, *Megaptera novaeangliae*; year-round, common: Indo-Pacific hump-backed dolphin, *Sousa chinensis*; Indo-Pacific bottlenose dolphin, *Tursiops aduncus*; more offshore: Bryde's whale, *Balaenoptera brydei*; Antarctic minke whale, *Balaenoptera bonaerensis*; short-beaked common dolphin, *Delphinus delphis*; orca, *Orcinus orca* • also: Cape fur seal, southern elephant seal; indigenous Cape vegetation
(23) Robberg MPA • located along the Robberg Peninsula, 5 mi (8 km) south of Plettenberg Bay, Western Cape • length of MPA is 5.6 mi (9 km)	• Jun–Nov: southern right whale, *Eubalaena australis*; Apr–Dec, migratory: humpback whale, *Megaptera novaeangliae* • also: Cape gannets, whitebreasted and Cape cormorants, Cape fur seal, blue duiker
(24) Dwesa-Cwebe MPA • located along 10.2 mi (16.5 km) of the coast extending 7 mi (11 km) out to sea, Eastern Cape • 68 mi² (176 km²)	• Jun–Nov: southern right whale, *Eubalaena australis*; Apr–Dec, migratory: humpback whale, *Megaptera novaeangliae*; year-round, common inshore: Indo-Pacific hump-backed dolphin, *Sousa chinensis*; Indo-Pacific bottlenose dolphin, *Tursiops aduncus*; more offshore: short-beaked common dolphin, *Delphinus delphis* • also: diverse bird species

Notes and rationale	For more information
• The De Hoop Nature Reserve was declared under the Nature and Environmental Conservation Ordinance 19/1974. The De Hoop MPA was created in 1986 and named as one of 19 MPAs in the Marine Living Resources Act No 18 of 1998. • The De Hoop MPA is one of the main breeding areas for the southern right whale, with some of the country's largest concentrations of mother–calf pairs. In addition, 13 other species of marine mammals regularly pass through these waters (Cockcroft and Joyce, 1998). Industries in the area include tourism and fishing. The coastline of the reserve is well known as a land-based whale watch site. • Rationale is to protect the largest remaining expanse of indigenous Cape vegetation, as well as the biodiversity of the marine component. • Managed by the Western Cape Nature Conservation Board (WCNCB) but a specific management agreement is required between WCNCB and Marine and Coastal Management (MCM). There is no formal management plan for the De Hoop MPA, only for the De Hoop Nature Reserve, but it does not include the MPA (Lemm and Attwood, 2003). Currently this MPA has limited active management.	• Attwood et al, 1997; Cockcroft and Joyce, 1998; Lemm and Attwood, 2003; Robinson and De Graaff, 1994 • Contact: Marine and Coastal Management, Ministry of Environmental Affairs and Tourism, Cape Town; email: tabane@iafrica.com; web: www.environment.gov.za • Vic Cockcroft, Centre For Dolphin Studies; email: cdsresearch@ worldonline.co.za • Western Cape Nature Conservation Board (WCNCB) web: www.capenature.org.za • management plan at www.capenature.org.za/ icdp/dehoopplan.html
• Site of a national monument (first European habitation in South Africa) as well as a land-based nature reserve with a marine component. • Located beside Robberg Nature Reserve, it was declared under the Nature and Environmental Conservation Ordinance 19/1974 and named as one of 19 MPAs in the Marine Living Resources Act No 18 of 1998. • Managed by the WCNCB at Plettenberg Bay but there is no management plan or zoning plan, nor formal agreement with MCM to manage this MPA, all of which are needed (Lemm and Attwood, 2003).	• Attwood et al, 1997: Lemm and Attwood, 2003; Robinson and De Graaff, 1994 • Contact: Robberg Nature Reserve, Plettenberg Bay; email: robkeur@mweb.co.za; web: www.cnc.org.za/ Nature_Reserves/html/ robberg.html
• MPA is located next to the Dwesa and Cwebe Nature Reserves, which are state forests, IUCN Category IV, established 1975; the MPA was set up under the Transkei Environmental Decree 10 of 1992 and named an MPA in the Marine Living Resources Act No 18 of 1998. • There is no zoning or specific MPA management plan (although the terrestrial area plan makes some references). At present the MPA is considered one zone where all fishing is prohibited. Eastern Cape Dept of Economic Affairs, Environment and Tourism (ECDEAET) is supposed to be responsible for species conservation and management of protected areas, but management agreement needs to be formulated between ECDEAET and the national MCM bodies (Lemm and Attwood, 2003). There is no active MPA management.	• Attwood et al, 1997: Lemm and Attwood, 2003; Robinson and De Graaff, 1994 • Contact: Marine and Coastal Management, Ministry of Environmental Affairs and Tourism, Cape Town; web: www.environment.gov.za

Table 5.11 *continued*

Name of MPA or sanctuary, location and size	Cetacean and other notable species
(25) Tsitsikamma MPA • located along 35.4 mi (57 km) east of Plettenberg Bay, spanning Western and Eastern Cape provinces • total size is 142.2 mi² (368.5 km²), of which 124.7 mi² (323 km²) is marine; the marine reserve extends 3.4 mi (5.5 km) offshore all along the coast	• Jun–Nov: southern right whale, *Eubalaena australis*; Apr–Dec, migratory: humpback whale, *Megaptera novaeangliae*; year-round, common: Indo-Pacific hump-backed dolphin, *Sousa chinensis*; short-beaked common dolphin, *Delphinus delphis*; Indo-Pacific bottlenose dolphin, *Tursiops aduncus*; also: Bryde's whale, *Balaenoptera brydei*; pygmy sperm whale, *Kogia breviceps*; dwarf sperm whale, *Kogia sima*; Risso's dolphin, *Grampus griseus*; striped dolphin, *Stenella coeruleoalba*; orca, *Orcinus orca*; various beaked whales • also: 400+ species of marine fish, almost 50 per cent of which are endemic and important spawning grounds; vervet monkey, Cape clawless otter, bushbuck, blue duiker
(26) Sardinia Bay MPA • located south of Port Elizabeth, along 4.3 mi (7 km) of shoreline, Eastern Cape • 5.1 mi² (13.2 km²)	• Jun–Nov: southern right whale, *Eubalaena australis*; Apr–Dec, migratory: humpback whale, *Megaptera novaeangliae*; year-round, common inshore: Indo-Pacific hump-backed dolphin, *Sousa chinensis*; Indo-Pacific bottlenose dolphin, *Tursiops aduncus*
(27) Mkambati MPA • located along 7.1 mi (11.5 km) of the coast, 25 mi (40 km) east of Flagstaff, Eastern Cape • 50 mi² (130 km²)	• Jun–Nov: southern right whale, *Eubalaena australis*; Apr–Dec, migratory: humpback whale, *Megaptera novaeangliae*; year-round, common inshore: Indo-Pacific hump-backed dolphin, *Sousa chinensis*; Indo-Pacific bottlenose dolphin, *Tursiops aduncus*; more offshore: short-beaked common dolphin, *Delphinus delphis* • also: Cape vulture, baboon

Notes and rationale	For more information
• The first marine park in South Africa, the marine portion of the Tsitsikamma Forest and Coastal National Park was initially established as a strict reserve in 1964 under the South African National Parks Act of 1962 as well as the National Parks Act No 57 of 1976. Today, it is still part of the Tsitsikamma National Park and is referred to as the Tsitsikamma MPA after being named as one of 19 MPAs in the Marine Living Resources Act No 18 of 1998 (see Regulation Gazette 6978 from 2000). • Managed by South African National Parks (SANParks), there is a management plan as of 2000 but it is considered not useful in its current form (Lemm and Attwood, 2003) and a new plan as well as an agreement is needed between MCM and SANParks to allow SANParks to take full responsibility for management of MPAs that are part of, as well as next to, national parks. • All fishing is currently prohibited; the park has high visitor numbers due to its location on the Garden Route but the marine section of the park is considered underutilized for tourism and there is very limited active management of the MPA (Lemm and Attwood, 2003). • The purpose of the park is to conserve a representative section of the southern Cape coastline with terrestrial and marine flora and fauna. One objective is to provide a breeding area for marine life so that it can repopulate exploited areas. The park itself specifies the southern right whales as part of its fauna. Rated IUCN Category II.	• Attwood et al, 1997; Lemm and Attwood, 2003; Robinson and De Graaff, 1994 • Contact: The Park Warden, Tsitsikamma National Park, PO Storms River 6308 South Africa; web: www.parks-sa.co.za/ frames.asp?mainurl=parks/ national_parks.html
• Adjacent to Sardinia Bay Reserve and Sylvic Nature Reserve which were declared under Ordinance 19 of 1974 Nature and Environmental Conservation Ordinance. Named as one of 19 MPAs in the Marine Living Resources Act No 18 of 1998, the Sardinia Bay MPA is managed on a day-to-day basis by the Nelson Mandela Metropolitan Municipality (NMMM). Lemm and Attwood (2003) recommend that Marine and Coastal Management (MCM) should make a formal agreement that would give more responsibility for management to NMMM.	• Attwood et al, 1997: Lemm and Attwood, 2003; Robinson and De Graaff, 1994 • Contact: Marine and Coastal Management, Ministry of Environmental Affairs and Tourism, Cape Town; web: www.environment.gov.za
• Located beside the Mkambati Nature Reserve, a State Forest under the National Forests Act; the MPA was set up under the Transkei Environmental Decree 10 of 1992 and named as one of 19 MPAs in the Marine Living Resources Act No 18 of 1998. • MPA has no management or zoning plan; at present it is considered to be one zone where all fishing is prohibited. • Eastern Cape Dept of Economic Affairs, Environment and Tourism (ECDEAET) is supposed to be responsible for species conservation and management of protected areas, but management agreement needs to be formulated between ECDEAET and the national MCM bodies (Lemm and Attwood, 2003). Currently, there is no active management of this MPA. • There are plans to expand this MPA and create a larger Pondoland MPA which would be jointly managed by ECDEAET and SANParks.	• Attwood et al, 1997: Lemm and Attwood, 2003; Robinson and De Graaff, 1994 • Contact: Marine and Coastal Management, Ministry of Environmental Affairs and Tourism, Cape Town; web: www.environment.gov.za

Table 5.11 *continued*

Name of MPA or sanctuary, location and size	Cetacean and other notable species
(28) Hluleka MPA • Mnenu River on the 'Wild Coast', Eastern Cape	• Jun–Nov: southern right whale, *Eubalaena australis*; Apr–Dec, humpback whale, *Megaptera novaeangliae*; year-round, common inshore: Indo-Pacific hump-backed dolphin, *Sousa chinensis*; Indo-Pacific bottlenose dolphin, *Tursiops aduncus*; more offshore: short-beaked common dolphin, *Delphinus delphis*
(29) Trafalgar MPA • 7.5 mi (12 km) south of Ramsgate near the southern end of the KwaZulu-Natal province • 1 mi² (2.5 km²)	• year-round, common inshore: Indo-Pacific hump-backed dolphin, *Sousa chinensis*; Indo-Pacific bottlenose dolphin, *Tursiops aduncus*; more offshore: short-beaked common dolphin, *Delphinus delphis*
(30) St Lucia MPA • near Cape Vidal, KwaZulu-Natal • 159.8 mi² (414 km²)	• Jun–Nov: southern right whale, *Eubalaena australis*; Apr–Dec, migratory: humpback whale, *Megaptera novaeangliae*; year-round, common inshore: Indo-Pacific hump-backed dolphin, *Sousa chinensis*; Indo-Pacific bottlenose dolphin, *Tursiops aduncus*; more offshore: short-beaked common dolphin, *Delphinus delphis* • also: leatherback and loggerhead turtles, coral reefs, coelacanth, crocodile (major breeding grounds)
(31) Maputaland MPA • KwaZulu-Natal • 157.5 mi² (408 km²)	• Jun–Nov: southern right whale, *Eubalaena australis*; Apr–Dec, migratory: humpback whale, *Megaptera novaeangliae*; year-round, common inshore: Indo-Pacific hump-backed dolphin, *Sousa chinensis*; Indo-Pacific bottlenose dolphin, *Tursiops aduncus*; more offshore: short-beaked common dolphin, *Delphinus delphis* • also: coral reefs, leatherback and loggerhead turtles

Notes and rationale	For more information
• The adjacent land-based reserve, IUCN Category IV, was established in 1977; the MPA was set up under the Transkei Environmental Decree 10 of 1992 and named in 1998 under the Marine Living Resources Act. • Special features include a unique swamp forest with some open grassland and ravines supporting a wide range of land, coastal and adjacent marine species. • MPA has no management or zoning plan; at present, it is considered one zone where all fishing is prohibited but there is no active management. Eastern Cape Dept of Economic Affairs, Environment and Tourism (ECDEAET) is supposed to be responsible for species conservation and management of protected areas, but management agreement needs to be formulated between ECDEAET and the national MCM bodies.	• Attwood et al, 1997: Lemm and Attwood, 2003; Robinson and De Graaff, 1994 • Contact: Marine and Coastal Management, Ministry of Environmental Affairs and Tourism, Cape Town; web: www.environment.gov.za
• IUCN Category II reserve set up to protect the remains of marine fossil beds. • Named as one of 19 MPAs in the Marine Living Resources Act No 18 of 1998, this small MPA may include cetacean habitat but studies need to be done. • Managed by Ezemvelo KwaZulu-Natal Wildlife, the public conservation agency of KwaZulu-Natal province. • Management plan is needed as there is currently very limited management of this MPA.	• Attwood et al, 1997: Lemm and Attwood, 2003; Robinson and De Graaff, 1994 • Contact: Marine and Coastal Management, Ministry of Environmental Affairs and Tourism, Cape Town; web: www.environment.gov.za • KwaZulu-Natal Wildlife; web: www.kznwildlife.com
• IUCN Category II, set up initially as a land-based park (dating from 1939) and game reserve (dating from 1897); it was named as one of 19 MPAs in the Marine Living Resources Act No 18 of 1998. • The MPA may include cetacean habitat, especially for dolphins; specific cetacean studies need to be done. • Part of and managed by the Greater St Lucia Wetland Park Authority, together with the Maputaland MPA (below) and a complex of other protected areas, through Ezemvelo KwaZulu-Natal Wildlife, the public conservation agency of KwaZulu-Natal province. • This zoned MPA was declared under Provincial Ordinance 15 of 1974 as well as the World Heritage Convention Act No 49 of 1999, initially to help protect turtles and coral. • The management plan needs to be revised (Lemm and Attwood, 2003).	• Attwood et al, 1997: Lemm and Attwood, 2003; Robinson and De Graaff, 1994 • Contact: Marine and Coastal Management, Ministry of Environmental Affairs and Tourism, Cape Town; web: www.environment.gov.za • KwaZulu-Natal Wildlife; web: www.kznwildlife.com
• Named as one of 19 MPAs in the Marine Living Resources Act No 18 of 1998, this MPA is part of and managed by the Greater St Lucia Wetland Park Authority, together with St Lucia MPA (above), through Ezemvelo KwaZulu-Natal Wildlife, the public conservation agency of KwaZulu-Natal province. • This zoned MPA was declared under Provincial Ordinance 15 of 1974 as well as the World Heritage Convention Act No 49 of 1999. • The management plan needs to be revised (Lemm and Attwood, 2003).	• Attwood et al, 1997; Lemm and Attwood, 2003; Robinson and De Graaff, 1994 • Contact: Marine and Coastal Management, Ministry of Environmental Affairs and Tourism, Cape Town; web: www.environment.gov.za • KwaZulu-Natal Wildlife; web: www.kznwildlife.com

Table 5.11 *continued*

Name of MPA or sanctuary, location and size	Cetacean and other notable species
(32) Helderberg MPA • located along 2.5 mi (4 km) of shore adjacent to Helderberg Coastal Reserve, northern False Bay, Western Cape	• Jun–Nov: southern right whale, *Eubalaena australis*; year-round: Indo-Pacific bottlenose dolphin, *Tursiops aduncus*; short-beaked common dolphin, *Delphinus delphis*
(33) Walker Bay Whale Sanctuary • Walker Bay, off Hermanus, Western Cape	• Jun–Nov: southern right whale, *Eubalaena australis*; year-round, common: Indo-Pacific bottlenose dolphin, *Tursiops aduncus*; short-beaked common dolphin, *Delphinus delphis*
(34) **West Coast National Park, including (35) Langebaan Lagoon MPA and (36) Sixteen Mile Beach MPA, as well as (37) Marcus, (38) Jutten and (39) Malgas MPAs,** *proposed* **for amalgamation** • located along Western Cape, north of Cape Town	• Jun–Nov: southern right whale, *Eubalaena australis*; year-round: Indo-Pacific bottlenose dolphin, *Tursiops aduncus*; Heaviside's dolphin, *Cephalorhynchus heavisidii*; dusky dolphin, *Lagenorhynchus obscurus*
(40) **Cape Peninsula MPA,** *proposed and in process*, **includes (41) Castle Rock MPA** • adjacent to Cape Peninsula National Park, False Bay, Western Cape • 2.5 mi^2 (6.6 km^2) at present for Castle Rock MPA only; expansion would be considerably larger	• Jun–Nov: southern right whale, *Eubalaena australis*; year-round: Indo-Pacific bottlenose dolphin, *Tursiops aduncus*; short-beaked common dolphin, *Delphinus delphis*

Notes and rationale	For more information
• Adjacent to the Helderberg Coastal Reserve which is managed by the Helderberg Municipality, the Helderberg MPA was named as one of 19 MPAs in the Marine Living Resources Act No 18 of 1998. • Currently there is no active management of this MPA but Lemm and Attwood (2003) suggest that MCM should forge an agreement with Helderberg Municipality to manage the MPA.	• Lemm and Attwood, 2003 • Contact: Marine and Coastal Management, Ministry of Environmental Affairs and Tourism, Cape Town; web: www.environment.gov.za
• In May 2000, the Minister of Environmental Affairs and Tourism set aside an area of Walker Bay to serve as a southern right whale sanctuary from 1 Jul to 15 Dec each year. Although not formally listed as an MPA under the Marine Living Resources Act, Walker Bay was made subject to regulation 58, published under Govt Notice No R-111 of 2 Sept 1998 (Gazette No 19205) that pertains to whale protection. No fishing boats, vessels, jetskis, kayaks or other craft are allowed in the sanctuary without permission. The only exceptions are legally permitted whale watch vessels that may operate subject to the relevant permit conditions and the closed areas for boat-based whale watching (see Govt Notice No 417 of 18 Feb 2000 – Gazette No 20877). • Rationale is to provide more protection for southern right whales in South African waters during whale season as well as greater recognition of their endangered status.	• Cockcroft and Joyce, 1998 • Contact: Marine and Coastal Management, Ministry of Environmental Affairs and Tourism, Cape Town; email: tabane@iafrica.com; web: www.environment.gov.za
• Langebaan Lagoon MPA was established under the National Parks Act No 57 of 1976 and named as one of 19 MPAs in the Marine Living Resources Act No 18 of 1998 (see Regulation Gazette 6978 from 2000). • Langebaan Lagoon and part of Sixteen Mile Beach MPAs are managed by South African National Parks (SANParks), but Marcus, Jutten and Malgas MPAs, located nearby, are not actively managed by SANParks which considers these MPAs to be MCM's responsibility (yet MCM doesn't actively manage them). Lemm and Attwood (2003) suggest the declaration of one large multiple-use MPA to manage the area as one management unit but MCM has not made a decision yet. • Lemm and Attwood (2003) point to the need for a management agreement between MCM and SANParks to allow SANParks to take full responsibility for management of all these MPAs that are part of, as well as next to, national parks. The areas are zoned. The draft 'West Coast National Park Integrated Environmental Management System – Strategic Management Plan 2003–2007' should help the process of managing Langebaan Lagoon MPA.	• Lemm and Attwood, 2003 • Contact: Marine and Coastal Management, Ministry of Environmental Affairs and Tourism, Cape Town; web: www.environment.gov.za • South African National Parks (SANParks); web: www.parks-sa.co.za
• Castle Rock MPA, named as one of 19 MPAs in 1998, is set to be included within the Cape Peninsula MPA which was gazetted in 2003 and has a draft management plan. Currently there is limited active management of Castle Rock MPA but this will change with its amalgamation into the Cape Peninsula MPA when SANParks expects to take an active role in management.	• Attwood et al, 1997; Lemm and Attwood, 2003 • Contact: Marine and Coastal Management, Ministry of Environmental Affairs and Tourism, Cape Town; web: www.environment.gov.za • South African National Parks (SANParks); web: www.parks-sa.co.za

Table 5.11 *continued*

Name of MPA or sanctuary, location and size	Cetacean and other notable species
(42) Betty's Bay MPA, *proposed for expansion as part of (43)* **Kogelberg MPA/Biosphere Reserve** • east of False Bay, Western Cape • 4.7 mi² (12.1 km²) at present; proposed expansion would be considerably larger	• Jun–Nov: southern right whale, *Eubalaena australis*; year-round: Indo-Pacific bottlenose dolphin, *Tursiops aduncus*; short-beaked common dolphin, *Delphinus delphis*; Indo-Pacific hump-backed dolphin, *Sousa chinensis* • also: abalone, rich fishing grounds
(44) Goukamma MPA, *proposed for expansion* • along 8.7 mi (14 km) of the coast in the heart of the Garden Route, Western Cape • 11.6 mi² (30 km²)	• Jun–Nov: southern right whale, *Eubalaena australis*; Apr–Dec, migratory: humpback whale, *Megaptera novaeangliae*; year-round, common inshore: Indo-Pacific hump-backed dolphin, *Sousa chinensis*; Indo-Pacific bottlenose dolphin, *Tursiops aduncus*; more offshore: short-beaked common dolphin, *Delphinus delphis*; Bryde's whale, *Balaenoptera brydei* • also: Cape gannets, whitebreasted and Cape cormorants, Cape fur seal
ST HELENA and ASCENSION (UK) (British overseas territory) **(45) St Helena Biosphere Reserve,** *proposed* • 1200 mi (1920 km) from the southwest coast of Africa • size undetermined	• resident: pantropical spotted dolphin, *Stenella attenuata*; other cetaceans sporadic or to be determined

Notes and rationale	For more information
• Betty's Bay MPA, adjacent to the existing Greater Betty's Bay Nature Reserve, set up in 1985 and named as one of 19 MPAs in 1998, has been actively managed by the Overstrand Municipality due to abalone poaching which had to be controlled. However, detailed arrangements and agreements with MCM need to be made to institute a comprehensive management regime for the MPA, including a multi-zone plan, but it may be best to wait for the decision on the proposed expansion to the larger Kogelberg MPA (Lemm and Attwood, 2003). For now, MCM has worked out an arrangement with Overstrand Municipality to enforce provisions of the Marine Living Resources Act in this area. • Although Betty's Bay is a small MPA at present, cetaceans are found in and around the area. Studies need to be done to determine if cetacean critical habitat has been partly protected by the MPA or if expansion into the much larger Kogelberg MPA could turn this into an effective MPA for cetaceans and other species as well. • Marine tourism possibilities include sea kayaking, and whale and seabird watching.	• Attwood et al, 1997; Lemm and Attwood, 2003 • Contact: Marine and Coastal Management, Ministry of Environmental Affairs and Tourism, Cape Town; web: www.environment.gov.za • Overstrand Municipality; web: www.overstrand.gov.za
• Located next to Goukamma Nature Reserve (declared under the Nature and Environmental Conservation Ordinance 19/1974), it was named as one of 19 MPAs in the Marine Living Resources Act No 18 of 1998. • Managed by WCNCB with a management plan, prepared in 2001, which does not consider the MPA but only the land-based reserve. The management plan needs to be reviewed along with the development of a zoning plan to manage the various activities within the MPA and the implementation of a formal management agreement with MCM (Lemm and Attwood, 2003). These authors also recommend the expansion of the MPA boundaries to include the entire reef and estuary. • Tourism, including whale and dolphin watching, is a key component of the MPA and needs to be managed wisely. At present this MPA has very limited management.	• Attwood et al, 1997; Robinson and De Graaff, 1994; Lemm and Attwood, 2003 • Contact: Marine and Coastal Management, Ministry of Environmental Affairs and Tourism, Cape Town; web: www.environment.gov.za • Western Cape Nature Conservation Board (WCNCB); web: www.capenature.org.za
• Conservation initiatives have focused on St Helena's unique terrestrial fauna and flora but Wells and Bleakley (1995) were the first to propose that the entire island be designated as a biosphere reserve to include at least nearshore waters. This could in effect provide habitat protection for a known resident nearshore spotted dolphin population. • Dolphin fishery here has ended and today schools on the island take dolphin watch tours. • Surveys should be conducted to determine distribution and habitat needs of other cetaceans and marine species.	• Wells and Bleakley, 1995

Table 5.11 *continued*

Name of MPA or sanctuary, location and size	Cetacean and other notable species
TRISTAN DA CUNHA (UK) (includes Tristan, Inaccessible, Nightingale and Gough islands) (British overseas territory) **(B) Tristan da Cunha Cetacean Sanctuary** • located 1240 mi (2000 km) south of St Helena, South Atlantic; includes islands of Tristan, Inaccessible and Nightingale in one group and Gough Island, which is 250 mi (400 km) to the southeast • size extends to the limit of the EEZ, 200 nm (371 km) from shore all around the islands	• Jun–Oct: southern right whale, *Eubalaena australis*; also: humpback whale, *Megaptera novaeangliae*; orca, *Orcinus orca*; false killer whale, *Pseudorca crassidens*; dusky dolphin, *Lagenorhynchus obscurus*; sperm whale, *Physeter macrocephalus*; beaked whales, possibly including Shepherd's beaked whale, *Tasmacetus shepherdi*; others
(46) Inaccessible Island Nature Reserve • 25 mi (40 km) southwest of Tristan da Cunha Island in the South Atlantic • size includes entire island of 5.4 mi² (14 km²) plus surrounding waters up to 12 nm (22.2 km) from shore	• Jun–Oct: southern right whale, *Eubalaena australis*; also: humpback whale, *Megaptera novaeangliae*; false killer whale, *Pseudorca crassidens*; dusky dolphin, *Lagenorhynchus obscurus*; sperm whale, *Physeter macrocephalus*; beaked whales, possibly including Shepherd's beaked whale, *Tasmacetus shepherdi*; others • also: southern elephant seal, subantarctic fur seal, some marine endemic species
(47) Gough Island Wildlife Reserve • located 250 mi (400 km) southeast of the main group of Tristan, Inaccessible and Nightingale • 25 mi² (65 km²) of land and marine area out to 3 nm (5.6 km)	• Jun–Oct: southern right whale, *Eubalaena australis*; year-round: dusky dolphin, *Lagenorhynchus obscurus*; others • also: rockhopper penguin (48 per cent of world numbers), wandering albatross, Atlantic petrel, little and greater shearwater, rare southern giant petrel

Notes and rationale	For more information
• National waters declared a cetacean refuge or sanctuary in Mar 2001; legal protection is under the Tristan da Cunha Fishery Limits Ordinance of 1983 (as amended 1991, 1992 and 1997). • Rationale is to ban hunting or causing harm to cetaceans: 'no person whatsoever shall hunt or capture, kill or harm in any way any species of cetacean'. • Tristan was site of former whaling station so historically there were many large whales around here, but further research is needed to determine cetacean species and populations currently present.	• Contact: The Administrator, Tristan da Cunha, South Atlantic; email: hmg@cunha. demon.co.uk
• Declared a nature reserve in Feb 1997 according to the terms of the Tristan da Cunha Conservation Ordinance (1976, as amended 1997). • Management plan completed and accepted by Tristan da Cunha government in Feb 2001 (Ryan and Glass, 2001) – sets out management as a strict nature reserve (IUCN Category I) in a zoned MPA; sustainable activities permitted in surrounding waters. • Rationale for protection is that it is one of the few temperate oceanic islands free of introduced mammals with many endemics and other features. • Further research would be needed to determine cetacean habitat use.	• Ryan and Glass, 2001 (available from UK Overseas Territory Dept, London) • Contact: The Administrator, Tristan da Cunha, South Atlantic; email: hmg@cunha. demon.co.uk • Peter Ryan, Percy FitzPatrick Institute, University of Cape Town, South Africa; email: pryan@botzoo.uct.ac.za
• This wildlife reserve became a World Heritage Site in 1995. • Rationale is that this stands as the least-disturbed cool-temperate island ecosystem in the South Atlantic and has important seabird colonies. • Whales and dolphins are reported; studies would need to be done to determine habitat use and degree of protection.	• web: http://whc.unesco.org/ sites/740.htm

MARINE REGION 9: SOUTH ATLANTIC

One of the first whale populations to be studied in the wild in the early 1970s was the southern right whale which is seasonally resident in the waters around Península Valdés, Argentina. Senior American whale researcher Roger Payne and his colleagues determined how to identify individual whales, observed their behaviour in detail and contributed to efforts to make the local waters of Península Valdés into an MPA. Over the past decade, work has focused on southern right whales in Uruguayan and southern Brazilian waters and their relationship to the overall population in the South Atlantic, as well as on the small cetaceans of the South America's southern cone. Researchers today from Argentina, Brazil and Uruguay, led by Miguel Iñíguez, José T Palazzo, Jr and others, continue to build on this work with southern right whales and other cetaceans.

More than 50 cetacean species are found in the region, 39 in Brazilian waters alone. Argentina has fewer species with 35, but has a number of cetacean species found mainly or only from Patagonia to Tierra del Fuego, three of which – Burmeister's porpoise and Peale's and Commerson's dolphins – range into Chilean waters of the Southeast Pacific Marine Region, with Commerson's also found in the Kerguelen Islands in the Antarctic. The spectacled porpoise and hourglass dolphin have a somewhat wider world range, extending to other marine regions in the southern hemisphere.

This region also has important river dolphin populations. Two are endemic: the completely riverine Amazon River dolphin of the Amazon and Orinoco (partly located in the Wider Caribbean, Marine Region 7) and the estuarine and nearshore franciscana that lives in and around the Rio de la Plata of Argentina and Uruguay. There is also the widespread riverine tucuxi, which is an oceanic dolphin (not in the group of river dolphins) with populations that live full time in the Amazon and Orinoco river basins.

In 2002 and again in 2003, the countries of the South Atlantic Marine Region, led by Brazil, took the lead in trying to have the South Atlantic declared an ocean-wide IWC whale sanctuary. There has been opposition from whaling countries and countries sympathetic to the whalers. However, the multi-country IWC initiative, as well as supporting cessation of whaling, might well lead to productive regional initiatives in favour of resident cetaceans and their critical habitat MPA conservation needs.

Four national governments have a role in the region, including Brazil, Uruguay and Argentina, as well as the offshore Falkland Islands (Malvinas) administered by the UK. The South Atlantic Marine Region borders the Greater Caribbean in the north and extends to the Antarctic in the South and includes the national waters and high seas of all but the northern part of eastern South America.

In the South Atlantic Marine Region, four large marine ecosystems (LMEs) have been identified: the North Brazil Shelf, East Brazil Shelf, South Brazil Shelf and the Patagonian Shelf. The overall oceanography is defined by the

South Equatorial Current which flows into the northern part of the region and divides into both northerly and southerly flows. The northern branch becomes the warm Guiana Current (which links with the Caribbean circulation system) while the southern flow turns into the warm Brazil Current which continues to have a strong influence as far south as the Rio de la Plata which forms the boundary between Uruguay and Argentina. Few areas of upwelling are found along the Brazilian coast, except for the Cabo Frio region near Rio de Janeiro, due to the strong stratification of the surface and deep water masses. South of the Río de la Plata, the main water mass influence is the cold Falkland (Malvinas) Current which flows up the coast of Argentina. The influence from the meeting and mixing of both of these two currents can be felt along all of Argentina (and as far north as Cabo Frio) and the mixing helps create productive marine ecosystems, including intense areas of upwelling along the edge of the continental shelf of Argentina. These are prime whale feeding areas.

Coral reefs in the South Atlantic are found in the tropical areas of Brazil, including offshore islands. The two main coral reef formations, at the offshore archipelago of Fernando de Noronha in Pernambuco State, the Rocas atoll in Rio Grande do Norte State and the Abrolhos archipelago in Bahia State, have cetacean habitat for, respectively, spinner dolphins and humpback whales, and both are protected as part of larger MPAs built around the coral reefs. Substantial mangroves, found especially around the Amazon River mouth in the north of Brazil, extend south, though in less dense formations, to Santa Catarina State. Further south, in Rio Grande do Sul State in southern Brazil, salt marshes are prevalent.

A UNEP regional seas programme has been initiated for the Southwest Atlantic, including Argentina, Uruguay and Brazil, but it is at an early stage and much work needs to be done if the programme is to function as a mechanism for bringing priority marine issues to the table and working out effective regional management plans. In 1995, there was a reported total of 19 MPAs of all kinds in this marine region (Diegues et al, 1995). This was seriously underreported, however, as a national Brazilian workshop in 1999 identified more than a hundred MPAs in Brazil alone (Augustowski, pers comm, 2004). The region is divided into five biogeographic zones all of which were represented by at least one MPA but four of which have only bare representation. As of 2004, according to Table 5.12 prepared for this book, there are 33 existing and 4 proposed MPAs which feature cetacean habitat. Two of the existing MPAs are proposed for expansion.

The IUCN 2002–2010 Conservation Action Plan for the World's Cetaceans recommends nine research and education initiatives for this region (Reeves et al, 2003):

- to investigate interactions between river dolphins and fisheries in Amazonia and Orinoquia (also applies to Marine Region 7);
- to assess existing and planned water development projects and gold mining in the Amazon and Orinoco basins (also for Marine Region 7);

BOX 5.6 BRAZIL: A WIDE VARIETY OF MPA DESIGNATIONS

Name	English Meaning

Full protection (indirect use) MPAs:

1 Reserva Biológica	biological reserve: IUCN Category Ia
2 Estação Ecológica	ecological station: restricted use area

MPAs for research and environmental education:

3 Parque Estadual Marinho	state marine park
4 Parque Nacional Marinho	national marine park

MPAs for 'sustainable' use (direct use):

5 Área de Proteção Ambiental (APA)	environmental protection area, usually comprising a broad area, designated as multiple use
6 Reserva Extrativista	designated for 'sustainable' use by traditional communities, including non-lethal uses of wildlife, such as ecotourism

- to develop a conservation strategy for South American river dolphins (also for Marine Region 7);
- to assess fishery interactions with cetaceans in Brazil;
- to identify threats and evaluate the status of marine tucuxi populations in Brazil;
- to monitor cetacean interactions with Argentine fisheries;
- to assess illegal use of small cetaceans for crab bait in southern South America (also for Marine Region 17);
- to investigate stock identity of endemic species in South America (also for Marine Region 17); and
- to conduct cetacean abundance estimation workshops in Latin America (also for Marine Regions 7 and 17).

There are also a number of IUCN initiatives recommended for franciscana, a species in the region rated 'data deficient', but with a restricted range and potentially endangered:

- to conduct aerial surveys to estimate franciscana abundance;
- to investigate stock identity of franciscana;
- to develop an overall management strategy to conserve the franciscana;
- for management authorities and all stakeholders to work together to modify fishing gear and practices, eg, by forcibly reducing the total fishing effort, imposing spatial/temporal closures, and possibly introducing new fishing methods;

BOX 5.7 ARGENTINA: PROVINCIAL AND NATIONAL LAWS DIRECTED TOWARDS WILD CETACEANS

There are a large number of laws at the provincial and national level that come into play in any discussion about protecting wild cetaceans in Argentina. At the national level are the following laws and resolutions:

- National Law Number 22344/80, Ley sobre el comercio internacional de especies amenazadas de flora y fauna silvestre;
- National Law Number 23094/84, Monumento Natural Ballena Franca Austral (*Eubalaena australis*);
- National Law Number 25052/98, Ley de conservación de Orcas (*Orcinus orca*);
- National Resolution 351/95, which prohibits the hunting, capture and transport of cetaceans within national jurisdiction ('Reglamento para establecimientos que albergan mamíferos marinos'); and
- Recommendation Number 10/00, a 'southern cone' initiative which designates *Eubalaena australis* as the 'MERCOSUR' whale (passed in 2000 by the MERCOSUR Parliament under the southern cone free trade agreement, the Asunción Treaty).

In Buenos Aires Province, there are two laws:

- Provincial Law 11477/94, Ley Provincial de Pesca, and
- Ordenanza 9702/94 (in Municipio General Pueyrredon).

Chubut Province has Provincial Law 2381/84, modified by Provincial Law 2618/85, with the Decreto Reglamentario Number 916/86, which prohibits all activity without official authorization and includes persecuting or approaching, sailing, swimming and diving near any marine mammals in the provincial jurisdiction on the coast and in the sea. The mandate of a provincial park in Chubut (Provincial Law 4617/00) is to protect and conserve natural ecosystems through native species, to restore habitats to their original state in places where they have been modified, and to work in accordance with scientific, economic and tourist objectives with conditions. Land inside the park is in the public domain. The park can be zoned for three uses: untouchable or highly protected; for conservation and commercial exploration; and for tourism and recreation.

Río Negro Province has Provincial Law 1960/85 which regulates research, conservation and use of biological resources of aquatic habitat, including cetaceans.

In Santa Cruz Province, provincial natural reserves can be designated to protect areas where the conservation of ecological systems or the preservation of transitional zones to provincial parks is important or when the area does not require the legal status of a provincial park. The conservation priorities in provincial natural reserves are protecting animals, plants, the main physiographic features and scenic beauty, and maintaining the ecological balance. In 2001 and 2003, Santa Cruz Provincial Laws 2582/2001 and 2643/2003 declared the Commerson's dolphin and southern right whale as provincial natural monuments, the highest conservation level in the province. These laws aim to protect these species in provincial waters against any kind of exploitation or habitat destruction.

Tierra del Fuego Province has Provincial Law 101/93 which prohibits the capture and commercialization of cetaceans and other animals.

- for management authorities to enforce existing fishery regulations and consider imposing new ones, such as gear modifications to restrict the length of gill nets;
- to do controlled studies on acoustic deterrents or pingers to determine effectiveness;
- to engage in a public information campaign to publicize the risks that gill-net fishing poses to franciscana as well as to the region's fish stocks; and
- for authorities to develop trilateral management arrangements to agree on a conservation strategy for franciscana.

The above IUCN initiatives provide an assessment of certain small cetacean priorities but cetacean policy-makers and researchers in the region, as well as the regional IUCN representative on the World Commission on Protected Areas (WCPA), have pointed out that the list fails to take account of many cetacean research needs, such as priorities for southern right, humpback and other whales.

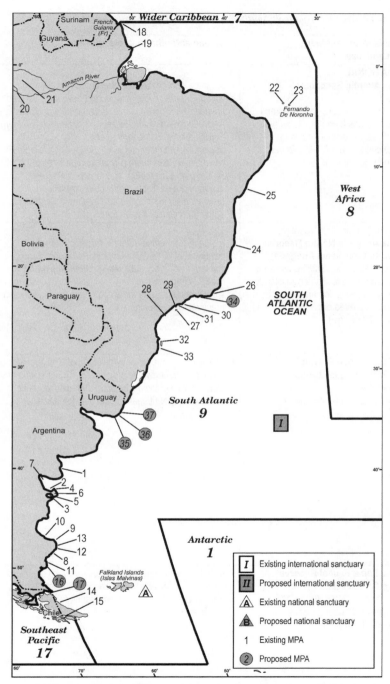

The roman numerals, letters and numbers correspond to the sanctuaries and MPAs listed and described in Table 5.12.

Figure 5.16 *Map of Marine Region 9: South Atlantic MPAs and sanctuaries*

Table 5.12 *Marine Region 9: South Atlantic MPAs and sanctuaries*

Name of MPA or sanctuary, location and size	Cetacean and other notable species
INTERNATIONAL **(I) South Atlantic Sanctuary, proposed** • South Atlantic Ocean, spread across Marine Regions 8 and 9 • size undetermined but goal is to protect entire South Atlantic Ocean from the Equator to 40°S	• southern right whale, *Eubalaena australis*; pygmy right whale, *Caperea marginata*; humpback whale, *Megaptera novaeangliae*; minke whale, *Balaenoptera acutorostrata*; Antarctic minke whale, *Balaenoptera bonaerensis;* pygmy Bryde's whale, *Balaenoptera edeni*; Bryde's whale, *Balaenoptera brydei*; sei whale, *Balaenoptera borealis*; fin whale, *Balaenoptera physalus*; blue whale, *Balaenoptera musculus*; sperm whale, *Physeter macrocephalus*. Protection would only extend to the great whales; in total, the South Atlantic Ocean has some 53 species of cetaceans.
ARGENTINA República Argentina **(1) Bahía Anegada Nature Reserve (Reserva Natural Bahía Anegada)** • located at 40°21'S, 62°23'W: includes Jabalí, Gamma and Flamengo islands as well as Bahía Union and Bahía San Blas, Buenos Aires province • 28.5 mi² (73.86 km²)	• resident: bottlenose dolphin, *Tursiops truncatus*; franciscana, or La Plata dolphin, *Pontoporia blainvillei*; sporadic: southern right whale, *Eubalaena australis*; orca, *Orcinus orca* • also: breeding areas for South American sea lion and many seabird colonies
(2) Golfo San José Provincial Marine Park (Parque Marino Golfo San José) • San José Gulf, Chubut province	• May–Dec: southern right whale, *Eubalaena australis*; dusky dolphin, *Lagenorhynchus obscurus*; orca, *Orcinus orca* • also: seabird colonies; sea lion rookeries, such as southern elephant seal and southern sea lion
(3) Punta Loma Faunal Reserve (Reserva Faunal Punta Loma) • Punta Loma (42°49'S, 64°53'W), Golfo Nuevo, Chubut province • 6.6 mi² (17.1 km²)	• May–Dec: southern right whale, *Eubalaena australis* • also: seabird colonies; year-round colonies of South American sea lions; important marine fossil deposits are found all over the reserve

Notes and rationale	For more information
• Rationale is to protect large whales from commercial whaling and to stimulate whale watching for the benefit of local communities as well as cetacean research and conservation. • First discussed in the IWC Scientific Committee in 2001, it was formally proposed by Brazil and Argentina in 2002 and by Brazil, Argentina and South Africa in 2003–2004; it has the dedicated support of countries in the region and will be proposed again.	• Government of Brazil, 2001 • Contact: Régis Pinto de Lima, Director, National Aquatic Mammals Center of Brazil, PO Box 1, 53900-000, Itamaracá, PE, Brazil; email: rplima@uol.com.br
• Rationale is to protect the ecology of the area, including the resident dolphins. • The area became a Provincial Natural Reserve in 1987 through Provincial Law 10492/87 (Buenos Aires). Within this reserve are a number of Natural Integral Reserves on the islands and banks. There is no management plan for the area – which should be done. • There has been a study for some years on the ecology and behaviour of the franciscana, or La Plata dolphin, *Pontoporia blainvillei*, by Pablo Bordino.	• Contact: María del Valle Fathala, Fundación Cethus, J De Garay 2861 Dto 3, (B1636AGK), Olivos, Prov Buenos Aires, Argentina; email: cethus@house.com.ar or machef@hotmail.com
• Rationale is to protect marine and coastal ecology including marine mammals, especially right whales. • The Golfo San José Provincial Marine Park was created by Chubut in 1974 under Provincial Law 1238/74 to give essential protection to a critical breeding area for southern right whales. The law was modified in 1979 and 1983 to allow economic activities such as whale watching which now attracts 80,000+ people a year. • The adjacent Golfo Nuevo is part of the right whale breeding area but not in the park and has been allowed to be developed industrially (aluminium and fish processing plants, boat traffic, raw sewage problems). Some say that Golfo Nuevo should have been part of the park, or that development should be limited. In 1983, with Provincial Law 2161, the adjoining land-based Península Valdés Tourist Reserve was created by Chubut. The Golfo San José Park is zoned as an untouchable or highly protected area within the larger Península Valdés reserve.	• Crespo, 2001; Iñíguez et al, 1998; Fundación Cethus, 1999 • Contact: Miguel A Iñíguez, Fundación Cethus, PO Box 126, 9310, Puerto San Julián, Pcia Santa Cruz, Argentina; email: tovera@sanjulian.com.ar • Claudio Campagna, Fundación Patagonia Natural, Casilla de Correo 160, 9120 Puerto Madryn, Argentina
• Rationale is to protect marine and coastal ecology including important seabird and marine mammal colonies. • The area was made a provincial untouchable faunal reserve in 1967 through Provincial Law 697/67. This is the highest level of protection which prohibits use of fauna, flora and land for commercial objectives, building in the reserve and sport hunting. The objective of the reserve is to preserve nature in all its aspects. • Existing conflicts include high numbers of visitors due to the proximity of the city of Puerto Madryn. Marine mammals may be affected by water contamination, shipping traffic and increasing fishing activity in the area.	• Contact: Miguel A Iñíguez, Fundación Cethus, PO Box 126, 9310, Puerto San Julián, Pcia Santa Cruz, Argentina; email: tovera@sanjulian.com.ar

Table 5.12 *continued*

Name of MPA or sanctuary, location and size	Cetacean and other notable species
(4) Punta Norte Provincial Faunal Reserve (Reserva Natural Turística Punta Norte) • Punta Norte (42°0'5S, 63°46'W) Chubut province • 0.023 mi^2 (0.06 km^2, or 6 hectares)	• Feb–May: orca, *Orcinus orca* • also: breeding rookeries for southern elephant seal and South American sea lion
(5) Punta Pirámide Nature Reserve (Reserva Natural Punta Pirámide) • Golfo Nuevo, Chubut province • 0.5 mi^2 (1.32 km^2)	• May–Dec: southern right whale, *Eubalaena australis*; dusky dolphin, *Lagenorhynchus obscurus*; orca, *Orcinus orca* • also: seabird colonies and rookeries for southern sea lion and southern elephant seal
(6) Península Valdés Nature Reserve (Reserva Natural Península Valdés) • Península Valdés (42°33'S, 63°54'W), Golfo Nuevo, Golfo San José, Chubut province • 1390 mi^2 (3600 km^2) including mostly land and some marine area	• May–Dec: southern right whale, *Eubalaena australis*; dusky dolphin, *Lagenorhynchus obscurus*; orca, *Orcinus orca* • also: seabird colonies and rookeries for southern elephant seal and southern sea lion
(7) Bahía San Antonio Oeste Hemispheric Reserve (Reserva Hemisférica Bahía San Antonio Oeste) • San Antonio Bay, San Matias Gulf, Río Negro province	• southern right whale, *Eubalaena australis*; orca, *Orcinus orca*; bottlenose dolphin, *Tursiops truncatus* • also: breeding area for seabird colonies and fishes
(8) Bahía Laura Provincial Nature Reserve (Reserva Natural Provincial Bahía Laura) • Bahía Laura (48°21'S, 66°27'W), along 6 mi (9 km) of coast between Cabo Guardián and Punta Mercedes, Santa Cruz province	• Peale's dolphin, *Lagenorhynchus australis*; Commerson's dolphin, *Cephalorhynchus commersonnii* • also: breeding areas for Magellanic penguins, cormorants and other seabirds

Notes and rationale	For more information
• Rationale is to protect marine and coastal ecology including important seabird and marine mammal colonies. • In 1967, Punta Norte was established by the Province of Chubut as a Provincial Faunistic Reserve mainly to protect southern sea lion and southern elephant seal rookeries (Provincial Law 697/67). In 1983, Provincial Law 2161 allowed the area to be considered as a Tourist Reserve. Some 50,000 tourists visit each year, many to watch orcas chasing and striking sea lion pups in the shallows. Fundación Cethus is studying the biology, behaviour, population dynamics and conservation of orcas in the area.	• Iñíguez, 2001; Iñíguez et al, 1998; López and López, 1985 • Contact: Miguel A Iñíguez, Fundación Cethus, PO Box 126, 9310, Puerto San Julián, Pcia Santa Cruz, Argentina; email: tovera@sanjulian.com.ar
• Rationale is to protect marine and coastal ecology including important seabird and marine mammal colonies. • The area was made a provincial nature reserve in 1974 according to Ministerial Resolution 9/74. Only 35,000 visitors are allowed each year to this relatively small area.	• Contact: María del Valle Fathala, Fundación Cethus, J De Garay 2861 Dto 3, (B1636AGK), Olivos, Prov Buenos Aires, Argentina; email: cethus@house.com.ar or machef@hotmail.com
• Rationale is to protect marine and coastal ecology including important seabird and marine mammal colonies, with tourism access. • The area was made a natural tourist reserve in 1983 with Provincial Law 2161/83. The Península Valdés Nature Reserve includes the land-based, highly protected core areas of the Golfo San José Provincial Marine Park, Punta Norte and Punta Pirámides, described above as reserves in their own right. Península Valdés currently limits tourists in the reserve to 140,191 a year (for more information, see also Golfo San José above).	• Contact: María del Valle Fathala and Miguel A Iñíguez, Fundación Cethus, J De Garay 2861 Dto 3, (B1636AGK), Olivos, Prov Buenos Aires, Argentina; email: cethus@house.com.ar or machef@hotmail.com
• In 1993, the Rio Negro provincial government passed Provincial Law 2670/93 creating a provincial hemispheric reserve primarily for coastal birds (Reserva Hemisférica de Reservas para Aves Playeras – RHRAP). Government agencies involved in the establishment and management of this area are Dirección de Fauna Río Negro Province, Instituto de Biología Marina y Pesquera 'Almirante Storni', and Red Hemisférica de Reservas de Aves Playeras. There is no biological inventory or management plan for the area, and there has been no research on local cetacean populations.	• Contact: María del Valle Fathala, Fundación Cethus, J De Garay 2861 Dto 3, (B1636AGK), Olivos, Prov Buenos Aires, Argentina; email: cethus@house.com.ar or machef@hotmail.com
• The Bahía Laura Nature Reserve was designated in 1977 through Provincial Decree 1561/77 to protect breeding bird colonies in the area. From 1986–94, researchers with Fundación Vida Silvestre Argentina made biological inventories of birds and marine mammals. Commerson's and Peale's dolphins are found but habitat use is unknown. • Fundación Cethus has been researching dolphins in this area.	• Perez et al, 1995 • Contact: Miguel A Iñíguez, Fundación Cethus, PO Box 126, 9310, Puerto San Julián, Pcia Santa Cruz, Argentina; email: tovera@sanjulian.com.ar

Table 5.12 *continued*

Name of MPA or sanctuary, location and size	Cetacean and other notable species
(9) Cabo Blanco Nature Reserve (Reserva Natural Intagible Cabo Blanco) • Cabo Blanco (47°12'S, 65°45'W), Santa Cruz province • 2.84 mi² (7.37 km²)	• southern right whale, *Eubalaena australis*; orca, *Orcinus orca*; Peale's dolphin, *Lagenorhynchus australis*; Commerson's dolphin, *Cephalorhynchus commersonnii* • also: seabird colonies and non-breeding pinniped rookeries for South American sea lions and South American fur seals. Three species of cormorants plus penguins and many other birds breed here.
(10) Monte Loayza Nature Reserve (Reserva Natural Monte Loayza) • Monte Loayza (47°49'S, 66°51'W), south of Golfo San Jorge, 75 mi (120 km) northwest of Puerto Deseado, Santa Cruz province	• southern right whale, *Eubalaena australis* • also: breeding area for cormorants, seagulls and other seabirds. Presence of southern elephant seal and breeding area for South American sea lion
(11) Península San Julián and Bahía de San Julián Nature Reserve (Reserva Natural Península San Julián y Bahía de San Julián) • San Julián peninsula and bay (49°15'S, 67°36'W) which includes Isla Cormoran and Justicia, Santa Cruz province • 40 mi² (104 km²)	• Sept–May: Peale's dolphin, *Lagenorhynchus australis*; Commerson's dolphin, *Cephalorhynchus commersonnii*; sporadic: southern right whale, *Eubalaena australis* • also: seabird colonies including Magellanic penguins and five species of cormorants; a non-breeding rookery of South American sea lions
(12) Complejo Bahía Oso Marino Nature Reserve (Reserva Natural Complejo Bahía Oso Marino) • Oso Marino Bay including Penguin Island (Isla Pingüino), Chata Island and Castillo Island, Santa Cruz province	• Peale's dolphin, *Lagenorhynchus australis*; Commerson's dolphin, *Cephalorhynchus commersonnii* • also: seabird colonies including Magellanic penguins, various cormorants and other seabirds; breeding rookery for the South American sea lion

Notes and rationale	For more information
• The Cabo Blanco Nature Reserve was designated in 1977 through Provincial Decree 1561/77 to protect pinniped rookeries and breeding bird colonies in the area. From 1986–94, researchers with Fundación Vida Silvestre Argentina made biological inventories of birds and marine mammals. There have been sporadic records of orcas, southern right whales and Peale's dolphins but aside from abundance and distribution studies, there has yet to be detailed study of their habitat use of the area. • Besides Fundación Vida Silvestre Argentina, Fundación Cethus and Fundación Patagonia Natural have been working in the area. The government agency is the Dirección de Fauna Provincia Santa Cruz and Dirección de Recursos Naturales y Áreas Protegidas. There is no management plan for the area.	• Perez et al, 1995 • Contact: Miguel A Iñíguez, Fundación Cethus, PO Box 126, 9310, Puerto San Julián, Pcia Santa Cruz, Argentina; email: tovera@sanjulian.com.ar • Jorge Perancho, Áreas Protegidas, Consejo Agario Prov, Roca 976, Río Gallegos, Pcia Santa Cruz, Argentina
• Rationale is to protect marine and coastal ecology including important seabird and marine mammal colonies. • The area was made a 'no go' natural reserve for scientific use in 1989 as part of Provincial Law 14/89. The inventories of birds and marine mammals made between 1986 and 1994 provide basic information. No management plan, but according to this type of reserve, no economic exploitation or recreational use is allowed. Only authorized visitors with certain scientific or educational objectives are allowed.	• Perez et al, 1995 • Contact: Miguel A Iñíguez, Fundación Cethus, PO Box 126, 9310, Puerto San Julián, Pcia Santa Cruz, Argentina; email: tovera@sanjulian.com.ar • Jorge Perancho, Áreas Protegidas, Consejo Agario Prov, Roca 976, Río Gallegos, Pcia Santa Cruz, Argentina
• San Julian Peninsula was made a natural reserve by Provincial Law 1821/86 (Decree 969) in 1986 to protect marine and coastal ecology including seabirds and marine mammals. In 1990, San Julian Bay became a 'no go' natural reserve for scientific use. The inventories of birds and marine mammals made between 1986 and 1994 has provided basic information. Another biodiversity inventory project is being carried out by Fundación Cethus and the municipality of Puerto San Julián. Area is considered a cetacean mating and breeding area based on studies of Commerson's since 1996. A resident group of Peale's dolphins is being studied by Fundación Cethus. • A management plan is being prepared by the Dirección de Áreas Protegidas y Recursos Naturales of Santa Cruz. According to this type of reserve, there is no economic expoitation; only authorized visitors with scientific or educational objectives are allowed.	• Contact: Miguel A Iñíguez, Fundación Cethus, PO Box 126, 9310, Puerto San Julián, Pcia Santa Cruz, Argentina; email: tovera@sanjulian.com.ar • Jorge Perancho, Áreas Protegidas, Consejo Agario Prov, Roca 976, Río Gallegos, Pcia Santa Cruz, Argentina
• Rationale is to protect marine and coastal ecology including important seabird and marine mammal colonies. • The area is a provincial nature reserve which includes several islands, coast and water. Penguin Island is a provincial reserve on its own. From 1986 to 1994, researchers with Fundación Vida Silvestre Argentina made detailed biological inventories in the province covering birds and marine mammals. • No research has been done on cetacean use of the area. • Penguin Island was made a provincial nature reserve in 1992 by Provincial Law 2274/92.	• Perez et al, 1995 • Contact: María del Valle Fathala, Fundación Cethus, J De Garay 2861 Dto 3, (B1636AGK), Olivos, Prov Buenos Aires, Argentina; email: cethus@house.com.ar or machef@hotmail.com • Jorge Perancho, Áreas Protegidas, Consejo Agario Prov, Roca 976, Río Gallegos, Pcia Santa Cruz, Argentina

Table 5.12 *continued*

Name of MPA or sanctuary, location and size	Cetacean and other notable species
(13) Ría Deseado Nature Reserve (Reserva Natural Ría Deseado) • Ría Deseado estuary	• Sept–May: Commerson's dolphin, *Cephalorhynchus commersonnii;* sporadic: southern right whale, *Eubalaena australis*; orca, *Orcinus orca*; Peale's dolphin, *Lagenorhynchus australis* • also: seabird colonies include Magellanic penguin, five species of cormorants, seagulls, flamingos and other seabirds; southern elephant seal and South American sea lion rookeries
(14) Costa Atlántica de Tierra del Fuego Nature Reserve (Reserva Costa Atlántica Tierra del Fuego) • Atlantic coast of Tierra del Fuego province, including San Sebastian Bay (between Punta Páramo and San Sebastian Cape), Rio Grande estuary, Península Mitre (northern coast including Bahía Tethis and Caleta Policarpo), part of Beagle Channel (seacoast including islands of Bahía Ushuaia and Puerto Harberton area) • 110 mi² (286 km²)	• Commerson's dolphin, *Cephalorhynchus commersonnii* (all areas); orca, *Orcinus orca* (Peninsula Mitre and sometimes in Beagle Channel); Peale's dolphin, *Lagenorhynchus australis* (Beagle Channel); Burmeister's porpoise, *Phocoena spinipinnis* (Beagle Channel); spectacled porpoise, *Phocoena dioptrica* (Rio Grande estuary) • also: seabirds, marine mammals including South American sea lions, South American fur seals and elephant seals
(15) Tierra del Fuego National Park and National Strict Reserve (Parque Nacional Tierra del Fuego y Reserva Nacional) • Beagle Channel, Tierra del Fuego province • 243 mi² (630 km²) (includes land area)	• Burmeister's porpoise, *Phocoena spinipinnis* • also: seabird colonies; sea otters, black-browed albatross, black-necked swan, great grebe

Notes and rationale	For more information
• Rationale is to protect marine and coastal ecology including important seabird and marine mammal colonies. • The area was made a provincial nature reserve in 1977 by Provincial Decree 1561/77. From 1986 to 1994, researchers with Fundación Vida Silvestre Argentina surveyed birds and marine mammals. In 1995, Miguel Iñíguez collected detailed information on local, cultural, historical and biological features. Since then he has led studies of Commerson's dolphins. The area is important as a cetacean feeding ground as well as a mating and breeding area. • A modest level of boat trips offers sea-based nature and dolphin watching. It is hoped that Commerson's dolphin research will increase public awareness and protection of the area.	• Iñíguez, 1995; Perez et al, 1995 • Contact: Miguel A Iñíguez, Fundación Cethus, PO Box 126, 9310, Puerto San Julián, Pcia Santa Cruz, Argentina; email: tovera@sanjulian.com.ar • Jorge Perancho, Áreas Protegidas, Consejo Agario Prov, Roca 976, Río Gallegos, Pcia Santa Cruz, Argentina
• Rationale is to protect marine and coastal ecology including important seabird and marine mammal colonies. • The area was made a provincial nature reserve in 1992 as part of Territorial Decree 2202/92. Since then, the area has been made a hemispheric site and in Oct 1995, it was included in the Ramsar list as a wetland of international importance. • This coastal reserve includes land and nearshore waters which are cetacean feeding grounds for dolphins and porpoises. Fundación Cethus researchers have studied the biology, ecology and conservation of Burmeister's porpoises in the area, but there is no management plan or formal biological inventory for the reserve. • Work has been done on cetacean habitat with Burmeister's porpoise but more could be done with Commerson's dolphins which are found throughout the area, as well as for the local spectacled porpoises and Peale's dolphins.	• Contact: María del Valle Fathala, Cecilia Gasparrou and Gabriela de Tezanos Pinto, Fundación Cethus, J De Garay 2861 Dto 3, (B1636AGK), Olivos, Prov Buenos Aires, Argentina; email: cethus@house.com.ar
• Rationale is to protect coastal ecology including wildlife and archaeological treasures, as well as scenic beauty and scientific interest, as a representative area of Argentina. • The area was made a national park in 1960 according to National Law 15554/60. According to National Park legislation, the area must be maintained without disturbance except as needed for visitor services, National Defence and park activities. Exploitation including commercial fishing, mining and other natural resources extraction, as well as human settlement, is prohibited except for tourism regulated by park authorities. A national strict reserve within the park ensures maximum protection of Argentine biodiversity. • Fundación Cethus has conducted recent Burmeister's porpoise research in the park; for many years Nathalie Goodall has maintained a research station near Ushuaia for studying local cetaceans.	• Contact: María del Valle Fathala, Gabriela de Tezanos Pinto, Fundación Cethus, J De Garay 2861 Dto 3, (B1636AGK), Olivos, Prov Buenos Aires, Argentina; email: cethus@house.com.ar

Table 5.12 *continued*

Name of MPA or sanctuary, location and size	Cetacean and other notable species
(16) Isla Monte León Provincial Reserve (Reserva Provincial Isla Monte León), *proposed as a national park* • Isla Monte Leon (49º55'S, 68º36'W), Santa Cruz province • 38.6 mi² (100 km²)	• Sept–May: Commerson's dolphin, *Cephalorhynchus commersonnii*; southern right whale, *Eubalaena australis* • also: seabird colonies (Magellanic penguin and others); South American sea lion breeding rookery
(17) Cabo Virgenes Nature Reserve (Reserva Natural Cabo Virgenes) *proposed for expansion* • Cabo Virgenes (52º22'S, 68º23'W), western mouth of Magellan Strait, Santa Cruz province • size of designated protected area is 4.75 mi² (12.3 km²); the proposed extension is 32.75 mi² (84.9 km²) which would make a total size of approximately 37.5 mi² (97.2 km²)	• resident Peale's dolphin, *Lagenorhynchus australis*; sporadic: Commerson's dolphin, *Cephalorhynchus commersonnii*; orca, *Orcinus orca*; southern right whale, *Eubalaena australis* • also: Magellanic penguins, seagulls, cormorants and other birds; southern sea lions. This area has historical and cultural value as the first settling of the Ciudad del Nombre de Jesus, founded by Sarmiento de Gamboa in 1584; there have been many shipwrecks here.
BRAZIL República Federativa do Brasil **(18) Cabo Orange National Park (Parque Nacional do Cabo Orange)** • Cabo Orange, Amapa State, northern tip of Brazil • 2389 mi² (6190 km²)	• bottlenose dolphin, *Tursiops truncatus*
(19) Lago Piratuba Biological Reserve (Reserva Biológica do Lago Piratuba) • Amapa State • 1525 mi² (3950 km²)	• boto, or Amazon River dolphin, *Inia geoffrensis*; tucuxi, *Sotalia fluviatilis*
(20) Mamirauá Sustainable Development Reserve (Reserva de Desenvolvimento Sustentável Mamirauá) • near Tefé, beside Solimões and Japurá rivers, Amazonas • 4339 sq mi² (11,240 km²)	• boto, or Amazon River dolphin, *Inia geoffrensis;* tucuxi, *Sotalia fluviatilis* • also: Amazonian manatee

Notes and rationale	For more information
• Rationale is to protect marine and coastal ecology including important seabird and marine mammal colonies. • The area was made a provincial nature reserve under Provincial Law 2445; now it is being proposed as a national park.	• Perez et al, 1995 • Contact: Miguel A Iñíguez, Fundación Cethus, PO Box 126, 9310, Puerto San Julián, Pcia Santa Cruz, Argentina; email: tovera@sanjulian.com.ar
• The core land area was declared a reserve in 1986 through Provincial Law 1806/86 (Decree 826) to protect the world's southernmost continental colony of Magellanic penguins. The inventories of birds and marine mammals made between 1986 and 1994 provide basic information. Fundación Cethus has also identified a resident population of Peale's dolphins as well as sporadic orcas, Commerson's dolphins, and southern right whales and the need for habitat protection (de Haro and Iñíguez, 1997; Anon, 1998). • Management plan was completed in 2001 according to the legal requirements for the reserve; plan identifies an important marine zone of 6 nm (11 km) radius around the lighthouse at Cabo Virgenes where a *Macrocystis* forest occurs with extensive feeding by Peale's dolphins, and marine and coastal birds. The current management plan has contingency plans for oil spills and mitigates against other conflicts; it needs to be put into action. • An expanded reserve is proposed to protect cetacean mating, breeding and feeding grounds in the area. More research on Peale's dolphins could further the legal move for expansion. The existing area and the area proposed for expansion do not interfere with commercial activity; boundaries were planned to avoid commercial fishing. Low-level marine- and land-based tourism would be allowed in the area.	• Anon, 1998; de Haro and Iñíguez ,1997; Perez et al, 1995 • Contact: Cristián de Haro, Fundación Cethus, Juan de Garay 2861 – Depto 3, Olivos, Prov de Buenos Aires, Argentina; email: cristiandh@hotmail.com • Carlos Albrieu, Universidad Nacional de la Patagonia Austral (UNPA), Belgrano 1828, 9400 Río Gallegos, Pcia Santa Cruz, Argentina • Jorge Perancho, Áreas Protegidas, Consejo Agario Prov, Roca 976, Río Gallegos, Pcia Santa Cruz, Argentina
• Established in 1980 by Federal Decree 84.913 to protect flora and fauna, including dolphins resident in the area.	• Contact: Parque Nacional do Cabo Orange; web: www.amazonia.org.br
• Established in 1980 by Federal Decree 84.914 to protect flora and fauna, including dolphins resident in the area.	• Contact: Reserva Biológica do Lago Piratuba; web: www.amazonia.org.br
• Established in 1990 by the government of the state of Amazonas as an ecological reserve and upgraded in 1996. • There is a management plan. • According to Reeves (2002), there is a 'strong research focus, [with] hunting and fishing by local people allowed'.	• Contact: RDS Mamirauá; web: www.mamiraua.org.br; www.amazonia.org.br

Table 5.12 *continued*

Name of MPA or sanctuary, location and size	Cetacean and other notable species
(21) Amanã Sustainable Development Reserve (Reserva de Desenvolvimento Sustentável Amanã) • between Rio Negro and Japurá and Solimões rivers, Amazonas • 8,878 mi² (23,000 km²)	• boto, or Amazon River dolphin, *Inia geoffrensis*; tucuxi, *Sotalia fluviatilis* • also: Amazonian manatee
(22) Atol das Rocas Biological Reserve (Reserva Biológica de Atol das Rocas) • 166 mi (267 km) east of Natal, 91 mi (148 km) west of Fernando de Noronha, Rio Grande do Norte State • 140 mi² (362.5 km²)	• spinner dolphin, *Stenella longirostris*; pantropical spotted dolphin, *Stenella attenuata*; rough-toothed dolphin, *Steno bredanensis* • also: seabird colonies and coral reefs
(23) Fernando de Noronha National Marine Park (Parque Nacional Marinho Fernando de Noronha) • offshore archipelago (3°54´S; 32°25´W) off coastal Pernambuco State, 224 mi (360 km) from Natal • 43.5 mi² (112.7 km²) – 15 per cent land and 85 per cent marine; land areas include Fernando de Noronha Island and 20 smaller islands and islets	• resident: spinner dolphin, *Stenella longirostris*; sporadic, Jul–Dec: humpback whale, *Megaptera novaeangliae*; sporadic, year-round: pantropical spotted dolphin, *Stenella attenuata*; offshore: sperm whale, *Physeter macrocephalus* • also: endemic lizards and birds, sea turtles, corals, fishes, sponges
(24) Abrolhos National Marine Park (Parque Nacional Marinho dos Abrolhos) • 36 mi (58 km) offshore from southern Bahia State • 352 mi² (913 km²) includes land areas and reefs	• Jul–Nov: humpback whale, *Megaptera novaeangliae*; occasionally: bottlenose dolphin, *Tursiops truncatus*; rough-toothed dolphin, *Steno bredanensis* • also: seabirds, coral, sponges, sea turtles
(25) Shelf of the Northern Coast Environmental Protection Area (Área de Proteção Ambiental da Plataforma Continental do Litoral Norte) • northern Bahia State near Forte Beach, from the coast to 1640 ft (500 m) depth, off Bahia State • 1398.3 mi² (3622.7 km²) includes land areas and reefs	• Jul–Nov: humpback whale, *Megaptera novaeangliae*; occasionally: minke whale, *Balaenoptera acutorostrata*; various small cetaceans • also: seabirds, coral, sea turtles

Notes and rationale	For more information
• Established by the government of the state of Amazonas. • There is a management plan.	• Contact: RDS Amanã; web: www.mamiraua.org.br; www.amazonia.org.br
• Existing biological reserve established by Government Decree 83.549 in 1979 to protect the special ecology of the atoll, including the marine ecosystems. • With Fernando de Noronha National Marine Park, this reserve comprises a Unesco World Heritage Site.	• Contact: Maurizélia Brito, Manager, Reserva Biológica Atol das Rocas; web: www1.uol.com.br/instaqua/info46.htm
• National marine park established by Government Decree 96.693 in 1988 to protect the special ecology of the archipelago, including marine ecosystems, and cultural features. • Offers more than 'nominal protection' (Reeves, 2002) as, according to José T Palazzo Jr, the Bay of Dolphins is entirely closed to vessel traffic except for authorized researchers, and this is fully enforced. Instead, dolphin watching is done from land.	• Lodi and Hetzel, 1994 • Contact: Parque Nacional Marinho de Fernando de Noronha, PARNAMAR, FN/IBAMA, Alameda Boldró, s/n Fernando de Noronha/PE, CEP 53990-000 Brazil; José Martins da Silva, Jr, Brazilian Spinner Dolphin Project, c/o Parque Nacional Marinho de Fernando de Noronha (see above)
• The first national marine park to be established, in 1984, protects coral reefs but also includes seasonal humpback whale calving area; park is divided into two sections. • Research on humpback whales has been conducted since 1988. • Additional measures to extend critical habitat protection for humpback whales and coral reefs were announced in 2003 with the creation of a new state APA covering the shelf of the northern coast (see below).	• Contact: Márcia Engel, Instituto Baleia Jubarte, Parque Nacional Marinho dos Abrolhos, Praia do Kitongo s/n, Caravelas – BA -45.900, Brazil; email: m.engel@terra.com.br; web: www.baleiajubarte.com.br
• This area to protect breeding humpback whales was the result of a campaign from the Instituto Baleia Jubarte in Brazil. It was designated June 2003 through a decree of Bahia State. The mandate is to help protect all marine life, including corals, fishes, turtles, as well as whales. • A management plan has not yet been prepared. • Whale watch guidelines are being established as this is potentially the main area for the development of whale watching in Bahia, due to easy access and good tourism infrastructure.	• Contact: Márcia Engel, Projeto Baleia Jubarte, Abrolhos National Marine Park (Parque Nacional Marinho dos Abrolhos), Praia do Kitongo s/n, Caravelas – BA -45.900, Brazil; email: m.engel@terra.com.br; web: www.baleiajubarte.com.br

Table 5.12 *continued*

Name of MPA or sanctuary, location and size	Cetacean and other notable species
(26) Arraial do Cabo Sustainable Reserve (Reserva Extrativista de Arraial do Cabo) • Arraial do Cabo, Rio de Janeiro State	• common: bottlenose dolphin, *Tursiops truncatus*; *Stenella* species; occasionally: Bryde's whale, *Balaenoptera brydei*; southern right whale, *Eubalaena australis*; humpback whale, *Megaptera novaeangliae*
(27) Laje de Santos State Marine Park (Parque Estadual Marinho da Laje de Santos) • 25 mi (40 km) offshore around a rock (named 'Laje') at 24°19´S , 46°11´W in São Paulo State, southeast Brazil • 19.3 mi² (50 km²)	• Bryde's whale, *Balaenoptera brydei*; southern right whale, *Eubalaena australis*; humpback whale, *Megaptera novaeangliae*; short-beaked common dolphin, *Delphinus delphis*; long-beaked common dolphin, *Delphinus capensis*; Atlantic spotted dolphin, *Stenella frontalis*; bottlenose dolphin, *Tursiops truncatus* • also: important nesting site for boobies and migratory terns; threatened reef fishes
(28) Tupiniquins Ecological Station (Estação Ecológica dos Tupiniquins) • São Paulo State • 0.2 mi² (0.4 km²)	• common: bottlenose dolphin, *Tursiops truncatus*; *Stenella* species; occasionally: Bryde's whale, *Balaenoptera brydei*; southern right whale, *Eubalaena australis*; humpback whale, *Megaptera novaeangliae*
(29) Tupinambás Ecological Station (Estação Ecológica de Tupinambás) • São Paulo State • 0.1 mi² (0.3 km²)	• common: bottlenose dolphin, *Tursiops truncatus*; *Stenella* species; occasionally: Bryde's whale, *Balaenoptera brydei*; southern right whale, *Eubalaena australis*; humpback whale, *Megaptera novaeangliae*
(30) Ilhabela State Marine Park (Parque Estadual Marinho da Ilhabela) • near Ilhabela, São Sebastião island, São Paulo State • 104 mi² (270 km²)	• common: bottlenose dolphin, *Tursiops truncatus*; *Stenella* species; occasionally: Bryde's whale, *Balaenoptera brydei*; southern right whale, *Eubalaena australis*; humpback whale, *Megaptera novaeangliae*
(31) Ilha Anchieta State Marine Park (Parque Estadual Marinho da Ilha Anchieta) • Ilha Anchieta, São Paulo State • 3.2 mi² (8.3 km²)	• common: bottlenose dolphin, *Tursiops truncatus*; *Stenella* species; occasionally: Bryde's whale, *Balaenoptera brydei*; southern right whale, *Eubalaena australis*; humpback whale, *Megaptera novaeangliae*

Notes and rationale	For more information
• This sustainable reserve created through IBAMA in 1997 includes dolphin habitat.	• Contact: IBAMA/Arraial do Cabo; web: www.arraialdocabo-rj.com.br/ atividades/resexmar.asp
• Designated in Sept 1993 under Instituto Florestal/Secretaria do Meio Ambiente do Estado de São Paulo. • Rationale is that this area has a high marine biodiversity, as well as being an important feeding area for the highest concentration of Bryde's whales in southeast Brazil (whales occur in austral spring–summer). • IUCN Category II MPA managed for ecosystem protection and recreation (diving, incipient whale watching, but no fishing), unzoned except for Category Ia protection for nesting sites on the rocks. • Lacks management plan and monitoring facilities; Bryde's whale research is currently being developed by CEMAR (Marine Conservation Research Centre).	• Contact: Laje de Santos Marine State Park; email: cemar@cetesb.sp.gov.br; web: www.ambiente.sp.gov.br/ cemar • Mabel Augustowski, Manager, Laje de Santos Marine State Park, Marine Conservation Research Center (CEMAR); email: mabelaug@uol.com.br; sma.mabela@ cetesb.sp.gov.br
• This small ecological station – a fully protected, restricted-use area – includes dolphin habitat, with occasional whale presence in the area.	• Contact: Danielle Paludo, Manager, Estação Ecológica Tupiniquins; web: www.estadao.com.br/
• Established under Government Decree 94.656 in 1987, this small ecological station – a fully protected, restricted use area – includes dolphin habitat, with occasional whale presence in the area.	• Contact: Estação Ecológica Tupinambás; web: www.estadao.com.br/ ciencia/noticias/2001/ out/03/127.htm
• This state park, designated for research and environmental education, includes dolphin habitat.	• Contact: Katia Regina Arean, Manager, Parque Estadual da Ilhabela; web: www.ilhabela.com.br/ parqueestadual/
• This state park, created in 1977, is designated for research and environmental education; it includes dolphin habitat.	• Contact: Parque Estadual da Ilha Anchieta; web: www.cunhambebe.org.br

Table 5.12 *continued*

Name of MPA or sanctuary, location and size	Cetacean and other notable species
(32) Anhatomirim Environmental Protection Area (Area de Proteção Ambiental do Anhatomirim) • North Bay of Santa Catarina Island (27°30'S, 48°31'W), Santa Catarina State, southern Brazil • about 11.6 mi² (30 km²)	• resident: *tucuxi Sotalia fluviatilis* (marine ecotype); occasional: bottlenose dolphin, *Tursiops truncatus*; May–Oct: southern right whale, *Eubalaena australis*; also: franciscana, *Pontoporia blainvillei* • also: otters
(33) Right Whale Environmental Protection Area (Area de Proteção Ambiental da Baleia Franca) • located between Santa Catarina Island, 81 mi (130 km) south to the Cape of Santa Marta and Rincão Beach, off central-southern Santa Catarina State • 600 mi² (1560 km²)	• May–Dec: southern right whale, *Eubalaena australis*; also, bottlenose dolphin, *Tursiops truncatus* (year-round residents near Laguna; work with artisanal fishermen to gather mullet in a symbiotic relationship) • also: important colonies of seabirds on coastal islands
(34) Marine Tucuxi Environmental Protection Area of Paraty Bay (Area de Proteção Ambiental da Botos-cinza do Baía de Paraty), *proposed* • northern Paraty Bay (Baía de Paraty) (23°56'S; 44°19'W) between Ponta do Boi and Ponta Grande de Timbuiba, in Rio de Janeiro State • proposed size is 19.64 mi² (50.87 km²)	• resident: tucuxi, *Sotalia fluviatilis*; common: pantropical spotted dolphin, *Stenella attenuata*; rough-toothed dolphin, *Steno bredanensis*; occasional: southern right whale, *Eubalaena australis*; humpback whale, *Megaptera novaeangliae*; pygmy Bryde's whale, *Balaenoptera edeni* • also: seabirds (brown boobies, terns, frigatebirds, cormorants)
FALKLAND ISLANDS (MALVINAS) (UK) **(A) Falkland Islands Marine Mammal Sanctuary** • located in the waters of the Falkland Islands, in the southwest Atlantic Ocean • size extends to the limits of the EEZ, 200 nm (371 km) around islands	• orca, *Orcinus orca*; Commerson's dolphin, *Cephalorhynchus commersonnii*; Peale's dolphin, *Lagenorhynchus australis*; pilot whale, *Globicephala* sp; others

Notes and rationale	For more information
• Designated by federal decree in 1992, comprising nearshore land and water under federal management, mainly for the tucuxi. • Photo-ID, habitat use and monitoring of strandings has been carried out mainly by Paulo Flores since early 1990s A group of 50+ tucuxi are sighted on a daily basis year-round near Enseada dos Currais and Anhatomirim Island. • In 1998 special regulations were made to protect tucuxi reproduction, resting and breeding at Anhatomirim which, says Reeves (2002), provides 'nominal protection from harassment'; a management/zoning plan with scientific and public input is needed.	• Flores, 1992, 1995 • Contact: Paulo Andre Flores, Sotalia Dolphin Project, International Wildlife Coalition/Brasil, CP 5087, 88040-970, Florianopolis, SC, Brasil; email: flores.p@terra.com.br web: www.baleiafranca.org.br
• A Sept 2000 federal decree protects this southern right whale birthing and nursery site off the central-southern coast of Santa Catarina state. Since 1995, the southern right whale has been a State Natural Monument and the species is on the National Endangered Species List. • This area was championed by José T Palazzo Jr and Projeto Baleia Franca of the International Wildlife Coalition after two decades of research showing need for habitat protection. • IBAMA, Brazil's national environmental authority, is working with researchers and other stakeholders on a management plan to define zoning and specific restrictions to protect the right whales.	• Contact: José T Palazzo, Jr, International Wildlife Coalition Brasil, Box 201, 88780-970, Imbituba, SC, Brazil; email: info@baleiafranca.org.br; web: www.baleiafranca.org.br
• The existing small environmental protection areas (EPAs) in Paraty Bay take no consideration of tucuxi and are not stopping habitat degradation and fishing bycatch; this new EPA proposed by Projeto Golfinhos in 2002 would protect resident tucuxi and develop zoning and regulations to ensure sensible tourism development. • Research into tucuxi habitat use, begun in 2000 by Liliane Lodi, will establish critical habitat areas and satisfy requirements of Brazilian Aquatic Mammals Action Plan (IBAMA, 1997).	• Lodi and Hetzel, 2000 • Contact: Liliane Lodi and Bia Hetzel, Projeto Golfinhos, CP 24075, Rio de Janeiro, Brazil 20530-000; email: lilodi@uninet.com.br, biahetze@uninet.com.br • Paulo Nogara, Environmental Protection Area of Cairuçu; email: nogara@zaz.com.br
• The Marine Mammals Ordinance 1992 has the effect of providing a sanctuary or refuge for all marine mammals in Falkland Islands fishing waters.	• Contact: RT Jarvis Government House, Stanley, Falkland Islands

Table 5.12 *continued*

Name of MPA or sanctuary, location and size	Cetacean and other notable species
URUGUAY República Oriental del Uruguay **[MPAs 35–37]** *(35)* **Punta Ballena – Bahía de Maldonado – José Ignacio MPA,** *proposed* • Punta Ballena, Bahía de Maldonado, José Ignacio, Maldonado department • 153 mi² (396 km²), along 31 mi (50 km) of Maldonado *(36)* **Cabo Santa María – La Pedrera MPA,** *proposed* • Cabo Santa María, La Pedrera, Rocha department • 92 mi² (238 km²), along 19 mi (30 km) of Maldonado *(37)* **Cabo Polonio – Punta del Diablo MPA,** *proposed* • Cabo Polonio, Punta del Diablo, Rocha department • 168 mi² (436 km²), along 34 mi (55 km) of Maldonado	• southern right whale, *Eubalaena australis*

Notes and rationale	For more information
• Three MPAs in process of being protected according to Law 17.234/00 with proposed biosphere reserve designation; regulations by Ministry of Environment to come. • Features critical habitat (reproductive behaviour) for the southern right whale as well as transition zones for environmental education and ecotourism including regulated whale watching. • Management of the three areas will be through the Dirección Nacional de Medio Ambiente (Ministerio de Medio Ambiente) – the Ministry of Environment – with participating institutions including the Comando General de la Armada, Prefectura Nacional Naval, Dirección Nacional de Recursos Acuáticos del Ministerio de Ganadería, Agricultura y Pesca and Intendencias Municipales. • In Sept 2002, the Symposium of Conservation and Sustainable Use of the Marine Fauna in Uruguay was held to discuss the proposed MPAs (see www.geocities.com/atneotropical/jornadasfaunamarina.htm).	• Contact: Rodrigo Garcia, OCC – Organización para la Conservación de Cetáceos, La Paloma, CP 27001, Rocha, Uruguay; email: info@ballenafranca.org web: www.ballenafranca.org • Protection of Fauna Marina (PROFAUMA); email: profauma@adinet.com.uy • Ecovoluntarios; email: ecovol@adinet.com.uy

MARINE REGION 10: CENTRAL INDIAN OCEAN

The Central Indian Ocean Marine Region has important habitats for most baleen whales, and many tropical and subtropical toothed whales and dolphins. Some of the baleen whales migrate into the region from the Antarctic, although the Indian Ocean may also have separate, completely resident populations. As part of the Indian Ocean Sanctuary, set up in 1979, this region and the adjoining Marine Regions 11, 12, 13 and 18 were protected from whale hunting. In a large ocean sanctuary, real protection for cetaceans is minimal, but it has helped promote research and conservation. In the early 1980s, a three-year research cruise crossed the region, finding large accessible populations of sperm, blue, Bryde's and other whales, as well as spinner, common and other tropical dolphins. The waters around Sri Lanka were identified as a hot spot for both large baleen whales and toothed whales (sperm whales and various dolphins). The cruise also exposed the widespread killing of dolphins in South Asia and opened up commercial whale watching in the area.

Since then, over the past decade, the Maldives have yielded a wide variety of cetacean sightings including rarely encountered beaked whales. An MPA is being designated at Addu Atoll which includes protection for melon-headed whales. For the most part, however, marine habitat protection for cetaceans in the region falls well short of providing even cursory coverage.

The region is also known for its endangered river dolphins. The Ganges and Indus river dolphins are endangered throughout their range in the rivers of India, Nepal, Bangladesh and Pakistan (included in Marine Region 11). Rice (1998) placed the formerly two river dolphins into one species *Platanista gangetica*; this makes the numbers higher but does not remove them from endangered species lists. Indeed, the two former species remain fully isolated populations. River dolphins are highly endangered due to their presence in rivers used by large human populations. Both India and Pakistan have set aside small protected areas of river and a similar area is proposed for Nepal. However, this may be too little protection coming too late. In addition, this region provides some of the key habitat worldwide for Irrawaddy dolphins, Indo-Pacific hump-backed dolphins and finless porpoises, which inhabit the estuaries, mangroves and inshore waters of substantial portions of the region.

A total of six national governments have a role in the Central Indian Ocean Marine Region (see Table 5.1 on p89). In addition, the rivers of land-locked Nepal, which is considered here because of the river dolphins, flow into the region. This region has three distinct areas: the Bay of Bengal, a portion of the Arabian Sea and a large area of the Indian Ocean south of India and Sri Lanka.

The Central Indian Ocean Marine Region has one large marine ecosystem (LME): the Bay of Bengal. The oceanography in the Bay of Bengal has clockwise circulation of its main surface currents throughout the year. The Arabian Sea, however, has surface water circulating clockwise only during the southwest monsoon from May to October. During this period, the surface currents feed both the Arabian Sea and the Bay of Bengal. With the northeast monsoon from November to April, the surface waters move counterclockwise. Both the Bay of

Bengal and the Arabian Sea are in the northern hemisphere. The Indian Ocean itself lies across the Equator but is largely in the southern hemisphere and has a broad counterclockwise movement of its surface waters.

The Central Indian Ocean Marine Region has substantial, diverse, relatively pristine coral reefs, including atoll, fringing and barrier reefs. These are most notable in the southern part of the region, while the mangrove forests are found along the northern part, especially Bangladesh and India which contain some of the world's most important mangroves.

This region has notable upwellings off the Andaman Islands, the west coast of Sri Lanka (seasonally during the northeast monsoon), and off northeast India.

A UNEP regional seas programme for South Asia includes India, Bangladesh, Sri Lanka, the Maldives and Pakistan (from Marine Region 11), but not Myanmar. Established in 1983, it has yet to develop a convention or action plan. The Indian Ocean Marine Affairs Cooperation (IOMAC), representing countries of the region, is poised to take a leadership role in the region with marine conservation issues. WDCS is also working actively in this area on cetacean surveys and management proposals for critical habitat protection, with the hope that such activities will contribute to the development of effective regional conservation agreements in the Bay of Bengal.

In 1995 there was a total of 15 MPAs of all kinds in this marine region – the lowest total for any marine region in the world (Wells et al, 1995). This region is divided into five biogeographic zones, but all zones have only marginal representation. In 2004, as shown in Table 5.13, there were five existing and four proposed MPAs which feature cetacean habitat. Two of the existing MPAs are proposed for expansion. Five of the MPAs are actually not marine but river-based, partly or wholly for freshwater river dolphins.

The IUCN 2002–2010 Conservation Action Plan for the World's Cetaceans recommends a number of research and education initiatives for this region (Reeves et al, 2003):

- to investigate deliberate and accidental killing of coastal cetaceans in India;
- to assess the status of cetaceans and threats from direct and indirect exploitation in Sri Lanka;
- to convene a workshop to develop an action plan for conserving freshwater populations of Irrawaddy dolphins (also applies to Marine Region 13); and
- to conduct intensive training courses on cetacean research techniques for scientists in South and Southeast Asia (also for Marine Region 13).

IUCN initiatives related to endangered species in the region, and thus of highest priority, are as follows:

- to investigate the impacts of reduced water levels on river dolphins in the Ganges and Indus rivers – India, Bangladesh, Nepal and Pakistan (also for Marine Region 11);
- to investigate the use of dolphin oil as a fish attractant in the Brahmaputra River and to conduct one or more experiments to test potential substitutes;

- to assess the distribution, abundance and habitat of Ganges River dolphins and monitor ongoing threats – India and Bangladesh; and
- to assess populations and habitat of Ganges dolphins (susus) and Irrawaddy dolphins in the Sundarbans of India and Bangladesh.

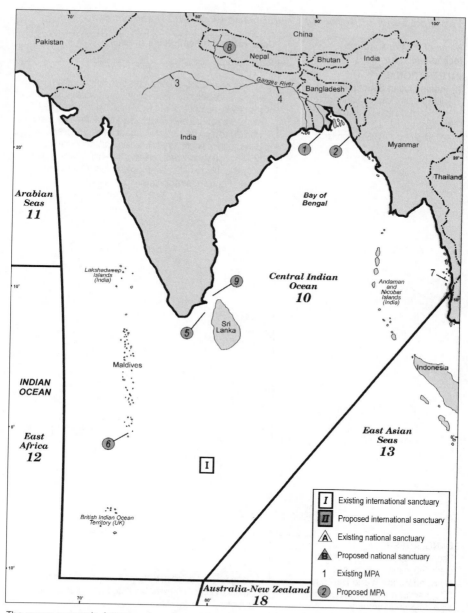

The roman numerals, letters and numbers correspond to the sanctuaries and MPAs listed and described in Table 5.13.

Figure 5.17 *Map of Marine Region 10: Central Indian Ocean MPAs and sanctuaries*

Table 5.13 *Marine Region 10: Central Indian Ocean MPAs and sanctuaries*

Name of MPA or sanctuary, location and size	Cetacean and other notable species
INTERNATIONAL **(I) Indian Ocean Sanctuary** • entire Indian Ocean southward to 55° S latitude spread across Marine Regions 10, 11, 12, 13 and 18 • 40 million mi² (103.6 million km²)	• at least 43 species of cetaceans including southern right whale, *Eubalaena australis*; pygmy right whale, *Caperea marginata*; humpback whale, *Megaptera novaeangliae*; minke whale, *Balaenoptera acutorostrata*; Antarctic minke whale, *Balaenoptera bonaerensis*; pygmy Bryde's whale, *Balaenoptera edeni*; Bryde's whale, *Balaenoptera brydei*; sei whale, *Balaenoptera borealis*; fin whale, *Balaenoptera physalus*; blue whale, *Balaenoptera musculus*; sperm whale, *Physeter macrocephalus*
BANGLADESH People's Republic of Bangladesh Gana Prajatantri Bangladesh **(1) Sundarbans World Heritage Site,** *part of it may be proposed as a dolphin sanctuary* • Sundarbans tidal mangrove forest (includes rivers of southwest Bangladesh and eastern India), southeast of Calcutta • no size data	• Ganges River dolphin, *Platanista gangetica*; Irrawaddy dolphin, *Orcaella brevirostris*; Indo-Pacific hump-backed dolphin, *Sousa chinensis*

Notes and rationale	For more information
• Rationale is to protect whales from commercial whaling and to stimulate cetacean research and conservation. • At the 1979 IWC meeting, the Republic of Seychelles proposed that the Indian Ocean be closed to commercial whaling and declared a sanctuary. With the support of most Indian Ocean states, this was voted in as a whale sanctuary, subject to review in ten years. In 1989, the sanctuary was renewed for three more years. In 1990, the Indian Ocean Marine Affairs Cooperation (IOMAC) declared a permanent Indian Ocean sanctuary for whales, later extended by resolution to all marine mammals. In 1992, the IWC agreed to make the sanctuary of 'indefinite duration'. A 2002 IWC review pointed to the research and conservation advantages of the sanctuary. • Research in the sanctuary started with the three-year WWF cruise led by Hal Whitehead, Jonathan Gordon and others. The cruise initiated some of the first studies of wild sperm whales, exposed the widespread killing of dolphins in South Asia, and opened up commercial whale watching in Sri Lanka and elsewhere (Whitehead, 1989). Other research is detailed in Leatherwood and Donovan (1991), with updates in Anon (1995) and de Boer et al (2002), the last of which highlights the role of the Indian Ocean Sanctuary in furthering research, management plans, conservation strategies and regional initiatives. • The IWC sanctuary designation falls short of providing comprehensive protection for cetacean habitat (Leatherwood and Donovan, 1991). The Indian Ocean remains the most heavily human-populated and the most neglected ocean for conservation programmes. Stone (1995) points to lack of infrastructure, capable country agencies and research labs to implement conservation programmes and suggests using IOMAC to coordinate work in the region through a single secretariat, supported by local conservation organizations with outside institutions to provide technical assistance and funding. • The approval of the IWC Southern Ocean Sanctuary in 1994 extended protection from hunting to the Antarctic, including both breeding and feeding habitats of Indian Ocean baleen whales. There has also been a proposal to extend the sanctuary to cover Indonesian waters in Marine Region 13.	• Anon, 1995; de Boer et al, 2002; Holt, 1984, 2000; Leatherwood and Donovan, 1991; Stone, 1995; Whitehead, 1989 • Contact: Mark Simmonds, WDCS; email: mark.simmonds@wdcs.org; web: www.wdcs.org • Hiran W Jayewardene, Indian Ocean Marine Affairs Cooperation (IOMAC), Suite 4-211-212 BMICH, Colombo 7, Sri Lanka; email: iomacs@lanka.ccom.lk
• In 2003, a study by representatives of the Wildlife Conservation Society (WCS), IUCN and WDCS surveyed dolphins in the Sundarbans delta and other Bangladesh rivers to determine if habitat protection could help reverse their decline. • Portions of the dolphins' habitat in the delta are being recommended for full protection as a sanctuary to aid recovery of these cetacean species which have disappeared from many of the regions' rivers. • Current problems for the dolphins include: accidental entanglement in gill nets; destruction of fish-spawning habitat through mangrove deforestation and toxic contamination from upstream cities such as Dhaka; non-selective catch of fish fingerlings and crustacean larvae in mosquito nets; growing ship traffic; and large-scale water engineering projects.	• More information: http://southasia.one world.net/article/view/71159/1/ • Contact: Brian D Smith, WCS and WDCS Asia; email: bsmith@wcs.org

Table 5.13 *continued*

Name of MPA or sanctuary, location and size	Cetacean and other notable species
(2) Sangu River, *may be proposed as a dolphin sanctuary* • southeast Bangladesh • size undetermined	• Ganges River dolphin, *Platanista gangetica*
INDIA Republic of India Bharat **(3) National Chambal Sanctuary** • Chambal River • no size information	• Ganges River dolphin, *Platanista gangetica* • also: gharial
(4) Vikramshila Gangetic Dolphin Sanctuary • middle Ganges River, Bihar • 31-mi (50-km) stretch of river	• Ganges River dolphin, *Platanista gangetica* • also: various turtles: the endangered red-crowned roofed turtle and Indian soft-shell turtle, gharial, smooth-coated otter, Indian skimmer, greater spotted eagle and other birds
(5) Gulf of Mannar Marine National Park, *proposed for expansion* • Gulf of Mannar and Palk Bay, waters between southeast India and northwest Sri Lanka • existing size is 4053 mi^2 (10,500 km^2); expansion undetermined	• Indo-Pacific bottlenose dolphin, *Tursiops aduncus*; finless porpoise, *Neophocaena phocaenoides*; spinner dolphin, *Stenella longirostris*; common dolphin, *Delphinus* sp • also: dugong; the area is rich in seagrass and coral reefs including 96 coral species from 36 genera (highest diversity in the region)

Notes and rationale	For more information
• In 2003, representatives of the Wildlife Conservation Society (WCS) and WDCS intensively surveyed dolphins in the Sangu River to assess the feasibility of establishing a protected area for conserving river dolphins, following a 1999 survey that had identified the lower reaches of the river as supporting a relatively high density of dolphins.	• Smith et al, 1999 • More information: http://southasia.one world.net/article/view/ 71159/1/ • Contact: Brian D Smith, WCS and WDCS Asia; email: bsmith@wcs.org
• Existing freshwater sanctuary located on the Chambal River, established in 1978 to protect gharial, also 'effectively protects small dolphin population' (Reeves, 2002). • Dolphins in the sanctuary number in only tens of animals, but this is one of the few viable populations still persisting in the smaller tributaries of the Ganges.	• Reeves, 2002; Reeves et al, 2000; Smith et al, 1994 • Contact: Alison Wood, Conservation Director, WDCS; email: alison.wood@wdcs.org; web: www.wdcs.org • Brian D Smith, WCS and WDCS Asia; email: bsmith@wcs.org
• This freshwater sanctuary, located in a river that is a spiritually and ecologically important part of India and Indian culture, was designated by the Bihar government in 1991 to protect endangered river dolphins. • WDCS has worked with the Vikramshila Biodiversity Research and Education Centre since 1999 to address problems, lobbying state and national governments to enforce laws that regulate fishing and hunting, as well as conducting dolphin research and monitoring, and developing a conservation plan (recommended in Report of the Second Meeting of the Asian River Dolphin Committee in 1997).	• Reeves et al, 2000; Smith et al, 1994 • Contact: Alison Wood, Conservation Director, WDCS; email: alison.wood@wdcs.org; web: www.wdcs.org • Sunil K Choudhary, Vikramshila Biodiversity Research and Education Centre (VBREC); c/o T M Bhagalpur University, Bhagalpur 812007, India • Brian D Smith, WCS and WDCS Asia; email: bsmith@wcs.org
• Declared Apr 1980 by Tamil Nadu state government, this MPA is protected under the Indian Wild Life Protection Act, 1972 (amended 1990); protection includes dugongs, sea turtles, coral reefs plus cetaceans. • Expansion into Sri Lanka waters where an adjoining reserve has been proposed, as suggested in Wells et al (1995), would form an ecological unit to improve conservation in the region with a jointly managed MPA. • Cetacean research to date has focused on abundance and distribution – area is a cetacean feeding and breeding area; biological inventory of the marine park has been done, and management plan, but public awareness programmes are needed to build MPA's long-term future.	• Wells et al, 1995 • Contact: RS Lal Mohan, Conservation of Nature Trust, 'Lagrace', 43C, Water Tank Rd, Nagercoil – 629 001, Tamilnadu, India • See also Palk Bay and the Gulf of Mannar Marine International Park, *proposed* under 'Sri Lanka' below

Table 5.13 *continued*

Name of MPA or sanctuary, location and size	Cetacean and other notable species
MALDIVES Republic of the Maldives Divehi Raajjeyge Jumhooriyaa **(6) Eidhigali Kulhi and Koattey Protected Area,** *proposed* • Addu Atoll, near Hithadhoo • 13.5 mi² (35 km²)	• melon-headed whale, *Peponocephala electra* (year-round, especially Dec–May)
MYANMAR Thammada Myanmar Naingngandaw (formerly Burma) **(7) Lampi Island Marine National Park** • Lampi Island and adjacent areas of Mergui Archipelago • 79 mi² (205 km²), including land areas	• Bryde's whale, *Balaenoptera brydei*; minke whale, *Balaenoptera acutorostrata*; spinner dolphin, *Stenella longirostris*; pantropical spotted dolphin, *Stenella attennuata*; striped dolphin, *Stenella coeruleoalba*; false killer whale, *Pseudorca crassidens*; long-finned pilot whale, *Globicephala melas* • also: dugong, sea turtles, whale shark
NEPAL Kingdom of Nepal Nepal Adhirajya **(8) Royal Bardia National Park,** *proposed* **for expansion to the Karnali Basin** • Karnali Basin, Nepal • size undetermined	• Ganges River dolphin, *Platanista gangetica* • also: tigers, rhinoceroses and elephants live in neighbouring Royal Bardia National Park; the adjacent Karnali Basin is home to endangered crocodiles, otters, turtles as well as the endangered river dolphins
SRI LANKA Democratic Socialist Republic of Sri Lanka Sri Lanka Prajathanthrika Samajawadi Janarajaya **(9) Palk Bay and the Gulf of Mannar Marine International Park,** *proposed* • Palk Bay, northwest Sri Lanka • no size data	• Indo-Pacific bottlenose dolphin, *Tursiops aduncus*; common dolphin, *Delphinus* sp; spinner dolphin, *Stenella longirostris*; finless porpoise, *Neophocaena phocaenoides* • also: dugong, seagrass, coral reefs (96 coral species from 36 genera – highest diversity in the region)

Notes and rationale	For more information
• This coastal protected area in the process of designation was proposed by the Ministry of Home Affairs, Housing and Environment; Charles Anderson, who leads whale watch cruises around the Maldives, helped draw the attention to the importance of this site and the threats it was facing; he has since assisted with coral reef and bird surveys. • The only cetacean research in the area has been a basic inventory indicating presence, relative abundance, but regular whale watch tours provide monitoring; still, more needs to be done to determine critical habitat.	• Contact: Ian Dight, Maldives Protected Areas System (MPAS) Project, Environment Research Centre; email: dight@attglobal.net • Charles Anderson, Marine Research Centre; email: anderson@ dhivehinet.net.mv
• Lampi Island was designated 1996 as a marine park to protect coral reefs, dense mangroves and turtle nesting beaches but it also includes some cetacean habitat. • Surveys in northwestern Myanmar, centred on the Ayeyarwady River, have turned up mainly Indo-Pacific bottlenose dolphin, *Tursiops aduncus*; Irrawaddy dolphin, *Orcaella brevirostris*; and spinner dolphin, *Stenella longirostris*.	• Smith et al, 1997b • Contact: WCS Myanmar Program Office; email: wcsmm@ mptmail.net.mm • Brian D Smith, WCS and WDCS Asia; email: bsmith@wcs.org
• WDCS supports river dolphin research here and has recommended that protection be extended to part of the river as a freshwater reserve for river dolphin habitat. • The Karnali Basin has hosted dolphin watch tours for some years; proposed construction of a high dam on the Karnali River hangs over the future of the river dolphins, ecotourism and the future of the area's Tharu communities.	• Contact: Alison Wood, Conservation Director, WDCS; email: alison.wood@ wdcs.org; web: www.wdcs.org • Brian D Smith, WCS and WDCS Asia; email: bsmith@wcs.org
• Rationale is that protecting the Sri Lankan part of the gulf, including Palk Bay, would make a complete ecological unit that, with a joint management agreement with India, would greatly improve conservation in the region. • The Gulf of Mannar is a dolphin and porpoise feeding and breeding area as well as an area frequented by dolphins on the move, but more detailed cetacean habitat studies need to be done.	• Wells et al, 1995 • Contact: Hiran W Jayewardene, Secretary General, IOMAC; email: iomacs@ lanka.ccom.lk; iomac@sltnet.lk • See also Gulf of Mannar Marine National Park, *proposed for expansion,* under India above.

MARINE REGION 11: ARABIAN SEAS

The Arabian Seas Marine Region has tropical and subtropical cetaceans including blue, humpback and Bryde's whales, as well as sperm whale, dwarf sperm whale and Cuvier's beaked whale. The region has no completely indigenous cetacean species but it does have several subspecies peculiar to the region, including long-beaked common dolphin and finless porpoise subspecies. It also has an important part of the range for various Indian Ocean and tropical small cetacean species such as the Indo-Pacific hump-backed dolphin, Indo-Pacific bottlenose dolphin and finless porpoise. Known habitat includes key baleen whale feeding areas in upwellings along the Oman coast and Gulf of Aden, as well as nearshore feeding areas for dolphins, such as around mangroves, coral reefs and especially along sandy shorelines. Current Oman researchers note some 21 species in national waters, although not the same 21 listed in Salm et al (1993), and there may be as many as 28 species of cetaceans living in the entire Arabian Seas Marine Region.

Most of the Arabian Seas are part of the Indian Ocean Sanctuary but, aside from the broad brush protection from whaling afforded by this IWC sanctuary, there are few actual cetacean conservation measures in this region. Only Oman has started on the process of considering cetacean habitat protection as an important element of marine conservation. Oman's interest and development in MPAs is shown in one existing and two proposed MPAs which feature cetacean habitat. These areas do not address the habitat needs of the range of cetaceans found in Oman, but they do provide a good starting point.

Inland and upstream, Pakistan has taken steps to protect some 600 remaining endangered Indus River dolphins with a reserve in the Indus River between the Sukkur and Guddu barrages.

A total of 11 national governments have a role in the Arabian Seas Marine Region (see Table 5.1 on p89). The Arabian Seas Marine Region includes all the seas around the Arabian Peninsula including the Red Sea, Gulf of Aden, the Persian Gulf, as well as parts of the Arabian Sea. There are two large marine ecosystems (LMEs) that have been identified: the Red Sea and the Arabian Sea. Here is a brief summary of these two LMEs as well as the Persian Gulf:

- The Arabian Sea has surface water currents which circulate clockwise during the southwest monsoon from May to October. During this period, the monsoon removes surface water and this is replaced by cooler, nutrient-rich upwelling water. The oceanic coasts of Yemen and Oman have large and productive oceanic upwellings which attract feeding baleen whales, dolphins and other marine species. With the northeast monsoon from November to April, the surface waters move counterclockwise.
- The Red Sea, some 1300 mi (2100 km) long from the Suez Canal to the Gulf of Aden, is the result of deep-ocean rifting. It has an average depth of 1640 ft (500 m) and a maximum depth of more than 6500 ft (2000 m).

Mostly isolated from world ocean circulation patterns, it contains some of the hottest, saltiest sea water in the world. The winds in summer flow down the Red Sea and reinforce the clockwise movement of air and water currents in the Arabian Sea.

- The Persian Gulf is a shallow basin with an average depth of only 102 ft (31 m) and strong tidal flows. The Gulf of Oman, which connects the Persian Gulf to the Indian Ocean is deep and open to the influence of the Arabian Sea.

Some of the most diverse, extensive and biologically significant coral reefs in the world are found in the central and northern Red Sea. Only a few coral species exist in the Gulf; further south in the region, coral communities become even less common. The mangroves in the region are modest in terms of diversity and extent.

There are UNEP regional seas programmes for the Red Sea and Gulf of Aden, as well as for the waters of all Gulf countries as part of the Kuwait Action Plan, also known as the Regional Organization for Protection of the Marine Environment (ROPME). The Red Sea, Persian Gulf, Gulf of Aden and Gulf of Oman are all declared Special Areas under Annex I and V of MARPOL.

This area has dominated world headlines with the two Gulf wars of 1991 and 2003 and other Middle East issues. Cetacean populations in the Gulf persisted despite the huge oil spill at the end of the 1991 war (Robineau and Fiquet, 1994a, 1994b) but long-term impacts from the 2003 conflict are as yet unclear. In any case, marine habitat management, research and conservation have been marginalized in the aftermath of these wars and in the face of concern over the production and supply of oil. It may be some years before those who care have the time and can harness the political will to begin to advance marine habitat protection.

In 1995, there was a total of 19 MPAs of all kinds in this marine region (Chiffings, 1995). This region is divided into 13 biogeographic zones, eight of which are represented by at least one MPA and five of which have no representation. As of 2004, according to Table 5.14 prepared for this book, there are two existing and two proposed MPAs which feature cetacean habitat; one of them is river-based.

The IUCN 2002–2010 Conservation Action Plan for the World's Cetaceans recommends a number of research and education initiatives for this region, particularly focusing on the endangered river dolphins (Reeves et al, 2003):

- to investigate and monitor the distribution, abundance and habitat quality of Indus River dolphins and address ongoing threats in Pakistan;
- to investigate the impacts of reduced water levels on river dolphins in the Ganges and Indus rivers – Pakistan, India, Bangladesh and Nepal (also applies to Marine Region 10); and
- to investigate the status of small cetaceans in the Indus Delta, Pakistan.

Table 5.14 *Marine Region 11: Arabian Seas MPAs and sanctuaries*

Name of MPA or sanctuary, location and size	Cetacean and other notable species
INTERNATIONAL **(I) Indian Ocean Sanctuary** • Indian Ocean, spread across Marine Regions 10, 11, 12, 13 and 18 • 40 million mi^2 (103.6 million km^2)	• at least 43 species of cetaceans
OMAN Sultanate of Oman Saltanat `Uman **(1) Daymaniyat Islands National Nature Reserve** • off Batinah Coast between Seeb and Barka, Gulf of Oman • 78.4 mi^2 (203 km^2) including water and land area (nine islands and shoals)	• year-round: long-beaked common dolphin, *Delphinus capensis*; bottlenose dolphin, *Tursiops truncatus*; spinner dolphin, *Stenella longirostris*; seasonal or infrequent sightings: Bryde's whale, *Balaenoptera brydei*; humpback whale, *Megaptera novaeangliae*; false killer whale, *Pseudorca crassidens* • also: Hawksbill turtles, various migratory bird species
(2) Bar al Hikman MPA, *proposed* • Masirah Channel and south, Arabian Sea • size undetermined **(3) Masirah Island MPA,** *proposed* • Masirah Island, Arabian Sea • size undetermined	• humpback whale, *Megaptera novaeangliae*; Bryde's whale, *Balaenoptera brydei*; and other species of baleen whales; Indo-Pacific hump-backed dolphin, *Sousa chinensis*; sporadic: long-beaked common dolphin, *Delphinus capensis*; spinner dolphin, *Stenella longirostris*; Cuvier's beaked whale, *Ziphius cavirostris*; orca, *Orcinus orca*; along west coast of Masirah only: Indo-Pacific bottlenose dolphin, *Tursiops aduncus*
PAKISTAN Islamic Republic of Pakistan Islami Jamhuriya e Pakistan **(4) Indus River Dolphin Reserve, or Sind Dolphin Reserve** • Indus River between Sukkur and Guddu barrages, Sind • no size data	• Indus River dolphin, *Platanista gangetica*

Notes and rationale	For more information
• Rationale is to protect large whales from commercial whaling and to stimulate cetacean research and conservation. • At the 1979 IWC meeting, the Republic of Seychelles proposed that the Indian Ocean be closed to commercial whaling and declared a sanctuary. With the support of most Indian Ocean states and the world, it was voted in as a whale sanctuary.	• See full account in Marine Region 10, Table 5.13.
• Rationale for protection is that the islands are of world importance for nesting hawksbill turtles and migratory bird species, and the surrounding waters have some of Oman's best coral reefs; the cetacean habitat is just being recognized. • Proposed as an MPA by IUCN in 1984, the Daymaniyat Islands National Nature Reserve was given legal recognition by Royal Decree 23/96 in 1996. • Current legal status provides blanket protection from potential threats, but it has not been enforced. • In particular, better regulation of artisanal fishing activities and careful tourism development will help safeguard this important marine habitat. In terms of effective cetacean habitat protection, the reserve would be greatly improved by expansion into offshore waters.	• Contact: Ali al Kiyumi, Ministry of Regional Municipalities and Environment, PO Box 323, Muscat, CPO 113, Oman; email: alialkiyumi@hotmail.com • For more information: Robert Baldwin, PO Box 2531, CPO 111, Oman; email: wosoman@omantel.net.om
• These two areas are thought to provide important humpback and other cetacean habitat, mainly for feeding. • Both areas are being considered for MPAs, depending on availability of resources in the near future. Inventory work needs to be done to evaluate cetacean use of the areas and other features worth conserving. To date, cetacean research has been largely opportunistic. Some cetacean sightings within the proposed MPAs have been recorded in the Oman Cetacean Database, maintained by volunteer researchers and held by the Oman Natural History Museum. • There is some discussion about making these two proposed MPAs into a single larger MPA. This would be more effective than individual MPAs, especially if protected waters could extend offshore at least to the 50 m contour and if fishing by gill nets and trawling can be carefully controlled.	• Contact: Ali al Kiyumi, Ministry of Regional Municipalities and Environment, PO Box 323, Muscat, CPO 113, Oman; email: alialkiyumi@hotmail.com • For more information: Robert Baldwin, PO Box 2531, CPO 111, Oman; email: wosoman@omantel.net.om
• In 2001, WWF Pakistan initiated efforts to revitalize the work to save some 600 dolphins which have shown no increase since the reserve was set aside in 1974. With help from the UN Development Programme and WDCS, a scientific-conservation expedition was organized to travel the 437 miles (700 km) of the river where the dolphins live. Part of the plan is an economic incentive for local people to protect dolphins through tourism. • Rationale is to protect the freshwater habitat of Indus River dolphins and, according to Reeves (2002), it does provide 'nominal protection to dolphins'.	• Contact: Alison Wood, Conservation Director, WDCS; email: alison.wood@wdcs.org; web: www.wdcs.org • WWF Pakistan; www.wwfpak.org/

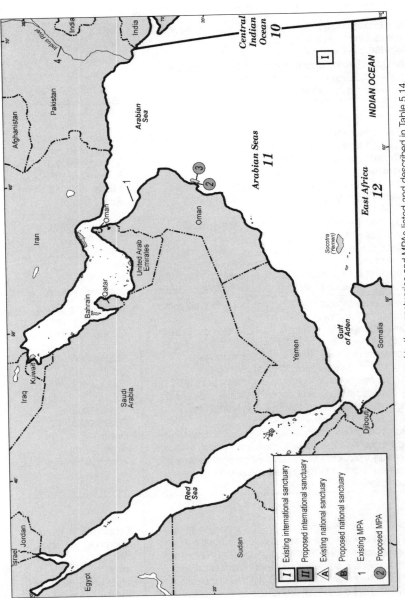

Figure 5.18 *Map of Marine Region 11: Arabian Seas MPAs and sanctuaries*

The roman numerals, letters and numbers correspond to the sanctuaries and MPAs listed and described in Table 5.14.

MARINE REGION 12: EAST AFRICA

The cetaceans of the East African Marine Region with known habitat are mainly humpback whales, inshore Indo-Pacific bottlenose and Indo-Pacific hump-backed dolphins. There are important breeding and calving areas for humpback whales, which have been identified and are protected, off southern Mozambique (Bazaruto Archipelago National Park) and off northeastern Madagascar (the Antafana Islands Marine Park which is part of Manannara North Biosphere Reserve, and three small marine reserves in the Masoala National Park). There is a larger proposed area off northeast Madagascar (Baie d'Antongil – Saint Marie Island Humpback Whale Sanctuary). Tanzania has taken the lead in the region with its MPA legislation and the designation of 12 existing and 3 further proposed MPAs, most of which have reported dolphin and humpback whale sightings but which require further study to determine the extent and location of significant cetacean habitat. In the Mohéli Marine Park in the Comoros, a programme to study humpback whales began in 2000 and a complete cetacean inventory has been conducted. In Mayotte, dolphin populations have been studied in two small coastal reserves.

For the most part, except for humpback whales and the two species of inshore dolphins in the region which have been studied, the distribution of cetaceans is little known. There are certainly blue, fin, Antarctic minke, Bryde's and sperm whales, along with spinner, pantropical spotted and other dolphins, mostly offshore in waters deeper than 325 feet (100 m), but research must be done to determine their habitat. Still, the Seychelles, without specifically protecting any cetacean habitat, has declared its national waters as a completely protected zone for marine mammals. Finally, the region is part of the Indian Ocean Sanctuary, as are Marine Regions 10, 11, 13 and 18, and this broad brush protection from whaling is at least some measure of international recognition, and could be a foundation to build upon.

The East African Marine Region includes eight countries and two French territories (see Table 5.1 on p89). Two large marine ecosystems (LMEs) have been identified: the warm (21°C+) southward-flowing Agulhas Current and the Somali Coastal Current. The oceanography of the region is complex as it spreads across either side of the Equator and in the south stretches all the way to the Antarctic Marine Region. In terms of upwellings and other potential, nutrient-rich cetacean feeding areas, strong offshore winds from the seasonal southeast monsoon from April to October contribute to productive cold-water upwellings particularly in the offshore waters of Somalia north of the Equator – the Ras Hafun upwelling. There are additional upwellings off the coast of Mozambique. Still, overall, the continental shelf here is narrow which is usually associated with lower productivity; indeed, the Western Indian Ocean is considered to be relatively fisheries-poor compared to other regions. However, extensive areas of both coral reefs and mangroves are spread throughout the northern and central part of the region.

There is an active UNEP regional seas programme for this region: MCEA – Convention for the Protection, Management and Development of the Marine and Coastal Environment of the Eastern African Region. On 21 June 1985, the Protocol Concerning Protected Areas and Wild Fauna and Flora in the Eastern African Region (Nairobi Convention) was signed. The protocol applies to regional waters and gives protection to listed species including migratory species (such as blue and humpback whales) and ecosystems.

In 1995, there was a total of 54 MPAs of all kinds in this marine region (Chiffings, 1995). The region is divided into five first-order biogeographic zones, three of which were represented by at least one MPA, while two have no representation. As of 2004, according to Table 5.15 prepared for this book, there are 28 existing and 5 proposed MPAs which feature cetacean habitat. Three of the existing areas are proposed for expansion. Many of these are small areas, such as in Tanzania, but they have the potential to be useful, particularly if they form part of an MPA network. More cetacean habitat work needs to be done in many of the areas.

The IUCN 2002–2010 Conservation Action Plan for the World's Cetaceans recommends only one conservation initiative for this region (Reeves et al, 2003): to investigate cetacean mortality in western Madagascar. However, in future editions of the action plan, there will be more focus on Africa.

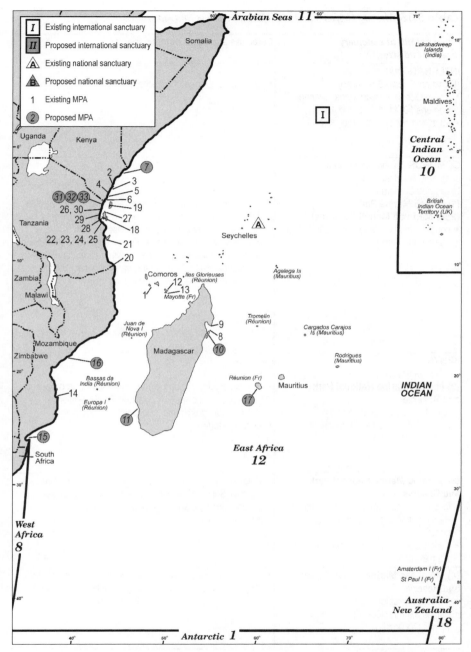

The roman numerals, letters and numbers correspond to the sanctuaries and MPAs listed and described in Table 5.15.

Figure 5.19 *Map of Marine Region 12: East African MPAs and sanctuaries*

Table 5.15 *Marine Region 12: East African MPAs and sanctuaries*

Name of MPA or sanctuary, location and size	Cetacean and other notable species
INTERNATIONAL **(I) Indian Ocean Sanctuary** • Indian Ocean, spread across Marine Regions 10, 11, 12, 13 and 18 • 40 million mi² (103.6 million km²)	• at least 43 species of cetaceans
COMOROS Jumhuriyat al-Qumur al-Itthadiyah al-Islamiyah Union des Comores **(1) Mohéli Marine Park** **(Parc Marin de Mohéli Comoros)** • south Comoros island, also called Mwali • 154 mi² (400 km²)	• humpback whale, *Megaptera novaeangliae*; also: spinner dolphin, *Stenella longirostris*; striped dolphin, *Stenella coeruleoalba*; Indo-Pacific bottlenose dolphin, *Tursiops aduncus*; pygmy killer whale, *Feresa attenuata*; short-finned pilot whale, *Globicephala macrorhynchus*; melon-headed whale, *Peponocephala electra*; sporadic: Indo-Pacific beaked whale, *Indopacetus pacificus*
KENYA Jamhuri ya Kenya **(2) Malindi Marine National Park and Reserve** • Kilifi district, north Kenya coast • park is 2.4 mi² (6.3 km²); reserve is 63.7 mi² (213 km²)	• dolphin sightings may include Indo-Pacific hump-backed dolphin, *Sousa chinensis* and Indo-Pacific bottlenose dolphin, *Tursiops aduncus*, possibly others • also: sea turtles
(3) Watamu Marine National Park and Reserve • located inside Malindi Marine National Reserve, Kilifi district, north Kenya coast • park is 3.9 mi² (10 km²); reserve is 3.9 mi² (10 km²)	• dolphin sightings may include Indo-Pacific hump-backed dolphin, *Sousa chinensis* and Indo-Pacific bottlenose dolphin, *Tursiops aduncus*, possibly others • also: sea turtles
(4) Mombasa Marine National Park and Reserve • Mombasa district • park is 3.9 mi² (10 km²); reserve is 77 mi² (200 km²)	• dolphin sightings may include Indo-Pacific hump-backed dolphin, *Sousa chinensis* and Indo-Pacific bottlenose dolphin, *Tursiops aduncus*, possibly others
(5) Diani-Chale Marine National Reserve • Kwale district • 96.5 mi² (250 km²)	• dolphin sightings may include Indo-Pacific hump-backed dolphin, *Sousa chinensis* and Indo-Pacific bottlenose dolphin, *Tursiops aduncus*, possibly others

Notes and rationale	For more information
• Rationale is to protect large whales from commercial whaling and to stimulate cetacean research and conservation. • At the 1979 IWC meeting, the Republic of Seychelles proposed that the Indian Ocean be closed to commercial whaling and declared a sanctuary. With the support of most Indian Ocean states and the world, it was voted in as a whale sanctuary.	• See full account in Marine Region 10, Table 5.13.
• MPA created in Apr 2001 for reefs (including black corals), mangroves and turtle nesting sties, but also includes breeding habitat of the humpback whale. • Managed by Direction Générale de l'Environnement and 12 communities with management plan under development which mainly focuses on turtles. • Part of a candidate World Heritage Site which would also include the proposed coelacanth MPA in Grand Comore and the Mt Ntringuni forest on Anjouane island. • Photo-ID work has been conducted here by the Association Megaptera from the Indian and South Atlantic Consortium on the Humpback Whale (ISACH).	• Contact: Michel Vély, l'association Megaptera; email: mvely@megaptera-oi.org; web: www.megaptera-oi.org • Howard Rosenbaum; email: hcr@amnh.org or hrosenbaum@wcs.org • ISACH; web: www.isach.org
• Gazetted in 1968, Unesco biosphere reserve status followed in 1979, with administration by the Kenya Wildlife Service. Mandate is to protect coral reef communities, but cetaceans are also present; cetacean habitat studies need to be done to determine if the reserve effectively protects cetacean habitat. • Tourism, including diving and dolphin watching, is an important mandate of Kenya's marine parks.	• Muthiga et al, 1998 • Contact: Kenya Wildlife Service; email: kws@kws.org; web: www.kenya-wildlife-service.org/marine.htm
• Gazetted in 1968, Unesco biosphere reserve status followed in 1979, with administration by the Kenya Wildlife Service. Mandate is to protect coral reef communities, but cetaceans are also present; cetacean habitat studies need to be done to determine if the reserve effectively protects cetacean habitat. • Tourism, including diving and dolphin watching, is an important mandate of Kenya's marine parks.	• Muthiga et al, 1998 • Contact: Kenya Wildlife Service; email: kws@kws.org; web: www.kenya-wildlife-service.org/marine.htm
• Gazetted in 1986, park and reserve are administered by the Kenya Wildlife Service. Mandate is to protect coral reef communities, but cetaceans are also present; cetacean habitat studies need to be done to determine if the reserve effectively protects cetacean habitat. • Tourism, including diving and dolphin watching, is an important mandate of Kenya's marine parks.	• Muthiga et al, 1998 • Contact: Kenya Wildlife Service; email: kws@kws.org; web: www.kenya-wildlife-service.org/marine.htm
• Gazetted in 1995, reserve is administered by the Kenya Wildlife Service. Mandate is to protect coral reef communities, but cetaceans are also present; cetacean habitat studies need to be done to determine if the reserve effectively protects cetacean habitat. • Tourism, including diving and dolphin watching, is an important mandate of Kenya's marine parks.	• Muthiga et al, 1998 • Contact: Kenya Wildlife Service; email: kws@kws.org; web: www.kenya-wildlife-service.org/marine.htm

Table 5.15 *continued*

Name of MPA or sanctuary, location and size	Cetacean and other notable species
(6) Kisite Marine National Park and Mpunguti Reserve • Kwale district, south Kenya coast • park is 4.2 mi² (11 km²) and reserve is 10.8 mi² (28 km²)	• common: Indo-Pacific hump-backed dolphin, *Sousa chinensis*; pantropical spotted dolphin, *Stenella attenuata*; occasionally: spinner dolphin, *Stenella longirostris*; common dolphin, *Delphinus* sp; Indo-Pacific bottlenose dolphin, *Tursiops aduncus*; Oct: humpback whale, *Megaptera novaeangliae*, possibly others
(7) Kiunga Marine National Reserve, *proposed for expansion as a World Heritage Site* • Lamu district • 15.5 mi² (25 km²); expanded World Heritage area would be 2341 mi² (6064 km²)	• humpback whale, *Megaptera novaeangliae*; sei whale, *Balaenoptera borealis*; sperm whale, *Physeter macrocephalus*; pilot whale, *Globicephala* sp; dolphin sightings may include Indo-Pacific hump-backed dolphin, *Sousa chinensis* and Indo-Pacific bottlenose dolphin, *Tursiops aduncus*, possibly others
MADAGASCAR Democratic Republic of Madagascar Repoblika Demokratika n`i Madagaskar **(8) Manannara North Biosphere Reserve, includes four small island MPAs in the Antafana Islands Marine Park** • Antafana Islands, northeast Madagascar • 4 mi² (10 km²)	• Jul–Nov: humpback whale, *Megaptera novaeangliae*; year-round: Indo-Pacific hump-backed dolphin, *Sousa chinensis*; Indo-Pacific bottlenose dolphin, *Tursiops aduncus*; spinner dolphin, *Stenella longirostris*
(9) Masoala National Park, including Itampolo, Masoala and Tanjona Reserves • Masoala Peninsula area, northeast Madagascar	• Jul–Nov: humpback whale, *Megaptera novaeangliae*; year-round: Indo-Pacific hump-backed dolphin, *Sousa chinensis*; Indo-Pacific bottlenose dolphin, *Tursiops aduncus*; spinner dolphin, *Stenella longirostris*
(10) Baie d'Antongil – Saint Marie Island Humpback Whale Sanctuary (Sanctuaire des Megapteres de la Baie d'Antongil – Ile Sainte-Marie), *proposed* • Masoala Peninsula area, northeast Madagascar • proposed size up to 27,000 mi² (70,000 km²) includes land and marine areas	• Jul–Nov: humpback whale, *Megaptera novaeangliae*; common: Indo-Pacific hump-backed dolphin, *Sousa chinensis*; Indo-Pacific bottlenose dolphin, *Tursiops aduncus*; spinner dolphin, *Stenella longirostris* • also: endemic rain forest species such as lemurs, various frogs and reptiles and a small declining population of dugong

Notes and rationale	For more information
• Gazetted in 1978, park and reserve are administered by the Kenya Wildlife Service. Mandate is to protect coral reef communities, but cetaceans are also present; cetacean habitat studies need to be done to determine if the reserve effectively protects cetacean habitat. • Kisite has well-established dolphin watch tours. • IUCN has been advising on a pilot project to develop stakeholder participation in MPA management at Kisite.	• Muthiga et al, 1998 • Contact: Kenya Wildlife Service; email: kws@kws.org; web: www.kenya-wildlife-service.org/marine.htm
• Gazetted in 1979, Unesco biosphere reserve status followed in 1980, with administration by the Kenya Wildlife Service. Mandate is to protect coral reef communities, but cetaceans are also present; cetacean habitat studies need to be done to determine if the reserve effectively protects cetacean habitat. WWF has been assisting the Kenya Wildlife Service in a pilot project for community-based management in this reserve. • Proposal for a World Heritage Site would allow substantial expansion to include all the Kiunga archipelago, Lamu and Ras Tenewi. • Tourism in the reserve includes dolphin watching.	• Muthiga et al, 1998 • Contact: Kenya Wildlife Service; email: kws@kws.org; web: www.kenya-wildlife-service.org/marine.htm
• These four modest-sized MPAs are part of the Antafana Islands Marine Park which forms the biosphere reserve and is part of the winter mating and breeding area for Indian Ocean humpback whales. • MEGAPTERA OI has worked in the area since 1994.	• Contact: Michel Vély, l'association Megaptera; email: mvely@megaptera-oi.org; web: www.megaptera-oi.org
• Three modest-sized MPAs which are part of the national park share winter mating and breeding habitat for Indian Ocean humpback whales. • MEGAPTERA OI has worked in the area since 1994.	• Contact: Michel Vély, l'association Megaptera; email: mvely@megaptera-oi.org; web: www.megaptera-oi.org
• Proposed MPA in process of probable designation includes nearshore and pelagic waters beside existing land-based protected area in the Masoala region. • Important mating and breeding area in the winter for Indian Ocean humpback whales. In Aug, mainly females with newborn calves reside in the bay, one of the few shallow, protected bays along the east shore of Madagascar (Rosenbaum et al, 1997). Antongil Bay has a resident population of about 100 bottlenose dolphins. • NGO working in the area, MEGAPTERA OI, deals with cetacean education, surveys and conservation in the western Indian Ocean and has operated from Saint Mari Island since 1994.	• Folkens and Voara, 1988; Hoyt, 1997b • Contact: Michel Vély, l'association Megaptera; email: mvely@megaptera-oi.org; web: www.megaptera-oi.org • Howard Rosenbaum; email: hcr@amnh.org or hrosenbaum@wcs.org

Table 5.15 *continued*

Name of MPA or sanctuary, location and size	Cetacean and other notable species
(11) **Toliara-Nosy Ve Candidate World Heritage Site,** *proposed for expansion* • southwest coast, Madagascar, including Toliara Barrier Reef and the island of Nosy Ve • 772 mi² (2000 km²), includes island and marine areas, approximately 10 per cent as IUCN Category I–III	• sperm whale, *Physeter macrocephalus*; other cetaceans • also: sea turtles, coral communities
MAYOTTE (France) (French territorial collectivity) **[MPAs 12–13]** **(12) Passe en S Reserve (Réserve de Passe en S)** **(13) Saziley Reserve (Réserve de Saziley)**	• Indo-Pacific bottlenose dolphin, *Tursiops aduncus*; Jul–Sept: humpback whale, *Megaptera novaeangliae*; also, Réserve de Saziley only: Indo-Pacific hump-backed dolphin, *Sousa chinensis*
MOZAMBIQUE People's Republic of Mozambique República Popular de Moçambique **(14) Bazaruto Archipelago National Park** • the Bazaruto archipelago (five islands) is about 20 mi (30 km) off the coast between the towns of Vilanculo and Inhassoro • marine component is 540 mi² (1400 km²)	• Jul–Sept: humpback whale, *Megaptera novaeangliae*; resident: Indo-Pacific hump-backed dolphin, *Sousa chinensis*; Indo-Pacific bottlenose dolphin, *Tursiops aduncus*; common: spinner dolphin, *Stenella longirostris*; occasional: Antarctic minke whale, *Balaenoptera bonaerensis*; other cetaceans • also: sawfishes, four species marine turtles, dugong (bay provides habitat for 150 individuals – largest known concentration left in East Africa)

Notes and rationale	For more information
• Two conservation areas have been created under local laws at Baie de Ranobe and Nosy Ve island and there is integrated coastal resource management (encompassing fisheries, mangroves and tourism). Proposed as a Unesco biosphere reserve as well as a World Heritage Site because of its outstanding marine biodiversity, the area has the largest barrier reef in the region high coral and fish diversity; high endemism in freshwater wetlands and coastal vegetation; seagrass beds, turtles, birds and marine mammals including sperm whales. • The coral reefs in the area have been monitored since 1997 and there have been numerous field surveys, though there has been little cetacean work in terms of habitat identification.	• Contact: Michel Vély, l'association Megaptera; email: mvely@megaptera-oi.org; web: www.megaptera-oi.org
• Photo-ID work on humpback whales has been conducted in and around these reserves by the Observatoire des Mamifères Marins (OMM) of the Direction de l'Agriculture et de la Forêt (DAF) and the Association Megaptera from the Indian and South Atlantic Consortium on the Humpback Whale (ISACH).	• Contact: Michel Vély, l'association Megaptera; email: mvely@megaptera-oi.org; web: www.megaptera-oi.org; Howard Rosenbaum; hrosenbaum@wcs.org • OMM-DAF; email: Daf.mayotte@wanadoo.fr • ISACH; web: www.isach.org
• In 1971, three of the islands, Bangue, Magaruque and Benguera, were proclaimed national parks, with modest marine waters included; in Dec 2001 the national government announced the expanded MPA. • MPA helps bring fishing in the area under sustainable management and protects diversity of ecosystems including pelagic waters, coral reefs, sandy beaches, tidal flats, mangroves and swamp forests. • Nature tourism industry employs some 2600 locals and could expand with whale watching in future. The Endangered Wildlife Trust (EWT), WWF and the South Africa Nature Foundation have funded the Bazaruto Archipelago Master Plan (BAMP) project to help guide the Mozambique government in developing sustainable tourism. • Research has started to determine resource inventory, distribution and occurrence of dolphins and other marine fauna, as well as impact of fisheries present in the bay.	• Dutton and Zolho, 1991; Engdahl and Motta, 2000 • Contact: Vic Cockcroft, Centre for Dolphin Studies; email: cdsresearch@ worldonline.co.za • More information, see web: http://ens.lycos.com/ ens/dec2001/2001L-12-17-03.html

Table 5.15 *continued*

Name of MPA or sanctuary, location and size	Cetacean and other notable species
(15) Maputo Bay-Inhaca Island Machangalo candidate World Heritage Site, *proposed for expansion* • Maputo Bay and Inhaca Island plus the Machangalo area close to the South African border • 1603 mi² (4153 km²), includes island and marine areas	• Jul–Sept: humpback whale, *Megaptera novaeangliae*; common: Indo-Pacific hump-backed dolphin, *Sousa chinensis*; northern limit: southern right whale, *Eubalaena australis* • also: dugong, whale shark, coral communities
(16) Zambezi River Delta candidate World Heritage Site, *proposed* • Zambezi River delta • 4811 mi² (12,464 km²) includes land and marine areas	• Jul–Sept: humpback whale, *Megaptera novaeangliae*; common: Indo-Pacific hump-backed dolphin, *Sousa chinensis*; Risso's dolphin, *Grampus griseus* • also: wattled crane, pelican, African skimmer
LA RÉUNION (France) (French overseas department) **(17) Réunion Marine Park (Parc Marin de La Réunion)** • La Réunion	• Indo-Pacific hump-backed dolphin, *Sousa chinensis*; Jul–Sept: humpback whale, *Megaptera novaeangliae*
SEYCHELLES Republic of Seychelles **(A) Seychelles Marine Mammal Sanctuary** • national waters of Seychelles to the limits of the EEZ	• humpback whale, *Megaptera novaeangliae*; fin whale, *Balaenoptera physalus*; sei whale, *Balaenoptera borealis*; Bryde's whale, *Balaenoptera brydei*; Antarctic minke whale, *Balaenoptera bonaerensis*; southern right whale, *Eubalaena australis*; sperm whale, *Physeter macrocephalus*; orca, *Orcinus orca*; Cuvier's beaked whale, *Ziphius cavirostris*; Gray's beaked whale, *Mesoplodon grayi*; Indo-Pacific beaked whale, *Indopacetus pacificus*; pilot whale, *Globicephala* sp; Risso's dolphin, *Grampus griseus*; pantropical spotted dolphin, *Stenella attenuata*; rough-toothed dolphin, *Steno bredanensis*; melon-headed whale, *Peponocephala electra*; Blainville's beaked whale, *Mesoplodon densirostris*
TANZANIA United Republic of Tanzania Jamhuri ya Muungano wa Tanzania **(18) Menai Bay Conservation Area** • Menai Bay, southwest of Unguja Island, Zanzibar • 181.4 mi² (470 km²)	• resident: Indo-Pacific hump-backed dolphin, *Sousa chinensis*; Indo-Pacific bottlenose dolphin, *Tursiops aduncus*; common: spinner dolphin, *Stenella longirostris;* Jul–Oct: humpback whale, *Megaptera novaeangliae*; sporadic: Risso's dolphin, *Grampus griseus*; possible: pantropical spotted dolphin, *Stenella attenuata* • also: sea turtles, whale shark

Notes and rationale	For more information
• Part of Inhaca Island forms the Ilhas da Inhaca e dos Portuguese Reserve but expanded area would include larger marine area. Identified as a national site and then proposed as a World Heritage Site because of its outstanding marine biodiversity, the site has feeding areas for turtles, dugong and migratory birds, as well as endemic fish and plant species and the southernmost coral communities in the region with high endemism of soft corals. • The area is experiencing pressure from urban and harbour development, dredging, pollution and tourism.	• Engdahl and Motta, 2000 • More information, see web: http://international.nos. noaa.gov/heritage/pdfs/ east_africa.pdf
• Proposed as a candidate World Heritage Site because of its outstanding marine biodiversity, the delta has the largest complex of mangroves in the western Indian Ocean and a globally important wetland with threatened wetland birds. • Area is under threat from upstream dam development controlled by Zambia and Zimbabwe, mariculture and national government development plans.	• More information, see web: http://international.nos. noaa.gov/heritage/pdfs/ east_africa.pdf
• Photo-ID work on humpback whales has been conducted here by Globice Réunion.	• Contact: Bernard Rota, GLOBICE; email: wanadoo.fr; web: www.globice.org
• Large refuge or sanctuary comprising entire national waters with ban on hunting cetaceans. • On 29 May 1979, the Seychelles government issued Decree 28 which established complete protection for marine mammals in Seychelles waters, specifically prohibiting any taking of marine mammals unless by permit granted from the president ('taking' is determined as killing, chasing with the intent to kill, harassing which would disturb natural behaviour or breeding habits, and taking dead or alive; there is some provision for accidental taking of marine mammals). • In the early 1990s, an Environmental Management Plan was adopted and all marine and other conservation initiatives are based on this. Some 22 protected areas in the Seychelles include marine and coastal habitat, with 15 of them covering coastal waters, but none are designed to protect cetaceans (Gaudian et al, 1995).	• Gaudian et al, 1995; Shah, 1993
• Gazetted as a conservation area in Aug 1997 by Zanzibar government to protect coral reefs, Menai Bay Conservation Area is managed jointly by the fisheries dept and local communities; rated IUCN Category VI. • Since 1998, a dolphin photo-ID project of Stockholm University, Sweden, and the Institute of Marine Sciences (IMS), Zanzibar, has found 160 resident Indo-Pacific bottlenose and 69 resident Indo-Pacific hump-backed dolphins in Menai Bay.	• Contact: Omar A Amir, Marine Mammal Education and Research Project, Institute of Marine Sciences; Zanzibar; email: omar@ims.udsm.ac.tz • Menai Bay Conservation Area, Fisheries Dept; email: wwfmenai@zitec.org; web: www.marineparktz.com

Table 5.15 *continued*

Name of MPA or sanctuary, location and size	Cetacean and other notable species
(19) Misali Island Conservation Area • 6 mi (10 km) off the west coast of Pemba Island, Zanzibar • 8.5 mi² (22 km²)	• Jul–Oct: humpback whale, *Megaptera novaeangliae*; dolphin sightings may include Indo-Pacific hump-backed dolphin, *Sousa chinensis* and Indo-Pacific bottlenose dolphin, *Tursiops aduncus*, possibly others
(20) Mnazi Bay Marine Park • Mtwara at far southern end of the Tanzanian coast on the border of Mozambique • 251 mi² (650 km²)	• Jul–Oct: humpback whale, *Megaptera novaeangliae*; dolphin sightings may include Indo-Pacific hump-backed dolphin, *Sousa chinensis* and Indo-Pacific bottlenose dolphin, *Tursiops aduncus*, possibly others
(21) Mafia Island Marine Park • about 75 mi (120 km) southeast of Dar es Salaam • 317 mi² (822 km²)	• Jul–Oct: humpback whale, *Megaptera novaeangliae*; dolphin sightings may include Indo-Pacific hump-backed dolphin, *Sousa chinensis* and Indo-Pacific bottlenose dolphin, *Tursiops aduncus*, possibly others
[MPAs 22–25] **Dar-es-Salaam Marine Reserves System (**northern Dar-es-Salaam) **(22) Mbudya Marine Reserve** • 3.4 mi² (8.9 km²) **(23) Bongoyo Marine Reserve** • 2.8 mi² (7.3 km²) **(24) Pangavini Marine Reserve** • 0.7 mi² (2.0 km²) **(25) Fungu Yasini Marine Reserve** • 2.9 mi² (7.5 km²)	• Jul–Oct: humpback whale, *Megaptera novaeangliae*; dolphin sightings may include Indo-Pacific hump-backed dolphin, *Sousa chinensis* and Indo-Pacific bottlenose dolphin, *Tursiops aduncus*, possibly others
(26) Maziwi Marine Reserve • Tanga, northern Tanzania	• Indo-Pacific hump-backed dolphin, *Sousa chinensis*; Indo-Pacific bottlenose dolphin, *Tursiops aduncus*; possibly others

Notes and rationale	For more information
• Declared in 1998, this conservation area is managed jointly by the Forest Dept and local communities; a small portion is land-based; rated IUCN Category VI. • Misali Island is surrounded by some of the finest coral slopes in the Indian Ocean. It is also a sea turtle nesting area.	• Contact: Omar A Amir, Marine Mammal Education and Research Project, Institute of Marine Sciences; Zanzibar; email: omar@ims.udsm.ac.tz; web: www.marineparktz.com
• Marine park declared Jun 2000 by Tanzanian parliament to protect coral reefs, following the Marine Parks and Reserves Act of 1995; rated IUCN Category VI.	• Contact: The Manager, Marine Parks and Reserves Unit, Dar es Salaam, Tanzania; email: marineparks@raha.com; web: www.marineparktz.com
• Gazetted in 1995 as a marine park with estuarine, seagrass, coral reef and mangrove ecosystems, an effective management structure is in place; rated IUCN Category VI. • Dolphin sightings reported but no distribution studies have been done yet to determine species and populations, and the extent and importance of cetacean habitat.	• Contact: Omar A Amir, Marine Mammal Education and Research Project, Institute of Marine Sciences; Zanzibar; email: omar@ims.udsm.ac.tz • The Warden, Mafia Island Marine Park, PO Box 74, Mafia, Tanzania; web: www.marineparktz.com
• The Dar es Salaam Marine Reserves – Mbudya, Bongoyo, Pangavini and Fungu Yasini – were established around four islands in 1975 under fisheries legislation to protect coral reefs. In 1998, they were transferred to Marine Parks and Reserves. They are rated IUCN Category II. • Dolphin sightings reported but no distribution studies have been done yet to determine species and populations, and the extent and importance of cetacean habitat. • Considered 'paper reserves', these MPAs would need to be refocused and rededicated, with cetacean research, to function as MPAs that would protect cetaceans. There are plans in progress to improve the success of the reserves. These include changing the status of the area from marine reserve to marine park. Conservation actions include coral reefs restoration in collaboration with local fishing communities and promotion of ecotourism.	• Contact: Omar A Amir, Marine Mammal Education and Research Project, Institute of Marine Sciences; Zanzibar; email: omar@ims.udsm.ac.tz; web: www.marineparktz.com
• Gazetted in 1981, but no management plan as yet; rated IUCN Category II.	• Contact: Omar A Amir, Marine Mammal Education and Research Project, Institute of Marine Sciences; Zanzibar; email: omar@ims.udsm.ac.tz; web: www.marineparktz.com

Table 5.15 *continued*

Name of MPA or sanctuary, location and size	Cetacean and other notable species
(27) Mnemba Island Marine Conservation Area • Off the northeast coast of Unguja island, Zanzibar • 0.06 mi² (0.15 km²)	• Indo-Pacific bottlenose dolphin, *Tursiops aduncus*; spinner dolphin, *Stenella longirostris*; Risso's dolphin, *Grampus griseus*; pantropical spotted dolphin, *Stenella attenuata*; Jul–Oct: humpback whale, *Megaptera novaeangliae* • also: sea turtles, whale shark
(28) Chumbe Marine Sanctuary • southwest of Zanzibar town • 0.12 mi² (0.3 km²)	• Indo-Pacific hump-backed dolphin, *Sousa chinensis*; Indo-Pacific bottlenose dolphin, *Tursiops aduncus*; Jul–Oct: humpback whale, *Megaptera novaeangliae*
(29) Mkwaja Saadani National Park • 31 mi (50 km) north of Bagamoyo town • 386 mi² (1000 km²), mainly land-based	• probably Indo-Pacific hump-backed dolphin, *Sousa chinensis* and Indo-Pacific bottlenose dolphin, *Tursiops aduncus*; possibly others
(30) Pangani MPA • Pangani, northern Tanzania	• probably Indo-Pacific hump-backed dolphin, *Sousa chinensis* and Indo-Pacific bottlenose dolphin, *Tursiops aduncus*; possibly others
[MPAs 31–33] **(31) Tanga Coral Gardens Marine Reserve and Marine Conservation Area,** *proposed* **(32) Kipumbwi Marine Conservation Area,** *proposed* **(33) Kigombe Marine Conservation Area,** *proposed* • all located in Tanga, northern Tanzania	• probably Indo-Pacific hump-backed dolphin, *Sousa chinensis* and Indo-Pacific bottlenose dolphin, *Tursiops aduncus*; possibly others

Notes and rationale	For more information
• Protected by a private investor, Conservation Corporation of Africa, since 1992, this small area aims to protect fragile coral reefs and marine life. It is operated by Mnemba Island management with local government and community involvement in management; rated IUCN Category VI. • Dolphin sightings reported but distribution studies have not been done to determine the extent and importance of cetacean habitat.	• Contact: Omar A Amir, Marine Mammal Education and Research Project, Institute of Marine Sciences; Zanzibar; email: omar@ims.udsm.ac.tz; web: www.marineparktz.com
• Coral reef area, also called Chumbe Island Coral Park, has been managed by a private investor, CHICOP, since 1994; rated IUCN Category II. • Dolphins are often reported passing by but no distribution studies have been done yet to determine species and populations, and the extent and importance of cetacean habitat.	• Contact: Omar A Amir, Marine Mammal Education and Research Project, Institute of Marine Sciences; Zanzibar; email: omar@ims.udsm.ac.tz; web: www.marineparktz.com
• Managed by Tanzania National Parks Authority, this former game reserve recently became Tanzania's 13th national park. The only coastal wildlife sanctuary, it contains distinctive, rare habitats, unique to East Africa, such as beaches with salt grass flats along the ocean. • Dolphins sighted but no studies have been done yet to determine the extent and importance of cetacean habitat.	• Contact: Omar A Amir, Marine Mammal Education and Research Project, Institute of Marine Sciences; Zanzibar; email: omar@ims.udsm.ac.tz; web: www.marineparktz.com
• Dolphin sightings reported but no distribution studies have been done yet to determine species and populations, and the extent and importance of cetacean habitat.	• Contact: Omar A Amir, Marine Mammal Education and Research Project, Institute of Marine Sciences; Zanzibar; email: omar@ims.udsm.ac.tz; web: www.marineparktz.com
• Proposed as marine conservation areas and some dolphin sightings reported but no distribution studies have been done yet to determine species and populations, and the extent and importance of cetacean habitat.	• Contact: Omar A Amir, Marine Mammal Education and Research Project, Institute of Marine Sciences; Zanzibar; email: omar@ims.udsm.ac.tz; web: www.marineparktz.com

MARINE REGION 13: EAST ASIAN SEAS

Some 30 species of cetaceans reside or pass through this crossroads region between the Pacific and Indian oceans. Straddling both sides of the tropics, the region is bounded by the Northwest Pacific region to the north and the Australia–New Zealand region to the south. To the west lies the Central Indian Ocean and in the east is the South Pacific Marine Region.

The region is dominated by the Indonesian archipelago – the largest archipelago nation in the world – the waters of which have been proposed as a marine mammal sanctuary. Various Indonesian national parks have cetacean habitat such as Komodo, Bunaken, Cendrawasih Bay and Wakatobi national parks, though none were designated for cetaceans. Recent field observations have revealed that the area of Alor-Solor (located at the eastern end of the Lesser Sunda Islands in the Nusa Tenggara Timur, Indonesia) is home for many species of cetaceans including orcas, sperm and blue whales, and this is part of a newly proposed MPA through WWF Indonesia. The Philippines archipelago covers much of the northeast of the region where there is important humpback whale mating and calving habitat, as well as year-round areas for various tropical and subtropical cetaceans. Certain lesser-known cetaceans are regularly found in the Philippines including dwarf sperm whales in Tañon Strait, melon-headed whales in Bohol and the northern Sulu Sea, and Fraser's dolphins in many locations. The Mahakam River in Kalimantan, part of Indonesia, and the inland Lao PDR and adjacent Cambodia, as well as several other areas in the region, provide important habitat for riverine Irrawaddy dolphins. In addition, the diverse Spratly Islands, consisting of some 26 islands and more than 600 coral reefs, are the subject of competing territorial claims from several countries, with no solution in sight. One proposed idea is to make the area an international peace park and biosphere reserve. The resident sperm whales and various tropical dolphins could be some of the flagship species of such an MPA.

The East Asian Seas Marine Region has four large marine ecosystems (LMEs) that have been identified: Gulf of Thailand, South China Sea, Sulu-Celebes Sea and the Indonesian Sea. The overall surface water masses of the region come from the Pacific via the North Equatorial Current which flows westward across the broad Pacific, hitting the Philippines and splitting into the northward Kuroshio or Japan Current and the southward Mindanao Current.

The region is a global centre for coral reef, seagrass bed and mangrove diversity – with probably the most diverse marine flora and fauna in the world (Bleakley and Wells, 1995). The region's oceanography is strongly influenced by monsoons. Upwellings during the southwest monsoon occur off the northeast Malay peninsula in the South China Sea; along the shelf edge west of Luzon and Palawan, Philippines; and in the Timor and Banda Seas. In the northeast monsoon, there is upwelling along the mainland shelf edge east of Vietnam and off Sarawak (Meth and Helmer, 1983).

Both the Philippines and Indonesia have a recent whaling history which continued into the 1990s to catch sperm, Bryde's and other whales from some of the more remote islands. Pamilacan Island, a village in the Philippines, has been converting to a tourism economy featuring whale watching, with snorkelling and an island community experience, and using an MPA as part of the conservation protection and ecotourism marketing strategy. There is some discussion about attempting the same conversion in Lamalera, Indonesia.

A UNEP regional seas programme has been set up in the region. The East Asian Seas Action Plan was adopted in 1981 by Indonesia, the Philippines, Singapore, Thailand and Malaysia. In December 2003, the Putrajaya Declaration was signed by 12 East Asian countries, representing their commitment to fulfilling the oceans and coasts requirements of the World Summit on Sustainable Development (WSSD) for the Seas of East Asia. These countries include most of those in Marine Region 13, as well as China, Japan, RO Korea and PDR Korea in the Northwest Pacific, Marine Region 16.

In 1995, there was a total of 92 MPAs of all kinds in this marine region (Bleakley and Wells, 1995). The region is divided into eight first-order biogeographic zones, all of which were represented by at least one MPA, but four of which have only bare representation. Four of the 22 second-order biogeographic zones have no MPA representation. As of 2004, as shown in Table 5.17 prepared for this book, there are 18 existing (2 of which are proposed for expansion) and 16 proposed MPAs which feature cetacean habitat.

The IUCN 2002–2010 Conservation Action Plan for the World's Cetaceans recommends a number of research and education initiatives for this region (Reeves et al, 2003):

- to investigate the status of cetaceans in the Indonesian archipelago;
- to assess the status of cetacean populations and levels of incidental mortality in the Philippines;
- to investigate the status of Irrawaddy dolphins in the Mekong River of Laos, Cambodia and Vietnam;
- to investigate the status of coastal small cetaceans in Thailand;
- to predict and investigate areas of high-density occurrence ('hot spots') for marine populations of Irrawaddy dolphins and identify focal areas for conservation effort;
- to convene a workshop to develop an action plan for conserving freshwater populations of Irrawaddy dolphins (also applies to Marine Region 10); and
- to conduct intensive training courses on cetacean research techniques for scientists in South and Southeast Asia (also for Marine Region 10).

There are also various IUCN Action Plan initiatives related to the critically endangered Mahakam River population of the Irrawaddy dolphin, as well as the more recently discovered geographically separate population in Malampaya Sound, Palawan, Philippines, which is thought to be in immediate danger of extinction due to low numbers, limited range and high mortality (Dolar et al, 2000; Reeves et al, 2003).

For the Mahakam River (Kalimantan, Indonesia) population of Irrawaddy dolphins, recommendations are:

- to monitor and evaluate ongoing threats;
- to eliminate accidental mortality by providing alternative employment options for gill net fishermen;
- to enforce regulations against destructive fishing methods, logging of riparian forests and intentional killing of the dolphins;
- to allow no captures for aquariums (as already proscribed by national law); and
- to replace large coal-carrying barges – which are degrading the habitat and displacing the dolphins – with smaller craft.

For the Malampaya Sound population of the Irrawaddy dolphins, the IUCN Cetacean Specialist Group (CSG) recommends that:

- dolphin mortalities in the crab fishery be dramatically reduced or eliminated;
- socioeconomic alternatives be promoted to reduce entanglement in gill nets; and
- long-term monitoring of dolphin abundance and mortality rate be initiated.

Case Study 8: Komodo National Park, proposed for expansion

Creating a place for cetaceans in Komodo National Park, Biosphere Reserve and World Heritage Site

Type: Existing national park with nearshore, pelagic and island components; biosphere reserve and world heritage area; now proposed for expansion.

Location: Eastern part of Nusa Tenggara island chain, just west of the island of Flores, between the Flores Sea and the Sumba Strait, Indonesia.

Cetacean species:

- Common or abundant in months surveyed – April, May, October: spinner dolphin, *Stenella longirostris*; bottlenose dolphin, *Tursiops truncatus*; pantropical spotted dolphin, *Stenella attenuata*.
- Uncommon in April, May, October: Fraser's dolphin, *Lagenodelphis hosei*; Risso's dolphin, *Grampus griseus*; melon-headed whale, *Peponocephala electra*; sperm whale, *Physeter macrocephalus*; pygmy Bryde's whale, *Balaenoptera edeni*; and other rorqual species.
- Rare: pygmy and dwarf sperm whales, *Kogia* spp; pygmy killer whale, *Feresa attenuata*; false killer whale, *Pseudorca crassidens*; common dolphin, *Delphinus* spp; rough-toothed dolphin, *Steno bredanensis*; Cuvier's beaked whale, *Ziphius cavirostris*; blue whale, *Baleanoptera musculus*; orca, *Orcinus orca*.

Additional species and other features: Rich fish habitat features 900–1000 fish species including spawning aggregations of regional conservation importance. There are two manta ray, *Manta birostris*, aggregations. There are some 70 sponge species and 253 reef-building coral species from 70 genera within the park and at nearby Banta Island. Hawksbill turtles, *Eretmochelys imbricata*, and green turtles, *Chelonia mydas*, use park beaches as nesting sites. There is a mix of coastal and marine habitat including mangrove forests, coral reefs, seagrass beds, with extraordinary diversity on adjacent land areas. Species include the Komodo dragon, *Varanus komodoensis*; Timor deer, *Cervus timorensis*; water buffalo, *Bubalus bubalus*; wild boar, *Sus scrofa*; and the long-tailed or crab-eating macacques, *Macaca fascicularis*.

Size of designated protected area: 701 square miles (1817 km^2), including 469 mi^2 (1214 km^2) of marine waters and 232 mi^2 (603 km^2) of land (includes Komodo, Rinca, Padar and various smaller islands).

Size of proposed extension: 9.6 square miles (25 km^2) of land (Banta Island) and 184.9 mi^2 (479 km^2) of marine waters. This extension would bring the total surface area protected to 896 mi^2 (2321 km^2).

Rationale: To protect rare, unique Komodo dragon and the rich diversity of land and marine species. According to recent surveys, the park also contains cetacean feeding areas, mating and breeding grounds and areas frequented by migrating cetaceans (Kahn et al, 2000). Park waters are part of the important corridor between the Pacific and Indian oceans. Proposed extension would specifically help protect more cetacean habitat.

In 1980, the Government of Indonesia decided to create the Komodo National Park to celebrate the unique Komodo dragon and the rich diversity of the area. In 1986, the park was declared a Unesco biosphere reserve and World Heritage Site. National and provincial governments share jurisdiction over the park. There are numerous laws and regulations that are effectively part of this protected area including: (1) some 33 national and regional laws, regulations and decrees pertaining to national parks (11 laws, 14 government regulations, 4 presidential decrees and 4 decrees of the Minister of Forestry); (2) seven laws and regulations pertaining specifically to Komodo National Park; and (3) ten legal regulations pertaining to the Komodo dragon. The key laws relating to the protection of cetaceans and cetacean habitat are listed in Table 5.16. Since 1995, The Nature Conservancy (TNC), following a request from the Ministry of Forestry, has assisted the Komodo National Park Authority with the preparation of a marine resource management plan as part of the process of developing the 25-year park management master plan. There have been extensive public consultations at the national, regional and local levels on the management plans and protected area zonations. In 2000, the plan was approved by the Indonesian government and it is now being implemented.

Cetacean surveys in the Komodo National Park began in April 1999 and are being conducted twice a year during the inter-monsoon periods of

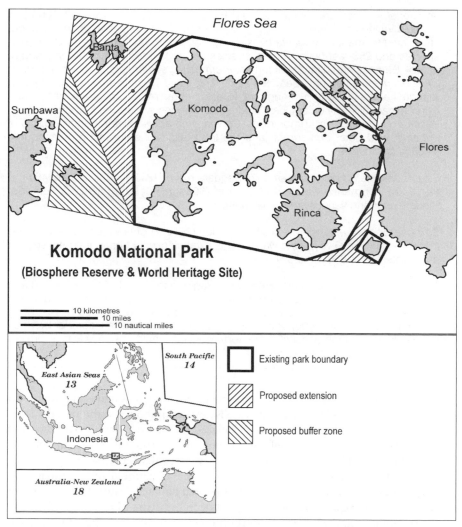

Komodo National Park, in Indonesia, was originally protected for its outstanding island biodiversity, but cetacean surveys have shown that the surrounding waters are an important habitat for many tropical cetaceans. More of the surrounding waters are now being proposed as an extension to the park as well as a buffer zone. See Case Study 8.

Figure 5.20 *Map of Komodo National Park*

April–May and September–October. The surveys address several park management priorities regarding cetaceans:

- to identify cetacean species and establish the abundance of their populations in the park and adjacent waters;

- to identify resident and transient populations including seasonal sighting patterns;
- to identify critical habitats, including preferred feeding and breeding habitats and migration corridors;
- to provide site and species information on the park's cetaceans for marine resource and management purposes, to assist in environmental awareness and educational programmes, and to help support the park's marine tourism and dive industry;
- to examine the major local and regional environmental impacts that threaten eastern Indonesia's whales and dolphins;
- to evaluate protective measures which can be implemented by park management authorities to minimize environmental impacts on cetacean habitats;
- to involve local communities, dive operators and tour guides to help monitor cetacean activity; and
- to share the survey results with the Indonesian park authorities, environmental groups and local communities.

Some research, such as work on pygmy Bryde's whales and sperm whales, features more detailed photo-ID and biopsy research. As a result of these studies, several whale and dolphin conservation measures have been incorporated in the park's 25-year management plan and are currently being implemented:

- the extension of the park's boundaries to shelter a wider variety of marine life;
- the creation of buffer zones to protect key migration routes;
- the training of a local cetacean team consisting of TNC field staff and park rangers to conduct periodic monitoring and survey activities; and
- additional regulations to prohibit activities inside the park that may harm migrating whales and dolphins, such as destructive fishing methods, gill and drift netting, as well as blasting and cyanide.

'The blasting activities', according to researcher Benjamin Kahn, 'have been significantly reduced within Komodo National Park due to the site conservation programme activities by the park authority, assisted by TNC. Nonetheless, reef bombing has been observed and heard underwater during several survey periods, especially in areas outside KNP, and this illegal fishing practice is considered a serious threat to KNP's whales and dolphins, with possible regional conservation implications.' Kahn says that the potential impacts of bombing in close proximity to sensitive cetacean habitats include: (1) fatal exposure to high pressure waves resulting from the blast, (2) permanently reduced sensory capabilities due to non-fatal exposure, (3) acoustic masking of environmental cues, (4) long-term abandonment of important habitats and (5) long-term alteration of migration routes. Reef bombing can also present a threat to the coral reef ecosystems. Other threats

Table 5.16 *Indonesian laws regarding cetaceans and cetacean habitat*

Date	Legislation	Description
1975	Ministerial Decree (Agriculture) No 35	Protection for wild animals including dolphins
1978	Presidential Decree No 43	Ratification of Convention on International Trade in Endangered Species of Wild Flora and Fauna (CITES)
1978	Ministerial Decree (Agriculture) No 327	Added protection for wild animals (whales, dolphins, crocodiles, leatherback turtles)
1980	Ministerial Decree (Agriculture) No 716	Added protection for wild animals (whales and turtles)
1985	Act No 17	Ratification of 'Principles of the Archipelagic Concept' and United Nations Convention on the Law of the Sea (UNCLOS)
1986	Presidential Decree No 26	Ratification of ASEAN Agreement on the Conservation of Nature and Natural Resources
1990	Act No 5	Conservation of living natural resources and their ecosystems
1990	Presidential Decree No 32	Management of protected areas
1999	Ministerial Decree (Forestry) No 7	Species protection

Source: Courtesy of Benjamin Kahn and Ketut Sarjana Putra

are plastic and chemical pollution, poaching, severe exploitation of resources in surrounding areas, which puts pressure on the park, and future mining activities and oil exploration. Finally, there are some problems with provincial boundary jurisdictions.

The research showing the habitat needs of cetaceans in Komodo National Park is reported in Kahn (1999, 2000, 2002e); Kahn et al (2000); and Kahn and Pet (2003). Following this work, the research programme has expanded from the rapid ecological assessments to include several focused ecological studies on Indonesia's resident and migratory cetaceans, especially in the Alor-Solor region, Bali and northern Sulawesi. The overall status of marine mammals in Indonesian waters is outlined in Kahn (2002f), while Kahn (2002b) details cetacean–fishery interactions.

Box 5.8 MPAs and cetaceans in Indonesia

The world's largest archipelagic state, Indonesia has within its national waters one of the world's most biologically diverse areas. As the gateway between the Indian and the equatorial Pacific Ocean, the deep passages between the islands are used by migrating cetaceans and other large, often migratory marine life (Kahn, 2002d, 2002f). The waters around the islands also provide habitat for feeding, mating and calving cetaceans. Indonesia's national waters, to the limits of its EEZ, are 2.2 million mi^2 (5.8 million km^2), two-thirds the size of Australia's vast national waters.

In 1982, at the III World Parks Congress (held in Bali), Indonesia began working towards the goal of establishing 39,000 mi^2 (100,000 km^2) in MPAs by 2000. This would only be 1.7 per cent of Indonesian national waters; still, it was an ambitious start. In 1984, Indonesian MPAs were described as designed for 'controlled development of the marine environment, sustainable utilization of Indonesia's diverse marine resources and protection of habitats critical to the survival of commercially valuable, endangered, vulnerable and other selected marine species' (Soegiarto et al, 1984). Indonesia's 200+ million population and an expanding national economy have placed increasing pressure on national waters and the emphasis of Indonesia's protected area programme has been to provide measured access to marine resources on a sustainable basis. Assessing the progress after a decade, Bleakley and Wells (1995) reported that most Indonesian MPAs partially or generally fail to meet management objectives and require management support, including more funding, local research, community environmental education and more trained managers, park naturalists and scientists.

In the late 1990s, two things happened which would have an important impact on the future of MPAs in Indonesia. The first was the mass bleaching of the coral reefs in 1998. This unforeseen environmental event caused the disintegration of many coral reefs in highly protected core zones and many reefs have not recovered. Unfortunately, a side effect of this event was that management resources allocated toward the core zones could not be shifted to areas or regimes where they could be of most benefit. An adaptive management strategy, with rapid reaction time, is now being planned, which would include a broader understanding of managing ecosystems (not just managing for coral reefs, seagrasses or other individual features alone) in order to make MPAs more resilient and ecologically functional in the long run.

The second crucial MPA development has been the decentralization of management which has allowed individual MPAs, and the NGOs working with them, to take more control of MPA management and their future mission. Instead of management from a single national institution, the Department of Forestry, Indonesia has seen the establishment of a collaborative management framework through the integration of park authorities, local communities, NGOs and the private sector. This initiative is now being realized in the national parks of Bunaken, Wakatobi and Komodo. In December 2003, Bunaken Marine National Park, in recognition of its success in developing sustainable marine tourism under the new management framework, was awarded the top prize at the British Airways Tourism for Tomorrow Awards.

As of January 2004, about 18,000 mi^2 (46,000 km^2) have been gazetted and partly managed in MPAs. The main ecological criteria used for MPA site selection has been the presence of coral reefs, mangroves, seagrass beds, turtle nesting beaches and coastal bird habitat. No MPAs have been established for the protection of cetaceans. It has only been by good fortune that some Indonesian MPAs, such as Komodo, Bunaken and Wakatobi, are large enough that they have been found, in the last few years, to contain cetacean habitat. In all, four existing and two proposed MPAs (or land national parks with a marine component) are known to have cetacean habitat (see Table 5.17 on p324). However, according to Ketut Sarjana Putra, Director of the Marine Program at WWF Indonesia, a further ten existing or formally proposed MPAs have portions of cetacean habitat and could offer significant protection for cetaceans, if their boundaries were to be expanded (also listed in Table 5.17). First of all, rapid ecological assessments are needed to determine cetacean presence and distribution, such as are described in Case Study 8 on the Komodo National Park (p316). Following that, more fine-grained cetacean habitat studies can be conducted to determine the precise habitat needs of the various populations and to suggest modifications of MPA boundaries.

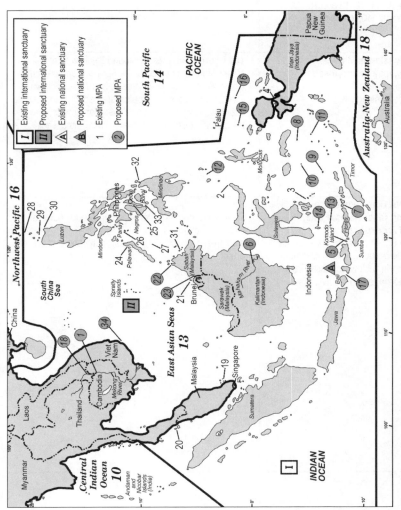

Figure 5.21 *Map of Marine Region 13: East Asian Seas MPAs and sanctuaries*

The roman numerals, letters and numbers correspond to the sanctuaries and MPAs listed and described in Table 5.17.

Table 5.17 *Marine Region 13: East Asian Seas MPAs and sanctuaries*

Name of MPA or sanctuary, location and size	Cetacean and other notable species
INTERNATIONAL **(I) Indian Ocean Sanctuary** • Indian Ocean, spread across Marine Regions 10, 11, 12, 13 and 18 • 40 million mi² (103.6 million km²)	• at least 43 species of cetaceans
(II) Spratly Islands Marine Sanctuary, *may be proposed* • south China Sea • size undetermined	• The following are present around Swallow Reef in the Malaysian-claimed area of the Spratly Islands: sperm whale, *Physeter macrocephalus*; bottlenose dolphin, *Tursiops truncatus*; pantropical spotted dolphin, *Stenella attenuata*; spinner dolphin, *Stenella longirostris*; melon-headed whale, *Peponocephala electra*; orca, *Orcinus orca*
CAMBODIA Roat Kampuchea **(1) Mekong River Ramsar Site,** *proposed for expansion* • Mekong River from a few miles south of the Lao border to a few miles north of the provincial town of Stung Treng • 30 mi (50 km) along the river	• year-round (common Dec–May): Irrawaddy dolphin, *Orcaella brevirostris* • also: freshwater fish (high biodiversity) and bird breeding areas

Notes and rationale	For more information
• Rationale is to protect large whales from commercial whaling and to stimulate cetacean research and conservation. • At the 1979 IWC meeting, the Republic of Seychelles proposed that the Indian Ocean be closed to commercial whaling and declared a sanctuary. With the support of most Indian Ocean states and the world, it was voted in as a whale sanctuary.	• See full account in Marine Region 10, Table 5.13.
• The rationale for this proposed park and sanctuary for biodiversity, including cetaceans, is to create an international peace park with valuable environmental protection for marine- and island-based ecosystems and species. • The Spratly Islands are currently one of the most hotly disputed island groups in the world, with conflicting claims (for all or part of the islands and surrounding waters) by China, Taiwan, Vietnam, Brunei, the Philippines and Malaysia. • Conflicts include legal question of ownership, fishing, oil and mineral resources.	• Jaaman, in prep • Contact: Saifullah A Jaaman, UMS, Marine Mammals and Whale Shark Research and Conservation Programme, Borneo Marine Research Institute, Universiti Malaysia, Sabah, Malaysia; email: saiful@ums.edu.my; s.jaaman@abdn.ac.uk
• The Irrawaddy dolphin was part of the rationale for protection, but the high biodiversity of freshwater fish and breeding birds makes this an important Ramsar site. • In 1994, the Asian Wetland Bureau (AWB) in Kuala Lumpur studied the Mekong River in Stung Treng province. In late 1995, David Ashwell from IUCN, working with the Ministry of Environment in Cambodia, looked at possible Ramsar sites, including this site. The Ramsar designation facilitates protection for fish and breeding birds but excludes key dry season dolphin habitat, including critical habitat a few miles north along the Lao border. Cetaceans are not the goal of wetlands habitat protection, but the Irrawaddy dolphin could benefit if the site were extended north to the Lao border. This Ramsar site could then become a transborder park if paired with Lao PDR sites. • Since 2001 the Mekong Dolphin Conservation Project has focused on studies of abundance, distribution, movements and mortality rates, in addition to working on conservation and management activities. The project plans to raise awareness with local communities about the dolphins and fisheries to improve the conservation.	• Baird and Mounsouphom, 1994, 1995; Baird et al, 1994; Roberts, 1993; Stacey, 1996; Baird and Beasley, in prep • Contact: Isabel Beasley, Mekong Dolphin Conservation Project, PO Box 9123, Kratie, Cambodia; email: psout@everyday.com.kh • David Ashwell, IUCN, 22, 222 St, Phnom Penh, Cambodia

Table 5.17 *continued*

Name of MPA or sanctuary, location and size	Cetacean and other notable species
INDONESIA Republik Indonesia *(A)* **Indonesian Marine Mammal Management Area (IM3A) (formerly called Indonesian Whale Sanctuary),** *proposed* • district, provincial and national waters to the limit of the 200 nm (371 km) Indonesian EEZ (marine area surrounding some 17,500 islands) • approximately 2.2 million mi² (5.8 million km²)	• at least 29 species of cetaceans (6 baleen whales, 3 sperm and at least 2 beaked whales, 15 dolphins and 1 porpoise) including: humpback whale, *Megaptera novaeangliae*; pygmy Bryde's whale, *Balaenoptera edeni*; fin whale, *Balaenoptera physalus*; blue whale, *Balaenoptera musculus*; sperm whale, *Physeter macrocephalus*; short-finned pilot whale, *Globicephala macrorhynchus*; orca, *Orcinus orca*; false killer whale, *Pseudorca crassidens*; pygmy killer whale, *Feresa attenuata*; melon-headed whale, *Peponocephala electra*; pantropical spotted dolphin, *Stenella attennuata*; common dolphin, *Delphinus* spp; Fraser's dolphin, *Lagenodelphis hosei*; Indo-Pacific hump-backed dolphin, *Sousa chinensis*; bottlenose dolphin, *Tursiops* sp; Irrawaddy dolphin, *Orcaella brevirostris*; finless porpoise, *Neophocaena phocaenoides* • also: dugong, fishes, turtles
(2) Bunaken Marine National Park • off Manado in Minahasa Province, on north Sulawesi • 305.2 mi² (790.6 km²); northern section consists of 239.9 mi² (621.5 km²) including 5 islands separated by deep channels; southern section is 65.3 mi² (169.1 km²), including the Arakan-Wawontulap coastal zone	• sperm whale, *Physeter macrocephalus*; pygmy sperm whale, *Kogia breviceps*; dwarf sperm whale, *Kogia sima*; short-finned pilot whale, *Globicephala macrorhynchus*; orca, *Orcinus orca*; false killer whale, *Pseudorca crassidens*; pygmy killer whale, *Feresa attenuata*; melon-headed whale, *Peponocephala electra*; spinner dolphin, *Stenella longirostris*; pantropical spotted dolphin, *Stenella attenuata*; rough-toothed dolphin, *Steno bredanensis*; Risso's dolphin, *Grampus griseus*; common dolphin, *Delphinus* spp; Fraser's dolphin, *Lagenodelphis hosei*; bottlenose dolphin, *Tursiops truncatus*; pygmy Bryde's whale, *Balaenoptera edeni* • also: land-based endemics such as crested black macaques, spectral tarsiers, black macaques and the red-knobbed hornbill

Notes and rationale	For more information
• In 1982, at the III World Parks Congress, held in Bali, Rod Salm (IUCN Marine and Coastal Conservation Programme) proposed the entire marine zone of Indonesia as a whale sanctuary to adjoin the Indian Ocean Sanctuary. The idea was accepted at the congress but formal gazettement was delayed for various reasons; it is still on hold. In 2002, however, APEX Environmental and The Nature Conservancy put the idea back on the agenda with a series of workshops and meetings. Upon request of the Minister for Marine Affairs and Fisheries, they developed an expanded marine mammal proposal. WWF Indonesia, as well as other organizations, have also provided support and the Indonesian Marine Mammal Management Area is currently positioned as a proposal within government and with the State Ministry of Environment as the coordinating ministry. • Rationale is to protect important migratory corridors for cetaceans between the Indian and Pacific oceans as well as to protect critical habitats for Indonesia's marine mammals and, in effect, to create an extension to the Indian Ocean Sanctuary in an area where little cetacean hunting occurs (Kahn, 2002c). • In 2000, Kahn et al pointed out that Indonesia was the only equatorial island nation where inter-oceanic exchange of marine flora and fauna occurs, including cetacean movements between the tropical Pacific and Indian Oceans through the Nusa Tenggara passages. This prime geographical location dictates 'an urgent need for additional protective measures for cetaceans in all seas under Indonesian jurisdiction'. The justification for an Indonesian national cetacean sanctuary is thus stronger than for most countries with marginal cetacean populations, or where cetaceans are already protected in various ways. Still, a national marine mammal sanctuary should not be seen as a substitute for creating a network of zoned MPAs or marine biosphere reserves, with IUCN Category I core areas, to protect critical habitats throughout the island archipelago.	• Alder et al, 1994; Kahn, 2002c, 2003b; Persoon et al, 1996; Soegiarto et al, 1984; Rudolph et al, 1997 • Contact: Benjamin Kahn, Indonesia Oceanic Cetacean Program Director, APEX Environmental Pty Ltd; email: bkahn@apex-environmental.com
• Set up in 1991, Bunaken was at first a paper park with few enforceable regulations but decentralization in Indonesia has helped; in 2000 Bunaken was allowed to start charging entrance fees with a third of the funds going to the 22 villages located on the various islands of the park and a sizeable portion going toward enforcement. • The extraordinary coral reef diversity is the key reason for protection. The park is positioned in the global centre of maximum marine biodiversity and includes an exceptional diversity of marine life within a range of coastal ecosystems featuring coral reefs, seagrass beds and mangroves. This high marine diversity extends outside the park along the scenic Sangihe-Talaud volcanic island chain that leads to the Philippines. • The park has commercial and artisanal fishing. There is also considerable coastal development with domestic and industrial wastes. Local gold mining uses submarine tailing disposal (STD) as the primary method of waste disposal. • In 2003, in recognition of its successes in developing sustainable tourism, the Bunaken Marine National Park was awarded the top prize at the British Airways Tourism for Tomorrow Awards.	• Contact: Benjamin Kahn, Indonesia Oceanic Cetacean Program Director, APEX Environmental Pty Ltd; email: bkahn@apex-environmental.com • Ian Dutton, Proyek Pesisir – CRMP Indonesia; email: crmp@cbn.net.id • Lembeh Strait Preservation Society, Yayasan Pelestarian Selat, Lembeh, Jl Sam Ratulangi 5, Bitung, Sulawesi Utara, Indonesia • Bunaken Marine National Park; web: www.bunaken.info

Table 5.17 *continued*

Name of MPA or sanctuary, location and size	Cetacean and other notable species
(3) Wakatobi Marine National Park • southeast Sulawesi in the Tukang Besi islands • 5000 mi² (13,000 km²)	• resident or regularly seen: pantropical spotted dolphin, *Stenella attenuata*; rough-toothed dolphin, *Steno bredanensis*; melon-headed whale, *Peponocephala electra*; short-finned pilot whale, *Globicephala macrorhynchus*; sporadic: sperm whale, *Physeter macrocephalus*; various dolphin species • also: marine turtles
(4) Cendrawasih Bay Marine National Park • southwest quarter of Cendrawasih Bay, Irian Jaya • 561 mi² (1453.5 km²) of which 504 mi² (1305.3 km²) is marine	• baleen whale species; short-beaked common dolphin, *Delphinus delphis*; various dolphin species • also: dugong, green and hawksbill turtles, white-tip reef shark, giant and other clams, Scleractinia corals
(5) Komodo National Park, Biosphere Reserve and World Heritage Site, *proposed for expansion* • eastern part of Nusa Tenggara island chain, just west of the island of Flores, between the Flores Sea and the Sumba Strait • 701 mi² (1817 km²), including 469 mi² (1214 km²) of marine waters and 232 mi² (603 km²) of land (Komodo, Rinca, Padar and various smaller islands) • proposed extension is 9.6 mi² (25 km²) land and 184.9 mi² (479 km²) water • Total area is 896 mi² (2321 km²) **See Case Study 8.**	• common in months surveyed – Apr, May, Oct: spinner dolphin, *Stenella longirostris*; bottlenose dolphin, *Tursiops truncatus*; pantropical spotted dolphin, *Stenella attenuata*. For complete cetacean species listed, see Case Study 8. • also: hawksbill and green turtles, 900–1000 fish species
(6) Semayang Lake National Park, *proposed* • Semayang Lake on east Kalimantan Island • size undetermined	• Irrawaddy dolphin, *Orcaella brevirostris*
(7) Alor-Solor MPA, *proposed* • eastern end of Lesser Sunda Islands in the Nusa Tenggara Timur • size undetermined but plans are to cover at least 85 mi (140 km) stretch from east to west along the Lesser Sunda Islands	• blue whale, *Balaenoptera musculus*; sperm whale, *Physeter macrocephalus;* bottlenose dolphin, *Tursiops truncatus*; pantropical spotted dolphin, *Stenella attenuata*; plus other cetaceans • also: manta ray, leatherback turtle

Notes and rationale	For more information
• Named a marine national park in 1997 mainly for the coral reef and to prevent threats from cyanide and blast fishing and extensive wildlife trade. • The park has zoned multi-user marine areas but to date has been largely a paper park; there is a management plan, now under revision, as it has not been implemented and has been largely ineffective. • The recent new impetus for protection has been based around tourism interest (two tourist resorts in the park) and due to pressure from WWF and Operation Wallacea following coral reef assessments in 1995–1996.	• Curran, 2001 • Contact: Sarah Curran, Operation Wallacea; email: sarahcurran00@hotmail.com • More information: web: www.opalwall.com/2004%20Wakatobi%20index.htm
• Named a marine national park (IUCN Category II) in 1993 through Decree from the Ministry of Forestry 472/Kpts-II/1993) for its relatively undisturbed, outstanding different reef types: fringing reef, barrier reef, patch reef, atoll and shallow water reef mound. • Problems include use of explosives by outside fishermen and overexploitation of certain species. • Biodiversity surveys were made in 1997.	• Contact: WWF Indonesia-Sahul Bioregion Programme; email: bmambai@wwf.or.id
• In 1980, the Government of Indonesia created the Komodo National Park. In 1986, the park was declared a Unesco biosphere reserve and World Heritage Site. • Cetacean surveys in the Komodo National Park began in Apr 1999 with greater recognition of the marine components of the park. • Rationale is to protect rare, unique Komodo dragon and the rich diversity of land and marine species. According to recent surveys, the park also contains cetacean feeding areas, mating and breeding grounds and areas frequented by migrating cetaceans (Kahn et al, 2000; Kahn and Pet, 2003). Park waters are part of the important corridor network between the Pacific and Indian oceans. • As of 2000, the 25-year park management master plan has been approved by the Indonesian government and is now being implemented. • Expansion proposal is mainly marine and will help protect more cetacean habitat; expansion proposal includes a buffer zone.	• Kahn, 1999, 2000; Kahn et al, 2000; Kahn and Pet, 2003 • Contact: Benjamin Kahn, Indonesia Oceanic Cetacean Program Director, APEX Environmental Pty Ltd; email: bkahn@apex-environmental.com • Komodo National Park Authority, Alamat Labuan Bajo Flores Barat 86554, Manggarai, NTT, Indonesia; web: www.komodo nationalpark.org/
• Proposed protected area in freshwater habitat. • In the early 1980s, the Directorate General for Forest and Nature Conservation of the Forestry Ministry of Indonesia proposed that Semayang Lake in east Kalimantan be made a national park to protect the Irrawaddy dolphin. Local conservationists have also been pressing for protection of the nearby Berambai Forest, which contains the watershed of the lake.	• Klinowska, 1991; Perrin, 1985, 1989 • Contact: Danielle Kreb; email: yk-rasi@samarinda.org
• In 1984, Rusa Island was proposed as a nature reserve for its mangroves, reef and rocky shores by the DG Forest Protection and Nature Conservation. Results from a 2002 area survey by WWF and The Nature Conservancy show that an MPA would help management and protection of fisheries as well as cetaceans. • The MPA would include Lamalera where traditional hunting of whales is still carried on; there is some discussion of proposing and assisting with a conversion to whale watching.	• IUCN/WWF and DG Forest Protection and Nature Conservation, 1984; Kahn, 2002a, 2003a • Contact: Ketut Sarjana Putra, Director, Marine Program, WWF Indonesia; email : kputra@wallacea.wwf.or.id

Table 5.17 *continued*

Name of MPA or sanctuary, location and size	Cetacean and other notable species
(8) Bandanaira and **(9) Gunungapi** (both located in the Moluccas), **Lucipara (10)** and **(11) Pulau Manuk** (both in the Banda Seas, Moluccas), **(12) Sangihe Talaud** (north of Sulawesi), **(13) Taka bone Rate** and **(14) Pulau Kakabia** (both south of Sulawesi), **(15) Kepulauan Asia** and **(16) Pulau Mapia** (both north of West Papua) and **(17) Bali-Lombok Strait,** *all proposed*	• wide variety of large and small cetaceans reported
LAOS Lao People's Democratic Republic (Lao PDR) Saathiaranagroat Prachhathippatay Prachhachhon Lao **(18) Community Fisheries Conservation Zones (FCZ) of Muang-Khong District,** *may be proposed* • Mekong River, Khong District, Champasack Province (adjacent to Stung Treng Province, Cambodia), Lao PDR • the FCZs are less than 0.07 mi^2 (0.18 km^2) each and range in depth from 8 feet (2.5 m) to 164 feet (50 m) in the dry season	• year-round (common Dec–May): Irrawaddy dolphin, *Orcaella brevirostris* (dolphin population lives solely in the Mekong and Sekong river basins in southern Laos and adjacent parts of Cambodia) • primarily for freshwater fish (high biodiversity)

Notes and rationale	For more information
• Proposed MPAs which are thought to have portions of cetacean habitat and could offer significant protection for cetaceans if their boundaries were to be expanded. • Rapid ecological assessments are needed to determine cetacean presence and distribution, followed by cetacean habitat studies to evaluate the precise habitat needs of the various populations and to suggest modifications of MPA boundaries.	• Contact: Ketut Sarjana Putra, Director, Marine Program, WWF Indonesia; email: kputra@wallacea.wwf.or.id
• Between 1993 and 1999, 63 communities established village-managed Fish Conservation Zones in the mainstream Mekong River and other aquatic resource management regulations for protecting fisheries resources. Of those villages, four (Ban Hang Khone, Ban Khone Tai, Ban Hang Sadam and Ban Veun Kham) include dolphins. However, the use of three of the areas by dolphins is rare, and in Ban Hang Khone, villagers on the Cambodian side would not agree to abide by their conservation zone, which straddled the border between Cambodia and Laos, so the conservation area had to be moved to a non-dolphin area. The 73 fish conservation zones in Khong have proved to be successful examples of community fish conservation, but they have had little impact on dolphins. • There is considerable potential for using fish conservation zones to protect dolphins, as they inhabitat relatively small geographical areas with deep water during the dry season. Perhaps such an area, especially designed to protect dolphins, can be established in partnership with the Cambodians who are now interested in such an initiative; local people already see the need for conservation of fishing resources. They also respect the dolphins – the only known cetacean from this land-locked country (villagers believe the dolphins are reincarnated humans). However, the original Lao Community Fisheries and Dolphin Protection Project has now ended and the idea needs to be revived among villagers in the Lao PDR. • Cetacean research by Baird et al since the early 1990s has focused on biopsy analysis for genetics, abundance and distribution studies, feeding, behaviour, migration and fish/dolphin ecological studies.	• Baird and Mounsouphom, 1994, 1995; Baird et al, 1994; Roberts, 1993; Stacey, 1996; Baird and Beasley, in prep • Contact: Ian G Baird, Global Association for People and the Environment (GAPE), PO Box 860, Pakse, Lao PDR; email: ianbaird@shaw.ca

Table 5.17 *continued*

Name of MPA or sanctuary, location and size	Cetacean and other notable species
MALAYSIA Federation of Malaysia Persekutuan Tanah Malaysia **(19) Johore Marine Park** • consists of 13 marine park islands in peninsular Malaysia, the centre of which is at Tinggi • total marine size for all 13 marine park islands is 766 mi² (1984 km²)	• short-beaked common dolphin, *Delphinus delphis*; spinner dolphin, *Stenella longirostris*; at least 5 other dolphin species, 1 porpoise species and blue whale, *Balaenoptera musculus*, have been recorded in peninsular Malaysia • also: dugong
(20) Langkawi Island Marine Park • peninsular Malaysia • no data on size	• short-beaked common dolphin, *Delphinus delphis*; Indo-Pacific hump-backed dolphin, *Sousa chinensis*; Indo-Pacific bottlenose dolphin, *Tursiops aduncus*; finless porpoise, *Neophocaena phocaenoides* • also: dugong
(21) Labuan Island Marine Park • Sabah, East Malaysia • no data on size	• Indo-Pacific bottlenose dolphin, *Tursiops aduncus* • also: dugong
(22) North Borneo Marine Park, *proposed* • Kudat, Sabah • size undetermined	• Irrawaddy dolphin, *Orcaella brevirostris*; Indo-Pacific hump-backed dolphin, *Sousa chinensis* • also: dugong
(23) Lawas Marine Park, *proposed* • Sarawak • size undetermined	• Irrawaddy dolphin, *Orcaella brevirostris*; Indo-Pacific hump-backed dolphin, *Sousa chinensis* • also: dugong

Notes and rationale	For more information
• Rationale is to protect coral reefs and fisheries resources but small numbers of dugong and inshore cetaceans may be found in the area; cetacean habitat studies would need to be done to determine if critical habitat is adequately protected.	• Jaaman et al, 2002; Jaaman, in press • Contact: Abdul Khalil Abdul Karim, Head of Marine Parks, Department of Fisheries, Malaysia; web: http://agrolink.moa.my/dof/index.html • Saifullah Jaaman; email: s.jaaman@abdn.ac.uk
• Rationale is to protect coral reefs and fisheries resources but small numbers of dugong and inshore cetaceans may be found in the area; cetacean habitat studies would need to be done to determine if critical habitat is adequately protected.	• Jaaman et al, 2002; Jaaman, in press • Contact: Abdul Khalil Abdul Karim, Head of Marine Parks; web: http://agrolink.moa.my/dof/index.html • Saifullah Jaaman; email: s.jaaman@abdn.ac.uk
• Rationale is to protect coral reefs and fisheries resources but small numbers of dugong and inshore cetaceans may be found in the area; cetacean habitat studies would need to be done to determine if critical habitat is adequately protected.	• Jaaman et al, 2002; Jaaman and Lah-Anyi, 2003; Jaaman, in press • Contact: Abdul Khalil Abdul Karim, Head of Marine Parks, Department of Fisheries, Malaysia; web: http://agrolink.moa.my/dof/index.html • Saifullah Jaaman; email: s.jaaman@abdn.ac.uk
• The rationale for protection is the seagrass and mangrove areas which include dugong and inshore cetaceans. • There is some cetacean habitat work by Saifullah Jaaman and colleagues (references at right).	• Jaaman and Lah-Anyi, 2003; Jaaman, in press • Contact: Ridzwan A Rahman, Borneo Marine Research Institute, Universiti Malaysia Sabah; email: ridzwan@ums.edu.my • Saifullah Jaaman; email: s.jaaman@abdn.ac.uk
• The rationale for protection is for the seagrass and mangrove areas which include dugong and inshore cetaceans. • There is some cetacean habitat work by Saifullah Jaaman and colleagues (references at right).	• Jaaman et al, 2000, 2001; Jaaman, in press • Contact: James Bali, Sarawak Forest Dept; email: jamesbali@sarawakforestry.com • Saifullah Jaaman; email: s.jaaman@abdn.ac.uk

Table 5.17 *continued*

Name of MPA or sanctuary, location and size	Cetacean and other notable species
PHILIPPINES Republic of the Philippines Republika ng Pilipinas **(24) Malampaya Sound Protected Land and Seascape** • Malampaya Sound, northwestern Palawan • 772 mi² (2001 km²) total; marine only is 430 mi² (1114 km²)	• Inner Sound: Irrawaddy dolphin, *Orcaella brevirostris*; Outer Sound: bottlenose dolphin, *Tursiops truncatus* • also: dugong, sea turtles; area includes some mangroves and modest coral reefs
(25) Tañon Strait Protected Seascape • Tañon Strait, between the islands of Negros and Cebu, shared by the provinces of Cebu, Negros Occidental and Negros Oriental, Central Visayas • approximately 800 mi² (2000 km²).	• Year-round: spinner dolphin, *Stenella longirostris*; pantropical spotted dolphin, *Stenella attenuata*; May–Sept: melon-headed whale, *Peponocephala electra*; bottlenose dolphin, *Tursiops truncatus*; short-finned pilot whale, *Globicephala macrorhynchus*; Risso's dolphin, *Grampus griseus*; Fraser's dolphin, *Lagenodelphis hosei*; rough-toothed dolphin, *Steno bredanensis*; false killer whale, *Pseudorca crassidens*; dwarf sperm whale, *Kogia sima* • also: sea turtles

Notes and rationale	For more information
• In 2000, Malampaya Sound was proposed as a protected area under the National Integrated Protected Areas System (NIPAS) and a general management plan for the area was issued (NIPAP, 2000). • Rationale for protection is the diverse land and marine tropical ecosystems, one of the richest fishing grounds in the Philippines. • Flagship species is the Irrawaddy dolphin, the only known population of the species in the country; WWF Philippines is designing a conservation programme for this rare population of more than 70 individuals as part of the management plan. • Following Malampaya Sound's designation as a protected seascape in 2000, the Malampaya Sound Ecological Studies Project has reported an 'uphill struggle to implement the policies being set by the Protected Area Management Board (PAMB)'. It has been noted that 'protected seascape' is the 'lowest possible prioritization' given to a protected area by the Department of the Environment and Natural Resources (DENR), yet there is no discussion of further or enhanced protection.	• Alcala, 2001; Dolar et al, 2000; NIPAP, 2000; Smith et al, in press • Contact: Joel Palma, WWF Philippines; email: jpalma@wwf.org.ph; web: www.wwf.org.ph • NIPAS, PAWB; email: biodiversity@ pawb.gov.ph; web: www.pawb.gov.ph • Maria Louella Dolar-Perrin; email: dolarperri@aol.com; William F Perrin, Southwest Fisheries Science Center, USA; email: wperrin@ucsd.edu
• Rationale for protection is the high cetacean density and diversity (with 10 species the second highest diversity in the Philippines), including mating, breeding and feeding areas, as well as coral reefs and mangroves; high concentration of dwarf sperm whales. • Research by Leatherwood et al (1994) and Tan (1995) led to formal proposals for protection from Silliman University Marine Laboratory. Presidential Proclamation No 1234 subsequently created a 'protected seascape'. According to this proclamation the entire Tañon Strait is protected and all resident cetaceans are accorded full protection by law. No development is allowed that might adversely affect the marine ecosystem. Yet, despite national laws delineating areas of the Strait exclusively for sustenance fishing, illegal commercial fishing continues with reports of cetacean bycatch as well. • A protected area management board is needed, with a management plan in place before legal and enforcement mechanisms can proceed. The jurisdiction over the area is unresolved (whether it would be federal, provincial or shared). In 2003, WWF began working on a conservation plan for the Strait, its fisheries and the cetaceans. • Future cetacean work should include obtaining data on genetics, contaminant loads, plus photo-ID research.	• Alcala, 2001; Leatherwood et al, 1994; Tan, 1995 • Contact: Joel Palma, Andrea Bautista, WWF Philippines; email: jpalma@wwf.org.ph; abautista@wwf.org.ph; web: www.wwf.org.ph • NIPAS, PAWB; email: biodiversity@ pawb.gov.ph; web: www.pawb.gov.ph • Maria Louella Dolar-Perrin; email: dolarperri@aol.com; William F Perrin, Southwest Fisheries Science Center, USA: email: wperrin@ucsd.edu

Table 5.17 *continued*

Name of MPA or sanctuary, location and size	Cetacean and other notable species
(26) Pamilacan Island Marine Mammal Sanctuary • Pamilacan Island, Quiniluban Islands, northern Cuyo Islands, west of Panay • no data on size	• Apr–May: Bryde's whale, *Balaenoptera brydei*; others mainly year-round: sperm whale, *Physeter macrocephalus*; melon-headed whale, *Peponocephala electra*; pygmy killer whale, *Feresa attenuata*; spinner dolphin, *Stenella longirostris*; Fraser's dolphin, *Lagenodelphis hosei*; Risso's dolphin, *Grampus griseus*; Blainville's beaked whale, *Mesoplodon densirostris* • also: manta ray, whale shark
(27) Tubbataha National Marine Park • Tubbataha Reefs, central Sulu Sea • 128 mi² (332 km²)	• spinner dolphin, *Stenella longirostris*; pantropical spotted dolphin, *Stenella attenuata*; bottlenose dolphin, *Tursiops truncatus*; Risso's dolphin, *Grampus griseus*; Fraser's dolphin, *Lagenodelphis hosei*; short-finned pilot whale, *Globicephala macrorhynchus*
(28) Batanes Islands Protected Land and Seascape • northernmost Philippines, Luzon Strait, 112 mi (180 km) southeast of Taiwan • 824.4 mi² (2135.8 km²)	• false killer whale, *Pseudorca crassidens*; short-finned pilot whale, *Globicephala macrorhynchus*; probably humpback whale, *Megaptera novaeangliae*
(29) Calayan Island Protected Area • Babuyan Islands, southern Luzon Strait, northern Philippines • 225 mi² (583 km²)	• Dec–May: humpback whale, *Megaptera novaeangliae*; year-round: sperm whale, *Physeter macrocephalus*; dwarf sperm whale, *Kogia sima*; melon-headed whale, *Peponocephala electra*; short-finned pilot whale, *Globicephala macrorhynchus*; Fraser's dolphin, *Lagenodelphis hosei*; spinner dolphin, *Stenella longirostris*; pantropical spotted dolphin, *Stenella attenuata*; bottlenose dolphin, *Tursiops truncatus*; rough-toothed dolphin, *Steno bredanensis*; false killer whale, *Pseudorca crassidens*; Risso's dolphin, *Grampus griseus*; others

Notes and rationale	For more information
• In Jul 1995, the Inter-Agency Task Force on Marine Mammals (Philippines) proposed the area as an MPA, with the rationale partly to protect cetacean diversity. • At Pamilacan Island, fishermen used to catch Bryde's whales. In the mid-1990s, the Dept of Tourism in the Philippines gave the villagers a grant to start up cetacean watching. Some 100 family members of the Pamilacan Island Dolphin and Whale Watching Organization (PIDWWO) began offering trips aboard refitted boats formerly used for hunting. Three-year funding for this community transition project was provided by WWF Philippines, the Philippine Dept of Tourism and Citibank NA. In 2001, PIDWWO was relaunched with new funding and tours that include various ecotour activities. According to Lory Tan, WWF Philippines director, the Pamilacan approach has been to 'directly address the livelihood concerns of the fishing community there, through ecotourism, thereby fueling a community interest in protecting cetaceans, their source of income … rather than simply creating a sanctuary on paper. This generates conservation action on the ground, rather than on paper.'	• Leatherwood et al, 1994 • Contact: Joel Palma, WWF Philippines; email: jpalma@wwf.org.ph; web: www.wwf.org.ph • NIPAS, PAWB; email: biodiversity@ pawb.gov.ph; web: www.pawb.gov.ph • Maria Louella Dolar-Perrin; email: dolarperri@aol.com; William F Perrin, Southwest Fisheries Science Center, USA: email: wperrin@ucsd.edu
• Established in 1988 and classified under the National Integrated Protected Area System (NIPAS) of the Philippines, this marine site may have critical cetacean habitat but more cetacean work needs to be done. • Research has identified at least six cetaceans present.	• Contact: Joel Palma, WWF Philippines; email: jpalma@wwf.org.ph; web: www.wwf.org.ph • NIPAS, PAWB; email: biodiversity@ pawb.gov.ph; web: www.pawb.gov.ph
• Established in 1994 and classified under NIPAS, this marine and forest site may have significant cetacean habitat but cetacean surveys and habitat work need to be done.	• Contact: Joel Palma, WWF Philippines; email: jpalma@wwf.org.ph; web: www.wwf.org.ph • NIPAS, PAWB; email: biodiversity@ pawb.gov.ph; web: www.pawb.gov.ph
• Established in 1999, this coastal and marine site in the Babuyan Chain of islands is classified under NIPAS; it is considered the most diverse cetacean area in the Philippines, with some 13 cetacean species having been identified. • Known habitat includes southernmost breeding and calving site for humpback whales in the western North Pacific. • Three years' work on photo-ID, biopsy and sound analysis of humpback whales indicates links to Ogasawara and Hawaii, as well as the possibility of genetic isolation (two new mitochondrial DNA haplotypes found here). • Threats include bycatch from illegal fishing activity (both local fishermen and poacher fleets) and shark fisheries that use dolphin meat as bait. • More cetacean habitat studies need to be done to determine cetacean use of the area. WWF is working on extending the protection to cover the cetaceans in this high-density, high-diversity cetacean site.	• Contact: WWF Philippines; web: www.wwf.org.ph • NIPAS, PAWB; email: biodiversity@ pawb.gov.ph; web: www.pawb.gov.ph

Table 5.17 *continued*

Name of MPA or sanctuary, location and size	Cetacean and other notable species
(30) Sierra Madre Natural Park • northeast Luzon, southeasterly portion of Babuyan Channel • 1233.3 mi² (3195.1 km²)	• humpback whale, *Megaptera novaeangliae*; sperm whale, *Physeter macrocephalus*; spinner dolphin, *Stenella longirostris*; pantropical spotted dolphin, *Stenella attenuata*; Indo-Pacific bottlenose dolphin, *Tursiops aduncus*; short-finned pilot whale, *Globicephala macrorhynchus*
(31) Turtle Islands Wildlife Sanctuary • extreme southwest of Philippines and Sulu Sea, 19 mi (30 km) northwest of Sandakan, Sabah • 2032.1 mi² (5264.5 km²)	• spinner dolphin, *Stenella longirostris*; stranded Irrawaddy dolphin, *Orcaella brevirostris* and Indo-Pacific hump-backed dolphin, *Sousa chinensis* (both probably from Borneo) • also: sea turtles
(32) Siargao Island Protected Land and Seascape • Siargao Island, off northeast Mindanao • 1076.6 mi² (2789.1 km²)	• false killer whale, *Pseudorca crassidens*; other cetaceans undetermined
(33) Apo Reef Natural Park • Apo Reef • 61 mi² (157.9 km²)	• melon-headed whale, *Peponocephala electra*; other cetaceans undetermined
VIETNAM Công Hòa Xã Hôi Chu Nghĩa Viêt Nam **(34) Hon Mun MPA, *proposed*** • east of the city of Nha Trang, south central Vietnam • size undetermined	• various dolphin species • also: high coral reef diversity, mangrove and seagrass beds

Notes and rationale	For more information
• Established in 1997, this marine and forest site is classified under the National Integrated Protected Area System (NIPAS) of the Philippines. • 2003 WWF Philippines survey of the northern Sierra Madre coastline confirmed the presence of the listed cetaceans; surprising sighting of a humpback mother and calf, south of the Babuyan Chain, indicates that the humpback calving may stretch even farther south than the Babuyan Chain (see Calayan Island Protected Area above). • More cetacean surveys and habitat work need to be done to define cetacean habitat use.	• Contact: WWF Philippines; web: www.wwf.org.ph • NIPAS, PAWB; email: biodiversity@ pawb.gov.ph; web: www.pawb.gov.ph
• Established in 1982 as a sea turtle protected area. • Classified under NIPAS, this coastal and marine site has various reports of cetaceans but more cetacean surveys and habitat work need to be done.	• Contact: WWF Philippines; web: www.wwf.org.ph • NIPAS, PAWB; email: biodiversity@ pawb.gov.ph; web: www.pawb.gov.ph
• This coastal and marine protected area is included in NIPAS. However, there is evidence of illegal activity here and very little active enforcement. • First report of false killer whales here was in the early 1990s, but there have been no substantial cetacean surveys. Surveys and habitat work would need to be done to determine whether there is important cetacean habitat to protect.	• Contact: WWF Philippines; web: www.wwf.org.ph • NIPAS, PAWB; email: biodiversity@ pawb.gov.ph; web: www.pawb.gov.ph
• This MPA is included in NIPAS, and it has active ranger presence but no specific focus on cetaceans. • There is a large, apparently resident group of melon-headed whales on Apo Reef, but more work needs to be done to determine precise habitat use and other cetacean presence.	• Contact: WWF Philippines; web: www.wwf.org.ph • NIPAS, PAWB; email: biodiversity@ pawb.gov.ph; web: www.pawb.gov.ph
• Hon Mun near Nha Trang was proposed by the Institute of Oceanography in Nha Trang in 1999 to protect the high diversity of coral (155 species in 44 genera). • The reef is currently threatened by dynamite and cyanide fishing activities. Cetaceans are not included in the current management plan but there may be modest cetacean habitat in the area. However, cetacean surveys have not turned up many sightings. • The Ministry of Fisheries and IUCN are cooperating as part of a GEF- and Danish (DANIDA)-funded initiative (2002–2006) to create the first MPA in Vietnam.	• Smith et al, 1997a, 2003 • Contact: Bui Dinh Chung; email: buichung@hn.vnn.vn

MARINE REGION 14: SOUTH PACIFIC

Cetacean habitat in the region includes important wintering habitat for humpback whale courtship and breeding activities, including singing, as well as nursery areas, both in the South Pacific (around Tonga and other islands) and extending as far north as the tropical North Pacific (around the Hawaiian Islands). Many Pacific island states (eg, in Tahiti, Samoa and Midway) have tropical dolphin populations such as spinner dolphins.

Notable MPAs here include the Hawaiian Islands Humpback Whale National Marine Sanctuary and Midway and Palmyra Atoll national wildlife refuges, all in US waters, and Aleipata and Safata MPAs in Samoan waters.

In recent years, a number of South Pacific countries and territories have declared, or announced their intention to declare, their entire national waters within the EEZ as whale or cetacean sanctuaries. The list includes American Samoa, Cook Islands, Fiji, French Polynesia, New Caledonia, Niue, Papua New Guinea, Samoa, Tonga and Vanuatu. More than half of all South Pacific waters are now in whale sanctuaries. (See Box 5.9: A whale sanctuary for the Cook Islands, p343.)

A total of 17 national governments have a role in the South Pacific Marine Region (see Table 5.1 on p89). This region is the most island-oriented of all the regions. It borders no continental areas and the only island with substantial non-coastal features is Papua New Guinea. The region is vast, covering more than 11 million mi^2 (29 million km^2) of the central to southern Pacific Ocean. The boundaries extend from the Chilean islands of Easter Island and Sala y Gomez in the east, to Palau and Papua New Guinea in the west. The southern boundary is just north of the subtropical Australian islands of Lord Howe and Norfolk and New Zealand's Kermedec Islands. In the north, the boundary extends into the North Pacific beyond the US Hawaiian Islands and includes Wake and Johnstone atolls and the northern Marianas. Despite its sprawling size, the region is considered to have just one large marine ecosystem (LME): the Insular Pacific-Hawaiian.

The major surface currents in the South Pacific Marine Region consist of the warm, westward flowing Equatorial Current (located between 5°N and 5°S), the North Equatorial Current (between 8°N and the Tropic of Cancer) and the South Equatorial Current (between 10°S and the Tropic of Capricorn). The North Equatorial Current is fed by the California Current and by return flows of the North Equatorial Counter Current and the North Pacific Current. The South Equatorial Current is fed by counterclockwise currents in the South Pacific. There are also subsurface currents that move in the opposite directions. There is little mixing between the warm surface waters and the much cooler deep waters.

This region has one of the lowest nutrient levels of any marine region. Some nutrients do flow into the area from upwellings off the coast of California and Peru but they are heated at the surface and quickly consumed by photosynthesis. Also, on the Equator, the Earth's rotation creates a divergence in the flow of the Equatorial Current, producing some upwelling of cool, nutrient-rich water from below the surface.

A cyclical influence on this marine region is the El Niño oscillation, which can cause dramatic fluctuations in currents and water temperature from year to year, with reversal in the ocean circulation for periods of more than a year. When this happens, any equatorial upwelling disappears and the low-nutrient surface waters become even lower in nutrients.

Most South Pacific islands come from volcanoes or coral reefs, or a combination of the two. The four main types of island here are atolls, raised coral islands, volcanic islands and continental islands. The biodiversity of the South Pacific is greater in the west and steadily decreases in the waters and around the islands toward the eastern South Pacific. In the west, the region has an almost continuous series of island arcs stretching from New Zealand, through Tonga, the Solomon Islands, the Bismarck Archipelago, Palau and the Marianas and on to Japan. To the east of the island arc are the deepest trenches in the world ocean including the Tonga Trench (35,704 ft or 10,882 m), the Kermadec Trench (32,964 ft or 10,047 m) and the Marianas Trench (35,801 ft or 10,915 m). Mangroves are mainly found in the western part of the region with diversity decreasing west to east, although they are found as far east as Samoa and a little beyond.

There is a high level of land-based species endemism, especially in the more isolated islands, but this does not apply to cetaceans, which can move between the islands and from inside and outside the atolls. The well-studied cetacean species around the Hawaiian archipelago, where some 24 cetacean species are found, and in the Cook Islands, with 25 species, probably represent the near upper-level for cetacean diversity in the region.

There is an active regional seas programme for the region under the umbrella of the South Pacific Region Environment Program (SPREP). The two significant environmental conventions are the Apia Convention (Convention on the Conservation of Nature in the South Pacific) and the SPREP Convention (Convention for the Protection of Natural Resources and Environment of the South Pacific Region). The SPREP Convention specifically deals with MPAs. SPREP's definition of the South Pacific, and thus its membership, differs from the South Pacific Marine Region as described above, with SPREP also including Australia and New Zealand from Marine Region 18.

In 1995, there was a total of 65 MPAs of all kinds in this marine region (Bleakley, 1995). The region is divided into 20 biogeographic zones with 12 represented by at least one MPA and 8 zones with no MPAs. As of 2004, according to Table 5.18 prepared for this book, there are 16 existing MPAs, three of which are proposed for expansion, as well as one proposed MPA, all of which feature cetacean habitat.

There are ten national whale sanctuaries as well as a proposed international cetacean sanctuary for the South Pacific, initiated through the IWC but yet to be approved. The proposal for a South Pacific Whale Sanctuary, including an IWC component, was endorsed by Pacific Island Forum members in 2001. The region is also considering a possible arrangement for marine mammal conservation management under the Convention on Migratory Species (CMS), and as part of this, WDCS is working toward the declaration of critical habitat. These efforts to recognize cetaceans in the South Pacific should be applauded, even if the resulting habitat protection to date is modest and unspecific. They have stimulated research and enhanced regional cooperation, and may well be the stepping stone to 'fine grain' cetacean critical habitat protection in future.

In the main southern part of the South Pacific Marine Region, cetacean research has been active for more than a decade through the South Pacific Whale Research Consortium and its extensive work in Tonga, the Cook Islands and other countries, with the active participation of researchers both within and outside the region and NGOs such as WhalesAlive, WWF South Pacific, IFAW and WDCS.

Cetacean research in the northern part of the region around the Hawaiian archipelago dates from the extensive humpback whale photo-ID and acoustic work in the 1970s which stretched across parts of Marine Regions 14, 15 and 16. Recently, this work has intensified with a cooperative international research effort called 'SPLASH' (Structure of Populations, Levels of Abundance and Status of Humpbacks, 2004–2007).

The IUCN 2002–2010 Conservation Action Plan for the World's Cetaceans has no specific research, education or conservation initiatives aimed at the South Pacific Marine Region.

Box 5.9 A whale sanctuary for the Cook Islands

On 19 September 2001, the Cook Islands government announced that it had established a whale sanctuary stretching to the limit of its EEZ in the South Pacific Ocean. Although called a whale sanctuary, the sanctuary covers all cetaceans.

Deputy prime minister of the Cook Islands, Robert Woonton (who became prime minister in 2002), said that the declaration of the sanctuary was a reflection of the high esteem in which whales are held by many Polynesian peoples.

'We have lived peacefully alongside whales for many centuries,' Woonton said. 'But the devastation wrought by the commercial whaling fleets of the last century has left us with only a few animals now returning to their traditional South Pacific breeding grounds each winter. For the past two years, Pacific Island nations have appealed to the International Whaling Commission to establish a whale sanctuary for our region, to secure the future for these leviathans, but we have been thwarted by the opposition of the whaling countries and their supporters. If the nations of the South Pacific wish to protect the breeding grounds which are so critical to the recovery of our depleted whale populations, then clearly we shall have to take matters into our own hands. We owe it to the Earth to support their survival.

'In establishing the Cook Islands Whale Sanctuary, we hope to encourage our friends and neighbours in the South Pacific to take similar actions. Together we can send a message to the whalers that their exploitation of our whales is now a thing of the past, and that the future lies in conservation.'

The seeds for this action were sown at the SPREP Ministerial and Regional Forum for a South Pacific Whale Sanctuary, which produced the Apia Statement in April 2001. Besides the Cook Islands, countries and territories represented included American Samoa, Australia, Fiji, French Polynesia, Kiribati, New Caledonia, New Zealand, Niue, Papua New Guinea, Samoa, Tonga, Tokelau, Tuvalu and Wallis and Futuna. The goal of the meeting was to advance the South Pacific Whale Sanctuary proposal, which would cover most of the Pacific Ocean south of the equator. It would adjoin the existing Southern Ocean Sanctuary to the south. However, at the July meeting of the IWC in London, despite the support of the Pacific Island nations and territories, and many other countries, the whaling nations and their allies were able to block the South Pacific whale sanctuary idea.

It was the reaction to this that led to the naming of the Cook Islands national waters as a whale sanctuary, with other Pacific island countries and territories soon to follow.

The Cook Islands sanctuary declaration states that it is designed to promote: non-lethal scientific research; collaboration for information exchange, education and awareness initiatives; monitoring of whales; identification of future threats to whales and appropriate action to counter those threats; and development of mechanisms for the regular evaluation of management programmes in terms of appropriate objectives.

Besides protection from whaling, the sanctuary restricts harassing cetaceans or catching them in nets and other fishing practices that would harm cetaceans. There are few real industrial, shipping or other threats to cetaceans due to the islands' isolation. Since 1998 whale research has been conducted in the Cook Islands and summaries of this research as well as details of the sanctuary were submitted in a paper to the 2002 IWC meeting in Shimonoseki, Japan (Hauser and Clapham, 2002). In April 2002, the Cook Islands Whale Center opened in Avarua, Rarotonga, featuring whale displays, interpretive programmes and educational displays for local and visiting tourists. There are plans to promote land-based whale watching in the sanctuary as the reef is very close to land and cetaceans can often be seen from shore. As the prime minister is fond of saying, 'We don't go to the whales, the whales come to us.'

Apart from the national sanctuary, Cook Islands has no marine protected areas which specifically include cetacean habitat, although there are local protected areas, called rauis, that protect fish and parts of the reef important as fish-rearing habitat. In 2002, the Department of Marine Resources began a comprehensive revision of fishing laws and at the same time was considering rules and regulations for the whale sanctuary including whale watch guidelines, penalties and management planning.

Since the creation of the Cook Islands Whale Sanctuary, a growing number of South Pacific nations and territories have designated or announced their intention to declare their waters a sanctuary, in solidarity with the other South Pacific nations and in defiance of the IWC refusal for the South Pacific Whale Sanctuary. As of 2004, there were nine others in the South Pacific Marine Region (American Samoa, Fiji, French Polynesia, New Caledonia, Niue, Papua New Guinea, Samoa, Tonga and Vanuatu), plus others in adjoining regions or in other parts of the world, who have taken the same steps. Through the protection of the national waters to the limit of the EEZs of ten countries, more than half of all South Pacific waters are now in whale sanctuaries (see Table 5.18 on p346 for sanctuaries in the South Pacific; see Table 1.2 on p17 for a world list of national whale sanctuaries).

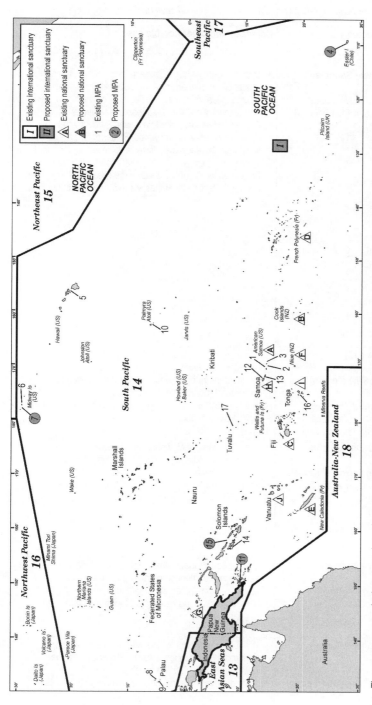

Figure 5.22 *Map of Marine Region 14: South Pacific MPAs and sanctuaries*

The roman numerals, letters and numbers correspond to the sanctuaries and MPAs listed and described in Table 5.18.

Table 5.18 *Marine Region 14: South Pacific MPAs and sanctuaries*

Name of MPA or sanctuary, location and size	Cetacean and other notable species
INTERNATIONAL **(I) South Pacific Whale Sanctuary, proposed** • entire South Pacific Ocean, spread across Marine Regions 14, 17 and 18 • size undetermined	• southern right whale, *Eubalaena australis*; pygmy right whale, *Caperea marginata*; humpback whale, *Megaptera novaeangliae*; minke whale, *Balaenoptera acutorostrata*; Antarctic minke whale, *Balaenoptera bonaerensis*; pygmy Bryde's whale, *Balaenoptera edeni*; Bryde's whale, *Balaenoptera brydei*; sei whale, *Balaenoptera borealis*; fin whale, *Balaenoptera physalus*; blue whale, *Balaenoptera musculus*; sperm whale, *Physeter macrocephalus*. Protection would only extend to the great whales; in total, the South Pacific Ocean has some 53 species of cetaceans.
AMERICAN SAMOA (US) (Unincorporated territory) **(A) American Samoa Whale and Turtle Sanctuary** • located in the waters of American Samoa and extending to the limits of the EEZ, 200 nm (371 km) away	• Jun–Oct: humpback whale, *Megaptera novaeangliae*; year-round: bottlenose dolphin, *Tursiops truncatus*; spinner dolphin, *Stenella longirostris*; other cetaceans • also: hawksbill and other sea turtles
(1) Fagatele Bay National Marine Sanctuary • located in a fringing tropical coral reef nestled within an eroded volcanic crater at Fagatele Bay • 0.25 mi² (0.66 km²)	• Jun–Oct: humpback whale, *Megaptera novaeangliae*; year-round: bottlenose dolphin, *Tursiops truncatus*; spinner dolphin, *Stenella longirostris* • also: crown-of-thorns starfish, blacktip reef shark, hawksbill turtle and giant clam
(2) National Park of American Samoa • American Samoa • 14.1 mi² (36.4 km²)	• Jun–Oct: humpback whale, *Megaptera novaeangliae*; year-round: bottlenose dolphin, *Tursiops truncatus*; spinner dolphin, *Stenella longirostris* • also: coral reef and associated fauna and flora
(3) Rose Atoll National Wildlife Refuge • American Samoa • 61.3 mi² (158.9 km²) nearly all marine (except for two islets totalling 0.02 mi² (0.06 km²)	• Jun–Oct: humpback whale, *Megaptera novaeangliae*; year-round: bottlenose dolphin, *Tursiops truncatus*; spinner dolphin, *Stenella longirostris* • also: coral reef and associated fauna and flora

Notes and rationale	For more information
• Rationale is to protect large whales from commercial whaling and to stimulate research and conservation. • First proposed in 1999, the South Pacific Sanctuary was turned down at the annual IWC meetings from 2000–2004. The idea has support from South Pacific nations, including Australia and New Zealand, and endorsement from SPREP and the Pacific Islands Forum, as embodied in the Apia Statement of 2001. The proposal is expected to be submitted again at future IWC meetings. This sanctuary would extend the Southern Ocean Sanctuary north to protect the heavily whaled populations of great whales still recovering in the South Pacific and allow protection of these species throughout their full migratory range. • The Apia Statement includes not only the regional agreement for the declaration of the sanctuary but provision for a broad suite of cetacean research, educational and conservation activities with support through SPREP's Regional Marine Mammal Conservation Programme (RMMCP). • In the original 1946 meeting agreement of the fledgling IWC, a sanctuary was established in the South Pacific sector of the Southern Ocean which applied to pelagic whaling of baleen whales only. Holt (2000) called it a symbolic sanctuary; it was abolished in 1955 when the whaling countries needed more whales.	• Holt, 2000 • Contact: WDCS – Australasia; email: info@wdcs.org.au; web: www.wdcs.org.au • WWF South Pacific Programme Whale Sanctuaries; web: www.wwfpacific.org.fj
• Designated 2003 according to Executive Order, this sanctuary provides full protection for all cetaceans and sea turtles in territorial waters. • All cetaceans are also protected through the US Marine Mammal Protection Act.	
• Identified in 1982 as a prime fringing tropical coral reef ecosystem and designated as an MPA in Apr 1986. • Management plan is oriented toward preserving and maintaining the tropical coral reef ecosystem of the bay while allowing compatible uses. • Education coordinator recently hired to conduct outreach and public awareness programmes. • Cetacean habitat not quantified; area is small and would need to be expanded to protect cetacean habitat effectively.	• NOAA et al, 1984 • Contact: Sanctuary Coordinator, Fagatele Bay, Box 4318, Pago Pago, American Samoa 96799 USA; web: www.fbnms.nos.noaa.gov
• All cetaceans are protected by the US Marine Mammal Protection Act. • Cetacean habitat not quantified; more research is needed.	• Contact: Park Superintendent, National Park of American Samoa, Pago Plaza, Pago Pago, AS 96799 USA; web: www.nps.gov/npsa
• A US National Wildlife Refuge (NWR) and IUCN Category I area established in 1973 to protect a coral atoll, this is the southernmost refuge in the NWR system. • All cetaceans are protected by the US Marine Mammal Protection Act. • Cetacean habitat is not quantified; more research is needed.	• Contact: US Fish and Wildlife Service; email; web: http://pacific islands.fws.gov/ wnwr/prosenwr.html

Table 5.18 *continued*

Name of MPA or sanctuary, location and size	Cetacean and other notable species
COOK ISLANDS (New Zealand) (Territory in free association) **(B) Cook Islands Whale Sanctuary** • located in the waters of the Cook Islands and extending to the limits of the EEZ, 200 nm (371 km) away • 1,324,000 mi² (3,430,000 km²)	• humpback whale, *Megaptera novaeangliae*; minke whale, *Balaenoptera acutorostrata*; Antarctic minke whale, *Balaenoptera bonaerensis*; sei whale, *Balaenoptera borealis*; blue whale, *Balaenoptera musculus*; sperm whale, *Physeter macrocephalus*; dense-beaked whale, *Mesoplodon densirostris*; Cuvier's beaked whale, *Ziphius cavirostris*; short-beaked common dolphin, *Delphinus delphis*; striped dolphin, *Stenella coeruleoalba*; spinner dolphin, *Stenella longirostris*; Peale's dolphin, *Lagenorhynchus australis*; short-finned pilot whale, *Globicephala macrorhynchus*; orca, *Orcinus orca*; 11 other cetacean species suspected
EASTER ISLAND (Chile) *(4) Parques Marinos de Rapa Nui, must be expanded to offer significant protection* • Easter Island: Coral Nui Nui, 0.037 mi² (0.095 km²) and Motu Tautara, 0.0006 mi² 0.0015 km²) both on the west coast, and Hanga Oteo, 0.59 nm (1.1 km) along northeast coast	• sperm whale, *Physeter macrocephalus*; short-beaked common dolphin, *Delphinus delphis*; *Stenella* dolphins
FIJI Republic of Fiji **(C) Fiji Whale Sanctuary** • national waters of Fiji • 486,000 mi² (1.26 million km²)	• spinner dolphin, *Stenella longirostris*; others
FRENCH POLYNESIA (French overseas possession) **(D) French Polynesia Marine Mammal Sanctuary** • located in the waters of French Polynesia to the limit of the EEZ • 2 million sq mi² (5.3 million km²)	• common: spinner dolphin, *Stenella longirostris*; rough-toothed dolphin, *Steno bredanensis*; Fraser's dolphin, *Lagenodelphis hosei*; melon-headed whale, *Peponocephala electra*; Jul–Nov: humpback whale, *Megaptera novaeangliae*; more than 20 cetacean species
HAWAII (US) **(5) Hawaiian Islands Humpback Whale National Marine Sanctuary** • located around the Hawaiian Islands centred on area between Maui, Molokai and Lanai • 1300 mi² (3368 km²)	• humpback whale, *Megaptera novaeangliae*; bottlenose dolphin, *Tursiops truncatus*; spinner dolphin, *Stenella longirostris*; pantropical spotted dolphin, *Stenella attenuata*; rough-toothed dolphin, *Steno bredanensis*; false killer whale, *Pseudorca crassidens*; short-finned pilot whale, *Globicephala macrorhynchus*; some 24 cetacean species in all • also: endangered Hawaiian monk seal, sea turtles, endemic coral reef fish

Notes and rationale	For more information
• Cetacean refuge or sanctuary to protect cetaceans from hunting, injury or harassment from fishing or other activities. • In 2002, the Dept of Marine Resources began revising fishing laws and considering rules and regulations for the whale sanctuary including whale watch guidelines, penalties and management planning. • Educational initiatives for the sanctuary include the Cook Islands Whale Center in Avarua, Rarotonga, featuring educational displays, a whale museum, and interpretive programmes for local people and visitors.	• Hauser and Clapham, 2002 • Contact: Nan Hauser, Cook Islands Whale Research, Box 3069, Takuvaine Valley, Rarotonga, Cook Islands, South Pacific; email: nan@whaleresearch.org; web: www.whaleresearch.org
• National park with cetaceans in coastal waters, • In Mar 2000 the Chilean Defence Ministry declared the first MPAs for Chile, mainly as a legal test and to show a profile for conservation. The sizes of these three MPAs on Easter Island are insignificant for any species or ecosystem management. Thus, there is legal protection but no biological importance attached to the three MPAs. • With research to define cetacean habitat, greatly increased MPA sizes, and a management plan put in place, there could be useful cetacean habitat protection.	• Contact: CMMR Leviathan; email: research@ leviathanchile.org; web: www.leviathanchile.org
• In 2003, the Fiji government approved the designation as a whale sanctuary, according to Fiji's Minister for Commerce, to 'help catalyze research and raise public understanding and ability to manage Fiji's marine biodiversity.'	• Hoyt, 2001; WWF, 2003 • Contact: WWF South Pacific Programme Whale Sanctuaries; web: www.wwfpacific.org.fj
• Sanctuary created in 2002 by French government, later approved by local government of French Polynesia with national legislation to bind the declaration. • Provides a sanctuary free from all hunting of marine mammals. • Gannier and Gannier (1998) found 70 per cent of cetacean sightings within 2 mi (3.2 km) of shore despite dedicated offshore effort.	• Gannier and Gannier, 1998; WWF, 2003 • Contact: WWF South Pacific Programme Whale Sanctuaries; web: www.wwfpacific.org.fj
• Rationale is specifically to protect humpback whales and their habitat. • This site extends to within the 100-fathom isobath and covers the warm, shallow waters which is the key humpback whale winter breeding habitat (for breeding, singing, calving and nursing) in the North Pacific. • Sanctuary management plan has been jointly developed by the public, NOAA's Sanctuaries and Reserves Division and Hawaii's Office of State Planning (OSP). • Final Environmental Impact Statement recommended expansion of the boundaries to include 100-fathom isobaths (183 m) around the big island of Hawaii, eastern Kauai and parts of Oahu. • Industries operating within or near sanctuary waters include commercial, recreational and subsistence fisheries, shipping, surfing, swimming, kayaking, diving, boating, whale watching and military activities.	• Sanctuaries and Reserves Division (NOAA), 1997 • Contact: Hawaiian Islands Humpback Whale Sanctuary, 726 South Kihei Rd, Kihei, HI 96753 USA; web: www.hihwnms.nos.noaa.gov/

Table 5.18 *continued*

Name of MPA or sanctuary, location and size	Cetacean and other notable species
NEW CALEDONIA (France) Kanaky **(E) New Caledonia Whale Sanctuary** • New Caledonia national waters, to the limit of its EEZ • 670,000 mi^2 (1.74 million km^2)	• Jul–Nov: humpback whale, *Megaptera novaeangliae*; year-round: spinner dolphin, *Stenella longirostris*; others
NIUE **(F) Niue Whale Sanctuary** • Niue national waters, to the limit of its EEZ • 150,000 mi^2 (390,000 km^2)	• Jul–Nov: humpback whale, *Megaptera novaeangliae*; year-round: spinner dolphin, *Stenella longirostris*; others • various turtles and world's largest coral island
NORTHWESTERN HAWAIIAN ISLANDS (US) (includes Midway Islands – unincorporated territory) **(6) Midway National Wildlife Refuge** • located at Midway Island in the Northwestern Hawaiian Islands • no size data	• spinner dolphin, *Stenella longirostris*
(7) Northwestern Hawaiian Islands Coral Reef Ecosystem Reserve and *proposed* national marine sanctuary • located in the Northwestern Hawaiian Islands • covers an area of 131,240 mi^2 (340,000 km^2)	• resident: spinner dolphin, *Stenella longirostris*; bottlenose dolphin, *Tursiops truncatus*; seasonal or migratory: humpback whale, *Megaptera novaeangliae*; pantropical spotted dolphin, *Stenella attenuata*; orca, *Orcinus orca*; striped dolphin, *Stenella coeruleoalba*; various beaked whale species • also: Hawaiian monk seal, green sea turtle, most extensive coral reefs in US
PALAU Republic of Palau; Belau **[MPAs 8–9]** **(8) Rock Islands Conservation Area** **(9) Ngeremendu Bay Conservation Area**	• various small cetaceans • also: dugong

Notes and rationale	For more information
• Sanctuary (not declared as such, but in effect and with legal sanction) created in late 1990s by New Caledonian government. • Humpback whale photo-ID studies have been active since the early 1990s; commercial whale watching started in 1995.	• Hoyt, 2001; WWF, 2003
• Designated in 2001; in 2002 Niuean Whale Sanctuary Regulations were passed to prohibit the killing or taking of all cetaceans with infringements carrying a maximum penalty of 3 months in prison. • Whale watching is a growing attraction and source of income.	• Constantine, 1998; Hoyt, 2001; WWF, 2003
• Existing US National Wildlife Refuge to protect fragile atoll habitat, Midway Atoll has been closed to the public but recently opened for ecotourism including dolphin watching. • The dolphin watching research is designed to assist management agencies in developing boater and visitor guidelines, as well as to provide new information on the ecology, behaviour and social organization of spinner dolphins in an atoll habitat.	• Hoyt, 2001 • Contact: Birgit Winning, Oceanic Society Expeditions, Fort Mason Center, Bldg E, San Francisco, CA 94123-1394 USA; email: winning@oceanic-society.org
• Created in 2000 to protect a relatively pristine coral reef ecosystem, the reserve was made permanent in 2001 and the Reserve Operations Plan is being circulated for public comment; the reserve is currently going through a process to become a US national marine sanctuary.	• Contact: Northwestern Hawaiian Islands Coral Reef Ecosystem Reserve, Honolulu, HI 96825 USA; email: hawaiireef@noaa.gov; bibliography and other information on the web at www.hawaiireef.noaa.gov/
• These two conservation areas were set up mainly to protect dugongs in Palau, but they also have dolphins. • As of 2003–2004, Palau was in the design phase, working on a comprehensive national network of MPAs.	• Contact: South Pacific Regional Environment Programme (SPREP), PO Box 240, Apia, Samoa; email: sprep@sprep.org.ws; web: www.sprep.org.ws

Table 5.18 *continued*

Name of MPA or sanctuary, location and size	Cetacean and other notable species
PALMYRA ATOLL (US) (Unincorporated territory) **(10) Palmyra Atoll National Wildlife Refuge** • located 1052 mi (1693 km) southwest of Honolulu, Hawaii in the tropical Pacific • MPA includes the lagoon and surrounding waters to the 12 nm (22 km) limit	• spinner dolphin, *Stenella longirostris*; other tropical dolphins • also: 1 million+ nesting birds, with 28 species of seabirds and migrating shorebirds, world's second largest colony of red-footed boobies and largest black noddy colony in central Pacific; hawksbill and green sea turtles, eagle rays and 125 species of stony corals
PAPUA NEW GUINEA **(G) Papua New Guinea Whale Sanctuary** • located in the national waters of Papua New Guinea, to the limit of its EEZ • 1.2 million mi² (3.1 million km²)	• sperm whale, *Physeter macrocephalus*; blue whale, *Balaenoptera musculus*; fin whale, *Balaenoptera physalus*; sei whale, *Balaenoptera borealis*; southern right whale, *Eubalaena australis*; pygmy right whale, *Caperea marginata*; Bryde's whale, *Balaenoptera brydei*; minke whale, *Balaenoptera acutorostrata*; humpback whale, *Megaptera novaeangliae*; dolphin species
(11) Milne Bay MPA, *proposed* • Milne Bay • size undetermined	• various cetacean species
SAMOA Malotutu'atasi o Samoa i Sisifo **(H) Samoa Whale, Turtle and Shark Sanctuary,** *announced but not formally declared* • located in Samoan national waters to the limits of its EEZ • 46,000 mi² (120,000 km²)	• year-round: spinner dolphin, *Stenella longirostris*; false killer whale, *Pseudorca crassidens*; sperm whale, *Physeter macrocephalus*; Sept–Nov: humpback whale, *Megaptera novaeangliae*; various other cetacean species
(12) Aleipata MPA • located from Tiavea south to Lalomanu, including 11 villages and all offshore islands; seaward boundary is 1 nm (2 km) off the reef slope	• spinner dolphin, *Stenella longirostris*; false killer whale, *Pseudorca crassidens*; sperm whale, *Physeter macrocephalus*; pilot whale, *Globicephala* sp; Sept–Nov: humpback whale, *Megaptera novaeangliae*; various other cetacean species

Notes and rationale	For more information
• Palymyra, privately owned since 1922, was purchased by The Nature Conservancy in Nov 2000 and is managed as a private reserve; in Jan 2001, the lagoon and surrounding waters were designated a National Wildlife Refuge. • Rationale for protection is that it is a rare undeveloped, unpopulated atoll in the tropical Pacific. • Oceanic Society Expeditions is offering a limited number of ecotours to the island.	• Contact: Birgit Winning, Oceanic Society Expeditions, Fort Mason Center, Bldg E, San Francisco, CA 94123-1394 USA; email: winning@oceanic-society.org
• In May 2002, Papua New Guinea's Prime Minister, Rt Hon Sir Mekere Morauta, Kt MP, declared their national waters as a sanctuary for all whales and dolphins. • Cetacean refuge or sanctuary covering national waters; ban on hunting; specifically mentions the protection of mating and calving grounds for various great whales. • National Museum has worked with whale researchers such as Roger Payne and Ingrid Visser to determine which cetaceans are in PNG waters. • Ocean Alliance conducted six months' research in Papua New Guinean waters in 2001: a total of six survey expeditions, with more than 350 sperm whale sightings, 84 sightings of other whales and 15 marine mammal species identified.	• Kahn, 2001 • Contact: Celine Godard, Woods Hole Oceanographic Institution, Biology Dept, Woods Hole, MA 02543-1049, USA; email: cgodard@whoi.edu • Ocean Alliance/Whale Conservation Institute, 191 Weston Rd, Lincoln, MA 01773 USA; web: www.pbs.org/odyssey; www.oceanalliance.org
• Community-based MPA set up through GEF funding and Conservation International. • Cetacean and other research need to be done to define habitat.	• Contact: Stephen Lindsay and Peter Mackay, Conservation International; email: slindsay@conservation.org; pmackay@conservation.org
• In 2002, the Samoan Ministry for Lands Survey and Environment announced its intention to declare a sanctuary for whales, dolphins, sharks and turtles to protect marine animals from hunting or harm. As of early 2004, it had yet to be declared. • In 2001, there was a new tourism strategy for Samoa, a marine mammal baseline survey and talks on the South Pacific Whale Sanctuary. • Two baseline national marine mammal surveys have been conducted by the South Pacific Island Whale and Dolphin Programme.	• Contact: Sue Miller; email: sue.miller@samoampa.com; web: www.sprep.org.ws • David Paton, South Pacific Island Whale and Dolphin Programme; email: d.paton@nbcnet.com.au
• Community-based MPA with core no-take reserves set up as a partnership between Aleipata district, Samoa government, IUCN and the World Bank, through GEF funding. • Project includes cetacean surveys for the waters of Samoa by the South Pacific Island Whale and Dolphin Programme (see contact details in above entry).	• Contact: Sue Miller, IUCN Project Manager; email: sue.miller@samoampa.com; • Latu Afioga, Aleipata District Officer; email: latu.afioga@samoampa.com; web: www.sprep.org.ws

Table 5.18 *continued*

Name of MPA or sanctuary, location and size	Cetacean and other notable species
(13) Safata MPA • located from Mulivai in the east, west to Saanapu, including nine villages; seaward boundary is 1 nm (2 km) off the reef slope	• spinner dolphin, *Stenella longirostris*; false killer whale, *Pseudorca crassidens*; sperm whale, *Physeter macrocephalus*; Sept–Nov: humpback whale, *Megaptera novaeangliae*; various other cetacean species
SOLOMON ISLANDS **(14) Marovo Lagoon World Heritage Area** • located in North New Georgia in the western part of the Solomon Islands	• tropical dolphin species
(15) **Arnavon Islands Marine Conservation Area,** *planned for* *expansion* • located around the Arnavon Islands, between Santa Isabel and Chioseul islands (7° 27' S; 158° E, in the Manning Straits • existing MPA is 31.9 mi^2 (82.7 km^2) including core about 12 mi^2 (31 km^2); proposed extension is undetermined but has been discussed and would grow out of management plan	• tropical dolphin species sighted but no studies or formal confirmation have been made of their presence • also: hawksbill turtles
TONGA Kingdom of Tonga Pule'anga Fakatu'i'o Tonga **(I) Tongan Whale Sanctuary** • Tonga national waters, to the limits of its EEZ • 270,000 mi^2 (700,000 km^2)	• humpback whale, *Megaptera novaeangliae*; sperm whale, *Physeter macrocephalus*; various dolphins
(16) Ha'apai Marine Conservation Area • located between 19°35' and 20°30' S and 174°15' and 175°06' W in Tongan waters • some 4000 mi^2 (10,000 km^2) of marine waters plus 64 islands in the Ha'apai group of islands	• humpback whale, *Megaptera novaeangliae*; sperm whale, *Physeter macrocephalus*; various dolphins

Notes and rationale	For more information
• Community-based MPA with core no-take reserves set up as a partnership between Safata district, Samoa government, IUCN and the World Bank, through GEF funding. • Project includes cetacean surveys for the waters of Samoa by the South Pacific Island Whale and Dolphin Programme (see contact details in above entry for Samoa Whale, Turtle and Shark Sanctuary).	• Contact: Sue Miller, IUCN Project Manager; email: sue.miller@ samoampa.com; Pulea Ifopo, Safata District Officer; email: pulea.ifopo@ samoampa.com; web: www.sprep.org.ws
• Existing World Heritage-listed area, Marovo Lagoon has had some dolphin watching and light marine and shore-based tourism, as well as fishing.	• Contact: Mavo Rest House, EcoTourism Resort (Village Stay), Ramata Village, Marovo Lagoon, North New Georgia, Western Province, Solomon Islands
• Formerly a wildlife sanctuary for breeding hawksbill turtles (since 1981), this area has recently become a community-based GEF-supported conservation area with the assistance of SPREP. • Coordinating committee comprises representatives from three local communities of Pasarae, Waghena and Kia who have management responsibilities for the area under the leadership of the Ministry of Forestry, Environment and Conservation.	• Contact: John Pita, CASO – Arnavon Islands, Marine Conservation Area, Dept of Forests, Environment and Conservation, PO Box G24, Honiara, Solomon Islands • South Pacific Regional Environment Programme (SPREP), PO Box 240, Apia, Samoa; email: sprep@sprep.org.ws; web: www.sprep.org.ws
• Sanctuary (not declared as such, but with legal sanction) is based on 1979 royal decree from the King of Tonga prohibiting whaling and the 1989 Tongan Fisheries Act banning the killing of all marine mammals in Tongan waters. • Includes prime mating and calving grounds for whales.	• WWF, 2003
• Existing community-based conservation area part of regional GEF Conservation Area programme; in the process of being formally declared an MPA. • Whale watching is big in Tonga but this is not in the prime whale watch locale. Still, there is interest in whale watching to help generate revenues for the MPA's sustainable management. • Area managed by a committee made up of all government departments on the islands under the leadership of the Land and Planning Unit, Ministry of Lands, Survey and Natural Resources.	• Hoyt, 2001; Orams, 1999 • Contact: CASO Ha'apai Conservation Area, Ministry of Lands, Survey and Natural Resources, Pangai, Ha'apai, Kingdom of Tonga • South Pacific Regional Environment Programme (SPREP); email: sprep@sprep.org.ws; web: www.sprep.org.ws

Table 5.18 *continued*

Name of MPA or sanctuary, location and size	Cetacean and other notable species
TUVALU South West Pacific State of Tuvalu **(17) Funufuti Conservation Area** • located in the SW Pacific in the former Ellice Islands	• various dolphin species
VANUATU Ripablik blong Vanuatu **(J) Vanuatu Marine Mammal Sanctuary** • Vanuatu's national waters, to the limits of its EEZ • 260,000 mi^2 (680,000 km^2)	• various cetacean species • also: dugong

Notes and rationale	For more information
• Existing community-based conservation area which is part of the regional GEF Conservation Area programme. • Cetacean surveys are needed to determine species and habitat use of area.	• Contact: South Pacific Regional Environment Programme (SPREP); email: sprep@sprep.org.ws; web: www.sprep.org.ws
• Fisheries Bill 2003 has protection measures for marine mammals and declares Vanuatu's national waters a sanctuary for all cetaceans. • Protection dates from 1982 when the Vanuatu Fisheries Act prohibited the killing of marine mammals.	• WWF, 2003

MARINE REGION 15: NORTHEAST PACIFIC

Cetacean habitat in the Northeast Pacific Marine Region ranges from desert coastal lagoons in México to glacial fjords in Alaska. This region contains both summer and winter habitat for a number of baleen whales, including substantial portions of the world populations of blue and gray whales. The population of blues in the region, found mainly off central California, is the world's largest and healthiest. Other cetacean species with portions of their habitat in the region include fin, Bryde's, minke, North Pacific right and sperm whales, as well as Pacific white-sided dolphins, Dall's and harbor porpoises. Since the early 1970s, the region has been the world centre for orca research. At least two of the known populations of orcas in US waters have very low, declining numbers and have been proposed for endangered species status. The region's humpback whales have also supported long-term research since the 1970s. This work has recently intensified with a cooperative international research effort called 'SPLASH' (Structure of Populations, Levels of Abundance and Status of Humpbacks, 2004–2007) to try to understand humpback whales in the North Pacific (applies to Marine Regions 14, 15 and 16).

One cetacean species endemic to the area is nearing extinction: the Gulf of California porpoise or vaquita. The Mexican government has created an MPA in the northern Gulf of California to try to save it, but it may well be too late. In 1972, the Mexican government created the world's first ever cetacean MPA at Laguna Ojo de Liebre (Scammon's Lagoon), the most important lagoon for mating and calving gray whales. Today this area, along with San Ignacio Lagoon, remains the core of El Vizcaino Biosphere Reserve which includes gray whale coastal habitat and several lagoons. These efforts by the Mexican government, together with international agreements through the IWC to refrain from killing gray whales, have helped the species rebound from close to extinction.

Other notable MPAs in the region are the National Marine Sanctuaries of Monterey Bay, Cordell Bank, Gulf of the Farallones and Channel Islands, which include substantial blue, humpback and other large whale feeding areas as well as year-round habitat for various dolphins. These California sanctuaries provide a good example of the beginnings of an MPA network that could protect cetacean species over much of their range, or at least in the key critical habitats. In Canada, the Robson Bight/Michael Bigg Ecological Reserve is a small reserve in Johnstone Strait for the resting and rubbing areas of resident orcas from the 'northern community'. There are proposals for expanded areas to protect orca and other cetacean habitat in British Columbia and Washington State waters.

The Northeast Pacific Marine Region features the US west coast and Alaska, western Canada and west coast México to the border of Guatemala. Sometimes referred to as 'Bering to Baja', the Northeast Pacific Marine Region has four large marine ecosystems (LMEs) that have been identified: the East Bering Sea, Gulf of Alaska, California Current and Gulf of California. Thus, it has portions of North Pacific subpolar, temperate, subtropical and tropical waters. It includes coastal waters within the 12 nm and EEZ limits, including the long Inside Passage of British Columbia and Alaska, and it extends to international waters beyond 200 nm (371 km) offshore.

The oceanography of much of the region is dominated by a cool water current, the North Pacific Drift, which flows east across the North Pacific, meeting the continental shelf and splitting into north- and south-flowing cool currents. The northward flow becomes the Alaska Current while the southward flow turns into the California Current. This influences most waters from the Aleutian Islands to southern California. Meantime, from the south, the extension of the warm Equatorial Counter Current moves north along the coast of Central America, bringing tropical water up the coast of México and to the Gulf of California, as well as warm water to as far north as southern California. This water flow then turns out to sea. Most of this water is warm except for the cooler water upwellings that occur, mainly in northern Mexican waters.

There is no UNEP regional seas programme for this region. However, national efforts by Canada, the US and México to address cetacean and other marine habitat needs are well advanced, and there is some international cooperation and collaborative work. The Commission for Environmental Cooperation (CEC) has recently established the North American MPA Network and has adopted the Northeast Pacific Marine Region as a pilot project. The CEC's North American MPA Network together with the Bering to Baja (B2B) Marine Conservation Initiative are currently evaluating and planning coordinated marine habitat protection within the Pacific coastal waters to the EEZ limits of continental US, Alaska, Canada and México. In 1995, there was a total of 167 MPAs of all kinds in this marine region – 108 in the US, 30 in México and 29 in Canada (Croom et al, 1995). This region is divided into nine biogeographic zones, all but one of which were represented by at least one MPA. As of 2004, according to Table 5.19 prepared for this book, there are 16 existing and 8 proposed MPAs specifically with cetacean habitat. Four of the existing MPAs are proposed for expansion. There is, in addition, a national cetacean sanctuary declared by México, which covers all of its national waters to the EEZ limit, as well as one proposed international sanctuary in British Columbia (Canadian) and Washington State (US) waters that would help protect cetaceans.

The IUCN 2002–2010 Conservation Action Plan for the World's Cetaceans recommends a number of research and education initiatives for this region, specifically in Mexican waters (Reeves et al, 2003):

- to develop a conservation plan for cetaceans in the Gulf of California (Sea of Cortés) and
- to assess potential impacts on cetaceans of México's planned 'Nautical Stairway' along the coasts of Baja California and the mainland.

IUCN initiatives related to the endangered species vaquita in the region, and thus of highest priority, are:

- to eliminate all fishing methods that result in the bycatch of vaquitas;
- to reduce the risk to vaquitas through fishery monitoring and enforcement;
- to monitor the vaquita population to detect trends in recovery or further decline over the next few decades (possibly through the use of acoustic instead of ship-board surveys); and
- to initiate socioeconomic alternatives for people whose incomes are affected by restrictions on gill net and other fisheries in the upper Gulf of California.

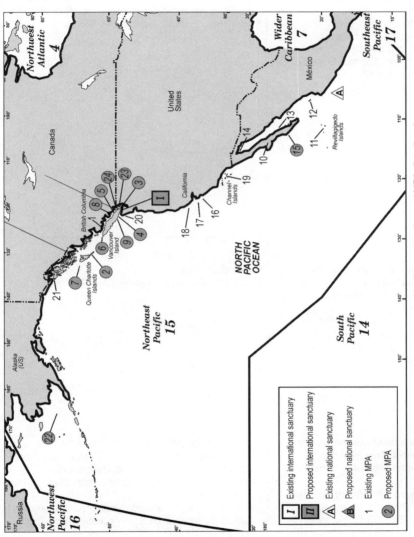

The roman numerals, letters and numbers correspond to the sanctuaries and MPAs listed and described in Table 5.19.

Figure 5.23 *Map of Marine Region 15: Northeast Pacific MPAs and sanctuaries*

Table 5.19 *Marine Region 15: Northeast Pacific MPAs and sanctuaries*

Name of MPA or sanctuary, location and size	Cetacean and other notable species
INTERNATIONAL **(I) Orca Pass International Marine Stewardship Area, proposed** • portions of Georgia, Haro and Juan de Fuca straits and Puget Sound, off southeastern Vancouver Island in Canadian and US waters • size undetermined	• orca, *Orcinus orca*; gray whale, *Eschrictius robustus*; minke whale, *Balaenoptera acutorostrata*; Dall's porpoise, *Phocoenoides dalli*; harbor porpoise, *Phocoena phocoena* • also: seals, sea lions, Pacific salmon species
CANADA **(1) Robson Bight/Michael Bigg Ecological Reserve** • Robson Bight, northeastern Vancouver Island • reserve includes 1.56 mi² (4.05 km²) of land and 4.69 mi² (12.14 km²) of water for a total size of 6.25 mi² (16.19 km²)	• orca, *Orcinus orca* • also: various species of salmon; Tsitika River estuary
(2) Gwaii Haanas National Marine Conservation Area Reserve, proposed for expansion to marine waters • located in South Moresby, southern Queen Charlotte Islands, west of northern British Columbia mainland • the existing national park boundary extends only to the high-tide line; the size of the NMCA would be 1177 mi² (3050 km²)	• gray whale, *Eschrictius robustus*; minke whale, *Balaenoptera acutorostrata*; humpback whale, *Megaptera novaeangliae*; orca, *Orcinus orca*; Dall's porpoise, *Phocoenoides dalli*; harbor porpoise, *Phocoena phocoena*; others sporadic • also: Steller sea lion rookeries; seabird breeding colonies such as rhinoceros and Cassin's auklets, tufted puffins and ancient murrelets

Notes and rationale	For more information
• Proposed in the late 1990s, this MPA is a transborder initiative of the Georgia Strait Alliance, People for Puget Sound and some 20 other NGOs in the Sounds and Straits Coalition; if successful, it would bring together two levels of government in two countries plus 'First Nations' (indigenous peoples). However, this initiative is not one advanced by agencies having a legislative instrument with which to establish an MPA. Thus, the initiative will depend on obtaining one or more legally designated MPAs on each side of the border (eg, state marine park or national marine sanctuary, plus a national marine conservation area (NMCA) or other MPA category on the Canadian side. • This proposed transborder, international MPA would include various core areas with zoned protection over a larger area. Rationale is to protect marine biodiversity including prime habitat for the southern orca community and transient orcas, as well as habitat of other marine mammals, seabirds, salmon and the ecosystem they all depend on. • This ambitious proposal could include or possibly be integrated with the proposed Southern Strait of Georgia National Marine Conservation Area (see below).	• Ford, 2002; Ford et al, 1994; Taylor, 2004 • Contact: Peter Ronald, Georgia Strait Alliance, email: Peter@GeorgiaStrait.org; web: www.georgiastrait.org/orcapass.php
• Established in 1982 as a provincial ecological reserve. • First MPA in Canada designed to protect cetacean habitat. Although the area is limited in size, it helps protect a prime summer resting, socializing and feeding area in Johnstone Strait, including a unique area where the orcas rub on smooth rocks, pebbles and sand. • Extensive summer salmon fishing (100+ commercial seine and gill net boats) occurs, although salmon stocks are depleted. • Reserve limits access by land; whale watchers, sports fishermen and other boat users kept out. • Value of reserve is questioned as provincial government reserves have no jurisdiction over marine fisheries and shipping (Baird, 2001; Duffus and Dearden, 1992).	See also Tables 5.3 and 5.7 for additional Canadian MPAs. • Baird, 2001; Duffus and Dearden, 1992; Ford et al, 1994; Hoyt, 1978, 1981, 1982, 1984, 1990a • Contact: Jim Borrowman, Stubbs Island Charters Ltd, PO Box 2, Telegraph Cove, BC VON 3JO Canada; web: www.stubbs-island.com
• Existing national park reserve in the South Moresby area of the Queen Charlotte Islands whose adjoining larger marine area has been proposed as an NMCA under Parks Canada legislation. • 1988 signing of a federal–provincial agreement committed both governments to work toward creation of NMCA (Mercier and Mondor, 1995), with the Department of Fisheries and Oceans (DFO) and Parks Canada developing a management plan and programme of research in collaboration with the Council of the Haida Nation.	• Hoyt, 1985b; Mercier and Mondor, 1995 • Contact: Parks Canada; web: www.pc.gc.ca/progs/amnc-nmca/index_E.asp

Table 5.19 *continued*

Name of MPA or sanctuary, location and size	Cetacean and other notable species
(3) Race Rocks Candidate 'Marine Protected Area', *proposed* • Race Rocks, southern tip of Vancouver Island, British Columbia • 0.85 mi² (2.2 km²)	• sporadic: orca, *Orcinus orca*; Dall's porpoise, *Phocoenoides dalli*; harbor porpoise, *Phocoena phocoena*; minke whale, *Balaenoptera acutorostrata* • also: harbor seal and California sea lion, diverse fish and invertebrate species
(4) Pacific Rim National Park Reserve, *proposed for expansion* • coastal and nearshore waters of southwestern Vancouver Island • approximately 85.1 mi² (220.5 km²) are marine waters, but area could be expanded to offer better protection to surrounding marine region	• gray whale, *Eschrictius robustus* (both migrating and summer residents); sporadic: minke whale, *Balaenoptera acutorostrata*; humpback whale, *Megaptera novaeangliae*; orca, *Orcinus orca*; Pacific white-sided dolphin, *Lagenorhynchus obliquidens*; Dall's porpoise, *Phocoenoides dalli*; harbor porpoise, *Phocoena phocoena* • also: Steller and California sea lions, harbor seal, six-gilled shark; sea otter; breeding seabirds, migrating shorebirds
(5) Southern Strait of Georgia National Marine Conservation Area, *proposed* • southern Strait of Georgia and Haro Strait, between southeastern Vancouver Island, the southern Gulf Islands and the San Juan Islands of Washington State, US • proposed size 367–463 mi² (950–1200 km²) includes some intertidal and land areas	• orca, *Orcinus orca*; Dall's porpoise, *Phocoenoides dalli*; harbor porpoise, *Phocoena phocoena*; minke whale, *Balaenoptera acutorostrata*; sporadic: humpback whale, *Megaptera novaeangliae*; gray whale, *Eschrictius robustus* • also: harbor seal, Pacific octopus

Notes and rationale	For more information
• Rationale for protection is the marine biodiversity. • Initially protected by British Columbia government in 1980 as a small ecological reserve – nine islets plus the bottom up to a depth of 120 feet (36.6 m) – but not the water column. • In 1998, Canada's DFO named Race Rocks as a pilot 'MPA'; DFO and BC Parks (British Columbia provincial parks agency) established an advisory board to represent stakeholder groups (federal and provincial agencies, aboriginal groups, scientists, divers, sports fishermen, NGOs, Dept of National Defense and others). • On 14 Sept 2000, DFO announced that the area would become an 'MPA', allowing for the integration of both federal and provincial initiatives. As of Jan 2004, the area still awaits resolution of issues raised by First Nations. • This site, located in an area where seals and seal lions were shot decades ago, affords only minimal habitat protection for orcas and other cetaceans because of the limited size; however, it may help protect some fish and marine mammals important to the diet of orcas.	• *MPA News*, 2000b • Contact: Kelly Francis, Dept of Fisheries and Oceans (DFO), South Coast Area Office; email: francisk@ pac.dfo-mpo.gc.ca; web: www.dfo-mpo.gc.ca/ canwaters-eauxcan/oceans/ mpa-zpm/mpa_e.asp • web: www.racerocks.com
• Mainly a terrestrial national park reserve but includes some nearshore marine habitat where gray whales reside and feed, especially during the summer – agreement initially signed in 1970, final agreement in 1987, proclamation in 2001; area is representative of the West Coast Vancouver Island Shelf Natural Marine Region (1 of 29 Parks Canada marine region designations). • Marine areas are managed under the Canada National Park Act which has a primary mandate to protect ecological integrity, as well as to offer opportunities for education, use and enjoyment. • Marine wildlife operators are required to follow species- and site-specific viewing guidelines. • Concerns exist over unknown cumulative effect of resource use on the whales (from whale watching, other boat traffic, increasing pollution, various fisheries, increasing kayak use and extensive crab traps which pose an entanglement hazard).	• Mercier and Mondor, 1995 • Contact: Pacific Rim National Park; Peter Clarkson; email: peter_clarkson@pc.gc.ca; www.pc.gc.ca/progs/ amnc-nmca/index_E.asp
• Feasibility study for NMCA status began in 1995 as part of the Pacific Marine Heritage Legacy (PMHL), a joint federal–provincial initiative to create a system of MPAs along British Columbia's coast; the PMHL programme is part of the Marine Protected Areas Strategy. • Southern resident orcas were listed as endangered in Canada by official government committee, COSEWIC. • Shared habitat for whales and dolphins includes known feeding areas but also frequented by migrating cetaceans; goal is to protect the ecological integrity of the area. • NMCA would stop dumping, dredging, exploration for and extraction of non-renewable resources such as natural gas, and ideally have input into fisheries management.	• Taylor, 2004 • Contact: Bill Henwood, Parks Canada; email: bill.henwood@pc.gc.ca; web: www.pc.gc.ca/progs/ amnc-nmca/index_E.asp

Table 5.19 *continued*

Name of MPA or sanctuary, location and size	Cetacean and other notable species
(6) Scott Islands Marine Wildlife Area, *proposed* • marine waters extending westward from 6 to 29 mi (10 to 46 km) offshore from the northwest tip of Vancouver Island, including the Scott Islands • 10,422 mi² (27,000 km²)	• blue whale, *Balaenoptera musculus*; fin whale, *Balaenoptera physalus*; sei whale, *Balaenoptera borealis*; minke whale, *Balaenoptera acutorostrata*; orca, *Orcinus orca*; Pacific white-sided dolphin, *Lagenorhynchus obliquidens*; Dall's porpoise, *Phocoenoides dalli*; • also: Cassin's and rhinoceros auklets, tufted puffin, black-footed albatross and many other seabirds; sea otter
(7) Bowie Seamount Candidate 'Marine Protected Area', *proposed* • 112 mi (180 km) west of the Queen Charlotte Islands • size undetermined, but recommendation from Bowie Workshop was 580 mi² (1500 km²)	• identified to date: orca, *Orcinus orca*; sperm whale, *Physeter macrocephalus*; North Pacific right whale, *Eubalaena japonica*; various dolphins • also: seals, sea lions, wide variety of seabirds, benthic invertebrates characteristic of deep water as well as intertidal and shallow subtidal
(8) Gabriola Passage Candidate 'Marine Protected Area', *proposed* • passage along Gabriola, Valdes and Breakwater islands and the Flat Top Island Group • size undetermined	• orca, *Orcinus orca*; Dall's porpoise, *Phocoenoides dalli*; harbor porpoise, *Phocoena phocoena*; minke whale, *Balaenoptera acutorostrata* • also: extensive marine invertebrate fauna, fishes, 230 species of algae
(9) Clayoquot Sound Biosphere Reserve, *proposed for greater protection* • Clayoquot Sound, from Esowista Peninsula in the south to just north of Estevan Point, west coast Vancouver Island • 1350 mi² (3500 km²), of which 425 mi² (1100 km²) are legally designated parks and ecological reserves	• gray whale, *Eschrictius robustus*; orca, *Orcinus orca*; Dall's porpoise, *Phocoenoides dalli*; harbor porpoise, *Phocoena phocoena*; minke whale, *Balaenoptera acutorostrata* • also: harbor seal, many others, plus extensive watershed and virgin rain forest

Notes and rationale	For more information
• The five islands that make up the group were originally designated as provincial ecological reserves to protect important seabird populations and pinniped rookeries, but in 2004 Environment Canada's Canadian Wildlife Service proposed the islands and a substantial marine seabird feeding area as the first Marine Wildlife Area (MWA) under the Canada Wildlife Act. • Focus is on seabirds, but there is recognition that this is a shared habitat for whales and dolphins including feeding and breeding areas and that it is also frequented by migrating cetaceans; three separate orca populations are listed as present at times of the year: the northern residents, West Coast transients and 'offshore' orcas. • Plans are to develop a management plan that will include consideration of First Nations issues, fisheries concerns, shipping, offshore oil and gas, and tourism.	• Contact: Greg Mallette, Canadian Wildlife Service; email: Greg.Mallette@ec.gc.ca • Canadian Parks and Wilderness Society; email: info@cpawsbc.org
• Proposed as a Dept of Fisheries and Oceans (DFO) 'MPA' under the Oceans Act, it became a pilot 'MPA' in Dec 1998 to protect its role as an offshore biological oasis and staging area supporting plant and animal communities, with productive oceanographic interactions due to its steep volcanic rise. • Bowie is one in a series of seamounts, thought to be representative; may be the richest, most vulnerable site. • Cetacean research is needed to determine all species present and if important habitat areas are included. • Recommendation is for a zoned area and for ecosystem-based management approach; there are no proposals for oil and gas exploration but some oil tanker traffic nearby.	• AXYS Environmental Consulting Ltd, 2000 • Contact: DFO, Pacific Region Headquarters; email: carsond@ pac.dfo-mpo.gc.ca; web: www.dfo-mpo.gc.ca/ canwaters-eauxcan/oceans/ mpa-zpm/mpa_e.asp
• Proposed as a pilot DFO 'MPA' in 1998 under the Oceans Act to protect abundance and diversity of local marine life. • In 1993, the Marine Life Sanctuary Society prepared a report revealing important biological and other stakeholder information on Gabriola Passage. • Cetacean records from DFO Pacific Biological Station should be able to quantify significant cetacean habitat.	• Contact: DFO, Pacific Region Headquarters; email: carsond@ pac.dfo-mpo.gc.ca; web: www.dfo-mpo.gc.ca/ canwaters-eauxcan/oceans/ mpa-zpm/mpa_e.asp
• Clayoquot Sound is the largest area of temperate rain forest left on Vancouver Island and has been the scene of numerous logging protests and blockades since 1983 when approval was first given to log 90 per cent of Meares Island, one of the sound's largest islands. • In Feb 2000, Unesco designated Clayoquot Sound as a biosphere reserve – important international recognition of the value of the region, yet the reserve does not confer additional provincial or federal protection. In fact, as of 2003, the battles continue in an effort to save a significant portion of the rain forest and the watershed, including the adjacent marine areas, and to usher in a 'green economy'. There is still no formal or official protection from logging, mining or fish farming. • As part of the biosphere designation, the Canadian government allocated $12 million CAD to seed a Biosphere Trust Fund for research, education and training. It is hoped that UN recognition will be a catalyst towards real protection for land and marine areas.	• Hoyt, 1990b • Contact: Friends of Clayoquot Sound; email: info@focs.ca; web: www.focs.ca/ 1clayoquot/biosphere.htm

Table 5.19 *continued*

Name of MPA or sanctuary, location and size	Cetacean and other notable species
MÉXICO Estados Unidos Mexicanos **(A) Mexican Whale Refuge** • national waters of México in Marine Regions 15 and 7, to the limits of its EEZ • 1,157,112 mi² (2,997,700 km²) *Also listed under Marine Region 7.*	• gray whale, *Eschrichtius robustus*; humpback whale, *Megaptera novaeangliae*; Bryde's whale, *Balaenoptera brydei;* sei whale, *Balaenoptera borealis*; fin whale, *Balaenoptera physalus*; blue whale, *Balaenoptera musculus*; bottlenose dolphin, *Tursiops truncatus*; and some 32 other cetacean species found mostly in the Pacific part of its national waters
(10) El Vizcaino Biosphere Reserve (La Reserva de Biosfera El Vizcaíno) • Pacific coast, Baja California Sur; includes the lagoons of Ojo de Liebre, San Ignacio and Guerrero Negro • 9,831 mi² (25,468 km²); protected marine area occupies a 3.1 mi (5 km) wide strip on both Pacific and Gulf sides of the reserve, plus coastal lagoons of Ojo de Liebre, San Ignacio, and most of Guerrero Negro **Laguna Ojo de Liebre (Scammon's Lagoon) National Gray Whale Refuge** **Laguna San Ignacio National Gray Whale Refuge** **Laguna Guerrero Negro National Gray Whale Refuge** The bottom three were originally separate protected areas but have since been integrated as part of El Vizcaino Biosphere Reserve.	• mainly gray whale, Dec–Mar: *Eschrichtius robustus*; year-round: bottlenose dolphin, *Tursiops truncatus*; sporadic: humpback whale, *Megaptera novaeangliae* (late Dec–Apr)*;* Bryde's whale, *Balaenoptera brydei;* fin whale, *Balaenoptera physalus*; blue whale, *Balaenoptera musculus*; common dolphin, *Delphinus delphis*; Pacific white-sided dolphin, *Lagenorhynchus obliquidens* • also: California sea lion, black turtle, green turtle
(11) Revillagigedo Archipelago Biosphere Reserve (La Reserva de Biosfera Archipiélago de Revillagigedo) • located 370–620 mi (600–1000 km) west of Baja California, Colima state • 2458 mi² (6367 km²) of which 67.1 mi² (173.7 km²) is land on the four islands	• Jan–Mar: humpback whale, *Megaptera novaeangliae*; also: Cuvier's beaked whale, *Ziphius cavirostris*; bottlenose dolphin, *Tursiops truncatus*; Pacific white-sided dolphin, *Lagenorhynchus obliquidens*; Fraser's dolphin, *Lagenodelphis hosei*; spinner dolphin, *Stenella longirostris*; orca, *Orcinus orca*; false killer whale, *Pseudorca crassidens*; common dolphin, *Delphinus* sp • also: marine turtles, many endemic bird species

Notes and rationale	For more information
• Rationale is for a refuge or sanctuary for cetaceans that protects them from hunting but may go further. • Designated in 2002; legislation published in Federal Register requires protection plan (equivalent to MPA management plan) to be defined for México's national waters under a new territorial species legal protection regime established by Wildlife Law in 2000 (which will take responsibility for maintaining necessary environmental conditions for whales). • Commercial and recreational activities will not be restricted inside the zone, but efforts will be undertaken to provide users with information on whale species and their significance in maintaining ecological balance.	See also Table 5.10 for more Mexican MPAs. • Contact: Jorge Urban; Universidad Autonoma de BCS; email: jurban@uabcs.mx; or Lorenzo Rojas-Bracho; email: lrojas@cicese.mx • Greenpeace México, México, DF 03400, México; web: www.greenpeace.org.mx
• This area of shared habitat for large whales and dolphins, frequented by migrating cetaceans (mainly in winter), serves as a cetacean mating and breeding area, and feeding ground for some species. Official decree stresses importance for annual gray whale migration and diversity of flora and fauna including endemic species at risk of extinction; Laguna San Ignacio, part of the biosphere reserve, is the only primary gray whale breeding/calving area in México that remains unaltered by industrial development. • In 1971 Laguna Ojo de Liebre was made a whale refuge by presidential decree; protection of Laguna San Ignacio and Laguna Guerrero Negro followed in 1979 and 1980; in Nov 1988, the entire lagoon complex was officially designated a MAB biosphere reserve and Unesco World Heritage Site status followed in 1993. • Whale watching tourism is a key source of income Dec–Apr; there are some protective restrictions on tourism and fishing, among other things. • Widely publicized conflict over building saltworks met with international protest and led to Mitsubishi withdrawing its expansion plans. • A partial biological and cultural inventory is available through the Center for Biological Research in La Paz, México; a more detailed inventory is in preparation. • Administered by Comisión Nacional de Áreas Naturales Protegidas (CONANP), a branch of the Secretaria de Medio Ambiente y Recursos Naturales (SEMARNAT). • In 2004 the area became a Ramsar protected wetland.	• Dedina and Young, 1995; El Vizcaíno management plan; web: http://conanp.gob.mx/anp/programas_manejo/vizcaino.pdf • Contact: Benito Bermudez, Director, Reserva de la Biosfera el Vizcaíno, AP #65 Guerrero Negro, CP 23940, Baja California Sur, México; email: bermudez@conanp.gob.mx • José Angel Sánchez Pacheco; email: jasanpa@telnor.net or jasanpa2000@hotmail.com
• Established in Jun 1994, this reserve has comparatively little human activity due to its remoteness from the North American mainland. Main activities are tourism and diving at a modest level; special permits are required for any human activity. Sport fishing and commercial activities are banned within the reserve waters. Surveillance posts on the islands enforce the regulations. • One of the key humpback whale breeding grounds in the North Pacific. In 1994, Urban estimated 957 (± 181) humpback whales use this area. • Administered by CONANP, a branch of SEMARNAT. • Management plan is currently under review.	• Anaya Reyna, 1996 • Contact: Jorge Urban, Universidad Autonoma de BCS; email: jurban@uabcs.mx

Table 5.19 *continued*

Name of MPA or sanctuary, location and size	Cetacean and other notable species
(12) Islas Marías Biosphere Reserve (La Reserva de Biosfera Islas Marías) • located 60 mi (100 km) west of Nayarit state • 2475 mi² (6413 km²) of which 2361 mi² (6116 km²) is land on the islands	• Jan–Mar: humpback whale, *Megaptera novaeangliae*; other cetaceans, but studies needed to quantify use of the area if any
(13) Loreto Bay National Park (Parque Nacional Bahía de Loreto) • Gulf of California, middle of Baja California Sur • 797.4 mi² (2065.8 km²) of which 702.5 mi² (1820 km²) is water	• mainly minke whale, *Balaenoptera acutorostrata*; fin whale, *Balaenoptera physalus*; Bryde's whale, *Balaenoptera brydei*; blue whale, *Balaenoptera musculus*; also: humpback whale, *Megaptera novaeangliae*; sei whale, *Balaenoptera borealis*; sperm whale, *Physeter macrocephalus*; various dolphin species; rare: gray whale, *Eschrichtius robustus*
(14) Upper Gulf of California and Colorado River Delta Biosphere Reserve (La Reserva de Biosfera Alto Golfo de California y Delta del Río Colorado) • located in the northern Gulf of California, México, and in the Colorado River Delta wetlands • 3700 mi² (9600 km²)	• vaquita, *Phocoena sinus* (total world population, estimated to be in the low hundreds, is mostly within the reserve) • also: totoaba, shark
(15) Bahía Magdalena National Gray Whale Refuge, *proposed* • Magdalena Bay, Pacific coast, Baja California Sur • size undetermined	• late Dec–late Mar: gray whale, *Eschrichtius robustus*

Notes and rationale	For more information
• Established in 2000, the Islas Marías are the site of a federal Mexican prison and access to the area is restricted; no fishing or navigation is permitted within the reserve's boundaries except under special permit. • This is a humpback whale breeding ground but due to the prison and restrictions over entering the area, little is known about the humpback whales. Prison status is due to end and Comisión Nacional de Áreas Naturales Protegidas (CONANP), a branch of SEMARNAT, will take over administration of the area. • Management plan is currently under review.	• Decree on web: http://conanp.gob.mx/ sig/decretos/reservas/ Islas%20Marias% 2027nov00.pdf • Contact: Victor Hugo Vazquez, CONANP; email: vvazquez@ conanp.gob.mx; Jorge Urban, Universidad Autonoma de BCS; email: jurban@uabcs.mx
• First established 1996, MPA may not include extensive cetacean critical habitat per se, but the park does benefit feeding grounds by stopping damaging fishing procedures, such as drag nets and other techniques, plus large-scale fisheries from outside countries. • Ecotourism, including whale watching, is prevalent but artisanal fisheries remain the primary economic activity of fishermen in the park. • Administered by CONANP, a branch of SEMARNAT.	• Contact: Gabriela Anaya, Área de Proteccion de Flora y Fauna, Islas del Golfo; email: ganaya@ conanp.gob.mx; Benito Bermudez; Reserva del Vizcaíno; email: bermudez@ conanp.gob.mx
• Established in northern Gulf of California in Jun 1993 to protect the endangered vaquita as well as the Colorado River Delta wetlands which provide reproduction and feeding habitat for various aquatic and migratory birds; now a MAB biosphere reserve under federal management. • A total ban on commercial and sport fishing in the nucleus of the reserve, as well as a prohibition on oil drilling and exploration, is designed to protect the vaquita; main known mortality has been accidental catches in totoaba and shark nets, but fishing is now supposed to be supervised in the reserve's buffer zone; however, Reeves (2002) reports 'nominal protection to vaquitas [that] fails to address main problem: bycatch in artisanal gillnet fisheries'. • Administered by CONANP, a branch of SEMARNAT.	• O'Connell, 1993; Rojas-Bracho and Taylor, 1999; management plan; web: http://conanp.gob.mx/ anp/programas_manejo/ alto_golfo.pdf • Contact: Lorenzo Rojas-Bracho; email: lrojas@cicese.mx; Silvia Manzanilla Naim, Asesora del C. Secretario; email: vita1@semarnat.gob.mx
• Proposed MPA to protect gray whale breeding and calving habitat in Bahía Magdalena. • The north zone has been specifically proposed for protection by Dedina and Young.	• Dedina and Young, 1995 • Contact: Francisco Ollervides, School for Field Studies, Bahia Magdalena; email: follervides@hotmail.com • Georgina Saad, Pronatura BCS; email: gsaad@pronatura-nmc.org

Table 5.19 *continued*

Name of MPA or sanctuary, location and size	Cetacean and other notable species
UNITED STATES OF AMERICA (USA) **[MPAs 16–17]** **(16) Monterey Bay National Marine Sanctuary** • situated along 300 mi (483 km) of north central California coast adjoining Gulf of the Farallones NMS • 5328 mi² (13,802 km²) – the largest US NMS **(17) Gulf of the Farallones National Marine Sanctuary** • west of San Francisco adjoining Monterey Bay NMS • 1255 mi² (3251 km²)	• Nov–May: gray whale, *Eschrictius robustus*; humpback whale, *Megaptera novaeangliae* (some resident year-round); Sept–Dec: blue whale, *Balaenoptera musculus*; Jun–Sept: fin whale, *Balaenoptera physalus* (some resident year-round); year-round: minke whale: *Balaenoptera acutorostrata*; Risso's dolphin, *Grampus griseus*; Pacific white-sided dolphin, *Lagenorhynchus obliquidens*; northern right whale dolphin, *Lissodelphis borealis*; common dolphin, *Delphinus* sp; and Dall's porpoise, *Phocoenoides dalli* (resident); in all, 26 species of cetaceans visit or inhabit sanctuary waters • also: sea otter, harbor seal, Steller and California sea lions; largest concentration of breeding seabirds in continental US
(18) Cordell Bank National Marine Sanctuary • 60 mi (97 km) NW of San Francisco • 526 mi² (1363 km²)	• gray whale, *Eschrictius robustus*; humpback whale, *Megaptera novaeangliae*; blue whale, *Balaenoptera musculus*; fin whale, *Balaenoptera physalus*; sei whale, *Balaenoptera borealis*; sperm whale, *Physeter macrocephalus*; Dall's porpoise, *Phocoenoides dalli*; and others • also: Steller sea lion, albatross and shearwater; four species of sea turtles (green, leatherback, Pacific Ridley, and loggerhead)
(19) Channel Islands National Marine Sanctuary • 25 mi (40 km) off Santa Barbara • covers 1658 mi² (4295 km²) including waters around San Miguel, Santa Rosa, Santa Cruz, Anacapa and Santa Barbara islands (from mean high tide to 6 nm offshore), and completely surrounds the Channel Islands National Park	• gray whale, *Eschrictius robustus*; humpback whale, *Megaptera novaeangliae*; blue whale, *Balaenoptera musculus*; Risso's dolphin, *Grampus griseus*; short-finned pilot whale, *Globicephala macrorhynchus*; Pacific white-sided dolphin, *Lagenorhynchus obliquidens*; common dolphin, *Delphinus* sp; bottlenose dolphin, *Tursiops truncatus*; Dall's porpoise, *Phocoenoides dalli*; in all, 27 cetacean species live in or visit sanctuary waters • additional species include harbor and elephant seals; California sea lions; 60 species of breeding birds

Notes and rationale	For more information
	See also Tables 5.7 and 5.10 for more US MPAs.
• Monterey Bay was established in 1992 and Gulf of the Farallones in 1981 as national marine sanctuaries (NMSs) under federal as well as state management. • Sites were designated to protect the variety of nearshore and offshore habitats – rocky shores, expansive kelp forests, wetlands, open ocean and one of the deepest underwater canyons within the 200 nm (371 km) EEZ of the US – up to more than 10,000 ft (3048 m) deep, the Monterey Canyon. Abundant cetacean and other marine mammals, birds, fish, invertebrates and floral and faunal communities depend on these habitats. • There are bans on oil and gas exploration, waste dumping and other discharges, but there are no special restrictions on fisheries. • Research activities include monitoring coastal ecosystem change, developing regional research priorities with 20 local marine science institutions, and evaluating scientific component of resource management issues. Cetacean research has included extensive blue whale studies (photo-ID and satellite tagging) and photo-ID of humpback whales, Pacific white-sided dolphins and others.	• Andersen, 1993 • Contact: Monterey Bay National Marine Sanctuary, 299 Foam Street, Suite D, Monterey, CA 93940 USA; web: www.mbnms.nos.noaa.gov • Contact: Gulf of the Farallones National Marine Sanctuary, Fort Mason, Bldg 201, San Francisco, CA 94123 USA; web: www.gfnms.nos.noaa.gov
• Designated in 1989 under federal NMS status and managed jointly with Gulf of the Farallones NMS. • Critical habitat for marine mammals and seabirds – a destination feeding ground on an offshore seamount where oceanic conditions combine with undersea topography to create a highly productive environment. • Research includes pelagic surveys for seabirds and marine mammals, sampling for state biotoxin monitoring programme, plus research on blue, humpback, gray and other whales. • Industrial activities include commercial and recreational fisheries, diving, whale and seabird watching, as well as regular naval operations. • Regulations prohibit disturbance of the seabed, depositing or discharging substances or materials; removing or injuring sanctuary resources, and hydrocarbon activities.	• Contact: Cordell Bank National Marine Sanctuary, Fort Mason, Bldg 201, San Francisco, CA 94123 USA; web: http://cordellbank.noaa.gov
• Established in 1980 to protect key habitats for marine mammals, including cetaceans, extensive pinniped rookeries and seabirds. • Network plans in process will create highly protected Category I core areas representing 10–25 per cent of the total area (up to 425 mi² (1100 km²). • Bans on oil and gas exploration, waste dumping and other discharges, but no special restrictions on fisheries; initial proposal for much larger sanctuary failed due to offshore oil and gas development conflicts. • In 2002, a network of ten no-take and two limited-fishing areas (comprising 10 per cent of sanctuary waters) were designated within state waters. As of 2004, more reserves/closures were set to follow in federal waters. In addition, boundary expansion of the sanctuary is also being evaluated.	• Leatherwood et al, 1987; Channel Islands NMS and University of Santa Barbara have a database with 4,000+ scientific references to the Channel Islands area • Contact: Channel Islands National Marine Sanctuary 113 Harbor Way, Santa Barbara, CA 93109 USA; web: www.channel islands.noaa.gov/

Table 5.19 *continued*

Name of MPA or sanctuary, location and size	Cetacean and other notable species
(20) Olympic Coast National Marine Sanctuary • situated along Washington's outer coast from Cape Flattery to the mouth of the Copalis River, averaging about 35 mi (56 km) seaward • 3310 mi² (8575 km²) including land and marine areas	• gray whale, *Eschrictius robustus*; humpback whale, *Megaptera novaeangliae*; Pacific white-sided dolphin, *Lagenorhynchus obliquidens*; Dall's porpoise, *Phocoenoides dalli*; 29 total cetacean species • also: sea otter, Steller sea lion, tufted puffin, many birds on Pacific flyway
(21) Glacier Bay National Park and Preserve • Glacier Bay, Alaska • 5000 mi² (12,955 km²) including land and marine; about 20 per cent is marine, or 1000 mi² (2591 km²); nearly 87 per cent is 'wilderness' but only 2 per cent of the marine area is included in 'wilderness' which is equivalent to IUCN Category I	• mainly humpback whale, *Megaptera novaeangliae*; also: minke whale, *Balaenoptera acutorostrata*; orca, *Orcinus orca* • other species: harbor seal, halibut, salmon, Tanner crab • the name 'Glacier Bay' refers to how the bay was made but there are no glaciers in the bay itself now, though in the surrounding area, even as they recede, they remain a big attraction
(22) **Southeastern Bering Sea Right Whale Critical Habitat,** *proposed* • 200 nm (370 km) north of Unimak Pass, eastern Aleutian Islands, southeastern Bering Sea, Alaska • size undetermined; main area is 60 x100 nm, or 7986 mi² (20,690 km²)	• summer: North Pacific right whale, *Eubalaena japonica*

Notes and rationale	For more information
• Designated in 1994 to protect the diversity of seabirds and marine mammals using pristine coastal waters for feeding and breeding, as well as rich fishing grounds, and historical and cultural resources such as Quinault, Hoh, Quileute, and Makah village sites, ancient canoe runs, artifacts, petroglyphs, and shipwrecks. • Environmental impact statement (EIS) and management plan was released in Dec 1993, creating comprehensive ecosystem-based management of natural as well as historical and cultural resources. • Research activities include marine archaeological and biological surveys and marine research coordinated with state and other federal agencies and universities.	• Taylor, 2004 • Contact: Olympic Coast National Marine Sanctuary, Port Angeles, WA 98362-2600, USA; web: www.ocnms.nos.noaa.gov
• Established 1925 as Glacier Bay National Monument, Glacier Bay has become a National Park and Preserve, as well as, in 1986, part of the Glacier Bay–Admiralty Island Biosphere Reserve and, in 1992, part of a Unesco World Heritage Site along with Wrangell–Mount St Elias National Park and Canada's Kluane National Park. • Both land and sea areas were protected originally as part of the national monument. With the growth of tourism since 1925 and the changing view of conservation, National Park Service (NPS) objectives now focus on conserving ecosystems and trying to manage fisheries and tourism threats to the park. • Some humpback habitat is in the park, NW of Bartlett Cove in NPS-dubbed 'whale waters', but most whales stay outside the park at Point Adolphus; MPA would need to expand considerably to include these. • Inside the park is controlled cruise ship and other tourism; commercial fishing (salmon trolling, halibut longlining, salmon seining, crab pot fishing) was banned in 1966 in the park and in designated wilderness areas, and is due to be discontinued.	• Contact: Superintendent Glacier Bay National Park and Preserve, PO Box 140, Gustavus, AK 99826 USA; web: www.nps.gov/glba
• In summer 1996, a group of four endangered North Pacific right whales were discovered summering in southeastern Bering Sea. Every year since then, the National Marine Fisheries Service (NMFS) has undertaken aerial, shipboard and/or acoustic surveys to study these whales, the only known 'concentration' of right whales in the North Pacific. By 2002, 13 individuals had been photo-IDed on these summer feeding grounds. • In Oct 2000, the Center for Biological Diversity petitioned NMFS to designate part of southeastern Bering Sea as a critical habitat for right whales under provisions of the Endangered Species Act. The petition was published in a Federal Register notice July 2001 but designation was postponed pending more information on the extent of the critical habitat and information about the species' essential biological requirements.	• More information: web: www.mmc.gov/ species/pdf/ar2002north pacrightwhale.pdf

Table 5.19 *continued*

Name of MPA or sanctuary, location and size	Cetacean and other notable species
(23) **San Juan Islands National Wildlife Refuge,** *proposed for expansion* • San Juan Islands including land, nearshore and intertidal (200 m seaward) but proposed to be extended out to sea • size undetermined	• if boundaries are extended out to sea, the refuge could include habitat for orca, *Orcinus orca*; minke whale, *Balaenoptera acutorostrata*; gray whale, *Eschrictius robustus*; Pacific white-side dolphin, *Lagenorhynchus obliquidens*; harbor porpoise, *Phocoena phocoena*; and Dall's porpoise, *Phocoenoides dalli*
(24) **Northwest Straits 'management area',** *unsuccessfully proposed as* **National Marine Sanctuary,** *now* **abandoned** • located in Puget Sound–Juan de Fuca Straits, northern Washington State waters • size undetermined	• orca, *Orcinus orca*; minke whale, *Balaenoptera acutorostrata*; gray whale, *Eschrictius robustus*; Pacific white-side dolphin, *Lagenorhynchus obliquidens*; harbor porpoise, *Phocoena phocoena*; Dall's porpoise, *Phocoenoides dalli* • also: harbor and elephant seals; Steller and California sea lions; salmon species, two of which are threatened under the Endangered Species Act

Notes and rationale	For more information
• Established 1914 to protect migratory birds, this IUCN Category Ia national wildlife refuge (NWR) covers 83 small islands and reefs in the San Juan Archipelago; the marine component, a 600 ft (183 m) buffer zone, is not enough to protect cetaceans but if extended could protect critical habitat. • Management authorities are Washington Dept of Fish and Wildlife (WDFW) and Dept of Natural Resources (DNR) but neither have implemented marine protection at NWR sites; collaboration might be sought with NMFS, US Coast Guard, Native tribes, local government, NGOs. This NWR could also be enhanced by the proposed Orca Pass International Marine Stewardship Area (see above).	• Don, 2002; Taylor, 2004
• First listed as a candidate site in 1983, it came under active consideration in 1988, but following public meetings and review and a draft EIS and Management Plan; NOAA dropped the NMS ideas in the late 1990s. • Despite the failed sanctuary idea, there has been interest in expanding the San Juan Islands National Wildlife Refuge or in considering a new, international initiative, such as the Orca Pass International Marine Stewardship Area (see above); some of the goals for protection of this area might be realized through these proposals. • In 1998, the Northwest Straits Commission was set up 'to restore and protect the marine habitats of the Northwest Straits'. • Programme is coordinated by Washington State and funded partly through the NMS Program. This 'bottom-up' approach may lead to future MPA initiatives.	• Don, 2002; Taylor, 2004 • Contact: Northwest Straits Commission, 10441 Bayview-Edison Rd, Mt Vernon, WA 98273 USA; web: www.nwstraits.org

MARINE REGION 16: NORTHWEST PACIFIC

Few cetaceans have received more international scientific and conservation attention, both within and outside of China, than the baiji, or Chinese river dolphin. Yet the species has continued to decline, largely due to local fishing methods – rolling hooks and electrofishing. The species probably numbers in the low tens now and may well become extinct over the next decade (Reeves et al, 2003).

Besides baiji, the Northwest Pacific Marine Region has important known populations with year-round habitat for toothed whales including Dall's and finless porpoises, sperm whales, Baird's beaked whales and orcas. The region also provides seasonal habitat for gray, humpback, Bryde's and minke whales and others. At least three highly endangered species or populations of baleen whales are resident in the region: the western Pacific, or Korean, stock of the gray whale, reduced to as few as 100 individuals which come to feed off Sakhalin, Russia; the bowhead whale in the Sea of Okhotsk; and the North Pacific right whale in the Bering Sea. For all three, habitat protection may well be too late to save the species, but highly protected MPAs may significantly help the prospects of these populations.

Several well-studied cetacean populations have received a measure of habitat protection: the Indo-Pacific hump-backed dolphin of the Pearl River delta and Hong Kong, China, and the finless porpoise in Japan, although both may be token gestures in view of the new airport and other developments around Hong Kong, and the reduced numbers of finless porpoises in the Sea of Japan. Elsewhere in the region, off eastern Taiwan, successful whale watch tours attract more than 238,000 people a year to see mainly tropical dolphins and small toothed whales. There is no habitat protection here but such predictable presence means that protection may well be warranted. Equally, none of the high-volume whale watch areas in Japanese waters have MPA status, although local operators and researchers have expressed interest in helping to create such protection (Hoyt, 2001). The Russian Far East, with its long coastline on the northwest Pacific, has a number of potentially valuable MPAs for cetaceans, although in most cases research needs to be done to define cetacean critical habitat and to assign and enforce IUCN Category I core protection. Off northeast Sakhalin, despite carefully defined cetacean critical habitat for the 'critically endangered' western Pacific population of gray whales, the Russian Ministry of Natural Resources seems poised to ignore scientists' recommendations, instead favouring the oil development industry in a 'compromise' reserve. The fate of these 100 gray whales may well depend on a well-managed MPA with adequate precautionary boundaries.

The Northwest Pacific Marine Region is under the jurisdiction of six national governments. The region's waters stretch from Far East Russia at the Bering Strait, past the Koreas, all the way to southern China and include Japan and Taiwan. The region has portions of North Pacific subpolar, temperate, subtropical and tropical waters.

The Northwest Pacific Marine Region has seven large marine ecosystems (LMEs) that have been identified: East China Sea, Yellow Sea, Kuroshio

BOX 5.10 DO MPAS REALLY EXIST IN JAPAN?

The meeting of the warm Kuroshio Current and the cold Oyashio Current in the northwest Pacific zone creates one of the world's most productive and diverse marine areas. Up to 1000 species of bottom-dwelling fishes are found with 2000 overall fish species for Japan (Simard, 1995). Adding this to rich bird populations and numerous, diverse invertebrates makes Japan an important area for world biodiversity. In terms of marine mammals, Simard (1995) calls the Northwest Pacific 'rich in cetaceans' although acknowledging that 'they have been hunted for a long time' by Japanese, Korean, Russian and American whalers.

The importance of the sea as the traditional support of society in Japan has had an enormous impact on the development of marine conservation in Japan. In terms of protected areas that have a bearing on marine waters, there are four main types of system: the natural parks, marine parks, nature conservation areas and the fisheries resources protection system.

Within the natural parks system, there are three categories and some subcategories: national parks, quasi national parks and prefectural parks. National parks can be special areas or special protection areas where protection is slightly stronger. The nature conservation system, viewed on a superficial level, would seem the best in the world. A large portion of the Japanese coast and marine waters is included in these 'protected' areas. In the prefectures of Iwate, Mie, Saga and Hyogo, for example, more than half the coastline is included. The prefectures of Fukui, Okayama and Kagawa have their entire coasts under protection. But according to Simard (1995), 'in reality, the Japanese Natural Park System is of little importance and has almost no influence on economic development along the coast.' Even with the special areas and special protection areas, which confer more protection on 62 per cent of the total area, there are extensive building, mining, quarrying and other industrial projects. Most extraordinary of all, only the water's surface is taken into account by law, not the water mass or the organisms present within it. Thus the role of natural parks for marine conservation is close to insignificant.

Japan also has a marine park system that does preserve underwater seascapes. These can be designated within national parks or quasi national parks as part of the so-called natural park system although they are totally marine. However, the marine parks (MPs) are tiny, with an average size in 2001 of only 0.16 square mile (0.41 km²). Even the larger ones are too small to make an impact for cetaceans or ecosystems. And excluded from protection in MPs are marine mammals and the target species of fisheries. According to Simard (1995), 'in most cases, the Japanese MPs cannot play the role of protecting a natural sea area. They only play an educational and touristic role, because they are not large enough to provide for effective management.'

A third type of nature conservation, outside the natural park system, is called the Nature Conservation Area. These areas are strictly protected but they are remote and, as of 2001, there was only one of them, designated in 1983, which covered a mere 0.5 mi² (1.28 km²).

Finally, Japan has an ancient, complex system of fisheries rights which gives fishing communities exclusive rights over the marine areas they exploit. These are managed by the more than 4000 fishermen's cooperative associations around Japan. With the exception of a few harbours, almost the entire Japanese coast is managed under this system which covers marine areas from the coast out to 3 to 13 miles (5 to 21 km).

One of the management tools to protect the reproduction of fish species is a system of Fisheries Resources Protection Areas (FRPAs) that are part of the fisheries resources system and are regulated under the 1951 Law on the Protection of Fisheries Resources, Article 14. FRPA management usually means a complete or seasonal ban on fishing or strict regulations on fishing gear. In 2002, there were 120 such areas (including freshwater fisheries areas) designated to protect particular fish species or groups of species. Of course, the function of the FRPAs is essentially to provide maximum harvesting of natural resources, but the system has arguably produced better management of certain fish species than many other countries over the past century or more. Still, Simard (1995), summarizing marine conservation in Japan, stated that 'The situation ... is therefore one where neither the marine park [nor the] fisheries resources system are adequate as a MPA system. Given the high human population density and the long tradition of exploitation of coastal fishing grounds, it would seem that a nature conservation orientated system may not be practical. Adaptation of the Fisheries Resources system, in the same way that has been achieved for forest protection by the Forestry Agency of the Ministry of Agriculture, Forestry and Fisheries, may provide a greater chance of success for conservation and sustainable development of Japan's coastal areas.'

Simard's comments notwithstanding, many MPA practitioners feel that Japan, as a signer of various international conservation treaties and a steward of world-important biodiversity, should institute a real MPA programme to a standard found in other parts of the world. The unofficial explanation for this state of affairs in Japan is that the Japanese government is unable to designate significant protected areas under its legal system because of personal rights over land and resources. Making MPAs, they contend, would breach the constitutional rights of individuals owning land or resources, or communities controlling fishing rights. But part of the explanation must be that designating protected areas is managed not by the Ministry of Environment but through the Fisheries Agency, a branch of the Ministry of Agriculture, Forestry and Fisheries whose main objective is protecting fisheries for exploitation. In fact, the only areas in Japan to receive real protection are forests and islands located in remote areas where there are no pre-existing personal rights or legal claims.

Perhaps not surprising in view of the emphasis on marine resource use, only two 'MPAs' in Japan can be said to protect cetaceans at even a modest level: the Seto-naikai National Park and the Finless Porpoise Gathering Area National Natural Monument (see Table 5.20 on p384). There are also several existing or potential areas associated with whale watching. Whale watching began in Japan in 1988 and has now spread to more than 25 coastal communities all over the country (Hoyt, 2001). There have been numerous discussions and debates in small communities associated with whale watching concerning various sorts of designations (Hoyt, 1993b, 1996). For example, the village of Zamami in Okinawa Prefecture (Ryukyu Islands) called its adjacent waters a 'sanctuary for whales' to celebrate the humpback whales that increasingly attract tourists to this diving paradise. There have also been informal proposals at Hayasaki Strait in Kumamoto Prefecture and Ogata in Kochi Prefecture (around Ino-Mizaki Point) to designate inshore areas as special 'reserves' for cetaceans. The extent of the real protection this would afford whales and dolphins, particularly species that are subject to being hunted in nearby areas, may be questionable, but the sentiment is positive.

With the natural park system intended to maintain natural underwater and terrestrial landscape, one might well argue that a landscape or scenic MPA should, by definition, protect and preserve any animal that is part of the natural scenery and is sought out by tourists. This would include marine mammals, and now that more than 100,000 Japanese a year are paying to take whale watch tours in Japan, cetaceans must qualify at minimum as 'natural scenery' and should be considered for protection from hunting. All that is needed is for a Fisheries officer to endorse this interpretation and enforce it!

Following the World Summit on Sustainable Development (WSSD) in Johannesburg in 2002 and the V World Parks Congress in Durban in 2003, there has been a rapidly growing world commitment to design and implement effective MPAs with strict core habitat conservation for ecosystems and species along with or as part of large biosphere-type reserves. Yet, as of 2004, Japan still had virtually no marine protected areas. Even when there is some protection, areas are small, and no protection is provided for free-moving species once they are out of a given area.

Current, Sea of Japan, Oyashio Current, Sea of Okhotsk and West Bering Sea. The oceanography of much of the region is dominated by the south-flowing, cold Oyashio Current and the warm, north-flowing Kuroshio Current. The Oyashio divides at the northern tip of Hokkaido and enters the Sea of Japan and the open North Pacific. The Kuroshio current, by contrast, comes up along the Ryukyu archipelago at up to 10 knots or faster, and splits at the southern tip of Kyushu, entering the Sea of Japan and the Yellow Sea as the Tsushima Current, as well as then continuing on as the Kuroshio Current which crosses the North Pacific. Along with the South Pacific Marine Region, the Northwest Pacific has an extensive series of deep trenches including the Vityaz depth off the Kuril Islands. The meeting of the Kuroshio and the Oyashio currents off the northeast coast of the main Honshu Island of Japan has created one of the most productive marine areas in the world.

This area has had only minimal regional cooperation in marine conservation and management (Simard, 1995). Recently, the countries of the region formed a UNEP regional seas programme for the Northwest Pacific, called NOWPAP. Priority issues are oil and chemical pollution, waste dumping and population pressure but it is hoped that it will also have a role in creating a representative system of MPAs.

In 1995, there was a total of 190 MPAs of all kinds in this marine region (Simard, 1995). This was the second highest number of MPAs for one marine region, but MPA practitioners have questioned the generally low quality of the protection. The region is divided into eight biogeographic zones, all but one of which were represented by at least one MPA. As of 2004, according to Table 5.20 prepared for this book, there are 22 existing and 11 proposed MPAs specifically with cetacean habitat. Two of the 22 existing MPAs are proposed for expansion.

The IUCN 2002–2010 Conservation Action Plan for the World's Cetaceans recommends the following research and education initiatives for this region (Reeves et al, 2003):

- to evaluate the status and levels of mortality of small and medium-sized cetaceans in Taiwan;
- to investigate and monitor the status of finless porpoises in the Yangtze River;
- to investigate the feasibility of establishing a natural reserve for finless porpoises in and near Dongting Lake or Poyang Lake, China;
- to establish a marine mammal stranding network in China; and
- to determine the migration route(s) and breeding ground(s) of western Pacific gray whales as a basis for their protection.

IUCN initiatives related to endangered species in the region, and thus of highest priority with regard to baiji in the Yangtze River, are to enforce the ban on the use of rolling hooks, to end electrofishing and to eliminate all other known threats to the survival of baiji in its natural habitat.

BOX 5.11 MPAS IN RUSSIA

The network of state zapovedniks, zakazniks and national parks provides the backbone of nature conservation in Russia, and these are the three main types of protected area that would have some application and importance to MPA conservation. According to the Russian Federal Law 'On Protected Natural Areas' which came into effect in March 1995, the state zapovedniks and national parks are meant to address not only nature conservation but environmental education as well. The distinctions drawn between the various types of protected area are as follows:

- A zapovednik, or strict nature reserve, is a federally managed area set up mainly to protect ecosystems. Zapovedniks are closed for all economic activity including ecotourism. Even the staff of the reserve cannot have their own farms. These are scientific reserves or 'strict nature reserves', IUCN Category Ia. Many zapovedniks are surrounded by a 1.2 mile (2 km) buffer zone which allows hunting and fishing but not large-scale resource extraction. Some zapovedniks are zoned biosphere reserves and several carry the official UN Man and the Biosphere label; usually in Russia this in effect confers greater protection. Zapovedniks were established in 1916 and strictly protected during the Soviet system except for a period of degradation for many reserves during the Stalin era (Shtilmark, 1996). Since the collapse of the Soviet system in 1991, the management of the zapovedniks has been turned over to the Ministry of Natural Resources. Zapovedniks form the greatest collection of scientific reserves in the world, representing 40 per cent of the world's Category Ia scientific reserves, but they are in trouble. Over the past decade, there has been intense pressure to exploit the timber, oil and other resources in the more than 100 zapovedniks across Russia (Webster, 2003). Some reserves are already being degraded by tourism pressures. Of course, well-managed ecotourism can be a useful sustainable strategy for helping to conserve nature, but there is a strong argument that tourism should be restricted to national parks, allowing zapovedniks to continue their important role as strict scientific reserves. Most zapovedniks are land-based only, but those in coastal or island areas can have marine components.
- A national park, IUCN Category II, is an area designed to protect ecosystems and cultural heritage but allowing for managed educational, recreational, cultural, as well as scientific activities. Thus, tourism and some types of economic activity that do not damage nature are permitted. Usually national parks are designed along the lines of modified biosphere reserves with core protected areas and other zones for tourism and limited commercial activity. National parks date only from 1983 and come under the federal Forest Service.
- A zakaznik, or temporary wildlife refuge, is designed to limit economic activity (often seasonally) to protect ecosystems or particular species. Most zakazniks have been set up to limit commercial hunting to conserve wildlife. These would be IUCN Category IV areas. Zakazniks can be federal or regional but most are regional. Unlike zapovedniks, which are 'permanent', zakazniks must be renewed every five years.
- A natural monument is IUCN Category III, a reserve to protect unique natural or man-made objects (special waterfalls, bird rookeries, caves). Natural monuments are small and are not designed to protect whole ecosystems.

- A prirodniye parky, or nature park, is a natural recreational area set aside for nature protection, education and recreation. This form of protection was established in 1995 to provide regional control of parks that would be mainly for the recreational use of Russian people.

On 22 April 2003, the Ministry of Natural Resources of the Russian Federation formally approved 'Fundamental directions for the development of the system of state zapovedniks and national parks in the Russian Federation until 2015.' This document announced that 12 new protected areas would be created between 2003 and 2006, including eight national parks and four zapovedniks. In summer 2003, *Russian Conservation News* produced a detailed ten-year review of Russia's zapovedniks, based in part on assessments by Vsevolod Stepanitskiy, deputy head of the newly created Department of Protected Areas and Biodiversity Conservation, in the Ministry of Natural Resources (RCN, 2003). The system of protected areas in Russia is the most extensive in the world and Russia also has by far the largest network of highly protected IUCN Category I areas. The challenge will be keeping the standards high, as well as extending the network of protected areas to cover the marine sector, which is much less represented. As of 2004, several proposals through WWF Russia and other groups are attempting to address the need for more MPAs in the marine sector, some of which will be important for cetacean habitat.

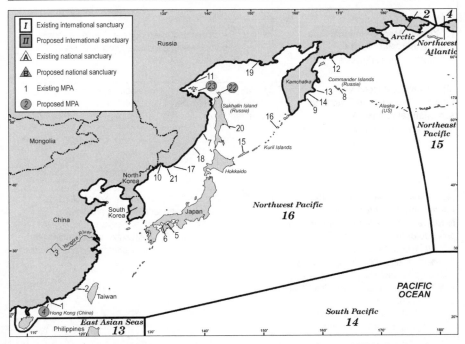

The roman numerals, letters and numbers correspond to the sanctuaries and MPAs listed and described in Table 5.20.

Figure 5.24 *Map of Marine Region 16: Northwest Pacific MPAs and sanctuaries*

Table 5.20 *Marine Region 16: Northwest Pacific MPAs and sanctuaries*

Name of MPA or sanctuary, location and size	Cetacean and other notable species
CHINA People's Republic of China Zhonghua Renmin Gonghe Guo (includes Hong Kong and Macao) **(1) Lung Kwu Chau and Sha Chau Marine Park** • Pearl River delta (estuarine waters) near Hong Kong • 4.6 mi² (12 km²)	• Indo-Pacific hump-backed dolphin, *Sousa chinensis*; finless porpoise, *Neophocaena phocaenoides* • also: soft corals
(2) Xiamen Marine National Park and Conservation Areas • Xiamen in Fujian Province	• Indo-Pacific hump-backed dolphin, *Sousa chinensis*; finless porpoise, *Neophocaena phocaenoides*
(3) Baiji Natural Reserve (and the Shishou and Tong Ling semi-natural reserves) • along an 81 mi (130 km) stretch of the Yangtze River at Honghu	• baiji, *Lipotes vexillifer*; finless porpoise, *Neophocaena phocaenoides* (shares habitat in the river though not endangered)
(4) Zhujiang (Pearl River) Delta Ecosystem Protected Area, *tentative name, proposed and in process of possible expansion* • Pearl River delta and adjacent waters (would include some smaller, mainly land-based protected areas as well as the Lung Kwu Chau and Sha Chau Marine Park (see above) • 178 mi² (460 km²) with a 54 mi² (140 km²) protected core area	• Indo-Pacific hump-backed dolphin, *Sousa chinensis*; finless porpoise, *Neophocaena phocaenoides* • also: many commercial and non-commercial fishes; third largest river in China with subtropical estuarine ecosystems including wetland, mangroves and islands

Notes and rationale	For more information
• Rationale is to protect the habitat of the 'pink dolphins'. • When the park was established in 1996, Brian Morton declared 'the proposal to establish a marine park sanctuary at Lung Kwu Chau and Sha Chau is ... largely a political decision and will probably not work as the dolphin population is already considered to be non-viable and the threats to its habitat can only increase.' As of 2003, the dolphins were holding their own, although more protective measures and enforcement would help ensure a future for the dolphins here. • Problems include considerable shipping traffic from one of world's busiest harbours, with oil barges and dredging inside park boundary (from building the airport) and (largely untreated) urban sewage and industrial effluents; one outfall is within half a kilometre of the park. • Regulations prohibit high-speed watercraft, trawling and sports fishing, although there are some abuses. • This MPA is considered insignificant and a sham by those who want a larger area with real protection; still, the MPA has helped alert many to the dolphins' plight.	• Würsig, 1995; Morton, 1996 • Contact: Tom Jefferson; email: Sclymene@aol.com; • More information: web: http://parks.afcd.gov.hk/newparks/chi/index.htm • Samuel Hung, Hong Kong Dolphin Conservation Society; email: samuel@hkdcs.org
• Several conservation areas have been set up specifically to help protect Indo-Pacific hump-backed dolphins. These areas were approved at the provincial level in 1997 and at the national level in Apr 2000.	• Contact: Prof Huang Zhongguo, Third Inst of Oceanography; email: hzg@public.xm.fj.cn
• This natural protected freshwater area was set aside specifically to protect the endangered baiji. • Recently, two 'semi-natural' reserves have been added at other points along the river at Shishou and Tong Ling. Because these are partly 'captive' and heavily managed areas, they are not considered in separate entries. Indeed, the wisdom of bringing additional baiji in from the wild to these semi-captive situations is questioned by many researchers and conservation groups.	• Contact: Tom Jefferson; email: Sclymene@aol.com
• In 1999 this proposal with the sizes described at left received provincial approval (Guangdong Province) to make it a national park with regulations to protect the dolphins. However, researchers have suggested much larger areas for a dolphin sanctuary – at least five times as large with even more substantial buffer zones (Duyuan and Qingchao, 1996). Another proposal (Simard, 1995) recommended an MPA covering the entire Zhujiang (Pearl River) delta to protect subtropical estuarine ecosystems including wetland, mangroves and islands (this proposal was rated as one of the six highest regional priorities for the NW Pacific). • Problems include extensive shipping, commercial fishing, dredging of marine sand for reclamation projects, and sewage disposal from several large cities.	• Contact: Huang Chuang-Liang, Ocean and Fisheries Dept, Resources and Environment Div; email: gdsczz@public.guangzhou.gd.cn • Tom Jefferson; email: Sclymene@aol.com • Samuel Hung, Hong Kong Dolphin Conservation Society; email: samuel@hkdcs.org

Table 5.20 *continued*

Name of MPA or sanctuary, location and size	Cetacean and other notable species
JAPAN Nippon **(5) Seto-naikai National Park** • Seto Inland Sea, between the islands of Honshu, Shikoku and Kyushu • 242 mi² (628 km²)	• finless porpoise, *Neophocaena phocaenoides* • also: important spawning and nursery grounds for many fish species
(6) Finless Porpoise Gathering Area National Natural Monument (Sunameri Kujira Kaiyu [Gun-ei] Suimen National Nature Monument) • waters surrounding Shironhana Rock, at southern tip of Awa-jima, near the city of Takehara, Hiroshima prefecture, in the Seto-naikai (Seto Inland Sea) • area is small, defined by less than 1 mi (1.5 km) radius	• finless porpoise, *Neophocaena phocaenoides*
RUSSIA Russian Federation Rossiskaya Federatsiya **(7) Botchinskiy Nature Reserve (Zapovednik)** • 170 mi (275 km) east of Khabaraovsk, Khabarovskiy, on the Sea of Japan • 1032 mi² (2674 km²), including land and marine areas	• probable cetacean habitat

Notes and rationale	For more information
<ul><li>Rationale is to protect natural scenery only at the surface.</li><li>This national park, created in 1934, includes a large portion of the marine waters of the entire inland sea of Japan as well as the coastline of ten prefectures. This park also contains a tiny national nature monument to the finless porpoise created in 1930, which, it has been claimed, was part of the reason for establishing the park. For more information, see entry (6) below.</li><li>Japan's Seto Inland Sea (Seto-naikai) also has about 20 FRPAs (Fisheries Resources Protection Areas) which include bans or gear restrictions on fishing in some areas.</li><li>IUCN Category VI and according to Simard (1995) a prime example of ineffective protection; Simard's suggestion for improving marine protection of high biodiversity is to create a real MPA for the entire Seto Inland Sea which includes 800 islands and measures 849 mi^2 (2200 km^2).</li></ul>	<ul><li>Simard, 1995</li><li>Contact: The Nature Conservation Society of Japan (NACS-J), Yamaji 3 – Ban-cho Bldg 3F, 5-24, 3 Ban-cho, Chiyoda-ku, Tokyo, 102-0075, Japan</li><li>WWF Japan, Nihon Seimei, Akabanebashi Bldg, 6F, 3-1-14, Shiba, Minato-ku, Tokyo, 105-0014, Japan; email: communi@wwf.or.jp; web: www.wwf.or.jp/</li></ul>
<ul><li>In 1930, Japan's Agency of Cultural Affairs (part of the Ministry of Education) made a national nature monument to celebrate the cultural tradition of finless porpoise-assisted community fishing in the waters of Takehara Hiroshima, a part of the Seto-naikai.</li><li>Rationale is to commemorate and protect the local cultural tradition of finless porpoise-assisted community fishing. In Japan, national nature monuments are mainly for the adoption of natural environments, ecosystems, and natural phenomena that have educational value and are important for Japanese cultural or social history.</li><li>As the only example of adopting cetacean species in Japan, this MPA should be celebrated yet the area protected is a fractional part of porpoise habitat. Sadly, the porpoise population in the area has dwindled in recent years and the seasonal gatherings that the monument was to protect are now a fading memory. The Agency of Cultural Affairs is charged with protecting the monuments, fixing problems and aiding recovery.</li></ul>	<ul><li>Simard, 1995</li><li>Contact: The Nature Conservation Society of Japan (NACS-J), Yamaji 3 – Ban-cho Bldg 3F, 5-24, 3 Ban-cho, Chiyoda-ku, Tokyo, 102-0075, Japan</li><li>WWF Japan, Nihon Seimei, Akabanebashi Bldg, 6F, 3-1-14, Shiba, Minato-ku, Tokyo, 105-0014, Japan; email: communi@wwf.or.jp; web: www.wwf.or.jp/</li></ul>
<ul><li>Established 1994, this coastal zapovednik includes marine areas (IUCN Category Ia).</li><li>Marine component is thought to include cetacean habitat; surveys and habitat assessments are required.</li></ul>	See also Tables 5.3, 5.6 and 5.9 for additional Russian MPAs. <ul><li>Contact: Kostomarov Sergey Vladimirovich, Sovetskaya Str, 28B, 90, Sovetskaya Gavan, Khabarovskiy Kray, 682880 Russia; email: botche@zapoved.sovgav.ru</li></ul>

Table 5.20 *continued*

Name of MPA or sanctuary, location and size	Cetacean and other notable species
(8) Komandor Islands Biosphere Reserve (Zapovednik) • around Komandorskiy (Commander) Islands, 155 mi (250 km) east of central Kamchatka peninsula • total size is 14,084 mi² (36,487 km²), including land areas; marine component is 13,368 mi² (34,633 km²)	• some 21 cetacean species including sperm whale, *Physeter macrocephalus*; orca, *Orcinus orca*; various beaked whales species • also: large colonies of some 300,000 fur seals and sea lions; spotted, harbor and ringed seals; northern elephant seal; sea otters; seabirds
(9) Nalychevo Nature Park and Marine Nature Reserve • Nalychevo, north of Petropavlovsk-Kamchatskiy, southeastern Kamchatka, from the mouth of the Nalycheva River to the Vakhil River • 47.5 mi² (123 km²)	• orca, *Orcinus orca*; others • various pinniped rookeries and seabird colonies
(10) Far Eastern Marine Nature Reserve (Zapovednik) • 37 mi (60 km) south of Vladivostok, Primorskiy Krai, Peter the Great Bay, Sea of Japan • 248 mi² (643 km²) includes land areas; marine area is 243 mi² (630 km²)	• minke whale, *Balaenoptera acutorostrata*; sei whale, *Balaenoptera borealis*; blue whale, *Balaenoptera musculus*; humpback whale, *Megaptera novaeangliae*; rare: North Pacific right whale, *Eubalaena japonica*; gray whale, *Eschrictius robustus* (w Pacific population); sperm whale, *Physeter macrocephalus*; Baird's beaked whale, *Berardius bairdii*; false killer whale, *Pseudorca crassidens*; orca, *Orcinus orca*; Dall's porpoise, *Phocoenoides dalli*
(11) Dzhugdzhurskiy Nature Reserve (Zapovednik) • Khabarovskiy, on the Sea of Okhotsk • 3319 mi² (8600 km²) includes land areas; marine area is 207 mi² (537 km²)	• Jul–Sept: orca, *Orcinus orca*; transient, Jun–Jul: beluga, *Delphinapterus leucas*; rare, Jun–Sept: fin whale, *Balaenoptera physalus*; sei whale, *Balaenoptera borealis*; humpback whale, *Megaptera novaeangliae*; North Pacific right whale, *Eubalaena japonica*
(12) Koryakskiy Nature Reserve (Zapovednik) • Koryakskiy, northeastern Kamchatka peninsula • 1263 mi² (3272 km²), includes land areas; marine area is 320 mi² (830 km²)	• probable cetacean habitat

Notes and rationale	For more information
• Designated 1993 to protect Komandorskiy Islands and the populations of birds and marine mammals. • Zapovednik (IUCN Category Ia), declared a biosphere reserve in 2003. • Protected marine zone extends for some 30 mi (50 km) around Komandorskiy Islands.	• Mamaev, 2002; Mironova et al, 2002 • Contact: Nikolay N Pavlov, Komandorskiy Zapoveduik, 29/1, Karla Marska St, 215, Petropavlovsk-Kamchatskiy, 683031 Russia; email: gpz_komandorskiy@mail.iks.ru
• Designated 2002 as an 'area of special protection adjacent to Nalychevo Nature Park'; IUCN Category I 'no-take' zone. • Rationale is mainly to protect marine mammals and seabird colonies. • Site which stretches 12 mi (20 km) along the coast will be administered by the regional fishing authority. • Cetacean surveys and habitat assessments required to determine cetacean habitat use.	• Contact: WWF Russian Programme Office; web: www.wwf.ru
• Designated in 1978 to protect marine shelf ecosystems and bird colonies. • Marine and coastal zapovednik which includes marine areas (IUCN Category Ia). • Cetacean surveys and habitat assessments required to determine cetacean habitat use.	• Newell and Wilson, 1996 • Contact: Kolmakov Peter Vasilyevich, Palchevskogo Str, Vladivostok, 690041 Russia; email: inmarbio@mail.primorye.ru
• Established 1990, this coastal zapovednik includes a relatively small marine area (IUCN Category Ia). • Marine component includes some cetacean habitat during the 3–4 months that the area is ice-free. • Cetacean observations are only incidental and there has been no dedicated cetacean work here. Surveys and habitat assessments are needed.	• Contact: Khrenova Galina Nikolaevna, Dzhugdzhurskiy Zapovednik, 30 let Pobedy Str, 2, Ajan Village, Ajano-Mayskiy Region, Khabarovskiy obl, 682571 Russia; email: nature@ajn.kht.ru or galicat@ngs.ru
• Established 1995, this coastal zapovednik is 25 per cent marine (IUCN Category Ia). • Marine component thought to include cetacean habitat; surveys and habitat assessments required.	• Contact: Bakushin Alexander Alexeevich, Naberezhnaya Str 8, Tilichiki village, Olyutorskiy region, Koryakskiy obl, 684800 Russia; email: koryak@mail.iks.ru

Table 5.20 *continued*

Name of MPA or sanctuary, location and size	Cetacean and other notable species
(13) Kronotskiy Biosphere Reserve (Zapovednik) • southern border is 62 mi (100 km) north of Petropavlovsk-Kamchatskiy, Kronotskiy Zaliv, in eastern central Kamchatka • 4409 mi² (11,421 km²) includes land areas; marine area is 521 mi² (1350 km²) extending 3 nm (5.5 km) out from the coast	• common or resident: orca, *Orcinus orca*; minke whale, *Balaenoptera acutorostrata*; gray whale, *Eschrictius robustus* (w Pacific population); Dall's porpoise, *Phocoenoides dalli*; rare: humpback whale, *Megaptera novaeangliae*; blue whale, *Balaenoptera musculus*; sei whale, *Balaenoptera borealis*; sperm whale, *Physeter macrocephalus*; Cuvier's beaked whale, *Ziphius cavirostris*; Baird's beaked whale, *Berardius bairdii*; harbor porpoise, *Phocoena phocoena*; others • also: sea otter; largha and common seals
(14) South Kamchatka Sanctuary • southern border is 62 mi (100 km) from Petropavlovsk-Kamchatskiy, Kronotskiy Zaliv, on eastern central Kamchatka • 869 mi² (2250 km²), extending along the coast for some 112 mi (180 km) from 1–3 nm (2–5.5 km) out from the coast	• common or resident: orca, *Orcinus orca*; minke whale, *Balaenoptera acutorostrata*; gray whale, *Eschrictius robustus* (w Pacific population); Dall's porpoise, *Phocoenoides dalli*; rare: humpback whale, *Megaptera novaeangliae*; blue whale, *Balaenoptera musculus*; sei whale, *Balaenoptera borealis*; sperm whale, *Physeter macrocephalus*; Cuvier's beaked whale, *Ziphius cavirostris*; Baird's beaked whale, *Berardius bairdii*; harbor porpoise, *Phocoena phocoena*; others • also: sea otter; largha and common seals
(15) Kurilskiy Nature Reserve (Zapovednik) • northern and southern parts of Kunashir Island, plus Demida and Oskolki islands, southern Kuril Islands (north of Japan) • 252 mi² (654 km²) is the size of land areas; MPA size is unknown; protection of coastal waters extends for 1 nm (2 km) around Kunashir and Oskolki islands	• common: minke whale, *Balaenoptera acutorostrata*; Dall's porpoise, *Phocoenoides dalli*; harbor porpoise, *Phocoena phocoena*; transient (resident offshore outside zapovednik): orca, *Orcinus orca*; sperm whale, *Physeter macrocephalus*; Baird's beaked whale, *Berardius bairdii*; Pacific white-sided dolphin, *Lagenorhynchus obliquidens*; others • also: Steller sea lion and other pinniped rookeries
(16) Maliy Kurils Wildlife Refuge (Zakaznik) • the 'Little Kurils', Kuril Islands (north of Japan) • 174 mi² (450 km²) total, with a 97 mi² (252 km²) marine area	• minke whale, *Balaenoptera acutorostrata*; sperm whale, *Physeter macrocephalus*; orca, *Orcinus orca*; Baird's beaked whale, *Berardius bairdii*; Pacific white-sided dolphin, *Lagenorhynchus obliquidens*; Dall's porpoise, *Phocoenoides dalli* • also: migratory waterfowl
(17) Lazovskiy Nature Reserve (Zapovednik) • Primorskiy Krai, Sea of Japan • total is 467 mi² (1210 km²) includes 22 mi (36 km) of marine coast and 2 islands	• common: orca, *Orcinus orca*; false killer whale, *Pseudorca crassidens*; sporadic: blue whale, *Balaenoptera borealis*; sperm whale, *Physeter macrocephalus* • also: Amur tiger and spotted deer

Notes and rationale	For more information
• Set up in 1934 but later dissolved and re-established in 1969, Kronotskiy has 12 active volcanoes and the famous Valley of the Geysers. • This coastal zapovednik includes substantial marine areas (IUCN Category Ia) – one of the largest marine reserves in Russia. • Cetacean observations are made as part of the reserve's activities, with most cetaceans observed in summer months; more research would be required to determine cetacean habitat use, particularly in winter.	• Nikanorov, 2000 • Contact: Alexander P Nikanorov, Ryabikova Str 48, Elizovo town, Kamchatskaya obl, 684000 Russia; email: zapoved@ elrus.kamchatka.su; web: www.wild-russia.org/ bioregion14/14-kronotsky/ 14_kro.htm
• South Kamchatka Sanctuary is a sub-section of Kronotskiy Biopshere Reserve, but the area of the sanctuary is not included in the boundaries of the reserve as listed above. • Coastal sanctuary (IUCN Category Ia). • Cetacean observations are made as part of the reserve's activities, with most cetaceans observed in summer months; more research would be required to determine cetacean habitat use, particularly in winter.	• Burdin et al, 2001 • Contact: Alexander P Nikanorov, Ryabikova Str 48, Elizovo town, Kamchatskaya obl, 684000 Russia; email: zapoved@ elrus.kamchatka.su; web: www.wild-russia.org/ bioregion14/14-kronotsky/ 14_kro.htm
• Established 1984 as a coastal zapovednik; extended to include marine waters in 1995 (IUCN Category Ia). • Since late 1990s, Russian–Japanese multidisciplinary expeditions (led by H Kato) have reported on cetacean sightings, as did two sea lion expeditions (led by V Burkanov). Despite these substantial surveys, more detailed habitat assessments are required to determine precise cetacean habitat use and needs; at present there is a pinniped specialist who is knowledgable about cetaceans, but there is no cetacean specialist on staff. • In recent years, poaching by Kuril islanders has been reported to be severe; also a gold mine excavation in the buffer zone of the reserve, may present various problems.	• Newell and Wilson, 1996 • Contact: Nevedomskaya Irina Alexandrova and Grigor'ev Evgeniy Mikhaylovich, Reserve 'Kurilskiy', Zarechnaya 5, Yuzhno-Kurilsk, Kunashir, Sakhalinskaya obl, 694500 Russia
• Managed by Kurilskiy Zapovednik, this zakaznik, or federal biological reservation, created in 1983, protects migratory waterfowl habitat and marine mammals including cetaceans. • Mainly a marine zakaznik with some land areas (IUCN Category IV).	• Contact: Nevedomskaya Irina Alexandrova and Grigor'ev Evgeniy Mikhaylovich, Reserve 'Kurilskiy', Zarechnaya 5, Yuzhno-Kurilsk, Kunashir, Sakhalinskaya obl, 694500 Russia; email: kurilsky@ostrov.sakhalin.ru
• Established in 1935 as a branch of Sikhote-Alinskiy Zapovednik; re-established on its own in 1957. • Coastal zapovednik, mainly land-based, which includes small marine area (IUCN Category Ia) and buffer zone. • Cetacean records show orcas common to the marine zone, especially in Proselochnaja Bay, Petrova Bay, 9–11 mi (15–17 km) north of Preobrazenie (42°52'N, 133°53'E); in Nov 2003, two blues were seen for more than an hour in the reserve near the coast.	• Contact: Voloshina Inna, Tsentralnaya Str, 56, Lazo village, Lazovskiy region, Primorskiy obl, 692890 Russia: email: lazovzap@mail.primorye.ru; voloshina@mail.primorye.ru

Table 5.20 *continued*

Name of MPA or sanctuary, location and size	Cetacean and other notable species
(18) Sikhote-Alinskiy Biosphere Reserve (Zapovednik) • central Sikhote-Alin mountains, 280 mi (450 km) north of Vladivostok, Primorskiy Krai, Sea of Japan • 1495 mi² (3873 km²) terrestrial core area with 241.4 mi² (625.5 km²) buffer zone; marine core area is 11 mi² (29 km²) with a 20 mi² (51 km²) buffer zone	• common: orca, *Orcinus orca*; Dall's porpoise, *Phocoenoides dalli*; gray whale, *Eschrictius robustus* (w Pacific population); sporadic: fin whale, *Balaenoptera physalus*; sei whale, *Balaenoptera borealis*; sperm whale, *Physeter macrocephalus*; false killer whale, *Pseudorca crassidens*; Baird's beaked whale, *Berardius bairdii* • also: Amur tiger and spotted deer
(19) Magadanskiy Nature Reserve (Zapovednik) • north and east of Magadan (city), Magadan Oblast, Sea of Okhotsk • total size is 3412 mi² (8838 km²) but marine area is only 147 mi² (381 km²), extending only 1 nm (2 km) from the coast of the Kony and P'yagina peninsulas and Yamsk Islands	• transient: orca, *Orcinus orca*; rare or offshore, outside of reserve: gray whale, *Eschrictius robustus* (w Pacific population); minke whale, *Balaenoptera acutorostrata*; Dall's porpoise, *Phocoenoides dalli* • also: Steller sea lion and Steller's sea eagles
(20) Poronayskiy Nature Reserve (Zapovednik) • eastern central Sakhalin, Terpeniye Peninsula, Sea of Okhotsk • total size is 219 mi² (567 km²), including mainly land areas	• orca, *Orcinus orca*; other cetaceans (some indication in Vladimirov, 2002) • also: Sakhalin musk deer, Steller's sea eagle
(21) Vostok Bay National Comprehensive Marine Sanctuary • Vostok Bay, Primorye • 7 mi² (18 km²) marine area	• probable cetacean habitat
(22) Northeast Sakhalin Whale Wildlife Refuge (Zakaznik), *proposed for expansion* • located off northeast Sakhalin, between the towns of Okha and Chaivo Bay, up to 24 nm (44.4 km) offshore, and in the Piltun Lagoon off northeast Sakhalin • final size undetermined; scientists and NGOs have recommended core protection of 5.4–12 nm (10–22.2 km) from shore, including the Piltun Lagoon, with a buffer zone of 21.6–24 nm (40–44.4 km), up to 3000 mi² (7770 km²) in all	• seasonally resident: gray whale, *Eschrictius robustus* (w Pacific population: critically endangered); sporadic: orca, *Orcinus orca* • also: the benthic food community used by gray whales

Notes and rationale	For more information
• Established in 1935; in 1997 a marine core area with a buffer zone was added. • Biosphere reserve as well as a zapovednik (IUCN Category Ia). • Cetacean records from the zapovednik reveal that gray whales migrate through the marine core area of the reserve. Some 18 whales were recorded in one month (Oct) about 0.9 mi (1.5 km) from the coast, near Terney Bay.	• Contact: Astafyev Anatoliy Alexeevich, Partizanskaya Str, 46, Terney village, Primorskiy obl, 692150 Russia; email: sixote@vld.global-one.ru • Voloshina Inna; email: voloshina@mail.primorye.ru
• Established 1982; coastal zapovednik includes small marine areas (IUCN Category Ia). • No cetacean studies have been conducted in the reserve but incidental sightings are recorded; cetacean surveys and habitat assessments would be required to determine cetacean habitat use of 'transient' orcas. • Comprised of four unconnected sections, two of which are inland. • Yamsk Islands have some of the Russian Far East's largest seabird colonies.	• Contact: Ivanov Vladimir Vladimirovich, Magadanskiy Zapovednik, Koltsevaya Str, 17, Magadan, Magadanskaya obl, 685000 Russia; email: zapoved@ online.magadan.su
• Established 1988 to protect conifer forest; land-based zapovednik which includes some minimal marine areas (IUCN Category Ia). • Marine component may include cetacean habitat; surveys and habitat assessments required; southern Sakhalin Island cetacean cruise by Vladimirov (2002) revealed 10 species of cetaceans with highest cetacean density in La Perouse Strait, northern and open-water parts of Aniva Bay and near Kril'yon and Aniva Capes; this may suggest productive expansion of MPAs around central and southern Sakhalin.	• Vladimirov, 2002 • Contact: Dushin Andrey Alexandrovich, Naberezhnaya Str, 15, Sakhalinskaya, Poronaysk town, Sakhalinskaya obl, 694220 Russia; email: zapovednik@sakhalin.ru
• Small area set aside for research, partly mariculture. • Marine component thought to include cetacean habitat; surveys and habitat assessments required.	• More information on the web at www.fegi.ru/ prim/range/zak-vost.htm
• In Feb 2003, the head of the Russian Natural Resources Ministry's Department for Highly Protected Natural Areas and Preserving Biodiversity announced that the first Russian national marine wildlife reserve would be established on the Sakhalin Shelf in 2004 specifically to protect the feeding habitat of the last known population of some 100 western Pacific gray whales. • Concerns about international oil company development include underwater noise from seismic surveys, drilling and production rigs, the possibility of oil spills and the traffic associated with industry vessels. The reserve would attempt to keep industry and the damaging effects of seismic work and traffic some distance from the whales, but Russian–American scientists and Sakhalin Environment Watch contend that the announced reserve is not large enough and does not follow key scientific recommendations about management and enforcement. • As it stands, the reserve proposal may simply help get oil and gas developers 'off the hook' while doing little to help the whales with meaningful protection.	• Weller et al, 1999, 2001 • Contact: Alexander M Burdin, Kamchatka Institute of Ecology and Nature Management, Petropavlovsk-Kamchatsky, 683024 Russia; email: graywhal@ mail.kamchatka.ru • David Weller; email: Dave.Weller@noaa.gov • Sakhalin Environment Watch, A Makarova St 27, Uzhno-Sakhalinsk, 693020, Russia; email: watch@dsc.ru

Table 5.20 *continued*

Name of MPA or sanctuary, location and size	Cetacean and other notable species
continued from pp392–393 **Northeast Sakhalin Whale Wildlife Refuge**	
**(23) Shantar Archipelago National Park (Shantarskie Ostrova), *proposed* • Shantar Archipelago, Khabarovsk Krai, southwest Sea of Okhotsk • size undetermined, but see notes at right	• common, May–Oct: bowhead whale, *Balaena mysticetus*; beluga, *Delphinapterus leucas*; sporadic: gray whale, *Eschrictius robustus* (w Pacific population) • also: walruses, seal rookeries, brown bear, wolf, lynx, many others
Various Russian Far East MPAs	• orca, *Orcinus orca*; gray whale, *Eschrictius robustus*; humpback whale, *Megaptera novaeangliae*; minke whale, *Balaenoptera acutorostrata*; Dall's porpoise, *Phocoenoides dalli*; others

Notes and rationale	For more information
• Researchers and NGOs propose increasing the core protected area and buffer zones, as well as moving the oil platform and the offshore–onshore pipeline farther away from the primary gray whale feeding area. • The endangered status of this population dictates the highest level of protection in this reserve. The reserve should specify and protect areas of critical habitat, and strive to eliminate impacts of underwater noise, oil and chemical contamination, and any potential effects on the feeding habitat and benthic food communities that these whales depend on. It is particularly important that exclusion zones specific to human activities and a comprehensive management plan with robust compliance provisions are developed for this MPA.	see page 393
• This former 18th–19th century whaling centre was called a biodiversity hot spot and proposed for protection (Newell and Wilson, 1996) for land and marine species including endangered populations of bowhead whales, as well as land mammals and birds; original proposal was for a 1160 mi² (3000 km²) island zapovednik surrounded by a 3860 mi² (10,000 km²) marine component (IUCN Category Ia); a limited area of the land is already protected in reserves; current proposal is for a national park to be set aside in 2010. • Boundaries may need to be adjusted to include the important bowhead whale habitat areas and possible use by critically endangered gray whales. • There was a threat from disturbance from electric power station project in the Tungur Gulf but it has been cancelled for now; area is little visited, but MPA would protect against future impacts.	• Brownell et al, 1997; Newell and Wilson, 1996; Stepanitsky, 2003; Vladimirov, 2000 • Contact: Alexander M Burdin, Kamchatka Institute of Ecology and Nature Management; email: graywhal@ mail.kamchatka.ru • Dept of Protected Areas and Biodiversity Conservation, Russian Ministry of Natural Resources; email: learn@nm.ru
• Some ten large new areas in the Russian Far East (including Anadyrskiy Zaliv, the surrounding waters of Karaginskiy Island and nearly the entire vast coastal waters of Chukotski Poluostrov) have been suggested as 'zones of marine mammals protection' or as 'marine protected areas' by WWF and other groups (see map published in *Arctic Bulletin*, no 4, 2003, p24). • Marine component would certainly include cetacean habitat; surveys and habitat assessments required.	• Contact: WWF Russian Programme Office; web: www.wwf.ru

MARINE REGION 17: SOUTHEAST PACIFIC

After spending the summer feeding around the Antarctic, humpback whales from the Southeast Pacific stock travel the entire length of this marine region, ranging north along the west coast of South America some 5176 miles (8334 km) and crossing the Equator to the waters off Colombia and Panamá. This is the longest migration of any whale.

This region also has southern right whales off Chile, and populations of sperm whales throughout the region, both offshore and close to shore. As well, there are blue, fin, sei, Bryde's and both Antarctic minke and (northern) minke whales in the region.

Rare cetaceans in this region include several small cetaceans with limited ranges. The Chilean dolphin is endemic. Two other species are found only in two regions – this region plus the South Atlantic Marine Region off eastern South America: Peale's dolphin and Burmeister's porpoise. The Burmeister's porpoise is the most common cetacean species to be found stranded or caught in nets along the Chilean coast. Three more species are found mainly in these two regions with some distribution in the adjacent Antarctic and other southern hemisphere regions: hourglass and Commerson's dolphins, and the spectacled porpoise.

This region has also produced findings of new cetaceans. In the 1990s, a new species of beaked whale was described from this region, together with new specimens of a rare beaked whale, electrifying whale researchers everywhere and causing them to wonder how many more cetacean species might yet be undescribed (eg, Reyes et al, 1991, 1995; van Helden et al, 2002). The pygmy beaked whale and the spade-toothed whale were both thought to be found only in the Southeast Pacific Marine Region until strandings turned up in the Australian–New Zealand Marine Region and (for the pygmy beaked whale only) in the southern part of the Northeast Pacific Marine Region.

In addition to the marine cetaceans, the rivers east of the Andes, in the countries of Peru, Ecuador and Colombia, have Amazon River dolphins and tucuxi, some of them in protected areas.

This region has one of the notable national parks of the world, the Galápagos Islands, which has been extended to surrounding marine waters. The Galápagos MPA is designated as both a 'Marine Resources Reserve' and a 'Whale Sanctuary'. It effectively forms the largest MPA in the region and one of the largest in the world with an area of 61,000 mi^2 (158,000 km^2). In addition, both Ecuador and Colombia have MPAs that include some coverage of humpback whale mating and calving areas, although the three main areas in Ecuador were designated before humpback whales were studied and became well known. Chile is developing various MPAs to protect cetaceans and ecosystems on its long coast, although there is some controversy as to the effectiveness of the government proposals, both in terms of ecosystem and cetacean habitat protection.

The Southeast Pacific Marine Region includes the jurisdictions of ten national governments (see Table 5.1 on p89). The region covers the waters along the entire Pacific coast of Central and South America. (Please note that in oceanographic and biogeographical studies, the Southeast Pacific is usually considered distinct from Central America, often referred to as the Eastern Pacific, but we treat both areas together here for consistency with the WCPA division into 18 marine regions that we have adopted.) Therefore, the Southeast Pacific features portions of the Pacific subpolar, temperate, subtropical and tropical waters, the latter two on both sides of the Equator. Notable offshore islands include the Galápagos Archipelago, Cocos Island and the Juan Fernández Archipelago. The Southeast Pacific Marine Region has two large marine ecosystems (LMEs): the Humboldt Current and the Pacific Central-American Coastal.

The surface oceanography of the northern hemisphere part of the region is determined by the warm North Equatorial Counter Current which enters the region at up to 10°N and splits off Costa Rica, flowing north and south along the coast and turning into a cyclonic eddy off Panamá and Colombia and an anti-cyclonic eddy off Nicaragua.

From the south, the cold, nutrient-rich waters of the Antarctic Circumpolar Current flow toward the southern tip of South America from the west, branching to the north and south. The northern section splits into the coastal Humboldt Current and the Peru Oceanic Current, both of which are separated by the warm, southward-flowing Peru-Chile Counter Current. The key productive current is the Humboldt Current, which is cold and rich in nutrients and has numerous gyres that give rise to local countercurrents and upwellings. The Humboldt Current supports some of the most productive fisheries in the world off Peru and Chile. Flowing north along the coast, when the Humboldt Current reaches about 6°S, it meets and mixes with warm, southward flowing currents as it veers west, turning into the South Equatorial Current.

The most important alteration in the oceanography of this region comes from the periodic El Niño event. When this occurs, the warm waters from the Equator dominate the Humboldt Current causing seawater temperature rises of 2–3° C and sea level rises of up to 1.6 ft (50 cm), with nutrient levels greatly reduced in the surface waters. El Niño causes declines in marine life dependent on these key productive areas of the region, and it is devastating to many local and commercial pelagic fisheries.

Coral reefs in the region are limited to Central America plus Colombia and are not nearly so extensive or diverse as on the Atlantic and Caribbean side of South and Central America. Mangroves extend a little further south to the border of Ecuador and Peru.

The most dominant factor for offshore cetacean presence is the occurrence of upwellings that attract feeding baleen whales, as well as various toothed whales and dolphins. Besides the Humboldt Current, there are large upwellings in the Gulf of Papagayo, the Gulf of Panamá and seasonal upwellings off the coast of Chile. The Galápagos upwelling is produced when the west underwater Cromwell Current meets the westernmost islands, Fernandina and Isabela; this most productive area of the Galápagos supports a large number of cetaceans, especially sperm whales and various baleen whales. The Peru-Chile Trench which parallels the coast at roughly 100 mi (160 km) from land, just off the continental shelf, plunges up to nearly 5 miles (8000 m) deep. In these deep waters, sperm and beaked whales, as well as certain squid-loving pelagic dolphins, can find abundant food.

The South American countries which form most of the region have agreed to a UNEP regional seas programme which includes a strong marine and protected area focus. The Convention for the Protection of the Marine Environment and Coastal Areas of the South-East Pacific (CPPS) has agreed to the Action Plan for Protection of the Marine Environment and Coastal Areas of the Southeast Pacific (1981), which includes a protocol for the conservation and administration of the coastal and marine protected areas of the region, as well as to the Action Plan for the Conservation of Marine Mammals in the Southeast Pacific (PNUMA, 1992). In the northern part of the region, the countries of Central America, plus México, have formed a separate association, signing the UNEP Convention for Cooperation in the Protection and Sustainable Development of the Marine and Coastal Environment of the Northeast Pacific (Antigua Convention).

In 1995, there was a total of 18 MPAs of all kinds in this marine region (Hurtado, 1995). The region is divided into six biogeographic zones in the coastal realm, three of which were represented by at least one MPA and the rest of which have no representation. As of 2004, according to Table 5.21 prepared for this book, there are 17 existing and 4 proposed MPAs which feature cetacean habitat. Three of the existing MPAs are proposed for expansion.

There is one national cetacean sanctuary here: in the waters of Ecuador. The region also includes a portion of a proposed international cetacean sanctuary for the South Pacific, initiated through the IWC, which has yet to be approved. It would serve as a sanctuary from whaling and could be a stepping stone here towards greater protection and recognition of cetacean habitat needs.

In 2000, marine mammal specialists at the VII Intergovernmental Meeting of the Action Plan reviewed the available scientific information to support the special declaration of a 'whale corridor' to protect large whales during the breeding migration along the Southeast Pacific coast (CPPS, 2000). The meeting, coordinated by the Southeast Pacific Action Plan office, did not find enough information to recommend the declaration but concluded that country members should promote studies in that direction.

The IUCN 2002–2010 Conservation Action Plan for the World's Cetaceans recommends a number of research and education initiatives for this region (Reeves et al, 2003):

- to monitor interactions between fisheries and cetaceans in Chile;
- to assess illegal use of small cetaceans for crab bait in southern South America (also for Marine Region 9);
- to investigate stock identity of endemic species in South America (also for Marine Region 9);

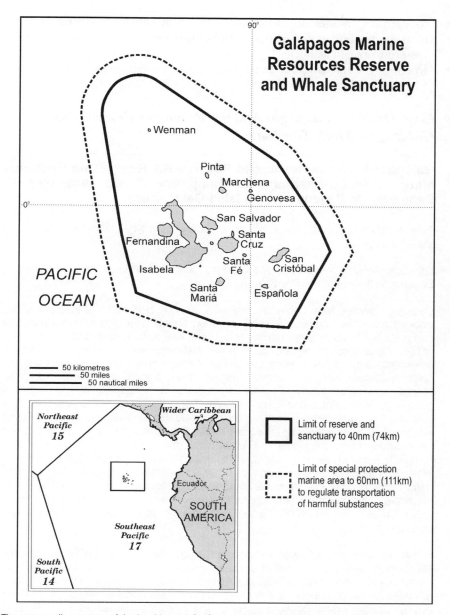

The surrounding waters of the land-based Galápagos National Park are protected in a marine resources reserve and whale sanctuary to the limits of 40 nautical miles (74 km) around the external borders of these islands owned by Ecuador. See Case Study 9.

Figure 5.25 *Map of the Galápagos Marine Resources Reserve and Whale Sanctuary*

- to monitor incidental and direct catches of small cetaceans in Peru;
- to assess the impacts of artisanal gill net fisheries on small cetaceans in the eastern tropical Pacific; and
- to conduct cetacean abundance estimation workshops in Latin America (also for Marine Regions 7 and 9).

Case Study 9: Galápagos Marine Resources Reserve and Galápagos Whale Sanctuary

Galápagos Marine Resources Reserve (La Reserva de Recursos Marinos de Galápagos) and Galápagos Whale Sanctuary (El Santuario de Ballenas en las Islas Galápagos)

Type: Existing national marine resources reserve and whale sanctuary within the same boundaries.

Location: Around the Galápagos Islands, located 600 miles (975 km) west of Ecuador, in the equatorial Pacific.

Cetacean species: Most common cetaceans seen are bottlenose, striped and short-beaked common dolphins, as well as short-finned pilot and sperm whales. A complete list is as follows: humpback whale, *Megaptera novaeangliae*; Bryde's whale, *Balaenoptera brydei*; sei whale, *Balaenoptera borealis*; blue whale, *Balaenoptera musculus*; bottlenose dolphin, *Tursiops truncatus*; pantropical spotted dolphin, *Stenella attenuata*; spinner dolphin, *Stenella longirostris*; striped dolphin, *Stenella coeruleoalba*; short-beaked common dolphin, *Delphinus delphis*; Fraser's dolphin, *Lagenodelphis hosei*; rough-toothed dolphin, *Steno bredanensis*; Risso's dolphin, *Grampus griseus*; melon-headed whale, *Peponocephala electra*; pygmy killer whale, *Feresa attenuata*; false killer whale, *Pseudorca crassidens*; orca, *Orcinus orca*; short-finned pilot whale, *Globicephala macrorhynchus*; beaked whales (possibly Hector's beaked whale, *Mesoplodon hectori*; ginkgo-toothed beaked whale, *Mesoplodon ginkgodens*; Blainville's beaked whale, *Mesoplodon densirostris*; pygmy beaked whale, *Mesoplodon peruvianus)*; sperm whale, *Physeter macrocephalus*; pygmy sperm whale, *Kogia breviceps*; dwarf sperm whale, *Kogia sima*; Cuvier's beaked whale, *Ziphius cavirostris* (Merlen, 1995; confirmed by Félix, pers comm, 2003).

Additional species and other features: Galápagos sea lion, *Zalophus wollebaeki*; Galápagos fur-seal, *Arctocephalus galapagoensis*; marine iguana, *Amblyrhynchus cristatus*. Also, there are the Galápagos penguin, waved albatross, Hawaiian (dark-rumped) petrel, Audubon's shearwater, white-vented (Elliot's) petrel, blue-footed booby, masked (white) booby and many other seabirds. The adjoining land-based national park has wildlife on the 19 main Galápagos Islands which is unique and world famous. Land birds include the various *Camarhynchus* finches and *Geospiza* ground finches; Galápagos tortoise, *Geochelone elephantopus*; Galápagos land iguana, *Conolophus subcristatus*; Barrington land iguana, *Conolophus pallidus*; and lava lizards, *Tropidurus* sp.

Size of designated protected area: Approximately 61,000 square miles (158,000 km²). Water area only extends from nearshore to pelagic between the 19 islands and 40 nautical miles (74 km) around the external borders of the islands.

Rationale: The islands, which are protected by the separate Galápagos National Park, are a natural laboratory for evolution and have been studied by evolutionary biologists dating back to Charles Darwin. It is fitting that the marine component of these islands be protected at a similar level. The waters around the Galápagos are a cetacean mating and breeding area as well as an area frequented by migrating cetaceans, and a feeding ground for dolphins and other mainly smaller whales. According to Hurtado (1995), the justification for conservation here 'includes ecological, economic, scientific, educational and political considerations'.

In 1959, all uninhabited land areas of the 19 Galápagos islands were protected as part of Ecuador's first national park. By 1970, the islands were opened to organized but controlled tourism and quickly became one of the first international ecotourism destinations. The land-based park achieved UN World Heritage status in 1979. A marine reserve, to include the waters for 15 nm (21 km) around the islands and covering 27,000 square miles (70,000 km²), was first proposed for marine protection in 1986.

In 1987, a draft zoning plan for the Galápagos Marine Resources Reserve proposed four zone types: (1) General Use Zone for sustainable use of the reserve; (2) Artisanal and Recreational Fishing Zones for the benefit of residents; (3) National Marine Park Zones for human activities where natural resources are neither damaged nor removed; and (4) Strict Nature Reserves where human access is not permitted. In 1992, the definitive version of this plan was approved and published as Government Decree No 3573. In 1997 this was revised by the National Institute of Forests and Natural Protected Areas (INEFAN) and staff at the Charles Darwin scientific base, in conformity with the terms of the Agreement for the Creation of the Biological Reserve. The new status of the reserve provides the Galápagos National Park Service legal authority to patrol the marine areas against illegal fishing.

In May 1990, Decree No 196, from the Ministerio de Industrias, Comercio, Integración y Pesca, declared all of Ecuador's waters protected for whales in a 'refugio natural' and 'prohibited all activity which goes against the life of these marine mammals'. As part of this law, a special whale sanctuary was created within the waters of the Galápagos Marine Resources Reserve (La Reserva de Recursos Marinos de Galápagos). The agreement was not very specific about what activities would be banned including whaling itself, although a prohibition was presumed. Only the whales were supposedly included in the whale sanctuary. In 2000, another decree (No 5), was issued that specifically prohibited whaling in Ecuador. Still, the status of dolphins needs to be clarified and confirmed to be included.

The whale watching around the Galápagos is minimal compared to coastal Ecuador. During a typical cruising tour, most visitors see various dolphin species as they move from island to island. Farther offshore from the islands are sperm whales and Bryde's whales, present year-round, but only cetacean-oriented trips go in search of them. Cetacean guidelines have been suggested for these waters, but the current relatively low level of effort does not appear to present a problem.

According to Hurtado (1995), management and administration of the Galápagos Marine Resources Reserve and Whale Sanctuary 'reflect the complex institutional situation in the management of marine and coastal resources. The management of the Marine Resources Reserve is the responsibility of a commission that represents several government bodies, while the Whale Sanctuary is established under fisheries laws.'

Researcher Fernando Félix from Fundación Ecuatoriana para el Estudio de Mamíferos Marinos (FEMM) opposed the provision of Decree No 196 to award the additional whale sanctuary and whale natural refuge designations to the existing Galápagos Marine Resources Reserve 'because at the same time two management categories about the same matter were created, one containing the other one. Of course this leads to problems when it comes to assign responsibilities for their control. We always had the idea that the Galápagos sanctuary was created to gain international image and not because a better protection for whales could be achieved. Also, Ecuador itself has never been a whaling nation. We have asked several times for a more precise definition about what is a whale (in Spanish the term "ballena" is more confusing than the English term "whale") and we have suggested to use in laws the term "cetacean", in an effort to include at least the small cetaceans in the regulation because they are the ones running great risk. Ecuador's [cetaceans have] a high rate of mortality in artisanal gillnets' (Félix and Samaniego, 1994; Samaniego and Félix, 1994).

In the mid-1990s, biologist Godfrey Merlen and other researchers and conservation organizations recommended that the reserve be enhanced through full protection for marine wildlife and restriction or elimination of commercial fisheries in these waters. Merlen suggested that the reserve be extended from 15 nm to 40 nm (74 km) around the islands. This is similar to what local small-time Galápagos fishermen have wanted in order to protect their interests and encroachment by mainland fishing vessels. Merlen thought it would take a focused campaign to stop the introduction of pelagic gill netting and longlining into Galápagos waters. Merlen and the National Parks also proposed that the protected area should be renamed a 'biological reserve' with a complete ban on industrial fishing, seining and longlining. Further restrictions to certain areas for local fishermen would be helpful, and it would be necessary for the area to be patrolled regularly by the National Parks Service. It is essential to monitor and have registered all boat movements entering and leaving the islands.

The main industries operating in or near the area and potential conflicts include shipping (eg, oil tankers), commercial fishing and tourism. The artisanal longline fisheries have been moving steadily more offshore and closer to the Galápagos in recent years as the fishing has become poor close to the mainland. They have found that various sea mounts just outside the protected area of the Galápagos are very productive for tuna. This intensive fishing could have a big impact on the Galápagos marine ecology without sufficient regulation and enforcement.

These and other matters have turned the conservation of the Galápagos into a worldwide concern in recent years. In April 1997, after the World Heritage Committee threatened to reclassify the islands as a World Heritage Site in Danger, Ecuador's president issued an emergency decree to try to eliminate illegal and non-artisanal fishing and to stop pollution and the introduction of non-native species all of which, along with human population increase, have been producing severe environmental impacts. The decree also required Ecuador's congress to draft a Special Law for the Galápagos, providing a clear legal framework for the management of the islands. A moratorium has been placed until the year 2005 on the authorization of new permits for cruise ships. In 1998, as part of the Year of the Ocean, Ecuador's government passed a new Special Law to strengthen the Galápagos Marine Reserve, extending the boundaries to 40 nm or 46 mi (74 km) offshore and outlawing industrial fishing in the area. This has gone some way toward the enhanced protection Merlen and others have asked for.

A management plan had been prepared for the marine reserve but may need to be modified in light of the above recommendations. There is also the problem of enforcement. There has been minimal budget available for government or park boats to patrol the waters of the Galápagos. For many years, Merlen, supported in some years by WDCS, has been the unofficial sanctuary 'warden', patrolling these waters for at least a week per month and reporting illegal fishing, invasive research activities, and collecting cetacean sightings and other data. But much greater monitoring and enforcement efforts are needed. For a time, help with enforcement of the reserve's fishing regulations came from the Sea Shepherd Society, better known for its active anti-whaling campaigns, as they teamed with the Ecuadorian Navy to monitor and arrest fishermen who broke the law. But the arrangement did not work out long term.

In January 2001, the Ecuadorian oil tanker *Jessica* struck a reef half a mile (800 m) off San Cristóbal Island inside the Galápagos Marine Resources Reserve, spilling some 240,000 gallons (875,000 litres) of heavy oil (bunker and diesel) into the sea. As the National Park Service and the Charles Darwin Research Station, aided by local fishermen, struggled to contain the 'major oil spill by Ecuadorian and US standards' (according to then research station director Robert Bensted-Smith), they tried to transport some of the threatened wildlife to unaffected islands. This was an Ecuadorian tanker familiar with the run to the islands, which is, like the rest of the world, dependent on oil. There have been worse spills in other corners of the world before and since, yet the question hangs in the air: how could this be allowed to happen in one of the most precious of all marine reserves? And: how can it be prevented from ever happening again?

In 2003, assessing more than a decade of whale natural refuges, marine resources reserves and whale sanctuaries in Ecuador, Fernando Félix declared that 'no practical measures to mitigate the problems that cetaceans face have been taken in the country other than to adopt ITTC (Inter-American Tropical Tuna Commission) regulations for the Ecuadorian tuna fleet'. In fact, there has not been a single government study of cetaceans in Ecuador. The declarations of whale refuges and sanctuaries 'sound good but don't mean much' and they have only 'masked other problems. They just pretend to show a government worried about the whales, working for their conservation and management, and probably some authorities really believe that, but the actual problems affecting the whales and dolphins – overfishing, bycatch (with thousands of dolphins dying every year as part of fisheries), habitat destruction and pollution in all its forms – remain hidden. I'm afraid that such political statements will continue in Ecuador with different names or forms but avoiding the core of the problem.'

These charges are damaging not only to the goal of good MPA conservation for cetaceans and other species in the region, but particularly in a country that sells itself as a world-class ecotourism destination, and as a regional leader in protection of the natural environment with the Galápagos Islands as its showcase to the world. Much more is expected from and for Ecuador.

In February 2004, the Eastern Tropical Pacific Seascape was agreed between the UN Foundation, Conservation International and the Unesco World Heritage Centre. Funded with US$3.1 million seed money, this ambitious marine conservation initiative links existing MPAs in Costa Rica, Panamá, Colombia and Ecuador, including the Galápagos to create an 814,500 mi^2 (2,110,00 km^2) marine conservation zone (see Table 5.21, p406). The hope is that this will lead to substantial marine conservation benefits for the Galápagos as well as for the region.

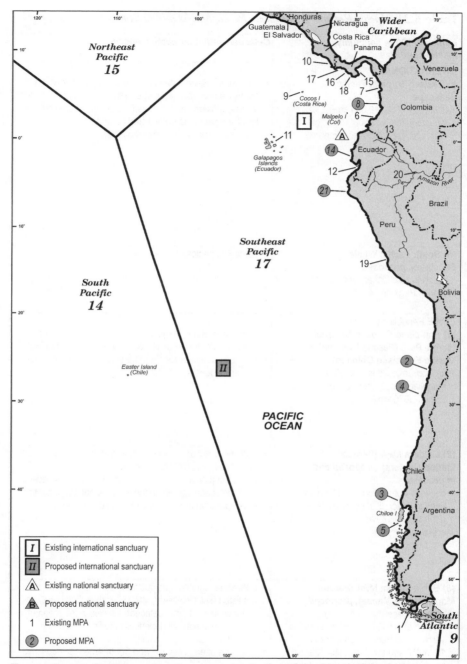

The roman numerals, letters and numbers correspond to the sanctuaries and MPAs listed and described in Table 5.21.

Figure 5.26 *Map of Marine Region 17: Southeast Pacific MPAs and sanctuaries*

Table 5.21 *Marine Region 17: Southeast Pacific MPAs and sanctuaries*

Name of MPA or sanctuary, location and size	Cetacean and other notable species
INTERNATIONAL **(I) Eastern Tropical Pacific Seascape** • 814,500 mi² (2,110,000 km²) • located in the waters of Colombia, Costa Rica, Ecuador and Panamá	• blue whale, *Balaenoptera musculus*; humpback whale, *Megaptera novaeangliae*; sperm whale, *Physeter macrocephalus*; many others (see cetacean species lists for most of the MPAs listed at right) • also: leatherback turtle, many others
(II) South Pacific Whale Sanctuary, *proposed* • South Pacific Ocean, spread across Marine Regions 14, 17 and 18	• some 53 species of cetaceans
CHILE República de Chile **(1) Francisco Coloane National Marine Park (Parque Nacional Marino Francisco Coloane)** • around Carlos III Island, Strait of Magellan, far southern Chile • 259 mi² (670 km²)	• humpback whale, *Megaptera novaeangliae*; Antarctic minke whale, *Balaenoptera bonaerensis*; other species • also: southern sea lions and fur seals, rockhopper and macaroni penguins
(2) Caldera MPA (Parque Marino Caldera), *proposed and in process* • between Punta Morro and Copiapó River in region III in northern Chile (27°14S, 70°57'W) • size undetermined	• bottlenose dolphin, *Tursiops truncatus*; other species but not listed by CONAMA; Centre for Marine Mammal Research (CMMR) Leviathan Database includes several other cetacean species in the area but habitat protection will depend on the final size of the protected area
(3) Bahía Mansa MPA (Parque Marino Bahía Mansa), *proposed and in process* • located at 40°40'S, 73°50'W, between Valdivia and Puerto Montt, about 12 mi (18 km) south of Bahía Mansa • size undetermined but located along 18 mi (29 km) of coast	• bottlenose dolphin, *Tursiops truncatus*; other species but not listed by CONAMA; CMMR Leviathan Database includes several other cetacean species in the area but habitat protection will depend on the final size of the protected area • also: sea otters, seabirds and South American sea lion

Notes and rationale	For more information
• Rationale is to link together existing MPAs and adjacent coastal parks to create a substantial marine conservation area as part of a broad conservation initiative. • This initiative is funded through US$3.1 million seed money from the UN Foundation and Conservation International in partnership with the Unesco World Heritage Centre. • An initiative to link together several existing protected areas with extensive marine components: Coiba Island National Park (Panamá), Gorgona National Park and the proposed Malpelo National Park (Colombia), Cocos Island Marine and Terrestrial Conservation Area and Baulas de Guanacaste National Park (Costa Rica), and Galápagos National Park, Marine Resources Reserve and Whale Sanctuary (Ecuador).	• Contact: Conservation International; web: www.conservation.org
• Rationale is to protect large whales from commercial whaling and to stimulate cetacean research and conservation. • Proposed in 1999, the South Pacific Sanctuary was discussed and later turned down at the IWC meetings from 2000–2004. The idea has overwhelming support from South Pacific nations.	• See full account in Marine Region 14, Table 5.18.
• In 2003, the first national marine park was declared with a rationale to conserve marine biodiversity including cetaceans and other marine mammals, seabirds, and marine turtles. • More cetacean surveys and habitat assessments are needed to determine cetacean habitat use, although there are several proposals from researchers, NGOs, universities and a draft proposal of priority sites prepared by the Chilean Environmental Agency (CONAMA). To help fund research and management, local government is investing more than US$1 million.	• Contact: CODEFF (National Committee for Defense of Fauna and Flora); email: biodiversidad@codeff.cl • CONAMA (Chilean Environmental Agency); email: areasmarinas@conama.cl
• This MPA is in process, to be officially declared before 2006; it was selected in part because of its wetland with migratory bird species. • Substantial tourism infrastructure is to be established, with expected investment of US$2.3 million. • Government believes that the bottlenose dolphins here may be Pod R (see entry 4, Los Choros MPA proposal, below), but osteological analysis from stranded animals shows a different ecotype (Sanino, pers comm 2003). More cetacean surveys and habitat assessments are needed to determine habitat use by other cetaceans.	• Contact: CONAMA (Chilean Environmental Agency); email: areasmarinas@conama.cl • Species database from Research Leviathan; web: www.leviathanchile.org
• This MPA is in process, to be officially declared before 2006; it was selected for its high diversity and representativeness of the Valdivian rain forest. • Substantial tourism infrastructure is to be established, with expected investment of US$2.6 million. • More cetacean surveys and habitat assessments are needed to determine cetacean habitat use.	• Contact: CONAMA (Chilean Environmental Agency); email: areasmarinas@conama.cl • Species database from Research Leviathan; web: www.leviathanchile.org

Table 5.21 *continued*

Name of MPA or sanctuary, location and size	Cetacean and other notable species
(4) Humboldt Penguin National Reserve (Reserva Nacional Pingüino de Humboldt), *proposed for expansion as Los Choros MPA* • system of five islands in north central Chile (between III and IV regions) including Chañaral, Damas, Choros and Gaviota islands and Pajaros Key • at present, actual national reserve includes only the terrestrial area of Chañaral, Damas and Choros totalling 3.3 sq mi (8.6 sq km); proposed size of terrestrial and marine expansion is undetermined	• resident: bottlenose dolphin, *Tursiops truncatus*; also, at least transient: Bryde's whale, *Balaenoptera brydei*; blue whale, *Balaenopter musculus*; fin whale, *Balaenoptera physalus*; sperm whale, *Physeter macrocephalus*; false killer whale, *Pseudorca crassidens*; orca, *Orcinus orca*; dusky dolphin, *Lagenorhynchus obscurus*; Cuvier's beaked whale, *Ziphius cavirostris*; pygmy beaked whale, *Mesoplodon peruvianus*; Burmeister's porpoise, *Phocoena spinipinnis*; has 43 per cent of the cetacean diversity recorded for Chile (see www.leviathanchile.org) • also: Humboldt penguins and South American sea lions
(5) Chiloe National Park (Parque Nacional de Chiloe), *proposed for significant expansion to marine waters, especially facing Golfo Corcovado* • Chiloe Island, especially off the south and west coast including Golfo Corcovado and the Guaitecas archipelago (43°20'S, 74°W) • size undetermined	• off north and east coast: several dolphin species including Chilean dolphin, *Cephalorhynchus eutropia*; Peale's dolphin, *Lagenorhynchus australis*; (possibly) Burmeister's porpoise, *Phocoena spinipinnis*; off the south and southwest: blue whale, *Balaenoptera musculus*; orca, *Orcinus orca*; pygmy killer whale, *Feresa attenuata*; various dolphins
COLOMBIA República de Colombia **(6) Isla Gorgona National Natural Park (Parque Nacional Natural Isla Gorgona)** • Isla Gorgona, 19 mi (30 km) off Departamento de Narino, on the Pacific coast • 190 mi² (492 km²) includes land area	• Jun–Nov: humpback whale, *Megaptera novaeangliae*; occasionally: sperm whale, *Physeter macrocephalus* • also: loggerhead and leatherback turtles

Notes and rationale	For more information
• In 1990, Humboldt Penguin National Reserve was created to protect terrestrial Humboldt penguin nesting sites and other bird species. • In 2000, after several studies and a workshop for local fishermen, a proposal from NGO-research group CMMR Leviathan suggested an expanded reserve and MPA for the system of five islands to give protection to surrounding waters, marine ecosystem and high marine biodiversity including seabirds, marine otters, resident bottlenose dolphins (mainly at Isla Choros) and other outstanding cetacean diversity, as well as to help manage uncontrolled dolphin watching activities. • At present the land reserve is administered by the Corporación Nacional Forestal (CONAF); there is considerable illegal traffic in molluscs and other animal products and some dolphin killings; tourism to the area (including dolphin watching at Isla Choros) is developing and must be managed at a sustainable level. The well-studied dolphin Pod R has shown high levels of stress (Sanino and Yáñez, 2000). • There have been photo-ID studies of the dolphins since 1991, but other studies are needed to assess the use and protection of the habitat and how best to protect and manage it. • The government is interested in the MPA proposal and it is expected to be declared an MPA under some category but there are considerable management and economic conflicts here and concerns about how the proposal is being developed.	• Contact: Gian Paolo Sanino, Centre for Marine Mammals Research Leviathan; email: research@ leviathanchile.org; web: www.leviathanchile.org • José Yáñez, National Museum of Natural History (MNHN); email: jyanez@mnhn.cl
• Coastal national park with cetaceans in surrounding waters and channels; if designation is extended to marine ecosystem, it could offer useful habitat protection. • No concrete proposal is yet on the table but a bold move would be to conserve cetacean habitat all around Chiloe Island with a greater extent out to sea off the southern and southwest coast where a recently discovered blue whale nursery has been found. The most important area according to CMMR Leviathan is the south facing the Golfo Corcovado including where the blue whales are found. Conflicts here, however, include large salmon aquaculture farm whose owners oppose protection. • Following the high profile announcement of the discovery of the Chiloe-Corcovado blue whale nursery and feeding area in 2003, the Chilean Environmental Agency CONAMA has reportedly endorsed the idea of declaring the area a protected marine park.	• Hucke-Gaete et al, 2003 • Contact: CONAMA (Chilean Environmental Agency); email: areasmarinas@conama.cl • Centre for Marine Mammals Research Leviathan; email: research@leviathanchile.org; web: www.leviathanchile.org • Centro Ballena Azul & Instituto de Ecología y Evolución, Universidad Austral de Chile; web: www.ballenazul.org
• Existing marine and offshore island-based protected area set up to conserve biodiversity; area includes humpback winter mating and calving grounds. • Protected area has land area on Isla Gorgona and three islets as well as surrounding marine area.	• Capella et al, 1995; Flórez-González and Capella, 1993 • Contact: Roberto Pardo Angel, PO Box 26513, Cali, Colombia; email: robepardoa@yahoo.com

Table 5.21 *continued*

Name of MPA or sanctuary, location and size	Cetacean and other notable species
(7) Ensenada de Utría National Natural Park (Parque Nacional Natural Ensenada de Utría) • Departamento de Chocó, on the Pacific coast • 206 mi² (534 km²), 20 per cent of which is the marine area	• bottlenose dolphin, *Tursiops truncatus*; Jun–Nov: humpback whale, *Megaptera novaeangliae* • also: marine turtles and coral reefs
(8) Malaga Bay MPA, *proposed* • Malaga Bay (including Negritos area)	• humpback whale, *Megaptera novaeangliae* • also: mangrove and wetland habitats
COSTA RICA República de Costa Rica	
(9) Cocos Island Marine and Terrestrial Conservation Area (Área de Conservación Marina y Terrestre Isla del Coco) • includes all of Cocos Island, 311 mi (500 km) SW of Costa Rica, eastern tropical Pacific and surrounding waters up to 9.3 mi (15 km) around the island • 385 mi² (997 km²) total; 376 mi² (973 km²) marine	• common: bottlenose dolphin, *Tursiops truncatus*; also: false killer whale, *Pseudorca crassidens*; humpback whale, *Megaptera novaeangliae*; others • also: California sea lion, hawksbill, green and olive Ridley turtles, various sharks (hammerhead, white-tip, whale), manta ray, nesting seabirds; various land-based endemics
(10) Ballena Marine National Park • extends 10 mi (15 km) from Uvita to Punta Piñuela and about 6 mi (9 km) out to sea • undetermined but 17.4 mi² (45 km²) by one estimate	• common: spinner dolphin, *Stenella longirostris*; bottlenose dolphin, *Tursiops truncatus*; common dolphin, *Delphinus* sp; Dec–Apr: humpback whale, *Megaptera novaeangliae*; sporadic: sperm whale, *Physeter macrocephalus*; orca, *Orcinus orca*
ECUADOR República del Ecuador **(A) Whale Natural Refuge (Refugio Natural de Ballenas)** • national waters of Ecuador, to the 200 nm (371 km) EEZ limit off the mainland as well as around the Galápagos Islands • 422,842 mi² (1,095,455 km²)	• humpback whale, *Megaptera novaeangliae*; Bryde's whale, *Balaenoptera brydei*; fin whale, *Balaenoptera physalus*; blue whale, *Balaenoptera musculus*; bottlenose dolphin, *Tursiops truncatus*; pantropical spotted dolphin, *Stenella attenuata*; spinner dolphin, *Stenella longirostris*; common dolphin, *Delphinus* spp; Fraser's dolphin, *Lagenodelphis hosei*; rough-toothed dolphin, *Steno bredanensis*; Risso's dolphin, *Grampus griseus*; orca, *Orcinus orca*; sperm whale, *Physeter macrocephalus*; various beaked whales; others

Notes and rationale	For more information
• Designated in 1987 to protect sandy beaches, marshes, mangrove and the largest coral reefs in Colombia. • More research is needed to define cetacean habitat.	• Contact: Roberto Pardo Angel, PO Box 26513, Cali, Colombia; email: robepardoa@yahoo.com
• Rationale would be to protect humpback whales, seabirds, fish, mangroves and wetlands, yet taking into account the local community – artisanal fishermen. • As of 2001, Environment Ministry was considering the idea of an MPA.	• Contact: Roberto Pardo Angel, PO Box 26513, Cali, Colombia; email: robepardoa@yahoo.com
• Rationale for protection is the many endemic species on the island and in surrounding waters. • In 1978, the land-based Isla del Coco National Park was created by Executive Decree 08748-A. In 1991, the park's limits were extended to include the marine component up to 9.3 mi (15 km) around the island. Under Executive Decree 20260, the entire area was made a 'zone of absolute protection', forbidding all extraction of marine resources or any commercial, industrial or agricultural activities. The 1995 Executive Decree 24652 made the whole area into a 'Conservation Area'. In 1997, it became a Natural World Heritage Area. Rating is IUCN Category II and IV. • Management plan was approved in 1995. • More detailed cetacean research would help clarify cetacean habitat needs.	See also Table 5.10 for more Costa Rican MPAs. • Contact: Isla del Coco National Park; web: www.costaricabureau.com/nationalparks/cocos.htm
• Designated in Feb 1990 to protect the shoreline of Bahía de Coronado and the marine waters around Isla Ballena.	• Contact: Ballena Marine National Park; web: www.costaricabureau.com/nationalparks/ballena.htm
• Refuge promises blanket protection for whales from activities that threaten their lives. • In May 1990, Official Decree (Acuerdo) No 196 from Ecuador's Ministry of Industry, Commerce and Fishing (Ministerio de Industrias, Comercio, Integración y Pesca) declared all national waters (to the limit of its EEZ) as a natural refuge for whales. • The main threat to whales and small cetaceans along the Ecuadorian coast is interaction with fisheries, especially the nets of artisanal and industrial fisheries including gill nets and purse-seiners which catch cetaceans accidentally. • The extent of real protection for cetaceans is unknown as the law is general and lacks clarity. Part of the problem is the use of the word 'ballenas' – which signifies only large whales. 'Cetaceos' would have at least offered protection in name to all cetaceans, including the dolphins which come into conflict with fishermen. Decree No 203, however, issued to prevent the tuna purse-seine fishery from operating around dolphins, may help to some extent.	• Félix and Samaniego, 1994 • Contact: Fernando Félix and Ben Haase, Fundación Ecuatoriana para el Estudio de Mamíferos Marinos (FEMM), PO Box 09-01-11905, Guayaquil, Ecuador; email: fefelix90@hotmail.com • Godfrey Merlen, c/o Estación Cientifica Charles Darwin, Isla Santa Cruz – Galápagos, Ecuador

Table 5.21 *continued*

Name of MPA or sanctuary, location and size	Cetacean and other notable species
(11) Galápagos Marine Resources Reserve (La Reserva de Recursos Marinos de Galápagos) and Galápagos Whale Sanctuary (El Santuario de Ballenas en las Islas Galápagos) • Galápagos Islands waters, 600 mi (975 km) west of Ecuador • about 61,000 mi² (158,000 km²) **See Case Study 9.**	• common: short-beaked common dolphin, *Delphinus delphis*; Risso's dolphin, *Grampus griseus*; striped dolphin, *Stenella coeruleoalba*; sperm whale, *Physeter macrocephalus*; for complete list, see Case Study 9. • also: Galápagos fur-seal, Galápagos sea lion, marine iguana and others
(12) Manglares-Churute Ecological Reserve (Reserva Ecológica Manglares-Churute) • southeast part of the inner estuary of the Gulf of Guayaquil • 191 mi² (494 km²)	• bottlenose dolphin, *Tursiops truncatus* • also: marine otters and aquatic birds
(13) Cuyabeno Faunistic Reserve (La Reserva de Producción Cuyabeno) • Ecuadorean Amazon basin in northeast Ecuador • 2328 mi² (6030 km²)	• boto, or Amazon River dolphin, *Inia geoffrensis*; tucuxi, *Sotalia fluviatilis* • also: Amazonian manatee, river otter and giant river otter
(14) Machalilla National Park (Parque Nacional Machalilla), extension *proposed* • Manabí province, central coast of Ecuador; reserve covers land along the continent, plus islands of La Plata and Salango, and 2 miles (3 km) of sea all around the islands • 212 mi² (550 km²); proposed extension of 135 mi² (350 km²) would create a total land and marine area of 347 mi² (900 km²)	• Jun–Sept: humpback whale, *Megaptera novaeangliae*; year-round: bottlenose dolphin, *Tursiops truncatus* and pantropical spotted dolphin, *Stenella attenuata*; most of the other cetaceans for Ecuador are possibilities • also: small sea lion colony on La Plata and some 350 bird species with colonies of blue- and red-footed boobies, masked boobies, frigate birds, pelicans and waved albatross

Notes and rationale	For more information
• The Galápagos Whale Sanctuary was decreed in 1990 and the Marine Resources Reserve plan approved in 1992. Formal protection of the waters around the Galápagos National Park came decades after the land park was created. These waters are a cetacean mating and breeding area as well as an area frequented by migrating cetaceans, and a feeding ground for dolphins and smaller whales. According to Hurtado (1995), the justification for conservation here 'includes ecological, economic, scientific, educational and political considerations'. • Special laws to protect wildlife include law banning industrial fishing throughout the reserve which is up to 46 mi (74 km) offshore. • Management plan in process may need to be modified.	• Day, 1994; Félix and Samaniego, 1994; Samaniego and Félix, 1994 • Contact: Godfrey Merlen, c/o Estación Cientifica Charles Darwin, Isla Santa Cruz – Galápagos Ecuador • Fundación Charles Darwin, PO Box 17-01 3891, Quito, Ecuador • More information on the web: www.unep-wcmc.org/ sites/wh/galapago.html
• Established in Nov 1979 to protect the mangrove ecosystem from agricultural expansion. The area is a typical estuarine zone with fresh water from several tributaries and sea water. Besides mangroves off the coast, the area includes salt marshes, lagoons, channels, islands and the river delta, and it constitutes a critical habitat for aquatic birds and other fauna associated with the mangrove, including bottlenose dolphins.	• Ministry of the Environment, P Icaza 203 y Pichincha, Guayaquil, Ecuador
• Existing national marine resources reserve designated by Ecuadorian government for its high biodiversity. • In the mid-1990s, Victor Utreras, followed by Judith Denkinger, began using photo-ID to determine conservation threats and status of the dolphins. • Industries operating in or near the area include transport of oil with attendant spills which have spoiled parts of the river. In 1998, Petroecuador, an Ecuadorian oil company with support from Shell, was planning to exploit oil in the protected area of Imuya, which is connected to the Lagarto Cocha River, the river with the highest density of river dolphins in the Cuyabeno Reserve and possibly in all of the Ecuadorian Amazon basin. According to Denkinger, Petroecuador's ITTI-Project will likely have a severe impact on the dolphins as well as on the ecology of the Rio Imuya.	• Denkinger et al, 1997; Utreras, 1996 • Contact: Victor Utreras Bucheli, Buenos Aires 12-38 y Panamá, Quito – Ecuador; email: aquatic@hoy.net • Judith Denkinger, Yaqa Pacha (Organization for the Conservation of Aquatic Mammals in South America), Casilla 17-17-51, Quito, Ecuador
• Existing combined marine and land-based national park, with extension proposed. • Machalilla National Park became a terrestrially focused protected area in 1979. In 1991, a humpback whale photo-ID study began. The area provides winter habitat for mating and calving (or newly born) humpback whales that spend Jun–Oct in the area. • Management is carried out by National Parks Service through Ecuadorian Institute for Forestry and Natural Areas (INEFAN) and Ministry of Agriculture and Livestock. • It has been suggested by researchers Fernando Félix and Ben Haase, as well as by authorities in Puerto López, that the marine part of the park be expanded to give more protection to humpback whales during the season, and to the year-round tropical dolphins and other cetaceans. • Future assessments and modifications of management plans must include provisions for the growing whale watch industry which offers the opportunity of expanded publicity for the park, as well as potential conflicts if not well managed.	• Félix and Haase, 1996, 2001; Félix and Samaniego, 1994; Samaniego and Félix, 1994 • Contact: Fernando Félix, Fundación Ecuatoriana para el Estudio de Mamíferos Marinos (FEMM), PO Box 09-01-11905, Guayaquil, Ecuador; email: fefelix90@hotmail.com • Carlos Zambrano, Machalilla National Park, Puerto Lopez, Manabí, Ecuador • Jorge Samaniego, Puerto Lopez Municipality, PO Box 770, Jipijapa, Ecuador

Table 5.21 *continued*

Name of MPA or sanctuary, location and size	Cetacean and other notable species
PANAMÁ República de Panamá **(15) Cerro Hoya National Park (Parque Nacional Cerro Hoya)** • southeast of the Azuero peninsula (7°N, 80°W), including the coast between the Restingue and Ventana rivers • 126 mi² (325.6 km²)	• bottlenose dolphin, *Tursiops truncatus*; plus several species of tropical dolphins and possibly the humpback whale, *Megaptera novaeangliae* (Jul–Oct)
(16) Coiba National Park (Parque Nacional Isla Coiba) • 15.5 mi (25 km) offshore from southwestern Veraguas province (7°30'N, 81°40'W) • total size is 1043 mi² (2701.1 km²), with 835.9 mi² (2165.4 km²) marine waters	• resident or regular, Jul–Oct: humpback whale, *Megaptera novaeangliae*; orca, *Orcinus orca*; pantropical spotted dolphin, *Stenella attenuata*; bottlenose dolphin, *Tursiops truncatus*; plus 19 more species of cetaceans occasionally found • also: whale shark, tiger shark, land and seabirds
(17) Golfo de Chiriquí National Marine Park (Parque Nacional Marino Golfo de Chiriquí) • western Panamá (8°08'N, 82°19'W) • 57 mi² (147.4 km²)	• several species of tropical dolphins and maybe humpback whale, *Megaptera novaeangliae* (Jul–Oct) • also: tropical birds and reptiles
(18) El Golfo de Montijo Wetland (Húmedad el Golfo de Montijo) • Veraguas province • 266.8 mi² (691.3 km²)	• several species of tropical dolphins and maybe humpback whale, *Megaptera novaeangliae* (Jul–Oct) • also: aquatic birds
PERU República del Perú **(19) Paracas National Reserve (Reserva Nacional de Paracas)** • Paracas district, Pisco province, Ica department (13°47'–14°17'S and 76°30'–76°00'W) • 1293 mi² (3350 km²) which includes water, islands and adjacent land on the coast; 65 per cent of the total is marine-based	• Jul–Nov: humpback whale, *Megaptera novaeangliae*; Jul–Sept: sperm whale, *Physeter macrocephalus*; year-round: bottlenose dolphin, *Tursiops truncatus*; Burmeister's porpoise, *Phocoena spinipinnis*; long-beaked common dolphin, *Delphinus capensis;* dusky dolphin, *Lagenorhynchus obscurus* • also: endangered marine otter; South American sea lion and fur-seal; 216 bird species including endangered Peruvian diving petrel and Humboldt penguin

Notes and rationale	For more information
• This national park was created in 1984 to protect coastal and marine habitat including endangered tropical land species; the diverse area includes two rivers and their estuaries, reefs, cays, islands and the continental shelf to 330 ft (100 m) depth. • More research is needed to define cetacean habitat.	• Contact: Cerro Hoya National Park; web: www.ipat.gob.pa/ ecoturismo/index.html
• National park created in 1991 to protect Coiba, the largest island in the Panamanian Pacific, plus 38 smaller islands with their surrounding waters. The outstanding biodiversity of Coiba includes 1450 species of plants and 120 species of birds. Surrounding Coiba are some of the few healthy coral reefs in the eastern Pacific. • A 2001 legal project proposes a type of co-management for the administration of the park. • More research is needed to determine cetacean distribution and define habitat.	• Contact: Coiba National Park; web: www.ipat.gob.pa/ ecoturismo/pnic.html
• National marine park created in 1994, this national park includes 22 islands with surrounding marine areas. • More research is needed to define cetacean habitat.	• Contact: Golfo de Chiriqui National Marine Park; web: www.ipat.gob.pa/ ecoturismo/pnmgc.html
• In 1994, this wetland MPA was created to include a coastal area, as well as marine, estuarine and fluvial waters, specifically to protect the fauna and flora typical of this transitional zone between marine and terrestrial ecosystems. • More research is needed to define cetacean habitat.	• Contact: El Golfo de Montijo Wetland; web: www.ipat.gob.pa/ ecoturismo/hrgolfomo ntijo.html; www.anam.gob.pa
• In Sept 1975, Paracas was declared a National Reserve by Supreme Decree No 1281-75-AG, due to the richness of the marine biomass. In addition, State Law 26585 protects dolphins, porpoises and other small cetaceans from direct catch, trade and utilization. • Potential conflicts include commercial fishing, illegal dolphin hunting (for human consumption), poor management due to the conflict between the Ministry of Fisheries and INRENA (part of Ministry of Agriculture). • In 1996 INRENA published a management plan with some zonification; plan and zonification will be reviewed every five years. • There has been little research into cetaceans in the MPA except for the resident bottlenose dolphins and small cetacean–fisheries interactions. The larger whales are either migratory or seasonal.	• Contact: Julio Reyes and Mónica Echegaray, ACOREMA; email: acorema@terra.com.pe • Instituto Nacional de Recursos Naturales (INRENA), Calle Los Petirrojos 355, Urbanización El Palomar, Lima 27, Peru • Carlos Obando, ProNaturaleza, San Andrés, Peru; email: proparac@qnet.com.pe • Stefan Austermühle, Mundo Azul; email: mundoazul@terra.com.pe

Table 5.21 *continued*

Name of MPA or sanctuary, location and size	Cetacean and other notable species
(20) Pacaya-Samiria National Reserve • near Iquitos, Peruvian Amazon • 8029 mi^2 (20,800 km^2)	• boto, or Amazon River dolphin, *Inia geoffrensis*; tucuxi, *Sotalia fluviatilis* • also: Amazonian manatee
(21) Peninsula Bayovar MPA, proposed • Peninsula Bayovar and north along the coast from 6°S, Dept of Piura, (northern) Peru • size undetermined	• humpback whale, *Megaptera novaeangliae*; sperm whale, *Physeter macrocephalus*; bottlenose dolphin, *Tursiops truncatus*; Burmeister's porpoise, *Phocoena spinipinnis*; possibly other cetaceans • also: many tropical and Humboldt Current fishes

Notes and rationale	For more information
• Created in 1972, this river-based reserve was enlarged in 1982; local people can hunt and fish and there is 'nominal protection to animals' (Reeves, 2002) with 'some restrictions on commercial exploitation and industrial activity'. • There are regular dolphin watch tours and research cruises by the Oceanic Society.	• Contact: Birgit Winning, Oceanic Society Expeditions, Fort Mason Center – E, San Francisco, CA 94123-1394 USA; email: winning@ oceanic-society.org
• Rationale for proposed protection is the great marine and land-based biodiversity due to the offshore meeting of the Humboldt and tropical currents. It appears to have diverse cetacean populations but how important this area is as cetacean habitat and how it should be zoned depends on definition through future research. National and world support are needed to obtain protection. • Best protection would be in zoned biosphere reserve or national park with buffering national reserves (IUCN Category I) to include coast, nearshore to deep water. • Most of Peru's cetaceans are likely found here; pre-1985, this was where whalers caught sperm (and historically blue and humpback) whales.	• Contact: Jorge Ugaz, ProNaturaleza, Parque Blume, Lima – Miraflores, Peru • Stefan Austermühle, Mundo Azul, Las Acacias 185 A, Lima – Miraflores, Peru; email: mundoazul@ terra.com.pe; web: www.peru.com/ mundoazul/ingles/index.asp

MARINE REGION 18: AUSTRALIA–NEW ZEALAND

The world's first whale sanctuary was designated in 1914 in the southeastern Indian Ocean, covering the nearshore waters of western Australia between Norwegian Bay and Point Cloates, an area used by a shore-based whaling station (Holt, 1984). The government in western Australia declared this small coastal marine sanctuary to protect a presumed humpback whale calving area. The 'management plan' included licensing, catcher boat limits, and bans on the killing of mothers and calves. Unfortunately, it did not last. Years later, at the 1979 IWC meeting, the Republic of Seychelles proposed that the Indian Ocean be closed to commercial whaling and declared a sanctuary. With the support of Australia, most Indian Ocean states and the rest of the world, this was voted in as the world's first ocean-wide sanctuary. Covering parts of Marine Regions 10, 11, 12, 13 and 18, the Indian Ocean Sanctuary offers broad brush protection from whaling and a measure of international recognition. In 2004, the Indian Ocean Sanctuary celebrated its 25th anniversary (see Table 5.13 on p288).

Before the early 1970s and the end of whaling in Australia, when the humpback whales migrated along the east and west coasts of Australia and the southern right whales brought their calves to the south coast, they were met with harpoons. Today, however, the whales inspire whale watchers and researchers who stand on shore or take to sea in small boats from these same coasts, as these populations attempt to return from commercial extinction. In recent years, blue whales have been studied as they come in to feed at the Bonney Upwelling in the waters of South Australia and Victoria, and off Perth in an area known as Rottnest Trench. Off northeastern Australia, a population of dwarf minke whales (a subspecies of minke whale) is now reliably encountered and studied.

The main southern hemisphere dolphins can all be seen in Australian waters but, close to shore, the sightings are mainly of bottlenose and common dolphins. In New Zealand, in nearshore waters, it is mainly dusky, bottlenose, common and Hector's dolphins.

Unique to the New Zealand part of the region is Hector's dolphin. In 2000, this species was reclassified on the IUCN Red List from 'vulnerable' to 'endangered'. Off South Island, the Banks Peninsula Marine Mammal Sanctuary is playing a role in the conservation of this dolphin but the area needs to be expanded, fishing activities including gill netting clearly need more restrictions, and enforcement is crucial. A separate population of fewer than a hundred Hector's dolphins, referred to as 'Maui dolphins', based around the west coast of the North Island, is listed separately as 'critically endangered'. A marine mammal MPA has been proposed there.

All lists of notable MPAs in Australia start with the Great Barrier Reef Marine Park (GBRMP). At 131,000 mi^2 (340,000 km^2), GBRMP is the largest MPA in the world managed on a zoned or biosphere reserve-type basis. In 2004, nearly a third of it, 43,116 mi^2 (111,700 km^2), was designated as a no-take, or highly protected, core area. GBRMP now has the world's largest and most substantial IUCN Category I core areas. Although created to protect the world's

Box 5.12 Australia's MPAs and Oceans Policy and the Implications for Cetacean Habitat

In 1990, the Australian Commonwealth government announced that it would establish the National Representative System of Marine Protected Areas (NRSMPA), although the follow-up, essential *Strategic Plan of Action for the NRSMPA* was not issued until 1999. The primary stated goal is to 'establish and manage a Comprehensive, Adequate and Representative (CAR) system of MPAs to contribute to the long-term ecological viability of marine and estuarine systems, to maintain ecological processes and systems, and to protect Australia's biological diversity at all levels' (ANZECC, 1999). A secondary goal of NRSMPA is to provide for the needs of threatened and migratory species, as well as species vulnerable to disturbance.

In 1998, the Commonwealth government launched Australia's Oceans Policy with a commitment to integrated and ecosystem-based planning and management. The Oceans Policy has the delivery of the NRSMPA as a key part of its focus, using Regional Marine Plans (RMPs). These RMPs are supposed to integrate MPAs into broader ecosystem-based management.

In 1999, the passage of the Environment Protection and Biodiversity Conservation Act (EPBC) provided some of the essential legislation for marine conservation as part of a broad Commonwealth act to address a wide variety of environmental matters.

Among other things, the marine aspects of the EPBC Act establish or enable the following:

- a biodiversity permit process to regulate actions in Commonwealth waters that harm or injure a cetacean (can be a member of a listed threatened species, ecological community or migratory species);
- the listing of threatened species, ecological systems and migratory species and the preparation of recovery plans (plans are being prepared for blue, southern right, humpback, sei and fin whales);
- the listing of key threatening processes and the development of targeted threat abatement plans; and
- the strategic assessment of management plans and policies concerning Commonwealth managed and export fisheries.

Australia has also signed nearly 50 international conventions and treaties, including CITES, CMS, CBD, CCAMLR, Ramsar and UNCLOS which commit it to fulfilling various provisions on marine conservation. The complete list and implications are described in Smyth et al (2003).

The mandate of the NRSMPA is to include at its core a network of MPAs of sufficient number and size to protect the full range of marine life and habitats on the regional scale, at different locations and at different stages in life cycles (Smyth et al, 2003). As of early 2004, some 14 MPAs have been set aside in the Commonwealth estate, plus many more in State and Territory waters, which extend 3 nm (3.5 mi or 5.6 km) from shore. Yet less than 4 per cent of Australia's marine estate is represented by any type of MPA, and most of that is in multiple use, IUCN Category VI protection.

The first RMP for Australia is now being developed for the Southeast Marine Region, to be followed by the Northern Regional Marine plan, but it will be some years before all 11 marine planning regions are able to complete their RMPs.

On paper, NRSMPA, Oceans Policy, Regional Marine Planning and the EPBC Act are pioneering advances, showing the talent and efforts of Australia's scientists, marine conservationists and policy-makers and demonstrating that Australia could lead the world in marine habitat conservation. Yet the implementation is not coming up to the potential. Criticism has been considerable – both in terms of the effectiveness for ecosystem-based management in Commonwealth waters, as well as the ultimate value for cetaceans (Smyth et al, 2003):

- Besides the delayed implementation, the NRSMPA is limited by lack of resources for declaration and management, lack of commitment to meeting international scientific standards for IUCN Category I protection, a reduced emphasis on species protection and difficulties in dealing with the steady expansion of industrial activities, especially fishing, petroleum, coastal development and shipping.
- Regarding Oceans Policy and the Regional Marine Planning, despite considerable time and money having been spent, not one regional marine plan has been finalized; the draft of the first plan proposed largely a business-as-usual, non-spatial approach to management, with a significant reduction in emphasis on ecosystem-based management.
- The existing protection, as embodied in the EPBC Act, is too narrowly applied by both proponents and government. Unfortunately, the act is generally not being used to protect all cetaceans, instead focusing on only those formally listed as threatened or migratory. On top of that, the cetacean provisions of the Act only apply in Commonwealth waters and do not address all the threats against cetaceans.

Smyth et al (2003) have called for urgent reform of the EPBC Act. In *Oceans Eleven*, a document endorsed by the 18 major NGOs in Australia, they recommended amendments:

- that would make all marine mammals either vulnerable or conservation-dependent species in recognition of their position within the marine ecosystem;
- to identify and list critical habitat for all marine mammals on the EPBC Act Register;
- to address the full range of threats experienced by marine mammals in Australian waters;
- to provide to the Environment and Heritage Minister increased powers to oversee and regulate the Petroleum and Submerged Lands Act over important cetacean habitat in both Commonwealth and state marine waters;
- to provide for the declaration and legal protection of all areas identified as critical habitat, and provide appropriate levels of protection for all such identified areas;
- to provide for the creation of a scientific register of government-accredited cetacean specialists for industry-observer coverage; and
- to provide for the creation of a National Cetacean Centre to manage industry-observer coverage, cetacean sighting reports and to promote and supervise cetacean research.

largest coral reef, GBRMP also contains cetacean populations including mating and calving humpback whales and various dolphins. Australia's national and state laws protect cetaceans in its waters (see Box 5.12, p419). Under the 1980 Whale Protection Act, now part of the 1999 Environment Protection and Biodiversity Conservation Act (EPBC), Australia created a national cetacean sanctuary in the country's state and Commonwealth waters to the limits of its EEZ, but there is still a long way to go to give critical habitat protection to resident and migratory cetaceans. New Zealand, too, with its protective national legislation for marine mammals protects cetaceans as part of the New Zealand Marine Mammal Sanctuary. Besides the Hector's dolphin MPA at Banks Peninsula, New Zealand has set aside the Auckland Islands Marine Mammal Sanctuary largely for southern right whales.

In the Australia–New Zealand Marine Region, eight large marine ecosystems (LMEs) have been identified: the North Australian Shelf, Northeast Australian Shelf–Great Barrier Reef, East-Central Australian Shelf, Southeast Australian Shelf, Southwest Australian Shelf, West-Central Australian Shelf, Northwest Australian Shelf and New Zealand Shelf. The region covers the waters of the southeast Indian Ocean, the southwest South Pacific, including the Tasman Sea, and a large band of the great Southern Ocean between the land masses of Australia and New Zealand and the Antarctic Polar Front. Politically, it includes the countries of Australia and New Zealand with their respective territories: Macquarie, Norfolk and Cocos (Keeling) islands (all part of Australia) and Kermadec, Chatham, Bounty, Antipodes, Auckland and Campbell islands (New Zealand). The Australian Antarctic territories of Heard Island and the MacDonald Islands are part of Marine Region 1.

There is no UNEP regional seas programme specifically for this region but Australia and New Zealand are active parties in SPREP (South Pacific Regional Environmental Programme) along with the countries in Marine Region 14. In 1995, there was a total of 260 MPAs of all kinds in this marine region representing nearly 20 per cent of all subtidal MPAs worldwide (Kelleher et al, 1995a). This is the highest number of MPAs in a single region of the world. Kelleher et al (1995a) divided the region into 40 biogeographic zones most of which were represented by at least one MPA. As of 2004, according to Table 5.22 prepared for this book, there are 40 existing and 12 proposed MPAs that feature cetacean habitat. Three of the existing MPAs are proposed for expansion.

The IUCN 2002–2010 Conservation Action Plan for the World's Cetaceans has only a limited number of research and conservation suggestions for this region, mainly for New Zealand (Reeves et al, 2003). In future editions of the Action Plan, there are plans to expand coverage within the Australian–New Zealand region. Until then, Bannister et al (1996) provides a starting point for cetacean conservation suggestions, supplemented by WDCS's Australian, New Zealand and Antarctic initiatives (see www.wdcs.org.au).

IUCN Action Plan points related to Hector's dolphin, an endangered species in the region, as well as directly related to marine habitat conservation, are:

- for management authorities to allow fishing only with methods known not to bother Hector's dolphins (replacing gill netting or trawling with line fishing) and to work to reduce pollution, boat strikes and other threats;
- to expand the size of MPAs which include habitat for Hector's dolphins;
- to implement an effective observer programme covering the species' range to verify whether and when bycatch has been reduced to sustainable levels; and
- to continue monitoring abundance and distribution of the species and to study population structure to assess the exposure to threats and the effectiveness of management.

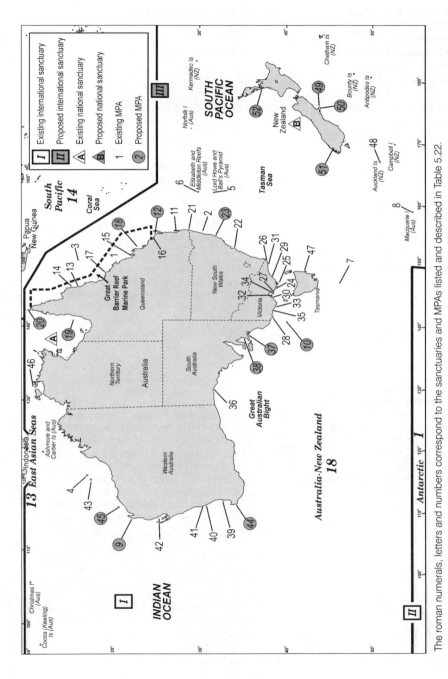

Figure 5.27 *Map of Marine Region 18: Australia–New Zealand MPAs and sanctuaries*

The roman numerals, letters and numbers correspond to the sanctuaries and MPAs listed and described in Table 5.22.

Table 5.22 *Marine Region 18: Australia–New Zealand MPAs and sanctuaries*

Name of MPA or sanctuary, location and size	Cetacean and other notable species
INTERNATIONAL **(I) Indian Ocean Sanctuary** • Indian Ocean, spread across Marine Regions 10, 11, 12, 13 and 18 • 40 million mi² (103.6 million km²)	• at least 43 species of cetaceans
(II) Southern Ocean Sanctuary • Southern Ocean • 19.3 million mi² (50 million km²)	• 7 baleen and 13 toothed whale species
(III) South Pacific Whale Sanctuary, *proposed* • South Pacific Ocean, spread across Marine Regions 14, 17 and 18 • size undetermined	• some 53 species of cetaceans
AUSTRALIA Commonwealth of Australia **(A) Australian Whale Sanctuary** • state and Commonwealth waters to the limits of the EEZ of Australia, including subantarctic territories and disputed Antarctic waters • 6.2 million mi² (16 million km²)	• some 44 species of cetaceans live all or part of the year in, or transit through, Australian waters, 5 of which are known to be endangered or vulnerable, 38 insufficiently known and 1 secure
Commonwealth MPAs (including joint Commonwealth–State MPAs) **(1) Great Barrier Reef Marine Park and World Heritage Area** • Great Barrier Reef, off Cape York, Queensland, including 940 islands and 2900 reefs • 131,000 mi² (340,000 km²), extending for 1400 mi (2250 km)	• Jul–Sep: humpback whale, *Megaptera novaeangliae*; Mar–Oct: minke whale (dwarf subsp), *Balaenoptera acutorostrata*; Antarctic minke whale, *Balaenoptera bonaerensis*; pygmy Bryde's whale, *Balaenoptera edeni*; sei whale, *Balaenoptera borealis*; fin whale, *Balaenoptera physalus*; year-round: sperm whale, *Physeter macrocephalus*; pygmy sperm whale, *Kogia breviceps*; dwarf sperm whale, *Kogia sima*; at least 4 beaked whale species; rough-toothed dolphin, *Steno bredanensis*; bottlenose dolphin, *Tursiops truncatus*; pantropical spotted dolphin, *Stenella attenuata*; spinner dolphin, *Stenella longirostris*; striped dolphin, *Stenella coeruleoalba*; common dolphins, *Delphinus* spp; Fraser's dolphin, *Lagenodelphis hosei*; Risso's dolphin, *Grampus griseus*; melon-headed whale, *Peponocephala electra*; pygmy killer whale, *Feresa attenuata*; false killer whale, *Pseudorca crassidens*; orca, *Orcinus orca*; long-finned pilot whale, *Globicephala melas*; short-finned pilot whale, *Globicephala macrorhynchus* • also: 500 fish species, 175 bird species, 6 sea turtle species, dugong; 359 types of hard coral

Notes and rationale	For more information
• Rationale is to protect large whales from commercial whaling and to stimulate cetacean research and conservation. • At the 1979 IWC meeting, the Indian Ocean was closed to commercial whaling and declared a sanctuary.	• See full account in Marine Region 10, Table 5.13.
• In 1992, a French proposal for an Antarctic whale sanctuary was first submitted to the IWC and it was approved by 3/4 majority in 1994. The Southern Ocean Sanctuary is part of a portfolio of treaties and other measures to protect Antarctica and its surrounding seas. • Australia's southernmost island territories are in the Southern Ocean Sanctuary.	• See full account in Marine Region 1, Table 5.2.
• Rationale is to protect large whales from commercial whaling and to stimulate cetacean research and conservation. • Proposed in 1999, the South Pacific Sanctuary was discussed and later turned down at the IWC meetings from 2000–2004. The idea has overwhelming support from South Pacific nations.	• See full account in Marine Region 14, Table 5.18.
• The Whale Protection Act 1980 created a cetacean refuge or sanctuary covering all Australian jurisdictional waters; this act has been melded into the Environment Protection and Biodiversity Conservation Act (1999) which provides protection for marine mammals from directed take (lethal and non-lethal) and deliberate harm. • There are calls to reform the act or introduce other legislation to cover such cetacean threats as noise, bycatch, climate change, pollution and cumulative impacts.	• Gill and Burke, 1999 • Contact: WDCS – Australasia; email: info@wdcs.org.au; web: www.wdcs.org.au
• Established in 1975, the Great Barrier Reef (GBR) is 'one of the most complex and biologically diverse ecosystems on earth'; it was inscribed on the World Heritage Area list in 1981. In 1990, the park was designated a PSSA, and it has a compulsory pilotage system as approved by IMO from the northern boundary to south of Cairns and also around the Whitsundays. There is also a park scheme in which all vessels over 50 m must report their position at points along the park's inner shipping route between the reef itself and the Queensland coast. Park management prohibits discharge of pollutants from ships within the GBR lagoon. • Rationale is to protect the world's greatest barrier reef and its ecosystem; this protection extends to the GBR's 'natural values through maintenance of its diversity of species and habitats ... including species conservation ... especially the protection of threatened species such as dugongs, turtles, whales and dolphins'. • Potential impacts of greatest relevance to cetacean populations in GBRMP, are 'noise, harassment and additionally, for Irrawaddy and Indo-Pacific hump-backed dolphins, entanglement in shark and fish mesh nets [followed by] pollution, habitat degradation, physical habitat degradation or destruction and displacement... Vessel strikes could become a concern for humpback whales as the numbers of whales increase.' The report says 'management measures ... should focus on gathering better information on	• Great Barrier Reef Marine Park Authority, 2000 • Contact: Great Barrier Reef Marine Park Authority; web: www.gbrmpa.gov.au/ • WDCS – Australasia; email: info@wdcs.org.au; web: www.wdcs.org.au

Table 5.22 *continued*

Name of MPA or sanctuary, location and size	Cetacean and other notable species
continued from pp424–425 **Great Barrier Reef Marine Park and World Heritage Area**	
(2) Solitary Islands Marine Reserve and Marine Park • Solitary Islands between Coffs Harbour and Plover Island, New South Wales • 336 mi² (870 km²) total; 274 mi² (710 km²) for the marine park and 62 mi² (160 km²) for the reserve	• Jul–Nov: humpback whale, *Megaptera novaeangliae*; Nov–Jan: melon-headed whale, *Peponocephala electra*; occasional: bottlenose dolphin, *Tursiops truncatus*; common dolphin, *Delphinus* sp; orca, *Orcinus orca*; pygmy killer whale, *Feresa attenuata*; long-finned pilot whale, *Globicephala melas*; sperm whale, *Physeter macrocephalus*; Antarctic minke whale, *Balaenoptera bonaerensis*; blue whale, *Balaenoptera musculus*; southern right whale, *Eubalaena australis*; others • also: grey nurse shark, black cod and marine turtles
(3) Coringa-Herald and Lihou Reef National Nature Reserve (referred to as Coral Sea NNR) • Coral Sea Islands territory to the east of the Great Barrier Reef; the two reserves are separated by 60 mi (100 km) of open ocean • 6677.8 mi² (17,300 km²)	• Jul–Sept: humpback whale, *Megaptera novaeangliae*; year-round, occasional: sperm whale, *Physeter macrocephalus*; striped dolphin, *Stenella coeruleoalba*; pantropical spotted dolphin, *Stenella attenuata*; bottlenose dolphin, *Tursiops truncatus*; Risso's dolphin, *Grampus griseus*
(4) Mermaid Reef Marine National Nature Reserve • part of the Rowley Shoals off NW Australia, 186 mi (300 km) northwest of Broome • 208.4 mi² (539.8 km²)	• listed as present, baleen whales seasonal: Bryde's whale, *Balaenoptera brydei*; Antarctic minke whale, *Balaenoptera bonaerensis;* humpback whale, *Megaptera novaeangliae*; sperm whale, *Physeter macrocephalus*; striped dolphin, *Stenella coeruleoalba*; common dolphin, *Delphinus* sp; spinner dolphin, *Stenella longirostris*; bottlenose dolphin, *Tursiops truncatus*; Risso's dolphin, *Grampus griseus*; short-finned pilot whale, *Globicephala macrorhynchus*; orca, *Orcinus orca*; melon-headed whale, *Peponocephala electra*; false killer whale, *Pseudorca crassidens*

Notes and rationale	For more information
cetacean distributions, abundances and threats, and taking prudent and appropriate measures to reduce impacts judged to be most significant. However, management also needs to take reasonable measures to anticipate and respond to future issues, such as disease outbreaks or unfavourable environmental change. Management measures should reflect the level of threat, the degree of certainty, and incorporate the precautionary principle' (Great Barrier Reef Marine Park Authority, 2000). • Intensively managed compared to most MPAs worldwide, this MPA has been rated IUCN Category VI with elements of Ia, Ib, II, III and IV. The entire park is off limits to mining and petroleum but allows tourism. Until 2004, only 4.6 per cent was protected from fishing. In 2004 highly protected no-take or 'green zones' were approved to bring the percentage to 33 percent IUCN Category I–II areas.	
• First proposed as a reserve by NSW Fisheries in 1989 for the benefit of fish and fish habitat and set aside in 1991; adjoining Commonwealth protection came in 1993. • Rationale is to protect a species-rich ecosystem around an open ocean, subtidal reef with soft substrate habitats; area is a mixing zone between tropical and temperate environments, with many species close to their northern or southern ranges. • Overall protection for the reserve is rated IUCN Category VI which includes a small sanctuary zone (Ia), a habitat protection zone (IV) and general use zone (VI). • Entire park in NSW and Commonwealth waters was placed on the Register of the National Estate in 1995 as an outstanding example of marine biodiversity. • Management plan has key habitat provisions for cetaceans. The increasing recreational and commercial boating traffic (including whale watching) is listed as a significant risk to cetaceans, as is entanglement in fishing gear, noise and depletion of prey species; cumulative impacts is listed as a management issue.	• Environment Australia, 2001c • Contact: Solitary Marine Reserve and Marine Park; web: www.ea.gov.au/coasts/mpa/solitary/index.html • WDCS – Australasia; email: info@wdcs.org.au; web: www.wdcs.org.au
• Commonwealth MPA with IUCN Category 1a protection. • Rationale is to protect coral reefs and there are no provisions for cetaceans, but highly protected management arrangements will benefit cetacean habitat.	• Environment Australia, 2001a • Contact: WDCS – Australasia; email: info@wdcs.org.au; web: www.wdcs.org.au
• Commonwealth MPA with IUCN Category 1a protection. • Rationale is to protect coral reefs and there are no provisions for cetaceans, but highly protected management arrangements will benefit cetacean habitat. • Cetacean species at left probably frequent the nature reserve, but cetacean surveys and habitat studies need to be done.	• Environment Australia, 2002b • Contact: WDCS – Australasia; email: info@wdcs.org.au; web: www.wdcs.org.au

Table 5.22 *continued*

Name of MPA or sanctuary, location and size	Cetacean and other notable species
(5) Lord Howe Island Marine Park and World Heritage Area • 435 mi² (700 km) northeast of Sydney, NSW • 1160 mi² (3005 km²)	• common: bottlenose dolphin, *Tursiops truncatus*; occasional: southern right whale, *Eubalaena australis*; humpback whale, *Megaptera novaeangliae*; fin whale, *Balaenoptera physalus*; sei whale, *Balaenoptera borealis;* blue whale, *Balaenoptera musculus*; spinner dolphin, *Stenella longirostris*; pantropical spotted dolphin, *Stenella attenuata*; dusky dolphin, *Lagenorhynchus obscurus*
(6) Elizabeth and Middleton Reefs Marine Nature Reserve • located in the Tasman Sea, 370 mi (600 km) east of Coffs Harbour, NSW • 725.7 mi² (1880 km²)	• various subtropical cetaceans probable (according to the management plan, cetaceans recorded in subtropical South Pacific waters would be expected to occur in the reserve)
(7) Tasmanian Seamounts Marine Reserve • 106 mi (170 km) south of Hobart, Tasmania • 150.1 mi² (388.9 km²)	• various cetaceans probable although none listed in the management plan, but large size alone offers probability of some importance to cetaceans
(8) Macquarie Island Marine Park and World Heritage Area • Macquarie Ridge, Tasman Sea, 930 mi (1500 km), southeast of Tasmania (54°29'S, 158°58'E) • 62,500 mi² (162,000 km²), including 22,400 mi² (58,000 km²) Category Ia area	• on migration, feeding: southern right whale, *Eubalaena australis*; humpback whale, *Megaptera novaeangliae;* sporadic or transient: Antarctic minke whale, *Balaenoptera bonaerensis*; sperm whale, *Physeter macrocephalus*; long-finned pilot whale, *Globicephala melas*; orca, *Orcinus orca*; Andrew's beaked whale, *Mesoplodon bowdoini*; strap-toothed whale, *Mesoplodon layardii*; Cuvier's beaked whale, *Ziphius cavirostris*; southern bottlenose whale, *Hyperoodon planifrons* • subantarctic fur-seal, grey and blue petrel, Antarctic tern, fairy prion, albatross species

Notes and rationale	For more information
• Commonwealth and NSW (state) MPA with IUCN Category Ia and IV protection, also a World Heritage area; largest MPA off NSW coast. • There are no specific provisions for cetaceans, but highly protected Category Ia and moderately protected Category IV management arrangements will benefit cetaceans and cetacean habitat.	• Environment Australia, 2002a • Contact: WDCS – Australasia; email: info@wdcs.org.au; web: www.wdcs.org.au
• Commonwealth MPA, with no IUCN Categories assigned; management plan is due to be updated according to EPBC Act requirements in 2003. • Currently no provisions for cetaceans in the management plan but provisions which prohibit commercial fishing and mining and limit recreational fishing would be beneficial to cetaceans. • Cetacean surveys need to be done to determine distribution and possible habitat.	• Contact: WDCS – Australasia; email: info@wdcs.org.au; web: www.wdcs.org.au
• Commonwealth MPA specifically designed to protect some 70 seamounts. • MPA includes IUCN Category Ia below a depth of 1640 ft (500 m) including the seamounts; the upper 1640 ft (500 m) of the reserve has Category VI protection. • Prohibition of trawls, as well as no mining below 1640 ft (500 m) would offer some benefit to cetaceans but cetacean surveys need to be done to determine distribution and possible habitat.	• Environment Australia, 2002d • Contact: WDCS – Australasia; email: info@wdcs.org.au; web: www.wdcs.org.au
• Rationale for protection is uniqueness of the geology: oceanic crust raised above sea level within an oceanic basin creating a barrier to the Antarctic Circumpolar Current plus the protection of various threatened species; designated in 2000. • Not designed specifically around cetacean habitat, but because of its size and location, it certainly contains cetacean habitat; cetacean distribution studies are needed. • Adjacent to the partly land-based Macquarie Island Nature Reserve, the park covers a third of Australia's territorial waters (to the limits of the EEZ) around Macquarie Island. • In 1997 the island and surrounding waters out to 12 nm (22.2 km) were listed as a World Heritage Area. • The 2001 Management Plan lists strategic objectives that include protecting the migratory, feeding and breeding ranges of marine mammals and threatened species that depend on the area. The plan notes that this park helps meet Australia's international objectives as a member of the IWC in terms of providing proper conservation of whale stocks. • Park includes IUCN Category Ia highly protected zone and Category IV habitat and species management zones.	• Environment Australia, 2001b; species list in Environment Australia, 2001a • Contact: WDCS – Australasia; email: info@wdcs.org.au; web: www.wdcs.org.au • Macquarie Island Marine Park; web: www.ea.gov.au/coasts/mpa/macquarie/index.html

Table 5.22 *continued*

Name of MPA or sanctuary, location and size	Cetacean and other notable species
(9) Ningaloo Marine Park *and proposed extension* • near Exmouth (21°40'S to 23°34'S), extending some 160 mi (260 km) along the coast and from the shoreline to the edge of the continental slope, Western Australia • existing size is 1771 m²i (4587 km²); proposed extension is 147 mi² (380 km²)	• year-round: Indo-Pacific bottlenose dolphin, *Tursiops aduncus*; May–Nov: humpback whale, *Megaptera novaeangliae*. Some of the 17 other cetacean species occasionally seen include: sei whale, *Balaenoptera borealis*; Bryde's whale, *Balaenoptera brydei*; sperm whale, *Physeter macrocephalus*; common dolphin, *Delphinus* sp; Risso's dolphin, *Grampus griseus*; false killer whale, *Pseudorca crassidens*; orca, *Orcinus orca* • also: whale shark, dugong, turtles, sea lions, southern elephant seals, manta rays, more than 460 species of reef-dwelling and pelagic fish • Australia's largest fringing reef, Ningaloo has the second largest barrier reef in Australia after the Great Barrier Reef
(10) Bonney Upwelling Blue Whale Feeding critical habitat MPA, *may be proposed* • continental shelf waters off southeast coast of South Australia and west coast of Victoria • size undetermined, but size of blue whale feeding area is 4632 mi² (12,000 km²)	• Dec–May: blue whale, *Balaenoptera musculus*; occasionally: sei whale, *Balaenoptera borealis*; fin whale, *Balaenoptera physalus*; southern right whale, *Eubalaena australis*; sperm whale, *Physeter macrocephalus*; bottlenose dolphin, *Tursiops truncatus*; short-beaked common dolphin, *Delphinus delphis*; various beaked whales • abundant marine wildlife in the area is linked to biological richness of upwelling where blue whales feed
Queensland MPAs **(11) Moreton Bay Marine Park** • Moreton Bay, around Moreton and Stradbroke islands • 132,292 mi² (342,725 km²)	• Jul–Nov: humpback whale, *Megaptera novaeangliae*; year-round: bottlenose dolphin, *Tursiops truncatus*; Indo-Pacific hump-backed dolphin, *Sousa chinensis*; occasionally: southern right whale, *Eubalaena australis*; minke whale, *Balaenoptera acutorostrata*; sperm whale, *Physeter macrocephalus*; common dolphin, *Delphinus* sp; spinner dolphin, *Stenella longirostris;* Risso's dolphin, *Grampus griseus*; orca, *Orcinus orca*; melon-headed whale, *Peponocephala electra*

Notes and rationale	For more information
• MPA from coast to pelagic, state and federal management, adjoins land-based Cape Range National Park; about half state and half Commonwealth waters. • Designated as a Commonwealth marine park in 1987, Ningaloo's large fringing reef, located close to land, is the main rationale for protection, but cetaceans are considered a major feature of the park, especially during the humpback whale migration. • Ningaloo Marine Park has three types of management zones: sanctuary zones (to provide special protection areas for wildlife; visitors can watch but not fish or collect anything), recreation zones (recreation consistent with conservation and with fishing allowed); and general use zones (allowing commercial fishing and recreational use); mostly IUCN Category II. Commonwealth waters are managed as Category II for ecosystem conservation and recreation. • Industries in the area include commercial fishing (trawling), sport fishing, resort development (leading to degradation of the reef), marine tourism, diving, mining, petroleum exploration (leases); key threat is the *Drupella* snail impact on the reef. • In July 2004, the WA government announced a Aus$5 million research programme into the reef and a draft plan to extend the state portion of the park by 147 mi^2 (380 km^3), mainly as sanctuary zones. There is a growing campaign for World Heritage listing of the area which would include Exmouth Gulf and preclude petroleum leases.	• Environment Australia, 2002c; Preen et al, 1995 • Contact: WDCS – Australasia; email: info@wdcs.org.au; web: www.wdcs.org.au • Ningaloo Marine Park; web: www.ea.gov.au/ coasts/mpa/ningaloo/ index.html
• Recognized as a blue whale feeding area in 1998. Specific areas within the upwelling are being considered for inclusion in the NRSMPA via multiple-use MPAs, potentially with some highly protected IUCN Category I areas. Area is also being considered for naming as a new 'Marine Park' and is to be the subject of a regional marine planning process (the Otway Multiple Use Management Model) under Australia's Oceans Policy. WDCS is trying to facilitate an agreement-based process with industry in the region with a view to protecting the endangered blue whales who feed in the area Dec–May. • Rationale for protection is that this massive upwelling provides a key seasonal feeding site for endangered blue whales, as well as other cetaceans. • The main potential industrial conflicts in the area stem from gas exploration and drilling, shipping and fishing.	• Gill, 2002 • Contact: WDCS – Australasia; email: info@wdcs.org.au; web: www.wdcs.org.au • Peter Gill; email: pcgill@ozemail.com.au
• There are whale watch operations in and around the park with regulations relating to use of 'personal water craft', to minimize harassment. Five zones, equivalent to IUCN Category I–VI, include a small no-take area, but 89 per cent of the park is IUCN Category IV and open to general use. The zoning plan, which is an Act of Parliament, includes the requirement for the authorities to consider cumulative impacts when giving permission for use. • More specific cetacean habitat protection needed; should be based on research into distribution and habitat needs in the park.	• Contact: Moreton Bay Marine Park; web: www.epa.qld.gov.au/ parks_and_forests/ marine_parks/moreton_bay/ • WDCS – Australasia; email: info@wdcs.org.au; web: www.wdcs.org.au

Table 5.22 *continued*

Name of MPA or sanctuary, location and size	Cetacean and other notable species
(12) **Hervey Bay Marine Park,** *proposed for expansion* • Hervey Bay, off central Queensland, along the north and western coast of Fraser Island, including Platypus Bay • 763 mi^2 (1978 km^2)	• Jul–Oct: humpback whale, *Megaptera novaeangliae*; occasionally: bottlenose dolphin, *Tursiops truncatus*; rarely: Risso's dolphin, *Grampus griseus*
[MPAs 13–17] **(13) Cairns Marine Park** • 2693 mi^2 (6978 km^2) **(14) Trinity Inlet–Marlin Coast Marine Park** • 149 mi^2 (386 km^2) **(15) Mackay Capricorn Marine Park** • 12,812 mi^2 (33,193 km^2) **(16) Woongarra Marine Park** • 41 mi^2 (107 km^2) **(17) Townsville Whitsunday Marine Park, including Hinchinbrook Management Area** • 2693 mi^2 (6978 km^2)	• Jul–Sept: humpback whale, *Megaptera novaeangliae*; Mar–Oct: minke whale (dwarf subsp), *Balaenoptera acutorostrata*; year-round: bottlenose dolphin, *Tursiops truncatus*; Indo-Pacific hump-backed dolphin, *Sousa chinensis*; Irrawaddy dolphin, *Orcaella brevirostris*; various other cetaceans possible; also: Risso's dolphin, *Grampus griseus* (Hinchinbrook Management Area in the Townsville Whitsunday Marine Park is the only one to specify protection of marine mammals including three dolphin species and several whale species) • also: dugong
[MPAs 18–20] *(18)* **Gumoo Woojabuddee Marine Park,** *proposed* *(19)* **Gulf of Carpentaria Marine Park,** *proposed* *(20)* **Torres Strait Indigenous Protected Area,** *proposed*	• various cetaceans probable • also: dugong

Notes and rationale	For more information
• Declared in 1989 to conserve the natural resources of the tidal lands and waters of Hervey Bay, as well as the humpback whales that migrate close to land and stop in the bay from Aug to Nov. • From Aug–Dec, the park is a Whale Management and Monitoring Area as set out in the zoning plan with active regulations in order to manage human activities in the vicinity of humpback whales and monitor the effect to ensure their protection. As part of the substantial whale watch industry, whale watchers visiting Hervey Bay pay a levy to help fund Queensland Dept of the Environment and Heritage management and research programmes. • Proposed additions include significant habitats in Hervey Bay, Great Sandy Strait and Tin Can Bay.	• Contact: Hervey Bay Marine Park; web: www.epa.qld.gov.au/ parks_and_forests/ marine_parks/ zoning_plans/; for background, see: www.epa.qld.gov.au/ publications?id=509 • WDCS – Australasia; email: info@wdcs.org.au; web: www.wdcs.org.au
• As of 2004, Queensland's protection regime for coastal waters is in a state of flux. Under draft legislation (Queensland Marine Parks Act), the 3 nm (3.5 mi or 5.6 km) state limit waters and adjacent tidal lands of Queensland will all essentially be named 'marine parks'. These will then be divided into management areas that are then zoned for special and higher protection including two types of Marine National Park zones, a Scientific Research Zone and a Preservation Zone. The zones range from IUCN Category I to VI and are being set up along the lines of the long-standing Great Barrier Reef MPA. While this approach holds a great deal of promise in terms of protecting marine fauna and ecosystems, and introducing sensible management of marine resources, there are big obstacles to overcome: (1) there is no attempt to use ecosystem-based management as a decision-making tool for the areas and zones that are put in place and how they are managed and monitored; (2) at present, only very small areas are being designated as IUCN Category I areas (on the order of 0.1 per cent of the total MPA); and (3) thus far in the two draft zoning plans (for Mackay Capricorn and Townsville Whitsunday marine parks), there has been no effort to identify and protect cetacean critical habitat either as Special Management Areas for whales or in IUCN Category I areas. • Cetacean research needs to be done to determine cetacean habitat needs and location of critical habitat with special management provisions to be applied.	• Contact: WDCS – Australasia; email: info@wdcs.org.au; web: www.wdcs.org.au • For Mackay Capricorn Marine Park zoning plans, see: www.epa.qld.gov.au/ parks_and_forests/ marine_parks/ zoning_plans/; for background, see: www.epa.qld.gov.au/ publications?id=511 • For Hinchinbrook Management Area of Townsville Whitsunday Marine Park zoning plans, see: www.epa.qld.gov.au/ parks_and_forests/ marine_parks/ zoning_plans/; for background, see: www.epa.qld.gov.au/ publications?id=569
• These are proposed marine parks under the Queensland Marine Parks Act which is being put in place within the 3 nm (3.5 mi or 5.6 km) state limit waters of the state (see Carins Marine Park and others above for more information). • Cetacean research needs to be done to determine cetacean presence, habitat needs and location of critical habitat with special management provisions to be applied.	• Contact: WDCS – Australasia; email: info@wdcs.org.au; web: www.wdcs.org.au

Table 5.22 *continued*

Name of MPA or sanctuary, location and size	Cetacean and other notable species
New South Wales MPAs **(21) Cape Byron Marine Park** **(including Byron Bay Sanctuary)** • Cape Byron, New South Wales • 88 mi² (227 km²)	• Jun–Oct: humpback whale, *Megaptera novaeangliae*; year-round: bottlenose dolphin, *Tursiops truncatus*; sporadic: orca, *Orcinus orca*, plus eight other cetacean species • also: meeting of Coral Sea waters and cooler southern currents produces rich marine ecosystem
(22) Jervis Bay Marine Park • Jervis Bay, New South Wales • 85 mi² (220 km²)	• year-round: bottlenose dolphin, *Tursiops truncatus*; occasional: southern right whale, *Eubalaena australis*; humpback whale, *Megaptera novaeangliae* (irregular Apr–Oct only); orca, *Orcinus orca*; long-finned pilot whale, *Globicephala melas*; sperm whale, *Physeter macrocephalus* • also: some 200 species of fish
(23) Port Stephens Marine Park, *may be proposed* • Port Stephens, Tasman Sea, New South Wales • approximately 54 mi² (140 km²) but exact size of MPA is not determined	• resident: bottlenose dolphin, *Tursiops truncatus*; may be resident: short-beaked common dolphin, *Delphinus delphis*; Jun–Nov: humpback whale, *Megaptera novaeangliae*; sporadic: orca, *Orcinus orca*; false killer whale, *Pseudorca crassidens*; Risso's dolphin, *Grampus griseus*; Antarctic minke whale, *Balaenoptera bonaerensis*; Bryde's whale, *Balaenoptera brydei* • also: turtles, penguins

Notes and rationale	For more information
• Created in 2002, this state marine park is the fourth multiple-use MPA in NSW waters. As of 2004, zoning is being developed with specific conservation mechanisms including whale watch permits and guidelines. A special 'Byron Bay Sanctuary' is being proposed within the park which would provide greater protection to 42.5 mi^2 (110 km^2). Other, less strict zones are proposed to restrict fishing to some extent, with even a general use zone set to phase out trawling within five years. • This is an important area for long-term monitoring of migrating humpback whales, as well as a refuge area for humpback mothers and calves on migration. • The Australian National Guidelines for Cetacean Observation and Areas of Special Interest lists Cape Byron as an area of special interest and comments that, 'As the area provides such high quality land-based whale watching, boat-based cetacean watching in the area could be discouraged.' One option is to exclude commercial boat-based whale watching from the park (or at least from sanctuary zone) to reduce harassment and stress; jet skis and commercial shipping should be excluded to reduce the danger of injuries.	• Contact: Cape Byron Marine Park; web: www.mpa.nsw.gov.au/ cbmp/cbmp.htm • WDCS – Australasia; email: info@wdcs.org.au; web: www.wdcs.org.au
• Jervis Bay is a large, nearly enclosed marine water body which contains diverse habitats: mangroves, seagrass, sandy and muddy sediments, rocky reefs and underwater cliffs which support a wide variety of marine life. • 1993 proposal for a marine reserve came from NSW Fisheries, and the area has since been expanded into an NSW state marine park. • MPA is zoned, with 20 per cent of the park in highly protected IUCN Category I area (no mining, fishing or aquaculture); 72 per cent is in a 'Habitat Protection' zone allowing recreational fishing but no trawling. • According to Margi Prideaux, Trevor Ward and others, 40 per cent no-take area is preferred for adequate conservation and to include critical habitat for dolphins. • Research on resident bottlenose dolphins has been going on since 1990; dolphins provide a focus for the public to learn about Jervis Bay Marine Park. • In 2003 an operational plan was put in place. Various measures are in place to control whale watching and other activities that might have an impact on cetaceans. Mandate is to 'develop appropriate management strategies to minimize potential impacts'.	• Marine Parks Authority, 2003; Sant, 1996 • Contact: Jervis Bay Marine Park; web: www.mpa.nsw.gov.au/ jbmp/jbmp.htm • WDCS – Australasia; email: info@wdcs.org.au; web: www.wdcs.org.au
• Discussed and informally proposed as a marine park. • Rationale would be primarily to protect an important marine ecosystem but also to help ensure management in the face of the growing dolphin watching industry and to protect dolphin critical habitat. • In this, the centre for dolphin watching on the east coast of Australia, dolphins and dolphin watch tours provide a focus for the public to get to know the proposed park, but dolphin watching needs to be managed (perhaps partly through a permit system) to help protect the core habitat of the dolphins; the park could help provide a legislative framework for licensing dolphin watching as well as for managing other threats such as Fisheries' planned expansion of the aquaculture industry.	• Allen and Moller, 1999 • Contact: WDCS – Australasia; email: info@wdcs.org.au; web: www.wdcs.org.au • Simon J Allen, Marine Mammal Research Group, Macquarie University; email: sallen@ ecosys.gse.mq.edu.au

Table 5.22 *continued*

Name of MPA or sanctuary, location and size	Cetacean and other notable species
Victoria MPAs **(24) Bunurong Marine National Park** • located along 3 mi (5 km) of coast, from 1.6 mi (2.5 km) east of Cape Patterson in Southern Gippsland to the eastern end of Eagles Nest Beach, Victoria • 8 mi² (21 km²)	• southern right whale, *Eubalaena australis*; bottlenose dolphin, *Tursiops truncatus*
(25) Wilsons Promontory Marine National Park • located along 43 mi (70 km) of coast near Wilsons Promontory, Victoria • 60 mi² (155.5 km²)	• May–Oct: southern right whale, *Eubalaena australis*; occasionally, Jun–Nov: humpback whale, *Megaptera novaeangliae*; occasionally: sperm whale, *Physeter macrocephalus*; bottlenose dolphin, *Tursiops truncatus*; short-beaked common dolphin, *Delphinus delphis*; Andrew's beaked whale, *Mesoplodon bowdoini*; short-finned pilot whale, *Globicephala macrorhynchus*
(26) Cape Howe Marine National Park • near NSW border, far eastern Victoria • 15.6 mi² (40.5 km²)	• May–Oct: southern right whale, *Eubalaena australis*; humpback whale, *Megaptera novaeangliae*; orca, *Orcinus orca*
(27) Churchill Marine National Park • south of Rhyll, in Western Port, Victoria • 2.6 mi² (6.7 km²)	• year-round: bottlenose dolphin, *Tursiops truncatus*
(28) Discovery Bay Marine National Park • 12 mi (20 km) west of Portland, Victoria • 11.7 mi² (30.5 km²)	• May–Oct: southern right whale, *Eubalaena australis*; occasionally: humpback whale, *Megaptera novaeangliae*; blue whale, *Balaenoptera musculus*
(29) Ninety Mile Beach Marine National Park • 19 mi (30 km) south of Sale adjacent to the Gippsland Lakes Coastal Park, Victoria • 10.6 mi² (27.5 km²)	• May–Oct: southern right whale, *Eubalaena australis*

Notes and rationale	For more information
• State MPA established after a decade-long process which resulted in 5.3 per cent of the Victorian marine estate being conserved in highly protected IUCN Category I MPAs. *Management Strategy 2003–2010*, prepared by Parks Victoria with public consultation, will guide the preparation of management plan (see: www.parkweb.vic.gov.au/resources/ma_0059.pdf). • Rationale for protection is not cetaceans but they are listed as present and may benefit from habitat protection.	• Contact: Bunurong MNP; web: www.parkweb.vic.gov.au/1park_display.cfm?park=254 • WDCS – Australasia; email: info@wdcs.org.au; web: www.wdcs.org.au
• State MPA established after a decade-long process which resulted in 5.3 per cent of the Victorian marine estate being conserved in highly protected IUCN Category I MPAs. *Management Strategy 2003–2010*, prepared by Parks Victoria with public consultation, will guide the preparation of management plan (see: www.parkweb.vic.gov.au/resources/ma_0059.pdf). • Rationale for protection is not cetaceans but they are listed as present and may benefit from habitat protection. • The largest state park in Victoria.	• Contact: Wilsons Promontory MNP; web: www.parkweb.vic.gov.au/1park_display.cfm?park=273 • WDCS – Australasia; email: info@wdcs.org.au; web: www.wdcs.org.au
• State MPA established after a decade-long process which resulted in 5.3 per cent of the Victorian marine estate being conserved in highly protected IUCN Category I MPAs. *Management Strategy 2003–2010*, prepared by Parks Victoria with public consultation, will guide the preparation of management plan (see: www.parkweb.vic.gov.au/resources/ma_0059.pdf). • Rationale for protection is not cetaceans but they are listed as present and may benefit from habitat protection.	• Contact: Cape Howe MNP; web: www.parkweb.vic.gov.au/1park_display.cfm • WDCS – Australasia; email: info@wdcs.org.au; web: www.wdcs.org.au
• State MPA established after a decade-long process which resulted in 5.3 per cent of the Victorian marine estate being conserved in highly protected IUCN Category I MPAs. *Management Strategy 2003–2010,* prepared by Parks Victoria with public consultation, will guide the preparation of management plan (see: www.parkweb.vic.gov.au/resources/ma_0059.pdf). • Rationale for protection is not cetaceans but they are listed as present and may benefit from habitat protection.	• Contact: Churchill MNP; web: www.parkweb.vic.gov.au/1park_display.cfm?park=274 • WDCS – Australasia; email: info@wdcs.org.au; web: www.wdcs.org.au
• State MPA established after a decade-long process which resulted in 5.3 per cent of the Victorian marine estate being conserved in highly protected IUCN Category I MPAs. *Management Strategy 2003–2010*, prepared by Parks Victoria with public consultation, will guide the preparation of management plan (see: www.parkweb.vic.gov.au/resources/ma_0059.pdf). • Rationale for protection is not cetaceans but they are listed as present and may benefit from habitat protection.	• Contact: Discovery Bay MNP; web: www.parkweb.vic.gov.au/1park_display.cfm?park=257 • WDCS – Australasia; email: info@wdcs.org.au; web: www.wdcs.org.au
• State MPA established after a decade-long process which resulted in 5.3 per cent of the Victorian marine estate being conserved in highly protected IUCN Category I MPAs. *Management Strategy 2003–2010*, prepared by Parks Victoria with public consultation, will guide the preparation of management plan (see: www.parkweb.vic.gov.au/resources/ma_0059.pdf). • Rationale for protection is not cetaceans but they are listed as present and may benefit from habitat protection.	• Contact: Ninety Mile Beach MNP; web: www.parkweb.vic.gov.au/1park_display.cfm?park=263 • WDCS – Australasia; email: info@wdcs.org.au; web: www.wdcs.org.au

Table 5.22 *continued*

Name of MPA or sanctuary, location and size	Cetacean and other notable species
(30) Point Addis Marine National Park • located along 6 mi (10 km) of coast between Anglesea and Jan Juc, Victoria • 17.8 mi² (46 km²)	• year-round: bottlenose dolphin, *Tursiops truncatus*; other dolphins
(31) Point Hicks Marine National Park • 16 mi (25 km) southeast of the Cann River, East Gippsland, adjacent to Croajingolong, Victoria • 15.4 mi² (40 km²)	• May–Oct: southern right whale, *Eubalaena australis*; occasionally: humpback whale, *Megaptera novaeangliae*
(32) Port Phillip Heads Marine National Park • close to Melbourne city at southern end of Port Phillip Bay, Victoria • made up of six separate areas which total 13.8 mi² (35.8 km²)	• May–Oct: southern right whale, *Eubalaena australis*; May–Jul, Nov: humpback whale, *Megaptera novaeangliae*; year-round: bottlenose dolphin, *Tursiops truncatus*; sporadic: common dolphin, *Delphinus sp*
(33) The Twelve Apostles Marine National Park • located along 10.6 mi (17 km) of coastline, Victoria (extends out to Twelve Apostles rock formations • 29 mi² (75 km²)	• May–Oct: southern right whale, *Eubalaena australis* • also: Twelve Apostles rock formations
(34) Yaringa Marine National Park • located between the Victorian mainland and Quail Island Nature Conservation Reserve, Victoria • 3.8 mi² (9.8 km²)	• occasionally, Jun–Nov: humpback whale, *Megaptera novaeangliae*
(35) Merri Marine Sanctuary • Warnambool, Victoria • 0.1 mi² (0.25 km²)	• May–Oct: southern right whale, *Eubalaena australis*

Notes and rationale	For more information
• State MPA established after a decade-long process which resulted in 5.3 per cent of the Victorian marine estate being conserved in highly protected IUCN Category I MPAs. *Management Strategy 2003–2010*, prepared by Parks Victoria with public consultation, will guide the preparation of management plan (see: www.parkweb.vic.gov.au/resources/ma_0059.pdf). • Rationale for protection is not cetaceans but they are listed as present and may benefit from habitat protection.	• Contact: Point Addis MNP; web: www.parkweb.vic.gov.au/ 1park_display.cfm? park=264 • WDCS – Australasia; email: info@wdcs.org.au; web: www.wdcs.org
• State MPA established after a decade-long process which resulted in 5.3 per cent of the Victorian marine estate being conserved in highly protected IUCN Category I MPAs. *Management Strategy 2003–2010*, prepared by Parks Victoria with public consultation, will guide the preparation of management plan (see: www.parkweb.vic.gov.au/resources/ma_0059.pdf). • Rationale for protection is not cetaceans but they are listed as present and may benefit from habitat protection.	• Contact: Point Hicks MNP; web: www.parkweb.vic.gov.au/ 1park_display.cfm? park=266 • WDCS – Australasia; email: info@wdcs.org.au; web: www.wdcs.org.au
• State MPA established after a decade-long process which resulted in 5.3 per cent of the Victorian marine estate being conserved in highly protected IUCN Category I MPAs. *Management Strategy 2003–2010*, prepared by Parks Victoria with public consultation, will guide the preparation of management plan (see: www.parkweb.vic.gov.au/resources/ma_0059.pdf). • Rationale for protection is not cetaceans but they are listed as present and may benefit from habitat protection.	• Contact: Port Phillip Heads MNP; web: www.parkweb.vic.gov.au/ 1park_display.cfm? park=268 • WDCS – Australasia; email: info@wdcs.org.au; web: www.wdcs.org.au
• State MPA established after a decade-long process which resulted in 5.3 per cent of the Victorian marine estate being conserved in highly protected IUCN Category I MPAs. *Management Strategy 2003–2010*, prepared by Parks Victoria with public consultation, will guide the preparation of management plan (see: www.parkweb.vic.gov.au/resources/ma_0059.pdf). • Rationale for protection is not cetaceans but they are listed as present and may benefit from habitat protection. Third most visited site in Australia. • Petroleum acreage granted 2003, but no seismic exploration is allowed, in addition to no mining or fishing, same as in other Victorian marine national parks.	• Contact: The Twelve Apostles MNP; web: www.parkweb.vic.gov.au/ 1park_display.cfm? park=271 • WDCS – Australasia; email: info@wdcs.org.au; web: www.wdcs.org.au
• State MPA established after a decade-long process which resulted in 5.3 per cent of the Victorian marine estate being conserved in highly protected IUCN Category I MPAs. *Management Strategy 2003–2010*, prepared by Parks Victoria with public consultation, will guide the preparation of management plan (see: www.parkweb.vic.gov.au/resources/ma_0059.pdf). • Rationale for protection is not cetaceans but they are listed as present and may benefit from habitat protection.	• Contact: Yaringa MNP; web: www.parkweb.vic.gov.au/ 1park_display.cfm? park=276 • WDCS – Australasia; email: info@wdcs.org.au; web: www.wdcs.org.au
• State MPA established after a decade-long process which resulted in 5.3 per cent of the Victorian marine estate being conserved in highly protected IUCN Category I MPAs. *Management Strategy 2003–2010*, prepared by Parks Victoria with public consultation, will guide the preparation of management plan (see: www.parkweb.vic.gov.au/resources/ma_0059.pdf). • Rationale for protection is not cetaceans but they are listed as present and may benefit from habitat protection. Though tiny, the site is listed as a right whale calving site.	• Contact: Merri Marine Sanctuary; web: www.parkweb.vic.gov.au/ 1park_display.cfm? park=261 • WDCS – Australasia; email: info@wdcs.org.au; web: www.wdcs.org.au

Table 5.22 *continued*

Name of MPA or sanctuary, location and size	Cetacean and other notable species
South Australia MPAs **(36) Great Australian Bight Marine National Park** • head of the Great Australian Bight, off South Australia, 683 mi (1100 km) west of Adelaide • 481 mi² (1247 km²) including an area previously set aside as 75.8 mi² (196.3 km²) whale sanctuary	• May–Oct: southern right whale, *Eubalaena australis*; year-round: bottlenose dolphin, *Tursiops truncatus;* sporadic: humpback whale, *Megaptera novaeangliae*; blue whale, *Balaenoptera musculus*; Bryde's whale, *Balaenoptera brydei*; Antarctic minke whale, *Balaenoptera bonaerensis*; sperm whale, *Physeter macrocephalus*; orca, *Orcinus orca*; various beaked whales and dolphin species • also: Australian sea lions, great white sharks, penguins
(37) Encounter Bay MPA, *proposed* • Encounter Bay, off Fleurieu Peninsula and Victor Harbour, South Australia • size undetermined	• May–Oct: southern right whale, *Eubalaena australis*; year-round: bottlenose dolphin, *Tursiops truncatus*; various others
(38) Adelaide Dolphin Sanctuary, *proposed* • in Port River, the North Arm, the Barker and Angas Inlets and Largs Bay, in Adelaide, South Australia • size undetermined	• resident: bottlenose dolphin, *Tursiops truncatus* • also: large tracts of mangroves that line the waterways providing habitat for various fish and birds • in more than a decade of research, 250+ bottlenose dolphins have been photo-IDed and 20–30 individuals are found in a concentrated area in the Port River estuary throughout the year
Western Australia MPAs **(39) Shoalwater Islands Marine Park** • 30 mi (50 km) south of Perth, Western Australia • 25.3 mi² (65.5 km²)	• year-round: Indo-Pacific bottlenose dolphin, *Tursiops aduncus*

Notes and rationale	For more information
• Marine national park declared in 1996 by State of South Australia, and extended to adjoining Commonwealth waters, outside the 3 nm (3.5 mi or 5.6 km) state limit, in 1998. • Designed to protect the winter mating and breeding ground of the southern right whale and the Australian sea lion, as well as to protect representative samples of the unique sediments and benthic fauna and flora, while attempting to manage for multiple use by industry. • Multi-use IUCN Category VI marine park has been strongly criticized for marginalizing conservation and failing to protect the significant natural features of the area; some temporal exclusion of fishing. • In 2003 the SA government banned mining in state waters of the park; it is hoped that Commonwealth will follow suit. • New management plan in process; with responsible review could lead to real critical habitat conservation.	• Environment Australia, 1999; Smyth et al, 2003 • Contact: GABMNP; web: www.deh.gov.au/coasts/mpa/gab/index.html • WDCS – Australasia; email: info@wdcs.org.au; web: www.wdcs.org.au
• Proposed MPA under the NRSMPA programme which would be the pilot MPA under the process; zoning options are being studied as of 2004. Compared to other states, SA has been very slow to implement MPAs, the only one being the somewhat disappointing Great Australian Bight Marine Park (see above). • This area would be relevant to cetaceans, although distribution and habitat research should be carried out to determine appropriate zoning and boundaries including the provision of highly protected core zones for right whale nursery and other key cetacean critical habitats.	• Contact: WDCS – Australasia; email: info@wdcs.org.au; web: www.wdcs.org.au
• Dolphins living in an estuary with diverse fish and bird species rarely occur in the heart of a city of 1 million+ people; this dolphin sanctuary could protect dolphins from adverse impacts as well as provide a framework for the development of well-managed tourism, educational and research activities. • In Nov 2000, a proposal was prepared for the Adelaide Dolphin Sanctuary in view of other initiatives such as the Gulf St Vincent Inquiry, state marine and estuarine policy, Australian MPA policy and Commonwealth government's whale and dolphin watching guidelines. A consultation paper on the sanctuary was released in 2002; if the sanctuary is approved, a management plan and process will also need to be considered. • Problems include sewage effluent, introduced marine pests such as fan worms, industrial discharges, thermal pollution and rubbish dumps near the river; local dolphin tissue analyses reveal elevated levels of PCBs, mercury and lead; there is some boat harassment of dolphins. • Draft bill and discussion paper released in 2003.	• Contact: WDCS – Australasia; email: info@wdcs.org.au; web: www.wdcs.org.au • Mike Bossley, Australian Dolphin Research Foundation; email: bossley@olis.net.au; web: www.environment.sa.gov.au/coasts/dolphin.html
• State marine park found only within the 3 nm (3.5 mi or 5.6 km) state limit. • Revised management plan is in progress, with some high-level protection, including 'look, no-take' sanctuary zones.	• Contact: Shoalwater Islands Marine Park; web: www.naturebase.net/national_parks/shoalwater.html • WDCS – Australasia; email: info@wdcs.org.au; web: www.wdcs.org.au

Table 5.22 *continued*

Name of MPA or sanctuary, location and size	Cetacean and other notable species
(40) Marmion Marine Park • north of Perth between Trigg Island and Burns Beach, Western Australia • 36.7 mi² (95 km²)	• year-round: Indo-Pacific bottlenose dolphin, *Tursiops aduncus*; striped dolphin, *Stenella coeruleoalba*; Jun–Jul, Sep–Nov: humpback whale, *Megaptera novaeangliae*
(41) Jurien Bay Marine Park • 124–186 mi (200–300 km) north of Perth, central west coast between Wedge Island and Green Head, Western Australia • along 60 mi (100 km) of coast	• Jun–Jul, Sep–Nov: humpback whale, *Megaptera novaeangliae*; May–Oct: southern right whale, *Eubalaena australis*; year-round: Indo-Pacific bottlenose dolphin, *Tursiops aduncus*
(42) Shark Bay Marine Park and World Heritage Area • Shark Bay, Western Australia • 8878 mi² (23,000 km²)	• year-round: Indo-Pacific bottlenose dolphin, *Tursiops aduncus*; Jun–Nov: humpback whale, *Megaptera novaeangliae* • also: dugong (healthy population of 10,000), green and loggerhead turtles
(43) Rowley Shoals Marine Park • located 160 mi (260 km) offshore from Broome, northwest Western Australia	• tropical cetaceans likely
(44) The Capes Marine Park, proposed • located along west coast of southwest Western Australia, between Busselton and Augusta • size undetermined	• Jun–Nov: humpback whale, *Megaptera novaeangliae*; May–Oct: southern right whale, *Eubalaena australis*; occasionally: blue whale, *Balaenoptera musculus*; Indo-Pacific bottlenose dolphin, *Tursiops aduncus*

Notes and rationale	For more information
• WA's first marine park, found only within the 3 nm (3.5 mi or 5.6 km) state limit, Marmion Marine Park includes an area which was the site of the former Marmion Whaling Station. The park now offers whale watching. • Management plan delineates small areas of high protection, sanctuary zones and other zones which restrict certain activities. • Management plan specifies marine mammal actions regarding strandings, interactions, education, monitoring and research. • Marmion Marine Park Management Plan 1992–2002 is available on the web at: www.naturebase.net/national_parks/management/pdf_files/marmion.pdf	• Contact: Marmion Marine Park; web: www.naturebase.net/national_parks/marmion.html • WDCS – Australasia; email: info@wdcs.org.au; web: www.wdcs.org.au
• State marine park found only within the 3 nm (3.5 mi or 5.6 km) state limit. • Various zones – mainly multiple use – include relatively small, high protection 'Sanctuary Zones' within the Park which prohibit all fishing. • Management Plan is in development.	• Contact: Jurien Bay Marine Park; web: www.calm.wa.gov.au/national_parks/marine/jurien/index.html| • WDCS – Australasia; email: info@wdcs.org.au; web: www.wdcs.org.au
• Inscribed on the World Heritage List in 1991, Shark Bay includes the famous Monkey Mia site where people have encountered resident bottlenose dolphins since the 1970s (100,000 people a year visit to watch the dolphins from shore). • Rationale is to protect an area of world biological importance due to the isolation of habitats on peninsulas and islands; the bay's unique hydrologic structure (hypersaline condition in southern parts of the bay leads to growth of stromatolites, ancient life form). • Bottlenose dolphins are resident in the bay year-round while humpback whales use the bay as a staging post in their migration along the coast.	• Preen et al, 1995 • Contact: WDCS – Australasia; email: info@wdcs.org.au; web: www.wdcs.org.au
• Declared as a state marine park; although far offshore, these are state islands so waters up to 3 nm (3.5 mi or 5.6 km) are state waters. • No management plan yet but some fishing restrictions have been created around the shoals. • Cetacean research needs to be done to determine cetacean presence and habitat use.	• Contact: Rowley Shoals Marine Park; web: www.naturebase.net/national_parks/rowley_shoals.html • WDCS – Australasia; email: info@wdcs.org.au; web: www.wdcs.org.au
• Proposed state marine park found within the 3 nm (3.5 mi or 5.6 km) state limit. • Popular whale watching site: humpbacks can be seen migrating past here twice a year. • Area includes critical habitat for cetaceans with possible calving and nursing areas for humpback whales as well as feeding areas for blues, and a special management zone has been mooted for this reason.	• Contact: The Capes Marine Park; web: www.naturebase.net/national_parks/marine/capes/index.html • WDCS – Australasia; email: info@wdcs.org.au; web: www.wdcs.org.au

Table 5.22 *continued*

Name of MPA or sanctuary, location and size	Cetacean and other notable species
(45) Monte Bellos/Barrow Island Marine Reserve, *proposed* • northwest shelf of Western Australia • size undetermined	• various tropical whales and dolphins possible
Northern Territory MPAs **(46) Garig Gunak Barlu National Park (also known as Cobourg Marine Park)** • 125 mi (200 km) northeast of Darwin, including Cobourg Peninsula, surrounding waters of the Arafura Sea and Van Diemen Gulf and nearby islands • 863 mi² (2236 km²) includes land and marine areas	• various tropical cetaceans probable including Indo-Pacific hump-backed dolphin, *Sousa chinensis* • also: dugong
Tasmania MPAs **(47) Governor Island Marine Reserve** • near fishing town of Bicheno, Tasmania • 0.2 mi² (0.5 km²)	• Jun–Jul, Oct–Nov: humpback whale, *Megaptera novaeangliae*; Jun–Oct: southern right whale, *Eubalaena australis*; year-round: bottlenose dolphin, *Tursiops truncatus*; various other cetaceans (species listings are in or near reserve)
NEW ZEALAND Dominion of New Zealand **(B) New Zealand Marine Mammal Sanctuary** • New Zealand national waters, to the limits of the EEZ • 1.86 million mi² (4.83 million km²)	• 30 resident or transient plus 7 rare cetacean species; 1 endemic • also: various seals and sea lions
(48) Auckland Islands Marine Mammal Sanctuary and Marine Reserve • located 12 nm (22.2 km) all around Auckland Islands, New Zealand subantarctic, 286 mi (460 km) south of New Zealand • 1868 mi² (4840 km²)	• May–Oct: southern right whale, *Eubalaena australis* • also: New Zealand sea lion and various endemic species of fauna and flora; birds include Gibson's albatross, southern royal albatross, sooty albatross, Antarctic prion, white-chinned petrel, subantarctic diving petrel, nothern giant petrel, white-fronted tern, white-faced storm petrel and the New Zealand falcon

Notes and rationale	For more information
• Proposed state marine reserve found within the 3 nm (3.5 mi or 5.6 km) state limit. • This proposed reserve may become WA's first 'Marine Management Area' with multiple use proscribed. • It is important to do studies to determine cetacean species found and habitat use in order to protect critical habitat areas.	• Contact: WDCS – Australasia; email: info@wdcs.org.au; web: www.wdcs.org.au
• First park in the world to be declared under the Ramsar Convention as a wetland of international importance (IUCN Category II). • Cetaceans are not listed but are almost certainly present in park waters; cetacean research needs to be done to determine cetacean presence and location of critical habitat with special management provisions to be applied.	• Contact: WDCS – Australasia; email: info@wdcs.org.au; web: www.wdcs.org.au
• State MPA declared 1991, rated IUCN Category IV. As of 2004, Tasmania is implementing its MPA strategy and is considering MPAs in the Davey and Twofold Shelf Bioregion, Port Davey/Bathurst Harbour area and in the Kent group of islands, but it is not known yet if cetaceans would be part of these proposals. • Rationale for protection is not cetaceans but they are listed as present. However, the area is very small. Cetacean distribution and habitat research should be carried out to determine if a larger area would be able to protect significant cetacean habitat.	• Contact: Governor Island Marine Reserve; web: www.dpiwe.tas.gov.au/ inter.nsf/WebPages/ RLIG-52Y7GV?open • WDCS – Australasia; email: info@wdcs.org.au; web: www.wdcs.org.au
• Sanctuary (not declared as such, but with legal sanction and strong protection for all marine mammals) is based on the 1978 Marine Mammal Protection Act.	• WWF, 2003
• Marine mammal sanctuary status under s.22 of the Marine Mammals Protection Act was obtained in 1993 under the Marine Mammals Protection Act 1978. Land areas of the islands are a reserve, accessed only by permit; marine area within the sanctuary was approved for higher level of protection (IUCN Category Ia) as NZ's second largest marine reserve in 2003. • New Zealand sea lion colony was the original rationale for protecting the islands, but area is now recognized as an important cetacean mating and breeding area particularly for an important stock of the southern right whales recently determined to be distinct from the Western Australian stock. • Cetacean research started in 1995 including photo-ID, biopsy darting for genetics and pollution studies, theodolite and acoustic tracking or recording (abundance-distribution studies). • Expansion of marine reserve has been suggested to cover all NZ's subantarctic islands (Bounty, Antipodes and Campbell, already named a World Heritage Area); Campbell also has southern right whale habitat.	• Baker et al, 1999; Donoghue, 1995, 1996; Patenaude and Baker, 2000; Patenaude et al, 1998, 2000 • Contact: Mike Donoghue, Dept of Conservation (DOC); email: donoghue@ icarus.ihug.co.nz; web: www.doc.govt.nz/ Conservation/Marine-and Coastal/Marine-Reserves/index.asp • Nathalie Patenaude, Univ of Auckland; email: n.patenaude@ auckland.ac.nz • Contact: WDCS – Australasia; email: info@wdcs.org.au; web: www.wdcs.org.au

Table 5.22 *continued*

Name of MPA or sanctuary, location and size	Cetacean and other notable species
(49) **Banks Peninsula Marine Mammal Sanctuary** and *proposed* **extension** • located around the Banks Peninsula, east coast, South Island • current size is 440 mi² (1140 km²); extension dimensions undetermined, could include additional protection within its boundaries (see Akaroa Harbour Marine Reserve, *proposed*)	• Hector's dolphin, *Cephalorhynchus hectori* (endemic) • also: small breeding population of endangered yellow-eyed penguin
(50) **Akaroa Harbour Marine Reserve,** *proposed* • southeastern part of Akaroa Harbour, South Island • no size data	• Hector's dolphin, *Cephalorhynchus hectori* (endemic)
(51) **Doubtful Sound Marine Sanctuary,** *proposed* • Doubtful Sound • no size data	• bottlenose dolphin, *Tursiops truncatus*
(52) **West Coast Marine Park,** *proposed* • west coast, North Island, at least between Port Waikato and Kaipara Harbour, some 62 mi (100 km) along the coast • size undetermined but should be at least 286 mi² (740 km²)	• Hector's dolphin, *Cephalorhynchus hectori* (endemic population or subspecies locally called Maui dolphins; critically endangered: fewer than 100 individuals left)

Notes and rationale	For more information
• Established in 1988 under federal jurisdiction (marine mammal sanctuary status under s.22 of the Marine Mammals Protection Act) with public and scientific support. • This sanctuary resulted from a survey which showed Hector's dolphin was declining and that Banks Peninsula was one of several key breeding areas remaining; dolphin entanglement in commercial and amateur sport nets set between Timaru and Motunau, which includes the Banks Peninsula area, was high and considered to have an adverse effect on numbers of dolphins in the area. • Sanctuary prohibits most gill netting (total set-net ban 1 Nov–28 Feb) but continuing problems with recreational fisheries and large number of mortalities suggest need for tighter regulations, possible expansion of the sanctuary or core marine reserves, and greater management. • Within sanctuary boundaries are the small, more stringently protected Pohatu Marine Reserve and the proposed Akaroa Harbour Marine Reserve.	• Dawson and Slooten, 1993; Donoghue, 1996 • Contact: Mike Donoghue and Rob Suisted, Dept of Conservation (DOC); email: donoghue@ icarus.ihug.co.nz; web: www.doc.govt.nz/ Conservation/Marine-and-Coastal/Marine-Reserves/ index.asp • WDCS – Australasia; email: info@wdcs.org.au; web: www.wdcs.org.au
• Proposed by Akaroa Marine Reserve Society in 1996 and decision from DOC still pending. • This proposed reserve, which includes habitat of the threatened Hector's dolphin, lies within the existing Banks Peninsula Marine Mammal Sanctuary and would apply a higher level of protection – IUCN Category I.	• Contact: Mike Donoghue, Dept of Conservation (DOC); email: donoghue@ icarus.ihug.co.nz • WDCS – Australasia; email: info@wdcs.org.au; web: www.wdcs.org.au
• Proposed in recent paper by Lusseau and Higham (in press) as a strategy to manage boat-based dolphin watching industry. Lusseau and Higham identified critical habitat areas through spatio-ecological analysis using observational data and recommended a multi-level (zoned) sanctuary.	• Lusseau and Higham (in press) • Contact: WDCS – Australasia; email: info@wdcs.org.au; web: www.wdcs.org.au
• In June 2003 all set netting was banned from Maunganui Bluff to Pariokariwa Point to protect the dolphins; ban should be extended to cover dolphins' full range. • Royal Forest and Bird Protection Society, among other groups, is proposing the creation of a marine park as well as extension of the fishing bans on set netting to include trawlers. MPA core area would need to cover a minimum of up to 4 nm (7.4 km) from the shore by 62 miles (100 km) along the coast in order to protect the main feeding habitat.	• Contact: Mike Donoghue, Dept of Conservation (DOC); email: donoghue@ icarus.ihug.co.nz • Royal Forest and Bird Protection Society of New Zealand Inc; web: www.forest-bird.org.nz/ • WDCS – Australasia; email: info@wdcs.org.au; web: www.wdcs.org.au

EPILOGUE

In the time it took to research and write this book, I am pleased to say that the number of marine protected areas (MPAs) with cetacean habitat, proposed and existing, more than quadrupled. Today, there are some 358 existing MPAs with cetacean habitat, 41 of which are proposed for expansion, plus 176 newly proposed MPAs with cetacean habitat, and the number grows every month (Table E.1). The worldwide total is 534 proposed or existing MPAs with cetaceans.

At least 102 countries and overseas territories, plus Antarctica, have existing or proposed MPAs with cetacean habitat, as listed in this book. Most countries and overseas territories have MPAs of some description, according to the UNEP-WCMC 2002 World Database of Protected Areas, although there is a huge discrepancy in the extent and degree of protection even among those with the largest MPA estate (UNEP-WCMC, 2002). Greenland, for example, has seven times more area in listed protected areas than Russia, yet Greenland's level of protection and enforcement has been strongly criticized in recent years while Russia has managed to keep the bulk of its large zapovedniks and national parks as IUCN Category I or II highly protected areas.

Some coastal countries still have no declared MPAs. However, virtually all of the coastal countries of the world have signed one or more conventions which commit them to participating in MPA conservation on a regional or international level, both in their own national waters to the limits of the EEZs as well as on the high seas.

In Durban, at the V World Parks Congress, in September 2003, delegates called for at least five ecologically significant MPAs to be designated on the high seas by 2008. Some 19 countries and territories have now declared or are in the process of declaring their national waters (including all the EEZ) as whale or cetacean sanctuaries (see Table 1.2, p17); there is hope that some of these areas may become real MPAs – managed multi-zone biosphere reserves with highly protected core areas that offer significant habitat protection for

Table E.1 Total sanctuaries and MPAs with cetacean habitat in each marine region

Marine region	Existing high-seas and multi-country sanctuaries and MPAs	Existing national sanctuaries	Existing MPAs (includes existing MPAs specifically proposed for expansion)	Existing MPAs specifically proposed for expansion	Proposed high-seas and multi-country sanctuaries and MPAs	Proposed national sanctuaries	Proposed or suggested MPAs (including MPAs under discussion)
1 Antarctic	1(s)	–	3	–	–	–	1
2 Arctic	–	–	23	2	3	–	16
3 Mediterranean	1	–	24	3	–	–	35
4 Northwest Atlantic	–	1	11	—	—	—	7
5 Northeast Atlantic	1	2	25	8	2	–	25
6 Baltic	–	–	1	–	–	–	4
7 Wider Caribbean	–	1(s)	33	2	–	1	15
8 West Africa	–	1	41	2	1(s)	1	6
9 South Atlantic	–	1	33	2	1(s)	–	4
10 Central Indian Ocean	1(s)	–	5	2	–	–	4
11 Arabian Seas	1(s)	–	2	–	–	–	2
12 East Africa	1(s)	1	28	3	–	–	5
13 East Asian Seas	1(s)	–	18	2	1	1	16
14 South Pacific	–	9	16	3	1(s)	1	1
15 Northeast Pacific	–	1(s)	16	4	1	–	8
16 Northwest Pacific	–	–	22	2	–	–	11
17 Southeast Pacific	1	1	17	3	1(s)	–	4
18 Australia–New Zealand	2(s)	2	40	3	1(s)	–	12
Totals	**5**	**19**	**358**	**41**	**9**	**4**	**176**

Notes:
(s) = shared with another marine region (counted more than once in separate marine regions).
Numbers in italics are proposed sanctuaries and MPAs. Proposed MPAs in the Arctic and the Northwest Pacific include 5 and 10 MPAs specifically proposed in Table 5.3, as well as 11 unnamed MPAs proposed in Russian waters. Totals for proposed high-seas and multi-country sanctuaries and MPAs do not include the proposed Global Whale Sanctuary.
Source: Table is based on data obtained for this book, as shown in Tables 5.2, 5.3, 5.6, 5.7, 5.8, 5.9, 5.10, 5.11, 5.12, 5.13, 5.14, 5.15, 5.17, 5.18, 5.19, 5.20. 5.21 and 5.22.

cetaceans. At the same time, accelerating technological advances such as GIS mapping, satellite tracking and biopsy research, paired with the photo-ID censuses of the past three decades, have increased our understanding and our ability to study, identify and monitor cetacean populations and to define their habitat needs.

All the newly established MPAs and MPA programmes represent the good intentions and hopes of many people. Still, few MPAs protect cetacean habitat as well as they could, or even adequately. Few have been set up using the guidelines suggested in this book which are built around core critical habitat protection in IUCN Category I areas. The consensus from MPA practitioners around the world at the V World Parks Congress was that at least 20 to 30 per cent of each marine and coastal habitat should be in highly protected IUCN Category I areas. At present, according to Roberts and Hawkins (2000), an estimated half a per cent, or one two-hundredth, of the world ocean has been designated as MPAs for all purposes, but only a very rough 0.0001 (one ten-thousandth) of the world ocean exists in fully or highly protected marine reserves.

As for ecosystem-based management, it is scarcely more than an abstract concept for most – if that. Few MPAs even have adequate management plans or provisions for enforcement. Networks of MPAs are being talked about in some areas and there are some fledgling networks, but they have barely started functioning. And there are many other concerns.

I debated whether to put my 'worry list' here in the Epilogue. I don't want these concerns to be taken as part of my key conclusions about cetacean MPAs. They are not. Still, I do think this list deserves consideration in this final section. Without being fully aware of many of the issues on this list, we have a greater risk of suffering the impact from them. Although, even with full awareness and considerable action, these worrisome developments are unlikely to disappear soon.

Here, then, is my list of concerns:

1 That the worldwide collapse of wild commercial fishing stocks, currently being talked about, may prove to be much less fixable and more long term even than imagined. Maybe it is 'permanent' and the future of the sea will only or largely be farmed fish, which brings it own ecological problems.

2 That protecting the recommended 20–30 per cent of the world ocean in IUCN Category I core areas will be impossibly too ambitious, and whatever smaller percentage is 'do-able' turns out to be too little, too late to make much of a difference.

3 That despite habitat protection, we will continue to suffer long-term declines of various cetacean species. It may be that cetacean time scales will prove so great, and cetacean needs so complex, that habitat protection and other conservation measures will make little or no difference in terms of the ultimate recovery of the great whale species that declined to a fraction of their original numbers.

4 That the long arm of industry will push for all-out development of the seabed and the water column, leading to an acceleration of development rather than a sustainable or precautionary approach.

5 That governments will be unable to come together to join, or even respect, other countries' efforts to protect significant portions of international waters, the global common, and that these open areas will be exploited even more intensively than before.

6 That previously progressive governments will 'turn their backs' on well-established protected areas and will weaken their MPA estate with multiple-use zones that provide little or no core protection.

7 That, as the existing commercial fish stocks are reduced to uncommercial levels, whaling and dolphin hunting will return, spoiling whale watching and marine protected areas and accelerating cetacean population declines.

8 That the key regional initiatives for cetacean and marine conservation, such as ACCOBAMS, the EU Habitats and Species Directive and the Cartagena Convention, among others, will not fulfil their promise, and that these efforts that have occupied the energies and passions of so many people for the past decade and more will be wasted or heavily diluted due to increasing development and political pressures.

9 That global warming will render many of the hard-won MPAs irrelevant as cetaceans and other species move out of their traditional habitats in search of adequate food sources and living conditions.

10 That the current effort to claim vast new areas of the high seas as part of national territories and EEZs will lead to uncertainty and greater exploitation of the sea.

11 That the 21st century focus on combating terrorism, paralleled by increasing military budgets and armament production, will dominate the political agendas of certain countries for the foreseeable future. The current reliance on waging war as a diplomatic tool stands as a huge waste of funds, human energies and potential. It is both passively and actively destructive of MPA and other conservation efforts. With the threat of military activities, conservation becomes marginalized, irrelevant, bordering on the hopeless.

As military activities begin (both preparations for war and actual war), in the marine environment alone, military traffic dominates the water, missiles and mines are fired or dropped and lost, harbours and coastal industries are savaged, oil wells and refineries bombed, sabotaged and left to leak or burn out of control. The human and environmental cost of such military folly can be catastrophic. Even one so-called 'limited' war can wipe out in weeks the hard-won conservation gains of decades. The implications of larger conflicts are staggering.

Still, in the face of these depressing prospects, we have no choice but to do what we can, locally and regionally, to choose optimistic problem-solving as our modus operandi. This applies to cetacean and marine habitat conservation, too. We have to continue to work 'as if'. We have no choice but to hope.

REFERENCES

Agardy, T (1997) *Marine Protected Areas and Ocean Conservation*, Academic Press, London, 224pp

Aguilar, A (2000) Population biology, conservation threats and status of Mediterranean striped dolphins, *Journal of Cetacean Research and Management* 2(1), pp17–26

Ainley, DG (2002) The Ross Sea, Antarctica: where all ecosystem processes still remain for study, but maybe not for long, *Marine Ornithology* 31, pp55–62

Airoldi, S, A Azzellino, B Nani, M Ballardini, C Bastoni, G Notarbartolo di Sciara and A Sturlese (1999) Whale watching in Italy: results of the first three years of activity, in *European Research on Cetaceans* 13, Proceedings of the annual conference of the European Cetacean Society, pp153–156

Alcala, AC (2001) *Marine Reserves in the Philippines: Historical Development, Effects and Influence on Marine Conservation Policy*, The Bookmark, Inc, Makati, Philippines

Alder, J, NA Sloan and H Uktolseya (1994) A comparison of management planning and implementation in three Indonesian marine protected areas, *Ocean and Coastal Management* 24, pp179–198

Allen, SJ and LM Moller (1999) Port Stephens Bottlenose Dolphin Population Survey, report to NSW National Parks and Wildlife Service (unpublished), 40pp

Anaya Reyna, G (1996) Status of marine protected areas in Mexico, graduate project, Marine Affairs Program, Dalhousie University, Halifax, Nova Scotia, 87pp

Andersen, J (1993) The Monterey Bay National Marine Sanctuary, *Whalewatcher* fall/winter, pp7–8

Angel, MA (unpublished) Case for a marine protected area in the regions of the Celtic Sea and South-western Approaches

Anon (ed) (1995) Proceedings of the First International Conference on the Southern Ocean Whale Sanctuary, Auckland, New Zealand, 15–16 October 1994, Department of Conservation, New Zealand, and Whale and Dolphin Conservation Society, Bath, UK, 119pp

Anon (1998) Observations about impact of petroleum activities in the south of Santa Cruz Province, report of the 3eras jornadas de preservación de agua, alre y suelo en la industria del petroleo y del gas, IAPG, pp157–176

Antarctic Division, Australian Department of Environment, Sport and Territories, and P Dingwall (1995) Marine Region 1: Antarctic, in G Kelleher, C Bleakley and S Wells (eds) *A Global Representative System of Marine Protected Areas. Vol I*, The Great Barrier Reef Marine Park Authority, The World Bank and IUCN, Washington, DC, pp45–59

ANZECC (1999) *Strategic Plan of Action for the National Representative System of Marine Protected Areas: A Guide for Action by Australian Governments*, Australian and New Zealand Environment and Conservation Council, Task Force on Marine Protected Areas, Environment Australia, Canberra

Arcangeli, A and L Marini (1999) Considerazioni sull'ecologia comportamentale di una popolazione di *Tursiops truncatus* nelle acque della Sardegna sud-orientale, poster presentato al 4 Convegno Nazionale sui Cetacei e sulle tartarughe marine, Museo Civico Storia Naturale, Milano, 11–12 November

Arcangeli, A, L Marini and S Nannarelli (1997) 'Progetto Tursiope': dati preliminari sulla presenza di *Tursiops truncatus* in Sardegna, atti del II Convegno Nazionale sui Cetacei, Napoli, December

Arnold, H (1997) The Dolphin Space Programme: the development and assessment of an accreditation scheme for dolphin-watching boats in the Moray Firth, a report for Scottish Wildlife Trust, Scottish Natural Heritage and EU LIFE Programme, Inverness

Attwood, CG, BQ Mann, J Beaumont and JM Harris (1997) Review of the state of marine protected areas in South Africa, *South African Journal of Marine Science* 18, pp341–367

Augier, H (1985) Protected marine areas. The example of France: appraisal and prospects, European Committee for the Conservation of Nature and Natural Resources, Council of Europe, Strasbourg, France, 134pp

Augustowski, M and JT Palazzo Jr (2003) Building a marine protected areas network to protect endangered species: whale conservation as a tool for integrated management in South America, presented at the V World Parks Congress, IUCN, Durban, South Africa, Sept 2003, 6pp

AXYS Environmental Consulting Ltd (2000) Bowie Seamount Pilot Marine Protected Area Workshop Summary, draft, 32pp

Baird, IG and I Beasley (in preparation) Paper on conservation of Irrawaddy dolphins in the Mekong River

Baird, IG and B Mounsouphom (1994) Irrawaddy dolphins (*Orcaella brevirostris*) in Southern Lao PDR and Northeastern Cambodia, *Natural History Bulletin of the Siam Society* 42(2), pp159–175

Baird, IG and B Mounsouphom (1995) National status of the Irrawaddy dolphin (*Orcaella brevirostris*) in Lao PDR, paper presented to the UNEP Workshop on Biology and Conservation of Small Cetaceans in Southeast Asia, 27–30 June, Dumaguete, Philippines

Baird, IG, B Mounsouphom and PJ Stacey (1994) Preliminary surveys of Irrawaddy dolphins (*Orcaella brevirostris*) in Lao PDR and northeastern Cambodia, *Report of the International Whaling Commission* 44, pp367–369

Baird, RW (2001) Status of killer whales, *Orcinus orca*, in Canada, *Canadian Field-Naturalist* 115(4), pp676–701

Baker, CS, NJ Patenaude, JL Bannister, J Robbins and H Kato (1999) Distribution and diversity of mtDNA lineages among southern right whales (*Eubalaena australis*) from Australia and New Zealand, *Marine Biology* 134, pp1–7

Baker, M, B Bett, D Billett and A Rogers (2001) The status of natural resources on the high-seas – an environmental perspective, WWF/IUCN, Gland, Switzerland, 68pp

Ballantine, WJ (1995) Networks of 'no-take' marine reserves are practical and necessary, in NL Shackell and JHM Willison (eds) *Marine Protected Areas and Sustainable Fisheries*, Proceedings of a symposium on marine protected areas and sustainable fisheries conducted at the Second International Conference on Science and the Management of Protected Areas, Dalhousie University, Halifax, Nova Scotia, 16–20 May 1994, pp13–20

Bannister, JL, CM Kemper and RM Warneke (1996) *The Action Plan for Australian Cetaceans*, Wildlife Australia, Endangered Species Program, Project No 380, Australian Nature Conservation Agency, Canberra, Australia, 242pp

Barlow, J (2002) Management, in WF Perrin, B Würsig and JGM Thewissen (eds) *Encyclopedia of Marine Mammals*, Academic Press, San Diego, pp706–709

Barr, BW (1995) The US National Marine Sanctuary Program and its role in preserving sustainable fisheries, in NL Shackell and JHM Willison (eds) *Marine Protected Areas and Sustainable Fisheries*, Proceedings of a symposium on marine protected areas and sustainable fisheries conducted at the Second International Conference on Science and the Management of Protected Areas, Dalhousie University, Halifax, Nova Scotia, 16–20 May 1994, pp165–173

Batisse, M (1990) Development and implementation of the biosphere reserve concept and its applicability to coastal regions, *Environmental Conservation* 17(2), pp111–116

Batisse, M and AJ de Grissac (1995) Marine Region 3: Mediterranean, in G Kelleher, C Bleakley and S Wells (eds) *A Global Representative System of Marine Protected Areas. Vol I*, The Great Barrier Reef Marine Park Authority, The World Bank and IUCN, Washington, DC, pp77–104

Baur, DC, MJ Bean and ML Gosliner (1999) The laws governing marine mammal conservation in the United States, in JR Twiss, Jr and RR Reeves (eds) *Conservation and Management of Marine Mammals*, Smithsonian, Washington, DC, pp48–86

Bearzi, G (1995) The Cres-Losinj dolphin reserve: modifications, update and further suggestions, document prepared for the Management Plan for the Conservation of the Cres-Losinj Archipelago, Tethys Research Institute Technical Report TRI/ADP 95-3, 6pp

Bearzi, G and G Notarbartolo di Sciara (1992) Preliminary observations of bottle-nosed dolphins near the island of Tavolara, Sardinia, *European Research on Cetaceans* 6, Proceedings of the annual conference of the European Cetacean Society, pp127–129

Bearzi, G and G Notarbartolo di Sciara (1997) Adriatic Dolphin Project, report 1987–1996, Tethys Research Institute Report TRI/ADP 97-01, 30pp

Bearzi, G, G Notarbartolo di Sciara and G Lauriano (1993) The Cres-Losinj dolphin reserve: proposal for the institution of a marine reserve in the waters adjacent to the east coast of Cres and Losinj, Tethys Research Institute Technical Report TRI/DP 93-01, 18pp

Bearzi, G, RR Reeves, G Notarbartolo, E Politi, A Cañadas, A Frantzis and B Mussi (2003) Ecology, status and conservation of short-beaked common dolphins (*Delphinus delphis*) in the Mediterranean Sea, *Mammal Review* 33(34), pp224–252

Belkovich, VM (2002) White whales of the European North: distribution and number, Marine Mammals of the Holarctic, Second International Conference, Baikal, 10–15 September, pp31–32

Bernstein, B (2002) MPA perspective: ways to ensure marine reserves get a fair test, *MPA News* 3(8), p5

Berrow, SD (2000) EU Habitats Directive and tourism development programmes in the Shannon estuary, Ireland, EU Conference on Sustainable Tourism, Berlin, 6pp

Berrow, S (2001) How effective is Ireland's whale and dolphin sanctuary? in PGH Evans and E Urquiola Pascual (eds) *Proceedings of the Workshop, Protected Areas for Cetaceans*, ECS Newsletter No 38 – special issue, pp44–47

Berrow, S (2003) An assessment of the framework, legislation and monitoring required to develop genuinely sustainable whalewatching, in B Garrod and J Wilson (eds) *Marine Ecotourism Issues and Experiences*, Channel View Publications, pp66–78

Berrow, SD and B Holmes (1999) Tour boats and dolphins: quantifying the activities of whalewatching boats in the Shannon estuary, Ireland, *Journal of Cetacean Research and Management* 1(2), pp199–204

Berrow, S and J Petch (1998) Pelagic yacht-based whale watching. Exploratory voyages off the west coast of Ireland, unpublished report from the Irish Whale and Dolphin Group, October, 26pp

Berrow, SD and E Rogan (1997) Cetaceans stranded on the Irish coast, 1901–1995, *Mammal Review* 27(1), pp51–76

Berrow, SD, B Holmes and O Kiely (1996) Distribution and abundance of bottle-nosed dolphins *Tursiops truncatus* (Montagu) in the Shannon estuary, Ireland, *Biology and Environment, Proceedings of the Royal Irish Academy* 96B (1), pp1–9

Berrow, SD, P Whooley and S Ferriss (2002) Irish Whale and Dolphin Group, Cetacean sighting review (1991–2001), Irish Whale and Dolphin Group, 34pp

Bérubé, M, A Aguilar, D Dendanto, F Larsen, G Notarbartolo di Sciara, R Sears, J Sigurjonsson, R Urbàn and P Palsbøll (1998) Population genetic structure of North Atlantic, Mediterranean Sea and Sea of Cortez fin whales, *Balaenoptera physalus* (Linnaeus, 1758); analysis of mitochondrial and nuclear loci, *Molecular Ecology* 7, pp585–99

Bigg, MA (1982) An assessment of killer whale (*Orcinus orca*) stocks off Vancouver Island, British Columbia, *Report of the International Whaling Commission* 32, pp655–666

Bigg, MA, GM Ellis, JKB Ford and KC Balcomb III (1987) *Killer Whales: A Study of Their Identification, Genealogy, and Natural History in British Columbia and Washington State*, Phantom, Nanaimo, BC, pp1–79

Birkun, AA and SV Krivohizchin (2000) Distribution and population change trends of cetaceans in Krym coastal waters, Marine Mammals of the Holarctic, First International Conference, Archangelsk, 21–23 September

Birnie, P and A Moscrop (2000) Report of the Workshop on the Legal Aspects of Whale Watching, Punta Arenas, Chile, 17–20 November 1997, IFAW, Yarmouth Port, MA, 48pp

Bjørge, A and G P Donovan (eds) (1995) Biology of the phocoenids: a collection of papers, *Report of the International Whaling Commission*, special issue 16, 552pp

Björgvinsson, A (1999) Iceland Whale Watching Report 1999, Húsavík Whale Center, Húsavík, unpublished, 14pp

Bleakley, C (1995) Marine Region 14: South Pacific, in G Kelleher, C Bleakley and S Wells (eds) *A Global Representative System of Marine Protected Areas. Vol IV*, The Great Barrier Reef Marine Park Authority, The World Bank and IUCN, Washington, DC, pp13–53

Bleakley, C and V Alexander (1995) Marine Region 2: Arctic, in G Kelleher, C Bleakley and S Wells (eds) *A Global Representative System of Marine Protected Areas. Vol I*, The Great Barrier Reef Marine Park Authority, The World Bank and IUCN, Washington, DC, pp61–76.

Bleakley, C and S Wells (1995) Marine Region 13: East Asian Seas, in G Kelleher, C Bleakley and S Wells (eds) *A Global Representative System of Marine Protected Areas. Vol III*, The Great Barrier Reef Marine Park Authority, The World Bank and IUCN, Washington, DC, pp107–136

Bledsoe, LJ, DA Somerton and CM Lynde (1989) The Puget Sound runs of salmon: an examination of the changes in run size since 1896, *Canadian Special Publication of Fisheries and Aquatic Sciences* 105, pp50–61

Bolaños, J and M Campo (1998) Aspects of the ecology and behavior of coastal cetaceans populations of the state of Aragua, central coast of Venezuela, abstract, The World Marine Mammal Science Conference, Monaco, p17

Bonnelly de Calventi, I (1994) *Mamiferos Marinos en la Republica Dominicana*, Talleres Materiales y Servicos Gráficos Armando, SA, Santo Domingo, RD, 77pp

Born, EW and J Böcher (eds) (1999) *Greenland's Ecology*, Atuakkiorfik Educational, Nuuk, 431pp (available in Greenlandic, Danish and English editions)

Bowles, AE, M Smultea, B Würsig, DP DeMaster and D Palka (1994) Relative abundance and behavior of marine mammals exposed to transmissions from the Heard Island feasibility test, *Journal of the Acoustical Society of America* 96(4), pp2469–2484

Boyd, IL (2002) Antarctic marine mammals, in WF Perrin, B Würsig and JGM Thewissen (eds) *Encyclopedia of Marine Mammals*, Academic Press, San Diego, pp30–36

Brady Shipman Martin, David Pryor & Associates and Natural Environmental Consultants (1999) Special Interest Marine Tourism in the West Clare Peninsula, interim report, 39pp

Brown, MW, JM Allen and SD Kraus (1995) The designation of seasonal right whale conservation areas in the waters of Atlantic Canada, in NL Shackell and JHM Willison (eds) *Marine Protected Areas and Sustainable Fisheries*, Proceedings of a symposium on marine protected areas and sustainable fisheries conducted at the Second International Conference on Science and the Management of Protected Areas, Dalhousie University, Halifax, Nova Scotia, 16–20 May 1994, pp90–98

Brownell, Jr, RL and GP Donovan (eds) (1988) Biology of the genus *Cephalorhynchus*, *Report of the International Whaling Commission*, Special Issue 9, Cambridge, UK

Brownell, Jr, RL, AM Burdin, AA Blokhin and AA Berzin (1997) Observations on bowhead whales (*Balaena mysticetus*) in the Shantar Archipelago, western Okhotsk Sea, IBI Reports (International Marine Biological Research Institute) No 7, pp1–7

Burdin, AM, E Hoyt, H Sato, K Tarasyan and O Filatova (2001) The ecology of *Orcinus orca* in southeast Kamchatka, Russia, abstract, 14th Biennial Conference on the Biology of Marine Mammals, Vancouver, BC, Canada, 28 November–3 December

Canada Gazette (1979) Beluga protection regulation amendment PC 1979-367, 15 February 1979, Registration SOR/79-169 Fisheries Act, *Canada Gazette*, part 2, vol 113, no 4, 28/II/79, p738

Canada Gazette (1993) Marine Mammal Regulations, DORS/93-56, part II, p930

Capella, JJ, L Flórez-González and GA Bravo (1995) Site fidelity and seasonal residence of humpback whales around Isla Gorgona, a breeding ground in the Columbian Pacific, abstract,

11th Biennial Conference on the Biology of Marine Mammals, Orlando, FL, USA, 14–18 December, p20

Caranto, TM and AJ Gonzalez-Fernandez (1998) Reproduction of the river dolphin (*Inia geoffrensis*) in the wildlife refuge Guaritico, Apure State, Venezuela, abstract, The World Marine Mammal Science Conference, Monaco, p23

Carlson, C (unpublished) Cetacean sanctuaries, 36pp

Carlström, J and P Berggren (1996) Bycatch rates of harbour porpoises (*Phocoena phocoena*) in Swedish bottom set gillnet fisheries obtained from independent observers, abstract, European Cetacean Society conference, 11–13 March

CEBSE (Centro para la Conservación y Ecodesarrollo de La Bahía de Samaná y su Entorno, Inc) (1993) Documento Sintesis: Propuesta descriptiva para la implementación de la reserva de biosfera Bahía de Samana su entorno

Chiffings, AW (1995) Marine Region 11: Arabian Seas, in G Kelleher, C Bleakley and S Wells (eds) *A Global Representative System of Marine Protected Areas. Vol III*, The Great Barrier Reef Marine Park Authority, The World Bank and IUCN, Washington, DC, pp39–70

Chiofalo, G, ME Quero, S Datta, A Di Natale, PY Dremiere and AD Goodson (2000) Applying acoustic telemetry techniques to the investigation of opportunistic feeding behaviour of dolphins around fishing nets, *European Research on Cetaceans* 14, Proceedings of the annual conference of the European Cetacean Society

Cockcroft, V and P Joyce (1998) *Whale Watch. A Guide to Whales and Other Marine Mammals of Southern Africa*, Struik, Cape Town, 104pp

Commission on Geosciences, Environment, and Resources (2000) Marine Protected Areas: Tools for Sustaining Ocean Ecosystems, report of the National Research Council, National Academy Press, Washington, DC, 181pp + appendices

Commonwealth of Australia (1998) *Australia's Oceans Policy*, Volumes I and II, Environment Australia, Canberra, 48pp

Consiglio, C, A Arcangeli, B Cristo, L Marini and A Torchio (1992) Interactions between *Tursiops truncatus* and fisheries along north-eastern coasts of Sardinia, Italy, *European Research on Cetaceans* 6, Proceedings of the annual conference of the European Cetacean Society, pp35–36

Constantine, R (1998) Whale, dolphin and turtle based tourism in Niue, final report to the Niue tourism & private sector development implementing agency of the Niue government and Niue Tourist Authority, 19pp (unpublished)

Cook, P and C Carleton (2001) *Continental Shelf Limits: The Scientific and Legal Interface*, Oxford University Press, London

Cooperation Francaise – Le Parc National du Banc d'Arguin (1993) Une visite au Parc National du Banc d'Arguin, pp119–131

Cortner, HJ and MA Moote (1999) *The Politics of Ecosystem Management*, Island Press, Washington, DC

Costanza, R, R d'Arge, R de Groot, S Farber, M Grasso, B Hannon, K Limburg, S Naeem, R O'Neill, J Paruelo, R Raskin, P Sutton and M van der Belt (1997) The value of the world's ecosystem services and natural capital, *Nature* 387, pp253–259

CPPS (Comisión Permanente del Pacífico Sur) (2000) Segunda Reunión de Expertos para Revisar las actividades del Plan de Acción para la Conservación de los Mamíferos Marinos del Pacífico Sudeste, Manta, Ecuador, 3–5 December, 17pp+ 6 annexes (unpublished)

Crespo, EA (2001) Interactions between humans and marine mammals and other wildlife in Patagone, The experience of coastal management of the last ten years, in PGH Evans and E Urquiola Pascual (eds) Proceedings of the Workshop, Protected Areas for Cetaceans, ECS Newsletter No 38 – special issue

Cripps, SJ and S Christiansen (2001) A strategic approach to protecting areas on the high-seas, in Expert Workshop on Managing Risks to Biodiversity and the Environment on the High-seas, including Tools such as Marine Protected Areas – Scientific Requirements and Legal Aspects, 27 February–4 March, Vilm, Germany

Croom, M, R Wolotira and W Henwood (1995) Marine Region 15: Northeast Pacific, in G Kelleher, C Bleakley and S Wells (eds) *A Global Representative System of Marine Protected Areas. Vol IV*, The Great Barrier Reef Marine Park Authority, The World Bank and IUCN, Washington, DC, pp55–106

Curran, S (2001) Cetacean Survey of Wakatobi Marine National Park, Operation Wallacea Survey Limited, unpublished report

Curran, S, B Wilson and P Thompson (1996) Recommendations for the sustainable management of the bottlenose dolphin population in the Moray Firth, *Scottish Natural Heritage Review*, No 56

Dalebout, ML, JG Mead, CS Baker, AN Baker and AL van Helden (2002) A new species of beaked whale *Mesoplodon perrini* sp n (Cetacea: Ziphiidae) discovered through phylogenetic analysis of mitochondrial DNA sequences, *Marine Mammal Science* 18(3), pp577–608

Darling, JD (1977) Aspects of the behavior and ecology of Vancouver Island gray whales, *Eschrictius glaucus* Cope, MSc thesis, University of Victoria, Victoria, BC

Darling, JD, KM Gibson and GK Silber (1983) Observations on the abundance and behavior of humpback whales (*Megaptera novaeangliae*) off west Maui, Hawaii, 1977–79, in R Payne (ed) *Communication and Behavior of Whales*, Westview Press, Boulder, CO, pp201–222

Dawson, SM and E Slooten (1993) Conservation of Hector's dolphins: the case and process which led to establishment of the Banks Peninsula Marine Mammal Sanctuary, *Aquatic Conservation: Marine and Freshwater Ecosystems* 3, pp207–221

Day, D (1994) List of cetaceans seen in Galápagos, *Noticias de Galápagos,* April, pp5–6

de Boer, MN and MP Simmonds (2001) Beaked whales in the Southern Ocean, paper submitted to the Scientific Committee of the IWC, SC/53/SM8

de Boer, MN, R Baldwin, CLK Burton, EL Eyre, KCS Jenner, M-NM Jenner, SG Keith, KA McCabe, ECM Parsons, VM Peddemors, HC Rosenbaum, P Rudolph and M Simmonds (2002) Cetaceans in the Indian Ocean Sanctuary: a review, paper submitted to the Scientific Committee of the IWC, SC/54/05, 60pp

de Fontaubert, AC (2001) The status of natural resources on the high-seas – legal and political considerations, WWF/IUCN, Gland, Switzerland, pp69–93

de Haro, JC and M Iñíguez (1997) Ecology and behaviour of Peale's dolphin (*Lagenorhynchus australis*) (Peale, 1848), at Cabo Virgenes (52°30'S, 68°28'W) in Patagonia, Argentina, *Report of the International Whaling Commission* 47, p723 (SC/48/SM37)

Dedina, S and E Young (1995) Conservation and development in the gray whale lagoons of Baja California Sur, México, US Dept of Commerce, NTIS Publication PB 96-113154

DeNardo, C (1998) Investigating the role of spatial structure in killer whale (*Orcinus orca*) behaviour, unpublished MSc Thesis, University of Aberdeen, Aberdeen, Scotland, 81pp

Denkinger, J (1998) Pink river dolphins in black trouble, *European Cetacean Society Newsletter* 33, pp2–3

Denkinger, J, V Utreras and I Araya (1997) Demographic studies on the Amazon River dolphin (*Inia geoffrensis*) in the Cuyabeno Reserve, Ecuador, Proceedings of the Annual Conference of the European Cetacean Society (ECS), Stralsund, Germany, March

Department of Canadian Heritage and Québec Department of Environment and Wildlife (1995) Crossroads of life, site of exchanges, wellspring of riches: the Saguenay-St Lawrence Marine Park master plan, Department of Canadian Heritage and Québec Department of Environment and Wildlife, 89pp

Diaz Lopez, B, B Mussi, A Miragliuolo, D Chiota, and L Valerio (2000) Respiration patterns of fin whales off Ischia, Arcipelago Campano, Mediterranean Sea, *European Research on Cetaceans* 14, Proceedings of the annual conference of the European Cetacean Society

Diegues, A, G Harris and A de Castro Moreira (1995) Marine Region 9: South Atlantic, in G Kelleher, C Bleakley and S Wells (eds) *A Global Representative System of Marine Protected Areas.*

Vol II, The Great Barrier Reef Marine Park Authority, The World Bank and IUCN, Washington, DC, US, pp71–85

Dixon, JA and PB Sherman (1990) *Economics of Protected Areas: A New Look at Benefits and Costs,* Island Press, Washington, DC, 234pp

Dolar, MLL, WF Perrin, JP Gaudiano, ASP Yaptinchay and JML Tan (2000) A small estuarine population of *Orcaella brevirostris* of uncertain status in the Philippines, paper presented to IWC, SC/52/SM29

Don, C (2002) Could the San Juan Islands National Wildlife Refuge serve to protect marine areas? Building on existing institutions and legal authorities to create marine protected areas, *Coastal Management* 30(4), pp421–426

Donoghue, MF (1995) New Zealand progress report on cetacean research, April 1993 to March 1994, *Report of the International Whaling Commission* 45, pp247–250

Donoghue, MF (1996) The New Zealand experience – one country's response to cetacean conservation, in MP Simmonds and JD Hutchinson (eds) *The Conservation of Whales and Dolphins: Science and Practice,* John Wiley & Sons, Chichester, pp423–445

Donovan, GP (1991) A review of IWC stock boundaries, *Report of the International Whaling Commission*, Special Issue 13, pp39–68

Donovan, GP, C Lockyer and AR Martin (eds) (1993) Biology of Northern Hemisphere pilot whales: a collection of papers, *Report of the International Whaling Commission*, Special Issue 14

Dorsey, EM, SJ Stern, AR Hoelzel and J Jacobsen (1990) Recognition of individual minke whales from the west coast of North America, *Report of the International Whaling Commission*, Special Issue 12, pp357–368

Drouot, V (2003) Ecology of sperm whales (*Physeter macrocephalus*) in the Mediterranean Sea, PhD Thesis, University of Wales, Bangor

Duffus, DA and P Dearden (1992) Whales, science, and protected area management in British Columbia, Canada, *George Wright Forum* 9, pp79–87

Dutton, TP and A Zolho (1991) The master plan for conservation and development of archipelago of Bazaruto (Plano director de conservaçao para o desenvolvimento do Arquipelago do Bazaruto), submitted to the Ministry of Agriculture, Maputo, 109pp

Duyuan, Y and C Qingchao (1996) Step up protection for *Sousa chinensis* (Osbeck) at the mouth of the Zhujiang

Engdahl, S and H Motta (eds) (2000) Proceedings from the Regional Workshop on the Nomination of World Natural Heritage Sites, Unesco/MICOA

Environment Australia (1999) Great Australian Bight Marine Park (Commonwealth Waters) Plan of Management, Environment Australia, Canberra (available on the web at: www.deh.gov.au/coasts/mpa/gab/index.html)

Environment Australia (2001a) Coringa-Herald National Nature Reserve & Lihou Reef National Nature Reserve (Commonwealth Waters) Management Plan, Environment Australia, Canberra

Environment Australia (2001b) Macquarie Island Marine Park Management Plan, Environment Australia, Canberra (available on the web at: www.deh.gov.au/coasts/mpa/macquarie/index.html)

Environment Australia (2001c) Solitary Islands Marine Reserve (Commonwealth Waters) Management Plan, Environment Australia, Canberra

Environment Australia (2002a) Lord Howe Island Marine Park (Commonwealth Waters) Management Plan, Environment Australia, Canberra

Environment Australia (2002b) Mermaid Reef Marine National Nature Reserve Plan of Management, Environment Australia, Canberra

Environment Australia (2002c) Ningaloo Marine Park (Commonwealth Waters) Management Plan, Environment Australia, Canberra (available on the web at: www.deh.gov.au/coasts/mpa/ningaloo/index.html)

Environment Australia (2002d) Tasmanian Seamounts Marine Reserve Management Plan, Environment Australia, Canberra

Esping, L and G Grönqvist (1995) Marine Region 6: Baltic, in G Kelleher, C Bleakley and S Wells (eds) *A Global Representative System of Marine Protected Areas. Vol I*, The Great Barrier Reef Marine Park Authority, The World Bank and IUCN, Washington, DC, pp153–183

Evans, PGH (1980) Cetaceans in British waters, *Mammal Review* 50(1), pp1–52

Evans, PGH (1999) Protected areas for cetaceans, Workshop on the criteria for the selection of species and habitats, OSPAR Convention for the Protection of the Marine Environment of the North-east Atlantic, Horta, 12–16 July

Evans, PGH and E Urquiola Pascual (2001) Introduction to marine protected areas: what are they designed to do and what criteria should be used in their selection? in PGH Evans and E Urquiola Pascual (eds) *Proceedings of the Workshop, Protected Areas for Cetaceans*, ECS Newsletter no 38 – Special Issue, pp4–11

Faucher, A and LS Weilgart (1992) Critical marine habitat in offshore waters: the need for protection, in JHM Willison, S Bondrup-Neilson, C Drysdale, TB Herman, NWP Munro and TL Pollock (eds) *Science and the Management of Protected Areas, Developments in Landscape Management and Urban Planning* 7, Elsevier, Amsterdam, pp75–78

Faucher, A and H Whitehead (1995) Importance of habitat protection for the northern bottlenose whale in the Gully, Nova Scotia, in NL Shackell and JHM Willison (eds) *Marine Protected Areas and Sustainable Fisheries*, Proceedings of a symposium on marine protected areas and sustainable fisheries conducted at the Second International Conference on Science and the Management of Protected Areas, Dalhousie University, Halifax, Nova Scotia, 16–20 May 1994, pp99–102

Félix, F and B Haase (1996) Study of the humpback whale off the Ecuadorian coast with an analysis of the whale watching operation during the season 1995, project report to Whale and Dolphin Conservation Society, 12pp

Félix, F and B Haase (2001) The humpback whale off the coast of Ecuador, population parameters and behavior, *Revista de Biologia Marina y Oceanografia* 36(1), pp61–74

Félix, F and J Samaniego (1994) Incidental catches of small cetaceans in the artisanal fisheries of Ecuador, *Report of the International Whaling Commission*, Special Issue 15, pp475–480

Ferreccio, P, I Milella, M Pedde, S Saba, PL Solinas and A Di Natale (1993) Contribution to the knowledge of the geographical distribution of *Tursiops truncatus* off the Coasts of north-west Sardinia, *European Research on Cetaceans* 6, Proceedings of the annual conference of the European Cetacean Society, pp121–126

Fisheries Joint Management Committee (2001) Beaufort Sea Beluga Management Plan, amended third printing, 29pp

Flores, PA (1992) Observações sobre comportamento, movimentos e conservação do golfinho ou boto *Sotalia fluviatilis* (Mammalia, Cetacea, Delphinidae) na Baía Norte de Santa Catarina, SC, Brasil, BSc monograph, Universidade Federal de Santa Catarina, Brasil, 48pp

Flores, PA (1995) Site fidelity and residence pattern of *Sotalia fluviatilis* at the environmental protection area (EPA) of Anhatomirim, North Bay, Santa Catarina, Southern Brazil, abstract, 11th Biennial Conference on the Biology of Marine Mammals, Orlando, FL, 14–18 December, p38

Flórez-González, L and J Capella (1993) Las ballenas, in P Leyva (ed) *Colombia Pacifico, Tomo I Fondo*, FEN, Bogotá, Colombia, pp38–47

Folkens, PA and R Voara (1988) A report on the diversity and status of the cetaceans of Madagascar with notes on other marine mammals (unpublished)

Fonteneau, A (2001) Potential use of protected areas applied to tuna fisheries and offshore pelagic ecosystems, in Expert Workshop on Managing Risks to Biodiversity and the Environment on the High-seas, including Tools such as Marine Protected Areas – Scientific Requirements and Legal Aspects, 27 February–4 March, Vilm, Germany

Forcada, J (1995) Abundance of common and striped dolphins in the southwestern Mediterranean, in *European Research on Cetaceans* 9, Proceedings of the annual conference of the European Cetacean Society, pp153–155

Forcada, J and P Hammond (1998) Geographical variation in abundance of striped and common dolphins of the western Mediterranean, *Journal of Sea Research* 39, pp313–325

Forcada, J, G Notarbartolo di Sciara and F Fabbri (1995) Abundance of fin whales and striped dolphins summering in the Corso-Ligurian Basin, *Mammalia* 59(1), pp127–140

Forcada, J, A Aguilar, P Hammond, X Pastor and R Aguilar (1996) Distribution and abundance of fin whales (*Balaenoptera physalus*) in the western Mediterranean Sea during the summer, *Journal of Zoology* 238, pp23–4

Ford, JKB (2002) Killer whale, in WF Perrin, B Würsig and JGM Thewissen (eds) *Encyclopedia of Marine Mammals*, Academic Press, San Diego, pp669–676

Ford, JKB, GM Ellis and KC Balcomb III (1994) *Killer Whales. The Natural History and Genealogy of Orcinus orca in British Columbia and Washington State*, UBC Press, Vancouver, Canada

Fossi, MC and L Marsili (1997) The use of nondestructive biomarkers in the study of marine mammals, *Biomarkers* 2, pp205–216

Fossi, MC, L Marsili, C Leonzio, G Notarbartolo di Sciara, M Zanardelli, and S Focardi (1992) The use of non-destructive biomarker in Mediterranean cetaceans: preliminary data on MFO activity in skin biopsy, *Marine Pollution Bulletin* 24(9), pp459–461

Fossi, MC, S Casini and L Marsili (1999) Nondestructive biomarkers of exposure to endocrine-disrupting chemicals in endangered species of wildlife, *Chemosphere* 39(8), pp1273–1285

Francese, M, P Zucca, M Picciulin, F Zuppa and M Spoto (1999) Cetaceans living in the north Adriatic Sea (Gulf of Trieste – Grado Lagoon) – intervention protocol for healthy and distressed animals, *European Research on Cetaceans* 13, Proceedings of the annual conference of the European Cetacean Society, pp410–415

Freitas, A and ME dos Santos (1999) A study of habitat use by bottlenose dolphins in the Sado Estuary, Portugal, *European Research on Cetaceans* 10, Proceedings of the annual conference of the European Cetacean Society, p210

Fundación Cethus (1999) The value of ecotourism of Bahía San Julián, Santa Cruz, Argentina, final report to the Whale and Dolphin Conservation Society, July 1999, 8pp

Gannier, O and A Gannier (1998) First results on the distribution of cetaceans in the Society Islands (French Polynesia), *European Research on Cetaceans* 12, Proceedings of the annual conference of the European Cetacean Society, pp54–58

Garcia-Martinez, J, A Moya, JA Raga and A Latorre (1999) Genetic differentiation in the striped dolphins *Stenella coeruleoalba* from European waters according to mitochondrial DNA (mtDNA) restriction analysis, *Molecular Ecology* 8, pp1069–1073

Gaspar, R (1999) Occurrence pattern of bottlenose dolphins in the Sado Estuary region, Portugal, *European Research on Cetaceans* 10, Proceedings of the annual conference of the European Cetacean Society, p211

Gaudian, G, A Koyo and S Wells (1995) Marine Region 12: East Africa, in G Kelleher, C Bleakley and S Wells (eds) *A Global Representative System of Marine Protected Areas. Vol III*, The Great Barrier Reef Marine Park Authority, The World Bank and IUCN, Washington, DC, pp71–105

Gerry E Studds Stellwagen Bank National Marine Sanctuary (2002) State of the Sanctuary Report, NOAA, 27pp

Gill, PC (2002) A blue whale (*Balaenoptera musculus*) feeding ground in a southern Australian coastal upwelling zone, *Journal of Cetacean Research and Management* 4, pp179–184

Gill, P and C Burke (1999) *Whale Watching in Australian & New Zealand Waters*, New Holland, Sydney, 147pp

Gjerde, KM (2001) Protecting particularly sensitive sea areas from shipping: a review of IMO's new PSSA guidelines, in Expert Workshop on Managing Risks to Biodiversity and the Environment on the High-seas, including Tools such as Marine Protected Areas – Scientific Requirements and Legal Aspects, 27 February–4 March, Vilm, Germany

Gjertz, I (1991) The narwhal, *Monodon monoceros*, in the Norwegian high Arctic, *Marine Mammal Science* 7(4), pp402–408

Gjertz, I and Ø Wiig (1994) Distribution and catch of white whales (*Delphinapterus leucas*) at Svalbard, in EW Born, R Dietz and RR Reeves (eds) Meddelelser om Grønland, *Bioscience* 39, pp93–97

Gordon, J, SD Berrow, E Rogan and S Fennelly (2000) Acoustic and visual survey of cetaceans off the Mullet Peninsula, Co Mayo, *Irish Naturalists' Journal* 26(7–8), pp251–259

Government of Brazil (2001) A South Atlantic Whale Sanctuary, IWC/53/7, 11pp

Gravestock, P (2002) Towards a better understanding of the income requirements of Marine Protected Areas, MSc Environmental Management for Business by Research, Cranfield University at Silsoe

Gray, J (1997) *Marine Biodiversity: Patterns, Threats and Conservation Needs*, GESAMP Reports and Studies No 62, International Maritime Organization

Great Barrier Reef Marine Park Authority (2000) Whale and dolphin conservation in the Great Barrier Reef Marine Park: policy document, Great Barrier Reef Marine Park Authority, Townsville, Qld, 68pp

Green, M and J Paine (1997) State of the world's protected areas at the end of the twentieth century, IUCN World Commission on Protected Areas (WCPA) symposium on protected areas in the 21st century: from islands to networks, Albany, Australia

Gubbay, S (1995) Marine Region 5: Northeast Atlantic, in G Kelleher, C Bleakley and S Wells (eds) *A Global Representative System of Marine Protected Areas. Vol I*, The Great Barrier Reef Marine Park Authority, The World Bank and IUCN, Washington, DC, pp127–151

Gubbay, S, CM Baker and BJ Bett (2002) The Darwin Mounds and the Dogger Bank. Case studies of the management of two potential Special Areas of Conservation in the offshore environment, report to WWF-UK

Hammond, PS, H Benke, P Berggren, A Collet, MP Heide-Jørgensen, S Heimlich-Boran, M Leopold and N Øien (1995) The distribution and abundance of porpoises and other small cetaceans in the North Sea and adjacent waters, final report of EC LIFE 92-2/UK/027, 240pp

Hansen, K (2002) *A Farewell to Greenland's Wildlife*, Bære Dygtighed, Klippinge and Gads Forlag, Copenhagen, 154pp

Hansson, R (2000) The best managed Arctic wilderness? *WWF Arctic Bulletin* 2, pp19

Harwood, J and B Wilson (2001) The implications of developments on the Atlantic Frontier for marine mammals, *Continental Shelf Research* 21, pp1073–1093

Hauser, N and P Clapham (2002) The Cook Islands Whale Sanctuary, paper submitted to the Scientific Committee of the IWC, SC/54/011

Heide-Jorgensen, MP and R Dietz (1995) Some characteristics of narwhal, *Monodon monoceros*, diving behaviour in Baffin Bay, *Canadian Journal of Zoology* 73(11), pp2120–2132

Hilton-Taylor, C (compiler) (2000) *2000 IUCN Red List of Threatened Species*, IUCN, Gland, Switzerland and Cambridge, UK

Holt, S (1984) Indian Ocean Whale Sanctuary, *Whalewatcher* Spring, pp17–19

Holt, SJ (2000) Whales and whaling, in CRC Sheppard (ed) *Seas at the Millennium: An Environmental Evaluation. Vol III, Global Issues and Processes*, Elsevier, Amsterdam, pp73–88

Hooker, SK and LR Gerber (2004) Marine reserves as a tool for ecosystem-based management: the potential importance of megafauna, *BioScience* 54(1), pp27–39

Hooker, SK, H Whitehead and S Gowans (2001) Marine protected area design and the spatial and temporal distribution of cetaceans in a submarine canyon, in PGH Evans and E Urquiola Pascual (eds) *Proceedings of the Workshop, Protected Areas for Cetaceans*, ECS Newsletter no 38 – Special Issue, pp48

Horstman, KR and JM Fives (1994) Ichthyoplankton distribution and abundance in the Celtic Sea, *ICES Journal of Marine Science* 51, pp447–460

Hoyt, E (1978) Friendly killer, in N Sitwell (ed) *Wildlife '78. The World Conservation Yearbook*, World Wildlife Fund and Danbury Press, Grolier Inc, Danbury, CT, pp38–45

Hoyt, E (1981) Battle of the Bight; when a log port threatened the killer whales' home bay, Canadian conservationists rushed to the rescue, *Defenders* (Washington, DC), December, pp23–30

Hoyt, E (1982) Orca: the sociable whale, *Equinox* 1(2), pp20–39

Hoyt, E (1984) The whales called 'killer', *National Geographic* 166(2), pp220–237

Hoyt, E (1985a) Masters of the Gulf. Life among the whales of the St Lawrence, *Equinox* 4(21), pp52–65

Hoyt, E (1985b) Paradise in peril. Battling to save South Moresby, Canada's Galápagos, *Equinox* 4(19), pp22–41

Hoyt, E (1990a) *Orca: The Whale Called Killer*, 3rd ed, Firefly, Toronto, pp1–291

Hoyt, E (1990b) The greening of Tofino, *Equinox* 9(50), pp103–117

Hoyt, E (1992) Designing marine reserves around whales and dolphins. Three case studies, IV World Parks Congress, Caracas, Venezuela, 16pp

Hoyt, E (1993a) Courting oblivion. Canadian researchers set sail to right the wrongs suffered by the most endangered of all whale species, *Equinox* 12(2), pp32–43

Hoyt, E (1993b) Kujira watching. Whales and dolphins: alive and being watched Japanese-style, Whale and Dolphin Conservation Society, Bath, UK, 16pp

Hoyt, E (1996) Whale watching and community development around the world, Keynote lecture to The International Whale Watching Festa '96, The International Whale Watching Forum (Japan), Zamami, Okinawa, Japan, 9 March 1996, in *Proceedings of the International Whale Watching Festa '96*, pp15–32

Hoyt, E (1997a) The potential of whale watching in Europe, Whale and Dolphin Conservation Society, Bath, UK, 34pp

Hoyt, E (1997b) The potential of whale watching in Africa, Whale and Dolphin Conservation Society, Bath, UK, 36pp

Hoyt, E (1999) The potential of whale watching in the Caribbean: 1999+, Whale and Dolphin Conservation Society, Bath, UK, presented as IWC/51/WW2 by the United Kingdom Government to the International Whaling Commission AGM, May 1999, Grenada, 81pp

Hoyt, E (2000) The status and potential of whale watching in the Caribbean, keynote lecture to The Turks and Caicos Islands Marine Mammals Conference, 3 March

Hoyt, E (2001) *Whale Watching 2001: Worldwide Tourism Numbers, Expenditures, and Expanding Socioeconomic Benefits*, International Fund for Animal Welfare, Crowborough, UK, 157pp

Hoyt, E (2002) Whale watching, in WF Perrin, B Würsig and JGM Thewissen (eds) *Encyclopedia of Marine Mammals*, Academic Press, San Diego, pp1305–1310

Hoyt, E (2003) *The Best Whale Watching in Europe*, WDCS, UK and WDCS – Germany, Unterhaching, Germany, 60pp

Hoyt, E and G Hvenegaard (1999) The development, value and study of whale watching in the Caribbean, paper submitted to the Scientific Committee of the IWC, SC51/WW4, 14pp

Hoyt, E and G Hvenegaard (2002) A review of whale watching and whaling with applications for the Caribbean, *Coastal Management* 30, pp381–399

Hucke-Gaete, R, LP Osman, CA Moreno, KP Findlay and DK Ljungblad (2003) Discovery of a blue whale feeding and nursing ground in southern Chile, *Proceedings of the Royal Society of London B (Suppl), Biology Letters*, 4pp

Humphreys, B and P Prokosch (eds) (2000) First response to the Svalbard – One National Park proposal, *WWF Arctic Bulletin*, no 1, p3

Hurtado, M (1995) Marine Region 17: Southeast Pacific, in G Kelleher, C Bleakley and S Wells (eds) *A Global Representative System of Marine Protected Areas. Vol IV*, The Great Barrier Reef Marine Park Authority, The World Bank and IUCN, Washington, DC, pp131–151

IBAMA (1997) Mamíferos aquáticos do Brasil: plan de ação, IBAMA, Diretoria de Ecossistemas/Departamento de Vida Silvestre (ed), Brasilia, DF 79pp

IFAW (1999) Report of the workshop on the socioeconomic aspects of whale watching, Kaikoura, New Zealand, 88pp

IFAW, WWF and WDCS (1997) Report of the international workshop on the educational values of whale watching, Provincetown, Massachusetts, 40pp

Iñíguez, M (1995) La Ria de Deseado, Provincia de Santa Cruz, Argentina, Report presented to the Escuela Argentina de Naturalistas, Fundación Cethus, Buenos Aires

Iñíguez, MA (2001) Seasonal distribution of killer whales (*Orcinus orca*) in northern Patagonia, Argentina, *Aquatic Mammals* 27(2), pp154–161

Iñíguez, MA, A Tomsin, CH Torlaschi and L Prieto (1998) Aspectos socio-económicos del avistaje de cetáceos en Península Valdés, Puerto San Julián y Puerto Deseado, Patagonia, Argentina, Fundación Cethus, Buenos Aires, 14pp

IUCN (1994) Guidelines for protected area management categories, CNPPA with the assistance of WCMC, IUCN, Gland, Switzerland and Cambridge, UK, 261pp (Available in PDF format at http://wcpa.iucn.org/pubs/pdfs/IUCNCategories.pdf)

IUCN (1997) The Isle of Sylt coastal waters as a harbor porpoise habitat, ASCOBANS 2nd Meeting of Parties, Bonn

IUCN (2000) Assessment of the macroeconomic impact of protected areas, IUCN Commission for Protected Areas, IUCN, Gland, Switzerland

IUCN (2001) IUCN Red List categories and criteria, Version 3.1, prepared by the IUCN Species Survival Commission, IUCN, Gland, Switzerland and Cambridge, UK

IUCN/UNEP/WWF (1979) Workshop on Cetacean Sanctuaries, México, February 1979

IUCN/WWF and DG Forest Protection and Nature Conservation (1984) *Marine Conservation Data Atlas Indonesia*, Department of Forestry, Indonesia

IWC (2001) Report of the working group on nomenclature, *Journal of Cetacean Research and Management* 3 (Supplement), pp363–367

IWDG (Irish Whale and Dolphin Group) (2000) SACs proposed for porpoise and dolphin, *The Irish Whale and Dolphin Group News*, summer, no 17, p7

Jaaman, SA (in preparation) Cetacean sightings around Layang-Layang Reef, The Malaysian Spratly, 16pp

Jaaman, SA (in press) A review of current knowledge on marine mammals in Malaysia and adjacent waters, *ASEAN Review of Biodiversity and Environmental Conservation (ARBEC)*, 40pp

Jaaman, SA and YU Lah-Anyi (2003) Dugongs (*Dugong dugon* Muller, 1776) in East Malaysian waters, *ASEAN Review of Biodiversity and Environmental Conservation (ARBEC) Online Journal* (available at: http://www.arbec.com.my/dugongs/index.htm)

Jaaman, SA, SA Ali, YU Lah-Anyi, CJ Miji, J Bali, JM Regip, R Bilang and R Wahed (2000) Research and conservation of marine mammals in Sarawak: current knowledge, in EL Bennett, CLM Chin and J Rubis (eds) *Hornbill Vol 4: Proceedings of the Fourth Annual Workshop of the National Parks and Wildlife Division*, Sarawak Forestry Department, pp17–28

Jaaman, SA, YU Lah-Anyi and Y Tashi (2001) Recent sightings of marine mammals and whale shark in Sarawak, in EL Bennett and CLM Chin (eds) *Hornbill Vol 5: Proceedings of the Fifth Annual Workshop of the National Parks and Wildlife Division*, Sarawak Forestry Department, pp64–81

Jaaman, SA, R Najib, AA Syuhaime and ULA Yuhana (2002) Records of marine mammals in peninsular Malaysian waters: a review, in FM Yusoff, M Shariff, HM Ibrahim, SG Tan and SY Tai (eds) *Tropical Marine Environment: Charting Strategies for the Millennium*, Malacca Straits Research and Development Centre (MASDEC), Universiti Putra Malaysia, Serdang, Malaysia, pp499–515

Jackson, JBC, MX Kirby, WH Berger, KA Bjorndal, LW Botsford, BJ Bourque, RH Bradbury, R Cooke, J Erlandson, JA Estes, TP Hughes, S Kidwell, CB Lange, HS Lenihan, JM Pandolfi,

CH Peterson, RS Steneck, MJ Tegner and RR Warner (2001) Historical overfishing and the recent collapse of coastal ecosystems, *Science* 293, pp629–638

Janik, VM and PM Thompson (1996) Changes in surfacing patterns of bottlenose dolphins in response to boat traffic, *Marine Mammal Science* 12(4), pp597–602

Jefferson, TA and SK Lynn (1994) Marine mammal sightings in the Caribbean Sea and Gulf of Mexico, summer 1991, *Caribbean Journal of Science* 30(1–2), pp83–89

Jefferson, T, S Leatherwood and MA Webber (1993) *FAO Species Identification Guide: Marine Mammals of the World*, Rome, FAO, 320pp

Kahn, B (1999) Visual and acoustic cetacean surveys in the waters of Komodo National Park, Indonesia, The Nature Conservancy Indonesia Coastal and Marine Program Report, 14pp

Kahn, B (2000) Komodo National Park cetacean surveys 1999 – A rapid ecological assessment of cetacean diversity, abundance and distribution, report to The Nature Conservancy Indonesia Coastal and Marine Program, 29pp

Kahn, B (2001) Important criteria for selecting/establishing protected habitat regions for cetaceans in Papua New Guinea, keynote presentation in transcripts of the New Guinea Marine Mammal Forum, 16–17 July 2001, Port Moresby, Papua New Guinea, pp6–8

Kahn, B (2002a) Alor Rapid Ecological Assessment – Visual and acoustic cetacean surveys and evaluation of traditional whaling practices, fisheries interactions and nature-based tourism potential: October 2001 and May 2002 survey periods, Alor Rapid Ecological Assessment (REA) Technical Report for WWF – Wallacea and TNC Coastal and Marine Program/Indonesia, 36pp

Kahn, B (2002b) Cetacean-fisheries interactions in the Indonesian Seas, keynote presentation to the expert workshop: Cetacean Interactions with Commercial Longline Fisheries in the South Pacific Region: Approaches to Mitigation, South Pacific Regional Environmental Program (SPREP), Apia, Samoa, 1–15 November 2002

Kahn, B (2002c) Discussion paper on the establishment of a Protected Marine Mammal Fisheries Area in Indonesia's national and EEZ waters, TNC Indonesia Program Technical Report prepared for the Government of the Republic of Indonesia – the Ministry of Marine Affairs and Fisheries, 55pp

Kahn, B (2002d) Indonesia's migratory corridors for large marine life: scientific and management perspectives, in Proceedings of the 1st Regional Session of the Global Biodiversity Forum for the Pacific (GBF): Global Forces and their Impacts on the Pacific's Biodiversity: Towards Local and Regional Response Strategies, Rarotonga, Cook Islands, 5 July–8, July 2002

Kahn, B (2002e) Komodo National Park Cetacean Surveys: April 2001 and 1999–2001 survey synopsis, Working paper CMS/SEAMAMSII/24, United Nations Environment Programme – Convention on the Conservation of Migratory Species of Wild Animals (UNEP/CMS) Second International Conference on the Marine Mammals of Southeast Asia, 22–23 July 2002, Demaguette, Philippines, 39pp

Kahn, B (ed) (2002f) Status of marine mammals of Indonesia, UNEP/CMS Technical Report, final draft submitted to the United Nations Environment Programme – Convention on the Conservation of Migratory Species of Wild Animals (UNEP/CMS), Second International Conference on the Marine Mammals of Southeast Asia, 24–26 July 2002, Dumaguete, Philippines, 13pp

Kahn, B (2003a) Alor rapid ecological assessment – visual and acoustic oceanic cetacean surveys and evaluation of traditional whaling practices, fisheries interactions and nature-based tourism potential: May 2003, APEX Environmental Technical Report for TNC SE Asia Center for Marine Protected Areas and the Wallace Research Foundation

Kahn, B (2003b) Conservation, socio-economic and policy benefits of Indonesia's Marine Mammal Management Area (IMMMA) – a national conservation and management initiative for Indonesia's marine mammals, TNC Indonesia Program/APEX Environmental Technical Report, 11pp

Kahn, B and J Pet (2001) Cetacean surveys and marine protected area management: Komodo National Park & World Heritage Area, Indonesia, abstract, 14th Biennial Conference on the Biology of Marine Mammals, Vancouver, BC, Canada, 28 November–3 December, p110

Kahn, B and J Pet (2003) Long-term visual and acoustic cetacean surveys in Komodo National Park, Indonesia 1999–2001: management implications for large migratory marine life, Proceedings and Publications of the World Congress on Aquatic Protected Areas 2002, Australian Society for Fish Biology, pp625–637

Kahn, B, Y James and J Pet (2000) Komodo National Park cetacean surveys – a rapid ecological assessment of cetacean diversity, distribution and analysis, *Jurnal Pesisir and Lautan* 3(2), pp41–59

Katona, SK and SD Kraus (1999) Efforts to conserve the North Atlantic right whale, in JR Twiss, Jr and RR Reeves (eds) *Conservation and Management of Marine Mammals*, Smithsonian, Washington, DC, pp311–331

Kelleher, G (1999) *Guidelines for Marine Protected Areas,* IUCN, Gland, Switzerland and Cambridge, UK

Kelleher, G (2001) MPA perspective: the development and establishment of coral reef marine protected areas, *MPA News* 2(7), pp5–6

Kelleher, G and R Kenchington (1992) Guidelines for establishing marine protected areas. A marine conservation and development report, IUCN, Gland, Switzerland, 79pp

Kelleher, G and C Recchia (1998) Editorial – lessons from marine protected areas around the world, *Parks* 8(2), pp1–4

Kelleher, G, C Bleakley, K Walls and P Dingwall (1995a) Marine Region 18: Australia/New Zealand, in G Kelleher, C Bleakley and S Wells (eds) *A Global Representative System of Marine Protected Areas. Vol IV*, The Great Barrier Reef Marine Park Authority, The World Bank and IUCN, Washington, DC, US, pp154–199

Kelleher, G, C Bleakley and S Wells (eds) (1995b) *A Global Representative System of Marine Protected Areas. Vol I–IV*, The Great Barrier Reef Marine Park Authority, The World Bank and IUCN, Washington, DC

Kelleher, G, C Bleakley and S Wells (1995c) Introduction, in G Kelleher, C Bleakley and S Wells (eds) *A Global Representative System of Marine Protected Areas. Vol I*, The Great Barrier Reef Marine Park Authority, The World Bank and IUCN, Washington, DC, pp1–44

Kimball, LA (1999) The Antarctic Treaty System, in JR Twiss, Jr and RR Reeves (eds) *Conservation and Management of Marine Mammals*, Smithsonian, Washington, DC, pp199–223

Kimball, LA (2001) *International Ocean Governance. Using International Law and Organisations to Manage Resources Sustainably*, IUCN, Gland

Klinowska, M (1991) *Dolphins, Porpoises and Whales of the World*, The IUCN Red Data Book, IUCN, Gland, Switzerland and Cambridge, UK, 429pp

Kochnev AA (2000) White whale migration in Wrangel Island waters, Marine Mammals of the Holarctic, First International Conference, Archangelsk, 21–23 September

Kraus, SD (1990) Rates and potential causes of mortality in North Atlantic right whales (*Eubalaena glacialis*), *Marine Mammal Science* 6, pp278–291

Kraus, SD and MW Brown (1992) A right whale conservation plan for the waters of Atlantic Canada, in JHM Willison, S Bondrup-Neilson, C Drysdale, TB Herman, NWP Munro and TL Pollock (eds) *Science and the Management of Protected Areas, Developments in Landscape Management and Urban Planning* 7, Elsevier, Amsterdam, pp79–85

Kraus, SD and RD Kenny (1991) Information on right whales (*Eubalaena glacialis*) in three proposed critical habitats in the United States waters of the western North Atlantic Ocean, National Technical Information Services Publication PB91-194431, Washington, DC, 71pp

Lauriano, G (1997a) Preliminary observations of fin whales in the north-western Sardinia, *European Research on Cetaceans* 11, Proceedings of the annual conference of the European Cetacean Society

Lauriano, G (1997b) Distribution of bottlenose dolphin around the Island of Asinara, *European Research on Cetaceans* 11, Proceedings of the annual conference of the European Cetacean Society

Lauriano, G and G Notarbartolo di Sciara (1995) The distribution of cetaceans off northwestern Sardinia, *European Research on Cetaceans* 9, Proceedings of the annual conference of the European Cetacean Society, pp104–107

Lauriano, G, L Tunesi, G Notarbartolo di Sciara, E Salvati and A Cardinali (1999) The role of cetaceans in the zoning proposal of marine protected areas: the case of the Asinara Island MPA, *European Research on Cetaceans* 13, Proceedings of the annual conference of the European Cetacean Society, pp114–117

Leaper, R and V Papastavrou (2001) The Southern Ocean as an example of a protected area, in PGH Evans and E Urquiola Pascual (eds) *Proceedings of the Workshop, Protected Areas for Cetaceans*, ECS Newsletter no 38 – Special Issue, pp31–35

Leatherwood, S and G Donovan (1991) Cetaceans and cetacean research in the Indian Ocean Sanctuary, UNEP Marine Mammal Technical Report, No 3, UNEP

Leatherwood, S, CB Peters, R Santerre, M Santerre and JT Clarke (1984) Observations of cetaceans in the northern Indian Ocean sanctuary, November 1980–May 1983, *Report of the International Whaling Commission* 34, pp509–520

Leatherwood, S, BS Stewart, and PA Folkens (1987) Cetaceans of the Channel Islands National Marine Sanctuary, Prepared for NOAA Channel Islands National Marine Sanctuary and NOAA National Marine Fisheries Service, 69pp

Leatherwood, S, MLL Dolar, CJ Wood and CL Hill (1994) A sea of jewels: whales and dolphins of the Philippines, *Whalewatcher*, pp16–21

Lemm, S and C Attwood (2003) State of marine protected area management in South Africa, WWF-SA and Marine & Coastal Management, South Africa, final report, 123pp

Lien, J (1999) When marine conservation efforts sink: what can be learned from the abandoned effort to examine the feasibility of a National Marine Conservation Area on the NE Coast of Newfoundland? Canadian Council on Ecological Areas (CCEA) l6th Conference, Ottawa, Canada, 4–6 October 1999

Lindberg, K (2001) MPA revenue generation and the user fee option, *MPA News* 2(9), April, pp5–6

Liret, C, B Le Goaziou and F Gourmelon (2001) How a marine national park in the Iroise Sea (Brittany) can contribute to coastal bottlenose dolphin conservation, in PGH Evans and E Urquiola Pascual (eds) *Proceedings of the Workshop, Protected Areas for Cetaceans*, ECS Newsletter no 38 – Special Issue, pp41–43

Lodi, L and B Hetzel (1994) *Golfinhos-rotadores do Arquipélago de Fernando de Noronha*, Fundação o Boticário de Proteção à Natureza, Rio de Janeiro, 31pp

Lodi, L and B Hetzel (2000) Cleptoparasitismo entre Fragatas (*Fregata magnificens*) e botos-cinza (*Sotalia fluviatilis*) NA Baía de Paraty, Rio de Janeiro, Brasil, *Biociências* (Porto Alegre) 8(1), pp59–64

López, JC and D López (1985) Killer whales (*Orcinus orca*) of Patagonia and their behavior of intentional stranding while hunting near shore, *Journal of Mammalogy* 66(1), pp181–183

Lusseau, D and JES Higham (in press for 2004) Managing the impacts of dolphin-based tourism through the definition of critical habitats: the case of bottlenose dolphins (*Tursiops* spp) in Doubtful Sound, New Zealand, *Tourism Management*

Lutz, W, W Sanderson and S Scherbov (2001) The end of world population growth, *Nature* 412, pp543–546

Malakoff, D (2002) Nations look for an edge in claiming continental shelves, *Science* 298, 6 December, pp1877–1878

Mamaev, EG (2002) Coast based observations of cetaceans near Commander Islands, Marine Mammals of the Holarctic, Second International Conference, Baikal, 10–15 September, pp168–170

Mann, J, RC Connor, PL Tyack and H Whitehead (eds) (2000) *Cetacean Societies. Field Studies of Dolphins and Whales*, University of Chicago, Chicago, 433pp

Marine Parks Authority (2003) *Operational Plan for Jervis Bay Marine Park*, Marine Parks Authority, Jervis Bay, NSW

Marini, L, G Villetti and G Consiglio (1995) Wintering areas of fin whales (*Balaenoptera physalus*) in the Mediterranean Sea: a preliminary survey, *European Research on Cetaceans* 9, Proceedings of the annual conference of the European Cetacean Society, pp126–128

Marini, L, C Consigio, A Arcangeli, A Torchio, M Casale, B Cristo and S Nannarelli (1996) Socio-ecology of *Tursiops truncatus* along the north-eastern coast of Sardinia (Italy): preliminary results, *European Research on Cetaceans* 9, Proceedings of the annual conference of the European Cetacean Society, pp139–141

Marmion Marine Park Management Plan 1992–2002, Department of Conservation and Land Management for the National Parks and Nature Conservation Authority, Perth, WA

Marsili, L, MC Fossi, G Notarbartolo di Sciara, M Zanardelli and S Focardi (1996) Organochlorine levels and mixed function oxidase activity in skin biopsy specimens from Mediterranean cetaceans, *Fresenius Environmental Bulletin* 5, pp723–728

Marsili, L, MC Fossi, G Notarbartolo di Sciara, M Zanardelli, B Nani and S Panigada (1998) Relationship between organochlorine contaminants and mixed function oxidase activity in skin biopsy specimens of Mediterranean fin whales (*Balaenoptera physalus*), *Chemosphere* 37(8), pp1501–1510

Martineau, D, P Beland, C Desjardins, and A Lagacé (1987) Levels of organochlorine chemicals in tissues of beluga whales (*Delphinapterus leucas*) from the St Lawrence estuary, Québec, Canada, *Archives of Environmental Contamination and Toxicology* 16, pp137–147

Martineau, D, S de Guise, M Fournier, L Shugart, C Girard, A Lagacé and P Béland (1994) Pathology and toxicology of beluga whales from the St Lawrence Estuary, Québec, Canada. Past, present and future, *Science of the Total Environment* 154, pp201–215

Mayer, S and MP Simmonds (1996) Science and precaution in cetacean conservation, in MP Simmonds and JD Hutchinson (eds) *The Conservation of Whales and Dolphins: Science and Practice*, John Wiley & Sons, Chichester, pp391–406

Mazzola, S, A Guerrini, A Bonnanno, B Patti, and GB Giusto (1995) Preliminary study on census data about the interaction between dolphins and fishing activity in the Sicilian fisheries, *European Research on Cetaceans* 9, Proceedings of the annual conference of the European Cetacean Society, pp256–259

McCloskey, M (1992) Protected areas on the high-seas, and the case for marine wilderness, IV World Parks Congress, Caracas, Venezuela, 12pp

McCloskey, M (1997) Protected areas on the high-seas and the case for marine wilderness, *Wild Earth*, spring, pp87–92

McQuaid, CD (1986) Post-1980 sightings of bowhead whales (*Balaena mysticetus*) from the Spitsbergen stock, *Marine Mammal Science* 2(4), pp316–318

Meffe, GK, WF Perrin and PK Dayton (1999) Marine mammal conservation: guiding principles and their implementation, in JR Twiss, Jr and RR Reeves (eds) *Conservation and Management of Marine Mammals,* Smithsonian, Washington, DC, pp437–454

Melnikov, VV and IA Zagrebin (2000) Minke whale (*Balaenoptera acutorostrata*) at Chukotkian coastal waters, Marine Mammals of the Holarctic, First International Conference, Archangelsk, 21–23 September

Mercier, F (1995) Report of a workshop to identify a potential national marine conservation area on the NE Coast of Newfoundland, in NL Shackell and JHM Willison (eds) *Marine Protected Areas and Sustainable Fisheries*, Proceedings of a symposium on marine protected areas and sustainable fisheries conducted at the Second International Conference on Science and the Management of Protected Areas, Dalhousie University, Halifax, Nova Scotia, 16–20 May 1994, pp240–248

Mercier, F and C Mondor (1995) Sea to sea to sea. Canada's national marine conservation area's system plan, Parks Canada, Department of Canadian Heritage, Ottawa, 106pp

Merlen, G (1995) *A Field Guide to the Marine Mammals of Galapagos*, Instituto Nacional de Pesca, Guayaquil, Ecuador, 130pp

Meth, N and R Helmer (1983) Marine environment and coastal resources in Southeast Asia: a threatened heritage, in EM Borgese and N Ginsburg (eds) *Ocean Yearbook 4*, University of Chicago Press, Chicago

Michaud, R and M-C Gilbert (1993) Les activités d'observation en mer des baleines dans l'estuaire du Saint-Laurent, situation actuelle et problématique, final report to Parcs Canada, Parc marin du Saguenay–Saint-Laurent, Tadoussac, Québec: Le Groupe de recherche et d'éducation sur le milieu marin, 31pp+ app

Mikkelsen, A (1996a) Conservation and resource management in Greenland: a challenge for the future, *WWF Arctic Bulletin*, no 4, p15

Mikkelsen, A (1996b) Important species in trouble: a need for joint efforts, *WWF Arctic Bulletin*, no 4, pp16–18

Mingelbier, M and R Michaud (1996) Étude des activités d'observation en mer des cétacés de l'estuaire maritime du Saint-Laurent, final report to Parcs Canada, Parc marin du Saguenay–Saint-Laurent, Le Groupe de recherche et d'éducation sur le milieu marin, Tadoussac, Québec, 64pp

Ministry of the Environment, The Government of Bermuda (2000) Marine resources and the fishing industry in Bermuda, discussion paper presented to the Legislature by The Minister of the Environment, Bermuda, 495pp

Mironova AM, AM Burdin, E Hoyt, EL Jikiya, VS Nikulin, NN Pavlov, H Sato, KK Tarasyan, OA Filatova and VV Vertyankin (2002) Killer whale abundance, distribution, predation and strandings in the waters around Kamchatka and the Commander Islands, Marine Mammals of the Holarctic, Second International Conference, Baikal, 10–15 September, pp85–86

Mondor, C, F Mercier, M Croom and R Wolotira (1995) Marine Region 4: Northwest Atlantic, in G Kelleher, C Bleakley and S Wells (eds) *A Global Representative System of Marine Protected Areas. Vol I*, The Great Barrier Reef Marine Park Authority, The World Bank and IUCN, Washington, DC, pp105–126

Moore, S, A Sirovic, D Thiele, J Hildebrand, M McDonald, A Frielaender, S Wiggins and E Hofman (2003) Mysticete whale acoustic and visual census in the SO GLOBEC West Antarctic region, paper submitted to the Scientific Committee of the IWC, SC/55/SH14

Mørkved, B and I Gjertz (1994) *In the Land of the Polar Bear*, Norsk Polarinstitutt, Svalbard, 23pp

Morton, B (1996) Protecting Hong Kong's marine biodiversity: present proposals, future challenges, *Environmental Conservation* 23(1), pp55–65

MPA News (2000a) Communications and MPAs: how practitioners are raising awareness of MPA issues, *MPA News* 2(4), p1

MPA News (2000b) MPA Update: Race Rocks to become Canada's First Official MPA, *MPA News* 2(4)

MPA News (2002a) Particularly sensitive sea areas: using a comprehensive planning tool to protect habitats from shipping, *MPA News* 3(8), pp1–3

MPA News (2002b) Gaps to be addressed in management: advice from Caribbean MPAs, *MPA News* 3(8), p4

MPA News (2003a) Balancing ecology and economics: lessons learned from the planning of a marine reserve network from the Channel Islands (US), *MPA News* 4(6), pp1–4

MPA News (2003b) Balancing ecology and economics, part II: lessons learned from planning an MPA network in Victoria, Australia, *MPA News* 4(7), pp1–4

MPA News (2003c) At World Parks Congress, target is set for high-seas MPAs: five to be designated by 2008, *MPA News* 5(4), pp1–3

MPA News (2004) Data available on hundreds of marine species, *MPA News* 5(8), p6

Mussi, B and A Miragliuolo (1999) Relazione per lo studio di fattibilita' della Riserva Marina 'Regno di Nettuno', Stazione Zoologica A Dohrn, Ischia, Italia

Mussi, B, A Miragliuolo and M Battaglia (1997a) Osservazioni sul comportamento di *Stenella coeruleoalba* (Meyen, 1833) nell'arcipelago Pontino campano, Tirreno centro meridionale, 3° Convegno Nazionale sui cetacei, abstracts, 5–6 Dicembre 1997, Napoli, Italia, Centro Studi cetacei della Società Italiana di Scienze Naturali

Mussi, B, A Miragliuolo and M Battaglia (1997b) Cetacei nell'arcipelago delle isole pontine e campane, in L Valerio (ed) Atti del 5° Seminario Internazionale di Studi sull'Ecosistema marino Gaeta, Napoli, Ustica, Oasi Blu del WWF Italia, Gaeta, Italia, pp157–167

Mussi, B, R Gabriele, A Miragliuolo and M Battaglia (1998) Cetacean sightings and interactions with fisheries in the Archipelago Pontino Campano, Southern Tyrrhenian Sea, 1991–1995, *European Research on Cetaceans* 12, Proceedings of the annual conference of the European Cetacean Society, pp63–65

Mussi, B, A Miragliuolo, E Monzini, B Diaz Lopez and M Battaglia (1999) Fin whale (*Balaenoptera physalus*) feeding ground in the coastal waters of Ischia (Arcipelago Campano), *European Research on Cetaceans* 13, Proceedings of the annual conference of the European Cetacean Society, pp330–335

Mussi, B, A Miragliuolo, M Battaglia and B Diaz Lopez (2000) Social structure and male parental care in a long-finned pilot whale (*Globicephala melas*) pod off Ventotene island (Mediterranean Sea, Italy), *European Research on Cetaceans* 14, Proceedings of the annual conference of the European Cetacean Society

Muthiga, N, L Bigot and A Nilsson (1998) East Africa: coral reef programs of eastern African and the Western Indian Ocean, *ITMEMS 1998 Proceedings,* pp114–143

Newell, J and E Wilson (1996) *The Russian Far East. Forests, Biodiversity Hotspots, and Industrial Developments*, Friends of the Earth, Tokyo, Japan, 200pp

Nijkamp, H and L Bijvoet (1996) Habitats and species protection in the OSPAR Convention Area, an overview of classification systems and protection programs, AID Environment, Amsterdam, The Netherlands, 65pp

Nikanorov, AP (2000) Marine mammals of Kronotskiy National Park, Marine Mammals of the Holarctic, First International Conference, Archangelsk, 21–23 September

NIPAP (2000) Malampaya Sound Protected Land and Seascape, General Management Plan, vol I and II, National Integrated Protected Areas Programme (NIPAP), a special project of the Department of Environment and Natural Resources supported by the European Community

NOAA, Sanctuary Programs Division, and Development Planning Office, American Samoa (1984) Final Environmental Impact Statement and Management Plan for the Proposed Fagatele Bay National Marine Sanctuary, NOAA, Washington, DC, 107pp+app

Norris, S (2002) Norway recognises Bear Island's importance, *Arctic Bulletin* 3, pp14–15

Norris, S (2003) Protected area boost for Svalbard, *Arctic Bulletin* 3, pp4, 11–13

Northridge, SP, ML Tasker, A Webb, JM Williams (1995) Seasonal distribution of harbor porpoises, white-beaked dolphins and minke whales in the waters around the British Isles, *ICES Journal of Marine Science* 52, pp55–56

Notarbartolo di Sciara, G (2000) Managing of whale watching in the International Sanctuary for Mediterranean Cetaceans, working paper presented at the 5th Workshop on Whalewatching, IFAW-ICRAM, Tuscany, Italy, 6–10 February (also in Report of the IFAW/ICRAM closing workshop to review various aspects of whale watching, IFAW, London, pp69–74

Notarbartolo di Sciara, G (2001) The Ligurian Sea International Sanctuary for Mediterranean cetaceans: rationale, history and current status, in PGH Evans and E Urquiola Pascual (eds) *Proceedings of the Workshop, Protected Areas for Cetaceans*, ECS Newsletter no 38 – Special Issue, pp28–30

Notarbartolo di Sciara, G (ed) (2002) Cetaceans of the Mediterranean and Black Seas: state of knowledge and conservation strategies, a report to the ACCOBAMS Secretariat, Monaco

Notarbartolo di Sciara, G and A Birkun, Jr (2002) Conservation needs and strategies, in G Notarbartolo di Sciara (ed) Cetaceans of the Mediterranean and Black Seas: state of knowledge and conservation strategies, a report to the ACCOBAMS Secretariat, Monaco, Section 18, 21pp

Notarbartolo di Sciara, G, F Ausenda, G Relini and L Orsi Relini (1991) Project Pelagos: proposal for a pelagic biosphere reserve in the Ligurian-Corsican-Provençal Basin (Mediterranean Sea), Proceedings of the 4th International Colloquy on coastal and marine parks of the Mediterranean, Bastia 1991, pp21–23

Notarbartolo di Sciara, G, F Ausenda, L Orsi Relini, and G Relini (1992) Una proposta di gestione dell'ambiente pelagico: la riserva della biosfera nel Bacino corso-ligure provenziale, *Oebalia* 17, Suppl, pp517–521

Notarbartolo di Sciara, G, M Zanardelli, S Panigada, M Jahoda and S Airoldi (2003) Fin whale, *Balaenoptera physalus* (L 1758), in the Mediterranean Sea, *Mammal Review* 33(2), pp105–150

O'Connell, K (1993) A meeting of minds in Mexico: the Upper Gulf of California Biosphere Reserve, *Whalewatcher*, Fall/Winter, pp9–10

O'Shea, TJ (1999) Environmental contaminants and marine mammals, in JE Reynolds III and SA Rommel (eds) *Biology of Marine Mammals*, Smithsonian Institution Press, Washington, DC, pp485–564

O'Shea, TJ, RR Reeves and AK Long (eds) (1999) Marine mammals and persistent ocean contaminants: Proceedings of the Marine Mammal Commission Workshop, Keystone, Colorado, 12–15 October 1998, Marine Mammal Commission, Bethesda, MD, 150pp

Offen, R (2003) Bringing in the cash: a short guide to fundraising, *MPA News* 5(1), p5

Ognetov, GN and ON Svetocheva (2000) White Sea as ecotope of seals and whales and summer marine mammal ecotours, Marine Mammals of the Holarctic, First International Conference, Archangelsk, 21–23 September

Orams, M (1999) The Economic Benefits of Whale Watching in Vava'u, The Kingdom of Tonga, Centre for Tourism Research, Massey University at Albany, North Shore, New Zealand, 64pp+ appendices

Osborn, D (2001) Challenges to conserving marine biodiversity of the high-seas through the use of marine protected areas – an Australian perspective, in Expert Workshop on Managing Risks to Biodiversity and the Environment on the High-seas, including Tools such as Marine Protected Areas – Scientific Requirements and Legal Aspects, 27 Feb–4 Mar, Vilm, Germany

Öztürk, B (1996) *Balinalar ve Yunuslar (Whales and Dolphins)*, Anahtar yayınevi, Istanbul, 119pp

Öztürk, B (1998) Black Sea biological diversity, *Environmental Series* 9, UN Publications, New York, p144

Öztürk, B and AA Öztürk (2003) Environmental problems of the Aegean Sea, in MH Nordquist, JN Moore and S Mahmudi (eds) *The Stockholm Declaration and Law of the Marine Environment*, Kluwer Law Int, Netherland, pp359–366

Pace, DS, M Pulcini and F Triossi (1998) *Tursiops truncatus* population at Lampedusa island (Italy): preliminary results, *European Research on Cetaceans* 12, Proceedings of the annual conference of the European Cetacean Society, pp165–169

Panigada, S, M Zanardelli, S Cabese, and M Jahoda (1999) How deep can baleen whales dive? *Marine Ecology Progress Series* 187, pp309–311

Patenaude, NJ and CS Baker (2000) Population status and habitat use of southern right whales in the sub-antarctic Auckland Islands of New Zealand, *Journal of Cetacean Research and Management*, Special Issue 2

Patenaude, NJ, CS Baker and N Gales (1998) Observations of southern right whales on New Zealand subantarctic wintering grounds, *Marine Mammal Science* 14, pp253–263

Patenaude, NJ, B Todd and R Stewart (2000) Movements of southern right whales between the sub-Antarctic Auckland and Campbell islands, *Journal of Cetacean Research and Management*, Special Issue 2

Pavan, G, JF Borsani, C Fossati, M Manghi and M Priano (1995) Acoustic research cruises in the Mediterranean – 1994, *European Research on Cetaceans* 9, Proceedings of the annual conference of the European Cetacean Society, pp85–88

Payne, R, V Rowntree, JS Perkins, JG Cooke, and K Lankester (1990) Population size, trends and reproductive parameters of right whales (*Eubalaena australis*) off Península Valdés, Argentina, *Report of the International Whaling Commission*, Special Issue 12, pp271–278

Perez, F, P Sutton, and A Vila (1995) Aves y mamíferos marinos de Santa Cruz: recopilación de los relevamientos realizados entre 1986 y 1994, Boletin Técnico No 26, Fundación Vida Silvestre Argentina

Perrin, WF (1975) Variation of spotted and spinner porpoise (genus *Stenella*) in the eastern tropical Pacific and Hawaii, *Bulletin of the Scripps Institution of Oceanography* 21, 206pp

Perrin, WF (1985) Refuge proposed for river dolphin, Newsletter of the Cetacean Specialist Group 1, p11

Perrin, WF (1988) *Dolphins, Porpoises and Whales. An Action Plan for the Conservation of Biological Diversity: 1988–1992*, IUCN Gland, Switzerland and Cambridge, UK

Perrin, WF (1989) *Dolphins, Porpoises and Whales. An Action Plan for the Conservation of Biological Diversity: 1988-1992*, 2nd edn, IUCN Gland, Switzerland and Cambridge, UK, 30pp

Perrin, WF, B Würsig and JGM Thewissen (eds) (2002) *Encyclopedia of Marine Mammals*, Academic Press, San Diego, 1414pp

Persoon, G, H de Iongh and B Wenno (1996) Exploitation, management and conservation of marine resources: the context of the Aru Tenggara Marine Reserve (Moluccas, Indonesia), *Ocean & Coastal Management* 32(2), pp97–122

Petersen, Æ and GA Gudmundsson (1995) A marine conservation area – Breidafjördur, West Iceland, *Arctic Bulletin*, March, pp20.

Petersen, Æ, G Porvaroardóttir, J Pagnan and S Einarsson (1998) Breidafjördur: West-Iceland: an Arctic marine protected area, *Parks* 8(2), pp23–28

Phillips, C (1996) Conservation in practice: agreements, regulations, sanctuaries and action plans, in MP Simmonds and JD Hutchinson (eds) *The Conservation of Whales and Dolphins: Science and Practice*, John Wiley & Sons, Chichester, pp447–465

Pingree, RD and GT Mardell (1981) Slope turbulence, internal waves and phytoplankton growth at the Celtic Sea Shelf-break, *Philosophical Transactions of the Royal Society of London A* 302, pp663–682

Pitman, R and P Ensor (2003) Three different forms of killer whales in Antarctic waters, *Journal of Cetacean Research and Management* 5(2), pp131–139

Platzoder, R (2001) The United Nations Convention on the Law of the Sea and Marine Protected Areas on the High-seas, in Expert Workshop on Managing Risks to Biodiversity and the Environment on the High-seas, including Tools such as Marine Protected Areas – Scientific Requirements and Legal Aspects, 27 February–4 March, Vilm, Germany

PNUMA (1992) Plan de Acción para la Conservación de los Mamíferos Marinos en el Pacífico Sudeste, Informes y Estudios del Programa de Mares Regionales del PNUMA, No 143, 13pp

Preen, AR, H Marsh, IR Lawler, RIT Prince and R Shepherd (1995) Winter distribution and abundance of dugongs, turtles, dolphins and other large vertebrate fauna in Shark Bay, Ningaloo Reef and Exmouth Gulf, Western Australia, report to Department of Conservation and Land Management, Western Australia, November 1995

Price, ARG, A Jeudy de Grissac and RFG Ormond (1992) Coastal assessment of Parc national du Banc d'Arguin, Mauritania: understanding resources, exploitation patterns and management needs, IUCN in collaboration with Parc National du Banc D'Arguin, Fondation Internationale de Banc d'Arguin and World Wide Fund for Nature, Gland, Switzerland, 44pp

Prideaux, M (2003a) Beyond the state: building regimes for species protection in all oceans, Hawke Institute, University of South Australia, Adelaide

Prideaux, M (2003b) Sheltering in deep water: cetacean critical habitat protection in all oceans, WDCS, UK

Prideaux, M (2003c) Small cetacea and world politics; developing regimes for species survival, University of South Australia, Adelaide

Prieto, R, MA Silva, M Sequeira, R Gaspar and F Tempera (2001) The implementation of marine protected areas in Portugal: implications to cetacean conservation, in PGH Evans and E Urquiola Pascual (eds) *Proceedings of the Workshop, Protected Areas for Cetaceans*, ECS Newsletter No 38 – special issue, p37

Prochnow, G (2001) A baseline study towards the protection of harbour porpoise in the waters off Amrum and Sylt (German Wadden Sea), in PGH Evans and E Urquiola Pascual (eds) *Proceedings of the Workshop, Protected Areas for Cetaceans*, ECS Newsletter No 38 – special issue, pp39–40

Prokosch, P (1999) All of Svalbard – one national park! *WWF Arctic Bulletin,* no 4, pp16–17

Quero, ME, G Chiofalo, S Datta, A Di Natale, PY Dremiere and AD Goodson (2000) Interaction between dolphins and artisanal gillnet fishery: methods of fishery and damages sampling, *European Research on Cetaceans* 14, Proceedings of the annual conference of the European Cetacean Society

RCN (2003) *Russian Conservation News,* summer, No 33 (available from Box 71, 117321, Moscow, Russia; email: rcn@igc.org)

Recchia, C, S Farady, J Sobel, and J Cinner (2001) *Marine and Coastal Protected Areas in the United States Gulf of Maine Region,* The Ocean Conservancy, Washington, DC, 96pp

Reeves, RR (1980) Spitsbergen bowhead whale stock: a short review, *Marine Fisheries Review* 42, pp65–69

Reeves, RR (2001) The value of sanctuaries, parks, and reserves (protected areas) as tools for conserving marine mammals, report to the Marine Mammal Commission

Reeves, RR (2002) Conservation efforts, in WF Perrin, B Würsig and JGM Thewissen (eds) *Encyclopedia of Marine Mammals,* Academic Press, San Diego, pp276–297

Reeves, RR and S Leatherwood (1994) *1994–1998 Action Plan for the Conservation of Cetaceans: Dolphins, Porpoises, and Whales,* IUCN, Gland, Switzerland and Cambridge, UK, 91pp

Reeves, RR, E Mitchell and H Whitehead (1993) Status of the northern bottlenose whale, *Hyperoodon ampullatus, Canadian Field-Naturalist* 107(4), pp490–508

Reeves, RR, BD Smith and T Kasuya (eds) (2000) Biology and conservation of freshwater cetaceans in Asia, IUCN/SSC Occasional Paper No 23, Gland, Switzerland and Cambridge, UK

Reeves, RR, BS Stewart, PJ Clapham, JA Powell and P Folkens (2002) *National Audubon Society Guide to Marine Mammals of the World,* Chanticleer Press and Knopf, New York, 527pp

Reeves, RR, BD Smith, EA Crespo and G Notarbartolo di Sciara (2003) *Dolphins, Whales and Porpoises: 2002–2010 Conservation Action Plan for the World's Cetaceans,* IUCN/SSC Cetacean Specialist Group, IUCN, Gland, Switzerland and Cambridge, UK, ix + 139pp

Reilly, SB, PC Fiedler, KA Forney and J Barlow (1997) Cetacean habitats in the California current: partitioning oceanographic and geographic patterns, paper submitted to the Scientific Committee of the IWC, SC/49/022, 22pp

Rejinders, PJH, A Aguilar and GP Donovan (1999) Chemical pollutants and cetaceans *Journal of Cetacean Research and Management,* Special Issue 1, Cambridge, UK

Relini, G, L Orsi Relini, A Siccardi, F Fiorentino, G Palandri, G Torchia, M Relini, C Cima and M Cappello (1994) Distribuzione di *Meganyctiphanes norvegica* e *Balaenoptera physalus* in Mar Ligure all'inizio della primavera, *Biologia Marina Mediterranea* 1(1), pp89–94

Reyes, JC, JG Mead and K Van Waerebeek (1991) A new species of beaked whale *Mesoplodon peruvianus* sp n (Cetacea: Ziphiidae) from Peru, *Marine Mammal Science* 7(1), pp1–24

Reyes, JC, K Van Waerebeek, JC Cárdenas and JL Yañez (1995) *Mesoplodon bahamondi* sp n (Cetacea, Ziphiidae), a new living beaked whale from the Juan Fernández Archipelago, Chile *Boletin del Museo Nacional de Historia Natural, Chile* 45, pp31–44

Reynolds, JE, III, and SA Rommel (1999) *Biology of Marine Mammals*, Smithsonian, Washington, DC, 578pp

Rice, D (1998) *Marine Mammals of the World. Systematics and Distribution*, Special Publication No 4, The Society for Marine Mammalogy, Lawrence, KS, 231pp

Ritter, F (1996) Abundance, distribution and behaviour of cetaceans off La Gomera (Canary Islands) and their interaction with whale watching boats and swimmers, Diploma Thesis to the University of Bremen, Faculty of Biology, 114pp

Ritter, F and B Brederlau (1999) Behavioural observations of dense beaked whales (*Mesoplodon densirostris*) off La Gomera, Canary Islands (1995–1997), *Aquatic Mammals* 25(2), pp55–61

Roberts, CM and JP Hawkins (2000) *Fully Protected Marine Reserves: A Guide*, WWF Endangered Seas Campaign, WWF-USA, Washington, DC and Environment Dept, University of York, York, UK, 108pp

Roberts, T R (1993) Artisanal fisheries and fish ecology below the great waterfalls of the Mekong River in Southern Laos, *Natural History Bulletin of the Siam Society* 41, pp31–62

Robineau, D and P Figuet (1994a) Cetaceans of Dawhat ad-Dafi and Dawhat al-Musallamiya (Saudi Arabia) one year after the Gulf War oil spill, *Courier Forsch Inst Senckenberg* 166, pp76–80

Robineau, D and P Figuet (1994b) The cetaceans of the Jubail Marine Wildlife Sanctuary, Saudi Arabia, in F Krupp, AH Abuzinada and IA Nader (eds) A Marine Wildlife Sanctuary for the Arabian Gulf: Environmental Research and Conservation following the 1991 Gulf War Oil Spill, National Commission for Wildlife Conservation and Development, Riyadh, Saudi Arabia, pp438–458

Robinson, R and G De Graaff (eds) (1994) *Marine Protected Areas of the Republic of South Africa*, National Parks Board, Pretoria, 203pp

Rogan, E and SD Berrow (1995) The management of Irish waters as a whale and dolphin sanctuary, in AS Blix, L Walløe and Ø Ulltang (eds) *Whales, Seals, Fish and Man*, Elsevier Science, Amsterdam, pp671–681

Rojas-Bracho, L and BL Taylor (1999) Risk factors affecting the vaquita (*Phocoena sinus*), *Marine Mammal Science* 15(4), pp974–989

Romero, A, AI Agudo and SM Green (1997) Exploitation of cetaceans in Venezuela, *Report of the International Whaling Commission* 47, pp735–746

Rosenbaum, HC, PD Walsh, Y Razafindrakoto, M Vely and R DeSalle (1997) First description of a humpback whale wintering ground in Baie d'Antongil, Madagascar, *Conservation Biology* 11(2), pp312–314

Rudolph, P, C Smeenk and S Leatherwood (1997) Preliminary checklist of cetacea in the Indonesian Archipelago and adjacent waters, *Zoologische Verhandelingen* 312, pp1–48

Ryan, PG and JP Glass (2001) Inaccessible Island Nature Reserve Management Plan, Govt of Tristan da Cunha, Edinburgh, Tristan da Cunha, 65pp

Salm, RV and JR Clark (1989) *Marine and Coastal Protected Areas: A Guide for Planners and Managers*, 2nd edn, IUCN, Gland, Switzerland, 302pp

Salm, RV and JR Clark (2000) *Marine and Coastal Protected Areas: A Guide for Planners and Managers*, 3rd edn, IUCN, Gland, Switzerland, 370pp

Salm, RV, RAC Jensen and VA Papastavrou (1993) Marine fauna of Oman: cetaceans, turtles, seabirds and shallow water corals, IUCN, Gland, 66pp

Samaniego, J and F Félix (1994) Study of the interactions of artisanal fisheries with small cetaceans in Ecuador, final report, March 1994, prepared for the United Nations Environment Program (UNEP) and Subsecretary of Fishery Resources (MICIP), Guayaquil, Ecuador, 30pp

Sanctuaries and Reserves Division (NOAA) (1997) Hawaiian Islands Humpback Whale National Marine Sanctuary, final environmental impact statement/management plan, February, 464pp

Sanino, GP and JL Yáñez (2000) Efectos del turismo de observación de cetáceos en punta de Choros, IV Región, Chile, *Revista Gestión Ambiental Chile* 6, pp41–53

Sant, M (1996) Environmental sustainability and the public: responses to a proposed marine reserve at Jervis Bay, New South Wales, Australia, *Ocean & Coastal Management* 32(1), pp1–16

Schandy, T (2000) Norwegian marine reserves in focus, *WWF Arctic Bulletin* 1, pp13–14

Schmidly, DJ (1981) Marine mammals of the southeastern US coast and the Gulf of Mexico, US Fisheries and Wildlife Service (USFWS), FWS/OBS-80/41, 165pp

Schmidt, RC and B Hussel (1994) Tourists and locals: seals and porpoises – friendly interaction and mutual endangering examples from the German Island Sylt, North Sea, *European Research on Cetaceans* 7, Proceedings of the annual conference of the European Cetacean Society

Schmidt, RC and B Hussel (1995) Observation of harbor porpoises (*Phocoena phocoena*) from ferry between the islands Rømø, Denmark, and Sylt, Germany, Summer 1994, *European Research on Cetaceans* 8, Proceedings of the annual conference of the European Cetacean Society

Scovazzi, T (ed) (1999) *Marine Specially Protected Areas,* Kluwer Law International, 296pp

Sea Around Us (in preparation for 2004) Millennium Ecosystem – Conditions and Trends Working Group Report (for more information, contact Jackie Alder; email: j.alder@fisheries.ubc.ca; dataset can be viewed at http://sedac.ciesin.columbia.edu/plue/gpw/index.html?main.html&2)

Sears, R (1983) The photographic identification of individual blue whales (*Balaenoptera musculus*) in the Gulf of St Lawrence, abstract, 5th Biennial Conference on the Biology of Marine Mammals, Boston, MA, USA, 27 November–1 December 1983

Shah, NJ (1993) Seychelles Country Report, Workshop and Policy Conference on Integrated Coastal Zone Management in East Africa and Island States, Arusha, Tanzania

Sherman, K and LM Alexander (eds) (1986) *Variability and Management of Large Marine Ecosystems,* AAAS Selected Symposium 99, Westview Press, Inc, Boulder, CO, 319pp

Sherman, K and LM Alexander (eds) (1989) *Biomass Yields and Geography of Large Marine Ecosystems,* AAAS Selected Symposium 111, Westview Press, Inc, Boulder, CO, 493pp (for more on LMEs, see http://na.nefsc.noaa.gov/lme/publications.htm)

Shtilmark, F (1996) *History of the Russian Zapovedniks: 1895–1995* (Translated, G Harper 2002, Russian Nature Press, Moscow) (see www.rusnatpress.org.uk)

Simard, F (1995) Marine Region 16: Northwest Pacific, in G Kelleher, C Bleakley and S Wells (eds) *A Global Representative System of Marine Protected Areas. Vol IV,* The Great Barrier Reef Marine Park Authority, The World Bank and IUCN, Washington, DC, pp107–130

Simila, T (1997) Behavioral ecology of killer whales in northern Norway, Dr Scient Thesis, Norwegian College of Fisheries Science, Univ of Tromsø, Tromsø, Norway

Simmonds, MP (1994) Saving Europe's dolphins, *Oryx* 28(4), pp238–248

Simmonds, MP and JD Hutchinson (eds) (1996) *The Conservation of Whales and Dolphins: Science and Practice,* John Wiley & Sons, Chichester, 476pp

Sissenwine, M and P Mace (2001) Governance for responsible fisheries: an ecosystem approach, paper presented to Reykjavík Conference on Responsible Fisheries in the Marine Ecosystem, Reykjavík, Iceland, 1–4 October

Smith, BD, RK Sinha, U Regmi and K Sapkota (1994) Status of Ganges River dolphins (*Platanista gangetica*) in the Karnali, Mahakali, Narayani and Sapta Kosi Rivers of Nepal and India in 1993, *Marine Mammal Science* 10(3), pp368–375

Smith, BD, H Thant, JM Lwin and CD Shaw (1997a) Preliminary investigation of cetaceans in the Ayeyarwady River and northern coastal waters of Myanmar, *Asian Marine Biology* 14, pp173–194

Smith, BD, TA Jefferson, S Leatherwood, DT Ho, CV Thouc and LH Quang (1997b) Investigations of marine mammals in Vietnam, *Asian Marine Biology* 14, pp111–143

Smith, BD, G Braulik, TA Jefferson, BD Chung, CT Vinh, DV Du, BV Hanh, PD Trong, DT Ho and VV Quang (2003) Notes on two cetacean surveys in the Gulf of Tonkin Vietnam, *Raffles Bulletin of Zoology* 51(1), pp165–171

Smith, BD, I Beasley, M Buccat, V Calderon, R Evena, J Lemmuel de Valle, A Cadigal, E Tura and Z Visitacion (in press) Status, ecology and conservation of Irrawaddy dolphins *Orcaella brevirostris* in Malampaya Sound, Palawan, Philippines, *Journal of Cetacean Research and Management*

Smith, TD, J Allen, PJ Clapham, PS Hammond, S Katona, F Larsen, J Lien, D Mattila, PJ Palsbøll, J Sigurjónsson, PT Stevick and N Øien (1999) An ocean-basin-wide mark-recapture study of the North Atlantic humpback whale (*Megaptera novaeangliae*), *Marine Mammal Science* 15, pp1–32

Smyth, C, M Prideaux, K Davey and M Grady (2003) *Oceans Eleven: The Implementation of Australia's Oceans Policy and Ecosystem-based Regional Marine Planning,* Australian Conservation Foundation, Melbourne, 63pp

Sociedad Española de Cetáceos (2000) Recopilación de áreas de especial interés para la conservación de la marsopa común (*Phocoena phocoena*), el delfín mular (*Tursiops truncatus*) y la tortuga boba (*Caretta caretta*), Reunión del Grupo de Expertos de la Red Natura 2000, Dirección General de Conservación de la Naturaleza, Madrid, 30 May

Soegiarto, A, Soewito and RV Salm (1984) Development of marine conservation in Indonesia, in JA McNeely and KR Miller (eds) *National Parks, Conservation and Development – The Role of Protected Areas in Sustaining Society*, Smithsonian Institution Press, Washington, DC

Sonntag, RP, H Benke, AR Hiby, R Lick and D Adelung (1999) Identification of the first harbor porpoise (*Phocoena phocoena*) calving ground in the North Sea, *Journal of Sea Research* 41, pp225–232

St Lawrence Beluga Recovery Team (1995) St Lawrence Beluga Recovery Plan, Department of Fisheries and Oceans and the World Wildlife Fund Canada, 73pp

Stacey, PJ (1996) Natural history and conservation of Irrawaddy dolphins, *Orcaella brevirostris*, with special reference to the Mekong River, Lao PDR, unpublished Master of Science thesis, 123pp

Stanley, S (1995) Marine Region 7: Wider Caribbean, in G Kelleher, C Bleakley and S Wells (eds) *A Global Representative System of Marine Protected Areas. Vol II*, The Great Barrier Reef Marine Park Authority, The World Bank and IUCN, Washington, DC, pp13–41

Stepanitsky, V (2003) The future we choose, *Russian Conservation News* 33, pp36–38

Sterrer, W (1992) *Bermuda's Marine Life*, Wiley-Interscience, New York, 742pp

Stewardson, CL (1997) *Mammals of the Ice*, an introductory guide to the seals, whales and dolphins in the Australian Subantarctic and Antarctica, based on records from ANARE voyages from 1977–1990, Sedona Publishing, ACT, Australia

Stone, G (1995) Indian Ocean marine mammal, turtle, coral reef and pelagic fisheries conservation programme, in Anon (ed) *Proceedings of the First International Conference on the Southern Ocean Whale Sanctuary*, Auckland, NZ, 15–16 Oct 1994, Dept of Conservation, New Zealand and Whale and Dolphin Conservation Society, Bath, UK, pp29–35

Szabo, M (1994) *State of the Ice: An Overview of Human Impacts in Antarctica*, Greenpeace International, Amsterdam

Tan, JML (1995) *A Field Guide to Whales and Dolphins of the Philippines*, Bookmark, Makati, Metro Manila, 125pp

Taylor, M (2002) Habitat degradation: contribution to extinction risk for southern resident killer whales, paper submitted to the Scientific Committee of the IWC, SC/54/E10, 19pp

Taylor, M (2004) Southern resident orcas: population change, habitat degradation and habitat protection, paper submitted to the Scientific Committee of the IWC, SC/56/E32, 13pp

Taylor, MFJ, K Suckling and JR Rachlinski (in review, 2004) The effectiveness of the Endangered Species Act: a quantitative analysis

Thiel, H (2001) MPAs for monitoring and scientific reference on the high-seas, in Expert Workshop on Managing Risks to Biodiversity and the Environment on the High-seas, including Tools such as Marine Protected Areas – Scientific Requirements and Legal Aspects, 27 February–4 March, Vilm, Germany

Tregenza, NJC, SD Berrow, PS Hammond and R Leaper (1997) Harbor porpoise (*Phocoena phocoena*) by-catch in set gill nets in the Celtic Sea, *ICES Journal of Marine Science* 54, pp897–904

Twiss, JR, Jr and RR Reeves (1999) *Conservation and Management of Marine Mammals*, Smithsonian, Washington, DC, 471pp

UNEP/CBD/SBSTTA (2003) Marine and coastal biodiversity: review, further elaboration and refinement of the programme of work, Subsidiary Body on Scientific, Technical and Technological Advice (SBSTTA) of the Convention on Biological Diversity (CBD), Eighth meeting, Montréal, 10–14 March

UNEP-WCMC (2002) World Database of Protected Areas (see www.wcmc.org.uk/cis)

Unesco (1974) Programme on Man and the Biosphere (MAB) Task Force on: Criteria and Guidelines for the Choice and Establishment of Biosphere Reseves, MAB Report Series No 22, Unesco, Paris, 61pp

Urquiola, E (1998) Ballenas y delfines de Canarias: Cetaceos en Tenerife, in *Tenerife y el Mar* (Excmo Cabildo Insular de Tenerife, ed), Canarias, España

Urquiola Pascual, E and PGH Evans (2001) Legislative instruments relevant to the establishment of marine protected areas for cetaceans, in PGH Evans and E Urquiola Pascual (eds) *Proceedings of the Workshop, Protected Areas for Cetaceans*, ECS Newsletter No 38 – special issue, pp12–22

Utreras, V (1996) Biología y ecología del Bufeo (*Inia geoffrensis*) en el Río Lagarto Cocha, Reserva de Producción Faunistica Cuyabeno, Ecuador, Master's Thesis, Pontifica Universidad Catolica, Quito, Ecuador

van Helden, AL, AN Baker, ML Dalebout, JC Reyes, K Van Waerebeek and CS Baker (2002) Resurrection of *Mesoplodon traversii* (Gray, 1874), senior synonym of *M bahamondi* Reyes, Van Waerebeek, Cárdenas and Yañez, 1995 (Cetacea:Ziphiidae), *Marine Mammal Science* 18(3), pp609–621

Van Waerebeek, K, E Ndiaye, A Djiba, M Diallo, P Murphy, A Jallow, A Camara, P Ndiaye and P Tous (2000) A survey of the conservation status of cetaceans in Senegal, The Gambia and Guinea-Bissau, WAFCET-1 Report, UNEP/CMS Secretariat, Bonn, Germany, 80pp

Vely, M, DA Tijane and R Ndiaye (1995) Biodiversite du littoral mauritanien: premieres données concernant l'inventaire des mammiferes marins du Parc National du Banc d'Arguin, Nouakchott, Mauritanie: Centre National d'Evelage et de Recherche Veterinaire (CNERV)

Viallelle, S (1997) *Dolphins and Whales from the Azores (Golfinhos e Baleias dos Açores)*, Espaço Talassa, Lajes do Pico, Açores, Portugal, 78pp

Vladimirov, VA (2000) Conservation of endangered gray and great polar whale populations at Okhotskoe Sea, Marine Mammals of the Holarctic, First International Conference, Archangelsk, 21–23 September

Vladimirov, VA (2002) On the distribution of cetaceans in the coastal waters of southern Sakhalin Island, Marine Mammals of the Holarctic, Second International Conference, Baikal, 10–15 September, pp65–66

Walton, MJ (1997) Population structure of harbour porpoises *Phocoena phocoena* in the seas around the UK and adjacent waters, *Proceedings of the Royal Society of London B* 264, pp89–94

Ward, N (1995) *Stellwagen Bank: A Guide to the Whales, Sea Birds, and Marine Life of the Stellwagen Bank National Marine Sanctuary*, Down East Books, Camden, Maine, 232pp

Ward, T, D Tarte, E Hegerl and K Short (2002) Policy proposals and operational guidance for ecosystem-based management of marine capture fisheries, WWF Australia, Sydney, 80pp

Warner, R (2001) Marine protected areas beyond national jurisdiction: existing legal principles and future legal frameworks, in Expert Workshop on Managing Risks to Biodiversity and the Environment on the High-seas, including Tools such as Marine Protected Areas – Scientific Requirements and Legal Aspects, 27 February–4 March, Vilm, Germany

Webster, P (2003) The wild wild east, *The Ecologist* 33(1), Feb, pp48–51

Weir, CR, C Pollock, C Cronin and S Taylor (2001) Cetaceans of the Atlantic Frontier, north and west of Scotland, *Continental Shelf Research* 21, pp1047–1071

Weller, DW, B Würsig, AL Bradford, AM Burdin, SA Blokhin, H Minakuchi and RL Brownell, Jr (1999) Gray whales (*Eschrichtius robustus*) off Sakhalin Island, Russia: seasonal and annual patterns of occurrence, *Marine Mammal Science* 15(4), pp1208–1227

Weller, DW, AM Burdin, and RL Brownell, Jr (2001) The western North Pacific gray whale: past exploitation, current status, and new threats, paper submitted to the Scientific Committee of the IWC, SC/53/BRG12

Wells, MP (1997) Economic perspectives on nature tourism, conservation and development, The World Bank, Washington, DC, Environment Department Paper No 55

Wells, RS, MD Scott, and AB Irvine (1987) Social structure of free-ranging bottlenose dolphins, in HH Genoways (ed) *Current Mammalogy*, Vol 1, Plenum Press, New York, pp247–305

Wells, S and C Bleakley (1995) Marine Region 8: West Africa, in G Kelleher, C Bleakley and S Wells (eds) *A Global Representative System of Marine Protected Areas. Vol II*, The Great Barrier Reef Marine Park Authority, The World Bank and IUCN, Washington, DC, pp43–69

Wells, S, SN Dwivedi, S Singh and R Ivan (1995) Marine Region 10: Central Indian Ocean, in G Kelleher, C Bleakley and S Wells (eds) *A Global Representative System of Marine Protected Areas. Vol III*, The Great Barrier Reef Marine Park Authority, The World Bank and IUCN, Washington, DC, pp13–37

Wheeler, B (2003) Nunavut whale project a success, *Arctic Bulletin* 4, p9

Whitehead, H (1981) The behaviour and ecology of the humpback whale in the Northwest Atlantic, PhD dissertation, Cambridge University, Cambridge, England

Whitehead, H (1989) *Voyage to the Whales*, Stoddart, Toronto, pp1–195

Whitehead, H, S Gowans, A Faucher, and SW McCarrey (1997) Population analysis of northern bottlenose whales in the Gully, Nova Scotia, *Marine Mammal Science* 13(2), pp173–185

Whitehead, H, A Faucher, S Gowans and S McCarrey (1998) Status of the northern bottlenose whale, *Hyperoodon ampullatus*, in the Gully, Nova Scotia, *Canadian Field-Naturalist* 111, pp287–292

Wilson, EO (2002) *The Future of Life*, Knopf, New York, 229pp

Würsig, B (1995) Potential effects of a proposed aviation fuel receiving facility at Sha Chau on the health and survivability of the Indo-Pacific humpback (Chinese white) dolphin, *Sousa chinensis*, in waters north of Lantau Island, Hong Kong territory, unpublished report to the Provisional Airport Authority, Hong Kong Government, Hong Kong

WWF (2003) South Pacific – gift to the Earth for whale conservation, Gift: 89, 13 Aug 2003, 8pp

Zanardelli, M, S Panigada, S Airoldi, JF Borsani, M Jahoda, G Lauriano and G Notarbartolo di Sciara (1998) Site fidelity, seasonal residence and sex ratio of fin whales (*Balaenoptera physalus*) in the Ligurian Sea feeding ground, *European Research on Cetaceans* 12, Proceedings of the annual conference of the European Cetacean Society, p124

INDEX

Italicized *(p)* indicates a marine protected area that is proposed, nominated or under discussion